# Sondheim in Our Time and His

# Sondheim in Our Time and His

*Edited by*

W. ANTHONY SHEPPARD

OXFORD

UNIVERSITY PRESS

# OXFORD
### UNIVERSITY PRESS

Oxford University Press is a department of the University of Oxford. It furthers
the University's objective of excellence in research, scholarship, and education
by publishing worldwide. Oxford is a registered trade mark of Oxford University
Press in the UK and certain other countries.

Published in the United States of America by Oxford University Press
198 Madison Avenue, New York, NY 10016, United States of America.

CIP data is on file at the Library of Congress
ISBN 978–0–19–760320–8 (pbk.)
ISBN 978–0–19–760319–2 (hbk.)

DOI: 10.1093/oso/9780197603192.001.0001

3 5 7 9 8 6 4 2

Paperback printed by Marquis, Canada
Hardback printed by Bridgeport National Bindery, Inc., United States of America

*In memoriam Stephen Joshua Sondheim (1930–2021).*
*This volume was already in press at the time of*
*Mr. Sondheim's death on November 26, 2021.*
*The editor and authors dedicate this book to his memory.*

# Contents

PART III.  VERSIONS, GENRES,
AND COLLABORATIONS

PART IV.  RECONCEIVED STRUCTURES
AND TECHNIQUES

# Contributors

**Kristen Anderson-Lopez** is an Oscar- and Grammy-winning songwriter. Along with her collaborator and husband Robert Lopez, she is the co-writer of Disney's animated features *Frozen* (Oscar and Grammy wins), *Frozen II* (Oscar and Grammy nominations), "Remember Me" from Pixar's *Coco* (Oscar win), and *Frozen* on Broadway. She is a co-writer of *In Transit*, the first-ever all a cappella musical on Broadway. Additional credits for stage and screen include *Finding Nemo: The Musical*, running at Disney World for more than ten years, Emmy-nominated songs for television's *87th Academy Awards* and *The Comedians*, songs for Marvel's *WandaVision*, Disney's *Winnie the Pooh*, and the original musical *Up Here*, featured at the La Jolla Playhouse. A recipient of the BMI Harrington Award and the 2014 Lily Award, Anderson-Lopez serves on the council of the Dramatists Guild. A graduate of Williams College, she currently resides in Brooklyn with her husband and two daughters.

**Geoffrey Block**, Distinguished Professor of Music History and Humanities, University of Puget Sound, emeritus, is the author of *Enchanted Evenings: The Broadway Musical from "Show Boat" to Sondheim and Lloyd Webber* (Oxford University Press, 1997; 2nd expanded ed., 2009), *The Richard Rodgers Reader*, ed. (OUP, 2002), *Richard Rodgers* (Yale University Press, 2003), and books about Ives, Beethoven, and Schubert. After serving as general editor of the Yale Broadway Masters Series, since 2010 he has been the series editor of Oxford's Broadway Legacies. Recent publications include essays in *The Oxford Handbook of Musical Theatre Adaptations* (OUP, 2019), the "Special Issue: Rethinking Sondheim" of *Studies in Musical Theatre* (2019), and a book about *Love Me Tonight* that is scheduled to appear in the forthcoming series Oxford's Guides to Film Musicals, edited by Dominic McHugh. Block is currently writing *A Fine Romance: Adapting Broadway to Hollywood in the Studio System Era*, also for Oxford.

**Andrew Buchman** has team-taught a range of interdisciplinary offerings at the Evergreen State College in Olympia, Washington, since joining the faculty in 1986. He earned a DMA degree in composition at the University of Washington's Seattle campus in 1987. Two previous studies of the genesis and dramaturgy of George Furth and Sondheim's *Merrily We Roll Along* (1981) appeared in Robert Gordon's *Oxford Handbook of Sondheim Studies* (2014) and a special issue of the journal *Studies in Musical Theatre* devoted to Sondheim (June 2019). A study of the 1979 film version of Ragni, Rado, and MacDermot's *Hair* is included in Dominic McHugh's *Oxford Handbook of Musical Theatre Screen Adaptations* (2019).

**Todd Decker** is Paul Tietjens Professor of Music at Washington University in St. Louis. He has published four books and more than twenty-five articles and book chapters on popular music and media in the United States in the twentieth and twenty-first centuries, including *"Show Boat": Performing Race in an American Musical* (Oxford University Press, 2013). His essay on the humanitarian ideals of Oscar Hammerstein II appeared in *Lincoln Center Theatre Review* for distribution at the 2015 Broadway revival of *The King and I*. Decker has lectured on the stage and screen musical at the Library of Congress and London's Victoria and Albert Museum and was featured in a 2019 BBC World Service documentary on the song "Ol' Man River." In the fall of 2016 he held a visiting International Chair at Labex Arts-H2H, a humanities center at Université Paris 8.

**Lara E. Housez** is adjunct professor of music at McMaster University. She holds BMus and MA degrees from Western University, and she completed her PhD in musicology at the Eastman School of Music, University of Rochester. Housez is the recipient of a doctoral fellowship from the Social Sciences and Humanities Research Council of Canada and the Music Library Association's Dena Epstein Award. She has presented papers on American musicals at the annual meetings of the American Musicological Society, the Society for American Music, the Canadian University Music Society, and Song, Stage, and Screen. Her publications include entries for the second edition of *The Grove Dictionary of American Music* and book reviews in *Notes*. She is currently writing an article on one of Sondheim's unfinished projects, *A Pray by Blecht*. Housez is also an accomplished singer. She has appeared on recordings and has performed in the Elora Festival Singers and Edison Singers.

**Kim H. Kowalke** is professor emeritus of musicology at the Eastman School of Music and the Turner Professor Emeritus in Humanities at the University of Rochester. He is the author of many articles and four books on twentieth-century music and theater, including *Speak Low: The Letters of Kurt Weill and Lotte Lenya*, which inspired the Broadway musical *LoveMusik*, directed by Hal Prince, and *Lenya-Story*, premiered in Vienna in 2017. He is a five-time winner of ASCAP's Deems Taylor Award for excellence in writing about music and two Irving Lowens Awards for the best articles on American music. Since Lotte Lenya's death in 1981 Kowalke has served as president of the Kurt Weill Foundation, founding both the Kurt Weill Edition and the Lotte Lenya Singing Competition. He has conducted dozens of musical theater productions and received the 2020 Erwin Piscator Honorary Award for his contributions to the international musical theater.

**Jim Lovensheimer** is associate professor of musicology at Vanderbilt University's Blair School of Music. He attended the University of Cincinnati College-Conservatory of Music and worked in the professional theater for almost twenty years, after which he returned to school and earned a BM in music history from the University of Tennessee at Knoxville and an MA and PhD from The Ohio State University. His book *"South Pacific": Paradise Rewritten* launched the Broadway Legacies series for Oxford University Press, and he is currently at work on *Oscar Hammerstein II and the American Century* for Oxford. Other publications include chapters on Sondheim and others for *The New Grove Dictionary of American Music*, 2nd ed., as well as entries in the *Encyclopedia of African American Music*, *The American Midwest: An Interpretive Encyclopedia*, and *The Oxford Handbook of the American Musical*. Still performing, Jim has done several cabarets, including evenings of Stephen Sondheim and Jacques Brel.

**Jeffrey Magee** is the author of *The Uncrowned King of Swing: Fletcher Henderson and Big Band Jazz* and *Irving Berlin's American Musical Theater*, both published by Oxford University Press. His work has been supported by the National Endowment for the Humanities and recognized with the Society for American Music's Irving Lowens Award for Best Book, as well as an award for Excellence in Historical Recorded Sound Research from the Association for Recorded Sound Collections. His commentary may be heard on the NPR documentary series *Leonard Bernstein: An American Life*, narrated by Susan Sarandon, and he has been interviewed by the *New York Times* and *Al Jazeera America* for news and features related to early twentieth-century American popular music. At the University of Illinois Urbana-Champaign, he is a professor of music in the College of Fine and Applied Arts and associate dean of the College of Media.

**Dominic McHugh** is professor in musicology at the University of Sheffield and the author or editor of seven books on musicals, including *Loverly: The Life and Times of "My Fair Lady"* (2012), *Alan Jay Lerner: A Lyricist's Letters* (2014), *The Letters of Cole Porter* (2019), and *The Big Parade: Meredith Willson's Musicals from "The Music Man" to "1491"* (2021). He co-edited a special issue of *Studies in Musical Theatre* focused on Sondheim and has convened four international conferences concerning musicals. He is also the series editor of Oxford's Guides to Film Musicals and has worked with leading organizations including the Library of Congress, Lincoln Center, and the Victoria and Albert Museum. He has made more than forty appearances on BBC radio and television, and his research has been used in several professional productions, as well as being covered by major outlets such as the *New Yorker*, the *Sunday Times*, and the *Washington Post*.

**James O'Leary** is Frederick R. Selch Associate Professor of Musicology at Oberlin College and Conservatory. Previous writing about musical theater has been published by the *Journal of Musicology*, the University of Illinois Press, and Sorbonne Université Presses. His book *Exit Right: The Middlebrow Musical of the 1940s* is forthcoming with Oxford University Press. O'Leary was awarded the prize for best essay by a scholar in the early stages of his or her career by the Transnational Opera Studies Conference, and he completed research for his contribution to this volume as a John W. Kluge Fellow at the Library of Congress.

**Ashley M. Pribyl** received her PhD in musicology from Washington University in St. Louis, where she was a Harvey Fellow in American Studies and a Graduate Fellow at the Center for the Humanities. Her dissertation, titled "Sociocultural and Antagonistic Collaboration in the Harold Prince–Stephen Sondheim Musicals, 1970–1979," analyzed the politics of Stephen Sondheim's musicals through a prism of collaboration. Pribyl's current book project, *Fifty Years of* Company: *Exploring Marriage, Gender, and Sexuality Through an American Musical, 1970–2020*, has received funding from the Society for American Music and the New York Public Library. She has also published work in *Studies in Musical Theatre*. Dr. Pribyl has taught at the University of Texas, Washington University in St. Louis, and Arizona State University. She currently serves as the director of education and outreach for the Missouri Symphony.

**W. Anthony Sheppard** is Marylin and Arthur Levitt Professor of Music at Williams College. His first book, *Revealing Masks: Exotic Influences and Ritualized Performance in*

*Modernist Music Theater*, received the Kurt Weill Prize, his article on *Madama Butterfly* and film earned the ASCAP Deems Taylor Award, an article on World War II film music was honored with the Alfred Einstein Award by the American Musicological Society, and "Puccini and the Music Boxes" received the AMS H. Colin Slim Award. His most recent book, *Extreme Exoticism: Japan in the American Musical Imagination*, received the AMS Music in American Culture Award and the Society for American Music Lowens Award. Sheppard's research has been supported by the National Endowment for the Humanities, the American Philosophical Society, the American Council of Learned Societies, and the Institute for Advanced Study, Princeton. He has served as editor-in-chief of the *Journal of the American Musicological Society* and is now the series editor of *AMS Studies in Music* (OUP).

**Steve Swayne** is Jacob H. Strauss 1922 Professor of Music at Dartmouth College. He has written two books—*How Sondheim Found His Sound* (University of Michigan Press, 2005) and *Orpheus in Manhattan: William Schuman and the Shaping of America's Musical Life* (Oxford, 2011; winner of the 2012 Nicolas Slonimsky Award for Outstanding Musical Biography in the concert music field)—and his articles have appeared in the *Sondheim Review*, the *Journal of the Royal Musical Association*, *American Music*, *Studies in Musical Theatre*, the *Indiana Theory Review*, and the *Musical Quarterly*. He has taught at the San Francisco Conservatory of Music, the University of California at Berkeley, and Quest University (Squamish, BC), and he has served on the board of the American Musicological Society as council secretary (2015–2019) and president (2020–2022). He is also an accomplished concert pianist.

**Elizabeth A. Wells** completed her doctorate in musicology at the Eastman School of Music and is former dean of arts and Pickard-Bell Chair in Music at Mount Allison University in Sackville, New Brunswick. Her work has appeared in *Cambridge Opera Journal* and the *Journal of the American Musicological Society*. She has won regional and national teaching awards, and her research has been supported by the Presser Foundation and the AMS-50 dissertation fellowship. Her book *"West Side Story": Cultural Perspectives on an American Musical* won the AMS Music in American Culture Award. Her research interests include American and British musical theater at mid-century and the scholarship of teaching and learning.

**Stacy Wolf** is professor of theater and American studies and director of the program in music theater at Princeton University. She is the author of *Beyond Broadway: The Pleasure and Promise of Musical Theatre Across America*, *A Problem Like Maria: Gender and Sexuality in the American Musical*, and *Changed for Good: A Feminist History of the Broadway Musical*, and is the co-editor of *The Oxford Handbook of the American Musical*. She has published extensively on issues of gender and sexuality in musical theater. In 2017 she received both a Guggenheim Fellowship and, at Princeton, the President's Award for Distinguished Teaching. Her work has also been honored with a Best Essay in Theatre Studies award from the Association for Theatre in Higher Education.

# Introduction

## Our Sondheim

*W. Anthony Sheppard*

The song "Our Time" occupies a peculiar Janus-faced position in Sondheim's 1981 *Merrily We Roll Along*. Three aspiring artists—Frank, Charley, and Mary—gaze at the night sky in wonder as Sputnik orbits the Earth in October 1957. The lyrics are focused both on this exciting present moment and on the promise of a bright future, and they speak of an energy and change that can be heard: "Something is stirring, / Shifting ground. / It's just begun"; "Hear what's happening." The lyrics are packed with invigorating alliteration, rhyme, and word repetition, pushing the song forward. Similarly, the strong, incessant bacchius (short-long-long) musical rhythm in the chorus section is assertive and optimistic. And yet we hear this song at the very end of the musical—or, in the original production, at the penultimate moment—after having traveled backward from 1980 through the lives of these three characters. In fact, as they sing of their promising futures, we cannot avoid looking back ourselves to the opening scenes of the show, in which we learn just how fraught and compromised their adult lives actually turned out to be.

Our knowledge—acquired through retrograde observation—of the disappointments, bitterness, and strained relationships that will mark the lives of these hopeful youths might lead us to mock the boundless optimism expressed in this song at the end of the show. They boast of being the "movers" and "shapers" of the future, of having "worlds to win," and of how their inevitable success will allow them one day to come back together and "buy the rooftop" on which they are standing and to install a plaque commemorating this night. Yet we neither mock nor laugh at their naiveté in our experience of this number. Indeed, Sondheim suggests through his lyric and musical setting that these young characters might very well intuit their own limitations, as they sing that imagined plaque's inscription: "'This is where we began / Being what we can.'" The first line is pure commemorative cliché, an assertion of pride. "Being what we can," however, is indicative of a more mature vision, a realistic view of what we are actually capable of in life, a distinct avoidance of the worn charge to "be all you can be." It is a realization that the older, disillusioned Frank, Charley,

W. Anthony Sheppard, *Introduction* In: *Sondheim in Our Time and His*. Edited by: W. Anthony Sheppard, Oxford University Press. © Oxford University Press 2022. DOI: 10.1093/oso/9780197603192.003.0001

and Mary have gradually and painfully come to during their lives. Sondheim's setting of these lines suggests a humanistic understanding of these characters and a worldly wisdom about how our lives tend to run. The assertive first phrase receives a *forte* dynamic with a high, sustained E♭ on the word "began." With the humbler second line, the music drops suddenly to *mezzo piano*, the meter loses a beat by shifting to 3/4, and the melody cascades down and lands on E♭ an octave lower, pausing on this supertonic pitch and a hollow dominant chord rather than coming to rest on a conclusive cadence. Thus, through melodic shape, register, meter, dynamics, and harmony, we are made to realize that "Being what we can" is a more accurate perception of life and its possibilities.

The humanistic resonance of "Being what we can," is, to my mind, of a piece with several other of Sondheim's most telling lyrics, such as "I'm a fragment of the day" ("Someone in a Tree," *Pacific Overtures*); "The choice may have been mistaken / The choosing was not" ("Move On," *Sunday in the Park with George*); and "Isn't it nice to know a lot! / And a little bit not" ("I Know Things Now," *Into the Woods*). The humanizing lyrical and musical twist of "Being what we can" is but one of many moments in which Sondheim displays a penetrating insight into the human condition and empathy for his characters, who often fall short in one way or another. Indeed, as early as *Climb High* (1953), the first musical he completed after college, Sondheim had explored the topic of unrealized aspirations and disillusionment. The title of this early work points to the text of an actual commemorative plaque placed at the bottom of some outdoor steps on the Williams College campus: "CLIMB HIGH / CLIMB FAR / YOUR GOAL / THE SKY / YOUR AIM / THE STAR." The song "When I Get Famous" from this early show expresses a character's immature, buoyant exuberance, one that, as in many of Sondheim's musicals, will be deflated throughout the course of the plot. David in *Climb High*, Gene in *Saturday Night*, Rose in *Gypsy*, Ben in *Follies*, Franklin Shepard in *Merrily We Roll Along*, George of onetime chromolume fame in *Sunday in the Park with George*, each assassin longing for recognition from American society in *Assassins*, the Mizner brothers in *Road Show*—all learn the hard way that art/life/success "isn't easy," that high hopes most often do not pan out.

Given the fact that Sondheim and his work have been so frequently honored (Tonys, Grammys, Oliviers, an Oscar, a Pulitzer, and the Presidential Medal of Freedom, not to mention a 1950 Hutchinson from Williams College), his gravitation to such characters and to the plot conceit of failed dreams and misplaced ambition is curious. As Sondheim and others have noted, *Merrily We Roll Along* resonates for him autobiographically.[1] The year 1957, of course, was not only the year of Frank, Charley, and Mary's fictional "Our Time;" it also marked Sondheim's propitious debut on Broadway at age twenty-seven with *West Side Story*. The high school graduation ceremony at the end of the original version of *Merrily We Roll Along* is set in both 1955, five years after Sondheim's Williams

College graduation, and in 1980. Two commencement moments are brought together as we see Franklin Shepard as both the young valedictorian of 1955 and
as his forty-three-year-old self delivering the 1980 commencement address, the
mid-life reflective moment at which the musical had begun in the original prologue. It is clear that writing this show also offered the fifty-year-old Sondheim
an opportunity to reflect back on his own career.

Sondheim and his musicals likewise occupy a Janus-faced position within the
history of American musical theater, connecting back to the origins of the genre
and ahead to its repeated reconceptualization. He was born but three years after
the premiere of *Show Boat* and five years before *Porgy and Bess*. He experienced
the Rodgers and Hammerstein "book musical" landmarks *Oklahoma!* (1943) and
*Carousel* (1945) and was famously mentored by Hammerstein during his formative
teenage years. As a college student in 1949, soon after Cole Porter's *Kiss Me, Kate*
had opened on Broadway in late 1948, he walked over to Porter's Williamstown
home to play a song from *All That Glitters* that parodied Porter's "Begin the
Beguine." His career flourished in the 1970s and 1980s, offering a distinct alternative to the rise of megamusicals, one pursued by the likes of William Finn, who
graduated from Williams in 1974 and whose *March of the Falsettos* (1981)/*Falsettos*
(1992) appears to pick up where Sondheim's *Company* left off. In the 1990s and the
early twenty-first century, Sondheim served as a mentor to such celebrated figures
as Jonathan Larson and Lin-Manuel Miranda.

Sondheim has been, and will be within this volume, celebrated as an innovator
who created works in which "edges are blurring" between genres, structures,
song types, and styles. But in addition to opening up the genre to new concepts
and prefiguring some of its more recent developments, Sondheim's works repeatedly look deep into Broadway's past. In his scores, "yesterday is [*not*] done" and,
instead, we hear numerous echoes of styles and forms from the musical past,
as he frequently redeploys the conventional in unconventional ways. Sondheim
clearly possesses an astonishing knowledge of Broadway history. He is also clearly
conscious of and deliberate in his engagements with the past, leading some to
classify him as the very model of a postmodern Broadway musical artist.[2]

In his commentary on *Merrily We Roll Along*, Sondheim relates that since the
show was about the careers of two songwriters active in the late 1950s, he decided
to use the thirty-two-bar song form:

> I knew this would make the score sound anachronistic; in fact, I hoped it
> would. . . . By 1981 the musical and theatrical language of Broadway had
> evolved considerably, but I hoped to write the score of *Merrily We Roll Along* as
> if I still believed in those conventional forms as enthusiastically as I had twenty-
> five years earlier, before I and my generation had stretched them almost out of
> recognition.[3]

Indeed, many of his shows contain music composed "as if" he were writing decades earlier. Many of his other musicals also openly display his love of pastiche in both lyrics and music, particularly when the plot occupies multiple time periods, either simultaneously or in succession: *Gypsy*, *Follies*, *Pacific Overtures*, *Sunday in the Park with George*, *Assassins*. Even in shows that are set more clearly in the contemporary moment, stylistic pastiche may suddenly appear for comic effect, as in the evocation of the Andrews Sisters in "You Could Drive a Person Crazy" and of vaudeville and soft shoe in "Side by Side by Side/What Would We Do Without You?," both from *Company*. In some cases his music appears to allude to, or at least surprisingly resemble, more contemporaneous music, as with "Unworthy of Your Love" from *Assassins* (1990), which recalls both the music of Karen Carpenter and "I Don't Know How to Love Him" from Lloyd Webber's *Jesus Christ Superstar* (1971), and "We Do Not Belong Together" from *Sunday in the Park* (1984), which resembles the well-known theme from the 1981 movie *Chariots of Fire*.[4]

Finally, Sondheim also clearly delights in referencing historical events in his works, as is evident in both the settings of several of his show's books and in numerous individual songs. These history numbers include "I'm Still Here" from *Follies* and "Bobby and Jackie and Jack" from *Merrily We Roll Along*, prefiguring such history-obsessed list songs as Billy Joel's 1989 "We Didn't Start the Fire." Commenting on the "Fourth Transition"—a number cut after the 1981 premiere of *Merrily We Roll Along* and one that, like the other transitions originally sung by the company, had offered lyrical historical signposts marking the passing years as we travel backward through time—Sondheim remarked: "As is apparent, *Merrily We Roll Along* allowed me to indulge myself in an orgy of history."[5]

\*\*\*

Our title, *Sondheim in Our Time and His*, suggests that much of our focus is likewise historical, as we uncover the aspects of biography, collaborative process, and contemporary context of his time that impacted the creation and reception of Sondheim's musicals. In addition, we explore in detail how his shows have been dramatically revised and adapted over time. Our title also reveals that several chapters will invite us to rethink his works from a distinctly 2020 critical perspective and to consider how these musicals are being reenvisioned today. We note that time and timing are of the essence for Sondheim, in the expression of temporal experience, in the musical timing of individual rhymes, and in the structures of his shows. Our temporal span extends from Sondheim's college theatrical experiences to productions of his musicals on college campuses today. Several of the chapters pursue a distinctly revisionary approach, challenging received critical opinion and, in several cases, Sondheim's own assessments of his works and techniques. Through chapters focused on individual musicals, and others that explore a specific topic as manifested throughout his entire career; by digging deep into the archives and focusing intently on his scores; from our interviews with performers and directors and close study of live and recorded productions–we have aimed throughout to bring together Sondheim's past with the present, thriving existence of his musicals.

The four authors represented in Part I, "Early Stages," identify formative influences and experiences that had a lasting impact on Sondheim's career and point to aspects of his early work that prefigure his later musicals and writings. In addition, these chapters illustrate his critical views and self-criticism. Building on intimate knowledge of Sondheim's stylistic formation and musical education, Steve Swayne provides a portrait of Williams College during Sondheim's time and details his activities, both in the theater and as a budding critic. Swayne also reports the reception of Sondheim's earliest efforts. This focus on institutional history and archival research enables Swayne to suggest the ways in which issues facing Williams in the postwar era shaped Sondheim, including the lack of racial diversity and the reception of Jewish students on campus, particularly given the fact that Sondheim apparently did not self-identify as Jewish at that time. (Knowledge about the fraternity milieu of this all-male college in the late 1940s may also help explain how Sondheim created such testosterone-infused numbers as "Exhibit A" from *Saturday Night* and "Have I Got a Girl for You" from *Company*.)

Basing his work on a detailed study of the surviving manuscripts, Dominic McHugh explores Sondheim's abandoned effort to adapt P. L. Travers's Mary Poppins stories for the musical stage, a project Sondheim pursued in his late college years. McHugh, pushing back at Sondheim's self-criticism, finds much to praise in this work and locates hints of Sondheim's later style and techniques. Though destined to be unfinished and unperformed, *Mary Poppins* displays his skill at transforming a complex literary source for the stage and his rather cinematic approach to constructing crucial scenes as a form of musical montage. Jeffrey Magee establishes the significant impact of Sondheim's encounter with the Actors Studio in the mid-1950s and the role of Arthur Laurents in the development of his dramatic sensibility. Magee uncovers, through archival work and musical analysis, the ways in which the Studio concept of acting with "subtext" shaped Sondheim's composition, pointing to multiple examples in which musical details suggest meanings not inherent in the lyrics. The impact of Laurents on Sondheim's development also proves crucial to James O'Leary's insightful analysis of the often-overlooked musical *Anyone Can Whistle* (1964), the show that Sondheim has deemed his breakout work and one that offered a pointed statement against multiple varieties of social and Broadway conformity. Concluding this section, O'Leary notes that the impact of these early dramaturgical and compositional ideas is evident throughout Sondheim's later career.

The second set of chapters, grouped under the heading "Staging Identities," considers Sondheim's own identity as a white gay Jewish man as well as the sexual, racial, and gendered dimensions of his characters, performers, and audiences, as these authors seek to understand the multitudes of meanings that his musicals have produced. These critical investigations focus our attention on the challenges that these shows present for twenty-first-century theater makers and audiences as revivals restage social attitudes and norms from decades ago. Calling on us to consider race in musical theater from a new perspective, Todd Decker thoroughly unpacks the construction of "whiteness" throughout Sondheim's oeuvre, taking into account aspects of musical style, setting, physical descriptions of characters, and "disposition of mind" as reflected in the lyrics. Decker notes the near total absence of characters of color and of Jewish representation in these musicals and argues that the representation of whiteness has been taken so much for granted in critical studies as to be invisible. In turn, Ashley M. Pribyl discusses the one Sondheim musical that emphatically sought to represent nonwhite characters in an exotic setting and to feature performers of color: *Pacific Overtures* (1976). Pribyl traces the early development of this show in John Weidman's multiple versions of the original script as well as how the message and focus of the musical shifted in the collaborative process of Weidman, Hal Prince, and Sondheim. She argues that the musical, and the original spoken play version in particular, resonated pointedly with the Vietnam War period, and reports on its reception by the Asian American community.

Andrew Buchman's and Stacy Wolf's chapters consider the representation and experience of gender and sexuality in Sondheim's musicals from two very different perspectives. Buchman documents in detail Sondheim's role in shaping the multiple versions of the script of *Company*, revealing the centrality of Sondheim's vision to the dramaturgical development process in his collaboration with George Furth and Prince. He also details the changes to the show that have been made with Sondheim's sanction over the past five decades. Buchman's focus is on how the representation of the central character's sexuality evolved through the numerous drafts and subsequent productions. Based on her extensive interviews and study of recent productions, Wolf explores what Sondheim's works signify on college campuses today, particularly in terms of his representations of female characters and with regard to issues of cross-gender and gender-neutral casting. Wolf notes the abiding popularity of Sondheim's works for college theater programs and presents telling statements made by student performers concerning their perceptions of women's roles in these musicals.

Many Broadway scholars, and, likely, many readers of this book, first experienced Sondheim's works during their college years. My initial intimate encounter with his musicals occurred in November 1987 during my first semester as a student at Amherst College, when I performed as a clarinetist in the pit for a production of *Sweeney Todd* directed by Douglas Anderson. I cherish two indelible memories of this production: first, in Anthony's gorgeous number "Johanna," dissonantly rubbing up against the second clarinet part played by John Cariani, who was inspired by the experience to go on to become a Broadway star, and second, glancing up as the student portraying Judge Turpin in his twisted version of "Johanna" convincingly mimed his masturbatory mea culpa at the apron's edge. I do not recall any cross-gender casting in this 1987 production. Consistent with Wolf's analysis of contemporary college productions, I note that in a 2017 Amherst production of *Sweeney Todd* the lead role was played by Ramona Celis. In the Amherst student newspaper's review of the production, Celis was consistently referred to with female pronouns, and no mention was made of this casting decision. The Smith College student newspaper reviewer, however, consistently employed male pronouns to refer to this performer. Clearly, the state of the art has healthily evolved on college campuses over the past thirty years with regard to gender and casting.[6]

Though we tend to reference individual titles of musicals as if they are fixed objects, holding still for our contemplation, and though we employ the term "Sondheim" and the singular possessive pronoun "His" in our title, most of the chapters in this book do consider the multiple versions and adaptations of these musicals and the collaborative creative processes from which they arose. We also note the divergent sources—short stories, movies, spoken plays—on which these musicals were based, and we discuss Sondheim's dramaturgical instincts and active role in shaping the books of his shows. This is particularly true of the chapters in Part III, "Versions, Genres, and Collaborations." Kim H. Kowalke's chapter is devoted to the astonishing career of *Sweeney Todd*. Kowalke traces this musical's hybridity right back to its relationship with its literary sources and to the divergent visions of Sondheim and Prince as they created the show. He convincingly identifies Brechtian elements, *pace* Sondheim, and discusses the multiple generic juxtapositions that exist between, and within, individual numbers. Finally, Kowalke chronicles the radical reworking of this musical through its numerous productions all the way to Tim Burton's 2007 screen adaptation, concluding that the work's rather protean relationship with genre is the very source of its astonishing success. Continuing this section's focus on individual landmark musicals, Geoffrey Block, countering received critical opinion and Sondheim's own negative views, comes to the defense of the 1978 film adaptation of *A Little Night Music*, a musical that was itself based on a film. Drawing on his archival investigations, Block details the deletions, revisions, and new material created by Sondheim that achieved this transformation of genre. He also considers the broader context of cinematic adaptations of stage musicals during this period and beyond. Block's chapter alerts us to an inherent bias against later adaptations and leads us to consider how received critical consensus tends to predetermine future criticism and our own experience of a work.

In the book's concluding section, "Reconceived Structures and Techniques," we discuss the various ways in which Sondheim repeatedly drew on Broadway's conventions and techniques, only to bend them nearly beyond recognition. His relation to the past seems to involve both a sense of homage and a competitive spirit, as he outdoes the past with more witty and complex rhyme schemes and transforms song types and conventional structures. The innovative approaches to narrative temporality found in many of his musicals established nonlinear plots, the coexistence of past and present on stage within a scene, and the presentation of a dramatic moment from multiple perspectives as perfectly kosher possibilities for the Broadway musical in the late twentieth and early twenty-first centuries. Similarly, in Sondheim's wake, apparently anything may now serve as a source for a musical, including a film, a historical event, fairy tales, a painting, a graphic novel, and a television cartoon.

Jim Lovensheimer explores Sondheim's treatment of time throughout his musicals, focusing on works in which time and memory are central topics and in which presentation of narrative time is anything but conventional and linear. *Company* may be understood as distending one specific moment in time, *Merrily We Roll Along* moves backward through time, *Pacific Overtures* fast forwards many decades at the end, and past and present appear to coexist in *Follies*. Lovensheimer's interpretive work reveals that our relation to time is a consistent philosophical topic in Sondheim's oeuvre. Lara E. Housez offers a highly detailed analysis of another musical that leaps historical time zones: *Sunday in the Park with George*. Housez discloses the intricate connections that exist at seemingly every level between the first and second acts of this musical. She also identifies parallels between Georges Seurat's painting techniques and Sondheim's score and traces Sondheim's penchant for creating intricate designs, in part, to his compositional studies with Milton Babbitt.

Elizabeth A. Wells, occupying the penultimate position in our volume, demonstrates how Sondheim manages to complicate even such a seemingly standard Broadway convention as the 11 o'clock number. Wells helpfully refers to Sondheim's creation of an "11 o'clock principle" as he turns the number into a multipart format in many of his shows. In fact, such numbers frequently do not appear at the penultimate moment at all, or he offers several in a row in this position. Wells's analysis and Sondheim's innovations spur us to realize that our terminology for Broadway numbers and structures is rather loose. With Sondheim we find ourselves repeatedly asking: When is an "I Want" song not just an "I Want" song? Is it possible to deconstruct the kickline? When is an overture not really an overture? (See *Company* for one set of answers.) In my chapter, I bring such an inquisitive spirit to one of the most fundamental features of song writing: rhyme. I start by identifying a few specific figures who shaped Sondheim's approach to rhyme and trace his discussion of this topic over the decades. Working from an investigation of all of Sondheim's shows, I attempt to describe his approach to rhyme and to the musical setting of rhymes, focusing particularly on the role of rhyme in characterization. I consider the differences between diegetic and nondiegetic rhyming and speculate on audience perception of the source of witty and elaborate rhyming within the experience of a live performance. I also address his use of poignant "phantom rhymes," moments when an expected rhyme fails to appear, and note a surprising allusion in *Sunday* to an opera by Stravinsky along the way. Finally, I briefly look to the work of more recent rhyming Broadway songwriters to illustrate Sondheim's profound and lasting impact on the sound and setting of lyrics.

***

As they sing "Our Time" on the rooftop, Frank and Charley are joined by Mary to form a trio. But the number begins with the "company" and ends with "All" singing of "Our dream coming true." Similarly, *Sondheim in Our Time and His* is the result of a collective effort and offers multiple distinct voices discussing Sondheim's work. Taken together, the chapters engage with almost all of his musicals, spanning his long career. Each author offers his or her particular take on Sondheim, on specific features of his work that they find compelling, on associations and meanings that his musicals have suggested to them. Our perspectives certainly differ, and an attentive reader will notice us disagreeing (amicably) in our interpretations here and there, both from chapter to chapter within these covers and even in relation to our prior Sondheim-focused publications.

   Scholars have claimed "our Sondheim" repeatedly over the past several decades. A simple database search (in Répertoire International de Littérature Musicale, for example) reveals that significantly more articles and books have been devoted to his work than to that of such figures as Cole Porter, Richard Rodgers, Jerome Kern, Irving Berlin, or Andrew Lloyd Webber. Like Sondheim, even in our most revisionary moments, we draw here on past exemplary scholarship; on, for example, the foundational work of Stephen Banfield and Joanne Gordon, on (in almost every chapter) the insightful interviews of Mark Eden Horowitz, based on his intimate knowledge of the manuscripts, and, of course, on the numerous commentaries offered by Sondheim himself throughout his long career.[7] And, like Sondheim, we have aimed throughout to "tell 'em things they don't know!" With a mere sixteen performances in its initial Broadway run, *Merrily We Roll Along* is one of Sondheim's least commercially successful shows. Yet, having traveled chronologically and emotionally backward from a rather dark and disillusioned position, the show ends with an anthem of hope and creative potential. Indeed, despite the typical darkness and ambiguities of their plots and characters, his works leave many audience members feeling artistically and intellectually invigorated and more fully alive to the human condition. With these shows, as for Sondheim scholars, "there's so much stuff to sing!"

Before raising the curtain, I would like to take the opportunity to whole-heartedly thank the contributors to this volume for their dedication and time-liness throughout the editorial process. Most of these contributions stem from the Sondheim@90@Williams symposium that was held in early March 2020 in celebration of Sondheim's ninetieth birthday and seventieth Williams College reunion year. In addition to the symposium, that weekend featured an alumni Sondheim recital, a production of *A Little Night Music* by Cap and Bells (the student-run theater group that had proved so central to Sondheim's own col-lege experience), and a new play produced by the Theatre Department titled *Our Time*, which was based on sources documenting the social life and contentious issues experienced at Williams during Sondheim's time there. I am particularly grateful to President Maud Mandel for her enthusiastic support of the entire project from its inception and to the Dean of the Faculty's office for generously funding these events. Rebecca Coyne provided crucial assistance in preparing the manuscript for submission, and Andrew Maillet set the music examples ex-pertly and efficiently. At Oxford University Press, I thank Sean Decker (Assistant Editor) and, particularly, Jane Zanichkowsky for her extraordinarily detailed copyediting. I would also like to thank Norm Hirschy at OUP for his sustained interest, from his attendance at the opening afternoon of the symposium all the way through to the publication of the book that you are now "on the brink" of experiencing in your own time.

## Notes

1. For example, Sondheim has repeatedly referred to the autobiographical aspects of this show, pointing particularly to the number "Opening Doors." Stephen Sondheim, *Finishing the Hat: Collected Lyrics (1954–1981) with Attendant Comments, Principles, Heresies, Grudges, Whines and Anecdotes* (New York: Knopf, 2010), 381–382, 419. On the autobiographical aspects of this musical, see also Andrew Milner, "'Let the Pupil Show the Master': Stephen Sondheim and Oscar Hammerstein II," in *Stephen Sondheim: A Casebook*, ed. Joanne Gordon (New York: Garland, 1997), 162–163.
2. On this subject, see, e.g., Scott Frederick Stoddart, "Visions and Re-Visions: The Postmodern Challenge of *Merrily We Roll Along*," in *Reading Stephen Sondheim: A Collection of Critical Essays*, ed. Sandor Goodhart (New York: Garland, 2000), 187–198; Robert L. McLaughlin, "Sondheim and Postmodernism," in *The Oxford Handbook of Sondheim Studies*, ed. Robert Gordon (New York: Oxford University Press, 2014),

25–38; and Robert L. McLaughlin, *Stephen Sondheim and the Reinvention of the American Musical* (Jackson: University Press of Mississippi, 2016).

3. Sondheim, *Finishing the Hat*, 379, 381. See also Mark Eden Horowitz, *Sondheim on Music: Minor Details and Major Decisions*, 2nd ed. (Lanham, MD: Scarecrow, 2010), 20.

4. Most surprising by far are the, surely coincidental, resemblances between Harry Partch's 1961 *Water! Water! An Intermission with Prologues and Epilogues* and Sondheim's 1964 *Anyone Can Whistle*. Both works are rather eccentric examples from the oeuvres of these two composer-lyricists. Both center on the schemes of a small-town female mayor facing a drought and hard times, and both offer a pointed political satire framed as a farce.

5. Sondheim, *Finishing the Hat*, 402.

6. I note that the Amherst reviewer also neglected to mention Sondheim. See Lorelei Dietz, "'Sweeney Todd' Confronts Audience with Their Inner Demons," *Amherst Student* 146, no. 15 (February 1, 2017). The Smith College reviewer reported: "Ramona Celis '19 played Sweeney Todd, adding depth and humanity to the inhumane actions of his character. His performance showed maturity and sophistication." Patience Kayira, "Murder, Mystery and Madness—A Review of Amherst Musical: *Sweeney Todd*," *Sophian* (February 1, 2017).

7. Stephen Banfield, *Sondheim's Broadway Musicals* (Ann Arbor: University of Michigan Press, 1993); Horowitz, *Sondheim on Music*. For a helpful overview of scholarship on Sondheim, see Robert Gordon, "Sondheim Scholarship: An Overview," *Studies in Musical Theatre* 13, no. 2 (2019): 197–204.

# PART I
# EARLY STAGES

# 1

# Williams College Before, During, and After Sondheim

*Steve Swayne*

Musicological writing about certain genres has often focused on how our under-standing of those genres has been shaped by extraordinary contributions from (almost exclusively) white men: the symphony and Beethoven; the opera and Wagner; popular song and Tin Pan Alley, Broadway, and Hollywood tunesmiths. Occasionally we reflect on how institutions shape artists: Johann Sebastian Bach and the Thomaskirche; Franz Joseph Haydn and Esterháza. In this chapter I at-tempt to wed these two approaches by looking at an institution that had reached a crossroads of its own at a time when an impressionable young artist entered its hallways and made it his home. In doing so, I aim to explore our understandings of that person, that institution, and that time—Stephen Sondheim and Williams College, 1946–1950—and recast them by drawing on writings from that era, compare them with subsequent retellings and recollections of those years, and position these alongside our received and imaginary narratives of the man, the college, and postwar America, as they all played out in northwestern Massachusetts.

## Establishing the Establishment

Williams, the second college founded in Massachusetts and the sixth in New England, has its own complicated genesis story.[1] Nearly forty years elapsed from the death of Ephraim Williams on September 8, 1755, near Lake George, New York, in the French and Indian Wars to the 1793 founding of the school that bears his name and was built on some of his property. The "appalling loneliness" or the "utter calm" found there (take your pick of contemporaneous quotations) was nearly disrupted when Williams president Zephaniah Swift Moore sought to move the school to Northampton, Massachusetts, in the late 1810s. This act, blocked by the state legislature, eventually led to the defection of Moore and some faculty with the founding of Amherst College in 1821. In response to what became known as the "Amherst Crisis," a group of Williams graduates came

Steve Swayne, *Williams College Before, During, and After Sondheim* In: *Sondheim in Our Time and His.*
Edited by: W. Anthony Sheppard, Oxford University Press. © Oxford University Press 2022.
DOI: 10.1093/oso/9780197603192.003.0002

together to start an alumni association, making Williams the first institution in America, and likely the world, to create such an entity.

Another feature of American life of the past two hundred years also found its start at Williams College. Most students of American Christendom have heard of the Haystack Meeting of 1806, which served as the impetus for U.S. involvement in foreign missionary work. Few recall that this meeting occurred near the Williams campus as five undergraduates, praying earnestly for the unconverted in other lands, sought shelter under a haystack from a summer thunderstorm. These men, captured by "the spirit of piety," were studying at a college founded during the French Revolution and devoted to secular study. This tension was felt through the decades as the liberality of New England Congregationalism and the dictates of evangelical Christianity stretched the sinews of the school up to and beyond its abandonment of required chapel attendance in the 1960s.

Until the 1960s Williams's most illustrious graduate was James Abram Garfield, Class of 1856. Garfield and other Williams alumni and friends of the college celebrated the holidays in 1872 at a dinner at Delmonico's in New York. That evening Garfield allegedly minted the mythology of alumnus-turned-professor-turned-president Mark Hopkins and the log: "The ideal college is Mark Hopkins on one end of a log and a student on the other." (Hopkins served as president from 1836 to 1872.) The truth, though, is more complicated. At the time Williams was suffering from the ennui and lack of focus attending its long-serving president, and Garfield felt compelled to counter any aspersions cast against the man who steered his alma mater. Garfield himself became a president—the twentieth president of the United States and the second to be assassinated. And, as fate would have it, he was commemorated in a musical by a fellow Williams alumnus, although there is no mention in *Assassins* that Garfield was apparently on his way to Williamstown to escape the summer heat of the district when Charlie Guiteau slowly sent Garfield to his Lordy. (Garfield lingered for two months before he died on September 19, 1881, of his gunshot wounds.)

The *Williams Pictorial History* states that on July 6, 1881, "the New Williams may be said to have begun," a reference not to Guiteau's July 2 act but to the inauguration of Franklin Carter, the first scholar-president in Williams's history, who inaugurated the new Williams, one that had scholarly aspirations. That new Williams, like the old one, would atrophy to a point where yet another resuscitation was necessary.

That jolt into a new reality began in the 1930s, when the Carter-inspired new Williams came face to face with the prejudices rife in Depression-era America. Although Williams had graduated non-white men before this decade, president Tyler Dennett (1934–1937) went out of his way to restrict matriculation to certain applicants. Indeed, he actively discouraged some categories of men from applying at all: Negroes, Catholics, and Jews. Dennett also wanted to reduce the number of "nice boy" matriculants—"nice boys" being his dismissive term for graduates of New England prep schools, who made up 81 percent of the freshman class in 1937—and given the discrimination already present in these prep schools, it wasn't difficult to keep the numbers of Jews, Catholics, and blacks down prior to Dennett's arrival. His push to include more public-school boys did not extend to those who weren't from White Anglo-Saxon Protestant (WASP) stock.[2]

In order to gain a sense about how successful this suppression was and how it infected nearly every element of American college life in the Northeast, consider this report from Stephen Birmingham, Class of 1950, who spoke fifty years after the fact about opening doors at Williams. He muses about his fraternity, Beta Theta Pi.

As the most forward-thinking social group on campus, it was natural that we Betas should want to be the first to break down all the old traditions and restrictions that had clung to college fraternities since the nineteenth century. Wouldn't it be swell, we told ourselves, if we could be the first fraternity at Williams to take in a black lowerclassman? It turned out, however, that there was only one black student in the freshman class that year, and this left us a very small pool to choose from. If he were invited to join Beta, it would look as though we were trying a bit too hard to make a political statement. Furthermore, this young man, a personable fellow to be sure, made it very clear that he did not want to be the token black in an all-white fraternity. Nor did he wish to incur the flood of national publicity that would certainly ensue if he were to be taken in.[3]

Robert Hickerson of Camden, New Jersey, may have been the black student to whom Birmingham was referring; Hickerson is easily identifiable as African American by thumbing through the 1950 *Gulielmensian* (the Williams yearbook) and spotting the photo of the sole Williams man who visibly looks black.[4] (Other fair-skinned blacks may have also been in attendance at the time.)

In its apparent monochromaticism, Williams looked like many other institutions of its day. At the George School, a prep school in Newtown, Bucks County, Pennsylvania, founded by Quakers, the first identified black student was a member of the Class of 1947; Sondheim, who attended the school as a day (nonboarding) student, was Class of 1946. Alongside Sondheim's upbringing in Manhattan and Bucks County, these truths help explain the nearly all-white world of a typical Sondheim musical. There simply weren't a lot of people of color in his early life. It remains to other scholars to investigate the race of the tenant farmers who grew alfalfa on Sondheim's mother's Doylestown farm and discover how many nonwhites were on the faculty and staffs of the George School and

Williams at this time. The college's bicentennial history tells of previous generations of black Williams students who traveled to North Adams for dances that were sponsored by the Pullman porters who came through town on the trains and who would, in turn, ferry the black students back to campus in private cars. The George School and Williams during Sondheim's time constituted a white, white, white, white world.[5]

The fact that Williams wholly gave itself over to the war effort in the first half of the 1940s did not change this whiteness in any appreciable way, given that the armed forces were segregated at the time, though this, too, would change by the end of the 1940s. World War II both saved and irrevocably altered Williams. Several Williams professors and staff decamped to help the federal government, including President James Phinney Baxter III, who served first as the research director for the Coordinator of Information and then as deputy director of the Office of Strategic Services. Moreover, Williams gave itself over to becoming a preflight training ground for the U.S. Navy beginning in 1943; in order to accommodate the cadets, Williams temporarily suspended all fraternities until after the war. Indeed, nearly four thousand Navy trainees were present during these years, when the graduating class of 1945 numbered four men, the fewest in 150 years. Even after the war had ended, Williams had a sizable number of G.I.s on campus who were not matriculated students, some of whom brought their wives.

Immediately after the war, Williams underwent a tremendous growth spurt. The college's March 1947 catalog provides the numbers. In March 1946, 511 students attended Williams. In June of that year, 80 additional students arrived. Four months later, when Sondheim entered, enrollment rose from 591 students to 1,059 students, a nearly 80 percent increase. For all intents and purposes, the Williams of fall 1946 was nothing like the Williams that every previous student had known. A new-new Williams was being born.

This did not stop some administrators, alumni, and students from trying to preserve the old-new Williams. These rearguard actions coalesced around the role that fraternities would play in the postwar Williams. In the spring of 1944, a year into the suspension of the fraternity system on campus,

> a substantial group of faculty members [wrote to] Baxter [outlining] detailed criticisms of the adverse scholastic and social influences of the prewar fraternity system. These criticisms were documented with factual data. A few of the faculty group at first advocated complete abolition of the fraternity system as the only solution.[6]

This information is contained in a January 1946 report filed by a committee convened to study the social climate at Williams generally and the role of fraternities specifically. The report concludes this recitation of the feelings of certain faculty members by noting that "after a year and a half of study, no one of this group is now actively advocating such abolition." Indeed, the committee's report makes it clear that it did not recommend this action, citing primarily the social and economic benefits to the college that the fraternity system afforded. But it did make one recommendation that, from this distance, seems somewhat petty: Move the fraternity rush period from the beginning of the freshman year to the beginning of the sophomore year. This recommendation received substantial pushback from some of the committee members, with fourteen in favor and ten opposed.

The overarching question was one of how much of Williams's social life would rest in the hands of the fraternities, which were controlled, by and large, by alumni who, in some cases, were eager to preserve Williams from infiltration by blacks, Catholics, and Jews. This is made explicit in the report's recommendation that "election to fraternity membership should be on the basis of individual qualities and without prejudice as to race, creed or color."[7] Although the *Beta Book* of 1927, the governing text of the national fraternity, says nothing that could be parsed as discriminating against members along such lines, it was well understood that national fraternities looked down on the idea of chapters' inducting members who did not resemble their predecessors; that is, there was a strong if unspoken understanding that a fraternity man was an upstanding WASP.[8] This lay behind Birmingham's conspiratorial conceit that inviting a black man to join Beta would elicit a conniption fit in the national office. Given that the most promising—and perhaps the only—black candidate turned Beta down, Birmingham took the conspiracy in another, and sadly predictable, direction. If inducting a black man wasn't in the cards, Birmingham opined,

> our next best idea was that our chapter of Beta Theta Pi would be the first Beta chapter in the country to take in a Jewish member—and not one of the upper-crust German-Jewish banking elite, as the Phi Gams had done. There was a largish group of Jewish freshmen to select from, and the young man picked was my classmate, Stephen Sondheim.[9]

With Birmingham's dramatic introduction of the man at the other end of the log, as it were, it is time to recount the history that brings Sondheim to this moment in Williams's history.

## "What Is a Jew, Anyway?"

In her biography of Sondheim, Meryle Secrest stated that Sondheim's reason for choosing Williams for his college experience revolved first and foremost around the Adams Memorial Theatre, completed in 1941 and underutilized during the war years for dramatic productions. It had state-of-the-art equipment, and it is easy to imagine that Sondheim and Oscar Hammerstein II discussed the hands-on theater experience that the former would gather at Williams. (Hammerstein owned a farm just outside of Doylestown, and from 1942 onward Sondheim became a regular fixture at the Hammerstein household by virtue of his friendship with Jamie Hammerstein, Oscar's son, who was one year younger than Sondheim.) But another reason why Sondheim selected Williams appears to be that he wasn't the only graduate of the George School who did so. Andrew Heineman, Sondheim's classmate and a graduate of Horace Mann in New York, recalled that "four of [the members of the Class of 1950] came from the George School. . . . The four of them decided to go to Williams together and I just never really thought much about it."[10] Actually, there were six newcomers in the fall of 1946 who made their way to Williams via the Quaker school in Pennsylvania:

- Jeremy Tyler Dresser, from Manhattan, who later joined the Garfield Club (the nonfraternity alternative at Williams in those days),
- Ralph Edward Gomory, from Brooklyn, who also joined the Garfield Club and who played on the football team,
- John Mason Jr., from Westport, Connecticut, a veteran who pledged Alpha Delta Phi and graduated in 1949,
- Walter Stabler, from Manhasset, New York, another veteran and a legacy who pledged Phi Gamma Delta,
- Christopher Wright, from Moylan, Pennsylvania, who also joined the Garfield Club,
- and Sondheim.[11]

Given that Mason and Stabler were veterans, it is unlikely that they graduated from the George School in the same year as did Dresser, Gomory, Sondheim, and Wright. Moreover, although Williams was still drawing heavily from private schools at this time—72 percent in September 1946[12]—having six members from this particular private school was unusual, not only for its physical distance from Williams but more for its theological distance: The Religious Society of Friends (Quakers) resides on the periphery of the mainline Protestantism that marked Williams for most of its history. Notwithstanding these distances, someone from the Williams admissions office paid a visit to the George School before applications came in for the Class of 1951 to see if the admissions office might repeat the success of the previous year. The result: the Class of 1951 included twenty-one men from Deerfield Academy, fourteen from Phillips Exeter, nine from Andover, six from St. Paul's in Concord, New Hampshire . . . and none from the George School.[13]

At this distance, determining whether Sondheim convinced his George School classmates to follow him to Williams or whether they decided collectively to head to northwestern Massachusetts may be a fool's errand. Yet I am reminded that the collegian who put on two musicals at Williams when no college musicals had been done there before was the same kid who put on *By George* at the George School. Sondheim got things done, in part because of his connections to theater royalty but also in part because of his ability to convince his classmates at both institutions to go along with his ideas.

Coming from Manhattan placed Sondheim squarely within the plurality of men who enrolled at Williams; New York, Massachusetts, and Connecticut—in that order—made up the top three home states for Williams men, so three more boys from Brooklyn and Manhattan was nothing new for the rural campus. But arriving at Williams at the age of sixteen unquestionably placed Sondheim on the young side of the ledger at a time when 73 percent of the student body in September 1946 consisted of veterans, sixty-nine of whom were married men (almost 20 percent of all new students).[14] The gap between prep school boys reliving their teenage exploits and men who served their country during wartime was wittily illustrated in a cartoon that appeared in the same newspaper issue where all 352 men in this record-breaking freshman class were individually named along with the city and high school they were coming from, their local housing arrangement, and their status as veterans and legacy admissions (see figure 1.1). Sondheim's young age and Manhattanite sophistication set him apart from both the old-money tweedy preppies and the skilled servicemen either returning to their college studies or embarking on them for the first time. His outsider status

"And Remember Last Spring at Deerfield, when . . . . ."

**Figure 1.1.** Smoking as a common denominator: veterans and preppies at Williams College. *Williams Record*, September 27, 1946, 3.

further extended to his association with two industries that, at the time, were marked as the province for Jews: the garment industry and the theater.

Secrest traced Sondheim's lineage back to Jewish immigrants from Germany (paternal) and Lithuania (maternal). By the time of Sondheim's birth, both of his parents were working in fashion design and manufacturing and had done well enough financially to allow for reconnaissance trips to Paris and relocation to the newly built San Remo on Central Park West. Herbert and Janet (who went by Foxy, derived from her maiden name of Fox) separated in the early 1940s and divorced later in the decade after Herbert had met Alicia Babé, a blonde Catholic Cuban American, and had fathered two sons with her. By Secrest's telling, neither Foxy nor Herbert did much to affirm their Jewish heritage, and Secrest's indication that Foxy "had her prominent nose reconfigured" at some point suggests that both of Stephen's parents sought to blend into the majority white American culture without having to address their Jewish roots.[15]

All this helps explain the revelation that, when Sondheim arrived in Williamstown, he did not understand himself to be Jewish at all. Evidence for this can be found, first of all, in his transcript, where "church affiliation of student" is recorded and the handwritten entry states "none."[16] More telling are the recollections of his fellow students and Sondheim's own attestation of his religious and ethnic understanding:

> Steve Sondheim, aware of the kerfuffle his proposed membership [in Beta Theta Pi] was causing, announced that he wasn't Jewish. "I'm a Quaker," he insisted. He based this on the fact that he had graduated from the George School, a Quaker prep school in Pennsylvania. "What is a Jew, anyway?" he demanded. I admitted that I didn't really know the answer to that one. Can you call Jewishness a race, when there are no real racial characteristics? . . . When Steve Sondheim asked me this, all I could say was, "Oh, for heaven's sake. Your father is a Seventh Avenue cloak-and-suiter. Of course you're Jewish!"[17]

If this sounds comical and uncomfortably stereotypical, consider Heineman's recollection:

> The Beta House, which didn't take Jews, had Steve Sondheim, who was my roommate. But Steve Sondheim didn't know he was Jewish. He thought he was a Quaker. And he came to me one day and he said, "I'm told I'm Jewish. Is that true?" I said, "Yes, it is." So we had a long discussion, which I mean, that happened in those days.[18]

These two reminiscences take us back to the 1946 George School contingent and their eventual associations at Williams. The two veterans pledged fraternities;

the three classmates of Sondheim joined the Garfield Club, the social option for men who, for whatever reason, did not join fraternities. And Sondheim became a Beta: a Jew to the goyim, someone whose family life did not lead him to self-identify as Jewish, and someone who respected the principles of Quakerism when he matriculated at Williams.[19]

## Criticism: Taking It in and Dishing It Out

The veneer of his Protestant prep school education appears to have allowed Sondheim to enter into the more prestigious social world of the fraternity system. And with that social springboard and the cachet he earned through his work in the theater, Sondheim literally made a name for himself on campus. During his four years there, he appears in the student newspaper no fewer than sixty times. Some of these mentions are perfunctory, such as his inclusion on various lists: new freshmen, inductees into Phi Beta Kappa, the dean's list, and graduates. Much more frequently his name appears in stories in which he is praised for his acting ability and lauded for his theatrical and literary contributions.[20] And in no fewer than three articles, the byline is "Steve Sondheim."[21]

His first article, a review of a theatrical adaptation of *Alice in Wonderland* that appeared during his sophomore fall semester, landed him in hot water. Peggy Lamson, an aspiring playwright and the wife of Roy Lamson, a professor in the English department, had already worked with Sondheim. He had appeared during his freshman spring semester as a spy in her play *Trade Name*, a "comedy-melodrama [that] deals with the top secret experiments the OSS conducted during the war to select agents for behind-the-lines duty," and he received plaudits for "convincingly act[ing] the part of an insurance salesman uneasy in his assumed role as a bandleader."[22] Six months later, Lamson lambasted Sondheim and his fellow contributors to the *Purple Cow*, a satirical magazine run by students:

> The PURPLE COW cannot boast of a point of view, a sense of humor or a literary style. Taken as a whole it adds up to approximately zero. It is therefore not surprising that contributors to the magazine are unable to raise their heads above a standard which sets mediocrity as its highest goal....
>
> Stephen Sondheim's "Cocktail Party" is a good example of bright forced, writing [*sic*] about three unrealistic and totally unbelievable people. Mr. Sondheim writes good descriptive prose and shows a marked facility with his pen, but his writing becomes lost in his inept characterizations.[23]

Less than a month later, the *Williams Record* ran two reviews of Lamson's adaptation of *Alice in Wonderland*. One, by Charles Klensch, is titled "wmsy," and its lowercase presentation and profusion of insider humor seemed to gloss over whatever shortcomings the reviewer had noticed ("the play was weakest throughout in the transitions between the carroll dialog").[24] The second was much more in the spirit of a theater critic:

> As a play, it turned out to be in part excellent, in a larger part dull, even boring. . . .
>
> The very fact that you can see Carroll's puns a mile of dialogue away is one of their charms and no charge can be made against the lines themselves. But it seems to me that the job of the adaptor is to prune unessential lines and parts of scenes which, however amusing in book form, lose life when presented on the stage where there is no prose description accompanying them. Such was the case during the first act of this Alice In Wonderland. . . .
>
> As Alice herself, ten-year-old Patsy Lamson had the most difficult role of the evening and I am sorry to report she was not successful in overcoming it. Alice is a very proper and sane little girl but she is nevertheless interesting and fun to know. Patsy managed to convey the first two qualities but not the latter, the result being that the character of Alice emerged as somewhat obnoxious. This was in part due to the direction of her opening scene[,] which stilted her gestures to the point of distraction (such as the foot-stamping and arm waving orgy which she indulged in) and in part due to the fact that it takes a more mature person than a ten-year-old to interpret Alice properly.
>
> As the fussy White Rabbit, Gordon Bullett was very funny, though he had a hard time keeping a straight face when he had to blow the trumpet in the Trial scene. Jerry O'Brien as the Caterpillar and Mr. Faison as the Frog Footman both got the most they could out of essentially dull parts. Mr. Pierson, of the Art Department appropriately enough, played the Mad Hatter. On the whole his was an enjoyable performance, but he indulged in a little too much mugging, and playing to the audience. . . .
>
> One thing more. I repeat that this review is personal and is probably contrary to a great many other opinions. The majority of comments which I heard after the play were most decidedly favorable, and the play did gross three hundred and fifteen dollars clear profit for a local charity, which deserves a hand even from those who didn't enjoy it unreservedly.[25]

With this review, the seventeen-year-old Sondheim made his writing debut on the pages of the student newspaper. And one can see him, at this early age, misjudging and overestimating his audience. Here he criticized the wife and daughter of a professor in whose department he intended, at that point, to earn his degree, and while the student veterans probably paid him no attention—they may not have come to the show or read theater reviews—the genteel worlds of women's faculty clubs and boarding school decorum found his review wanting (notwithstanding the fact that a professor's wife had previously publicly disparaged the work of students).[26]

A letter to the editor asked for clarification concerning why two reviews were deemed necessary in the first place. Then, after comparing the two reviews, the writer gets to his point:

> Almost everyone except Mr. Sondheim seems to have thought very well of the performance of the title role. But even if his remarks on it were justified on a purely critical basis, few persons would be proud to have written them.
>
> I am wondering what moved Mr. Sondheim to feel this second review was desirable. I can only suggest that he, like others of your correspondents, suffers from digital diarrhea.

The paper's editors appended a lengthy note:

> Despite Reader Faison's expressed satisfaction with the Wmsy review of the ALICE production, the editorial board of the Record and columnist Klensch felt that the production merited a fuller, more thorough-going review than the one originally printed.
>
> The Record then asked Steve Sondheim to write a full review. We felt that Sondheim was qualified to write such an article, for, though he has not contributed to this newspaper before, he has written a number of articles for the Purple Cow and has worked in several Adams Memorial Theatre productions—including, incidentally, the trial run of Peggy Lamson's "Trade Name" last spring.
>
> What Sondheim had to say about the play, as Faison points out, was "purely personal." The Record policy has been, and will continue to be, to allow reviewers a free hand in their criticisms.
>
> We believe the what-is-the-story-on-the-Record-policy query is legitimate. The Sondheim review should have been explained. In the future, Record reviews will be featured articles, rather than sidelines of personal columns.[27]

Klensch was one of the paper's editors at the time. Another, Josiah T. S. Horton, would play a prominent role in returning Sondheim to the good graces of the Williams community. For his part, Sondheim mined the controversy for laughs.

In "The Pail Runneth Over," Sondheim composed a mock review of the *Record* for the *Purple Cow*. His writing had appeared in the *Cow* as early as December 1946, just four months after his arrival on campus. Less than a year later, he answered Lamson's brickbat with one of his own.

(LAMSON) If the Cow wants to be a funny magazine it must be funnier—much
     funnier. If it wants to be a literary magazine its literary content must be greatly
     strengthened, and if it wants to be a magazine of undergraduate opinion it must
     establish itself as such by presenting a reasonably wide cross-section of stu-
     dent views on matters of collegiate importance. If on the other hand the Cow
     wants to continue as a pot-pourri it must somehow contrive to use topnotch
     ingredients instead of the very mediocre fare which makes up the current issue.
(SONDHEIM) If the Record wants to be funny, it must be funnier—much funnier.
     If it wants to be literary, it must be literarier—much literarier. You cannot put
     sports stories next to the editorial page. In fact, anything and everything the
     Record does is wrong. The cartoons are bad, the paper is bad, the print is bad,
     the masthead is bad. . . .
(LAMSON) It would have been pleasant and agreeable to give the magazine and its
     editors a better send off on its new season. But unfortunately the only send off
     this reviewer can honestly recommend for the Purple Cow is one which will lead
     it to extinction and make way for a fresh literary magazine of a calibre worthy of
     the abilities which must and do exist on the Williams College campus.
(SONDHEIM) I would *so* much have liked to give the Record a good review, but my
     honest opinion would only send it into oblivion and make way for the Cow to
     take over all Williams journalistic efforts.[28]

Birmingham called Sondheim "a smarty-pants. The genius at the putdown or send-
up. He had professors scared of him."[29] And perhaps professor's wives as well.

Yet there was no denying Sondheim's prodigious talents in the classroom, on the
boards, and between the pages. His sophomore spring semester arguably represented
his high-water mark in terms of his esteem across the campus, based primarily on his
work at the Adams Memorial Theatre. He had turned heads with his performances
in two different productions in which he played the blind seer Tiresias: Sophocles's
*Oedipus Rex* and Jean Cocteau's *Infernal Machine*.[30] And then he and Horton brought
something to the campus no one had ever experienced before.

## A Star Is Born

On Friday, April 30, 1948, *Phinney's Rainbow* opened at the Adams. With music
by Sondheim and book and lyrics by Sondheim and Horton, it received encomia
for its ambition before the curtains parted. "The musical's cast of 52 students is the
largest since 'Marco Millions' celebrated the opening of the AMT in 1941," noted
the *Williams Record*.[31] And its four-performance run—including two shows that
were part of house party weekend (that is, when women came to campus)—was
greeted enthusiastically by Klensch, who penned an effusive review:

"Phinney's Rainbow," the Sondheim and Horton musical comedy which pokes gentle fun at our dandy little school, thinly disguised as Swindlehurst Prep, is the biggest thing that has hit the campus since the April Fool issue of The Record. . . . It has been argued that singing songs is not the way to achieve that elusive quality known as "school spirit," but "Phinney's Rainbow" has demonstrated that it damn sure helps.[32]

Sondheim capped off the year by starring in *Night Music Fall* by Emlyn Williams, earning the best reviews he was to receive as an actor at Williams, as exemplified by Paul K. Barstow:

[He] gave a vivid and credible characterization in the difficult role of the murderous Dan. For the first time on the A. M. T. stage, he gave rein to the high talents which have previously been confined. Here at last, is an actor who knows how to use his whole body dramatically. His gestures, movements, and even the angles of his body anticipated, participated in and completed his vocal presentation of the character. His hands were never idle or awkward, but beautifully expressive at all times. He was acting every minute he was on the stage, and acting very well.[33]

And in the next issue of the school newspaper, which appeared at the start of Sondheim's junior year, readers discovered that not only was Sondheim elected to the Cap and Bells Council as the representative for acting but that, over the summer, he had written a second musical that, if all went well, would be for that year what *Phinney's Rainbow* was for the preceding one.[34]

Secrest quoted Sondheim as saying that, after having played Dan, his interest in becoming an actor faded.[35] He appeared onstage in three more Cap and Bells productions, and immediately after leaving Williams he worked in summer stock at the Westport, Connecticut, Country Playhouse.[36] He continued on the Cap and Bells Council in his junior and senior years, and he was listed along with David C. Bryant, director of the Adams Memorial Theatre, as the producer for *Where To From Here?*, the hastily assembled revue that Cap and Bells produced in May 1950 after plans to mount *High Tor*, Sondheim's second "apprentice" musical, were scrapped because Maxwell Anderson would not give Sondheim the rights to his play.[37] For that revue, noted the *Williams Record*,

two very considerable talents were brought together when Miss Virginia Knapp, an artist with an extraordinarily rich and beautifully modulated mezzo-soprano, sang Stephen Sondheim's "No Sad Songs For Me." It was an achievement of a high order, belonging well outside the recognized limits of a college musical.[38]

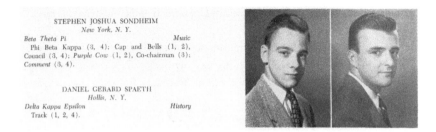

**Figure 1.2.** Sondheim's entry in the *Gulielmensian* 1950, 73.

Knapp and Sondheim reprised their performance a week later at a two-and-one-half-hour outdoor festival ("Main Street Jamboree") at which Sondheim further regaled the audience by (according to the *Record*) playing the score of *High Tor*, "which was scheduled to have been produced on the AMT stage this season."[39] And the yearbook entry for his senior year runs longer than those for most of his classmates (see figure 1.2). On graduation, he was esteemed and estimable.

Before I circle back to Sondheim's junior-year exploits, I invite the reader to notice the continued high esteem in which various writers for the *Record* held Sondheim all the way through to his graduation. Moreover, in his junior and senior years, Sondheim worked closely with Bryant. All this complicates Heineman's report that Sondheim "had a rough time in many ways" in Williams's theater community, especially Heineman's assertion that Bryant was jealous of Sondheim because of the latter's talents.[40]

Certainly, Sondheim had connections that Bryant could well have envied, most notably Hammerstein, who had laid out for Sondheim a syllabus to hone his abilities as a writer of musical theater: Adapt a play you admire (Sondheim chose Kaufman and Connelly's *Beggar on Horseback*); adapt a play you think would be improved in a musical treatment (Anderson's *High Tor*); adapt a non-dramatic work such as a novel or short story (Travers's *Mary Poppins*); and write an original work (*Climb High*).[41] Between Hammerstein's likely encouragement and the apparent ease with which Sondheim acquired the rights to *Beggar* from Kaufman and Connelly, *High Tor* would have premiered in the spring of 1950 at Williams had Anderson given his permission. And Bryant seemed poised to direct this second apprentice musical. Instead, the *Review* announced,

the AMT musical production of 1950, "Where To From Here?" [will have] its three-night stand May 11–13. The producers anticipate a sell-out performance, if last year's acclaim is any indication.

"Where To From Here?" takes up where "Phinney's Rainbow" left off, in presenting the experiences of a typical Williams alumnus. The time sequence covers commencement to class reunion. Original music and lyrics appear throughout this comedy. . . .

The book is a series of skits, connected by the central theme "what happens to the Williams man after graduation." Ida Kay will do the choreography, and Edward Farrow '50 will provide the piano accompaniment.[42]

Three things about this story stand out. First and foremost, its subheading—"Student Comedy Sequel to 'Phinney's Rainbow'"—references a musical that had been performed in 1948, *two years prior* to *Where To From Here?* Second, the musical that was performed in 1949 apparently was well received in some quarters (note the mention of "last year's acclaim") but remains unnamed. Third, Sondheim is not mentioned at all in this notice. Now we can return to Sondheim's first apprentice musical, for the events surrounding its production, its unexpected reincarnations and champions, and a hazing of sorts that occurred soon after its closing collectively suggest that *All That Glitters* and Sondheim's junior year at Williams made for "a rough time in many ways."

## Supernova

The anticipation on campus concerning *All That Glitters* feels palpable even from this distance: "A hot rumor around the AMT has it that Steve Sondheim has written a new musical which will be produced later in the year," reported the *Williams Review*.[43] No fewer than twenty-one stories in the *Record* mention Sondheim by name during his junior year: one announces a radio play he wrote (*The Rats in the Walls*) that aired just days before the musical, two are about his work for the *Purple Cow* (with one indicating that he had been named its co-chairman), four review his acting, and thirteen cover various aspects of *All That Glitters*:

- the "hot rumor" printed in the year's first issue
- the decision about its name and a précis of the musical's materials[44]
- the disappointment at discovering that the gift from Hammerstein of the Broadway sets for *Annie Get Your Gun* could not be accepted due to moving costs that involved union workers[45]
- an interview with Sondheim[46]
- a feature on the dance sequence[47]
- the assurance that the musical was a social highlight for a weekend during which the sophomores invited women to "invade" the campus[48]
- a review of the musical (the headline suggests that everyone received a "shiner"—a black eye—for their efforts)[49]

- a mention of *Variety*'s review of the musical[50]
- a letter to the editor from Irwin Shainman, one of Sondheim's music professors[51]
- three announcements and one review that mention the song "When I See You" from the musical, which was performed in concert by the Williams and Wellesley joint choral ensembles in an arrangement by Robert Barrow, another of Sondheim's music professors.[52] (The third, Joaquín Nin-Culmell, was on sabbatical that year.)

Professors support students in ways too numerous to count, but seeing two of Sondheim's bring public attention to his "excellent score" (Shainman) so soon after its performance suggests that they felt the need to bolster their star student. For his part, Shainman expressed frustration that, to him, so few students turned out to support the efforts of so many others, although the attendance figure that he promulgated would represent more than 40 percent of the student body. As for Barrow, Shainman later said, "I doubt Bob Barrow ever attended a performance of a Sondheim show while he was at Williams, and I don't think he ever went to one in New York, either."[53] That may be true, but there is no evidence that Sondheim, who wasn't involved in the Williams choral scene, asked Barrow to arrange a song from his newest musical for the spring concert. Instead, it appears that, at a minimum, Sondheim showed Barrow the song, and Barrow agreed to take the time to cast it for men's chorus. Given the shiner that Sondheim suffered in the public eye, it seems just as likely that Barrow saw the promotion of his arrangement as a way of signaling his approval of Sondheim's art.

The entry in the 1949 yearbook calls *All That Glitters* a "resounding success," and by the numbers it was successful, in no small part due to how well Sondheim's musical of the previous year had done.[54] Most attendees must have entered the theater expecting a night like the one a year earlier, and few at Williams questioned Sondheim's creativity and fecundity. But after the final curtain had come down, the majority opinion appeared to be that the show missed the mark.

In his review of *All That Glitters*, Edwin N. Perrin foreshadowed countless future critics who have had to write about a Sondheim musical, writing,

The best basis of comparison for this play would probably be last year's hit, "Phinney's Rainbow"—and in such a comparison the 1949 entrant comes out a clear loser. The reason, I think, is not entirely that "Phinney's Rainbow" had local reference while "All That Glitters" is more ambitious in its scope. It is not even that Josiah T. S. [Horton, Sondheim's collaborator on *Phinney*'s book and lyrics] has graduated. The answer, I think, is this: "Phinney's Rainbow" made no attempt to be Serious Art; it was satirical throughout, and even poked fun at its love interest. Sondheim's new musical, on the other hand, seeks to mix parody and social significance, to combine a straight romantic love affair with biting satire. To me it seems an unstable compound, and I believe that the play would have been better had it stuck to parody.[55]

The alchemy that Sondheim pursued in 1949 struck most theatergoers, then and now, as a fool's errand. But it is an alchemy that Sondheim unrelentingly pursued, as can be seen in his remarks twelve years later to a writer for the *Record* who sought to capture that year's top stories, the undisputed one being Baxter's retirement after twenty-four years as Williams's president:

4 MARCH—"Musical theatre is heading away from the classic style of musical comedy. I think that serious characters can be integrated with serious music and the result will be entertaining."
—Stephen Sondheim '50, lyricist for
**West Side Story** and **Gypsy**.[56]

So said the Williams prodigy who, when these words appeared, had yet to have his music performed on Broadway. As for the musicals he composed and performed on the Adams Memorial Theatre stage, there was no question: His audience in 1949 wanted a sequel to 1948's *Phinney's Rainbow*, and they would get one in 1950's *Where To From Here?*, for which Sondheim was only one participant of many.

If Bryant and Sondheim had been thinking of mounting *High Tor*, notwithstanding the reception of *All That Glitters*, it makes some sense that Sondheim would not become president of Cap and Bells in the spring of 1949. For one student to commandeer the college's main performance space for three evening-long performances of original work boggles the mind; for that student also to take the reins of its student-run organization might have been a bridge too far for everyone. Sondheim was not snubbed at the theater. But he was snubbed by his classmates during the Gargoyles' public initiation ceremony.

Twenty men from the class of 1950 were tapped this afternoon by Gargoyle, senior honorary society, to fill its fifty-sixth delegation. Reviving to the customary Memorial Day tapping, today's exercises closely approximated the original ceremony in 1895.

After the class of 1950 marched to the fence led by its class officers, the Gargoyle delegation clad in caps and gowns . . . emerged from Jesup Hall and marched the length of the fence before the second term juniors. Returning in the same manner, the Gargoyles formed a circle in front of the laboratory, between the audience and the class to be tapped.

Each Gargoyle then withdrew from the ring, again walking the length of the fence before the juniors, and on his return, he pulled his man from the fence and led him into the circle.[57]

Sondheim, who was not chosen, watched as classmate Daniel Pynchon received the Grosvenor Memorial Cup, "bestowed each year on that member of the junior class who 'best exemplifies the traditions of Williams.' A committee from the retired undergraduate council makes the selection."[58] Pynchon played hockey, lacrosse, and football at Williams; just as important, he was a member of the Williams Christian Association and served on the Chapel Committee.

In his sophomore year Sondheim's star was approaching its zenith; a successful second musical in his junior year would have made him indisputably a Big Man on Campus. Yet by the end of that junior year, he had been slighted for two of Williams's highest honors, and those doing the slighting were his peers. A year later, the faculty made their opinions known by awarding Sondheim the Hubbard Hutchinson Prize, which came with a total purse of $6,000 (worth almost $65,000 in 2020) over the course of two consecutive years.[59]

Taking stock of Williams's social pecking order as revealed in its student newspaper is relatively easy. Gauging Williams's anti-Semitism at a distance of seventy years is much harder, and those who wish to argue that Sondheim's being taken down a peg had to do with his being Jewish have Williams's own history—before and during Sondheim's studies there—to make their case. And yet the evidence that Williams was putting its anti-Semitic practices behind it appears in plain view: Sondheim wasn't tapped for Gargoyles, but Andrew Heineman, who made no secret of his Jewish heritage, was.

Moreover, Sondheim's identification with Quakerism on his arrival in Williamstown and his disinclination after graduation to assert his Jewish identify befuddle many, including those within the Jewish community. In his 2010 review of the revue *Sondheim on Sondheim*, Tim Merwin underwent quite a bit of agony trying to place Sondheim in that community. Merwin does a better job than I ever could of sketching Sondheim's situation and situating it within a larger American Jewish music and theater history:

What the show never mentions, for those of us on the lookout for it, is Sondheim's Jewish background—or whether he still considers himself to be Jewish at all. There is certainly nothing new about American Jewish composers and other artists being assimilated; in fact, they were so secular that they secularized the whole country, including its Christian majority. As Philip Roth famously said of Irving Berlin, only a Jew could have taken Christmas out of "White Christmas" and taken Easter out of "Easter Parade," making one a holiday about snow and the other a holiday about a clothing pageant. Indeed, Sondheim has almost no overt Jewish content in any of his work; one would have to argue for a Jewish sensibility somehow inherent in his use of conflicted, neurotic characters or in the ways that his music, deriving from a place of marginalization, provides a discordant antidote to mainstream American theater music. Connecting this to Jewishness would be quite a stretch.

Why do we need to claim him as Jewish? Is it intolerable for us that many of our nation's geniuses want little to do with Judaism or the Jewish people? In Sondheim's case, as "Sondheim on Sondheim" makes abundantly clear, it is his collaborators in theater that have become both family and community to him. His sense of outsiderness, which he has expressed in interviews, seems to stem mostly from his homosexuality rather than any kind of religious or ethnic identity.[60]

And perhaps the most humorous truth of all is that Sondheim wasn't the only member of the Williams class of 1950 whose intersections with Jewish life have marked him: Stephen Birmingham, fellow Beta and rival thespian, wrote a trilogy of novels about American Jewish life, the best-known being *Our Crowd: The Great Jewish Families of New York*, which was on the *New York Times* Best Sellers list for a remarkable forty-seven weeks. Of Hotchkiss, his prep school, Birmingham said: "There were no blacks, maybe one Chinese person, who was the son of a missionary, and a quota on Jews."[61] Birmingham sought to break the Jewish quota at Beta by getting Sondheim to pledge; instead, he got a quasi-Quaker who bested him on the Williams stage and was his peer if not his superior in popular acclaim.

In his final year at Williams, Sondheim's name appeared about a dozen times in the *Record*. He was elected to Phi Beta Kappa; he made the dean's list; and in the final issue of the school year, his graduation with distinction— PBK and *magna cum laude*—and the Hutchinson Prize were noted.[62] Twice his byline appeared: Once for a review of a performance by the New England Opera Company under the direction of Boris Goldovsky; and the second time for a review of the Paganini String Quartet in a recital of works by Haydn, Schubert, and Williams's own Robert Barrow.[63] Barrow's choral arrangement of "When I See You" from *All That Glitters* was performed as part of an NBC broadcast of the Williams Glee Club from Adams Memorial Theatre on November 20, 1949; the arrangement was repeated at part of their spring home concert, their first solo engagement in four years.[64] In addition to his notices for "No Sad Songs for Me" and travails with *High Tor*, Sondheim was singled out for his final stage performance at Williams, a relatively small role, Harold Goff in Irwin Shaw's *Gentle People*, considering his star turn as Dan at the end of his sophomore year. "Steve Sondheim, replete in black homberg and chesterfield[,] carried off the villainous role of Goff with a little less than Bogartlike conviction," noted the *Record*, "but was completely competent for the demands of the part."[65]

The *Record* that year also announced that the music major would no longer fall under a composite academic unit:

> The music major has been removed from the Department of Art and Music and a new Music Department has been created, with Joaquin Nin-Culmell, associate professor of music, appointed as chairman, the Board of Trustees of Williams College announced after a meeting October 8.
>
> . . . Nin-Culmell, a composer, pianist, and conductor, has been a member of the Williams faculty since 1940. He is also the founder and conductor of the Berkshire Community Orchestra. Last year, he was visiting Professor of Music at the University of California.[66]

One imagines that Sondheim was present when Nin-Culmell's Concerto for Piano and Orchestra in C major received its premiere at Williams on December 6, 1946, with the composer as soloist and with the Rochester Philharmonic Orchestra under the baton of Erich Leinsdorf.[67] With Nin-Culmell's return in Sondheim's final year, the department's star student had someone to review his writing about twentieth-century music and comment on his senior thesis, his own attempt at a multimovement work: a piano sonata, also in C major.[68]

And just as his review in the *Record* of *Alice in Wonderland* swept Sondheim up into a debate between a prominent faculty member and the editorial board, so did he reappear as a stalking horse in his last semester. The student body was engaged in a debate about whether a new student fee should be levied to help underwrite the performing arts on campus. A letter to the editor from Hilbert Schenck Jr., Class of 1950, decried the creeping socialism that such taxation implied; in response, Alexander M. Clement, Class of 1949, browbeat Schenck for his shortsightedness and then proceeded to proffer Schenck's classmate as an example of the fact that the college didn't care about those in their midst who made art. "Steve Sondheim, who is perhaps one of the most significant people to attend Williams for a long time[,] has not only been ignored, but chastised, criticized and generally treated in a manner which is disgusting. And he's one of your own!" Schenck demurred: "It seems unfortunate that [Clement] didn't read my letter of April 29, since he would have seen that I said nothing against the AMT, Steve Sondheim, the Glee Club, the Lecture Committee, the Art Department, and the Thompson Concert Committee, which I think are doing a good job, **under the present system**."

The pages of the *Record* are silent as to what Sondheim thought about the student fee or his classmates' exchange.[69]

## The Hills of Tomorrow

Birmingham and Heineman and Pynchon and Schenck and Sondheim undoubtedly left Williams with different degrees of affection toward the school and their classmates.[70] Their president—James Phinney Baxter III, Williams Class of 1914 and president of the Gargoyles in his senior year—helped usher in a new Williams, one that might have tried to continue Dennett's bigotry and sectarianism had the war not intervened. The wave of new students arriving in the fall of 1946 may have included only one black, but there would soon be more. A press release about the Class of 1955, when "Williams College open[ed] its 159th year . . . with the heaviest freshmen enrollment in five years" (that is, since Sondheim's class arrived), crowed that "more than 20 percent of the entering class will study at Williams under scholarships, including Herbert E. Kinds, 18-year-old Cleveland boy who is the first Negro ever granted a Tyng award good for four years of study at Williams and three years of post-graduate work elsewhere." (The Stephen H. Tyng Scholarship is Williams's most prestigious award for incoming students.) Language that sounds cringeworthy today—Kinds as a Negro boy—was laudatory back then: Williams was unapologetically welcoming black men to campus.[71]

Jews and Catholics were also already present in the servicemen's community; now their numbers would increase in the traditional undergraduate ranks as admissions focused less and less on prep school matriculants. And even the WASPs were tiring of their WASP-y manners: in a survey released during Sondheim's final month as an undergraduate, 66 percent of Williams men called for the end of compulsory chapel.[72] It would be up to Phinney's successor, John Edward (Jack) Sawyer, to end compulsory chapel (1962), disband the fraternities (1968), and make permanent invasions of women to Williamstown by bringing coeducation to the campus (1969).

A photograph from 1972 shows Sawyer with that year's recipients of honorary degrees. In the back row on the far left is Sondheim (see figure 1.3).[73] He would return again in 2010 with the dog-and-pony show that he and Frank Rich took around the nation, making Williamstown just another evening on their whistle-stop tour.[74] These two events comprise the totality of Sondheim's post-baccalaureate physical visits to Williams. A videoconference with a class taught by the editor of this volume and a videorecording of an interview conducted as part of his ninetieth birthday celebration at Williams round out his returns to his alma mater.

**Figure 1.3.** Honorary degree recipients, Williams College, June 1972 (courtesy Williams College archives). *Front row, l–r:* Eugene W. Goodwillie, lawyer and senior trustee of the Clark Art Institute in Williamstown, MA; Barbara Tuchman, American historian; Williams president John Edward Sawyer; Barbara McClintock, American scientist; Mamie Phipps Clark, American psychologist who, with her husband Kenneth, focused on the development of self-consciousness in black preschool children (perhaps in response to the racial unrest at Williams in the late 1960s). *Second row, l–r:* Sondheim; Rev. Morris F. Arnold, suffragan bishop of the Episcopal Diocese of Massachusetts and Williams Class of 1936; S. Dillon Ripley II, secretary of the Smithsonian Institute; and Ulrich J. Franzen, architect and Williams Class of 1942.

Notwithstanding the fervid love that many Williams graduates, students, and friends have for the college, and notwithstanding an alma mater replete with references to sound and music—

> The mountains! The mountains! We greet them with a song,
> Whose echoes rebounding their woodland heights along,
> Shall mingle with anthems that winds and fountain sing,
> Till hill and valley gaily, gaily ring.

—Sondheim has been relatively quiet about his time at Williams. Surely any talk about his hating the college seems to be greatly overblown; perhaps it would be more in line to say, to alter a lyric of his, "Reune me a little." But word does get out: Another composer-lyricist—William Finn, Class of 1976—found his way there in part because of Sondheim's successes there. And Finn is not alone.[75]

Depending on the circles in which one travels, Sondheim cannot be said to be Williams's most notable alumnus. President Garfield is most likely the most famous early alumnus; presidential historians James MacGregor Burns and Michael Beschloss also call Williams their alma mater. Just as Sondheim placed his fellow alumnus Garfield in *Assassins*, perhaps Dmitri Weismann (*Follies*) slyly references Frederick Wiseman (Class of 1951), whose documentary *Titicut Follies* came out in 1967 and who, oddly enough, got into theatrical work a decade after Sondheim's musical appeared. Photographer and photojournalist Walker Evans may be the college's most famous dropout. Elia Kazan, Dominick Dunne, John Frankenheimer, John Sayles, Chris Collingwood, Wang Leehom, Mika Brzezinski, Erin Burnett, Norah Vincent, Jon Lovett, Kristen Anderson-Lopez, and others join Sondheim among Williams graduates who found their way in theater, film, music, television, literature, and criticism.

But few of these women and men found themselves and their alma mater simultaneously at a crossroads, and even fewer used those circumstances to forge their artistic personae. The works that Sondheim produced at Williams foreshadowed his post-collegiate career and the criticisms that accompanied it: the runaway hit in which his contributions took a back seat to others' (*Phinney's Rainbow* and *A Funny Thing Happened on the Way to the Forum*); the spectacular flop that temporarily hobbled his career (*All That Glitters* and *Anyone Can Whistle*); the stillborn shows and the songs written for creative efforts in which the spotlight fell on someone other than him; the acclaim for his brilliance and wit married to complaints that his reach exceeded his grasp.[76] Williams alone did not make Sondheim, just as Esterháza alone did not make Haydn. The wealth of opportunities and resources afforded both men and the isolated location of their creative workbenches allowed them to take risks within a supportive environment. And though sometimes the cloistered world disapproved of their efforts, the wider world periodically looked in and smiled. Perrin's review of *All That Glitters* was brutal, yet the notice in *Variety* gave Sondheim every reason for hope: "The music and lyrics have been composed as an integral part of the play, and Stephen Sondheim displays great potential as a lyricist-composer."[77] The flowering of that potential should make everyone associated with Williams College proud—and the rest of us grateful—for what Sondheim did and became during his stint in northwestern Massachusetts.

# Notes

1. Unless otherwise noted, I rely on the bicentennial history of the college as my primary source for quotations related to, and facts about, the college: *Williams 1793–1993: A Pictorial History*, ed. R. Cragin Lewis, Williams Class of 1941 (Williamstown, MA: Williams College Bicentennial Commission, 1993).

2. John W. Chandler, *The Rise and Fall of Fraternities at Williams College: Clashing Cultures and the Transformation of a Liberal Arts College* (Williamstown, MA: Williams College Press, 2014), 60–65. For an example of the question of Jews and Williams, see the 1938 correspondence between H. C. Byrd, president of University of Maryland, College Park, and J. Phinney Baxter III, president of Williams. Byrd addressed his March 28, 1938, letter to Tyler Dennett, thinking that Dennett was still president of the college. Baxter responded on April 5, 1938, that, though there was no restriction on Jews at Williams and though there was "no quota or restriction of any kind based on race or religion and that there are several Jewish boys in every entering class at Williams," Baxter felt compelled to add that "there is little likelihood of their being invited to join a fraternity." Williams College Archives and Special Collections.

3. Stephen Birmingham '50, in Benjamin Aldes Wurgaft, *Jews at Williams: Inclusion, Exclusion, and Class at a New England Liberal Arts College* (Williamstown, MA: Williams College Press, 2013), 19.

4. "Gulielmensian is intended to be an archaic linguistic reference to Williams. The Old French 'Guillemin' and the modern 'Guillaume' anglicize to 'William.' Notably, the first official professor of Williams was a scholar of the French language." https://unbound. williams.edu/islandora/object/gulielmensian%3Ayearbooks, accessed August 19, 2020.

5. See Todd Decker's chapter in this volume.

6. Report to the Board of Trustees of Williams College from the Committee on Post-War Extracurricular Activities (commonly known as the Shriver Report), January 1946, 2. Williams College Archives and Special Collections.

7. Ibid., 11. For more on fraternities at Williams, see Chandler, *Rise and Fall of Fraternities*. As the fraternity system pertained to Jewish students, see note 2 and Wurgaft, *Jews at Williams*, 73–75, 84–85.

8. See Francis W. Shephardson, *The Beta Book: The Story and Manual of Beta Theta Pi* (Menasha, WI: George Banta, 1927), 447: "[Beta Theta Pi] shall be constituted as hereinafter provided, and shall have for its objects the promotion of moral and social culture of its members, the establishment of confidence and friendly relations between the universities and colleges of the United States, in securing unity of action and sympathy in matters of common interest between them, and the building up of a fraternity that recognizes mutual assistance in the honorable labors and aspirations of life, devotion to the cultivation of the intellect, unsullied friendship, and unfaltering fidelity, as objects worthy the highest aim and purpose of associated effort."

9. Wurgaft, *Jews at Williams*, 19.

10. Interview with Andrew Heineman '50 (Pete Rosenfeld, interviewer), [9], in Williams College Jewish Oral History Project, Williams College Archives and Special Collections.

11. "352 Veterans and Civilians Bring Enrollment to 1060," *Williams Record* (hereafter *WR*), September 27, 1946, 3. I thank Sylvia Kennick Brown, archivist at Williams College, and Elizabeth Kimmelman Schwartz, the Director of Alumni and Parent Engagement at the George School, for their assistance in tracking down this information.

12. J. Phinney Baxter, "Williams in 1950: A Report from the President," 2, Williams College Archives and Special Collections.

13. Frederick C. Copeland, "Report of the Director of Admissions, 1946–1947," October 10, 1947, Williams College Archives and Special Collections. For Sondheim's class, Copeland wrote, "Deerfield has the largest delegation with 24 men, while Exeter follows close by with 22. Choate with 16, Loomis with 11, and Hotchkiss with 10 are also high on the list. Other schools with large representation are: Kent, 9; Andover, 9; Taft, 7; Lawrenceville 6, and St. Paul's, 6." "Freshmen Arrive as Williams Reaches Top Enrollment," *WR*, September 27, 1946, 6.

14. "Freshmen Arrive," 1.

15. Meryle Secrest, *Stephen Sondheim: A Life* (New York: Knopf, 1998), 11.

16. In 2001 Mr. Sondheim granted the author permission to obtain a copy of his Williams transcript.

17. Stephen Birmingham '50, in Wurgaft, *Jews at Williams*, 20.

18. Heineman interview, [8]. Heineman's poignant comment about the kinds of discussions that roommates had seems to touch upon Sondheim's young age in comparison with other Williams men. Heineman also talked extensively about the place of Jews at Williams and the role that the Garfield Club played in the college's social life.

19. Sondheim spent at least one summer at Camp Androscoggin in Wayne, Maine. According to an undated flyer from mainejews.org, "in [their] earlier history Camp Androscoggin and Tripp Lake Camp advertised themselves as Jewish camps, but the word 'Jewish' is no longer found on their current web sites." Camp Androscoggin was founded in 1907. https://mainejews.org/docs/DMJ/SummerCamps1-2.pdf, accessed on August 15, 2020. Sondheim's attestation of respect for the principles of Quakerism come from an email exchange between him and the author in February 2020.

20. For more on Sondheim's theatrical career at Williams, including a listing of all the shows in which he acted, see Steve Swayne, *How Sondheim Found His Sound* (Ann Arbor: University of Michigan Press, 2005), 139–141.

21. He appears as "Steve" in at least seventeen mentions; "Stephen" is far more common.

22. For more on Lamson's career, see "*Undersigned* To Give *Trade Name*, New Play Script by Mrs. Lamson," *WR*, March 27, 1947, 1. The Undersigned, according to David C. Bryant, assistant director of the Adams Memorial Theatre, was created by "individuals who wanted an opportunity for acting in addition to the regularly scheduled productions": *WR*, January 10, 1947, 1. For the description of *Trade Name* and the review of Sondheim's performance in it, see Charles Klensch, "First-Night Crowd Enjoys 'Trade Name,' Despite Its Faults," *WR*, April 3, 1947, 1, 6.

23. Peggy Lamson, "Peggy Lamson Pans COW: Calls for Better Editing, Revised Policy, Originality," *WR*, October 8, 1947, 1.

24. Charles Klensch, "wmsy," *WR*, October 29, 1947, 4. The term "wmsy" may mean "whimsy" or "Williams-y" or both.

25. Steve Sondheim '50, "Alice in Wonderland Review," *WR*, November 1, 1947, 2.

26. The Williams Women's Faculty Club sponsored the presentation, and the "charity" receiving the proceeds was the Williamstown High School Music Fund. "AMT Will Produce '*Alice in Wonderland*,'" *WR*, October 11, 1947, 1.

27. S. Lane Faison Jr., "Letter to the Editor" and Editor's Note, *WR*, November 8, 1947, 2. Faison, himself a Williams alumnus, was a famed art professor and museum director.

28. Lamson, "Peggy Lamson Pans COW, 1, 6; Stephen Sondheim, "The Pail Runneth Over," *Purple Cow*, November 1947, 33. See Bob Taylor, "Review Praises *Purple Cow* for 'Coherence, Balance,'" *WR*, November 22, 1947, 1: "Steve Sondheim really takes the bull by the shovel in a parody of a Record review of the Cow and provides a presentable number of chuckles." See also John D. O'Neill, "A Christmas Guide to Broadway," *WR*, December 15, 1949, 5, where in his mention of Sondheim, O'Neill—then assistant professor of English—sounds as though he wished to curry Sondheim's favor and acknowledge Sondheim's wit: "[re: *Touch And Go*] Steve Sondheim, who speaks with some authority in the matter of the musical stage, says he would have stayed for the second show, had there been one."

29. Secrest, *Sondheim: A Life*, 77.

30. Paul K. Barstow, "Lasell, Kelly Perform 'Brilliantly' in 'Fine Production' of 'Oedipus Rex,'" *WR*, January 28, 1948, 1: "Stephen Sondheim as the blind seer showed remarkable vocal sensitivity, and by his restraint made the contrast between Oedipus' violent fury and his calm contempt particularly striking." Paul K. Barstow, "Cap and Bells Production of 'The Infernal Machine' Weak," *WR*, March 31, 1948, 1: "Stephen Sondheim as Tiresias again showed that he has all the emotional and vocal power necessary for fine acting, but seemed held back by a fear of over-acting, or of reaching too high a pitch before his climaxes. When he let himself go he was strikingly effective, but through most of the play he let dramatic opportunities pass unrealized, and seemed only half into his role." In this review Barstow criticized the performance of Sondheim's castmate, classmate, and sometimes critic Stephen Birmingham (Oedipus).

31. "'Phinney's Rainbow' Opens Friday with 52 Man Cast" (lead story), *WR*, April 28, 1948, 1.

32. Charles Klensch, "Undergrad-Penned 'Rainbow' Gives Biz to Local Yokels," *WR*, May 8, 1948, 1, 8.

33. Paul K. Barstow, "'Night Must Fall' Ends Fine Season at AMT This Week," *WR*, June 2, 1948, 3. The article's subheading reads: "Direction by Bryant, Sondheim's Acting in Role of Hero, Tops."

34. "Steinbeck Hit Cap and Bells First Play," *WR*, September 25, 1948, 1. Cap and Bells began their season that year with an adaptation of Steinbeck's *Of Mice and Men*.

35. Secrest, *Sondheim: A Life*, 82.

36. For the reviews of his performances in the *Record*, see Robert Scott Taylor, "'Auto-da-fe' Interpretation Hit by Critic; 'Lefty' Uneven," *WR*, December 18, 1948, 6 (Agate Keller in Odets's *Waiting for Lefty*); Robert Scott Taylor, "Critic Commends

Continuity of 'Julius Caesar'; Lasell, Sondheim, Dissell Praised," *WR*, February 23, 1949, 2 (Cassius in Shakespeare's *Julius Caesar*); and Stuart Robinson, "Reviewer Finds AMT Play Entertaining; Luthy, Gushee Praised for Performances," *WR*, March 4, 1950, 1 (Harold Goff in Irwin Shaw's *The Gentle People*). For the notice of his appearance at the Westport Country Playhouse, see Elem., "Strawhat Reviews: *The Life of the Party*," *Variety*, July 19, 1950, 52.

37. "Special awards to the incomparable Schumanns; to Dave Bryant and Steve Sondheim for their direction." Raymond F. Smith '51, "Reviewer Praises Musical; Acting, Directing, Cited in 'First-Rate' Show," *WR*, May 17, 1950, 4. "Steve Sondheim was supervising a group of amateurs in the production of another Masse musical, following Maxwell Anderson's axe of his HIGH TOR adaptation": *Gulielmensian* [Yearbook] 1950, 92. Bryant came to Williams sometime in mid-1946—in other words, shortly before Sondheim matriculated. He began as the assistant director of the Adams Memorial Theatre (see *WR*, July 26, 1946, 1) and, less than a year later, is listed as the director (see *WR*, April 24, 1947, 3). Bryant would go on to become the founding director of the Williamstown Theatre Festival in 1954. For more on Sondheim's apprentice musicals, see Swayne, *How Sondheim Found His Sound*, 125–126.

38. Smith, "Reviewer Praises Musical," 1.

39. "Featured Local Talent Amuse Estimated 1200 at Jamboree," *WR*, May 24, 1950, 4.

40. "[Sondheim] had a run-in with the faculty member who ran the Adams Memorial Theater (not over the fact that he was Jewish), and clearly Steve should've been made the head of Cap and Bells and was not. That was denied to him. . . . Sondheim had written two musicals up there, etc. . . . I think [Bryant] felt clearly threatened by Steve because Steve even at that age was a much more talented person than he was, and they had run-ins about all kinds of things. He just black-balled Steve and made sure that everybody up there knew that he detested Steve and they should vote for this other guy if they wanted to still get parts in the plays and so on. So Steve had a rough time in many ways." Heineman interview.

41. See Swayne, *How Sondheim Found His Sound*, 126.

42. "AMT Musical Opens May 11," *WR*, May 10, 1950, 1, 4.

43. "Steinbeck Hit Cap and Bells First Play," *WR*, September 25, 1948, 1. For more on *All That Glitters*, see Stephen Banfield, *Sondheim's Broadway Musicals* (Ann Arbor: University of Michigan Press, 1993), 16–18; Swayne, *How Sondheim Found His Sound*, 129–135.

44. "Musical's Title Finally Settled," *WR*, March 5, 1949, 1–2.

45. "Varied Sets in AMT Musical," *WR*, March 9, 1949, 1, 4.

46. "Sondheim Interview," *WR*, March 12, 1949, 2.

47. "Ida Kay Directs Two Dances in New Sondheim Musical," *WR*, March 16, 1949, 1.

48. "Sophs Assure 'Healthy Blast'" (subheading: "Entertainment Features Dance, New Musical"): "Two top entertainment opportunities will be available to weekenders. On Saturday evening from 8:30 to 12 Bill Lawson's orchestra will provide some very danceable music for Williams men and their dates, while on both Friday and Saturday nights Cap and Bells will present Stephen Sondheim's new musical 'All That Glitters.'" *WR*, March 16, 1949, 1.

49. Edwin N. Perrin, "'All That Glitters' Shiner for Cap and Bells, Cast," *WR*, March 23, 1949, 1, 4.
50. "'Variety' Covers 'All That Glitters': Lauds Bryant Direction, Cites Music, Lyrics," *WR*, March 31, 1949, 1.
51. "Letters to the Editor," *WR*, March 26, 1949, 2.
52. "Glee Club Plans Home Appearance," *WR*, April 20, 1949, 1; "Williams Glee Club, Wellesley Choir to Give Joint Concert," *WR*, April 27, 1949, 1; "Wellesley Sends 83 for Concert Tonight," *WR*, April 30, 1949, 1; S. H. Graybill Jr., "Wellesley Choir, Williams Glee Club Combine to Present Superb Concert, Thrilling Large Chapin Hall Audience," *WR*, May 4, 1949, 1. The arrangement was also performed in concert the following year. See "Glee Club to Give First Home Solo Concert in Four Years," *WR*, March 18, 1950, 1.
53. Secrest, *Sondheim: A Life*, 69.
54. "The sophomores decided that things were going too slowly and came out with the news that they were sponsoring a dance on the weekend of March 19, which was received with much acclaim by the rest of the college. This was the same weekend that Cap and Bells was presenting its second production of the year, *All That Glitters*, a musical written by Steve Sondheim. Both the dance and the musical were resounding successes, and as everyone expected, there was a slight snowfall." *Gulielmensian* 1949, 73.
55. Perrin, "'All That Glitters' Shiner," 4. Perrin also wrote a sentence that Sondheim seemed to mine twice more in his work: "In the second act, Mr. Cady proclaims that the unwashed masses want tunes they can whistle" (1). Compare *Anyone Can Whistle* and "Opening Doors" from *Merrily We Roll Along* ("There's not a tune you can hum").
56. "Editors Select Year's Outstanding Stories: Baxter Resignation; Honor System," *WR*, January 23, 1961, 2–3.
57. "Gargoyle Society Taps Twenty Men in Traditional Lab Campus Exercise," *WR*, May 30, 1949, 1.
58. "Class of '50 Gives Pynchon Grosvenor Cup," *WR*, May 30, 1949, 1.
59. "In memory of her son, the late Hubbard Hutchinson '17, Mrs. Eva Hutchinson, of Columbus, Ohio, provided in her will for an annual scholarship of $3,000, to be awarded to that member of the graduating class at Williams 'most talented in creative work in music, writing, or painting.' The award, which will be known as the Hubbard Hutchinson Memorial Scholarship, is nearly twice the amount of any previous Williams scholarship and ranks with the highest in the United States. The winner of this award, who will be chosen by a committee consisting of the head of the fine arts department, a member of the English department, and the faculty member in charge of music, will receive the grant for the two years following his graduation, with no restrictions upon its use. 'He shall be entirely free to study, travel, or loaf, as he may see fit,' the terms of the award state. In addition, he may apply for a year's renewal at the end of two years, which may be granted at the discretion of the college authorities." "New Scholarships," *Williams Alumni Review*, February 1940, 76–77. The 1951 college prospectus lists Sondheim as the recipient of the 1950 scholarship.

60. Tim Merwin, "Sondheim, Unrevealed," *New York Jewish Week*, April 27, 2010, https://jewishweek.timesofisrael.com/sondheim-unrevealed/, accessed August 15, 2020. See also Benjamin Ivry, "Getting Sick of Sondheim?," *Forward*, March 3, 2010, https://forward.com/culture/126411/getting-sick-of-sondheim/, accessed August 15, 2020. For more on Sondheim's sexuality, see David LaFontaine, "Merrily He Strolled Along," *Gay & Lesbian Review* 26, no. 2 (March/April 2019): 19–22.

61. Sam Roberts, "Stephen Birmingham, Chronicler of the Rich and Other Elites, Dies at 86," *New York Times*, November 19, 2015, sec. B, p. 14.

62. "Junior Class Sets Record; 20 Phi Betes," *WR*, September 21, 1949, 1; "Seniors Lead Dean's List; 22% of Total Enrollment Net 'B' Average or Better," *WR*, March 18, 1950, 2. In the June 18, 1950, issue he appears on pp. 1 (PBK) and 2 (Hutchinson, *magna cum laude* and a music major).

63. "Opera Singing, Text Praised by Sondheim," *WR*, November 5, 1949, 1, 4; "Paganini Quartet Plays Haydn, Barrow, Schubert in Chapin," *WR*, November 30, 1949, 1.

64. "NBC Concert by Glee Club," *WR*, November 19, 1949, 1; "Glee Club to Give First Home Solo Concert in Four Years," *WR*, 1.

65. Stuart Robinson, "Reviewer Finds AMT Play Entertaining; Luthy, Gushee Praised for Performances," *WR*, March 4, 1950, 1; see also "Experienced Cast Selected for Play," *WR*, January 14, 1950, 1.

66. "New Department of Music Created," *WR*, October 15, 1949, 1.

67. Frederick H. Moore, '49–N, "Premier [*sic*] Performance of Nin-Culmell's Work Receives High Praise," *WR*, December 13, 1946, 1, 10.

68. See Steve Swayne, "*Music for the Theatre*, the Young Copland, and the Younger Sondheim," *American Music* 20, no. 1 (Spring 2002): 80–101; Steve Swayne, "Sondheim's Piano Sonata," *Journal of the Royal Musical Association* 127 (2002): 258–304.

69. Hilbert Schenk Jr., '50, "No Blanket Tax" (Letters to the Editor), *WR*, April 29, 1950, 2; Alexander M. Clement, "49, No Culture?" (Letters to the Editor), *WR*, May 10, 1950, 2; "Schenck Answers Clement" (Letters to the Editor), *WR*, May 24, 1950, 2 (emphasis in the original).

70. On the "Class Elections" page of the 1950 *Gul*, Heineman ranks no. 1 as most respected (45 votes vs. Pynchon's 12, 3rd place), most likely to succeed (42 vs. Sondheim's 29, 4th place, and Pynchon's 27, 5th place), done most for Williams (42 vs. Pynchon's 27, 3rd place, and Sondheim's 4, 8th place), and class politician (117; the person in 2nd place received 25 votes). Sondheim also received votes for most versatile (22, 3rd place, vs. Pynchon's 46, 1st place), most brilliant (14, 6th place, vs. Heineman's 12, 7th place), and most original (32, 2nd place). Heineman received 19 votes for most popular (4th place; "Me" received 3 votes, 10th place) and 3 votes for being the handsomest (9th place; "Me" is in 6th place with 10 votes); Pynchon did not receive enough votes to merit mention as best athlete; and neither Birmingham nor Schenck appears in any category. In light of Sondheim's later work on *Gypsy*, it's worth noting that Gypsy Rose Lee received 2 votes for being most entertaining. *Gulielmensian* 1950, 80.

71. "From the President's Office" (Press release), September 18, 1951, Williams College Archives and Special Collections.

72. "Poll Shows 66% Oppose Compulsory Chapel," *WR*, May 24, 1950, 1. When I asked him about compulsory chapel, Sondheim had no memory of attending chapel. Pers. corr., February 24, 2020.

73. I thank Sylvia Kennick Brown for identifying the individuals in figure 1.3 for me. See also [Williams College] *Record Advocate*, June 4, 1972, 1: A photo of Sondheim is there (Clark, Tuchman, and Franzen also have photographs) and his first name in the article and caption appears as "Steven."

74. Sondheim befriended Rich after reading Rich's review in *The Crimson* (Harvard University) of the out-of-town tryout of *Follies* (see https://www.thecrimson.com/article/1971/2/26/theatre-the-last-musical-pthese-are/, accessed August 24, 2020). Rich subsequently worked for the *New York Times* as drama critic from 1980 to 1993 and as an op-ed columnist from 1994 to 2001. His rave reviews and championing of *Sunday in the Park with George* set him apart from most of his colleagues at the time. See Frank Rich, *Hot Seat: Theater Criticism for the* New York Times, *1980–1993* (New York: Random House, 1998), 113–114, 314–317, 341–353, and 974–975. For more on the show that Rich and Sondheim took across the nation, see A. M. Homes, "On The Road: Rich Evenings with Sondheim," *Vanity Fair*, February 22, 2008, https://www.vanityfair.com/news/2008/03/ontheroad200803, accessed January 9, 2021; Frank Rich, "The Sondheim Puzzle," *New York*, November 30, 2013, https://nymag.com/news/frank-rich/stephen-sondheim-2013-12/, accessed January 9, 2021.

75. See Liz Leyden, "In Good Company," *Williams Magazine*, https://magazine.williams.edu/2020/spring/feature/in-good-company/, accessed August 28, 2020.

76. See Swayne, *How Sondheim Found His Sound*, xiii–xvi.

77. Russ., "College Show: *All That Glitters*," *Variety*, March 23, 1949, 52; "'Variety' Covers 'All That Glitters,'" 1. See also Stephen Banfield, "Sondheim's Genius," in *The Oxford Handbook of Sondheim Studies*, ed. Robert Gordon (Oxford: Oxford University Press, 2014), 12–13.

# 2

# Fragments of Fairyland

## Sondheim's Abandoned Adaptation of *Mary Poppins*

### *Dominic McHugh*

It is with some disdain that Sondheim writes of his earliest attempts at song-writing in *Look, I Made a Hat*, his second volume of collected lyrics:

> I don't consider that the phrase "Collected Lyrics" on the covers of these books
> obliges me to display all my juvenilia—in particular, school and college songs,
> and the ones I wrote under the tutelage of Oscar Hammerstein. . . . [H]owever, it
> occurred to me that a small sampling of my first fumblings might be helpful to
> other fumblers. . . . Here then is a small feast of clichés, redundancies, inappro-
> priate and infelicitous words, cutenesses and confusions (I leave the pleasure of
> discovering which are which to the reader), all excusable for beginners.[1]

Yet he goes on to confess that "juvenilia can be fascinating to fans and researchers"
and admits that there is "every now and then a graceful image, a fresh rhyme, a
surprising joke, all recognizable buds of someone who was meant to be a lyric
writer, and a lyric writer for the theater." In this, Sondheim acknowledges that
his early work is of interest and seems to invite scholars to consider it, even if
he is not proud of it. He may cringe at the idea of putting it on display in his
published lyric books, but he has preserved the early works in the archive of the
Wisconsin Historical Society alongside his professional work up to *Do I Hear a
Waltz?*, rather than destroying them or keeping them in his possession; he knows
they are significant as the seeds of a major writer's later career. Nonetheless, he
denied permission to reproduce in this chapter any of the music or lyrics from
his manuscripts for his incomplete early show *Mary Poppins*.

Sondheim makes a qualitative distinction between the songs he wrote
at the George School and the slightly later musicals he wrote at Williams
College or under the tutelage of his mentor Oscar Hammerstein II in his late
teens, explaining, "The curtain will fall at my sophomore year at Williams. My
prep school years will have to remain shrouded in total obscurity."[2] The four
"Hammerstein" musicals are of special interest because they were written on the
cusp of Sondheim's professional career—indeed, I have argued elsewhere that

Dominic McHugh, *Fragments of Fairyland* In: *Sondheim in Our Time and His*. Edited by: W. Anthony Sheppard,
Oxford University Press. © Oxford University Press 2022. DOI: 10.1093/oso/9780197603192.003.0003

the last of the four, *Climb High*, might be considered to signal the beginning of his career rather than the end of his apprenticeship.[3] In this chapter I turn my attention to the third of Hammerstein's developmental challenges to the young Sondheim, written around 1949–1950, directly before *Climb High*: an adaptation of a nontheatrical work. Sondheim explains his choice of P. L. Travers's series of novels about Mary Poppins and the Banks children: "I had loved the Mary Poppins books since I was a child and thought it would be a useful challenge to try to make a coherent whole out of a group of short, interrelated stories. It was, but I couldn't meet the challenge and gave up about a third of the way through."[4] He reproduces the lyrics to one song, "The Sun Is Blue," in *Look, I Made a Hat*, but otherwise Sondheim offers little commentary on his abandoned adaptation.

Others have also given the show little space. For instance, Stephen Banfield notes that "The Sun Is Blue" is "a study in wistful heartache disguised as a child-like naïveté, achieved as a nursery list song with a French flexibility of rhythm and phrase structure in the melody,"[5] observing the influence of Sondheim's interest in French music on the score, while Steve Swayne merely comments that "of the four apprentice musicals, *Mary Poppins* is the least complete."[6] Yet the remaining fragments of this project are fascinating, not least because they provide a striking glimpse of how Broadway's most influential composer-lyricist of the second half of the twentieth century was thinking about a property that went on to be one of the most popular and successful movie musicals in others' hands.[7] Indeed, on the surface *Mary Poppins* seems like an unusually commercial choice for Sondheim, whose mission is to push the envelope. But the extant materials—however in-complete—reveal that Sondheim saw exactly that kind of unusual potential in this musical, a reminder of how the popular but saccharine Disney version by no means captures the essence of Travers's work even before one takes into account what Sondheim wanted to do with it. In this chapter I consider Sondheim's notes about the order and content of scenes, three script fragments that encompass material for four scenes, and fifteen musical sketches to reveal how his thinking, if not "practically perfect," showed elements of the innovative perspective on music drama that would become the hallmark of his career.

## Adaptive Choices

Although the materials in the Wisconsin archive are not extensive, they in-clude some fragments that are telling with regard to the underlying challenges that Sondheim faced when turning the Mary Poppins books into a musical. Travers had written only three of her six Poppins volumes by the time Sondheim worked on his adaptation in 1950: *Mary Poppins* (1934), *Mary Poppins Comes Back* (1935), and *Mary Poppins Opens the Door* (1944). Each book deals with the arrival of Mary Poppins at a time when the Banks children are badly behaved or restless, followed by ten or so adventures and her departure. Some of the adventures scarcely involve the children, and several chapters focus on Mary's reciting moralistic fables to them on a park bench or in the nursery rather than engaging in an activity; their static nature makes them particularly challenging to dramatize. There is little connection or progression between the stories other than the return of a few familiar characters. Even Travers started to have doubts about this nonlinear format: When she wrote *Mary Poppins in the Park* in 1962 (more than a decade after Sondheim's work) she offered a preface explaining that "the adventures in this book should be understood to have happened during any of the three visits of Mary Poppins to the Banks Family. . . . She cannot for ever [*sic*] arrive and depart."[8]

Although the children are touched by their experiences of living with Mary Poppins, their household does not seem to have been permanently changed. She comes back twice, and when Travers felt that she should come back no more, the author saw no problem in writing more and more short stories, all of which could have happened at any time. By extension, any of the stories could have occurred in any of the books. No doubt that is, in part, why Sondheim remarked, "It was very difficult to structure a play out of a group of short stories, and I wasn't able to accomplish it."[9] On another occasion, he went a little further: "I realized I couldn't complete it because I could not solve the problem of taking disparate short stories, even though they are interconnected, and making a larger form."[10] Of course, later in his career Sondheim would successfully exploit nonlinear narratives with breathtaking results (for example, in *Company*), in collaboration with a bookwriter. In a slightly different way, his problems with *Poppins* also call to mind his remarks about the initial challenge of writing *Into the Woods*: "When you have infinite choices and no point to make, every plot is possible and every character arbitrary except for the principals."[11] But at the point when he was working on *Poppins*, the novelty of writing a musical in which the episodes could have come in almost any order (and none of which progresses a broader plot) was an intriguing problem rather than something for which he had a solution.

This is apparent from the two scenic plans that Sondheim considered for the show, reproduced in tables 2.1 and 2.2, complemented by a list of the surviving song sources in table 2.3. Sondheim's notes are shown in the first line of each cell, and the chapter or chapters to which they refer have been added to the transcription for clarity; also, it is unclear which version came first, so the order may be the opposite of the one given here. Common to both versions is the decision to base the opening on the first chapter of the first book, which details the Banks's need for a nanny and Mary Poppins's arrival. Both versions feature "The Day Out" (the chapter liberally adapted by Disney into the "Jolly Holiday" sequence in the movie) in Act I, but each uses it in a different position. Sondheim also

**Table 2.1.** Sondheim's layout of the Mary Poppins stories across two acts (version 1, marked "Probabilities"). The source (which is in pencil) contains numerous markings and ticks, showing that this is a working draft.

| Act 1 | Act 2 |
|---|---|
| Opening<br>*Mary Poppins*, Ch. 1: "East Wind" | Return—Kite or <u>Fireworks</u><br>*Mary Poppins Comes Back*, Ch. 1:<br>    "The Kite"<br>Or<br>*Mary Poppins Opens the Door*, Ch. 1:<br>    "The Fifth of November" |
| Bert, Afternoon Tea, In the Picture<br>*Mary Poppins*, Ch. 2: "The Day Out" | Miss Andrew's Lark<br>*Mary Poppins Comes Back*, Ch. 2:<br>    "Miss Andrew's Lark" |
| The Red Cow<br>*Mary Poppins*, Ch. 5: "The Dancing Cow" | The New One (Baby)<br>*Mary Poppins Comes Back,* Ch. 5:<br>    "The New One" |
| Bad Tuesday—Around the World<br>*Mary Poppins*, Ch. 6, "Bad Tuesday" | The Dirty Rascal—Robertson Ay<br>*Mary Poppins Comes Back*, Ch.<br>    6: "Robertson Ay's Story" |
| Twink—Fanny, Annie, Mrs. Corry, Dance<br>*Mary Poppins*, Ch. 8: "Mrs Corry" | Balloons—mates from balloon mix-up<br>*Mary Poppins Comes Back*, Ch.<br>    8: "Balloons *and* Balloons" |
| John and Barbara teeth, 1st Birthday—<br>    Starling, Mrs. Banks<br>*Mary Poppins*, Ch. 9: "John and Barbara's<br>    Story" | Mr. Twigley's wishes—change wishes<br>*Mary Poppins Opens the Door*, Ch. 2:<br>    "Mr Twigley's Wishes" |
| Departure—West Wind or <u>Carousel</u><br>Bert can't go.<br>*Mary Poppins Comes Back*, Ch.<br>    10: "Merry-go-round"<br>Or<br>*Mary Poppins*, Ch. 12: "West Wind" | The Cat at King—tour de force—Story +<br>    Pantomime<br>*Mary Poppins Opens the Door*, Ch. 3:<br>    "The Cat That Looked at a King" |
| | New Year Crack<br>*Mary Poppins Opens the Door*, Ch. 7:<br>    "Happy Ever After"<br>Departure with Bert—The Other Door<br>*Mary Poppins Opens the Door*, Ch. 8:<br>    "The Other Door" |

Note: At some point, Sondheim crossed this line out in ink (the outline is in pencil, so this is probably a later amendment).

**Table 2.2.** Sondheim's layout of the Mary Poppins stories across two acts (version 2). The source is in ink, suggesting a more definite draft.

| Act 1 | Act 2 |
|---|---|
| Opening<br>*Mary Poppins*, Ch. 1: "East Wind" | Return<br>*Mary Poppins Comes Back*, Ch. 1: "The Kite"<br>Or<br>*Mary Poppins Opens the Door*, Ch. 1:<br>"The Fifth of November" |
| Mary arrives<br>*Mary Poppins*, Ch. 1: "East Wind" | Bad Tuesday<br>*Mary Poppins*, Ch. 6, "Bad Tuesday" |
| Miss Andrew<br>*Mary Poppins Comes Back*, Ch. 2:<br>"Miss Andrew's Lark" | The Dancing Cow, The Dirty Rascal, etc.<br>*Mary Poppins*, Ch. 5: "The Dancing Cow"<br>and/or<br>*Mary Poppins Comes Back*, Ch. 6: "Robertson<br>Ay's Story" |
| Day Out<br>*Mary Poppins*, Ch. 2: "The Day Out" | Mr. Twigley<br>*Mary Poppins Opens the Door*, Ch. 2:<br>"Mr Twigley's Wishes" |
| Combo: Balloons and Mrs Corry<br>*Mary Poppins Comes Back*, Ch. 8:<br>"Balloons *and* Balloons"<br>*Mary Poppins*, Ch. 8: "Mrs Corry" | The Twins<br>*Mary Poppins*, Ch. 9: "John and Barbara's<br>Story" |
| Departure<br>? | Birthday<br>*Mary Poppins*, Ch. 10: "Full Moon"<br>Departure<br>? |

**Table 2.3.** Extant song sources for *Mary Poppins* in the Wisconsin collection

**Extant musical numbers in sketch or piano-vocal**
"The Sun Is Blue," piano-vocal score (music and lyrics)
"Miss Andrew," piano-vocal (music only)
"Miss Andrew," melodic sketch, 1 p. (music only)
"Tea," piano-vocal, 12 pp. (music only, matches lyrics from script)
"Indian," melodic sketch (music only, matches lyrics from script)
"Bali Ha'i," melodic sketch (music only, matches lyrics from script)
"Mandarin," melodic sketch (music only, matches lyrics from script)
"Incidental Indian," piano sketch (music only, matches lyrics from script)
"Mary's Parting Shot," melodic sketch (music only, matches lyrics from script)
"Mary to Ellen," melodic sketch (music only, matches lyrics from script)
"End of Serv. Song," melodic sketch (music only)
"Dancing Cow Themes," melodic sketch (music only)
"Verse—Nanny," melodic sketch (music only, matches lyrics from script)
"Nanny" (refrain), melodic sketch (music only, matches lyrics from script)
"Ad," piano-vocal score (music only, matches lyrics from script)

*(continued)*

Table 2.3. Continued

---

**Numbers with lyrics in script for scenes 1–3 (46 pp.)**
"When Children Reach That Difficult Age"
"Minus-Rally"
"Advertisement" (Wanted, a Nurse)
"What a Life We Lead (Sing a Song of Servants)"
"Softly, Now Hear My Heart"
"Nanny"
"Mary Poppins, Welcome"
"Suddenly the Sunlight"
"Once in a Color I Saw My Love"

**Numbers in untitled annotated scene fragment based on *Bad Tuesday* (13 pp.)**
"What a Life We Lead (Sing a Song of Children/Servants)"
The Eskimo Song
The Mandarin Song
The Hawaii Song
The Indian Song
"The World Is Yours" reprise

**Numbers in *Bad Tuesday* script (29 pp.)**
"You're the Only One Awake (The World Is Yours)"
"What a Life We Lead (Sing a Song of Children/Servants)"
"My Dear Mrs. Brill"
The Eskimo Song
The Mandarin Song
The Hawaii Song
The Indian Song

---

knew he wanted to adapt the striking "Bad Tuesday" episode from Chapter 6 of the first book, in which Michael Banks is in a bad temper and Mary Poppins takes the children around the world using a magic compass found in the park, but this is the centerpiece of Act I in version 1 and the first major episode of Act II in version 2. Similarly, "Miss Andrew's Lark," a chapter that reveals the unhappy truth about the sadistic nanny by whom Mr. Banks was raised, moves from Act II to Act I.

Another example of interchangeability is the opening of Act II. Cameron Mackintosh explains that when he was planning his own stage musical of *Mary Poppins* in 2004, it was a challenge to create "a dramatic structure that would make theatre audiences want to come back for a second half. The answer of course lay with Pamela [Travers] herself. In the books Mary Poppins leaves the family twice and comes back only until she's no longer required. This gave me the clue where the interval should be."[12] Sondheim had already made this discovery (namely, that Mary should depart at the intermission as a cliff-hanger and return in Act II) half a century earlier, but the fact that both of his outlines indicate that the first chapters of *either* the second or the third book could be used to bring her back reinforces how little was at stake in the choice; it did not matter which was chosen as long as Mary returned.

A further commonality of the outlines is that, with a couple of important exceptions, most of the episodes chosen by Sondheim are particularly dramatic. For example, Chapter 8 of *Mary Poppins Comes Back*, in which Mary and the children buy a balloon each and are able to fly with them, is there in both; no doubt Sondheim saw the potential for spectacle here. The dancing cow episode (Chapter 5) from *Mary Poppins* was identified as a dance number (for which some musical sketches survive). In the book, a star lands on one of the cow's horns and she cannot stop dancing until the King advises her to jump over the moon (in the manner of the nursery rhyme). In the version shown in table 2.2, however, Sondheim notes that this story might be combined with or replaced by "Robertson Ay's Story" from *Mary Poppins Comes Back*, in which Mary reveals to the children that the reason their manservant is lazy is that he is secretly living a double life as the Dirty Rascal from the "King of the Castle" nursery rhyme. Sondheim also considered using "The Cat That Looked at a King" from *Mary Poppins Opens the Door* in one of the outlines. Travers was enormously enthusiastic about the importance of fairy tales, commenting that they are "concerned with the nature of the world and man's relation to it. In these matters no one of us is too old to be involved. Fairy-tale is at once the pattern of man and the chart for his journey."[13] In his way, Sondheim seemed in *Poppins* to be attracted to this sort of sentiment, too, even if he would later take a more sophisticated view of fairy tales in *Into the Woods*; there was no need to focus on three of Mary's story-telling chapters, in which the bulk of the prose is devoted to her narration of a fairy tale and therefore awkward to absorb into the plot of a musical, so Sondheim's choice of these tricky chapters represents a gesture.

In addition to these outlines, the Wisconsin archive includes some general notes about ideas for the adaptation. After the outline reproduced in table 2.1, Sondheim has written six ideas or characters from other stories to add: scenes for the parents; the maid Ellen and the Policeman (who are a couple); Admiral Boom and Binnacle (a former pirate); the Sweep (unnamed in the books), next to which Sondheim adds "good luck," foreshadowing the importance of the latter in the Sherman Brothers' "Chim Chim Cher-ee";[14] Mary and Bert (who is the Match Man rather than the chimney sweep in the books); and the birthday scene, which takes place at the zoo in *Mary Poppins* but for which Sondheim notes: "Big no., but no animals" (it is unclear how this would have worked, given the centrality of the animals and their relationship to Mary in this episode in the book). Another note also covers ground that the Disney film would later explore in "A Spoonful of Sugar": Sondheim notes that Mary could have a "takeoff on song gestures" and a "song to window or mirror—self-compliments." There are also some ideas for smaller elements of some of the scenes, for example, that the "Miss Andrew" episode should include reactions to Mary from the "Bad Tuesday chapter."

## Developing the Script

Sondheim does not consider himself to be a bookwriter, as he has stated on numerous occasions, for example, in reference to his initial attempts to write *Sweeney Todd*.[15] Further, the extant script materials for four of his scenes for *Mary Poppins* are drafts rather than finished products. Therefore, it is both unreasonable and meaningless to critique them too harshly: They are, after all, the product of an abandoned "training exercise" that his mentor set him to help him develop into a writer, not the fruits of a polished professional stage production. Collaboration is key to Sondheim's process, and there is evidence that even on *Mary Poppins* he considered taking what he had written of the score and developing it to fit a book by someone else: Among the papers at Wisconsin is an undated thirteen-page treatment of the musical for either stage or television production (options are given for both) by Richard S. Bacharach, whose identity is unclear. It makes reference to Sondheim's score, listing the songs currently written and to be written, and explains how Bacharach would break down the scenes, but there are clear differences between Bacharach's ideas and those in Sondheim's draft scenes, and it outlines Bacharach's vision for the musical rather than Sondheim's. For the purposes of this chapter, therefore, no further reference will be made to this treatment.

Sondheim's completed scenes are all the more interesting in light of his subsequent development as a composer-lyricist, for they illustrate part of his evolution as a writer for the theater, unmediated by a collaborator's thoughts. It was natural that a training course set by Hammerstein would involve Sondheim's writing the books for the four musicals rather than just the scores; Hammerstein's career had been based on writing both dialogue and lyrics, though sometimes he would have co-writers in one or both roles. What the four scenes show is how this exercise helped Sondheim think about the structure of a musical scene, where the songs are spotted, and how to put characters across. The project does not merely hint at what might have become of Sondheim's career had he pursued the auteur model of writing book, music, and lyrics, but more important, represents a space in which he could experiment with musico-dramatic ideas.

The main surviving document is a script with dialogue, lyrics, and stage directions for Act I, scenes 1–3. It is forty-six pages long, an exceptional length if this represents only about half of the scenes intended for Act I. Hammerstein's reaction to Sondheim's work on *Mary Poppins* is unrecorded (if indeed he looked at it), but his comment on the ninety-nine pages of Act I of the lengthy *Climb High*—"Boy!"—clearly applies here, too (Sondheim has often told this story and added that *South Pacific* is only ninety pages in total).[16] The main reason for this length is the way in which Sondheim crams so much detail into each scene. Table 2.4 shows an analysis of what happens in each scene, with scene summaries and a breakdown of each part of the scene below each summary. Immediately, the problem with the work becomes clear: Sondheim does not make enough progress on each page. The first five pages are a particularly slow exposition of the dysfunctional nature of the Banks household, and it seems that Sondheim is too inclined to tell parts of the story twice, that is, in both dialogue and song. The opening number, "When Children Reach That Difficult Age," is effective in setting the scene, particularly as regards the disagreement between Mr. and Mrs. Banks as to whether the children should have more freedom or more discipline, but their discussion of the topic goes on too long. It is notable that Sondheim develops the personalities of the Banks parents in order to give more depth to the story—it sets up the "problem" of the show so that there can be an overarching narrative. The character of Mr. Banks is sterner than he is in the Travers stories, even referring to the children in one song as "normal little bastards," whereas Mrs. Banks is more assertive and engaged than her counterpart, if intellectually pretentious—she refers several times to "Dr. Frederic Bukofzer's *Manual of Infant and Child Care*," a fictitious volume whose author Sondheim must have modeled on the German American musicologist Manfred Frederick Bukofzer (1910–1955). This dispute between Mr. and Mrs. Banks cleverly creates a question that presumably would have been resolved had the show been finished, as well as introducing a much more adult conversation about nature versus nurture than we see in the Travers books.

The song "When Children Reach That Difficult Age" is also interesting in that it shows Sondheim creating a narrative kind of number that could recur later in the scene both to provide musical cohesion and to tell a different part of the story. Its use is not unlike use of the "You're a Queer One, Julie Jordan" theme from Rodgers and Hammerstein's *Carousel* (1945), which is similarly deployed flexibly across two separate conversations (Julie–Carrie and Julie–Billy), the second of them as an introduction/verse to a new song ("If I Loved You" in the case of *Carousel*). In *Mary Poppins*, Mrs. Banks sings a bit of "When Children Reach" with new words ("When Servants Reach That Difficult Age") near the end of

**Table 2.4.** Breakdown of scene structure, Sondheim's *Mary Poppins*, Act I, scenes 1–3.

| Scene no. | Pages | Content |
|---|---|---|
| 1 | 1–13 | **The Banks family advertises for a nanny** |
| | 1–5 | Mr. and Mrs. Banks discuss parenthood. Song: "When Children Reach That Difficult Age." |
| | 58 | Jane and Michael appear and are naughty. Mr. and Mrs. Banks tell them they are going to advertise for a new nanny. Jane and Michael sing a nonsense song they have written (Song: "Minus-Rally"). |
| | 9–11 | Mrs. Brill announces that the kitchen flue is on fire and Ellen the maid tells Mrs. Banks she intends to take the next day off. |
| | 12 | Mrs. Banks tells Robertson Ay he only polished one of Mr. Banks' shoes and asks Jane and Michael to take the twins to the park. Song: "When Servants Reach That Difficult Age" (reprise). |
| | 13 | Mrs. Banks writes the advertisement for a new nanny. Song: "Ad." |
| 2 | 14–32 | **Mary Poppins arrives and is introduced to the Banks family** |
| | 14 | Through the window, the children see Mary Poppins arrive. |
| | 15–19 | Mary Poppins arrives in the house. She discusses her terms of employment with Mrs. Banks and meets the children. |
| | 19–23 | Mr. Banks returns home and learns that Mrs. Banks has hired Mary Poppins. Song: "Softly Now, Hear My Heart." |
| | 23–27 | Mary Poppins unpacks her bag in the nursery. Song: "No Ordinary Nanny Am I." |
| | 27–29 | Mr. Banks comes to the nursery with Mrs. Banks to say goodnight to the children. He meets Mary Poppins. |
| | 29–32 | Jane and Michael ask where Mary comes from. She explains that she has friends and relatives close by. They sing to her (Song: "Mary Poppins, Welcome"). The children ask her to sing them to sleep and she responds with their nonsense song (Song: "Minus-Rally" [reprise]). She explains that she will stay until the wind changes. |
| 3 | 33–46 | **Mary and Bert go out for afternoon tea in a pavement picture** |
| | 33 | Mary leaves the children for her day out. |

**Table 2.4.** Continued

| Scene no. | Pages | Content |
|---|---|---|
| | 33–35 | Mary meets Bert and learns he does not have enough money to take her out for afternoon tea. |
| | 35–36 | They decide to step into Bert's pavement picture to have tea there instead. Song: "Suddenly the Sunlight." |
| | 36–43 | The waiter asks them to sit down. Bert wants to skip tea because he wants to make love to Mary; she insists on having tea. Song: "Tea." |
| | 43–44 | Mary and Bert ride on the merry-go-round but have to leave at six o'clock. |
| | 44–46 | Back in the real world, Mary and Bert say goodbye. Song: "Suddenly the Sunlight" (duet reprise). They kiss and Bert is left alone. Song: "Once in a Color I Saw My Love." |

the first scene and, a little like the Bench Scene in *Carousel*, underscoring keeps the music going under dialogue into a new song, "Wanted: A Nurse" (the music manuscript is titled "Ad"). The parallels with the Disney version in the decision to set the latter to music are fascinating because Travers does not put the advertisement into words in the book (though it must be noted that Sondheim makes a song from Mrs. Banks's advertisement, whereas the Sherman Brothers use Jane and Michael's version in the Disney adaptation).

This reveals that finding moments for song in a musicalization of *Mary Poppins* actually meant creating *new* moments. It should also be emphasized that Sondheim realizes much more dramatic impact from the number than the Disney writers do: The lights dim after the climax of "Ad" and the clock strikes six before a cinematic segue into scene 2 (Sondheim's well-documented love of cinema, with the exception of film musicals, is evident here). If the opening scene was too long, and bogged down by dialogue from the books combined with new ideas from Sondheim, its completion is beautifully written, underlining the point of the scene: The Banks family needs a new nanny, and Mrs. Banks has now advertised for one. This leads very nicely into the opening of the second scene, in which Sondheim gets much more rapidly to business. On its first page, the children look out of the window, see Mary Poppins arrive on the east wind, and describe her appearance. The next part of the scene is much more drawn out, however, taking more than four pages for Mrs. Banks to hire Mary and escort her to the nursery (as in both Travers's book and the Disney film, Mary glides up the bannister to the nursery without Mrs. Banks' seeing).

In itself, this highlights a problem with the way the scene is written out: In effect, the different constituents of scene 2 provide material for several separate scenes in different rooms of the house and probably should have been written as such. Sondheim writes them as one continuous scene with his cinematic perspective; because these moments happen consecutively, they are conveyed as one scene. Dividing them up might have given him more focus and even led him to drop some of them. This is especially true of the passage on pages 19–23, in which Mr. Banks returns home and learns that Mary Poppins has been hired. This information could have been related to the audience in a couple of lines. But not only does Sondheim draw out this process into a comical back-and-forth between Mr. and Mrs. Banks, he also adds a song to probe the psychology of their marriage, "Softly Now, Hear My Heart."[17] Their relationship has cooled ("Conversation melted to a silent stare," sings Mrs. Banks), and after they have a mild argument about the fact that Mrs. Banks has hired a nanny who refuses to provide references, Sondheim's script tells us that they "sit, occasionally looking at each other furtively. Neither can think of anything to say, so they sing their thoughts, each unaware of what the other is thinking."

Perhaps it is going too far to suggest a direct emulation, but it is possible that Sondheim was trying (if unconsciously) to copy his mentor Hammerstein's "Twin Soliloquies" from *South Pacific* (1949), in which we hear the unspoken thoughts of Emile and Nellie through the medium of song. As for the content of the number, the depiction of an affectionate marriage in which the passion has cooled is remarkably astute for a writer of nineteen or twenty (there are no dates on any of the materials, so we can only estimate the period of composition; Sondheim gives 1950 in *Look, I Made a Hat*). It is cleverly done and extends the embellishment of the Banks marriage from the opening of the first scene to form part of the core problem of the plot. The lyric itself reads like something the mature Sondheim would mock in Hammerstein's work—what he called in a 2010 interview with Adam Guettel "Oscar's obsession with . . . nature imagery,"[18] which he regards as "wet and embarrassing." Therefore, it is not clear whether Sondheim is being ironic in using lines such as "Now by moonlight, moss and mimosa" in this number from *Mary Poppins* or whether he had not yet "learned to be himself," a maxim of Hammerstein's that Sondheim related in the same interview. What really matters is that although there are signs of Sondheim's insightfulness about human relationships in this section of the scene, it slows down the momentum in a way that is uncommon in Sondheim's mature shows.

Later segments of the scene are much more on message, especially when Mary interacts with the children. Sondheim makes the most of the passage in the Travers story where Mary uses her magic thermometer to "read" Jane and Michael's personalities, and he also exploits the section about the magical medicine bottle that delivers a different liquid to each person. In this regard it is worth briefly comparing Sondheim's approach to those of the Sherman Brothers in the 1964 Disney film and of George Stiles and Anthony Drewe in the 2004 Disney/Cameron Mackintosh stage adaptation. In the film, the Sherman Brothers set this medicine bottle moment to music in "A Spoonful of Sugar," but the sweetness alluded to in the lyric spills over into the dramatic effect; the song itself is saccharine, even if Julie Andrews's delivery is irresistibly charming. For the lyricist Robert Sherman, the song (and therefore Mary Poppins) is about "finding fun" in work by adding sugar. Stiles and Drewe relocate and rearrange this song for a later episode in their stage adaptation and instead write a new song called "Practically Perfect" for Mary's first scene in the nursery, in which Mary describes herself as the "perfect" nanny, a reference to the children's advertisement. But Sondheim attempts to characterize her in much more detail in a song called "Nanny." The verse illustrates Mary's mysterious, contradictory nature: she tells the children not to ask her any questions if they want to know things about her. Syncopations on two instances of the word "you" ("Do not ask me where I dwell. You / mustn't ask me who I am. / And if you don't then I will tell / you") and unexpected flatted sevenths in the whirling melody go much further than the equivalent songs from the familiar Disney film and stage productions in communicating the supernatural in Mary's persona. The song has three verses and three refrains, and between each hearing is a piece of dialogue between Mary and the children in which the thermometer and medicine episodes take place over underscoring.

In this part of the scene, Sondheim's sophisticated approach to song, story, and dialogue is well developed. Following this, Mr. and Mrs. Banks come to say goodnight to the children, and at the end Mary astonishes Jane and Michael by singing a song called "Minus Rally" that the children had "invented" in the first scene, long before Mary first arrived. Because she knows the words and lyrics to something she cannot have heard, they start to suspect her magical powers. It is a cute idea but a cumbersome extension of the scene that would surely have been cut had the show been developed further.

## Experimenting with Form and Drama: "Time for Tea" and a Lovers' Quarrel

By far the most significant item from the *Poppins* project is a number called "Time for Tea," the centerpiece of scene 3. In line with the chapter "The Day Out" from the first Poppins book, Mary meets up with Bert, the Match Man, on her day off, in the hope that he will take her out for tea. But he has not made enough money from his pavement drawings that week, so Mary and Bert step inside one of the pictures and go for tea (for which they do not need to pay) there instead. Sondheim follows Travers more closely than the Disney movie does, because Jane and Michael do not join the adults on the excursion. When the set magically changes into the park within the painting, Mary bursts into the song "Suddenly the Sunlight," the lyrics for which are in the script but the music for which has not been discovered in the Wisconsin archive. Though the imagery in the lyrics is fairly generic, there is a lovely third stanza indented along the page as if it were an interlude in which Mary sings wistfully in the *carpe diem* mode about the beauty of the temporary world that Bert has painted and which will disappear: "Like a summer's day, it is / Just a transient gaiety." Without the music it is impossible to properly assess the impact of the song, even if it seems like a strong idea to have a big vocal item immediately after the lights have come up to reveal the brightly painted scene within the pavement picture. Sondheim's theatrical instincts regarding this are good.

In Travers's *Mary Poppins*, there is a gentle suggestion that Mary and Bert are a romantic item. For example, when Bert cries Mary's name on first seeing her in Chapter 2, Travers notes that "you could tell by the way he cried it that Mary Poppins was a very important person in his life."[19] Later, he takes her hand and "squeezes it hard,"[20] and she "puts her hand through the Match Man's arm."[21] But these are no more than suggestions of tenderness. Sondheim makes Bert's desire to have sex with Mary the focus of the tea scene, retaining most of Travers's dialogue but considerably embellishing it in a musical number that is highly unusual in form and nature for its time. Before the song starts, Mary and Bert have what amounts to a lovers' quarrel, completely without precedent in the book. Mary complains that with so many people about, they will never be alone (the one place where she implies that she, too, desires time alone with Bert); Bert responds that they should therefore skip the meal, but Mary insists that she *never* misses her tea, and this becomes the basis for an argument that takes place in the "Time for Tea" number.

This is a trio that involves the Waiter as well as the other two, and the poor Waiter is constantly confused as Mary orders lots of things while Bert sulkily rejects everything. Over the course of 145 measures they argue, and of course Mary has her way. The first striking aspect is that Sondheim uses unpitched rhythmic dialogue in the opening fifteen measures of the number, making the move from dialogue to full-on song smoother (no wonder he would later express admiration for Meredith Willson's "Rock Island" number from *The Music Man*;

Sondheim himself had used such a technique in *All That Glitters*).[22] He begins with a rhythmic introduction in the orchestra that grows from two pitches to become a dense chord within the space of a few bars. Fragments of this introductory motif recur regularly through the opening vocal section (Waiter: "Modom [*sic*]; sir; tea is served;" Mary: "Four o'clock, Bert, tea is served") along with a freer (but still highly rhythmic) theme in the treble line from m. 8. The contents of m. 15 also recur in several places: as Mary rebukes Bert for his sulkiness (beat 1: "Bert!"), the Waiter expresses confusion ("Sir?" beat 2), Bert pleads with Mary (beat 3: "Mary . . ."), and the Waiter declares "Tea!" (beat 4). At m. 16, a new section begins and Mary starts to sing for the first time ("I don't want you making love to me now"). The tessitura of the vocal writing in this number is puzzlingly wide, requiring Mary to have strength across two full octaves, but the placement of her first entrance is certainly effective; she sings in a "chesty" place below the staff in what seems to communicate controlled anger with Bert's inappropriate flirtation (if such a mild word can be used to describe his obvious desire for them to go off and make love). Although new, this section's melodic material is obviously related to the accompaniment figure in m. 8, showing Sondheim's sophisticated approach to providing both coherence and structural divisions.

At m. 49 ("No, I am drinking my tea!"), Mary starts to lash out more, singing a high A above the staff in a short figure that repeats, like the others, at appropriate moments in the dialogue (that is, whenever Bert asks her to come away with him or declare love to him). This gives way to new material at m. 50, when Bert sings in a more lyrical style, signifying the ardent lover ("Now we're alone can't we talk of something gay?"); a sequential figure is used to raise the temperature and urgency of his argument, but she still responds in a monotone (at m. 57) with "Not while I'm drinking my tea."

An abrupt modulation descending from A major to A♭ at m. 62 signals a new part of the discussion. Mary reminds him that afternoon tea is an important British tradition, but Bert replies "Not for me" and even asks to drink some Guinness, much to Mary's horror (mm. 74–77). The key of A major resumes in m. 105, and from m. 123 to m. 125 Mary sings a chromatically rising passage to lead into a contrapuntal conclusion with all three characters stating their fixed positions at the same time (Bert still wants Mary, Mary rejects Bert, the Waiter continues to offer them tea). It is a terrific number that may represent the birth of Sondheim's musico-dramatic instinct, foreshadowing the great ensemble writing of his mature musicals ("Your Fault" from *Into the Woods* comes to mind).[23] In addition, his personal slant on the story—bringing an adult sensibility to an innocent children's short story—demonstrates how innate his particular vision for the musical theater is, without the influence of collaborators.

## Around the World with Mary Poppins

The remainder of scene 3 is, admittedly, less interesting. Back in the real world, Mary and Bert sing a reprise of "Suddenly" and they kiss before Mary returns to the house and Bert sings what must be a ballad (the music is missing), "Once in a Color I Saw My Love." It is a shame that the eyebrow-raising satire of "Tea" is afterward dissipated through the conventions of the kiss, the love duet, and the ballad. This scene forms the end of the main script draft in the Wisconsin materials. But there are two versions of another scene, based mainly on the chapter "Bad Tuesday," which represent significant additional work. One copy is a complete draft of the scene, twenty-nine pages long, and the other has a nine-page span that is identical to pp. 19–28 of the complete version, plus four other draft pages with Sondheim's working notes on them.

The complete draft of this scene indicates exactly the same problem that was earlier highlighted in connection with scene 2: It contains enough material for several separate scenes, a situation made all the more obvious in this example by a dimming of the lights to change the scene from one room of the house to another on pp. 4 and 9 and a blackout to change again to an exterior set on p. 15.[24] The purpose of pp. 9–15 is to illustrate life among the motley collection of servants in the Banks household, a conflation of small details about their personalities and relationships from across the Poppins books welded together by a mock nursery rhyme number called "Sing a Song of Servants," while pp. 1–9 and 15–29 relate the main story about Michael Banks's bad temper, "Bad Tuesday." There is certainly a logic to the way in which Sondheim has constructed the scene as a whole: Mary encounters chaos in the nursery when Michael wakes up in a naughty mood (pp. 1–9), finds equal disfunction in the kitchen when she goes to collect the children's breakfast from Mrs. Brill (9–15), and then takes the children on an adventure around the world to cure Michael of his bad mood (15–29).

The kitchen episode provides amusement about the grumbles of the working characters and amplifies Mary Poppins's mysteriousness by having the servants discuss her unfathomable powers. The highlight of the scene is perhaps the section of the song when Mary confronts Mrs. Brill about her cooking skills, the choppy alliterative lines and rhyme scheme hinting at what was to come much later in the Witch's rap from *Into the Woods* and Mrs. Lovett's songs from *Sweeney Todd* (for example, "I could baste in haste / Without any kind of waste / And my gravy didn't taste / Like paste"). The music has not been located for this passage, but this extant lyric certainly has an air of the wit and multiple rhyming of later Sondheim. Nevertheless, this part of the scene significantly slows the momentum of the show and adds nothing meaningful to the plot.

Much more convincingly laid out is the main "Bad Tuesday" storyline. As with other scenes, Sondheim is perhaps a little too inclined to add songs where a couple of lines of dialogue would do. For example, he begins with Michael's "inner voice" (played by an offstage actor referred to as the Voice) persuading him to be naughty and then, quite unnecessarily, singing a duet with Michael, essentially to persuade him again (albeit offering more detailed images of the naughty things he could do). In total, this takes up 10 percent of the script for the scene, which is too much for so little progress. Michael then proceeds to be naughty, with the Voice instructing him what to do. Sondheim makes him naughtier than he is in the Travers story; for example, in the book Michael bathes himself when he refuses to allow Mary Poppins to bathe him, but in Sondheim's script he puts on his best suit without washing at all. The Voice is also an invention of Sondheim's. In the book, Michael doesn't know why he is being naughty, but Sondheim turns the first part of the scene (pp. 1–9) into a deconstruction of Michael's psyche, a conversation between two different parts of his brain. Although the concept is overdone, again it is a fascinating example of Sondheim's creative experimentation at this point in his career, without obvious precedent in the musical theater canon.

As noted, the main part of the scene is based on the adventure that Mary takes the children on in the "Bad Tuesday" chapter of Travers's book. The episode in the original book is highly problematic for its culturally stereotyped portrayals of the people Mary and the children visit during their journey, so much so that in 1967 Travers removed some of the most offensive language and in 1981 rewrote the unacceptable chapter to replace the people with animals from the different countries (Mary Shephard also revisited her original illustrations at this point). Ironically, given Travers's well-known dislike of it, this brought the chapter closer to the 1964 movie: the new paragraphs in which Mary chats with a polar bear, a panda, a dolphin, and a macaw are the cutesy stuff of a Disney cartoon. But of course, Sondheim's version was based on the only source available to him, the original novel, in which Mary and the children meet Indigenous Alaskans, Chinese, sub-Saharan Africans, and Native Americans. It is not surprising that Sondheim takes most of the dialogue from the novel and supplements it with a brief song in each place. The script for the journey round the world makes for uncomfortable reading, precisely because these are mainly Travers's words, which were later rightly condemned and modified.

Yet the scene is of scholarly importance for the way it reflects and reveals Sondheim's cinematic interest and instinct, which are at the fore of the extant materials. There are quick changes of set from the park to the north, the south, the east, and the west, taking the form of cinematic dissolves from location to location (something that had a precedent in *Lady in the Dark*, 1941). By employing music and song in each segment of the journey, Sondheim made it like a musical montage of the types seen in Hollywood musicals (for example, *Easter Parade*, 1948), rather than four short theatrical scenes with a song in the middle of each. The songs are used to teach the children the different customs of greeting in each culture, and Sondheim writes a few extra lines that are not in the Travers book to depict Michael refusing to respect the different cultures and being quickly reprimanded by Mary Poppins; this is clearly the writer's attempt to address the problematic aspects of the source novel. He also seems to gently lampoon cultural stereotypes as depicted in other musical dramatic works. For example, the Mandarin's song evokes the "bow down" section of "Behold the Lord High Executioner" from *The Mikado*, while the southern episode pokes fun at Hammerstein's "Bali Ha'i." The episode with the Native Americans even more strongly lampoons a previous work associated with Sondheim's mentor, namely the "I'm an Indian, Too" scene from Irving Berlin's *Annie Get Your Gun* (1946), a work co-produced on Broadway by Hammerstein. Making subtle connections between (and comments on) his work and that of his forebears would become a cornerstone of Sondheim's later shows, especially *Follies* (1971), but the technique was already in play in this early project.

## Down on Sweetness, up on Satire

That Sondheim's *Mary Poppins* cannot and should not be performed should be obvious. Too little of it was written, and what survives has the inevitable flaws of style, content, and structure of an abandoned work. His stated intention, in connection with this chapter, that nobody will ever be allowed to reproduce the show's music and lyrics will ensure that it is never heard. On the other hand, it is also obvious from the treatment by Richard S. Bacharach alluded to earlier that, at some point in the initial stages of his career, Sondheim seriously considered pitching the project to professional producers. He even did further work on the show, writing some melodic ideas for the "Dancing Cow" episode mentioned in Bacharach's outline, as well as the songs "Miss Andrew" and "The Sun Is Blue," neither of which feature in Sondheim's script drafts. "The Sun Is Blue" is the most refined and compelling of these, with the contradictions and oxymorons in the lyric and little quirky features in the music (for example, a diminished seventh chord after the word "small" in m. 6, underlining the contradiction in Mary's sentiment): "The universe is small, the sun is blue, / And summer follows fall while spring is freezing."

Yet we need not join Sondheim in deriding his "first fumblings" for the theater, or characterize them as such. We have seen that although the pieces did not fit together, these fragments of fairyland not only offer a glance at roads not taken but also prove that his remarkable creativity and technical flair were already well developed by his late teenage years (his frustrated attempts to get his work staged before *West Side Story* mask his prodigious talent). As I have previously remarked in connection with *Climb High*, Sondheim's personal division of his canon into before and after *Saturday Night* (1955, first performed 1997) gives the impression that what came before was of no value. But the sense of personal vision apparent in *Mary Poppins* and *Climb High* indicates that these unperformed works should be regarded not as juvenilia but, rather, as the beginning of Sondheim's overall artistic project.

The fact that his initial ideas for *Mary Poppins* are so much at odds with the Disney version seems also to carry the implication that it was at odds with what Rodgers and Hammerstein might have done with Travers's work. Though he may not have been able to crack the *Mary Poppins* project, one final source in the Wisconsin papers—a handwritten note—suggests that he was well aware of what he needed to do to make it better:

PROBLEMS:
(1) Continuity (via story-line?)
(2) Variety + non-repetition.
    a)  Non-repetition of scenic form.
    b)  Non-repetition of episode type.
(3) Feet on the ground via humor.
(4) Cut down on sweetness, up on satire.

The last two of these emphasize the divergence from the Rodgers and Hammerstein model. The lofty nature imagery that Sondheim so deplored in the aforementioned interview typifies a stylistic difference between the two generations of writers, and it is clear from the "feet on the ground via humor" remark that this distance was already being created in *Mary Poppins*. The mention of satire in the fourth item on the list also demonstrates the cementing of Sondheim's aesthetic approach; not for nothing would one of his greatest later works, *Sweeney Todd*, also be a London musical with social commentary at its heart. Thus, even if its lack of completeness means that it does not have the potential for reconsideration as a part of the professional Sondheim canon as I have argued in relation to *Climb High*, perhaps *Mary Poppins* deserves to be recognized as a milestone (and his four "Hammerstein project" musicals recognized as more than juvenilia): In its most innovative moments of adaptation, such as the "Time for Tea" trio, it reveals a breakthrough in Sondheim's ability to bring a personal view of the world to his writing.

# Notes

1. Stephen Sondheim, *Look, I Made a Hat* (New York: Knopf, 2011), 419.
2. Ibid.
3. Dominic McHugh, "*Climb High*: Sondheim at the Gateway to His Career," *Studies in Musical Theatre* 13, no. 2 (June 2019): 103–115. Acting as Sondheim's mentor, Hammerstein asked the young writer to create four musicals based on specific challenges: "an adaptation of a good play, an adaptation of a flawed play, an adaptation of something not written for the stage and, finally, an original." See Sondheim, *Look, I Made a Hat*, 419.
4. Sondheim, *Look, I Made a Hat*, 422.
5. Stephen Banfield, *Sondheim's Broadway Musicals* (Ann Arbor: University of Michigan Press, 1993), 19.
6. Steve Swayne, *How Sondheim Found His Sound* (Ann Arbor: University of Michigan Press, 2005), 139.
7. The sources for *Mary Poppins* are found in the Stephen Sondheim papers at the Wisconsin Historical Society, Madison, Wisconsin, Box 14, Folders 11–13.
8. P. L. Travers, *Mary Poppins: The Complete Collection* (London: HarperCollins, 2008), 503. It is noteworthy that two other contemporary musicals were based on collections of loosely connected short stories: Hammerstein's *South Pacific* (1949) and Loesser's *Guys and Dolls* (1950).
9. Quoted in Martin Gottfried, *Sondheim* (New York: Harry N. Abrams, 1993), 18–19.
10. Quoted in Meryle Secrest, *Stephen Sondheim: A Life* (New York: Knopf; London: Bloomsbury, 1998), 79.
11. Sondheim, *Look, I Made a Hat*, 57.
12. Cameron Mackintosh, "Why You'll Love This Book," introduction to P. L. Travers, *Mary Poppins—The Complete Collection* (London: HarperCollins, 2008), 5. Mackintosh's adaptation uses "The Kite" from *Mary Poppins Comes Back*.
13. P. L. Travers, "The Fairy-Tale as Teacher," in *A Lively Oracle: A Centennial Celebration of P. L. Travers*, ed. Ellen Dooling Draper and Jenny Koralek (New York: Larson, 1999), 200.
14. Robert and Richard Sherman were prolific writers for the screen and stage, known especially for their scores of some of the Disney films, including *Mary Poppins* (1964) and *Chitty Chitty Bang Bang* (1968).
15. He explains this at length in Mark Eden Horowitz, *Sondheim on Music: Major Details and Minor Decisions*, 2nd ed. (Lanham, MD: Scarecrow, 2010), 148–149. For example, he comments: "I got panicky. I wish I hadn't—I wish I'd stuck to my guns and just done it myself, but I couldn't. . . . [With] Hugh [Wheeler] aboard I felt confident again."
16. See Swayne, *How Sondheim Found His Sound*, 126.
17. No music has been discovered for this number, though the lyrics are complete in Sondheim's script.
18. See https://www.youtube.com/watch?v=TofC3KD-h8M, especially 0:18:30.
19. Travers, *Mary Poppins*, 23.

20. Ibid., 24.
21. Ibid., 28.
22. Sondheim describes the number as "surely one of the most startling and galvanic openings ever devised," going on to analyze the "rhythmic chatter" of the salesmen. Sondheim, *Look, I Made a Hat*, 309.
23. Thanks to Geoffrey Block for this observation.
24. By implication, Sondheim must have had in mind a large set for the house, showing different rooms that could be framed by having the lights move on and off them. The blackout implies a change to an exterior set of the park, where the rest of the scene takes place.

# 3

# "Nearly everything I wrote"

## Sondheim and the Actors Studio

*Jeffrey Magee*

None of Stephen Sondheim's formative experiences has become as legendary as Oscar Hammerstein II's lessons: the one-day tutorial analyzing the faults in his ambitious fifteen-year-old protégé's first musical, and the four-part musical-writing assignment that followed, a project that took Sondheim six years to complete. In the forty-five years since Sondheim first related that story in print, it has been duly cited in almost every account of his early years and has assumed a mythical aura.[1] Stephen Banfield has gone so far as to describe him as Hammerstein's "conscious creation, fulfilling a deep need and offering a unique opportunity to pass on his art."[2] We are a short step away from the musical theater's *The Creation of Adam*, with Hammerstein's outstretched finger animating Sondheim's creative spirit.

Yet just as that iconic panel covers but a fraction of the Sistine Chapel ceiling, the Hammerstein project must be seen in a broader context of ongoing experiences that shaped Sondheim's genesis as a musical dramatist.[3] Musicologist Steve Swayne has shown in unprecedented detail the courses that Sondheim took at Williams College in music, English, and drama, and the plays and musicals in which he performed, thirteen in all, indicating an almost constant cycle of auditions, rehearsals, and productions over the course of his four years there, ranging from *Oedipus Rex* to his own creations.[4] The story of Sondheim's postgraduate studies of music composition with Princeton University professor and avant-garde composer Milton Babbitt is well known.[5] Sondheim counted Babbitt, along with Hammerstein, high school Latin teacher Lucille Pollack, and Williams College music professor Robert Barrow as the four teachers who "changed and saved" his life.[6] And Sondheim has cited two others besides Hammerstein who influenced his lyric-writing for the stage: Burt Shevelove and Arthur Laurents, whose impact on Sondheim's artistic sensibility far exceeded the realm of lyrics.[7]

Sondheim has also mentioned, repeatedly, another crucial experience that deserves attention: his visit with Laurents to the Actors Studio in the mid-1950s, a visit that lodged two important concepts in his mind and continued to resonate

Jeffrey Magee, *"Nearly everything I wrote"* In: *Sondheim in Our Time and His*. Edited by: W. Anthony Sheppard, Oxford University Press. © Oxford University Press 2022. DOI: 10.1093/oso/9780197603192.003.0004

in his work for decades. Recognizing the visit's importance provides a necessary reminder of the constant creative flows between people and forces that are too often segregated in our stories about them, between so-called legitimate theater and musical theater, between artistic and commercial pursuits, between performers and writers, and even between words and music. It is also a reminder that Sondheim, like many of us, may not be the most reliable narrator of his own story.[8] This chapter takes a closer look at Sondheim's visit, at the ways Sondheim has reported it, at the ways its long-term impact resonates through his work, and, finally, at several figures in his creative circles in the 1950s and 1960s who were closely associated with the Actors Studio. Altogether, rediscovering Sondheim's connections to the Actors Studio adds a new dimension to studies that place him in the company of the shapers of modern American drama in the postwar period, while remaining attuned to details of musical composition that distinguish him from playwrights.

## Establishing the Studio

At the time of the visit, the Actors Studio had reached a pinnacle of hard-won stability and unsought notoriety, so it behooves us to retrace its path to that point. It had been founded in 1947 by directors Robert Lewis and Elia Kazan and producer Cheryl Crawford to provide a refuge for actors seeking to refine their craft free from the demands of production and of the commercial theater. It grew and blossomed from what Studio chronicler David Garfield called "the nurturing subsoil of the formative twenties and thirties."[9] Founded on American adaptations of the principles and techniques developed by Russian actor and director Konstantin Stanislavsky with the Moscow Art Theatre (MAT), the Actors Studio followed in the wake of the American Laboratory Theatre (1924-1930), led by Stanislavsky's protégés Richard Boleslavsky and Maria Oulenskaya, and the Group Theatre (1931-1941), led by their American students Harold Clurman and Lee Strasberg, with support from Crawford, then a young casting director. Politically charged with a desire to reimagine Depression-era America while drawing out the actor's inner life, the Group Theatre's decade of existence formed "the fervent years," as Clurman dubbed them in a book that would become seminal in the history of American theater.[10]

A belief in truth in acting anchored the line of descent from Stanislavsky to Boleslavsky and Oulenskaya to Clurman and Strasberg, who would assume artistic directorship of the Actors Studio in 1948 and become the target of Sondheim's and Laurent's ire. Stanislavsky distinguished between "the art of representation" and "the art of living the part" and developed his system in order to steer actors toward rigorous pursuit of the latter.[11] He and his protégés conducted many exercises to bring their students closer to living the part, and none became so famous and controversial as one called *affective memory*, which Stanislavsky developed from his readings of the work of the French psychologist Théodule Ribot concerning the experience of emotional recall. He came to believe that reviving memories, and the strong emotions they summoned, were the "golden keys" to great acting.[12] Clurman called affective memory Stanislavsky's "root discovery."[13]

The effort to tap affective memory could be intensely personal and revealing, so the Actors Studio, like Stanislavsky's studio, strove to sustain privacy and intentional dissociation from the mandates of production and commerce. Stanislavsky had developed his studio, later known as the First Studio, only after applying his increasingly systematic techniques for actor preparation in the MAT's 1909 production of Ivan Turgenev's *A Month in the Country*. He established the studio apart from the MAT in 1912, and then instituted a policy of shielding his actors from public view as they developed their craft in the Stanislavsky System.[14]

Like its American predecessors, the Actors Studio had shuttled among various venues in order to conduct its work. Unlike them, it ultimately settled in a permanent home where it continues to flourish to this day: the former United Presbyterian Church at 432 West Forty-Fourth Street in Manhattan, where it opened in October 1955. Less than a month later, in November 1955, the first Studio-incubated work to reach Broadway, titled *A Hatful of Rain*, opened a few blocks away at the Lyceum Theatre to strong reviews that included attention to its Studio links.[15] Soon thereafter celebrity drop-ins became more frequent, and newspaper columnists quoted their observations and raised the Studio's profile in the public's consciousness. By late 1955 the Studio had become a fishbowl. It had not been conceived as a showcase. Now it was one.[16]

Visitors knew that the Studio only accepted a small cadre of the best: In a period of less than three years between 1948 and 1951, more than two thousand actors auditioned and only about thirty were offered membership, an acceptance rate of 1.5 percent.[17] Visitors also knew that actors such as Marlon Brando, Montgomery Clift, Paul Newman, Kim Stanley, and renowned film director and Studio co-founder Elia Kazan, to name a few, had passed through; and some continued to return, signaling that successful professionals had something more to learn there under Lee Strasberg, the voluble guru of whom it was said, "That man uses twenty words where one would do."[18]

It was also during the Studio's first season in its new home that Marilyn Monroe began visiting regularly. Having studied privately with Strasberg, she witnessed sessions in the fall of 1955 and performed her first and only scene there in early 1956.[19] As Harold Clurman reflected, "Everyone wanted to know what the Actors Studio was that the phosphorescent Marilyn should be concerned with it."[20] (In mid-1956, during the period when Monroe strove to be recognized as a serious actress, she married playwright Arthur Miller.) And just weeks before Sondheim and Laurents's visit, James Dean, another Studio product, had died in a dramatic car accident at the age of twenty-four, adding to the aura of the Studio as a place where artists pushed the boundaries to dangerous limits in both art and life.

The media attention coincided with a sense that the Studio might not hold together. It all concerned Strasberg deeply and personally. In a rambling lecture preserved on tape, Strasberg notes that the publicity had come as they "tried to eradicate it" and that he feels "helpless" because of what he viewed as the irresponsible, even "destructive" behavior of several Studio members. He chides them for the "waste" of talent that Dean's death represented, and adds pointedly, "It isn't just Jimmy. Jimmy is just a symbol. . . . I see personal problems here, and outside. I wish there was something we could do."[21] Still, and surely *because* Studio members' behavior had become fuel for gossip columnists, the spotlight intensified.

In 1956 two notable public responses to the increased notoriety followed. One of them was an article that Strasberg published in the *New York Times* attempting to demystify, perhaps to normalize, the Studio's inner workings by citing the naturalistic film performances of such stars as Gary Cooper, John Wayne, and Spencer Tracy as public manifestations of the kind of "authenticity, even at moments of technical insecurity," the Studio sought to cultivate in its members.[22] It is telling that he did not mention Studio members and film stars Marlon Brando and the late James Dean in that list. The other public response followed soon thereafter. Late November saw the Broadway opening of the musical *Bells Are Ringing*, which includes in one scene a parody of Studio acting in which "several 'Brandos,' all dressed alike in jeans and leather jackets . . . exchange inarticulate grunts."[23] In one stage direction, Betty Comden and Adolph Green captured what would become the clichés that clung to Studio acting for decades. Until the fall of 1955 the Studio had not received much public attention, but, as Garfield has put it, the establishment of "permanent headquarters changed all that. The world began to take notice."[24] It was in this context of growing attention, even mythologizing, that Laurents and Sondheim made their visit.

## Visiting the Studio

There is a compelling reason *not* to overestimate that visit: Sondheim always describes it with contempt. He has mentioned it in print at least three times, however, each time with more nuance and a perceptible shift in tone, and he has been very clear about its impact on him. In every telling, Arthur Laurents was the instigator. In a 1985 essay Sondheim recalled, "[he] dragged me to two sessions of the Actors Studio while we were writing *Gypsy*."[25] Two decades later, he wrote that Laurents "took me" to the Studio "when I first started to work on *West Side Story*."[26] A few years after that he claimed that Laurents "suggested that I accompany him to a session" at that time.[27] Laurents's influence changes with the telling: The coercive "dragged me"—connoting Sondheim's unwillingness—yields to the more neutral "took me," and then evolves to the more courteous "suggested that I accompany him." Each successive telling grants Sondheim more agency in his visit to the Studio.

Factual details also change with the telling. In the first account Sondheim mentions going to the Studio while writing *Gypsy*, which would suggest the last half of 1958 or early 1959; the later accounts indicate that the visit occurred at least three years earlier. It appears that those correct a faulty memory in the initial account, which would thus place the visit in late 1955 or perhaps early 1956, soon after Sondheim signed on to work on *West Side Story*—in October 1955, the same month the Studio opened its permanent home and began to receive more public attention.[28]

But one thing is clear: The visit triggered an abiding disdain for the work of the Actors Studio. Sondheim writes of the "horrifying Actors Studio sessions which were nothing but group therapy,"[29] of actors who "took themselves much too seriously, over-analyzing and indulging themselves,"[30] and of his own "embarrassment" at bearing witness to actors "hyperanalyzing both their lives and their craft" in a manner that "seemed to me to be self-indulgent and pretentious."[31] Sondheim's most recent account offers particularly pointed scorn for Strasberg, whom he describes as the "grand panjandrum . . . (who, as demonstration of his status, had a chair-boy following him to support him wherever he chose to land)."[32] Sondheim's published views of the Studio tend to be in synchrony with those of Laurents, who also skewered what he perceived as Strasberg's pretentions: "When he [Strasberg] spoke and only when he spoke, a recording machine was turned on. . . . Moses, he was, and he looked at me with disdain."[33] Laurents reiterates the most common critique of the Studio's work, from the *Bells Are Ringing* spoof to later testimonials and scholarly accounts: that the actors mumbled and could not be understood.[34] The critique is fair enough when addressing production before an audience but perhaps beside the point when describing an exercise to develop the actor's craft. What Laurents does not note is that, as a guest, his open critique of the session he visited was, at the very least, inappropriate and unproductive. If he held it in such open contempt, why visit at all?

It is not difficult to understand why the Studio and its method discomfited writers such as Sondheim and Laurents: The goals of the work in the Studio placed script and character a distant second to whatever acting challenge the actor was striving to address in any given exercise. Scenes written by playwrights, including some from librettos for musicals, were mere vehicles for the actor's journey as the actor, under Strasberg's "priest-like" tutelage, sought "solutions" to particular technical, physical, or expressive "problems."[35] This stood among Strasberg's departures from the master's teachings: Stanislavsky and his protégés had emphasized building character from the "given circumstances" of the play.[36] Strasberg, more a teacher than a director, placed the actor in a uniquely privileged position. The Wisconsin Center for Film and Theater Research contains hundreds of audio tapes of Strasberg's commentary on actors' work—thanks to the "recording machine" that Laurents noticed—and in a sampling of more than a dozen of them, one rarely hears mention of the names of characters, playwrights, or plays, except when an assistant softly announces the scene into the recording microphone prior to Strasberg's remarks.

Strasberg's search for solutions to the actors' problems, which came to be known as The Method, usually invoked one or more of his three prized pedagogical techniques: improvisation, based either on a scene or on an invented situation; the "private moment exercise," in which an actor performed an everyday activity usually done alone behind closed doors;[37] and what Strasberg called "sense memory"—the recollection of a smell, sound, look, feel, or taste associated with a significant life event—which led to affective memory, or emotional recall, the holy grail of Stanislavsky's System and Strasberg's Method.[38] For a beginner, sense and affective memory might take a half an hour to summon; the goal was to reduce the preparation to a "golden minute," as it came to be called among Studio members.[39] To some observers these memory exercises looked like a form of psychotherapy; this would lead Strasberg to take pains to distinguish his work from that of the analyst. He did so even as he continued to work to unveil the actor's "inner" self and tap the "unconscious," often by urging the actor to dredge up painful memories, much as Freud—whose reputation and ideas enjoyed a peak of prestige and popularity in the United States in the mid-1950s—had done for different purposes.[40] In this context, it seems likely that the hype surrounding the Studio at the very moment of Sondheim and Laurents's visit intensified their distaste for what happened there.

## The Studio's Lessons

Yet Sondheim also makes it clear that the Actors Studio taught him two important lessons. For one, Laurents, he said, "wanted me to understand acting from an actor's point of view, how they approached a role," and Laurents believed that visiting the Studio would provide that insight.[41] Sondheim reports asking Laurents why he took him there. "'You've got to know the instruments you're working with,' [Laurents] explained in a tone somewhere between scorn and admiration."[42] The other lesson Sondheim learned was about *subtext*, which he describes as "what is not being said, the counterpoint underneath a scene," which "is what keeps the scene alive."[43] He concluded that "those two lessons—the idea of the actor as an instrument, and the uses of subtext—informed nearly everything I wrote after that session at the Studio."[44]

The phrase "informed nearly everything I wrote" makes a powerful claim that deserves elaboration. Fortunately, Sondheim himself has provided a great deal of that elaboration—so much so, in fact, that a reader might be forgiven for feeling strong-armed into accepting both the claims and the evidence. Resonating with the notion of actor-as-instrument, for example, Sondheim regularly situates his artistic muse among the performers for whom he has written, noting, "I really don't want to write a score until the show's cast." This is because "instead of writing Madame Rose you write for Madame Rose as played by Ethel Merman. . . . Joanne as played by Elaine Stritch. . . . [and] Mrs. Lovett as played by Angela Lansbury. . . ,"[45] a list to which he added Alexis Smith for "Lucy and Jessie" and Glynis Johns for "Send in the Clowns."[46] He continued: "It's not so much that you tailor the material, but you hear the voice in your head whether you want to or not."[47] Of course, Broadway (and Hollywood) composers had long written for particular performers: That was the basis for the star vehicles that carried the likes of Al Jolson, Ethel Merman, Fred Astaire, Gertrude Lawrence, and many others. The bespoke tailoring of material for 1920s performers led Bruce Kirle to dub them "co-creators" of the musicals in which they starred.[48] Sondheim's work tended to steer performers to extend their star personas and become actors. For example, Laurents asked Merman during the writing of *Gypsy*: "Rose is a monster. . . . How far are you willing to go?"[49] In his published memoirs and in his private datebook, Laurents wrote of meeting Merman for the first time over a drink at Sardi's. In the datebook Laurents wrote that "she really wants to act," which was likely the catalyst for his question.[50] But in his memoirs Laurents did not concede that Merman could act, claiming that she was "a voice, a presence, and a strut, not an actress."[51] Much later, Sondheim would concede that she was, and that the show had brought it out: "To our surprise and delight, Ethel could act."[52]

Following the Studio visit, Sondheim and Laurents talked about what they had witnessed, and Sondheim has elaborated on what he learned there about actors:

Suddenly everything I'd witnessed seemed, if no less silly, much more focused: I began to understand something about what actors require. Just as a composer shouldn't write for the piano without knowing something about how to play it, so a playwright (and by implication a lyric writer) shouldn't write for the musical theater without understanding acting from an actor's point of view. Writing for actors, you have to ask yourself: How do they approach a role? How do they see themselves? How, in fact, do they *think*? Not every actor uses the Stanislavsky techniques on which the Actors Studio is based, but that afternoon was an invaluable, if unsettling, experience.[53]

As for the second lesson, its impact is evident in Sondheim's repeated use of the word *subtext,* a keynote in his discussions of a variety of numbers and shows in his books of lyrics, although the word is not indexed in them. Tracking its use provides another gauge of the ongoing resonance of the Actors Studio visit.

It is worth recalling that when Sondheim first heard it in the mid-1950s the English word *subtext* was of recent coinage, at least within the theater. Its first appearance in print in a theatrical context seems to have been the English translation of Stanislavsky's *Building a Character,* published in 1949.[54] In the late 1960s, Shakespeare scholar John Russell Brown tried to trace the term's etymology and reported not finding it in an English dictionary.[55] Nor does the term appear in the *Oxford English Dictionary* as late as 1971. It may now be found in the OED online, where it is defined as "an underlying and often distinct theme in a conversation, piece of writing, etc. Also in later use: *spec.* the subjective reality drawn on by a performer and underlying his or her interpretation of a role."[56] That "later use" refers to Stanislavsky's book and its aftermath.

In *Building a Character* Stanislavsky provides a loftier, more discursive definition, which is delivered through the voice of Stanislavsky's avatar Tortsov:

> What do we mean by subtext? What is it that lies behind and beneath the actual words of a part? . . . It is the manifest, the inwardly felt expression of a human being in a part, which flows uninterruptedly beneath the words of the text, giving them life and a basis for existing. The subtext is a web of innumerable, varied inner patterns inside a play and a part, woven from "magic ifs," given circumstances, all sort of figments of the imagination, inner movements, objects of attention, smaller and greater truths and a belief in them, adaptations, adjustments and other similar elements. It is the subtext that makes us say the words we do in a play.[57]

Subtext, then, can forge an intimate bond between the writer, the actor, the character, and the context. It connotes an implicit understanding that an author conjures through "patterns inside a play and a part" and which an actor can realize in a number of ways. For a composer, however—at least for Sondheim—subtext connotes something different than it does for playwrights and actors. For subtext may be conjured by music in relation to words and plot context.

## "Subtextual Writing"

Sondheim invokes the term *subtext* many times in his writings and interviews, especially throughout his books of collected lyrics *Finishing the Hat* and *Look, I Made a Hat.* He seems particularly intent on making the subtextual connotations explicit, as he eagerly offers clues about how his music creates subtext for actors to play. For Exhibit A, we might begin with a passage that Sondheim calls "a class-room example of subtextual writing": "The Road You Didn't Take" from *Follies*. The number features what he calls a "recurrent dissonant note in the music" that "contradicts the blitheness of what Ben is saying."[58] What Ben is saying is that he is content with his lot, that the choices he has made and not made have led to success and formed "the famous Benjamin Stone." He sings the song to impress his former lover, Sally, who is clearly still smitten with him. The song leads us to see that he is actually anguished by visions of "the Ben I'll never be." The recurrent dissonant note stands a tritone way from the tonic, but it is more than just a *note*, as Jonathan Tunick's original orchestration shows. (See example 3.1.) Tunick italicizes the dissonance with a unique, other-worldly blend of instruments that sharpens the note's stabbing impact.

A closer look shows that dissonant note played in unison by a horn, stopped and *cuivré*, that is, "forced" or "overblown"; three muted trumpets; and a vibraphone marked "no vibr[ato]" and played "loud with soft mallets." Could there be a clearer indication of Ben's repressed existential sadness and rage than the muffled cries of the stopped and "forced" horn,[59] the muted trumpets, and the straight-toned vibraphone for which the player must produce a loud dissonance by overcompensating for "soft mallets"? These are more than just score indications. They are metaphors for Ben's psychological state, straining to fortify the shaky dam that contains his emotions. His psychological state becomes more explicit in the dramatic contrast between the words of the song and the brief flashbacks inserted between its refrains. In the song, Ben insists that he doesn't remember the roads not taken, but the flashback shows that he does remember his younger self, making choices—to borrow money and a car from his friend and take his future wife Phyllis on a date that led to his proposal of marriage, which he later claims to have been "the one impulsive thing I ever did."[60]

**Example 3.1.** "The Road You Didn't Take," mm. 33–34, brass and percussion only, from Stephen Sondheim, *Follies (Orchestrations by Jonathan Tunick)*, edited by Jon Alan Conrad, Music of the United States of America 33 (Middleton, WI: A-R Editions, forthcoming).

That Sondheim cites this passage from "The Road You Didn't Take" as a "classroom example of subtextual writing" raises questions about unmentioned composers and models that should come readily to the minds of musicians, and to that issue we shall return. For now, Sondheim's description invites us to look for comparable places where the music casts doubt on the denotative and connotative meanings of words. At the end of "Epiphany," for one, as Sweeney Todd has cemented his understanding of his life mission to embark on class warfare by killing his customers, he sings, "The work waits, I'm alive at last, and I'm full of joy!" On "joy" Todd sings an F♯ that joins a dissonant cluster with the orchestra. The ensuing final cadence parts the curtain on the pensive sadness underlying that "joy" in the work, because he has by now abandoned the notion of finding his wife and daughter. Two measures of quiet dissonance (marked *p*)—with a piercing tritone and major seventh—alternate with loud, triumphant chords (marked *ff*).[61] (See example 3.2.) Sondheim speaks explicitly about this passage in *Finishing the Hat*, where he addresses the issue of whether the soft, dissonant chords at the end would dissipate the ovation following the song,[62] or "kill the hand," as he has put it in another context.[63]

**Example 3.2.** "Epiphany," ending, from the piano-vocal score of Stephen Sondheim and Hugh Wheeler, *Sweeney Todd* (n.p.: Rilting Music, Inc. and Warner Bros., 1997).

That other context was a comparable scene from *Gypsy* twenty years earlier. In the course of reflecting on the *Sweeney* passage, Sondheim mentions a number whose soft ending posed a threat to the ovation that the actor deserved after a rousing mad scene, namely, "Rose's Turn." The familiar ending in the published score and every performance ever since the Broadway premiere was loud and climactic and begged for a big hand. (See example 3.3.) But the original ending, as preserved in a manuscript piano-vocal score in Sondheim's papers, reveals Rose's psychological interior in a final cadence that sounds like a premonition of the dark side of Sweeney's epiphany. Here, the piano part's right hand reveals a source for the dissonant musical intervals that Sondheim hereafter would summon with regularity: a tritone (G–D♭) and a minor second (C–D♭). (See example 3.4.) The final cadence is unlike any music that Jule Styne wrote before or after *Gypsy*, so it is likely by Sondheim, or, at least, suggested by him, because Sondheim has claimed that Styne "followed my instructions" in the writing of the song.[64] In an interview with the composer Adam Guettel, Sondheim tipped his hand about the chord's authorship, including its orchestration: "I had written a high violin harmonic" at the end of "Rose's Turn."[65]

**Example 3.3.** "Rose's Turn," ending, from the piano-vocal score of Jule Styne, Stephen Sondheim, and Arthur Laurents, *Gypsy* (Milwaukee: Hal Leonard, n.d.).

**Example 3.4.** "Mama's Turn" [*sic*], ending, from the manuscript piano-vocal score dated March 14, 1959 (Wisconsin Center for Film and Theater Research, Stephen Sondheim Papers, Box 13, Folder 3).

As in *Gypsy*, the script and songs of *Merrily We Roll Along* reiterate the word *dream* many times. The recurring title song, for example, brings it back repeatedly, and three instances can serve to show how harmonic anomalies on the word *dream* undermine the confidence projected by the words and the company that sings them. See, for instance, the harmonic slip that occurs just after the phrase "Bursting with dreams" in the song's first iteration (example 3.5). The bass sinks, in effect, "too far" to C♭ when its predictable "proper" resolution should have been the C♮ that follows, establishing a cadential sonority known as a dominant seventh suspended-4 chord (a familiar chord in jazz and rock referred to as "dominant sus 4 chord") setting up the next phrase's return to the tonic. It is a brief moment, but one that signals to keen ears that "rolling along" through life will not always be merry.

In a later reprise Sondheim creates even more shadows following the phrase "Gathering dreams," now with more dissonance in the bass—as revealed in the left hand's crunching major sevenths in the piano-vocal score, where the earlier passage had consonant octaves (example 3.6) Transition 4 begins, "Dreams don't die, / So keep an eye on your dream," and Sondheim underscores "dream" with a piercing dissonance on an F♯ that corrupts an otherwise "normal" E♭ seventh

**Example 3.5.** "Merrily We Roll Along," mm. 11–13, from the piano-vocal score of Stephen Sondheim and George Furth, *Merrily We Roll Along* (1981; Milwaukee: Hal Leonard, 1991).

**Example 3.6.** "Transition 3," mm. 10–12, from the piano-vocal score of Stephen Sondheim and George Furth, *Merrily We Roll Along* (1981; Milwaukee: Hal Leonard, 1991).

Example 3.7. "Transition 4," mm. 3–4, from the piano-vocal score of Stephen Sondheim and George Furth, *Merrily We Roll Along* (1981; Milwaukee: Hal Leonard, 1991).

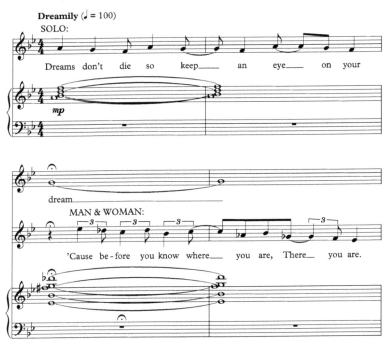

chord with a G in the melody. (See example 3.7.) Earlier in the show, Sondheim had introduced the same passage without the infecting F♯.

These moments provide aural reminders of the characters' pain and defenses as their dreams get sidetracked or slip away, and it's interesting that they appear in the "fills" between vocal phrases so as to offer unimpeded hearing of the underscore. They also remind us that a full understanding of Sondheim's dramaturgy requires understanding words and music together.[66] If, as Sondheim has said, "God is in the details," we might more aptly claim that the *Devil* is in these details. Together, these examples suggest that in some contexts the dissonant sonorities of a minor second, a major seventh, and a tritone should be read as signals of Sondheimian subtext. This is not to claim that such passages exist only because Sondheim visited the Actors Studio. There exists a lot of musicological and theoretical literature about how music can say what words cannot or do not say or how music may contradict the words, as Edward Cone has shown in his seminal book *The Composer's Voice*.[67] Moreover, it is surely undeniable that Sondheim learned many of the ways music can italicize, nuance, or contradict text in his music studies at Williams; at least a few of the sixteen music courses that he took would have included study of the music dramas of Richard Wagner and of lieder by the likes of Franz Schubert and Robert Schumann among the nineteenth-century European composers who brought innovative nuance to the merger of music and words. Indeed, Stephen Banfield, throughout his pioneering analytical study of Sondheim's music, regularly invokes Wagner's work as a precedent and potential model for Sondheim,[68] if one whose dramatic pace was anathema to his theatrical aesthetic.[69] Closer to home, Sondheim had the model of Rodgers and Hammerstein in such extended numbers as "If I Loved You" from *Carousel*, in which the words, in effect, say "maybe" while the music says "yes." Further, Sondheim seems already to have applied subtext, as he conceives it, to his early unproduced show *Climb High*—the last project in his six-year Hammerstein assignment—which includes a number titled "When I Get Famous," in which, as Dominic McHugh has written, "the character (David) is singing an ironic waltz: the superficial 3/4 represents the character's naive certainty that he's going to become famous, but there are numerous little moves to the minor or small chordal gestures (e.g. on 'dream' near the end) that help us realise that it's not going to happen. It's a very Sondheimian song, because although it in theory uses an old-school Rodgers device (the waltz), other musical gestures tell us that the waltz is in inverted commas, so to speak."[70] All of these precedents surely prepared Sondheim for understanding subtext, yet the concept of *subtext* that Sondheim learned from the Actors Studio seems to have given him an intellectual framework for writing music that summons the unspoken emotional and psychological force behind the words.

Dissonant musical intervals may call attention to Sondheimian subtext, but in Sondheim's shows subtext is much more than such details. The dual number sequence in *Follies* that includes both Ben's "The Road You Didn't Take" and Sally's "In Buddy's Eyes" sets up a major subtext for the entire show: Their long-suppressed yearning for one another (which later emerges in the big regretful love duet, "Too Many Mornings") flares up in Sally's torch song "Losing My Mind," and is extinguished by the end of Ben's musical breakdown, "Live, Laugh, Love." That song rips away his veneer of alpha-male success as he yells for his wife Phyllis—a yell that some actors have unleashed as an animalistic roar that echoes Stanley's "Stella!" in *A Streetcar Named Desire*. Judging by the number of musical scenes they have together, Ben and Sally form the principal couple in *Follies*.

Melody alone can also signal subtext. Act I, scene 4, of *A Little Night Music* depicts the married lawyer Fredrik Egerman visiting his former lover Desiree, an actress, backstage after a performance. The scene is rich with Chekhovian pauses as it slowly emerges that Fredrik seeks a sexual reunion with Desiree, which she ultimately grants. Before that, however, the conversation reaches a cul-de-sac, so Fredrik redirects:

FREDRIK (*artificially bright*): Well, I think it's time to talk about my wife, don't you?
DESIREE: Boast or complain?
FREDRIK: Both, I suspect.

He launches the number "You Must Meet My Wife," with its list of (mostly) endearing qualities sung to a melody whose recurring main motif circles within a cramped, narrow range for several measures, more like a strained cringe than a soaring paean to marriage. (See example 3.8.)

Subtext also informs Sondheim's preliminary work on musical numbers. Among the manuscripts that survive for "Send in the Clowns," Mark Eden Horowitz found what he identifies as "the first step" in Sondheim's songwriting process: "a one-page interior monologue discussing Desiree's thoughts and feelings—her subtext."[71] This, in Horowitz's re-creation of the creative process, led to two pages of monologue for Desiree in which she "uses everything in her power to convince Fredrik that he's made a mistake by marrying Anne and that it makes more sense for the two former lovers to be reunited" using "logic, flattery, self-deprecation and honesty."[72] All of this informs the songwriting; little of it may be found in the show itself.

"Irony is a form of subtext," Sondheim has written, in a seeming non sequitur to a snarky comment about *The Sound of Music* in his second book of lyrics, *Look, I Made a Hat*.[73] He develops that notion nearly 250 pages later in a long disquisition on the ironic use of vaudeville pastiche in the early versions of the musical that became *Road Show*. To have characters deliver truths about themselves during or through numbers that are strong on show-business glitz has in fact stood at the core of Sondheim's musical theater aesthetic throughout his career, from "Rose's Turn" to "You Could Drive a Person Crazy," the entire sequence of "Follies"—a "group nervous breakdown"[74]—for the four principals in *Follies*, and *Assassins*. As he has noted,

Metaphoric irony, the kind that sets a show about presidential assassins in a shooting gallery, has become such a useful cliché in musicals that it will

Example 3.8. "You Must Meet My Wife," mm. 8–12, from the piano-vocal score of Stephen Sondheim and Hugh Wheeler, *A Little Night Music* (n.p.: Warner Bros., 1974).

She   light - ens   my   sad - ness.   She   liv - ens   my   days.

probably never be abandoned. Its attraction persisted with me for a long time, but the use of vaudeville—the practice of applying an inappropriate style to an idea, sentiment, or situation—had peaked for me in *Assassins*.[75]

Despite an abiding disdain for the work of the Actors Studio, Sondheim has accepted and articulated its impact on him in ways that serve, in retrospect, to enhance the dramatic legitimacy of his work. He credits it with developing his understanding of actors and with teaching him the meaning and value of subtext, a word that occupies a prominent place in his writings, where he eagerly and regularly calls attention to examples. On some level, Sondheim resonated with the Studio's psychological probes to help the actor learn "the art of living the part."

## Studio Company

Another indicator of the Studio's impact on Sondheim's work remains unremarked-on by him: the recurring presence of Studio members and practices among the artistic company that Sondheim kept in the late 1950s and 1960s. Chief among them is Jerome Robbins, director and choreographer of *West Side Story* and *Gypsy*. Robbins was an original member of the Studio when it opened in the fall of 1947. Commentary on *West Side Story*, much of which stems from Robbins, attributes the show's original concept to Robbins's efforts to advise Montgomery Clift, another Studio member, how to play Romeo as a contemporary,[76] although Elizabeth A. Wells has offered equally compelling sources of inspiration for the show.[77] Likewise, the offstage separation of Jets and Sharks in the rehearsal process to strengthen their tribal bonding and mutual hatred, and the offstage isolation of the character of Anybodys, are regularly described as an extension of Actors Studio methods. Studio co-founder Elia Kazan was notorious for obtaining sharper performances of conflict by inciting off-stage friction between actors.[78]

Gerald Freedman, Robbins's assistant director for *West Side* and *Gypsy,* was also associated with the Actors Studio, becoming a member after returning to New York from Hollywood in 1956 to work as Robbins's assistant on *Bells Are Ringing*. "I learned about letting actors breathe from my work at the Actor's [*sic*] Studio," he said. "I came to respect the actor's process and be a 'guider' rather than a 'director'; a collaborator in the true sense of the word. This is what I observed and learned from [Actors Studio co-founder] Bobby Lewis and Lee Strasberg. . . . It was a wonderful learning experience, at the same time, I was working commercially on Broadway."[79] Freedman's coaching of actors under Robbins's direction of *West Side* and *Gypsy* owed much to his work at the Studio.[80] In a 2018 interview he recalled that Arthur Laurents resented the "Actors Studio tactics"

Freedman used to coach actors in *Gypsy*: "It intimidated him, he didn't understand it, and [he] made fun of it, but [he] would change his mind as he got older
and started to direct himself."[81]

Two Studio members would also count among the original cast of
*Gypsy*, and, perhaps not coincidentally, both would disappoint the creative collaborators. Sandra Church, cast as older Louise, began studying with
Strasberg in 1955. Recalling *Gypsy* rehearsals, she did not mention Freedman
but noted that "Jack [Klugman] and I worked on sense memories and all the
other techniques that came from Lee Strasberg at the Actors Studio."[82] Laurents
claimed that Church's association with the Studio carried weight with Robbins
and accounted for her being cast in the role; Laurents would come to disdain
Church and her Actors Studio connections.[83] "Jerry was happy with her in
the first act," Laurents recalled. "She was lovely, quietly touching, a frightened
doe at the curtain. The second act, alas, begins with the first signs that Louise
can be as tough as her mother. Sandra shrank; her Method training was of no
help."[84] Still frustrated during the show's Philadelphia tryout, Robbins depu-
tized Laurents to work with her on her scenes. But "whatever progress Sandra
made" disappeared when she went back to rehearse with Robbins: "Her terror
blocked her."[85]

Laurents wanted Church in the role more than he implies in his memoirs. In
a letter to the producers and creative team from his writing retreat in Acapulco
while *Gypsy* auditions were in progress, he insisted, "It is ABSOLUTELY IM-
PERATIVE that the role of Louise be played BY AN ACTRESS," and named Carol
Lawrence and Church as the only possibilities.[86] Then he named another Actors
Studio member as his image of Louise: "Ideal casting, for me," he wrote, "would
be Anne Bancroft—if you ever saw her in one of her B pictures where she played
chic sophisticates." Bancroft, however, was already committed to *The Miracle
Worker*, for which she would receive a Tony Award for Best Actress. As the letter
continues, Laurents urges his colleagues to beat the bushes for good actors. He
recommends contacting the Actors Studio and insists that Herbie must be played
by an actor—a word he consistently capitalizes for emphasis.[87] Despite Laurents's
avowed distaste for the Studio's approach, he appears to have been more than
happy to cast its members, because he viewed them as actors of quality. And yet
he would publicly state in 1960 that "the 'Method' school has been a blight."[88] All
told, Laurents appears to have held a deep ambivalence about the Studio, one that
Sondheim carried into old age.

Lane Bradbury, the original June in *Gypsy*, had the distinction of being
among the youngest actors ever admitted to the Studio, having been accepted
soon after moving to New York, probably in 1957, when she was nineteen.[89]
Bradbury has said, "Being at the Actor's [*sic*] Studio was a godsend. You could go

and work on different scenes and experience different characters and I learned on my feet. I worked with some incredible people including Lee Strasberg, and it was really an amazing and creative time in my life."[90] The Actors Studio tapes archived in Wisconsin provide fascinating glimpses of Strasberg's work with Bradbury before, during, and after her time in the cast of *Gypsy*. Her identification with character roles was so intense as to have blurred for her the boundary between herself and her role. On the tapes, Strasberg admires her "natural sensitivity" but also regularly uses words such as "nervous," "self-conscious," "uncomfortable," and "embarrassed" to describe her efforts to perform. Two or three times, she seems to have become so overwhelmed by her emotions that she stopped performing in the middle of a scene eliciting Strasberg's anger.[91] "But," he adds about her nervous discomfort, "it doesn't throw a bad light on Lane. On the contrary, it throws a rather nice and pathetic light." By the time Strasberg said that, in October 1959, the writing was on the wall for Bradbury in *Gypsy*. Robbins checked in on the show in early December, a little more than six months into the run, and wrote a memo to the collaborators including the observation that "Lane Bradbury, with whom none of us were too pleased to begin with, hasn't gotten better."[92] She made her last appearance as June on January 13, 1960. On reflection, Bradbury recalled, "It was tough to be fired like that but I was tired of it anyway." As Church had felt "terror" in rehearsals with Robbins, Bradbury "found him to be really, really frightening," although she had "absolutely worshipped" him before that.[93] Perhaps that fright helps explain why Bradbury had interrupted her own Studio scene work, much to Strasberg's consternation.

Sondheim continued to collaborate with Studio protégés beyond *West Side Story* and *Gypsy*. One other connection between the Studio and Sondheim's early work includes George Furth and Kim Stanley. The literature about *Company* regularly mentions that show's origins in the eleven one-act plays that Furth wrote with Kim Stanley in mind for the eleven leading roles.[94] Less well known is that Furth was a life member of the Actors Studio and that Stanley, an active member of the Studio for fifteen years, was recognized for emotionally nuanced and authentic performances that made her, in the words of Arthur Laurents, "the Goddess of the Actors Studio."[95] A recent biography dubbed her the "female Brando."[96] This Studio icon, then, would appear to embody the original incarnation of what would become Bobby. Laurents's disdain for the Studio did not seem to interfere with his interest in its goddess's participation in his own work: Stanley was cast in the leading role of Laurents's psychological drama *A Clearing in the Woods*, which ran for a month in early 1957. She had made her reputation in the original productions of William Inge's plays *Picnic* (1953–1954) and *Bus Stop* (1955–1956), coached by Strasberg.

## "a scene in a play"

Inge stood among the playwrights favored for scene work at the Studio along with Williams and O'Neill for their focus on the psychological dimensions of domestic and family drama. (Not surprisingly, Shakespeare and Chekhov were the writers whose works were most frequently chosen for scene work.)[97] But the Studio did not insist on spoken drama alone. That scenes from musicals were occasionally used may come as a surprise to those who associate Strasberg and the Studio with uncompromising artistic ideals and a strong antipathy to the commercial pressures of Broadway and Hollywood. In fact, Studio members did scenes from *Carousel*, *Guys and Dolls*, and *My Fair Lady*. And in a session recorded in 1966, Strasberg comments on exercises and performances by Madeleine Sherwood as Rose and Hilda Brawner as Louise in the last two scenes of *Gypsy*, including Sherwood performing a private moment exercise based on "Rose's Turn." Curiously, Strasberg's musings in this case venture beyond the actors and their challenges to commentary on the show itself. He is clearly surprised to find dramatic value in a musical. In what may serve as an indirect tribute to Sondheim and Laurents, he observes that the scene was so "moving and dramatic" that it was worthy as "a scene in a play, not in a musical."[98] For the doyen of the Actors Studio and its Method, that was high praise indeed, and, what is unusual for Strasberg the teacher, it accords with the writers' intentions.

## Notes

1. I would like to thank Jason Witt for preparing the musical examples and Samantha Lampe for double-checking many of the citations. Thanks also to Andrew Kuster, executive editor of Music of the United States of America, and Jon Alan Conrad, editor of its *Follies* volume, for permission to use an excerpt from the forthcoming publication of the show's full score. For questions, comments, and insights that informed the writing and research, I am grateful to Geoffrey Block, Maya Cantu, Todd Decker, Gerald Freedman (and his assistant Robert Beseda), Liza Gennaro, Ray Knapp, Gayle Magee, Dominic McHugh, James O'Leary, Doug Reside, David Savran, Jessica Sternfeld, Dominic Symonds, Stacy Wolf, Tamsen Wolff, and Liz Wollman. Thanks also to Tony Sheppard for inviting my participation in the Sondheim@90@Williams symposium.

   Stephen Sondheim, "Theatre Lyrics," in *Playwrights, Lyricists, Composers on Theater*, ed. Otis L. Guernsey (New York: Dodd, Mead, 1974), 62–63; Craig Zadan, *Sondheim & Co.* 2nd ed., updated (New York: Da Capo, 1994), 4–5; Stephen Banfield, *Sondheim's Broadway Musicals* (Ann Arbor: University of Michigan Press, 1993), 13–14; Andrew Milner, "'Let the Pupil Show the Master': Stephen Sondheim and Oscar

Hammerstein II," in *Stephen Sondheim: A Casebook*, ed. Joanne Gordon (New York: Garland, 1997), 154–155; Meryle Secrest, *Stephen Sondheim: A Life* (New York: Knopf, 1998), 72; Stephen Citron, *Sondheim and Lloyd Webber: The New Musical* (New York: Oxford University Press, 2001), 36–37; Steve Swayne, *How Sondheim Found His Sound* (Ann Arbor: University of Michigan Press, 2005), 125–127; Geoffrey Block, *Enchanted Evenings: The Broadway Musical from 'Show Boat' to Sondheim and Lloyd Webber*, 2nd ed. (New York: Oxford University Press, 2009), 341; Dominic Symonds, "'You've Got to Be Carefully Taught': Oscar Hammerstein's Influence on Sondheim," in *The Oxford Handbook of Sondheim Studies*, ed. Robert Gordon (New York: Oxford University Press, 2014), 39; Ethan Mordden, *On Sondheim: An Opinionated Guide* (New York: Oxford University Press, 2016), 4; Dominic McHugh, "*Climb High*: Sondheim at the Gateway of His Career," *Studies in Musical Theatre* 13, no. 2 (2019): 103–104.

2. Banfield, *Sondheim's Broadway Musicals*, 14.

3. Swayne, *How Sondheim Found His Sound*, 127.

4. Ibid., 139–141. Until Sondheim took his first music class at Williams, he claimed, his goal was to be a mathematician, in Lonny Price, dir., *The Best Worst Thing That Could Have Ever Happened* (2016). But according to Secrest, he began his Williams College career as an English major (Secrest, *Sondheim: A Life*, 65). Zadan claims he considered both math and English as possible majors until taking a music course in his freshman year (Zadan, *Sondheim & Co.*, 6). Swayne details the numerous courses in English (ten) and music (sixteen) that Sondheim took as an eventual music major, culminating with an honors project in music composition (Swayne, *How Sondheim Found His Sound*, 141).

5. See, e.g., Banfield, *Sondheim's Broadway Musicals*, 21–23; Secrest, *Sondheim: A Life*, 85–88; Stephen Sondheim, *Finishing the Hat: Collected Lyrics, 1954–1981* (New York: Knopf, 2010), 303–304.

6. Quoted in Secrest, *Sondheim: A Life*, 344. Sondheim later wrote that those four teachers "guided and changed" his "intellectual life, and to some extent my personal one as well," and referred to Hammerstein as "my immediate mentor" (*Finishing the Hat,* xxii).

7. Sondheim, "Theatre Lyrics," 66–72. On the formative influence of Laurents on Sondheim, also see James O'Leary's chapter in this volume.

8. On Sondheim as master of "disavowal" whose work, interviews, and prose reveal a "persistent pattern of contradiction," see David Savran, "'You've Got That Thing': Cole Porter, Stephen Sondheim, and the Erotics of the List Song," *Theatre Journal* 64, no. 4 (2012): 544. For Sondheim as an unreliable narrator of musical theater history, see Geoffrey Block, "The Last Word: Rewriting Musical Theatre History with Sondheim," *Studies in Musical Theatre* 13, no. 2 (2019): 133–150.

9. David Garfield, *A Player's Place: The Story of the Actors Studio* (New York: Macmillan, 1980), 1.

10. Harold Clurman, *The Fervent Years: The Group Theatre and the '30s* (1945; repr., New York: Da Capo, 1983).

11. Garfield, *Player's Place*, 13.

12. Ibid., 15.
13. Clurman, *Fervent Years*, 44. For more on the American reception and development of Stanislavsky's system, see Mel Gordon, *Stanislavsky in America: An Actor's Workbook* (New York: Routledge, 2010) and chapters in *The Routledge Companion to Stanislavsky*, ed. R. Andrew White (New York: Routledge, 2014), esp. David Krasner, "Stanislavsky's System, Sense-Emotion Memory, and Physical Action/ Active Analysis: American Interpretations of the System's Legacy" (chap. 12), and Yasen Peyankov, "In Search of Truth: Stanislavsky and Strasberg" (chap. 17), which emphasizes the common ground between the System and the Method from a personal standpoint.
14. Mel Gordon, *Stanislavsky in America*, 9–10. Even then, First Studio members soon ventured into "a series of laboratory productions" (11). The American extensions of Stanislavsky's studio likewise embraced production. The American Laboratory Theatre (the Lab, for short), as its name suggests, focused both on actor development per se and on rehearsals, scene preparation, and public productions (27–29). The Group Theatre alternated between retreats in rural Connecticut and upstate New York for intensive work on acting technique and returns to New York for productions (Gordon, chap. 3).
15. Ibid., 110–111. The work's playwright, Michael V. Gazzo, was a Studio member who became better known as an actor, especially for his Oscar-nominated performance as mob boss Frankie Pentangeli in *The Godfather: Part II* (1974), which also featured two other Studio legends as competing mob bosses: Lee Strasberg and Al Pacino.
16. Strasberg had allowed reporters to visit before 1955. For example, Arthur Gelb refers to his glimpse of a phenomenon that had previously occurred only "behind closed doors": Arthur Gelb, "Behind the Scenes at the Actors Studio," *New York Times*, April 29, 1951. Two years later, Herbert Mitgang noted that the Studio's work had been shut off from public view "until now": Herbert Mitgang, "Actors' Studio: Classroom for Our Stars," *Town & Country*, May 1953. But such visits by nonmembers in order to report the Studio's work to the public seem to have been comparatively rare until 1955. On the difficulties faced by actors and the Studio's uneasy relationship with publicity, see Garfield, *Player's Place*, 98–99.
17. Garfield, *Player's Place*, 90.
18. Quoted in ibid., 118.
19. Ibid., 119–122.
20. Quoted in ibid., 119.
21. Wisconsin Center for Film and Theatre Research, Actors Studio, New York, N.Y., Recordings, Box 339A/10 (UCD Box 11), Side 2: "Discussion of Death of James Dean" (dated October 5, 1956 [sic; just over a year after his death in September 1955]). For an edited transcript of the speech that launched the Studio's 1956 season, including the passages about James Dean, see Robert H. Hethmon, ed., *Strasberg at the Actors Studio* (New York: Viking, 1965), 27–30. It is possible that the tape is mislabeled 1956 and that Hethmon repeated that error. (In fact, my research visit on January 9–10, 2020, turned up other mislabeled recordings.) Strasberg begins as if the Studio had just established its new residency: "We now have a place, you see. That

gives us a symbol, a feeling that it's permanent." Then he launches into his reflections on James Dean, intermittently weeping—all of which strongly suggests that the session took place in October 1955, when the new venue opened, soon after Dean's death (Hethmon, *Strasberg at the Actors Studio*, 27). Indeed, the sense of permanence offered by the new venue, coupled with a belief in the historic significance of the moment, may well have inspired Strasberg's decision to have the sessions recorded.

22. Lee Strasberg, "View from the Studio," *New York Times*, September 2, 1956.
23. Betty Comden, Adolph Green, and Jule Styne, *Bells Are Ringing* (New York: Random House, 1957), 90.
24. Garfield, *A Player's Place*, 114.
25. Stephen Sondheim, "The Musical Theater," in *Broadway Song and Story: Broadway Playwrights, Lyricists, Composers Discuss Their Hits*, ed. Otis L. Guernsey (New York: Dodd, Mead, 1985), 247.
26. Craig Carnelia, "In Conversation with Stephen Sondheim," *Sondheim Review* 15, no. 1 (Fall 2008): 15.
27. Sondheim, *Finishing the Hat*, 56.
28. Burton, *Leonard Bernstein*, 255.
29. Sondheim, "Musical Theater," 247.
30. Craig Carnelia, "In Conversation with Stephen Sondheim," *Sondheim Review* 15, no. 1 (Fall 2008): 15.
31. Sondheim, *Finishing the Hat*, 57.
32. Ibid. That account omits what Sondheim told his biographer Meryle Secrest: that when he first met Strasberg during his summer stint as an assistant stage manager for a show under Strasberg's direction at the Westport County Playhouse, he recalled thinking: "He's the most brilliant man I've ever heard in my life" (Secrest, *Sondheim: A Life*, 91).
33. Arthur Laurents, *Original Story By: A Memoir of Broadway and Hollywood* (New York: Random House, 2000), 4.
34. See, e.g., for example, Garfield, *Player's Place*, 67.
35. Morris Carnovsky called Strasberg "priest-like." Quoted in ibid., 31.
36. Bruce McConachie, *American Theater in the Culture of the Cold War* (Iowa City: University of Iowa Press, 2003), 90–91.
37. The "private moment" was Strasberg's distinctive realization of Stanislavsky's requirement that the actor learn to be "private in public" (Garfield, *Player's Place*, 172).
38. Lee Strasberg, *A Dream of Passion: The Development of the Method*, ed. Evangeline Morphos (Boston: Little, Brown, 1987), esp. 106–115.
39. Garfield, *Player's Place*, 26.
40. See Wisconsin Center for Film and Theater Research, Actors Studio Tapes A54/2, pt. 1 (March 18, 1966) for just one example of Strasberg's use of the words *inner* and *unconscious*, and Garfield, *Player's Place*, 146–147 and 174–175, on Strasberg, the Studio, and psychoanalysis. Strasberg himself addresses both the commonalities and the distinctions between Method work and psychoanalysis in Strasberg, *Dream of Passion*, 103–105, after citing illustrative cases of working with unnamed specific actors on relaxation. All of the cases share the theme of uncovering a

traumatic experience from the actor's past much the way psychotherapy might do (96–100, 109). The concurrence of Freud's and Strasberg's peak of ascendency in the mid-1950s, and Sondheim's engagement with the ideas of both, resonates with what Aleksei Grinenko has aptly written: that the period of the late 1940s to the early 1960s comprised a "double 'golden age,' defined by the concurrent reign of psychoanalysis and the Broadway musical in US culture." Aleksei Grinenko, "Madness and the Broadway Musical, 1940s–2000s," PhD diss., City University of New York, 2019, 21.

41. Carnelia, "In Conversation," 15.
42. Sondheim, *Finishing the Hat*, 57.
43. Ibid. It is interesting to note that the first time Sondheim wrote about subtext, he did not mention a *visit* to the Actors Studio but only that he heard "Actors Studio types" talk about it, and that he learned what it meant from Laurents: "The major thing I got from Arthur was the notion of sub-text. Now, this is a word that I had heard tossed around by Actors Studio types for a long time and really rather sneered at; but what it means simply is, give the actor something to act. I think this is a real secret; if I had to sell secrets about lyric writing I would sell this secret about sub-text." See Sondheim, "Theater Lyrics," 71.
44. Sondheim, *Finishing the Hat*, 57.
45. Quoted in Secrest, *Sondheim: A Life*, 134.
46. Sondheim, *Finishing the Hat*, 238, 277–278.
47. Secrest, *Sondheim: A Life*, 134.
48. Bruce Kirle, *Unfinished Show Business: Broadway Musicals as Works-in-Process* (Carbondale: Southern Illinois University Press, 2005), chap. 2.
49. Laurents, *Original Story By*, 378.
50. Library of Congress Music Division, Arthur Laurents Papers, Box 130, datebook entry of June 16, 1958.
51. Laurents, *Original Story By*, 378.
52. Sondheim, radio interview with Terry Gross, *Fresh Air*, October 28, 2010, www.npr.org/templates/story/story.php?storyId=130732712.
53. Sondheim, *Finishing the Hat*, 57 (emphasis in original).
54. Konstantin Stanislavsky, *Building a Character*, trans. Elizabeth Reynolds Hapgood (1949; repr., London: Methuen, 2001), 113. Secondary sources often mistakenly cite the publication date as 1950.
55. John Russell Brown, *Shakespeare's Plays in Performance* (New York: St. Martin's, 1967), 52–53.
56. OED online, accessed May 5, 2020: https://www.oed.com/view/Entry/193161?redirectedFrom=subtext#eid. An earlier and more literal usage of the word *subtext* precedes that definition: "text or a text appearing below other text on a page, etc. Now *rare*."
57. Stanislavsky, *Building a Character*, 113.
58. Sondheim, *Finishing the Hat*, 217.
59. My colleague Bernhard Scully, associate professor of music at the University of Illinois Urbana-Champaign as well as a former horn player with the Canadian Brass and former principal horn with the St. Paul Chamber Orchestra, called the

combination of stopped and *cuivré* unusual and noted that "Adding *cuivré* . . . suggests an extra nastiness in the sound." He added that "*cuivré* is the most nasal and nasty sounding of all the stopped horn sounds possible." Email communication, February 29, 2020.

60. James Goldman and Stephen Sondheim, *Follies* (New York: Theatre Communications Group, 2001), 42.

61. Steve Swayne finds an operatic precedent for this moment in the third act of Benjamin Britten's *Peter Grimes*, in the contrast between the townspeople's loud roars for "Peter Grimes" and the soft response of muted horns (Swayne, *How Sondheim Found His Sound*, 38). On this chord and moment in *Sweeney*, also see Kim H. Kowalke's chapter in this volume.

62. Sondheim, *Finishing the Hat*, 355.

63. Ibid., 77.

64. See Jeffrey Magee, "Whose Turn Is It? Where *Gypsy*'s Finale Came from, and Where It Went," *Studies in Musical Theatre* 13, no. 2 (2019), esp. 121–122.

65. "The Art of Songwriting with Stephen Sondheim and Adam Guettel" (Dramatists Guild Foundation, ca. 2010), accessed December 16, 2020 at https://www.youtube.com/watch?v=TofC3KD-h8M. The statement appears at 14:04.

66. The perils of interpreting Sondheim's work through his words alone becomes painfully evident in Ian Bradley's discussion of the reprises of "Merrily We Roll Along," which, in his view, show that "even for the cynical Sondheim in the 1980s, the message is still essentially what it was for the idealistic and optimistic Rodgers and Hammerstein in the 1940s and 1950s—following your dreams." See Ian Bradley, *You've Got to Have a Dream: The Message of the Musical* (Louisville: Westminster John Knox Press, 2004), 171.

67. Edward T. Cone, *The Composer's Voice* (Berkeley: University of California Press, 1974). Cone does not use the term *subtext* to describe what the composer or performer brings to the musical interpretation or enhancement of words.

68. See, e.g., Banfield, *Sondheim's Broadway Musicals*, 281, 302–303, 305, and 347–351.

69. See Swayne, *How Sondheim Found His Sound*, 7.

70. Dominic McHugh, email to the author, March 25, 2020. See also McHugh's chapter, "Fragments of Fairyland: Sondheim's Abandoned Adaptation of *Mary Poppins*," in this collection, especially his insights concerning the musical number "The Sun Is Blue," with its "contradictions and oxymorons," and which Banfield, quoted by McHugh, has characterized as "a study in wistful heartache disguised as a childlike naïveté."

71. Mark Eden Horowitz, "Biography of a Song: 'Send in the Clowns,'" *Sondheim Review* 11, no. 3 (Spring 2005): 15.

72. Ibid.

73. Stephen Sondheim, *Look, I Made a Hat* (New York: Knopf, 2011), xx. The full context for the quotation is: "**Hits** There is a tonic in the things men do not wish to hear, it's been said. But not much money. The biggest hit shows always tell you stories you want to hear. You can be true to your calling as a nun and marry the richest man in the country and still escape from the Nazis into a lucrative show business future. Who

can't identify with that?" A paragraph break ensues, followed the single-sentence paragraph: "**Irony** is a form of subtext" (boldface in original).

74. Sondheim, *Finishing the Hat*, 231.

75. Sondheim, *Look, I Made a Hat*, 244.

76. For example, Burton, *Bernstein*, 187.

77. Elizabeth A. Wells, *"West Side Story": Cultural Perspectives on an American Musical* (Lanham, MD: Scarecrow, 2011), 29.

78. Garfield, *Player's Place*, 85. See also 104.

79. Gerald Freedman, "My Life in Art: A 21st Century Riff on Stanislavsky," address presented at the John F. Kennedy Center for the Performing Arts, April 20, 2008, 3. I thank the late Mr. Freedman and his assistant Robert Beseda for sharing the written text of the speech.

80. Ibid.

81. Gerald Freedman, Skype interview with the author, December 18, 2017.

82. Brad Hathaway, "Church Had a Real Good Time in *Gypsy*," *Everything Sondheim*, October 10, 2017, https://www.everythingsondheim.org/church-real-good-time-gypsy/.

83. This contradicts Laurents's claim that "the final choices" for Louise were Church and Suzanne Pleshette. Laurents, *Original Story By*, 391.

84. Ibid.

85. Ibid., 391–392.

86. Laurents to "Gypsies" [Leland Hayward, David Merrick (?), Jerome Robbins, Jule Styne, and Stephen Sondheim], n.d., New York Public Library for the Performing Arts, Billy Rose Theatre Collection, Leland Hayward Papers, T-Mss 1971-002, Box 12, Folder 9.

87. Ibid.

88. Thomas Lask, "Seed of a Comedy," *New York Times*, October 23, 1960. Thanks to James O'Leary for bringing this article to my attention.

89. In recounting her career for a 2008 interview, Bradbury did not consistently offer dates, but she recalled moving to New York as a teenager, being accepted into the Actors Studio, and making her first television appearance in [May] 1958, just short of her twentieth birthday. See John O'Dowd, "Lane Bradbury: A Life of Meaning and Purpose" (2008), http://www.john-odowd.com/portfolio/lane-bradbury-a-life-of-meaning-and-purpose/. Actors Studio tapes housed at the Wisconsin Center for Film and Theater Research feature Lee Strasberg's commentary on several scenes and exercises in which Bradbury took part, the earliest of them in January 1958, over a year before she was cast in *Gypsy*. The finding aid for the tapes is available online at https://search.library.wisc.edu/catalog/999465350802121.

90. O'Dowd, "Lane Bradbury."

91. For Strasberg's observations of Bradbury's "embarrassment" and "sensitivity" after a scene from Arthur Miller's *View from the Bridge*, see Wisconsin Center for Film and Theater Research, Actors Studio, New York, NY, Recordings, Tape 50/2, March 14, 1958. Two tapes date from October 1959, when Bradbury was performing in *Gypsy*. In one, Strasberg praises her "awareness and confidence" then regrets that she

"stop[s] short" even, he says, "when something right is happening, because then you feel uneasy, you feel uncomfortable, you feel insecure, you feel embarrassed" (Tape 87/1, October 9, 1959). In the other, Strasberg becomes very angry because Bradbury and her scene partner stopped their scene although he thought it was "hard-hitting" and going well (Tape 90/1, October 27, 1959).

92. Robbins to Hayward, Merrick, Laurents, Styne, and Sondheim, December 8, 1959, New York Public Library, Jerome Robbins Papers MGZMD 130, Series 1, Box 25, Folder 3.

93. O'Dowd, "Lane Bradbury."

94. See, e.g., Zadan, *Sondheim & Co.*, 116; Joanne Gordon, *Art Isn't Easy: The Achievement of Stephen Sondheim* (Carbondale: Southern Illinois University Press, 1990), 38; and Sondheim, *Finishing the Hat*, 165, which does not even mention Stanley.

95. Laurents, *Original Story By*, 4.

96. Jon Krampner, *Female Brando: The Legend of Kim Stanley* (New York: Back Stage Books, 2006).

97. Hethmon, *Strasberg at the Actors Studio*, 410.

98. Wisconsin Center for Film and Theater Research, Actors Studio, New York, NY, Recordings, UCD 339A, Tape A60/1, April 8, 1966.

# 4

# Breakout from the Asylum
# of Conformity

## Sondheim, Laurents, and the Dramaturgy
## of *Anyone Can Whistle*

*James O'Leary*

The form that Rodgers and Hammerstein developed tells a story
through character and song. It expands the character, and the
characters therefore cause the things to happen in the story, and
it goes song-scene, song-scene, song-scene, song-scene. I'm very
proud of *Gypsy*, but when it was all over I thought, "That's the last
one of those I want to do." Now let's try different things.

                                           Stephen Sondheim (1978)

The historiography of Stephen Sondheim's work typically places a dramaturgical gulf between his early musicals from the late 1950s and his major shows
of the 1970s. In the familiar telling, his early works, including *West Side Story*
(1957) and *Gypsy* (1959), tend to fall into the Rodgers and Hammerstein "integrated" mode, in which score, script, and production combine as coherently
and naturalistically as possible to portray a story and its characters while still
toggling back and forth between speech and song.[1] His later works, beginning
with *Company* (1970) and *Follies* (1971), tend to be grouped with so-called
concept musicals, which critic Martin Gottfried defined as shows "whose
music, lyrics, dance, stage movement and dialogue are woven through each
other in the creation of a tapestry-like theme (rather than in support of a
plot)."[2] Spanning these two poles is what musicologist Stephen Banfield termed
Sondheim's "decade of uncertainty," a period when Sondheim transitioned
from a precocious young lyricist to the composer-lyricist of genre-defining
scores; from a Broadway journeyman who supported his stage work with odd
jobs (writing for television, devising crossword puzzles, writing one-off novelty songs) to a leader in the field (president of the Dramatists Guild, Tony

James O'Leary, *Breakout from the Asylum of Conformity* In: *Sondheim in Our Time and His.* Edited by: W. Anthony Sheppard,
Oxford University Press. © Oxford University Press 2022. DOI: 10.1093/oso/9780197603192.003.0005

Award winner); from a collaborator on integrated shows to an auteur composer of concept musicals.[3]

In this prevailing historical narrative, *Anyone Can Whistle* (1964) appears as
neither fish nor fowl. The show tends to squirm away from Sondheim narratives,
emerging most often as a short-lived flop (or cult classic) that closed after only
nine performances, as part of the menagerie of oddball transitional works nes-
tled between Sondheim's landmark productions. This assessment is not un-
founded. Few shows have matched it for sheer eccentricity: It is a madcap story
(in three acts, no less) of a corrupt mayoress and her cronies who save their poor
town with a fake miracle, water spurting from a rock by means of a hidden pump.
When the head nurse of the local insane asylum demands that her patients
("cookies") take the waters, the sane and insane mix, and the rest of the show's
action involves trying to separate those who are sane from those who are not. It
has been equally hard to place from a dramaturgical standpoint: Although the
show's numbers more or less conform to the song-story song-story *structure* of
a Rodgers and Hammerstein show, many of the songs do not fulfill the typical
*function* of such songs. Instead of expressing the characters' emotions or developing the plot, as they would in a more conventional integrated show, Sondheim
has maintained that the songs in *Anyone Can Whistle* "commented on the action
instead of advancing it," often trading in show-biz pastiche that evaded direct
or sincere expression, supplying instead a layer of detached authorial winking,
a self-referential perspective that more closely aligns to the typical features of a
concept musical.[4]

Although the typical historiographical model has had trouble accommo-
dating *Anyone Can Whistle*, Sondheim himself has not. "I think my breakout
score was *Whistle*," he claimed. When he said this his interviewer, librarian Mark
Horowitz, pressed him on the subject, suggesting that the true watershed was in
fact *Company*, in keeping with the familiar historical narrative.[5] Sondheim, however, persisted: "*Company* was the first time I got good notices. But no, I think
finding my voice happened in *Whistle* . . . long before *Company*."[6] On one level,
this amounts to a reappraisal of Sondheim's career. It changes the shape of the
Sondheim narrative, placing the central breakout halfway through his so-called
decade of uncertainty, rather than at the beginning of the 1970s. Also at play
here, however, is another reappraisal: a dramaturgical one. After all, even though
*Anyone Can Whistle* does not exactly resemble an integrated musical, neither
does it resemble a concept musical in any straightforward way, suggesting that
whatever breakout Sondheim had was not predominantly due to the attainment
of the concept-musical form. He was explicit about this in other interviews. He
maintained, for example, that he never actually abandoned the Rodgers and
Hammerstein show after *Gypsy* but instead was "carrying it on, making variations;" he also claimed that he "loathed" the term "concept musical," which he

found to be merely a "vogue word" that "[reduced] things to simplicities."[7] Taken together, his historical and dramaturgical reappraisals suggest that the familiar narrative has not quite captured how his musicals changed after *Gypsy*. They also suggest that coming to terms with *Anyone Can Whistle* could indeed capture more precisely the idiosyncrasies of what Sondheim was trying to achieve during this period. Finally, they suggest some of the foundational principles that would also underlie his later scores from the 1970s.

Yet however frustrated Sondheim may have been (and may still be) with the familiar terminology and historical narratives surrounding his work, he has never abandoned them entirely. After all, he acknowledged that something did change in his writing after *Gypsy* and that this change was somehow bound up in moving away (to whatever degree) from the Rodgers and Hammerstein style of show. Rather, one gets the sense that Sondheim has had different cultural and aesthetic priorities than those that usually stand at the center of the stories told about his career. Therefore, the preliminary step to devising a historiography that would capture the idiosyncrasies of his approach must first ascertain which aesthetic, cultural, social, or biographical values should form its backbone. The existing model, charting Sondheim's gradual attainment of the concept musical, generally prioritizes the formal relationship between script and score, which historians describe as wavering over time. Without abandoning these insights, what follows prioritizes different values: Sondheim's evolving opinion of the institution of Broadway, its conventions, and its norms, alongside his growing frustration with what he perceived the musical to represent more broadly in postwar America.[8]

His opinions about these matters emerged in collaboration with playwright Arthur Laurents. He and Sondheim probably met in 1953 or 1954, and over the course of the next decade they maintained an intense friendship built on mutual admiration: "on the phone daily, dinners, theatre, weekends in Quogue [at Laurents's weekend house]," as Laurents described it.[9] They ultimately collaborated on six major Broadway productions including the musicals *West Side Story* (1957), *Gypsy* (1959), *Anyone Can Whistle* (1964), and *Do I Hear a Waltz?* (1965, based on Laurents's 1952 play *Time of the Cuckoo*).[10] Sondheim also wrote incidental music for Laurents's plays *Invitation to a March* (1960) and *The Enclave* (1973). Sondheim regarded Laurents's work with "awed respect" and learned from him that the "book writer is the source from which the songwriter—in this particular case, me—takes character, diction, tone and style, and sometimes dialogue."[11]

Laurents emerged in the late 1950s as an advocate for experimentation in the Broadway musical. For example, in 1957 he argued in the *New York Times* that "our popular musical stage is probably the best and most advanced in the world, artistically as well as technically," and his goal was to develop its potential.[12] He did this by prodding the Broadway musical toward new subject matter: a critique of postwar American society as suffering in an age of disillusion, a period when seemingly stable values and morals had become oppressive, evacuating them of any potential virtue and making them tools of "conformism." Sondheim and Laurents explored this topic explicitly in two productions, *Invitation to a March* and *Anyone Can Whistle*. The nature of their exploration, however, was not merely a matter of the shows' content. As will become clear, Laurents and Sondheim also sought to devise a style of theater that would knock Broadway out of its conformist aesthetic rut. Most contemporary reviews considered their effort to have failed. (Howard Taubman began his *New York Times* review of *Anyone Can Whistle*, "There is no law against saying something in a musical, but it's unconstitutional to omit imagination and wit."[13]) Nevertheless, the bedrock principles of Sondheim's dramaturgy emerged from these collaborations, and he carried them with him for decades.

## Off-Broadway, Anti-Broadway: Early Drafts of *Anyone Can Whistle*

The earliest surviving sketches for *Anyone Can Whistle* date from March 1957, seven years before the musical opened in New York. At this point the show existed as a cluster of drafts for two separate projects, which Laurents eventually merged. The first was called "Bridge" or "Bridge Play," and of it only a rough three-page typewritten scenario of the stage action and a small handwritten note (designated simply as "play") remain.[14] The second was "The Novel of Mort," but Laurents changed its name (and genre) to "Play About Love."[15] Laurents called the combined version "An Hour Before Closing."[16] The proposed show was to take place in a small mountain town somewhere in Europe, *Brigadoon*-like in its remoteness. The central character was to be an American entrepreneur who hoped to build a bridge that would connect the town to the rest of the world.[17] He was to fall in love with a local marquesa who ultimately, with the help of the townspeople, would scuttle the bridge in order to protect the town from the hurly-burly of modern society.[18]

Although this plot bears little resemblance to what eventually became *Anyone Can Whistle*, these early drafts do share some points of similarity with the musical, small details that Laurents would eventually weave together in the final version that premiered on Broadway. The first and clearest point: in "Bridge" and "An Hour Before Closing," the townspeople thwart the entrepreneur by faking a miracle on the exact spot where the bridge was supposed to be built. "The bell starts to ring: miracle; water spurting from very rock on which bridge span to rest on. He is depressed but town goes wild with joy," a sequence that remains in *Anyone Can Whistle*.[19] In both shows, too, Laurents included a scene that would reveal the fake miracle's pumping mechanism. In "Bridge," the water "trickles down the rock, then begins to spurt with a curiously regular rhythm. This awaken[s] [the entrepreneur's] curiosity. He starts to examine it, [the marquesa] tries to stop him—but he [discovers] that villagers are pumping water in thru the back."[20] In the final version of *Anyone Can Whistle*, the mayoress's henchmen are still tasked with pumping the water by hand until an electric mechanism can be set up (and Sondheim even wrote "pumping music" to accompany them).[21]

Second, in both shows, Laurents described the main female character as a hybrid or a split personality. In "Bridge," she is "part elegant sophisticated marquesa; part young town girl." According to the sketches, during an early scene she speaks to the American entrepreneur as an elegant marquesa, "but as they talk [she has an] argument with her young brother during which hair tumbles down, [she] throws [her] shoe, and presto chang[e-]o."[22] In *Anyone Can Whistle*, the character of Nurse Fay also has a hybrid personality, prim and orderly on the one hand, wild and uninhibited on the other. She marks the difference between the two sides of her personality not by letting her hair down but by putting on a wig. "Eight years ago, at the hospital where I was training, we put on a graduation play," she explains in one scene. "I was what I still am—control and order—so everyone thought it would be funny to make me be a French *soubrette*. This was the dress; zis was ze accent; and (*She holds up the wig*) I put it on; I wore it to the party afterwards. A week later I woke up in a hotel room in Cleveland with an interne."[23]

Third, there exists in these early drafts what may be called an anti-Broadway attitude, a pose that Laurents struck against that institution. Years later, Sondheim would describe himself and Laurents as coming across like "the two smartest kids in the class (in the back row, of course), wittily making fun of the teacher as well as our fellow students, demonstrating how far ahead of established wisdom we were."[24] Laurents's frustration with the institution of Broadway was of long standing, however. Before writing these drafts, and before he ever met Sondheim, Laurents had already inveighed against Broadway for producing very few plays of actual merit. "Critics and public alike may complain that they are damned lucky if they see even three plays during a season which try to be more than good shows. You can't argue with that complaint; it is certainly justified," he wrote in a 1946 article for the *New York Times*. He heaped blame in all directions—on critics, on playwrights, on audiences—but at the heart of his critique sat the commercial foundation of the New York theater. "The term 'Broadway play' does not stand for a good play; it stands for a handsomely wrapped, generously perfumed piece of store cheese. In other words, the equivalent of a Hollywood movie—the very same type of merchandise which Broadway is so quick to criticize." He tried to enlist his contemporaries to stand against the Broadway crowd ("the danger is compromise," he warned), to dare something untested, to risk a flop.[25] However, stifled by Broadway, Laurents turned his attention toward Off-Broadway in

1958, allowing four of his plays to be revived in a series at the Sheridan Square Playhouse.[26]

Laurents made this shift not simply to escape the commercial pressures of large Broadway houses but also because he believed that the intimate Off-Broadway theaters allowed for a different aesthetic, and thereby drew audiences who "demand less literalness and accept more challenge to the imagination."[27] When he began work on the early drafts of *Anyone Can Whistle* from March 1957, he stipulated a nonliteral approach: "Play should have the quality of a once-upon-a-time fable."[28] He continued: "Action should be fluid: settings simulated, not real. Characters speak to the audience in character as narrators or explaining themselves, etc.; helping tell and explain the tale. (Easier in the musical theater where they sing to the audience anyway.)"[29] Eight months later, in November 1957 (less than two months after *West Side Story* opened), Laurents expanded on this idea in an article he published in the *New York Times*. "The easiest way for audiences to journey the farthest from the conventional reproductions of naturalism to the unconventional illusions of theatricality is to introduce music, song and dance," he wrote, and he used his script for *West Side Story* as an example.[30] The operative word is "conventional." Laurents's critique against the institution of Broadway could only be met by finding a different mode of expression, one that seemed far outside the Broadway orbit. By his own account, Laurents was drawn to similarly unconventional shows; he admired Jule Styne's score for Brecht's *Resistible Rise of Arturo Ui* (1963), William Bolcom's "Dynamite Tonite" (1964), Margarite Monnot's *Irma la Douce* (Broadway, 1960), and Leslie Bricusse and Anthony Newley's *Stop the World—I Want to Get Off* (Broadway, 1962) and *The Roar of the Greasepaint—The Smell of the Crowd* (Broadway, 1965).[31]

Sondheim shared Laurents's frustration with Broadway. Following his lead, Sondheim would also write for Off-Broadway shortly after working on *Anyone Can Whistle*. He contributed to the long-running, irreverent, and satirical revue *The Mad Show* (1966), which, shortly before it opened, his co-composer Mary Rodgers described in terms that would resonate with anybody who complained about conformity in the musical theater: "There's not a thing in it that sounds as though it belongs in a Broadway musical."[32] Like *Anyone Can Whistle*, the show largely avoided topical humor, instead spoofing modern culture more broadly: "Television commercials inevitably come under assault, as do idiotic tv kiddie shows, pro football announcers, hypocritical parents, selfish teenagers, square elements of pop culture and neurotics great and small," wrote one reviewer.[33]

The final feature of *Anyone Can Whistle* that appears in the early drafts is its broad condemnation of modern society. For Laurents, writing such a critique did not mean writing a play that was merely controversial, politically charged, shocking, or titillating. "The inclusion of an important idea (social, political, economic, etc.) unfortunately does not of itself make a play either important or good. Too often, these ideas seem to have been sprayed over a script just to give it an air of importance; other times, the play form has merely served as a medium for the exposition of an idea," he wrote. "But plays dealing with fundamentals of human behavior, plays motivated by people rather than dramatis personae, plays which try to dig even a few fractions of an inch beneath the surface—where are they?"[34] He was keen to supply them. In the sketched prologue to "An Hour before Closing," for example, the characters turn outward and tell the audience what the play will be about, as in a classic French drama. "Man is over-civi-lized, over-analyzed, over philosophized," one character says. "The more he has progressed, the more miserable he has become. Instinct and heart are so buried that a man isn't sure what he feels, if he feels at all. And if he does feel, he doubts whether he feels what he feels for the right reasons and whether it is what he should feel anyway."[35] Although this prologue would not appear in *Anyone Can Whistle*, Laurents would develop these basic ideas over the years that separated these drafts from the Broadway premiere, and the final lyrics and libretto still offered the audience thoughts about freedom in the modern world, the poten-tial dangers of idealism, and what it means to be mad or sane in contemporary America (especially in songs such as "Everybody Says Don't," "Take One Look," and "With So Little to Be Sure of").

Taken together, what emerges from these early drafts is an institutional view of Broadway that linked the practical, concrete side of show business with its prevailing conventions and dramaturgy. For Laurents and Sondheim, commer-cialism and "naturalism" went hand in hand, and their goal with *Anyone Can Whistle* would be to critique the former by subverting the latter. More than that: Laurents also sought to indict a broader segment of society, which fostered the commercial institution of Broadway and stifled experimentation. At this stage, however, what exactly this critique would entail remained unclear.

## *Invitation to a March* Against Conformity: Interim Work (1957–1962)

Laurents appears to have done no work on *Anyone Can Whistle* between 1957, when he wrote notes and sketches for "An Hour before Closing," and 1962, when he began drafting dialogue for the first version of the musical's script. In the in-terim, however, he collaborated with Sondheim on a project in which he cul-tivated themes that would eventually appear in *Anyone Can Whistle*. This was his play *Invitation to a March*, the story of a Sleeping Beauty–like character who nods off whenever her purported Prince Charming speaks of their impending conventional life together. On a broad level, according to an interview Laurents gave to the *New York Times*, this play addressed "the problem of individualism, of standing up against those forces that try to fashion man in one mold," and he continued (in words that resemble "Everybody Says Don't" from *Anyone Can Whistle*), "Everybody . . . wants to be right. People are afraid to dare; they're afraid to fall on their faces."[36] This general idea would allow him to gather all the disparate elements of his early drafts for *Anyone Can Whistle*—the idealism of the entrepreneur, the rigidity of the marquesa, the desire to be free and escape modern society—and fashion them into a coherent theme, which the creative team would describe in the early press materials as a "comedic attack on conformity."[37]

Conformity and individuality have remained prevalent themes on Broadway in the many musicals that promote marching to the beat of one's own drum. Yet "conformity" meant something different for the creative team of *Anyone Can Whistle*.[38] Between the 1940s and the 1960s the word gave rise to a veritable cottage industry of popular and scholarly books that described the subtle ways in which purportedly free and open postwar societies nonetheless pressed their members into docility. As Herbert Marcuse wrote in his 1954 epilogue to *Reason and Revolution*, "The defeat of Fascism and National Socialism has not arrested the trend towards totalitarianism. Freedom is on the retreat—in the realm of thought as well as society."[39] The causes of this retreat were myriad. Erich Fromm described conformity as a psychological result of the anonymous power of modern democracy in *Escape from Freedom* (1941); David Reisman argued that a society of abundance produced a generation of "other-directed" people, attuned (at times overly so) to the opinions of others in *The Lonely Crowd* (1950); Irving Howe mourned the ways in which intellectual enthusiasm for modern capitalism and modern government obliterated radical thinking in "This Age of Conformity" (1954); William Whyte detailed how applying scientific analysis to society produced a "social ethic" of "belongingness" in *The Organization Man* (1956); and Marcuse warned that advanced capitalism destroyed the possibility of radical, critical, dialectical thought in *One-Dimensional Man* (1964).[40]

In the literature about conformity, the focus tended to be on the "well-adjusted" individual, a term (often pejorative) for somebody whose character was more or less aligned with the modes, fashions, and norms of the day.[41] Often adjustment was portrayed as neither conscious nor chosen but, rather, as a form of automatic orthodoxy—and such religious language was not uncommon in the literature. Whyte, for example, compared conformity positively to "a utopian faith," negatively to a kind of "idolatry."[42] More broadly, he argued that the problem of modern America was that people too readily adhered to a "belief in the group as the source of creativity, a belief in 'belongingness' as the ultimate need of an individual, a belief in the application of science to achieve the belongingness," which he labeled "scientism," another form of quasi-religious belief.[43] The result was a generation of "Organization Men," "blood [brothers] to the seminary student," whose fault lay "not in organization, [but rather] in [their] worship of it."[44]

This quasi-religious concept of conformity linked a number of details that had been unconnected in the early drafts. For example, in "Bridge," the fake miracle was enough to save the town from development by the American entrepreneur, who could not build on a holy site; in *Anyone Can Whistle*, however, the town sells its miracle waters for their purported curative abilities, marketing them to those who do not fit in but want to. Sondheim's lyrics for the "Miracle Song" in Act I exhort, "Come and take the waters / And with luck you'll be / Happy and successful / Liked and loved and beautiful and perfect. / Healthy, rich, handsome, independent, / Wise, *adjusted*, and secure, and athletic," making the connection between the miracle and conformity explicit.[45]

It was common to use religious language to describe conformists, but it was equally common to use scientific language to describe those who engineered the conformist society. This was the era of the personality test, a tool used by social scientists to determine who was well-adjusted and who was not. The literature about conformity tends to relish pointing out how absurd such tests could be. (One sample question that Whyte cites: "Do you prefer serious motion pictures about famous historical personalities to musical comedies?"[46]) In debunking these metrics, critics of conformity often demonstrated how contradictory the postwar well-adjusted life could be for those who paused long enough to think about it. Whyte, for example, on thrift: "The same man who will quote from Benjamin Franklin on thrift for the house organ would be horrified if consumers took these maxims to heart and started putting more money into savings and less into installment purchases."[47] On self-reliance: "The upward path toward the rainbow of achievement leads smack through the conference room. . . . the committee way simply can't be equated with the 'rugged' individualism that is supposed to be the business of business."[48] *Anyone Can Whistle* was no different. Sondheim described the final interrogation scene of Act I as a series of "paradoxical sketches" written by Laurents and "syllogisms" written by him ("The opposite of left is right, / the opposite of right is wrong, / So anyone who's left is wrong, right?"), bringing to mind the agitprop tone of Marc Blitzstein's prewar musicals but taking aim at postwar logical absurdity.[49] At the end of Act I, the protagonist, Hapgood, delivers a string of pseudo-psychological personality tests that are meant to distinguish the sane from the insane but invariably end in blatant contradiction. For example, he turns his attention to members of the town council:

Most of your money goes to the government in taxes. What does the government do with most of the money? Makes bombs. . . . But you say to make a product and not to use it is crazy. . . . And doesn't that make you crazy for letting them waste your money, Treasurer Schub? . . . But perhaps the government is making bombs because it means to use the product. Which means everyone will be killed . . . Which means you are paying most of your money to have yourself killed. Which means . . . you are the maddest of all![50]

In the "Bridge" drafts, *Invitation to a March*, and eventually *Anyone Can Whistle*, Laurents focused, not on the well-adjusted characters, but instead on the characters who could not or would not fit in. This, too, was common in the literature about conformity. Flipping expectation on its head, authors often described the well-adjusted as suffering from a malady—in Reisman's memorable phrasing, they are "ambulatory patients in the ward of modern culture" who exhibit "too much compliance and too little insight."[51] This short sentence could summarize the plot of *Anyone Can Whistle*, which revolves around asylum inmates who, to the dismay of the town council and asylum orderlies trying to assert control, appear indistinguishable from the rest of society.

Reisman described two different kinds of maladjusted people: the "anomic," who cannot function because they are either paralyzed by the expectations of others or misread others' cues, and the "autonomous," who are capable of conforming but choose not to.[52] "Modern industrial society has driven great numbers of people into anomie, and produced a wan conformity in others," Reisman wrote, "but the very developments which have done this have also opened up hitherto undreamed-of possibilities of autonomy."[53] *Anyone Can Whistle* is a veritable study in anomie and autonomy. Nurse Fay, for example, is "anomic," paralyzed by fear, incapable of happiness. In a notebook that Laurents kept while writing the musical, he described her as having thought she was free in society: "Thought piano [could] be played by ear; Thought 'Whistling Boy' poem <u>was</u> free; Thought because [she] felt, like Peter Pan, her spirit was free, she soared, she [could] dance." But she realized at some point in her life this was untrue: "[She] says she is no one."[54] As suggested by these notes, the title song, which Nurse Fay sings in Act II, is a response to James Whitcomb Riley's children's poem "The Whistling Boy" (1916):

> O happy boy with untaught grace!
>   What is there in the world to give
>   That can buy one hour of the life you live
> Or the trivial cause of your smiling face![55]

Sondheim's lyric for the title song takes the original poem's central image of whistling as "untaught grace" and turns it into a futile plea for freedom in the age of conformity.

What's hard is simple,
What's natural comes hard.
Maybe you could show me
How to let go
Lower my guard,
Learn to be free.
Maybe if you whistle,
Whistle for me.[56]

The last two lines of the lyric are especially appropriate for a character suffering from anomie. So excessively is she tuned into what others think that her version of freedom involves another person acting freely—whistling—in her stead.

If Nurse Fay is an example of anomie, Hapgood is the paragon of freedom. Reisman describes the "autonomous" as a variation on the "hero." "The autonomous are not to be equated with heroes. Heroism may or may not bespeak autonomy; the definition of autonomous refers to those who are in their character capable of freedom, whether or not they are able to, or care to, take the risks of overt deviation."[57] Laurents and Sondheim likewise cast Hapgood as an unconventional hero, and explicitly so, during the Act I song "There Won't Be Trumpets": "He may not be the cavalier, / Tall and graceful, fair and strong / Doesn't matter, just as long as he comes along." For Whyte, the autonomous hero possesses a mind that does not fit with convention, a mind that questions old norms—and Whyte believes that it is this kind of mind that harbors true genius. "Look, we are told, how the atom bomb was brought into being by the teamwork of huge corporations of scientists and technicians. Occasionally somebody mentions in passing that what an eccentric old man with a head of white hair did back in his study forty years ago had something to do with it," he wrote.[58] In *Anyone Can Whistle*, at the end of Act II, Fay names her inmates, the other people who seemed crazy in the eyes of the well-adjusted because they did not conform, Anthony, Susie B.; Freud, Harriet; Gandhi, Salvatore; Kierkegaard, Mac.[59]

As Laurents's critique of modern society sharpened, moving from a general displeasure with "over-philosophized" postwar culture and toward an attack on conformity, the script gradually took shape. By 1962 Laurents had drafted an outline for a show he called "O Cockeyed World!," which appeared at first to be distinct from any previous draft from 1957. The earliest fragments of the story run as follows: "All the patients of a mental institution are released and their records gone," he wrote; "the sane try to act sane and seem crazy. Then some enjoy the release, act as they have wanted to—mad—and seem sane." The main characters are "an aging idealist" and a head nurse who fall in love with one another. As the insane run amok in the town, the chief of police finds the head nurse and forces her to name her charges so they can be locked up again.[60] Over the course of the next year, however, Laurents merged this new show with characters and situations he had been holding onto for years from his earlier drafts, and, in broad outline, by March 1963 the plot of *Anyone Can Whistle* began to take shape: The town is bankrupt, so it stages a miracle to drum up business; the head nurse represents control and order but dons a wig and a French accent in order to let herself go; the roving, idealistic hero becomes an escaped inmate who ultimately would teach the nurse how to be free.

### "A Moderately Pretentious Show": The Harmonic Idiom of *Anyone Can Whistle*

If Laurents used his play *Invitation to a March* to explore ideas of conformity onstage, Sondheim, who supplied the incidental music, explored musical analogues for this topic. In his incidental music for *Invitation*, Sondheim differentiated the accompaniments for characters who were well-adjusted and those who refused to conform. For example, in his notes for the score, he identifies one theme as the Aaron theme and another the Tucker theme.[61] Aaron is a young man who chooses to live unconventionally and unapologetically (that is, he does not want to marry, adding another peripatetic character to the roster of such men in Laurents's and Sondheim's work); Tucker (who, it turns out, is Aaron's father) once was given the choice to break convention and be happy, but instead left his life behind, settled down, got married, and lives regretfully. Aaron's theme is created from thirds, while Tucker's is built of fourths. Having set up their themes separately, Sondheim places them on top of one another when the two characters come into conflict.[62] (See example 4.1.)

When Sondheim turned his attention to *Anyone Can Whistle*, he adapted this strategy from *Invitation to a March* to his new score, at least in part. He suggested as much in a 1978 article in which he referred to something along the lines of a stacked-fourth approach. "*Anyone Can Whistle* is sort of a music student's score," he said, claiming that "the whole score is based on the opening four notes of the overture, which is a second going to a fourth."[63] Previous researchers have taken this to mean that the score Sondheim composed was sui generis, and they rooted out the transformations of the opening motive across the entire score. They have also expanded this into a historical claim that unified construction and extended musical scenes (most notably "Simple," the end of Act I) signaled sophistication or maturity, which differentiated this show from his earlier ones, and which Sondheim would carry over into later productions.[64] Yet musicologist Stephen Banfield also sounded a note of doubt. "Given the finitude of musical intervals, everything could be derived

**Example 4.1.** Stephen Sondheim, Suite from *Invitation to a March* (Milwaukee: Hal Leonard, 2016), 21–22.

from everything else in a multiplicity of ways," he wrote.[65] A little more than a decade later, Sondheim followed suit, saying,

> But if I said that about the *Whistle* score, I'm afraid I was—"There Won't Be Trumpets"—I'm afraid I was blowing my own horn. It's possible. . . . I wouldn't be surprised if I did, because I was still very heavily under the influence of Milton Babbitt, and this was going to be a moderately pretentious show. So it's very possible that I tried to do that. But when I look back on the score as you speak, I don't really see anything going on among the songs that has any kind of consistency. . . . And the fact is a number of numbers were replaced, so I don't think it was very much of a conceived score.[66]

The aesthetic import of this statement is that the score is most likely not organic or unified in the ways previously thought. The historiographical implications of this immediately follow: The claim that Sondheim's career consists of steps toward ever greater musical coherence is most likely untrue, or at least not true in any straightforward way.[67]

Yet what could Sondheim have meant when he said that the entire score could be derived from "a second going to a fourth"? The key idea that he retained in *Anyone Can Whistle* was that a stacked-third language could be *placed into conflict* with a stacked-fourth language.[68] The clearest example is the song "Everybody Says Don't," which is built around two contrasting sections of lyrics—the "don't sections" and the "do sections." First, the "don't sections" (mm.

1–4) feature melodies and accompaniments (above a functional bass line) built largely on stacked fourths and major seconds (with a recurring syncopated rhythmic punch). Second, the "do sections" (mm. 11–14) are built largely on stacked thirds. In the middle section of the song, when Hapgood tries to coax Fay into taking a risk (mm. 29–44), Sondheim combines the two logics: The repeated, syncopated stacked-fourth accompaniment also contains a third, while the melody features two ascending fourths, each a major second apart, followed by a falling minor third. (See examples 4.2a–c.) Almost the same strategy pertains to the opening song, "Me and My Town." The mayoress begins wailing about the troubles of her town, accompanied by lush stacked thirds. Yet in the middle of the song, as her bluesy wail becomes a sardonic mambo, the accompaniment switches to stacked fourths. At the end of the song, when her opening melody returns, Sondheim once again combines the stacked-fourth harmony with an extra third. (See examples 4.3a–c.)

A slightly different strategy, yet one with a similar effect, is at play in "There Won't Be Trumpets." The first section of the chorus begins with a lush chord built in B♭.[69] Between each phrase of the chorus, however, is an eighth-note triad from a completely different key, C major (with a strongly projected dissonant E♮, doubled in the vocal score's orchestrated version), with a rhythm, texture, and orchestration that are foreign to this context—as if a fanfare from another world. (See example 4.4.) If the song is about how a real hero will not need a conventional trumpet flare to announce his arrival, then these sounds from a distant key suggest a struggle to keep convention at bay—and immediately following the song, a large, ironic brass fanfare announces the purported hero's arrival.

On the one hand, there was much about the musical syntax of *Anyone Can Whistle* that was perfectly in keeping with Broadway convention. For example, just about every song in the musical (with the major exception of the first-act finale) conforms to a standard thirty-two-bar form, which typically comprises phrases of an expected length (usually eight bars) that arrive at clearly etched cadences.[70] Similarly "standard" was Sondheim's approach to harmonic function. He tended to sketch songs in roman-numeral notation (albeit, a slightly idiosyncratic approach to it), and the function of each chord was determined by the bass: "Musical harmony, as you know, moves by bass line," he stated. "That is the motive that changes things. And it doesn't matter how you screw around with the notes on top; if the bass remains solidly consistent, it's going to sound that way throughout."[71]

Yet above this functional bass line and between these cadential moments was where Sondheim's music took its own unconventional approach to melody and harmony. Most often, the upper voices in his harmonies tend to derive from elaborately stacked thirds. But he would vary the quality of the thirds, as if he

**Example 4.2.** Stephen Sondheim, "Everybody Says Don't," *Anyone Can Whistle*, vocal score (New York: Burthen Music), 136, 137, 138.

**Example 4.2.** Continued

**Example 4.3.** Sondheim, "Me and My Town," *Anyone Can Whistle*, vocal score, 13–14, 16, 23–24.

**Example 4.3.** Continued

**Example 4.4.** Sondheim, "There Won't Be Trumpets," *Anyone Can Whistle*, vocal score, 50.

could adjust the clarity of a key by turning a dial that would tweak the accidentals of the chord extensions.[72] For example, regarding a scene in *Passion* (1994), he described "the kind of chord in which you take a triad and lay on top of it another triad and it's all within the same key. It's sort of a jazz chord is really what it is. And it's unresolved which is what's nice about it," and then he pointed to a particular chord. "Ordinarily, in D minor, that would be a C♯, but by making it a C♮ it has a softer more fluid sound. And it's just something I like a lot."[73] In *Anyone Can Whistle*, most of the score deploys stacked-third harmony, but there are moments that slip out of his accustomed, "normative" musical practice, and slip instead into stacked seconds and fourths. By playing these two different kinds of composition off one another, Sondheim could both wink in the direction of

**Example 4.5.** Sondheim, "Interrogation—Part I," *Anyone Can Whistle*, vocal score, 57 (mm. 1–7).

Broadway convention and at the same time stand outside it, thereby giving a sonic emblem to his theme of conformity and autonomy.[74]

With this in mind, it becomes clearer what Sondheim meant when he referred to the opening four notes of the overture: This is one of the moments in the score when he aggressively deploys nontriadic harmonies. Although it is unlikely that Sondheim wrote the overture himself (most often arrangers and musical directors cobbled together overtures, and no sketches for it survive in Sondheim's archives), its music derives from music that he did write: the interrogation scene at the end of the first act, in which the unconventional hero deploys his special logic to prove that most of the purportedly sane are actually mad. (See example 4.5.) When Sondheim reflected back on the score in 1978, the closing of the Act I finale probably stood out as germinal or emblematic of the entire score in his memory for two reasons: first, because it was one of the first sections he composed, and lyrics survive for this piece in some of the earliest drafts of the script; and second, because it is a moment when the overall theme of conformity clearly takes over the plot, and the unconventional harmony takes over the score—the kind of writing that Sondheim first explored in *Invitation to a March*.

## A Spotlight on Whom? Song Form in *Anyone Can Whistle*

Sondheim's and Laurents's goal in *Anyone Can Whistle* was not merely to stand apart from convention, however. Their goal was also to turn around and critique the institution of Broadway for the role it played in modern, commercial, conformist society. Two other features of the score explain how they achieved this.

First, in later interviews, Sondheim described experimenting with what might be called the "shape" of the songs in the musical.

> Most of the score of *Whistle* is, in a sense, my experimenting with things. "There Won't Be Trumpets" is an experiment in form. And I'm not just talking about when it turns into a waltz, I'm talking about the structure of it, and the constant acceleration, that sort of stuff.[75]

Taken separately, each large section of "There Won't Be Trumpets" conforms roughly to a familiar thirty-two-bar pattern, the parallel-period (AB||AC) format.[76] In the first half of this standard format, A sections tend to be tonic-prolongational, whereas B sections move away from the tonic toward a cadence (almost always a half cadence or dominant arrival).[77] Such is the case in "There Won't Be Trumpets": The first twelve measures sway hypnotically back and forth between tonic and dominant, at which point a stacked-fourth chord built over scale degree 3 unsettles the repeating pattern and launches it from its harmonic home. (See table 4.1.) The B section begins by prolonging a IIsus4 chord, which Sondheim transposes upward chromatically, reaching a moment of maximum harmonic tension, a #IVsus4 chord. Through stepwise voice leading, Sondheim settles into a rumbling dominant, which in turn relaunches the A section. At this point, aside from its harmonic sophistication (stacked fourth chords, whole-step sequences, embellished dominants), the underlying harmonic structure has followed convention.

Normally the second half of the standard AB||AC form would begin with a repetition of the tonic-prolongational A phrase, and the following measures would travel away from the tonic toward a pungent dominant, leading ultimately to an authentic cadence. In "There Won't be Trumpets," however, despite some differences in surface figuration, the second section simply repeats the under-lying harmonic structure of the first half, arriving once again at an expectant dominant. From a broad, diachronic point of view, the song has shifted away from a binary parallel-period format and has become a song in three large rotations: AB||AB||AB||coda. Considered synchronically, however, the arrival of the second dominant creates a compositional problem: How does one end a piece that could simply repeat ad infinitum?

In his interview, Sondheim's phrase "constant acceleration" gives some sense of his solution. The surface figuration in "There Won't Be Trumpets" is more than merely decorative; it creates an overall sense of acceleration: the first rotation's ac-companiment is mainly in whole notes, the second's is in quarter-note oom-pah figures, and the third's is in triplets. In addition, the recurring fanfare increases in prominence, speed, and orchestral weight as the song progresses. The effect, essentially, is that the song avalanches ever faster toward its final conclusion—a formal shape not dissimilar to that of a number of works by Maurice Ravel, one of Sondheim's favorite composers and the subject of his senior thesis at Williams College. Many of Ravel's works swirl around a repeating passage, only to launch out of them with a moment of "breakdown"—an abrupt shift in meter, an ab-rupt change in key—which isolates and emphasizes the cadence that follows: for example, the final, stumbling duple-meter bars of *La Valse* (1920), the sudden lurch to E major in *Boléro* (1928), and the intrusion of the military tattoo in the final bars of the Piano Concerto for the Left Hand (1930).[78] A similar strategy

**Table 4.1.** Stephen Sondheim, "There Won't Be Trumpets." Measure numbers correspond to the printed piano-vocal score.

| Rotation 1 | | Rotation 2 | | Rotation 3 | | |
|---|---|---|---|---|---|---|
| A Section (m. 30) | B section (m. 46) | A Section (m. 62) | B Section (m. 78) | A Section (m. 94) | B Section (m. 110) | Coda (m. 127) |
| "There won't be trumpets…" | "He may not…" | "But not with trumpets…" | "We can wait…" | "Don't look for trumpets…" | "Don't know when…" | "You won't need trumpets!" |
| 𝄴 | | | | | 𝄵 | 𝄵 |
| Whole-note accomp. | | Eighth-note accomp. | | Triplet accomp. | | Tremolo end |
| | | ("Constant acceleration") | | | ("Breakdown!") | |
| | I : HC | | I : HC (!) | | I : HC | I : PAC |

m. 46    m. 52    m. 54    m. 61

IIsus4

V7

pertains to "There Won't Be Trumpets." In the song's headlong rush through the third rotation, the final B section retains the same basic structural harmonies as previous sections (a IIsus4 chord that ascends stepwise and lands on an active dominant) but stumbles into triple time, breaking the repetition, and thereby emphasizing the final repeated tonic-dominant toggling. It ultimately screeches to a close with a brassy tonic marked "*sffz*," overlain with a dominant seventh, ninth, and eleventh, as if the once distant fanfare had finally arrived.[79]

A similar kind of formal experiment, with different implications, appears in the mayoress's opening number, "Me and My Town." The background model in this song is not the parallel-period form but rather the thirty-two bar "lyric bi-nary" (AABA) form. Traditionally, these standard choruses tend to be "end ac-cented": The final A section comprises what musicologist James Hepokoski has termed a "double spotlight," in which the "truth" of the song is revealed in both music and lyrics.[80] This sonic spotlight usually appears as a series of evaded cadences (the "one-more-time effect"), large leaps, and other special effects—ul-timately creating a moment of musical emphasis to accompany the final, most important words.[81]

In "Me and My Town," however, Sondheim has created an extra composi-tional problem. The overall structure of the song, as indicated earlier, comprises two choruses stitched together (forming what musicologist Graham Wood has termed a "macrochorus"): a first chorus built largely over stacked thirds, a second chorus built largely over stacked fourths, and then a final section that purports to wrap up both by superimposing elements of the first chorus over elements of the second.[82] This final section amounts to the "double spotlight" moment: From a lyrical angle, this is the moment of truth in which Cora reveals naked ambition, unencumbered by faux concern for the "poor, starving, cold, miserable, dirty, dreary, depressing peasants" that live in her town: She sings, "Give me my coat, give me my crown, / Give me, give me your vote and hurry on down."[83] This is also the moment of truth in the music, leading to a cadence emphasized to the point of frenzy by repetitions of the A-section material that continually evade cadence. What follows these repetitions, and what ultimately brings the song to a halt, is another "breakdown": A large stepwise lead-in in the low brass and bass saxophone with dramatic ritardando prepares the moment when Cora calls for her coat and crown. (See table 4.2.) After that lead-in, how-ever, what music accompanies this moment? A vulgar, brassy "strut" reminiscent of Mama Rose's final runway prowl from *Gypsy*: naked ambition accompanied by stripper's music.

If this is a moment of "double spotlight," what kind of truth does the music re-veal? On the one hand, "Me and My Town" functions as what has been dubbed an "I want" number, the kind of song that often appears early on in many Rodgers

**Table 4.2.** Stephen Sondheim, "Me and My Town," "double spotlight" ending. Measure numbers correspond to the printed piano-vocal score.

| A section returns | | A section returns | A section returns |
|---|---|---|---|
| "Last week a flood" (m. 142) | "A friendship is lovely" (m. 158) | "What'll we do?" (m. 166) | "Give me my coat" (m. 174) |
| Mambo | | | Strut |
| | | | ("Double spotlight") |
| E♭ major | C minor | E♭ major (Low brass lead-in) | E♭ major (cadential) |

and Hammerstein shows in which a character sincerely discloses what he or she hopes to achieve—in Cora's case, power. On the other, the strut seems far removed from "I want" conventions; after all, Cora does not consider herself to be vulgar. Rather, what emerges is the author's and composer's ironic, sardonic external commentary on the character. In interviews, both Sondheim and Laurents have stated that they found her character to be "venal." In fact, at times the writers were so contemptuous of the character that the original actress, Angela Lansbury, found the role difficult to play. She said, "[Laurents] loved all the surface, kind of overt camp qualities of the character and he wanted her played as the nastiest thing on two feet. And I simply could not find this lady in myself. . . . I felt that there needed to be some vulnerability in a character like that, that would be far more interesting than playing her as an out-and-out bitch which would merely be a caricature."[84] Laurents tried to resist adding any vulnerability or depth to her role, preferring instead something that was obviously fictitious or false. Eventually, however, he and Sondheim relented and inserted the song "There's a Parade in Town" to round her out. Yet this, too, may have been a wink in the direction of pastiche: The musical *Hello, Dolly!* contains a very similar song, "Before the Parade Passes By." This show premiered on January 16, 1964, the day after *Anyone Can Whistle* began rehearsals and just before Sondheim considered writing this song. Laurents would later write in the *New York Times* that the character of Dolly Levi "has been reduced to what is almost a caricature" of the character in Thornton Wilder's original play, representing "a triumph of frenetic staging and a performance by a larger-than-life actress," a description that could apply equally well to his vision of the mayoress in *Anyone Can Whistle*.[85]

Beyond commenting on Cora, the breakout of the strut at the end of "Me and My Town" also achieves the final level of commentary that Sondheim and Laurents were making: the critique of the institution of Broadway. *Anyone Can Whistle* is a show-biz show, a production steeped in past Broadway productions and styles. This winking aspect of the production was conceived early on, even before the mayoress appeared in Laurents's drafts. Originally, before the patients at the asylum were called cookies, Laurents had planned to call them "Brazilians," and wrote: "Brazil: where the nuts come from."[86] This refers to a recurring gag from Brandon Thomas's popular comedy *Charley's Aunt* (1892), which became Frank Loesser's musical *Where's Charley?* (1948 Broadway, 1952 film). In the summer of 1963 (about six months before rehearsals began), Laurents wrote to his producer that the nurses in the asylum (characters he later cut) should be given the "Helzapoppin' treatment," referring to the zany, long-running musical revue from 1938, and in his earliest draft of the script (probably dating from the summer of 1962), he described the mayoress as singing a "Kay-Thompson-and-the-Boys" number, referring to the actress and choreographer who fronted a famous nightclub act with the Williams Brothers.[87]

The show-biz quality goes further. As Raymond Knapp has noticed, the plot of *Anyone Can Whistle* bears striking similarities to the plot of another musical, *The Music Man* (1957).[88] Both tell the stories of outsiders who appear in town, who win over the townspeople with a revivalist ensemble number, and who encourage prim women (in the one a librarian, in the other a nurse) to "let go." (Perhaps it is no coincidence that Kermit Bloomgarden produced both *The Music Man* and *Anyone Can Whistle*, that Don Walker orchestrated both, and, as discovered by librarian Mark Horowitz, somebody noticed the link between the two shows and drew a cartoon about it on one of Walker's scores.[89]) (See figure 4.1.) The plot also resembles that of the musical *110 in the Shade*, which opened in 1963, just as Laurents was finishing his rehearsal draft of *Anyone Can Whistle*. This musical also told the story of an outsider who appears in a town ruined by drought, wins over the inhabitants in a revivalist number about water, and encourages a prim woman (in this case a self-described "old maid") to let go. (Perhaps it is no coincidence that Laurents had earlier approached Robert Horton to star in *Anyone Can Whistle*, but Horton turned him down to appear as Starbuck in *110 in the Shade*.[90]) With these allusions squarely at the center, *Anyone Can Whistle* becomes an indictment, not only of the mayoress's crassness but also of venality, the shallowness of the Broadway musical.[91]

**Figure 4.1.** A cartoon pointing to the similarities between *The Music Man* and *Anyone Can Whistle*. Originally printed in Mark Eden Horowitz, "Really Weird: The Story of *Anyone Can Whistle* with Lots of Details," *Sondheim Review* 17, no. 2 (Winter 2010): 9. The "Think System" is the musical method Harold Hill purports to teach the children of River City in *The Music Man*.

\*\*\*

Repositioning *Anyone Can Whistle* from transitional work to breakout moment in Sondheim's career has meant identifying the aspects of his "voice" that he supposedly discovered in this show. In his words, the production was "unconventional and inventive and, above all, playful. It allowed me to use pastiche for comment on character and style, as in Cora's songs and 'The Cookie Chase'—devices I continued to experiment with in subsequent shows. It was a laudable attempt to present something off-center in mainstream musical theater."[92] Sondheim thereby linked his experiments in form to pastiche, to the institutional norms of Broadway, and to a critique of modern society writ large. All of these features would reappear in Sondheim's musicals in the decades to come.

There is, however, one other important aspect of Sondheim's voice that emerged in *Anyone Can Whistle*. He never articulated it explicitly, but it has appeared consistently around the edges of his commentary for decades. Consider, for example, which songs from *Anyone Can Whistle* Sondheim claimed expressed his unique voice: "The 'Interrogations' [that is, 'Simple,' the finale to the first act] is my voice; Cora's songs—those Kay Thompson numbers—and 'With So Little to Be Sure of,' those are my own voice."[93] It is striking how different these songs are. The "Interrogations" and Cora's songs trade in the kind of ironic commentary that is typical of other concept musicals, whereas "With So Little to Be Sure Of" is the complete opposite: genuine, heartfelt, a duet for two characters who are struggling to find meaning in an increasingly conformist society and who resolve to struggle together against Weltschmertz: "Crazy business this, this life we live in / Can't complain about the time we're given, / With so little to be sure of in this world, / Hold me, hold me."[94]

The quality of Sondheim's voice that emerges in *Anyone Can Whistle* is rooted in a conflict between the two. When Sondheim described turning away from the Rodgers and Hammerstein song-scene, song-scene production, he found its formal features to be inseparable from its typical expressive modes: sentimental, straightforward, sincere integrated musicals stood opposed to the more sardonic concept musical. Describing Hammerstein's legacy, he said, "Oscar's lyrics are often flat-out sentimental, lacking in irony, which is the favorite mode of expression of the latter part of the 20th century. And I happen to love irony."[95] Yet another part of him also rejected this ironic tone. He said, "Irony gives you an excuse to say anything, no matter how crass or banal or pretentious, and get away with it. Irony is a made-to-order refuge from emotion or criticism." He criticized John Kander, Fred Ebb, and Bob Fosse's *Chicago* (1975) for taking it too far: "Almost every number is a manifestation of vaudeville, no matter what the character, subject or dramatic moment."[96] Over the years, when he denied turning away entirely from the Rodgers and Hammerstein model toward the concept musical, this is what he most likely meant: that although the form of his musicals may look different from that of the integrated musical, he did not entirely abandon the heartfelt, sentimental, sincere expression that went with it. On one hand, in a world where the Broadway musical had become yet another tool of conformism, remaining outside the musical's sentimental sway was a sign of independent, critical thought—of "autonomy," to use Reisman's word. On the other, even as cultural critics attacked received social values as oppressive, Sondheim found it difficult to move entirely into a world that dismissed stable social or moral values as merely the tools of conformity.

Coming to terms with *Anyone Can Whistle* as a show means coming to terms with this kind of conflicted expression. Coming to terms with *Anyone Can Whistle* as a historiographical watershed in Sondheim's career suggests seeing this conflicted expression as central to his dramaturgy. Rather than positioning the show as falling uneasily between the integrated musical and concept musical, conceived in terms of the relationship between song and spoken word, it instead marks the first time that Sondheim found a manner of expressing himself that spoke to a crisis of meaning in modern society, which he would take up in the decades that followed.

In Act II of *Anyone Can Whistle*, Hapgood turns to Nurse Fay and says, "Until this morning, I was probably the craziest man in the world. Because I was not only an idealist, I was a practicing idealist. Now *that is mad*; it's thankless; and it's absolutely exhausting."[97] Whether or not one believes him, Hapgood declared himself finished with futile idealism. One wonders whether Sondheim ever did the same.

## Notes

1. The author wishes to thank W. Anthony Sheppard, Danielle Ward-Griffin, Christopher Mirto, Kathy Li, and Julie Vatain-Corfdir for their comments on earlier drafts of this chapter.

     For a summary, see Geoffrey Block, "Integration," in *The Oxford Handbook of the American Musical*, ed. Raymond Knapp, Mitchell Morris, and Stacy Wolf (New York: Oxford University Press, 2011), 97–110; Scott McMillin, *The Musical as Drama: A Study of the Principles and Conventions Behind Musical Shows from Kern to Sondheim* (Princeton: Princeton University Press, 2006), 6–10, 31–33; see also Hannah Lewis, "*Love Me Tonight* (1932) and the Development of the Integrated Film Musical," *Musical Quarterly* 100, no. 1 (2017): 5, in which she describes integration as an "ideal." For some, the term "naturalism" is so strained in relation to the Broadway musical that they describe the style in other ways. Raymond Knapp, for example, calls this "Musically Enhanced Reality Mode" in the American film musical; see Knapp, *The American Musical and the Formation of National Identity* (Princeton: Princeton University Press, 2005), 67–70. Andrea Most calls it an "anti-theatrical bias"; see Most, *Making Americans: Jews and the Broadway Musical* (Cambridge, MA: Harvard University Press, 2004), 103–104; Jeffrey Magee, "Rodgers and Hammerstein's Musical Metatheatre, or: Why Billy Bigelow Had to Die," *Studies in Musical Theatre* 8, no. 3 (2014): 215–223.
2. Martin Gottfried, "Flipping over 'Follies,'" *New York Times*, April 25, 1971. For a history of the term see Thomas P. Adler, "The Musical Dramas of Stephen Sondheim: Some Critical Approaches," *Journal of Popular Culture* 12, no. 3 (Winter 1978): 513–525; Larry Stempel, *Showtime: A History of the Broadway Musical Theater* (New York: Norton, 2010), 517–518; Steve Swayne, *How Sondheim Found His Sound* (Ann Arbor: University of Michigan Press, 2005), 257–259; and John Bush Jones, *Our Musicals, Ourselves: A Social History of the American Musical Theatre* (Hanover, NH: Brandeis University Press, 2003), 270–271.
3. Stephen Banfield, *Sondheim's Broadway Musicals* (Ann Arbor: University of Michigan Press, 1993), 38.
4. Quoted in Robert Gordon, "Old Situations, New Complications," in *The Oxford Handbook of Sondheim Studies*, ed. Robert Gordon (New York: Oxford University Press, 2014), 65. Sondheim contrasts this to the songs in *A Funny Thing Happened on the Way to the Forum*, which offer "respites from the action," and *Company*, in

which "the songs were respites and comments." See also Stephen Citron, *Sondheim and Lloyd Webber: The New Musical* (New York: Oxford University Press, 2001), 127. Likewise, Banfield describes the score to *Anyone Can Whistle* as a "comprehensive musical structure [which] distinguishes it sharply from *Forum*." Banfield, *Sondheim's Broadway Musicals*, 123.

5. Eugene K. Bristow and J. Kevin Butler, "*Company*, About Face! The Show That Revolutionized the American Musical," *American Music* 5, no. 3 (Autumn 1987): 241–254; Samuel G. Freedman, "The Words and Music of Stephen Sondheim," *New York Times Magazine*, April 1, 1984, 25; Wendy Smith, "Good Thing Going: Stephen Sondheim Only Looks Better with Time," *American Scholar* 76, no. 4 (Autumn 2007): 111; Stempel, *Showtime*, 531; Geoffrey Block, *Enchanted Evenings: The Broadway Musical from* Show Boat *to* Sondheim and Lloyd Webber (New York: Oxford University Press, 2009), 336.

6. Mark Eden Horowitz, *Sondheim on Music: Minor Details and Major Decisions* (Lanham, MD: Scarecrow Press with the Library of Congress, 2010), 191 (ellipses original).

7. Guy Flatley, "When Stephen Sondheim Writes Words and Music, Some Critics Don't Leave the Theater Humming," *People*, April 5, 1976, 69–70.

8. Two other studies have taken pioneering steps along these lines. See David Savran and Daniel Gundlachtt, "*Anyone Can Whistle* as Experimental Theater," in *The Oxford Handbook of Sondheim Studies*, ed. Robert Gordon (Oxford: Oxford University Press, 2014), 81–94; Raymond Knapp, "Sondheim's America; America's Sondheim," in *The Oxford Handbook of Sondheim Studies*, ed. Robert Gordon (New York: Oxford University Press, 2014), 432–450. As will be seen, this chapter builds on their insights while reaching different conclusions.

9. Arthur Laurents, *The Rest of the Story: A Life Completed* (Milwaukee: Applause Theatre and Cinema Books, 2011), 138. For slightly differing accounts of their meeting, see Stephen Sondheim, "Theater Lyrics," in *Playwrights, Lyricists, Composers on Theater*, ed. Otis L. Guernsey (New York: Dodd, Mead, 1974), 63; Meryle Secrest, *Stephen Sondheim: A Life* (New York: Knopf), 111–112. On the formative influence of Laurents on Sondheim, also see Jeffrey Magee's chapter in this volume.

10. Arthur Laurents, *Original Story By: A Memoir of Broadway and Hollywood* (New York: Knopf, 2000), 369–370. They also collaborated on the aborted "A Pray by Blecht," for which Laurents was brought in as a consultant. They were also slated to collaborate on the political satire *Hot Spot*, for which Sondheim provided the songs "Don't Laugh" and "That's Good, That's Bad." Laurents signed a contract to direct in March 1963 but pulled out of the production. See Arthur Laurents Papers, Music Division, Library of Congress, Washington, DC (hereafter LoC-AL), Box 53, Folder 3, "Contracts—Hot Spot (1963)."

11. Quoted in John M. Clum, *The Works of Arthur Laurents: Politics, Love, and Betrayal* (Amherst, NY: Cambria, 2014), 51.

12. Arthur Laurents, "Musical Adventure," *New York Times*, November 3, 1957.

13. Howard Taubman, "Theater: A New Musical," *New York Times*, April 6, 1964. Contemporary reviews of *Anyone Can Whistle* have been collected in the Kermit Bloomgarden Papers, Wisconsin Historical Society, Madison, WI (hereafter WHS-KB), Microfilm 1021, Reel 3. (In the library's finding aid it is listed as Reel 2.)

14. All of these early drafts are contained in LoC-AL, Box 6, Folder 3, "Bridge." In the same folder are other sheets with notes on them, but it is unclear what relation, if any, they have to these drafts.

15. Some fragmented penciled notes on a single piece of paper describe the proposed content: "Two people throughout the play fall in love, sexual love, affairs, out of love, but loving, loving always."

16. At some point Laurents jotted down another note on a separate sheet and labeled it "Story—or scene for Love Play (or Bridge?)," suggesting that the two separate stories, "Play About Love" and "Bridge," were beginning to merge in his mind. LoC-AL, Box 6, Folder 3.

17. Laurents indicated that "there should be no specific place names or last names or language," but at one point he described the local restaurant as a "buca," suggesting that Italy served as a background model. Laurents himself was an avid traveler, and before he wrote these notes, he had written a few times about the topic of the clash of cultures or estrangement one experiences while abroad, especially in Italy. This was, for example, the subject of *The Time of the Cuckoo* and also the subject of his article "But It Has Been Lovely, Just Lovely," *New York Times*, February 22, 1953. It is possible that Laurents initially envisioned this as the inverse of his 1952 play *The Time of the Cuckoo* (which eventually became the musical *Do I Hear a Waltz?*). *The Time of the Cuckoo* followed Leona Samish, an older American woman, who eventually succumbs to the charms of an Italian man. "The Novel of Mort" (or "Play About Love") focuses instead on the story of an older Italian man who seduces an American woman.

18. The combined version added two more characters. Although the bridge remains central to the plot, the focus shifts to the wavering relationships among two couples: The entrepreneur's wife is dissatisfied with her marriage and begins to fall in love with the marquesa's partner, Mort, which in turn pushes the jilted entrepreneur toward the marquesa, who ultimately rejects him.

19. "Bridge," LoC-AL, Box 6, Folder 3, 2.

20. Ibid.

21. Stephen Sondheim, *Anyone Can Whistle: Vocal Score* (New York: Burthen Music, 1968), 45; the melody in the flute and oboe derives from the cut song "The Lame, the Halt, and the Blind," which was planned for this point in the show.

22. "Bridge," LoC-AL, Box 6, Folder 3, 2.

23. Arthur Laurents and Stephen Sondheim, *Anyone Can Whistle: A Musical Fable* (New York: Random House, 1965), 104. No mention of the marquesa's hair or wig exists in the combined draft, "An Hour before Closing."

24. Stephen Sondheim, *Finishing the Hat: Collected Lyrics (1954–1981) with Attendant Comments, Principles, Heresies, Grudges, Whines and Anecdotes* (New York: Knopf, 2010), 111.

25. Arthur Laurents, "Writer's Dilemma: The Dramatist Should Choose Honesty Rather Than Compromise," *New York Times*, August 25, 1946.

26. Savran and Gundlachtt argue that Off-Off-Broadway experiments may also have influenced *Anyone Can Whistle*. See "*Anyone Can Whistle* as Experimental Theater," 81–85.

27. Arthur Laurents, "Laurents Off Broadway," *New York Times*, October 12, 1958.

28. "Bridge," LoC-AL, Box 6, Folder 3, [1].

29. Ibid.

30. Laurents, "Musical Adventure."

31. Laurents discusses these musicals in two main sources: Arthur Laurents to Goddard Lieberson, May 1, 1964, LoC-AL, Box 104, Folder 1; Arthur Laurents, "'Look, Girls, There's the Man with Our Tap Shoes!'" *New York Times*, September 11, 1966.

32. Stuart W. Little, "An Irreverent Revue Just for the Holidays," *New York Herald Tribune*, December 23, 1965.

33. Tomo, "The Mad Show," *Variety*, January 19, 1966.

34. Laurents, "Writer's Dilemma."

35. "Points and Bits," LoC-AL, Box 6, Folder 3.

36. Thomas Lask, "Seed of a Comedy," *New York Times*, October 23, 1960.

37. "Theater: Anyone Can Whistle," *New York Herald Tribune*, March 22, 1964, 23.

38. For another study about conformity in the context of *Anyone Can Whistle*, see Savran and Gundlachtt, "*Anyone Can Whistle* as Experimental Theater," 84.

39. Quoted in Douglas Kellner, "Introduction to the Second Edition," in *One-Dimensional Man: Studies in the Ideology of Advanced Industrial Society*, by Herbert Marcuse (London: Routledge Classics, 2002), xxiv.

40. Erich Fromm, *Escape from Freedom* (New York: Avon, 1941); David Reisman with Nathan Glazer and Reuel Denny, *The Lonely Crowd: A Study of the Changing American Character* (New Haven: Yale Nota Bene, 2001); Irving Howe, "This Age of Conformity: Notes on an Endless Theme, or, a Catalogue of Complaints," *Partisan Review* 21, no. 1 (January–February 1954): 7–33; William H. Whyte, *The Organization Man* (Philadelphia: University of Pennsylvania Press, 2002); Marcuse, *One-Dimensional Man.*

41. See, e.g., Whyte, *Organization Man*, 173.

42. Ibid., 8, 23, 171.

43. Ibid., 7, 23.

44. Ibid., 3, 14.

45. Sondheim, *Anyone Can Whistle*, 37, 39–40 (emphasis added).

46. Whyte, *Organization Man*, 180.

47. Ibid., 17.

48. Ibid., 18.

49. "Paradoxical sketches," "syllogisms": Sondheim, "Theater Lyrics," 91; "The opposite of left is right": Laurents and Sondheim, *Anyone Can Whistle*, 83–84.

50. Laurents and Sondheim, *Anyone Can Whistle*, 78.

51. Reisman, *Lonely Crowd*, 244.

52. Ibid., 242ff.

53. Ibid., 251.

54. Arthur Laurents Papers, Robert R. Farber University Archives and Special Collections Department, Brandeis University, Waltham, MA (hereafter RRF-AL), Box 1, Folder 5, notebook titled "'Anyone Can Whistle' Preliminary Notes," [14].

55. James Whitcomb Riley, *James Whitcomb Riley's Complete Works* (Indianapolis: Bobbs-Merrill, 1916), 1:32.

56. Sondheim, *Finishing the Hat*, 129.

57. Reisman, *Lonely Crowd*, 250.

58. Whyte, *Organization Man*, 206.

59. Laurents and Sondheim, *Anyone Can Whistle*, 171–172.

60. RRF-AL, Box 1, Folder 5, notebook, 1.

61. "Notes for Recording," Stephen Sondheim Papers, Wisconsin Historical Society, Madison, WI (hereafter WHS-SS), Box 14, Folder 1, 2.

62. Sondheim may have derived this strategy by pulling apart the opening notes of "Taps," the tune which begins the play and consists of a perfect fourth followed by a major third.

63. Sondheim, "Musical Theater," 14.

64. Banfield describes the structural features as a forerunner to *Follies* in *Sondheim's Broadway Musicals*, 123. See also Swayne, *How Sondheim Found His Sound*, 245.

65. Banfield, *Sondheim's Broadway Musicals*, 125.

66. Horowitz, *Sondheim on Music*, 188–189.

67. For example, musicologist Steve Swayne notes that sui generis motivic development had been a feature of Sondheim's composition from his student days at Williams. See *How Sondheim Found His Sound*, 227, 230; see also Steve Swayne, "Sondheim's Piano Sonata," *Journal of the Royal Musical Association* 127, no. 2 (2002): 263ff.

68. Swayne discusses a similar "stacked-seconds and -fourths" musical language in the context of *Sunday in the Park with George*. See Swayne, *How Sondheim Found His Sound*, 243–245.

69. Sondheim's original manuscript score spells this opening chord as a series of stacked fourths, rather than the lush thirds in the printed, orchestrated version. Sondheim, "There Won't Be Trumpets," WHS-SS, Box 2, Folder 2.

70. Sondheim has called these moments "thumbtacks" or "bedposts." He said: "One of the great things I loved when I went to the Library of Congress and saw the Gershwin sketch for the trio at the end of *Porgy and Bess* was he knew where he was going. He would just put little thumbtacks all along the way to remind himself: Okay, I gotta reach the C-major chord over here. And he's spinning out the melodic line and he thinks: I'll fill in the harmony later. I won't worry about how I get from here to here. I just want to be sure that I get *there*. That's in a sense, what these are—these are bedposts." Horowitz, *Sondheim on Music*, 10.

71. Ibid., 17. "Motive" here is not a musical term but rather a dramatic one, i.e., the thing that drives change is the bass.

72. This is what Sondheim said: "So, if you want to stay in C major, and you want some variety, why not go to a C I$^6$? Now the instability of first inversions is something that's very hard to deal with when you're so used to block harmony. I get scared sometimes when I use a I$^6$ that it's all going to fall apart. Because, you know, it's so easy and satisfying to pound away at the I–V–I–V–I–V, as most songs do. But when you get to the I$^6$ chord, it becomes a little more interesting. Because the I$^6$ chord tends not to want to go back to the V, but to lead to a IV or even, sometimes, to a VI chord." Ibid., 17.

73. Ibid., 29–30.

74. Ibid., 19–20: "To write a thirty-two-bar song that has freshness and style to it and tells the story is really hard," he claimed. Decades later, when Sondheim said this, he believed that "sung-through" composition had become the norm on Broadway. "Everybody writes so-called 'sung-through' pieces, and it's because anybody can write sung-through pieces. It's all recitative, and they don't develop anything, and it just repeats and repeats and repeats."

75. Ibid., 191.

76. The fast cut-time meter in this song produces sixty-four bars instead of the customary thirty-two. Each section, however, conforms to exactly double the familiar proportions. In William Caplin's terminology, the number of "real" measures is half the number of notated measures. See Caplin, *Classical Form: A Theory of Formal Functions for the Instrumental Music of Haydn, Mozart, and Beethoven* (Oxford: Oxford University Press, 1998), 35. The most detailed explanation of "default" procedures in the AB||AC format remains Graham Wood, "The Development of Song Forms in the Broadway and Hollywood Musicals of Richard Rodgers, 1919–1943," PhD diss., University of Minnesota, 2000, 109–121.

77. In Broadway music, the functional distinction between a dominant arrival and a half cadence tends to be less pronounced than it is in other kinds of music. Put differently, there is often a functional equivalent of a "medial caesura" at the moment of dominant arrival, effectively producing a half cadence embellished by a seventh scale degree or other triadic extensions.

78. For a summary of Sondheim's statements about Ravel, see Swayne, *How Sondheim Found His Sound*, 10–20. Especially suggestive in Swayne's account is his discussion of vamps on p. 18.

79. Immediately following the song, in fact, is a brass fanfare announcing Hapgood's arrival.

80. Hepokoski's term appears in Wood, "Development of Song Forms," 65.

81. This term is taken from Janet Schmalfeldt, "Cadential Processes: The Evaded Cadence and the 'One More Time' Technique," *Journal of Musicological Research* 12, nos. 1–2 (1992): 1–52.

82. The "macrochorus" precedent that Wood cites is Richard Rodgers's and Lorenz Hart's "Jonny One Note." Yet the "second" AABA chorus in "Me and My Town" contains some additional unusual local features that require explanation. First, and most obviously, the final A of this chorus differs from the first two As, thereby following an AABC model along the lines of what Sondheim did in the song "Free" from *A Funny Thing Happened on the Way to the Forum*. Second, the second A phrase transposes up a whole step, following the precedent set by Bernstein's "Tonight" (which transposes up a minor third) and "Gee, Officer Krupke!" from *West Side Story* (in which every verse moves up by a whole step), and, once again, the song "Free" (in which the second A section of the chorus moves up by a major third).

83. Laurents and Sondheim, *Anyone Can Whistle*, 24.

84. Craig Zadan, *Sondheim and Co.* (New York: Harper and Row, 1986), 90.

85. Laurents, "'Look, Girls.'"

86. RRF-AL, Box 1, Folder 5, notebook, [3].

87. Arthur Laurents to Kermit [Bloomgarden], dated "Sunday" [probably 28 July 1963], WHS-KB, Box 2, Folder 2, 3; WHS-SS, Box 2, Folder 1, "The Nut Show," 5. In fact, Sondheim wrote a number for her act called "The Night Is the Best Time of the Day." See Stephen Sondheim, *The Almost Unknown Stephen Sondheim: 39 Previously Unpublished Songs from 17 Shows and Films* (New York: Rilting Music, 2016), viii.

88. Knapp, "Sondheim's America; America's Sondheim," 437–439.

89. Mark Eden Horowitz, "'Really Weird': The Story of *Anyone Can Whistle* with Lots of Details," *Sondheim Review* 17, no. 2 (Winter 2010): 9.

90. The telegram, dated July 31, 1963, where Laurents responded to Robert Horton is in RRF-AL, Box 1, Folder 10. See also Lara Housez, "Becoming Stephen Sondheim: *Anyone Can Whistle, A Pray by Blecht, Company*, and *Sunday in the Park with George*." PhD diss., Eastman School of Music, University of Rochester, 2013.

91. Harry Partch's *Water! Water!* (produced in 1962 at the University of Illinois, Urbana-Champaign) also bears striking similarities to *Anyone Can Whistle*: the zany plot about a mayor who tries to end a drought by using jazzmen to summon rain, the broad critique of modern society, the pastiche (in this case, alluding often to West Coast jazz of the 1950s), and so on. Indeed, scholars have described this piece as being "as close as [Partch] ever came to writing a Broadway musical." Partch did try in 1962 to mount this show Off Broadway, but to no avail, and shortly thereafter he all but disavowed the work. See Andrew Granade, "Decoding Harry Partch's Aesthetic: Satire, Duality, and *Water! Water!*," *American Music* 35, no. 2 (Summer 2017): 173, 187. Laurents never mentioned it in any of his correspondence, but further research may indicate some link between the works. The author thanks W. Anthony Sheppard for bringing this connection to his attention.

92. Sondheim, *Finishing the Hat*, 139.

93. Horowitz, *Sondheim on Music*, 191.

94. Laurents and Sondheim, *Anyone Can Whistle*, 230–231.

95. Frank Rich, "Conversations with Sondheim: On His 70th Birthday, the Broadway Musical's Last Great Artist Takes Measure of the Theater and of Himself," *New York Times Magazine*, March 12, 2000, 38–43, 60–61, 88–89.

96. Stephen Sondheim, *Look I Made a Hat: Collected Lyrics (1981–2011) with Attendant Comments, Amplifications, Harangues, Digressions, Anecdotes and Miscellany* (New York: Knopf, 2011), 244.

97. Laurents and Sondheim, *Anyone Can Whistle*, 128 (emphasis in original).

# PART II
# STAGING IDENTITIES

# 5

# Sondheim's Whiteness

*Todd Decker*

Stephen Sondheim's *Sunday in the Park with George* (1984, book by James Lapine) begins with the polysemous word *white*. Intoned with world-making authority by the first of two title characters—in Act I, an imagined version of the French pointillist painter Georges Seurat—a definition of white operative for the show follows: "White. A blank page or canvas." After defining the "blank" and "white" space open to him as a creator, *Sunday*'s Seurat speaks aloud his aesthetic goal and principles: "The challenge: bring order to the whole. Through design. Composition. Balance. Light. And harmony."[1] The George of Act II—a fictional white male American artist struggling to find his way creatively—ends the show as it began on an empty white stage. He reads aloud *Sunday*'s final words: a note left behind by Seurat's (fictional) lover, Dot, who refines the show's definition of *white* a bit more and from a point of remove from the creative act and the creative agent: "White. A blank page or canvas. His favorite. So many possibilities."[2]

The notion of an empty, "blank," "white" space open to a radically individual and male subject is more philosophical ideal—or conceit—than historical reality. All around the edges of any blank page or canvas lie other artists' creations, not to mention the natural world and human society itself, which crowd in on any artist heeding *Sunday*'s call to "let it come from you / then it will be new." And the material reality of, not to mention access to, any such "blank page or canvas" (or, much more rarely, the commercial musical stage) carries its own history that limits the "many possibilities" available to any given artist. The notion named by the word *white*, celebrated in *Sunday* as the artist's starting point of radical freedom, elides any and all such baggage.[3]

The word *white* also carries racial meanings synonymous with power for many centuries—power of the political, military, social, and economic kind, but also power of the conceptual and philosophical kind that arguably undergirds all the others. *Sunday*'s blank white page and stage and the pair of Georges who strut and fret there find their larger grounding in the concrete facts of racial whiteness across global history. Sondheim's output for the Broadway stage, discussed here as a whole, claims genuine white imperial reach: His shows and songs, almost all sung by racially white characters, stretch in their settings from the Americas to Europe to Asia and from Ancient Greece and Rome to the postwar

Todd Decker, *Sondheim's Whiteness* In: *Sondheim in Our Time and His*. Edited by: W. Anthony Sheppard, Oxford University Press. © Oxford University Press 2022. DOI: 10.1093/oso/9780197603192.003.0006

Pax Americana. Sondheim's musicals—created for the Broadway stage from the late 1950s to the mid-1990s—are staged across a similarly wide geography into the present. As a body of work, they form a celebrated part of the often un(re)-marked cultural representation of whiteness of the past sixty years.

Whiteness as a powerful racial category defined by conceits of blankness or emptiness—registered perhaps only in (tacit) contrast against a nonwhite other—is, in fact, a varied and tangible thing, made specific in time and place across overlapping axes of identity. The Georges' shared intersectional identities underscore how the power of whiteness is reinforced and amplified by other categories: As white, (apparently) straight men doing high-status, self-expressive creative work, this pair of artists, played by one virtuoso actor, is legible as the implicitly raced and gendered type known as the "genius," a class of strong individuals with tremendous agency over the social imaginary and a category of persons into which Sondheim himself might be put.[4]

This chapter brings a measure of visibility and audibility to whiteness of the racial kind as represented across the breadth of Sondheim's Broadway musicals. While Sondheim himself resists broad considerations—"overviews [of my work] are anathema to me," he has said—I adopt the strategy here and employ whiteness as a category of analysis applicable at all levels to this group of highly praised and much-studied musicals.[5] My goal is to open a conversation about whiteness on the American commercial musical stage more generally.

## Naming the White-Cast Musical

My approach builds on Richard Dyer's foundational study *White*. Following Dyer, I am interested in "how white people are represented, how we represent ourselves"—a sentence I quote as my own since I am, like Dyer and like Sondheim, white.[6] Dyer continues, "As long as race is something only applied to non-white peoples, as long as white people are not racially seen and named, they/we function as a human norm. Other people are raced, we are just people."[7] He goes on: "Moreover . . . , to focus exclusively on those texts that are 'about' racial difference and interaction risks giving the impression that whiteness is only white, or only matters, when it is explicitly set against non-white, whereas whiteness reproduces itself as whiteness in all texts all of the time."[8]

The first step is to conceptualize and to name white-cast Broadway musicals as such according to the homogeneous racial makeup of their performers and characters—in exactly the way we have understood black-cast shows for the past century. Scholarship concerning the musical remains a tacitly segregated endeavor: The black-cast musical, a vibrant, century-long tradition, has largely been neglected (the last book-length survey, Allen Woll's *Black Musical Theater:*

*From "Coontown" to "Dreamgirls,"* was published in 1989),[9] and the white-cast musical has, with very few exceptions, not been considered as a site of racial representation or construction.[10] The relative handful of musicals with interracial casts, such as *Show Boat* (1927), have been the typical site of scholarly engagement with "racial difference and interaction" as represented and performed on the American musical stage.[11] In short, scholarship has replicated the tacit segregation of the musical into a named racial other (blackness) and an unmarked, unnamed racial norm (whiteness). Harry Newman, cofounder of the Non-Traditional Casting Project, wrote in 1989, "If someone said, 'I saw a terrific white play last night,' it would sound ludicrous. Why is it acceptable the other way around?"[12] White scholars have labored far too long to reify the all-white cast as a racially unmarked, Platonic ideal. The long overdue moment has arrived for scholars of the musical, especially white scholars like me, to find it acceptable, indeed essential, to name white-cast shows by the racial makeup of their casts and the racial world and identities they represent, perform, and re-perform. Black music research begins with the acknowledgment of blackness. The musicologist Loren Kajikawa has recently noted that white classical music research is still typically figured as simply and unproblematically *music* research; the same is true for musical theater scholarship.[13]

The needed and necessary naming of white as a racial category with a constitutive relation to an artistic repertory—the white-cast musical—acknowledges the power of the black-white binary in Broadway history and the foundational social, economic, and political structures of the United States. Black-cast and white-cast musicals alike find their origins and history in the pervasive practices of racial segregation, an enduring phenomenon from the birth of Broadway to the present, whether de facto or de jure, that continues to create black and white schools, churches, neighborhoods, and life chances in the United States. Appropriate nomination of white-cast musicals according to their race of performers and characters begins the process of seeing, hearing, and recognizing whiteness in Sondheim and across the Broadway musical, the United States' unique and (unsurprisingly) sharply racially segregated contribution to global theater culture.

Thinking in racial terms, there are, of course, several sorts of shows besides the foundational white-cast and black-cast categories, although this binary serves a primary structuring purpose across American theater history. A handful of musicals have nonwhite casts that are not black, among them Sondheim's *Pacific Overtures* (1976, book by John Weidman), one of only three musicals in Broadway history to 2020 to feature an all-Asian cast.[14] The bulk of *Pacific Overtures* concerns the nineteenth-century encounter between Japan and a group of white imperialist aggressors (the United States, Britain, France, Russia, the Dutch) who forced open the Japanese economy. In several scenes,

*Pacific Overtures* requires performers of Asian descent to play white characters who act out European and American imperial aggression using exaggerated versions of white national musical styles ("Please Hello") and pidgin or awkward English. Other scenes present Japanese characters adopting white Western ways ("A Bowler Hat" explores issues of class familiar in any bourgeois context). The finale, "Next," confronts the Broadway audience (invariably strongly majority white) with Japan as a defining force within contemporary Western culture. *Pacific Overtures*—a very rare instance of white theater makers reaching, successfully or not, across the white-Asian color line—has, to put it mildly, not been the norm in the commercial space of the Broadway musical.[15] Critical consideration of such shows as *Pacific Overtures*, always the exception, cannot bear the weight of a scholarly project that takes racial representation in the musical seriously. Whiteness is at the core of the Broadway musical, and whiteness outside any contrast with a nonwhite other—in short, in white-cast musicals—must be the site of any such work.

Another type of musical that troubles the binary of the black-cast and white-cast musical juxtaposes racially or ethnically distinct performers playing similarly distinct characters. *Show Boat* is the already noted exemplar; others include Tony Award winners for Best Musical *Big River* (1985), *Hairspray* (2003), and *The Book of Mormon* (2011).[16] Sondheim's first Broadway show, *West Side Story* (1957, book by Arthur Laurents, music by Leonard Bernstein), can also be understood within the frame of interracial confrontation and would seem to force questions of racial representation (although not necessarily for Sondheim himself, as shown below). The nonwhite other in *West Side Story* is a specific ethnic group defined by a particular moment in U.S. immigration: Puerto Rican immigrants to New York in the 1950s. The resource of "Latin" music—a generalized category of exotic otherness audible against the norms of U.S. music (in Bernstein's hands a mix of black [jazz] and white [classical])—sets the show's Puerto Rican gang, the Sharks, in specifically musical contrast against the Jets, a gang made of "an anthology of what is called American" and cast with only white-presenting actors in the original production and 1961 film.[17] Over time, *West Side Story* has moved toward uniform authenticity in casting (only Latinx performers playing the Sharks, whereas the original cast had just a small group) and in language (Spanish translations of dialogue and lyrics by Lin-Manuel Miranda were used for the Sharks in the 2009 revival directed by Laurents).

Reflecting on *West Side Story* in *Finishing the Hat* (2010, volume 1 of his collected lyrics), Sondheim critiqued his lyrics as overwrought and overly poetic (qualities, he says, Bernstein encouraged): "It almost worked, but when I hear it today I wish it were in a foreign language in an opera."[18] The use of Spanish lyrics in 2009 likely relieved Sondheim of the persistent embarrassment he has expressed over "I Feel Pretty." The lyric's delight-filled "inner rhymes and trick rhymes" strike Sondheim as too clever, too composed, "drawing attention to the lyric writer rather than the character," a young woman recently arrived from San Juan. This feeling goes back to 1957, when Sondheim tried, unsuccessfully, to get his collaborators to accept a revision using simpler language. They insisted, however, on his initial effort and, Sondheim noted in 2010, "I have blushed ever since."[19]

Thinking back to the invitation to work on *West Side Story*, one argument Sondheim mustered against saying yes relates to personal experience as the ground from which creative work springs: "I've never been that poor and I've never even *known* a Puerto Rican."[20] (Sondheim's mentor Oscar Hammerstein II, with much experience writing nonwhite characters, urged him to join the project anyway.) Sondheim has described his artistic practice as grounded on acting: "I've discovered over a period of years that essentially I'm a playwright who writes with song, and that playwrights are actors. And what I do is I act."[21] In another context he noted, "When I write a song, I try to become the character— or more accurately, I try to be the actor who has to play the character."[22] These repeated formulations suggest that a strong identification between Sondheim and his characters fuels his work, a sense that on some conceptual level he can see himself being cast as the characters he writes. Beyond the fact that Sondheim was still a very young lyricist, his concern about acting as a "poor . . . Puerto Rican" can be read as a kind of expressive probity about crossing the color line, a sense that to be authentic to himself and his creative voice, he should avoid writing (and acting) as certain types of characters. Indeed, *West Side Story* is an atypical Sondheim show: Almost all of his long creative life has entailed writing whiteness, usually of an upper-middle-class, slightly cerebral sort. My consideration of Sondheim's whiteness intends no critique of his general career-long focus on white characters and contexts—a focus that can be seen as a perhaps praiseworthy reluctance on his part to ventriloquize nonwhite characters. My goal, instead, is to directly address Sondheim's work as the representation of whiteness it manifestly is and to begin the process of understanding what this whiteness concretely is in his musicals.

Sondheim opens the chapter on *West Side Story* in *Finishing the Hat* with a startling claim: "For most people *West Side Story* is about racial prejudice and urban violence, but what it's really about is theater: musical theater, to be more precise. It's about the blending of book, music, lyrics and, most important, dance into the seamless telling of a story."[23] A symptomatic reading of this preemptive correction might diagnose a classic slip: anxiety about *West Side Story* as a musical centered on racial prejudice and racialized urban violence—the police in the show notably seek alliances with the white Jets, not the nonwhite Sharks— generates an explicit disavowal of the show's manifest content in favor of an aesthetic, thoroughly modernist appeal to purely formal matters (the integration of theatrical elements, bringing "order to the whole . . . through design"). I do not necessarily disagree with such an interpretation, and I wonder why a show as important as *West Side Story* cannot be about both content and form (as it was for Laurents in his late-life thoughts about the show).[24] I am not, however, interested in how Sondheim thinks about issues of racial prejudice and urban violence. I am, instead, interested in the content of racial whiteness as represented on the musical stage in (primarily) the musical and lyrical texts of Sondheim's shows, although some attention is paid to performance choices as captured in recordings and videos. To better understand Sondheim's texts, in particular, how he conceptualizes issues of racial identity and representation in his own work, I draw throughout on late-career reflections by Sondheim as found in his collected lyrics (published in 2010 and 2011) and in Mark Eden Horowitz's invaluable series of interviews with Sondheim, conducted between 1997 and 2009 and published in the book *Sondheim on Music*.

## Sondheim's (and Others') Whiteness (and Jewishness)

Beyond the aforementioned two shows that include nonwhite characters played (eventually in the case of *West Side Story*) by nonwhite performers, Sondheim's output is entirely white-cast musicals—with the single-scene exception of a minor character in *Anyone Can Whistle* (1964, book by Arthur Laurents).[25] In this, Sondheim's whiteness is far from an outlier: Many of his white contemporaries of similar stature generally chose not to represent nonwhite racial others in their work. Brief mention of a few prominent figures in adjacent creative realms offers parallel examples of how specific intersectional and generational nuances shape powerful creative whitenesses in U.S. arts and letters. For example, the whiteness of filmmaker Martin Scorsese (born twelve years after Sondheim, active 1967 to the present) frequently dwells in the off-white edge zones of Italian American and Irish American history. Scorsese often represents New York as an all-white city, and he has almost never included a black character with even minimal speaking lines in his films.[26] His capacious filmography encompassing hypermasculine films such as *Taxi Driver* (1976) and meditations on spirituality like *Silence* (2016), remains tightly focused on white subjects and subjectivities.

In the literary domain, the novelist and critic Jess Row, in his 2019 book *White Flights: Race, Fiction, and the American Imagination*, has measured the extent to which white American literary fiction writers of the past fifty years have created representations of the United States that ignore racial difference or the existence of nonwhite others. He notes, for example, that the novelist Anne Tyler's Baltimore is an entirely white city (Sondheim's *Company* [1970, book by George Furth] offers a parallel version of New York). Row models how to read race back into such carefully constructed whitenesses and maps more broadly the extent to which the constructed "emptiness" within which white characters in such fictions move and find their being relies on strategic acts of forgetting and forgotten acts of exclusionary violence towards racial others.[27] This is all, Row insists, white people's "sheer wishful thinking . . . wishful thinking as a way of life, a way of seeing, and a way of making art."[28] The philosopher Shannon Sullivan similarly characterizes such "white solipsism" as "living as if only white people existed or mattered."[29]

Row's analysis can be expanded to include two of Sondheim's direct contemporaries. The output of the prolific novelist John Updike (born two years after Sondheim, active 1958 to 2009) centers almost without exception on white, middle-class suburbanites and their marriages.[30] Updike and Sondheim are alike praised for being master stylists, with virtuoso and distinctive styles whether in prose or lyrics. The playwright Edward Albee (born two years before Sondheim, active 1958 to 2007) is another relationship-obsessed writer known for a singular verbal style and for bringing an experimental edge into commercial theater where, as with Sondheim, commercial failure has not precluded enduring artistic stature. Sondheim (born 1930, active 1957 to [at this writing] 2008)[31], Updike, and Albee offer a triptych of powerful creators who, while each offering a distinct variety of whiteness, have not been framed as white creative figures and instead emerged as norms of creative achievement. From the other side of the color line, James Baldwin, Toni Morrison, Spike Lee, and August Wilson (among others) have not escaped being conscripted into the representation of blackness.

Along the intersectional axis of religious identity, Updike's frequent exploration of Christian faith and Albee's professed fascination with Christ figures locate their whitenesses in a decidedly WASPish register: Both men come from Christian backgrounds. Their origins and elite educations in the northeastern United States —which Sondheim shares—add a further regional whiteness that, given New York's cultural power in literary publishing and theater, masquerades as a historic white norm. Sondheim's utterly nominal Jewishness is not a constituent element in his work—a surprising statement, perhaps, given the strong identification between Jewishness and Broadway. (In a spontaneous comment to Horowitz, Sondheim noted, "I'm German by ancestry, and I have a Germanic neatness sense, and I make lists.")[32] Indeed, direct evidence for Sondheim's Jewish background proves exceedingly thin on the ground: in his interviews, in the occasional "Oy"; in his lyrics, as rare as the declension "Bobby bubi"—the *only* such Yiddishism in any of his lyrics—that bounces around in *Company*'s obsessive repetition of the central character's name.[33] The poetic resource of this alliterative phrase, often paired with "Bobby baby," seems more important than the use of it to lend a Jewish identity to any single character.[34] In conversation with Horowitz about *Into the Woods* (1987, book by James Lapine), Sondheim responded to Horowitz's saying the phrase "I wish" (in Horowitz's description, "with an inflection and a shrug") by imagining a "Jewish version" of Cinderella's "I wish": Instead of the score's rising whole step, Sondheim heard "a minor second . . . or it could actually go down."[35] This exchange shows Sondheim managing his musical materials to ensure an audibly white (and not Jewish) sonic identity for his Cinderella (a figure from Christian European folklore, first published in the seventeenth century and tightly folded into the aristocratic imaginations of Italian, French, and German national traditions). The minor second—for Sondheim, in this context—would indicate Jewishness; racial and ethnic representation often inheres in such small choices.[36]

However, to follow the performance studies scholar Henry Bial, we might ask of any character in a Sondheim show, "Could this character be Jewish?"[37] In the overview of Sondheim's work that follows, I return to this question, which Bial formulates as the prerogative of audiences with the requisite knowledge of Jewish codes to engage in a "Jewish reading" of a creative text. Bial notes, "It is not necessary to be or identify as Jewish in order to be a Jewish reader; it is simply necessary to be literate in the requisite codes."[38] Such codes are subtle and, in addition to textual cues, also reliant on the choices made by individual performers and productions. Imagine, for instance, if the frequently sarcastic and brash Mary in *Merrily We Roll Along* (1981, book by George Furth) spoke with a thick New York (Jewish) accent—an unlikely choice given that her last name in the script is Flynn. Indeed, *none* of the character surnames in Sondheim shows set in the United States directly indicate Jewishness, although some might hint at typical Jewish American name changes (Mr. Goldstone perhaps conceals a Mr. Goldstein in *Gypsy* [1959, book by Arthur Laurents, music by Jule Styne]). This chapter stays close to Sondheim's texts, with only select comparisons of different interpretations of Sondheim's work. Meanings made in performance are, of course, essential to the critical appraisal of theater and the bringing to light of whiteness as a constitutive, always intersectional category. But in this look at the entirety of Sondheim's Broadway work, I remain mostly focused on the texts. Furthermore, my own Protestant background makes me a less than ideal analyst of latent Jewish content. Still, asking, if not conclusively answering, Bial's question is crucial: In my provisional reading, Sondheim's whiteness proves to be predominantly and often explicitly *not* Jewish, ruling out the possibility of a Jewish reading much of the time.[39] Whiteness, like any racial identity category, cannot be understood in isolation or as monolithic. The apparent lack of Jewishness in Sondheim's musicals proves an important part of his representation of a whiteness always embedded in an intersectional as well as historical context.

The substantive content of Sondheim's whiteness can be located in (at least) four sorts of evidence: (1) the settings of his shows; (2) indications of white bodies in his lyrics; (3) the racial histories of his musical style choices; and (4) a disposition of mind in Sondheim's white characters toward epistemological reflection through an Enlightenment individualist lens understood historically and stereotypically to be the property of white subjects. Before examining these aspects of whiteness as represented in Sondheim's work, one caveat remains.

Sondheim works in collaboration, and his shows only come to life in performance. In *Finishing the Hat*, Sondheim elegantly positions himself, as a songwriter, between the book writer, "the collaborator who makes something out of nothing," and the director, whose task is to "enhance the playwright's work, to explore the characters and intensify the situations." The songwriter, he writes, sits "halfway between creator and interpreter."[40] Sondheim continues, "I don't create those characters, the book writer does. What I do is inhabit them as best I can."[41] Thus, Sondheim's whiteness is a composite of his and others'. In a longer study, it would be important to explore the specific whitenesses of Sondheim's collaborators, particularly his book writers, as Sondheim does in an aside about James Lapine that mentions archetypal figures in the literary history of whiteness: "All of Lapine's writing has a touch of the formal (the ghosts of writers like Henry James and Edith Wharton visit him quite often)."[42] Indeed, in interviews Sondheim has parsed the differences between his book writers and has noted of the opening words of *Sunday* (and of this chapter), "That's all James."[43] Still, Sondheim's voice is unmistakable in his shows' music and lyrics and is the primary reason his musicals (even the flops) survive in performance into the present.

## Whiteness in Milieu

Race as represented on the musical stage begins with the foundational choice of setting. The time and place of a show, typically tersely announced in the opening pages of a libretto and in playbills, sets the possibilities for racial content—even if known racially diverse settings, such as New York City, might end up represented as entirely white (the original 1964 *Hello, Dolly!*) or entirely black (the 1967 *Hello, Dolly!* starring Pearl Bailey). Settings are selective, limited, historical, and almost invariably raced and classed. *In the Heights* (2008), set in the Latinx neighborhood of Washington Heights, relies on Manhattan's racially segregated neighborhoods every bit as much as *Company*, set in "New York City NOW" but more precisely located in "various high-rise Manhattan apartments," and so, likely, around midtown and Central Park.[44] Whiteness in setting, or milieu, provides the foundation for the whiteness evident across Sondheim's Broadway output (excluding from here forward *West Side Story* and *Pacific Overtures*). Of these fourteen shows (three with lyrics but not music by Sondheim), six are set in Europe, six in the United States, and two in the ancient Western world. Each of these larger categories opens different possibilities for the representation of whiteness.

The six Sondheim shows in a European milieu present exquisitely calibrated British and Continental whitenesses, each more or less familiar to American audiences of a certain educated class. *A Little Night Music* (1973, book by Hugh Wheeler), an adaptation of a film by the iconic Swedish director Ingmar Bergman, is set in "Turn of the [Twentieth] Century Sweden."[45] *Sweeney Todd: The Demon Barber of Fleet Street* (1979, book by Hugh Wheeler) takes place in London, in the neighborhood around Fleet Street, in "The 19th Century," a rather vague indicator as to time when compared with *Passion* (1994, book by James Lapine), set "in Milan and a remote military outpost in 1863."[46] Riffing freely on a well-known monumental masterpiece on permanent view at the Art Institute of Chicago (Seurat's *Un dimanche après-midi à l'Île de la Grande Jatte*), *Sunday*, Act 1, is precisely located in a park and in Seurat's Paris studio from 1884 to 1886. (*Sunday*, Act II, set in the 1984 present of the original production, returns to the park in Paris after beginning in a generic "American art museum.")[47] *Into the Woods*, set in a mythic and vaguely Germanic forest, draws on multiple fairy tales collected by Jacob and Wilhelm Grimm (published in multiple editions between 1812 and 1857).[48] Counting *Into the Woods* and, for the moment, *Pacific Overtures*, six of the thirteen shows for which Sondheim wrote both lyrics and music are set outside the United States in the nineteenth century—before the profound twentieth-century shifts initiated by the world wars, the development of mass media, and the global juggernaut of syncopated (black) American popular music. (In the Horowitz interviews, Sondheim refers to his musical persona by saying, "I'm about 1890.")[49] Of all these shows, only *Pacific Overtures*, with its leap to its 1976 present for the closing number "Next"—in Sondheim's words "vaguely rock music"—makes any nod toward an American popular sound.

*Do I Hear a Waltz?* (1965, book by Arthur Laurents, music by Richard Rodgers), the sole show in a European milieu to be set in the present at its premiere, uses the tourist destination of Venice to draw persistent distinctions between national whitenesses. The plot turns on American tourists interacting romantically with Italians. Sondheim's lyrics for the number "This Week, Americans" leverage the setting to broaden the range of national types: To supposedly comic effect, an Italian *pensione* owner delivers a veritable travelogue of white stereotypes, praising "generous Americans" over Germans (who "sweat a lot"), the English ("all those teeth"), Parisians ("over-groomed"), and a string of white others. In this case, various national whitenesses are described rather than performed (as in *Pacific Overtures*' "Please Hello," which unfolds with an American brass band march, a British Gilbert and Sullivan patter song, a Dutch clog dance, and so on). Contrasts, stated or implied, between different varieties of whiteness prove an important element of several of Sondheim's European shows. For example, Fosca's family in *Passion* is inordinately impressed with her scoundrel husband's Austrian background. Sondheim reinforces their attraction by having them repeat "Count Ludovic of Austria" again and again. (Austria ruled northern Italy at the time this scene is set; enthusiasm for the count betrays the longing of Fosca's family for an alliance with the occupier.) The shaving standoff between Sweeney Todd and the Italian barber Pirelli is fueled by the latter's thick accent—later revealed to be fake—and affected manner. Todd silences Pirelli twice over: He outshaves him, then slashes his throat. Long-standing stereotypes as to relative national manhood are rehearsed here as Pirelli's effete Italian tenor pomposity falls to Todd's mocking British baritone menace. The differing varieties of whiteness in several of these European shows reveal Sondheim using white national stereotypes to effect quick and broad characterization, sometimes in the service of generating laughs.

Two Sondheim shows purport to represent the classical era: Roman in *A Funny Thing Happened on the Way to the Forum* (1962, book by Burt Shevelove and Larry Gelbart) and Greek in *The Frogs* (a 1974 show produced at Yale University [book by Burt Shevelove] and mounted on Broadway in 2004 [book revised by Nathan Lane]). But *Forum* and *Frogs* alike are, of course, Broadway versions of these reciprocal, reputed sources of modern whiteness. Indeed, the combination of classical trappings and Broadway tropes allows for a peculiar sort of American whiteness, especially in *Forum*'s "Free" (a solo for the slave Pseudolus with no precedent in Plautus, the Roman comic playwright and the show's source of inspiration). The setting allows Sondheim to discourse on "the necessary nature of democracy" and the repugnance and attractions of slavery without engaging with the facts of African chattel slavery in the modern West—even though this long history, and its segregated aftermath in American entertainment, shaped the vaudeville and burlesque sources underpinning *Forum*'s entire comic world. In "Free," the historical hypocrisies of American democracy are elided even as the heritage and individual glories of the U.S. political system are heralded—by a slave. "Free" escapes any resonance with Broadway's segregated American context while also celebrating abstract notions of "freedom" that ignore the actual history of the concept. Such are the ideological effects available when setting a white-cast show in the distant past.

Whoopi Goldberg's replacement star turn as Pseudolus in the 1997 Broadway revival of *Forum* potentially problematized "Free"—although Goldberg's performance, as captured on video, makes no indication that she explored her own blackness in relation to Pseudolus's slave status in this key number.[50] Goldberg's Pseudolus can be read as a typical instance of colorblind casting that, while including nonwhite performers in a previously white-cast context, requires reception that ignores race and supports the notion that whiteness is somehow not, itself, a racial marking (in this case a marking directly tied to the concept and lived fact of human freedom).[51]

The six Sondheim musicals set in the United States, and thus directly implicated in the nation's history of racial inequality, fall into two groups: historical and contemporary. The four historical shows are all deeply embedded in the history of popular entertainment. Three of the four are book shows that restage American popular culture history in the milieu of live entertainment across several early to mid-twentieth-century decades. *Gypsy* explores small- and medium-time vaudeville and burlesque milieus across the country "from the early twenties to the early thirties."[52] *Follies* (1971, book by James Goldman), while set in the year the show premiered, offers multiple conceits of time travel to Broadway's past by way of featured numbers from stars of yesteryear (1918 to 1941) as well as flashbacks to the younger selves (1920s) of the story's central couples and high-concept musical numbers for each of the four leads that evoke (and somewhat deconstruct) earlier showbiz styles. *Merrily We Roll Along* centers on songwriting and showmaking while working backward over a quarter century from its 1981 premiere present to around 1957. *Gypsy*, *Follies*, and *Merrily* alike figure the world of American popular entertainment as entirely white, though all these forms of mass musical entertainment included black performers and creators.

The remaining historical show—*Assassins* (Off-Broadway 1990, Broadway 2004, book by John Weidman)—puts a disparate collection of actual presidential assassins into the conceptual zone of the revue. Given the range of assassins included, from John Wilkes Booth (who killed Abraham Lincoln in 1865) to John Hinckley (who shot Ronald Reagan in 1981), this decidedly theatrical space allows Sondheim to dip into a broad range of popular music styles, from close harmony (pseudo-barbershop) to 1970s singer-songwriter ballads. Among the assassins is Giuseppe Zingara (who attempted to shoot Franklin D. Roosevelt in 1933). With a Pirelli-like Italian accent, Zingara offers a leftist critique of capitalism while insisting to no avail, "No left. No right. No anything. Only American." In "The Ballad of Booth," Booth's thick southern accent (a performance choice) and his use of the N-word to slur Lincoln (an element in the text) combine to represent a specific regional whiteness delivered in a high rhetorical style recalling nineteenth-century declamatory acting. The show's presiding voice, the Balladeer, frames Booth's big moment with a fast-paced, highly contrasting narrative ballad that shrugs this assassin off as an aberration—"what he was was off his head," we are assured. But there's no denying the powerful space that *Assassins* gives to a repugnant American whiteness in Booth's melodramatic and, in context, deeply serious turn in the spotlight. Booth's still-pertinent historical stature as the first successful presidential assassin and as the murderer of Lincoln, the white president who issued the Emancipation Proclamation, only adds to the character's theatrical resonance. Performance and direction choices fundamentally shape how Booth's whiteness is performed; still, *Assassins* grants southern "Lost Cause" ideology, an enduring and malignant U.S. whiteness, a Broadway hearing.[53]

Two remaining Sondheim shows set in the United States (as well as part of *Sunday*, Act II) represent the contemporary moment of their premiere date. *Company* features white, upper-middle-class New Yorkers circa 1970 seen, mostly, in their apartments. Other Broadway slices of New York life from the turn of the 1970s such as *Hair* (1968) and *Ain't Supposed to Die a Natural Death* (1971) staged a very different street-level city—the former, somewhat interracial (downtown); the latter, entirely black (uptown).[54] *Company*, like countless white-cast shows across Broadway history, imagines and makes theatrically actual a racially homogeneous, all-white United States. This consistent aspect of white-cast musicals—a lingering product of the practices and fantasies of Jim Crow—must be acknowledged and named. As Angela C. Pao has noted (while borrowing Ruth Frankenberg's influential theorization of whiteness), "The centuries-old tradition of all-white casting [is] one of the most effective of [the] processes" that render "whiteness as 'un-marked marker,' as empty signifier . . . whiteness as norm, as transparency, as national/natural state of being."[55]

The 1964 of *Anyone Can Whistle*, a "Musical Fable" set in "a not too distant town," features the only named black character in a Sondheim show: Martin, described as "A Negro" in the original edition of the libretto and called "An African American" in *Finishing the Hat*.[56] Appearing only in the extended scene "Simple," Martin interacts cryptically (and briefly) with Hapgood, a white male doctor granted absolute freedom to sort the townsfolk into the sane and the crazy and allowed to play with epistemological and ontological categories, leading to an utter breakdown in meaning and social chaos onstage and, by implication, in the theater. Hapgood—the show's handsome, romantic hero, originally announced with trumpets just before his entrance in the song "There Won't Be Trumpets" (a typical Sondheim subtlety)[57]—is a charismatic and opaque exemplar of white, masculine (purported) expertise (or genius) being given command of society: His private admission of doubt in the song "With So Little to Be Sure Of" only adds to Hapgood's stature as a self-reflexive thinker (more on this strain of Sondheim's whiteness later). Martin steps into Hapgood's view singing and repeating the cliché "You can't judge a book by its cover." When Hapgood questions Martin as to his occupation (a spoken exchange by book writer Laurents), Martin replies, "Going to schools, riding in buses, and eating in restaurants," a pointed reference to direct, frequently dangerous nonviolent civil rights protests of the time. Hapgood replies, "Isn't that line of work getting rather easy?" Martin retorts, "Not for me. I'm Jewish." The brief sung exchange between Hapgood and Martin that follows (penned by Sondheim) plays further with racial stereotypes and signals: Hapgood arrives syllogistically at the conclusion "anything that's dark is dumb;" Martin repeats the phrase with him, adding "but they [those who are 'dark'] sure can hum"; Hapgood dismisses Martin with the phrase "simple as NAACP," at which point Martin's role is over. The upshot of the exchange, as with just about anything in "Simple," is far from simple (although a direct critique of the nuclear arms race is evident later in the number when Comptroller Schub is interrogated). Hapgood's full embrace of ambiguity and his total control of the conversation is part of his power. So, too, of course, for Sondheim. Still, Martin's deflection of his evident blackness onto a professed Jewishness is striking: This is one of only two times the word *Jew* or *Jewish* appears in a Sondheim show, and it's in relation to a character who does not immediately seem Jewish in context (although perhaps a now-obscure joke about the well-known black American Sammy Davis Jr., a convert to Judaism, is being made).[58] This short encounter between Hapgood and Martin is the only moment when the United States as a racially diverse, black and white nation—or a nation with a significant Jewish minority—is directly and explicitly represented in the music and lyrics of Sondheim.[59]

To continue with the question of a possible Jewish reading and Sondheim's milieus, historical and contemporary settings in Europe (as well as the Japan of *Pacific Overtures*) eliminate the likelihood (or possibility) that any of the characters could be Jewish. The broad burlesque of *Forum* and *The Frogs* opens the way to possible Jewish readings; Zero Mostel, a well-known Borscht Belt comedian, the original Pseudolus, and, in his next Broadway role as the milkman Tevye in *Fiddler on the Roof*, likely spiked *Forum* with a fair measure of recognizably Jewish stage manner (even if his performance on the cast album seems not to head in that direction). Sondheim's three showbiz shows (*Gypsy*, *Follies*, and *Merrily*) would all seem to keep open the option to read individual characters as potentially Jewish even when the texts of these shows never make such identities manifest. Bial productively frames Jews in the entertainment industry as a "dominant minority"—as a group that, on the whole, is historically cautious about directly acknowledging their overrepresented numbers to the mass audience they address, a "mainstream" audience understood as gentile, but only as such within a context of Jewish as Other.[60] Furthermore, as the American Studies scholar Stephen Whitfield notes, "No epicenter of American Jewish culture exists. . . . But if there were such a locale, it would be Broadway."[61] And while this holds for *Gypsy* (the real family profiled in the show was Jewish) it does not so easily apply to *Follies* and *Merrily*. In both, the last names of major characters seem to foreclose Jewish backgrounds: Sally Durant Plummer and Benjamin Stone (not Stein) in the former; Mary Flynn, Charley Kringas, and Franklin Shepard in the latter. Actor Lonny Price, the original Charley in *Merrily*, mutters a quiet "Oy" in response to his creative struggles before the vocals start in "Opening Doors" (a number, Sondheim noted, that "describes what the struggle was like for me and my generation of Broadway songwriters"). This "Oy"—a tiny marker of Jewishness, also heard a few times in Sondheim's interviews with Horowitz—is indicated in the script for *Merrily* as "CHARLEY: (Grunts in displeasure)."[62]

Sondheim's contemporary U.S. shows are more challenging to read as Jewish given their location outside the entertainment industry and their contrastingly vague and specific social and political contexts (*Company*'s detached couples and singles and *Anyone Can Whistle*'s town officials and doctors). The latter's plot dwells on the very Catholic notion of a miracle drawing pilgrims to a shrine—Sondheim's lyrics for "The Miracle Song" reference the miracles ("Water that you walk on / Water that you turn to wine"), stories ("No room / At the inn now!") and sayings ("Blessed be . . .") of Jesus. He clearly has knowledge of the Gospels. *Company* includes several Christian references: The soprano in "Getting Married Today" is listed as "Church Lady" and the wedding described in the lyric is recognizably Christian (it is to take place in a church with an "apse," and Amy suggests that her guests might instead "catch a christening"), though Amy says in dialogue that she's not having a Catholic wedding and notes that her fiancé Paul is Jewish. More significant, just before the big tempo change in "Side by Side by Side," Robert repeats the nursery rhyme "Here is the church, here is the steeple." The "crazy married people" who rush forward on his cue are, by implication, pouring out of a Christian house of worship.

Apart from Paul in *Company*, the only identifiably Jewish character in any Sondheim show is Emma Goldman, an important turn-of-the-century political activist, in *Assassins*. Goldman appears in one scene to inspire the man who killed William McKinley. She does not sing.

## Whiteness in Lyrics

Blackness as represented in U.S. popular culture appears concretely in the often racist descriptions and stereotypes attached to black bodies in song lyrics from minstrelsy onward. Whiteness and white bodies are similarly apparent in popular song lyrics, although in this case the stereotypes tend toward the idealized and the sentimental, and whiteness (as is often the case) can go unmentioned in specific terms. A frequently ironic lyricist such as Sondheim might critique or trouble white stereotypes, but invoking them—an often necessary first step—inevitably rehearses, re-performs, and recirculates them as well.

Some lyrical indications of whiteness are phenotypical. For instance, white skin, blonde hair, and blue eyes appear with regularity in *Sweeney Todd*. The first thing we learn about the endlessly described title character is that "his skin was pale." Todd, Anthony, and Judge Turpin—the three men who love or lust after Johanna—all continually describe, and perhaps fetishize, her by reference to her yellow hair and white skin. Todd's rehearsal with Anthony of all the words for blonde—"tawny, golden saffron, flaxen"—doubles as a catalog of white bodies. By contrast, Giorgio in *Passion* only exalts Clara's overdetermined whiteness in their opening coital duet, singing, "Your skin so white, so pure, so delicate." Clara's foil, Fosca, is never described as dark, although the point is made in her costuming, hair, and makeup.

White bodies also appear in lyrics that describe experiences associated with or historically limited to white individuals. For example, Turpin and Todd's "Pretty Women" praises a typical nineteenth-century Angel of the House, a white woman posing prettily in a domestic space while doing light and decorative tasks. George, the first to face Hapgood in "Simple," mentions almost every signifier of suburban whiteness except whiteness. The *Follies* feature numbers "I'm Still Here" and "Broadway Baby" both track historical pathways for white women in show business; Sondheim claimed he modeled the former on white movie star Joan Crawford.[63] The showbiz anthem from *Follies*, "Beautiful Girls," reactivates the white archetype of the stately strolling showgirl as the pinnacle of beauty, exemplifying "what beauty can be" and assuming audience assent that this white type is "the best you'll agree."[64]

Another type of Sondheim song precisely describes specific class-related varieties of whiteness. These sociological numbers revel in sharply observed details. "The Ladies Who Lunch" (from *Company*) parses white upper-middle-class women making (or not making) an effort to fill their days. "A Little Priest" (from *Sweeney Todd*) assesses mostly middling white men as potential white meat. "By the Sea" (*Sweeney*) and "The Miller's Son" (*A Little Night Music*) alike voice the aspirations of a lower-class white woman for domestic security and pleasure, if from either end of the life cycle. "Liaisons" (*Night Music*) laments a lapsed social practice among white Continental elites. Each of these numbers adds texture and specificity to the whiteness milieu of their respective shows and, in the process, also affords a rich representation of the nuances of whiteness, a social field defined as containing great variety and individuality within its types.

Sondheim has decried chorus numbers that assume a group of people are all thinking the same thought.[65] Two group numbers in *Merrily We Roll Along* use the dramaturgical technique of single-line solos to voice a buzzing whiteness that defines the show's white showbiz milieu: "Rich and Happy" (with the noxious line "so we found this little Chinese gardener") and "Now You Know" (mostly group therapy platitudes after a divorce). "The Blob" describes its fashionable collectivity as "The bodies you read about. The ones who know everyone that everyone knows"—to which the crowd responds "Albee! Warhol! Kurosawa!" The show's anthem, "Our Time," makes the same claim—"we're the names in tomorrow's paper"—expressed as a confident hope by the story's now-young white characters that the future, for them, will be "a blank page or canvas"—which it mostly is in professional terms, even if the show dwells on failures in friendship and marriage.

Many of these sociological numbers match what Sondheim identifies in *Look, I Made a Hat* as "my upper-middle-class DNA."[66] The category "white" might be added here for specificity, whereas Jewish (or not) remains a persistent open question.

## Whiteness in Musical Style

Whiteness also inheres in musical styles and tropes, especially in Sondheim's pastiche numbers, which tap identifiable earlier popular styles for dramatic purposes. Only one Sondheim pastiche, the entrance of the Witch in *Into the Woods*, claims a direct black popular music model. Sondheim notates the vocal line with x's instead of noteheads but indicates rhythmic values precisely. The section begins with the indication "*(conversational)*," but after three measures it shifts to "*('Rap' style)*"; cast recordings with the white star Bernadette Peters (original) and the black star Vanessa Williams (2002 revival) show no evident change in vocal style at the latter indication.[67] The introduction of a percussion line for the synthesizer in Jonathan Tunick's orchestration does, however, hint at "'Rap' style" for an effect perhaps not unlike a hip-hop beat. In other words, neither Peters nor Williams drops into a recognizable facsimile of rap timbre. And though Peters articulates clearly in the manner of the spoken patter in *The Music Man* (1957)—a source likely closer to Sondheim than was 1980s rap—Williams, surprisingly, affects an unmistakable nasal, almost Jewish but not black accent that forestalls any audible sense of her Witch as African American (especially at the lyric "your father cried, your mother died"). Subsequent sections that are spoken in rhythm (such as the Witch's instructions for reversing the curse) use other styles that are clearly not rap. Notably, the character is "ugly" at this point in the story: After her transformation near the end of Act I into a beauty she never "raps" or speaks in time again. The Witch's "rap," situated within a range of spoken vocal styles proves a vaguely defined, highly exceptional moment in Sondheim's output.

A few pastiche numbers evoke popular music blacknesses already once removed—such as Cora's "Me and My Town" (*Anyone Can Whistle*), which Sondheim identifies as "jazzy showbiz" *à la* Kay Thompson (a white nightclub singer with an eccentric scat-singing style seen in the film *Funny Face* [1957]). Sondheim describes Buddy's "The God-Why-Don't-You-Love-Me Blues" (*Follies*) as "vaudeville music for chases and low comics, but with a patter lyric." The word *blues* in the title originated, Sondheim continues, with the Gershwins' "The Half of It, Dearie, Blues" (itself a white version of the blues composed for Fred Astaire,

as "Father of the Blues" W. C. Handy noted when he included the tune as an example of white use of black music in his 1926 book *Blues: An Anthology*).[68]

Repeated use of the word *Lord* in Stella Deems's "Who's That Woman?"
(*Follies*) hints at 1920s song lyrics that, in their day, drew on black pop music
slang (although Sondheim has identified Cole Porter and Rodgers and Hart, who
are not known for use of black slang, as inspirations for the song).[69] The tune's
jaunty syncopation, including clear nods to the Charleston, adds further jazzy
energy evocative of the 1920s, as does the tap routine performed by the entire
female cast. The casting of black women as Stella in twenty-first-century revivals
suggests strategic efforts to moderate the whiteness of the cast of *Follies* and the
show's larger tribute to showbiz as an historically all-white realm. Revival cast
recordings of Terry White (2011, Broadway) and Dawn Hope (2017, London
National Theater) reveal both women adding a decided if subtle black style (such
as scooped pitches and rhythmic alteration) to their vocals that is not heard when
white women sing the part (Mary McCarty in the 1971 original; Phyllis Newman
in the 1985 Avery Fisher Hall concert version). The African American actress E.
Faye Butler played Stella in a 2016 production at the St. Louis Repertory Theater
that I attended. Butler used Stella's short cadenza at the close of "Who's That
Woman?"—five iterations of the word *Lord* in a descending pattern—to insert
unmistakable black gospel energy that, entirely predictably for the almost entirely white crowd, activated tremendous and demonstrative audience response.
The moment was a reminder of how lone black performers singing gospel vocals
in otherwise white-cast shows have, since the 1990s, been a consistent part of the
Broadway scene.[70] Sondheim's shows seem to be no different in this respect, if
only *Follies*—with its, for Sondheim, rare invocation of a whitened black style—
offers an opportunity for this sort of vocal excess, marked consistently as also
blackness.[71]

While Jerome Kern, the canonic Broadway composer with the most distant
connection to the black musical styles of his time, provides the most frequent
point of reference for Sondheim in the Horowitz interviews, Sondheim's several
and laudatory mentions of Harold Arlen, a composer with close links to black
music and musicians, indirectly raise the question of blackness, notably by way
of familiar code words of an earlier generation of popular culture. The musicologist Steve Swayne, in his consideration of Arlen's influence on Sondheim,
has described Arlen's location between black and white composers as being in
"a crease in American culture; he became neither Richard Rodgers nor Duke
Ellington, neither Cole Porter nor Fats Waller."[72] While discussing *Sunday* with
Horowitz, Sondheim said:

> I usually have one Arlen song in every show, and "Children and Art" is my
> Arlen song in *Sunday*.[73] And there's a reason for it; George's grandmother is

talking about how she was brought to America into the deep South, and that's where she grew up as a child. So I wanted to echo that, and when I think of the deep South, I think of Arlen. It's unfair since he comes from Buffalo or some-place in New York State and was the son of a cantor, but still, he wrote those bluesy songs. You listen to "Blues in the Night" and you think: Gee, that guy must have been born in Georgia. But he wasn't.[74]

In this remarkable statement, Sondheim substitutes region for race—"Georgia" for black—and employs a racial code word, *bluesy*, that keeps his appraisal of Arlen's music a step removed from the African American genre *the blues*. Both of these rhetorical moves date to the pre-war regime of popular songwriting that Arlen exemplifies: an expressive, highly commercial practice in which white, mostly Jewish songwriters based in New York created popular songs about a mythical South, a moonlight-and-magnolias, cabin-in-the-cotton, blues-in-the-night ethos that Arlen (often in collaboration with the lyricist Johnny Mercer, a white Episcopalian and Georgia native) cultivated at a very high aesthetic level.[75] Sondheim draws on the discourse of popular music before rock and roll; he is, decidedly, a composer rooted in the pre-1960s popular culture dispensation, which was, itself, enmeshed in a racial regime predicated on segregation.

Sondheim's use of black musical models at a decided and white-mediated remove continues and expands in another mention of Arlen in the Horowitz interviews. Sondheim notes, "If I had my choice, in every show I write, there would be one bossa nova and one Harold Arlen tune, because those are my two favorite modes." Bossa nova, a moderate-tempo 1960s Brazilian popular style forged in collaboration with white American jazz musicians and popular with middle-class white listeners in the United States, turns up in one of Sondheim's best-known numbers, "The Ladies Who Lunch." Sondheim and Horowitz re-flect a bit on why this choice does or does not make sense, Sondheim concluding without real resolution, "God, of all of the things that don't characterize the char-acter [Joanne, introduced by Elaine Stritch]. But on the other hand, she goes to a lot of nightclubs, and you know, these are the days when they were popular."[76] The relationship between character, musical style, and milieu comes together around Joanne (a well-to-do white character, likely the oldest of the bunch in *Company*), context (bossa nova as music to relax [and drink] by), and time period (*Company*'s late-1960s moment). As the scholar of Brazilian popular music K. E. Goldschmitt notes, by the end of the decade, bossa nova, as exemplified by Sergio Mendes's "The Look of Love" (1968), was "easy listening" music, "the essence of cutting-edge fashion for the privileged—predominantly white—elite" and "a pop [sound] with references to Latin music, rather than the reverse. Whatever stereotypical Brazilian musical elements were left . . . likely escaped public atten-tion through most listeners' awareness."[77] As a construction of elite whiteness,

Joanne's bossa nova can be heard to gently push against the white women she mocks in her first two verses—ladies chasing after concert music (Mahler) and experimental theater (Pinter)—and, when she turns to her own set, lend Joanne herself a glib, edgy self-image, secure among the "ones who just watch" (and drink). A totally appropriate, synthetic, quasi-Latin, quasi-jazzy, imported beat successfully marketed to middle-class and upper-middle-class white people in the United States is about all Joanne can muster in the way of rebellion against her own "upper-middle-class DNA." Bossa nova fits Joanne perfectly and finds a comfortable home in Sondheim's *Company*.

Most of Sondheim's pastiches, however, work from distinctly white models, such as a pair of numbers from early and late in his career: "The Miracle Song" (*Anyone Can Whistle*) and "The Ballad of Guiteau" (*Assassins*). Both communicate religious fervor and use the word *Lord* or *Lordy*—a word that might indicate blackness.[78] But the music evokes instead the rousing white revival hymns of the nineteenth century, and off-beat hand claps that might activate a black aesthetic are contained. The choice of white rather than black gospel is unsurprising: *Anyone Can Whistle* predates the introduction of black-cast gospel on Broadway (in *Purlie*, 1970); *Assassins* similarly pre-dates white-cast production numbers that push the black gospel edge (like "Run, Freedom, Run" in *Urinetown*, 2001). Sondheim's musical choices reflect their historical context and the safe assumption—given abundant evidence from his writings and interviews—that he engages primarily with the music of Broadway and, in his words, "so-called concert music" (of which more later).[79] Musical representations of blackness and whiteness have changed over time on Broadway. Sondheim's work, however highly personal, is part of this history.

Sondheim frequently evokes the waltz—a broad category of tempos and characters that, since the ragtime-era advent of black-inspired syncopated popular music, has indicated a flexible cluster of related associations: the nineteenth century, Europe (home of white culture), white American respectability and propriety, and "traditional" (meaning conservative white) values—even if the waltz was a scandal in its day. Waltzes come as no surprise in *A Little Night Music* or the full-on operetta mode of "One More Kiss" (*Follies*). But waltzes also resound in unlikely and significant spots in other Sondheim shows. The following examples demonstrate that the waltz—a white-identified musical register—is a core component of Sondheim's style regardless of milieu. In *Anyone Can Whistle*, Cora, who begins as a jazzy diva, gleefully rounds up the errant cookies to a snappy patter waltz, her kooky brand of fascism doing its work to a Viennese beat. The Witch in *Into the Woods* follows a similar path; beginning with a "'Rap' style" patter, she ends with the self-aggrandizing grandeur of "Last Midnight." In *Sunday*, Jules and Yvonne share their snobbery in the ponderous waltz "No Life." *Company* and *Into the Woods* alike put waltz in conversation with duple meter.

Bobby falls into a rare romantic reverie in "Someone Is Waiting" and lyrically lists the endearing qualities of the wives in the cast. This shamelessly sentimental waltz is prepared musically by the husbands, who shift to triple meter just before "Someone Is Waiting" with the carousing collective gripes of the "Whaddya like" passage, a style and tempo transition that itself moves out of the husbands' Pandarus-like offers in "Have I got a girl for you." There's a progression backward in time, musical styles, and stereotypes of white women across this stretch of *Company*: we move from edgy and urgent whispers of breaking news from the sexual revolution sung to a driving contemporary beat through a muscular, almost drinking-song waltz of masculine complaint, into Bobby's uber-traditional slow waltz, which names not one but two "blue-eyed" women: Sarah and Amy. *Into the Woods* tracks a reverse trajectory: "Any Moment" has Cinderella's Prince using old-fashioned adulterous waltz time to seduce the Baker's Wife; the start of the ensuing solo, "Moments in the Woods," has the Baker's Wife relishing, then rejecting waltz time in favor of leaving the woods and returning to house, husband, and duple meter (only to die). A final waltz, telling and creepy, warrants mention: "The Gun Song" (*Assassins*) features four white characters extolling, fondling, and accidentally firing their firearms in a medley of triple-meter tunes with a four-part quasi-barbershop refrain that stacks one whiteness atop another.

Apropos of *A Little Night Music*, Sondheim has noted that his inspiration for the show's waltz-laden score was not pastiche of early twentieth-century Broadway operetta by the likes of Victor Herbert and Sigmund Romberg but instead "stealing" from European concert composers such as Maurice Ravel and Sergei Rachmaninoff: "Once you decide you're going to do it in three: Ravel!"[80] Drawing on art music exemplars—often directly—puts into practice Sondheim's persistent discursive orientation toward establishing ranked categories of art, an approach with deep roots in European aesthetics, themselves rooted in and supportive of pernicious racial hierarchies. The ranking and sorting of art and artists permeates Sondheim's *Finishing the Hat* and *Look, I Made a Hat*, which, in addition to definitive (for now) versions of his lyrics, include highly opinionated "thumbnail observations about the men and woman (yes, just one) who by general consensus comprise the Pantheon of Great Lyricists in the English-speaking musical theater."[81] (All the lyricists mentioned are white, with the exception of passing notice given Langston Hughes's lyrics for the opera *Street Scene* [1946]. Admittedly, there *were* no other black lyricists writing for Broadway in the period Sondheim covers.)[82]

In the Horowitz interviews, Sondheim persistently sorts his own shows into two types: song forms and extended forms. The former—working from recognizable popular music styles—are generally found in his American milieu shows and, in Sondheim's view, are challenging to write owing to the aesthetic constraints of the models (such as thirty-two-bar song form). Extended forms, often constitutive of thematically integrated scores like *Sunday* and *Passion*, make up the warp and woof of his European milieu shows and are, he states, rather easier to put together. Beyond such extended forms lies "the land of opera," a place Sondheim at times seems to gaze toward longingly, even as he professes little interest in specific operatic repertoire. (From his youth, Sondheim's tastes have run toward instrumental music generally.)[83] Putting these categories into conversation, Sondheim conveys a thoroughly conventional, white view of musical taste—"To analyze a Kern tune or to analyze an Arlen tune is not more than a rung below analyzing the Mozart 39th [Symphony]; it's the same process"— and locates his own work rather precisely somewhat between popular Broadway "classics" (scare quotes mine) and European art music: "I lean toward writing arty salon songs—that's what I like to do."[84] This declaration rhymes with Sondheim's self-proclaimed "upper-middle-class DNA" but, again, the decidedly white status of "arty salon songs" might be added for greater social and historical specificity. I will return to Sondheim's aesthetic categories—song forms, extended forms, "the land of opera," and "arty salon songs"—in a closing discussion of the long-term reception of his shows in American, British, and European musical theatrical culture. These categories prove pertinent to an assessment of Sondheim's twenty-first-century audiences.

Sondheim's music, as well as his own words about his music, establish clear lines of descent from European art music ("I'm about 1890") and white American popular music models.[85] Sondheim's whiteness is not built on the appropriation of recognizable blacknesses—as is the case with, for example, George Gershwin or Arlen. Understanding Sondheim's whiteness as such in relation to other white musics is hence essential to this project and to any larger understanding of how racial categories and histories operate in musical theater and beyond.

## Whiteness as Philosophical Disposition

Sondheim's unfailingly smart lyrics generally grant his white characters a verbally virtuoso interiority. This common characteristic—mistakenly applied to Maria in *West Side Story*, Sondheim believes—constructs a gallery of musical theater roles centered on singing more than dancing (or even minimally moving): theatrical figures defined by their often elaborate words and thoughts, not by their bodies and actions. A number added to the 2004 Broadway version of *The Frogs* pokes self-reflexive fun at dramatic characters made mostly of thoughts and words. Just after the arrival of George Bernard Shaw, a playwright known for his verbose, cerebral characters and a central figure in *The Frogs*, a chorus of "Shavians" demonstrate how one can "dance to Shaw." The lyrics to the Shavians' "dance" list intellectual acts (thinking, commenting, discussing, reading, making a quip) as if they were danceable. Sondheim's musical setting of his lyrics includes several stoppings of the beat filled with mumbled (no doubt very smart) discussion that disrupts any sustained connection between music and bodily movement—in short, any real dancing. A subsequent lyric uses the verbs *dance*, *waltz*, and *samba* metaphorically with relation to what words, thoughts, and syllables do in the mind. Everything Sondheim says of Shaw in this broadly funny (and gently self-mocking) number obtains for Sondheim's own talky, analytically minded characters. Such solely verbal construction of character alone speaks volumes for Sondheim's whiteness, given the persistent historical connections made by white thinkers between white subjectivity and the mind and nonwhite subjectivity and the body, a legacy of racist European and American thought with particular purchase in the history of the musical stage.[86]

This collective bent among Sondheim's white characters has yielded lyrics that, though thoroughly integrated into their respective shows, frequently find their way to general statements on the order of "the situation's fraught / fraughter than I thought" (*Forum*, "Impossible"). One Sondheim character concludes, "why look for answers when none occur," only to opine—circularly—about the coupled self, "you always are what you always were which has nothing to do with, all to do with her" (*Company*, "Sorry-Grateful"). Ending the search for general truth with such a paradox counts as a conclusion across much of Sondheim's output. Arriving at points of studied indecision is goal enough, as in the infinite reiterations inherent in a conclusion like "A person like Bob doesn't have the good things but he doesn't have the bad things but he doesn't have the good things" (*Company*, "Side by Side by Side"). Such cogitation can happen alone, in pairs, or in groups. Solo reflections include the oscillating desires of "That Dirty Old Man" or the catalog of symptoms matched to cultural common sense in "Love, I Hear" (both in *Forum*). Pairs or groups of similar characters working over the same idea from subtly different perspectives form a common format, repeated in "Impossible," "Sorry-Grateful," "It Would Have Been Wonderful" (*A Little Night Music*) and "Agony" (*Into the Woods*), among others. The duet "Pretty Women" (*Sweeney Todd*) works this trope in a perverse manner driven by details of character and plot. Similarly, these white characters share an impulse to think through a concept by exploring its opposite or reverse side, as in "There's Won't Be Trumpets" (*Anyone Can Whistle*) and "The Road You Didn't Take" (*Follies*). In these numbers, whiteness is consistently attached to a detached ability to see "all sides," in contexts where reason is consistently taken up as the tool of choice for self-reflection. Such solitary or simultaneous cogitation—done with wit and spectacular word choice—again gives whiteness (of a certain class) as represented in Sondheim's shows a glossy sheen of subtlety and nuance.

The Cartesian mind-body split central to Western thought plays out in two numbers that explore female perspectives attended to by a concerned male onlooker. Philia's "That'll Show Him" (*Forum*) mixes concerns about masculine control over female bodies with an (in-context) ironic celebration of a white female's ability to separate sex from love (Philia enthusiastically details her plans to give her body to Miles Gloriosus, who paid for it, while remaining true in her heart to Hero, who looks on aghast at Philia's idea that he will "enjoy it"). And Phyllis in "Could I Leave You?" (*Follies*) hedges any final answer to the title's question (she ends her tirade with a shouted "Guess!") and pauses, mid-song, to consider whether, in her head, she's already long gone. Sondheim's whiteness is made of such philosophizing—in the above two numbers delivered from a gendered perspective—but is not limited to its pieties: There is room to hear critique of white Western subjectivities, but such critiques are from safely inside the system.

There are, to be sure, exceptions, such as the more conclusive final solos of Giorgio and Fosca in *Passion* and some of the pithy lessons arrived at by thoughtful fairytale characters in some solos from *Into the Woods*, such as Red Riding Hood's insightful conclusion that "nice is different than good" ("I Know Things Now"). Still, most of the solos in *Into the Woods* are, in Sondheim's words, about "ambivalence . . . about being in between—liking and disliking the adventure," reaching conclusions that diagram rather than resolve a situation on the order of "how can you know what you want till you get what you want and you see if you like it?" ("Moments in the Wood").[87] Reveling in the luxury of such reasoned ambivalence comes easy to Sondheim's characters, who mostly enjoy enough control over their physical lives and social contexts to make their own reasoned decisions and, perhaps, to conclude that internal and intellectualized ambiguity is, on the whole, a tolerable state of being. *Anyone Can Whistle*'s "Everybody Says Don't" and the show's title song similarly long "to be free" in a context where freedom means simple self-expression or actualization, the ability to "relax" like everyone else or to "walk on the grass" when convention says "don't." Such problems—especially for characters in a show like *Anyone Can Whistle*, set in 1964 in a generic town rocked by social confusion over who is sane or not—register as white people's problems.

Sondheim's white characters share a disposition of mind and a verbal ability to parse and define their situations in abstract terms as if their dilemmas can be drawn (if not solved) like geometrical proofs on a blank page or canvas. The notion that human problems can be understood in this way is elegantly staged in *Sunday*'s repeated coup de theater: Both Georges, in turn, speak the incantatory, even mystical words *order*, *design*, *tension*, *composition*, *balance*, *light*, *harmony*, which silence social chaos and still the voices of self-doubt. Such solemnly intoned abstractions—a veritable list of modernism's mantras—contain the assumption that philosophical categories and principles of form, divorced from historical and human contexts and content, can be leveraged to control the messiness of life. Such thoughts in Sondheim's hyperarticulate characters are the property of white, usually economically privileged subjects.

In short, Sondheim's characters are powerful exemplars of white, Western philosophical concepts, grounded in Enlightenment rationalism, of the radically free and solitary individual. The social and the ethical, community-oriented dimensions of human life, prominent in Jewish thought and practice and in some strains of the Christian tradition, are notably lacking and, when present, are often ironicized in context or qualified in expression. *Into the Woods*—part of his "warmer" period (mostly working with Lapine), as Sondheim puts it—includes two quasi anthems; neither makes a definitive social or utopic statement.[88] "No One Is Alone" centers on the individual's task to decide what is "right" and "good" (the community, by implication, does not), and "Children Will Listen" merely councils probity around the young (no suggested content is given to the example that adults inevitably set). Sondheim seems to recognize that centering on the self can be a limiting perspective: he admits that the conclusion at which *Sunday* arrives ("let it come from you / then it will be new") offers a "weak mantra."[89] This pointed lack of utopic utterance marks much of Sondheim's output—indeed, a paranoid reversal of the utopic seems the more likely upshot in some cases ("Isn't that Sweeney there beside you?"). Of course, for some audiences Sondheim's ambivalent, intellectual, at times solipsistic, anti-utopic, frequently satiric or parodic whiteness serves as evidence for his greatness, a stature defined as his transcendence (note the metaphorical elevation) above the overemphatic, simplistic, optimistic, sentimental, communitarian, utopian, enthusiastic whiteness of most of the Broadway musical tradition. If that tradition—as exemplified by figures such as Irving Berlin, Jerry Herman, and Rodgers and Hammerstein—is understood as chiefly the work of Jewish American creators then, once again, Sondheim's Jewishness in the Broadway context is slight indeed.

In her description of "Jewish whiteness from the late 1940s to the mid-1960s," Sondheim's formative years as well as the period when Jews were folded decisively into white America, the anthropologist Karen Brodkin identifies three ways in which "Jewish whiteness became American whiteness." Brodkin's second way—"when Jews spoke as white and spoke for whites, whether as Ken and Barbie [archetypal white dolls created by Jewish toymakers] or as artists and intellectuals"—maps closely on to Sondheim's whiteness. Brodkin continues, "To ask, But is this a Jewish point of view? is to miss the point that Jews were helping to define whiteness as they became part of it." Still, Sondheim's whiteness, predicated on the individual mind thinking through its problems, falls decidedly outside Brodkin's view of Jewishness, even after ambiguous assimilation into whiteness, as still characterized by "an earthly system of morals and meaning somehow embodied in good works and social justice."[90]

# Conclusion

Sondheim's whiteness is unusual in the Broadway context. His shows have not, on the whole, been particularly successful in commercial terms in their original time or later. Such a statement functions as either criticism or praise, depending on your position. And the ever more distant historical position of Sondheim's Broadway output further locates his whiteness as of an earlier phase in American social, economic, and political history. *Passion*, his last original Broadway score, closed shortly before the momentum to reclaim Forty-Second Street for family entertainment kicked in; the twenty-first-century Broadway of jukebox musicals, film adaptations, and *The Lion King* is distinctly different from the quarter century between *Company* and *Passion*. Sondheim's whiteness is—from the contemporary point of view—historical.

Here we might juxtapose Sondheim's whiteness with that of the composer Andrew Lloyd Webber (born 1948, active on Broadway from 1971 to the present). Lloyd Webber's thoroughly commercial whiteness can be summarized as British (not American); rock-referencing (prominent synths and electric guitars, even in a European period show such as *The Phantom of the Opera* [1986, London]); tunefully predictable; reliant on spectacle, often involving dance; expressive in very broad, mostly musical (rather than lyrical) terms; and engineered (and stunningly managed) to run seemingly forever.

By contrast, Sondheim's whiteness has come, in the decades since *Passion*, to occupy various noncommercial or modestly commercial spaces adjacent to commercial Broadway:

- limited-run Broadway and Off-Broadway revivals produced by nonprofits (benefiting the return of *Pacific Overtures*, *Assassins*, *The Frogs*, and *Merrily We Roll Along*),
- cabaret shows and concerts (including recurring tributes to Sondheim on notable birthdays),
- symphony "pops" concerts perfect for PBS (the New York Philharmonic has presented *Sweeney Todd* and *Company* in semi-staged concert versions),
- university, high school, and even junior high theater programs (see Stacy Wolf's chapter in this volume), and
- opera houses and other theaters where the American musical is rarely seen (as part of a multi-year effort to introduce French audiences to Broadway musicals, Paris' Théâtre du Châtelet produced a lavish Sondheim cycle in the 2010s, including all five of his European-milieu shows, featuring *Passion* with opera star Natalie Dessay as Fosca and *Sunday* reorchestrated for an orchestra of forty-six instead of the original eleven).

These spaces, all largely elite and white, have welcomed and nurtured Sondheim's whiteness for its opening of a liminal zone between the crassness of twenty-first-century commercial Broadway and the pretentions and, by comparison, genuine aesthetic difficulties of opera and classical music. In many of these sites, "the land of opera" expands its borders to annex Sondheim's extended-form musicals. This aspect of Sondheim's whiteness—neither mainstream fluff, nor snooty high art, poised in the space between mass and elite whitenesses—bears acknowledgment in any history of Sondheim's large place in the history of the American musical and the representation of whiteness of a certain social class in our time.

Throughout this chapter, I have avoided comparing white and black to better foreground the content of whiteness on its own terms. To close, I juxtapose two startlingly similar quotations: one by Sondheim, one by Toni Morrison (born eleven months after Sondheim, active 1970 to her death in 2019). In *Look, I Made a Hat*, Sondheim spends two pages on critics and their uses. The conclusion he comes to is this: "That's the most pernicious thing about critics: they cause you to waste your time."[91] In her 1975 speech "A Humanist View," Morrison said, "The very serious function of racism . . . is distraction. It keeps you from doing your work."[92] Comparing Sondheim's and Morrison's words reminds us how the sentiments contained in the lines "White. A blank page or canvas. His favorite. So many possibilities" represent the experience of white (and male) artists. Whiteness is inherent in this view of the very notion of creative possibility.

Near the end of *Sunday*, Act I, Seurat sings "I am what I do," a claim that works fine for white male subjects who begin with blank pages seemingly but never in fact unmarked by history. Morrison's words do more than hint at how that blank page is impacted by racism for black artists. They also express the impossibility of separating art from life and material circumstances for artists in marginalized groups. Looking to Sondheim's whiteness, as I have tried to do, situates the freedom to imagine the possibility of a blank page as perhaps the ultimate gift whiteness bestows on those given the chance to claim it as their own.

# Notes

1. My warmest thanks to Dan Fister, Rachel Jones, Paige McGinley, Ashley Pribyl, Tony Sheppard, Robert Snarrenberg, Steve Swayne, and Stacy Wolf for invaluable input on this chapter.

   James Lapine and Stephen Sondheim, *Sunday in the Park with George: A Musical* (New York: Dodd, Mead, 1986), 21.

2. Ibid., 202.

3. The politics and economics of the art world are critiqued in the Act II song "Art Isn't Easy," during which George carefully maintains the distance between the artist and his work.

4. Stephen Banfield, "Sondheim's Genius," in *The Oxford Handbook of Sondheim Studies*, ed. Robert Gordon (New York: Oxford University Press, 2014).

5. Mark Eden Horowitz, *Sondheim on Music: Major Decisions and Minor Details*, 2nd ed. (Lanham, MD: Scarecrow, 2010), 164.

6. Richard Dyer, *White* (London: Routledge, 1997), xiii.

7. Ibid., 1.

8. Ibid., 13.

9. George Gershwin's folk opera *Porgy and Bess* has received the lion's share of scholarly attention to black-cast musical theater. Theater scholar Donatella Galella has given close consideration to *Raisin* (1973, music by Judd Woldin, lyrics by Robert Brittan, book by Robert B. Nemiroff and Charlotte Zaltzberg) in *America in the Round: Capital, Race and Nation at Washington, DC's Arena Stage* (Iowa City: University of Iowa Press, 2019), chap. 4, and "Playing in the Dark: Musicalizing *A Raisin in the Sun*," *Continuum Journal* 1, no. 2 (January 2015). See also Todd Decker, "'Big, as in Large, as in Huge': *Dreamgirls* and Difference in the Performance of Gender, Blackness, and Popular Music History," in *Twenty-First Century Musicals from Stage to Screen*, ed. George Rodosthenous (New York: Routledge, 2018).

10. Scholarship concerning whiteness in the Broadway musical includes Raymond Knapp, "History, *The Sound of Music*, and Us," *American Music* 22, no. 1 (Spring 2004): 133–144; and Carol J. Oja, "*West Side Story* and *The Music Man*: Whiteness, Immigration, and Race in the US During the late 1950s," *Studies in Musical Theater* 3, no. 1 (2009): 13–30. On racial performance more generally on the musical stage since about 1910 see Todd Decker, "*Show Boat*": *Performing Race in an American Musical* (New York: Oxford University Press, 2013); Warren Hoffman, *The Great White Way: Race and the Broadway Musical* (New Brunswick: Rutgers University Press, 2014); Jeffrey Magee, *Irving Berlin's American Musical Theater* (New York: Oxford University Press, 2012); Carol J. Oja, *Bernstein Meets Broadway: Collaborative Art in a Time of War* (New York: Oxford University Press, 2016); and Elizabeth A. Wells, "*West Side Story*": *Cultural Perspectives on an American Musical* (Lanham, MD: Scarecrow, 2011).

11. Even *Show Boat*, however, has not always been "about" race for those who write about musical theater. See Todd Decker, "'Do You Want to Hear a Mammy Song?': A Historiography of *Show Boat*," *Contemporary Theater Review* 19, no. 1 (2009): 8–21.

12. Harry Newman, "The Theater's Resistance to Non-Traditional Casting," *Drama Review* 33, no. 3 (Autumn 1989), 27.

13. Loren Kajikawa, "The Possessive Investment in Classical Music: Confronting Legacies of White Supremacy in U.S. Schools and Departments of Music," in *Seeing Race Again: Countering Colorblindness Across the Disciplines*, ed. Kimberlé Williams Crenshaw, Luke Charles Harris, Daniel Martinez HoSang, and George Lipsitz (Berkeley: University of California Press, 2019).

14. These include *Flower Drum Song* (1958, revived 2002), *Pacific Overtures* (1976, revived 2004), and *Allegiance* (2015, with several supporting white characters). African American actress Juanita Hall, who won a Tony award for the Asian role Bloody Mary in *South Pacific* (1949), again appeared in yellowface as Auntie Liang in the original production of *Flower Drum Song*. Hall reprised both roles on film.

15. W. Anthony Sheppard, *Extreme Exoticism: Japan in the American Musical Imagination* (New York: Oxford University Press, 2019), 375–380, subtly and critically situates *Pacific Overtures* in the long history of exoticist representations of Japan in American culture. See Ashley Pribyl's chapter in this volume for more on *Pacific Overtures*.

16. See Decker, *"Show Boat"*, epilogue.

17. Stephen Sondheim and Arthur Laurents, *West Side Story* (New York: Random House, 1958), 3. For discussion of the "Latin" music informing *West Side Story*, see Wells, *West Side Story*, chap. 3.

18. Stephen Sondheim, *Finishing the Hat: Collected Lyrics (1954–1981)* (New York: Knopf, 2010), 28.

19. Ibid., 48. The similarity and contrast between "I Feel Pretty" and "A Little Priest" (*Sweeney Todd*) is worth noting. In the latter, lower-working-class characters banter "inner rhymes and trick rhymes" for verse after verse, demonstrating and delighting in poetic virtuosity. Perhaps the assumption behind the number's success is a white American bias granting to all white British subjects a quasi-Shakespearean mastery of the English language.

20. Wells, *West Side Story*, 33.

21. Horowitz, *Sondheim on Music*, 79.

22. Sondheim, *Finishing the Hat*, 186.

23. Ibid., 25.

24. Laurents called *West Side Story* "a musical about love destroyed by the bigotry and violence of gangs" and located "its real contribution to American musical theater" in the fact that "it showed that any subject—murder, attempted rape, bigotry—could be the subject of a popular musical." Arthur Laurents, *Mainly on Directing: "Gypsy," "West Side Story" and Other Musicals* (New York: Knopf, 2009), 93, 145.

25. The African American performer Myrna White appeared as the courtesan Vibrata in the original cast of *A Funny Thing Happened on the Way to the Forum* (1962). Introduced by Lycus as "exotic as a desert bloom . . . lithe as a tigress . . . for the man whose interest is wild life," Vibrata does not appear in the (cut) lyrics for this scene as given by Sondheim in *Finishing the Hat*. Stephen Sondheim, Burt Shevelove, and Larry Gelbart, *A Funny Thing Happened on the Way to the Forum/The Frogs* (New York: Dodd, Mead, 1985), 36. While in *Forum*, White integrated the regular dance troupe on the *Ed Sullivan Show* in 1963. See "Myrna White Scores Dance Success," *Ebony*, April 1963, 59–64.

26. *Gangs of New York* (2002) presents a powerful exception with its representation of the Civil War–era draft riots, including depictions of white mobs lynching black men on the streets of New York.

27. Jess Row, *White Flights: Race, Fiction, and the American Imagination* (Minneapolis: Gray Wolf, 2019), 109.

28. Ibid., 9.

29. Shannon Sullivan, *Revealing Whiteness: The Unconscious Habits of Racial Privilege* (Bloomington: Indiana University Press, 2006). 10.

30. Updike's novels *The Coup* (1978), *Brazil* (1994), and *Terrorist* (2006) are notable exceptions; only the last is set in the United States.

31. Sondheim's last New York production of a new musical was the Off-Broadway *Road Show* at the Public Theatre in 2008.

32. Horowitz, *Sondheim on Music*, 91. On Sondheim's not self-identifying as Jewish during his college years, see Steve Swayne's chapter in this volume.

33. The cut number "The Wedding Is Off" (*Company*, replaced by "Getting Married Today") includes the word *kvelling* but also mentions a preacher, putting the Jewish nature of the ceremony in question. Sondheim, *Finishing the Hat*, 185.

34. "Bobby bubi" occurs in both *Company*'s opening number, sung by his "married friends," and in "You Could Drive a Person Crazy," a trio for Robert's three girlfriends, who sing the phrase together. The phrase's possible relation to any one character in the show is, thereby, diluted.

35. Horowitz, *Sondheim on Music*, 83.

36. In an analogous exchange with Horowitz about *Sweeney Todd*, Sondheim identifies his setting of the word *London* in the opening duet for Anthony and Sweeney as "an appoggiatura on the downbeat. That, to me, is characteristic of British music, and it shows up a lot in [William] Walton and in [Benjamin] Britten. So when I heard 'London,' I thought: Yeah, that's very British" (Horowitz, *Sondheim on Music*, 130). Here, a detail of musical style speaks to a white national identity as constructed by composers with strong, reception-defining national identifications.

37. Henry Bial, *Acting Jewish: Negotiating Ethnicity on the American Stage and Screen* (Ann Arbor: University of Michigan Press, 2005), 57.

38. Ibid., 64.

39. Bial offers a periodization of Jewish content and characters in U.S. commercial culture after World War II. While Sondheim is mentioned only once (in passing, in relation to the well-known Jewish performer Zero Mostel), his musicals find their most comfortable fit in the chapter of Bial's book covering the years 1947 to 1955—the period *before* Sondheim's Broadway career began. Like Arthur Miller's *Death of a Salesman*, Sondheim's shows raise the question of Jewish identity in a context lacking almost any explicit indicators of Jewish presence.

40. Sondheim, *Finishing the Hat*, 112. Studies of Sondheim as collaborator include Ashley M. Pribyl, "Collaborative and Sociocultural Antagonism in the Stephen Sondheim–Harold Prince Musicals, 1970–1979" (PhD diss., Washington University in St. Louis, 2019), and Theodore Chapin, *Everything Was Possible: The Birth of the Musical "Follies"* (New York: Applause Books, 2003), among many.

41. Sondheim, *Finishing the Hat*, 408.

42. Stephen Sondheim, *Look, I Made a Hat: Collected Lyrics (1981–2011)* (New York: Knopf, 2011), 17.

43. Horowitz, *Sondheim on Music*, 114.

44. George Furth and Stephen Sondheim, *Company: A Musical Comedy* (New York: Random House, 1970), 3.

45. Stephen Sondheim and Hugh Wheeler, *A Little Night Music* (New York: Applause Books, 1991), 18.

46. Hugh Wheeler and Stephen Sondheim, *Sweeney Todd: The Demon Barber of Fleet Street; A Musical Thriller* (New York: Dodd, Mead, 1979); James Lapine and Stephen Sondheim, *Passion: A Musical* (New York: Theater Communications Group, 1994).

47. Notably, *Pacific Overtures* begins in "Japan in July of 1853" and concludes, after several skips in time, like *Sunday* in the present. Sondheim noted of *Pacific Overtures* in relation to *Sweeney Todd*: "Same period. Different country." Horowitz, *Sondheim on Music*, 155.

48. Sondheim, *Finishing the Hat*, 58. Only the Baker and his Wife are not drawn from Grimm.

49. Horowitz, *Sondheim on Music*, 117.

50. See https://www.youtube.com/watch?v=f6twfrbUstA.

51. Select Sondheim roles have been cast (in some cases repeatedly) with performers of color in major revivals, including the following: Carol Woods (2001) and Terry White (2011) as Stella Deems in Broadway revivals of *Follies* (as well as Dawn Hope in the 2017 National Theater production in London) lead the up-tempo number "Who's That Woman?," which, unusual for Sondheim, includes black popular music slang (the word *Lord*); La Chanze (1995) and Angel Desai (2006) as Marta, the edgy girlfriend who sings "Another Hundred People" in Broadway revivals of *Company* (as well as Anika Noni Rose in the New York Philharmonic's televised 2013 concert version); Vanessa Williams's turn as the Witch in the 2002 revival of *Into the Woods*; and British actor Adrian Lester (son of Jamaican immigrant parents) as Bobby in the 1995 revival of *Company* at London's Donmar Warehouse. In the 2021 Broadway revival, three of the ten performers in *Company*'s five married couples were of color; thus, three of the five couples were interracial and one of the remaining two was same-sex.

52. Arthur Laurents and Stephen Sondheim, *Gypsy: A Musical* (New York: Random House, 1959).

53. To Sondheim's and Weidman's credit, they do not soft-pedal the antiblack racism of southern American whiteness as, in contrast, is apparent in the sympathetic (and largely tacit regarding slavery) representation of slaveholding American founding fathers in *1776* (1969) and *Hamilton* (2015).

54. Todd Decker, "Remembering the American Tribal Love-Rock Musical Before It Got Old: Broadway's 'Hair' in Its Times Square Time," March 2, 2021, https://commonreader.wustl.edu/c/remembering-the-american-tribal-love-rock-musical-before-it-got-old/.

55. Angela C. Pao, *No Safe Spaces: Re-casting Race, Ethnicity, and Nationality in American Theater* (Ann Arbor: University of Michigan Press, 2010), 136.

56. Arthur Laurents and Stephen Sondheim, *Anyone Can Whistle: A Musical Fable* (New York: Leon Amiel, 1965).

57. The song was cut before opening but was included on the cast album.

58. In the dialogue scene after "Getting Married Today" in *Company*, Amy reveals that she is Catholic and her fiancé Paul is Jewish. Amy says, "I mean I didn't even *know* anybody who was Jewish," and Paul replies, "About three-quarters of your friends are Jewish." Furth and Sondheim, *Company*, 65.

59. An unnamed black minister appears in a dialogue scene in the 1981 version of *Merrily We Roll Along*, facilitating a racist comment by an old white minor character (Beth's father). Black actress Tonya Pinkins was credited in the role of Gwen Wilson in the 1981 cast list. No lines or lyrics for this role are present in the 1981 script, and the role is eliminated in all subsequent versions of *Merrily*. George Furth and Stephen Sondheim, *Merrily We Roll Along*, rental typescript, Music Theatre International, New York, NY, Act II, scene 3, p. 34.

60. Bial, *Acting Jewish*, 8.

61. Stephen J. Whitfield, *In Search of American Jewish Culture* (Hanover, NH: Brandeis University Press, 1999), 59.

62. Furth and Sondheim, *Merrily We Roll Along*, Act II, scenes 3–4, p. 36.

63. Chapin, *Everything Was Possible*, 236.

64. Black chorus girls, by contrast, were famous for vigorous dancing.

65. Sondheim, *Finishing the Hat*, 345; Horowitz, *Sondheim on Music*, 106.

66. Sondheim, *Look, I Made a Hat*, xix.

67. Stephen Sondheim, *Into the Woods* (Secaucus, NJ: Warner Bros. Publications, 1987), 29f. Vocal score.

68. Sondheim, *Finishing the Hat*, 235. On the Gershwin song's use of blackness and blues, see Todd Decker, "Broadway in Blue: Gershwin's Musical Theater Scores and Songs," in *The Cambridge Companion to George Gershwin*, ed. Anna Harwell Celenza (New York: Cambridge University Press, 2019), 97–98.

69. Sondheim, *Finishing the Hat*, 219.

70. For more on this phenomenon, see Todd Decker, "Race, Ethnicity, Performance," in *The Oxford Handbook of the American Musical*, ed. Raymond Knapp, Mitchell Morris, and Stacy Wolf (New York: Oxford University Press, 2011), 208–209.

71. Dan Dinero, "A Big Black Lady Stops the Show: Black Women, Performances of Excess and the Power of Saying No," *Studies in Musical Theater* 6, no. 1 (March 2012): 29–41.

72. Steve Swayne, *How Sondheim Found His Sound* (Ann Arbor: University of Michigan Press, 2005), 78.

73. The bluesy setting of the lyric "I'm just quoting Mama" supports Sondheim's description of "Children and Art" as Arlenesque. My thanks to W. Anthony Sheppard for this detail.

74. Horowitz, *Sondheim on Music*, 100.

75. Karen Cox, *Dreaming of Dixie: How the South Was Created in American Popular Culture* (Chapel Hill: University of North Carolina Press, 2013), chap. 1.

76. Horowitz, *Sondheim on Music*, 192.

77. K. E. Goldschmitt, *Bossa Mundo: Brazilian Music in Transnational Media Industries* (New York: Oxford University Press, 2020), 25, 73.

78. Racial performance by way of musical style in "The Ballad of Guiteau" is complicated by the use of a ragtime rhythm at the chorus ("Look on the bright side"), a passage where the script indicates that Guiteau should "[cakewalk] cheerfully up and down the gallows steps." Stephen Sondheim and John Weidman, *Assassins* (New York: Theater Communications Group, 1991), 66. Audience knowledge of the cakewalk as a ragtime dance done by African Americans and originating in black spoofing of white high society manners potentially complicates this moment of physically exuberant gallows humor. My thanks to Steve Swayne for drawing my attention to this detail.

79. Horowitz, *Sondheim on Music*, 231.

80. Ibid., 213.

81. Sondheim, *Finishing the Hat*, ix.

82. Andy Razaf mainly wrote for the popular song market.

83. Swayne, *How Sondheim Found His Sound*, chap. 1.

84. Horowitz, *Sondheim on Music*, 168, 187.

85. Horowitz, *Sondheim on Music*, 117; Swayne, *How Sondheim Found His Sound*, chaps. 1 and 2.

86. Among the many scholars of whiteness, Thomas DiPiero, *White Men Aren't* (Durham: Duke University Press, 2002), 96–97, locates the origins of the specious equation of whiteness with rationality and intellect in the eighteenth century. Karen Brodkin, *How Jews Became White Folks and What That Says About Race in America* (New Brunswick: Rutgers University Press, 1998), 82–83, points towards the evolutionary thinking of Herbert Spencer.

87. Horowitz, *Sondheim on Music*, 190.

88. Sondheim, *Look, I Made a Hat*, 6.

89. Ibid., 55.

90. Brodkin, *How Jews Became White Folks*, 138, 168, 172.

91. Sondheim, *Look, I Made a Hat*, 41.

92. Toni Morrison, "A Humanist's View," May 30, 1975. Speech delivered at Portland State University. Recording in Portland State Library Special Collections and available at https://soundcloud.com/portland-state-library/portland-state-black-studies-1 (quotation at 36:00).

# 6

# Politics, Representation, and Collaboration in *Pacific Overtures* (1976)

*Ashley M. Pribyl*

*Pacific Overtures* (1976), a show about Commodore Matthew Perry's 1853–1854 expedition to Japan, remains an outlier in Sondheim's oeuvre—his only non-white musical, it lacks the traditional American and European musical theater topics of love and relationships, and focuses instead on the complicated connections between cultures, time, and progress while invoking a decidedly non-Western milieu. Thomas Adler declared this work "the first Broadway musical directly spawned by our involvement in Vietnam."[1] While Adler overlooks a few musicals, including *Hair* (1968) and *The Lieutenant* (1975), *Pacific Overtures*, though focused on nineteenth-century Japanese–American relations, resonates with the role of the United States in Southeast Asia during the 1970s.[2] Whereas according to bookwriter John Weidman, the connection to the Vietnam War was never explicitly brought up by any of the collaborators while working on the project, *Pacific Overtures* appeared at a time when many Americans were questioning the traditional narrative of the United States as savior of foreign nations.[3]

The project began as a straight-play collaboration between Weidman, who was interested in Japanese history, and Harold Prince, who focused on current political and extratheatrical issues—topics that Sondheim had little interest in.[4] These two, then, set the initial tone for the work. Once Prince convinced Sondheim to participate in the project, however, the three men together came to the conclusion that *Pacific Overtures* would combine Broadway and *kabuki* aesthetics while attempting to avoid Orientalist stereotypes by reimagining the historical events through the eyes of a fictional Japanese creative team making a Broadway musical. The term *Occidental*, used throughout this chapter, is meant to denote this attempt to reverse the norms of Orientalism by centering the point of view of the East and "othering" the West. In *Pacific Overtures,* this meant othering the American characters and centering the Japanese ones. With an all-white creative team, though, such an attempt was destined to fall short of this concept, a point that Weidman continually emphasized during my interview with him.[5]

Ashley M. Pribyl, *Politics, Representation, and Collaboration in* Pacific Overtures *(1976)* In: *Sondheim in Our Time and His.* Edited by: W. Anthony Sheppard, Oxford University Press. © Oxford University Press 2022. DOI: 10.1093/oso/9780197603192.003.0007

As this chapter reveals, by trying to make a kabuki-Broadway hybrid in which the aesthetic and narrative sympathies align with Japan and not the United States, the creators engaged with discourses surrounding the Vietnam War, the Asian American movement, and more general concerns with American imperialism, even if they themselves might not have been directly aware of it at the time. Archival documents indicate that Weidman originally wrote a more political play, and many of his overt political ideas were maintained throughout the collaborative process, in part because Sondheim relied heavily on Weidman for research and content. Furthermore, by trying to achieve a certain type of authenticity, the creators inadvertently made an overtly political and contemporary experimental musical. *Pacific Overtures* critiqued past conventions regarding representation of Asians on the Broadway stage and cracked a door for later works by actual, rather than imagined, Asian American authors.

## Weidman's Anti-Imperialist "Untitled Play About the Opening of Japan"

The unique subject and style of *Pacific Overtures* was a product of intense and sometimes contradictory collaborations. This dependence on collaboration is typical of Sondheim's works—the composer himself continues to insist on viewing his musicals as products of multiple authors, as illustrated by his recent defense of George Furth in the *New York Times*.[6] *Pacific Overtures* clearly demonstrates the value of such collaborations, as this is not a work Sondheim would have proposed or been able to create on his own. Prince and Weidman were clearly the primary instigators and authors. Yet Sondheim's interest in characterization, aesthetic integration, and clever lyrical and musical techniques added nuance to the foundation laid by Weidman and Prince, creating a complicated analysis of the impact of Western imperialism on East Asia generally and Japan specifically.[7]

In the early 1970s Weidman began writing what at that time he called "An Untitled Play About the Opening of Japan" as a distraction from law school and an attempt to find a career outside law.[8] Intending to focus on modern European history while an undergraduate at Harvard, he took a course on East Asian history which so fascinated him that he decided to make East Asian history and culture his concentration instead. According to Weidman, at that time, especially on the East coast, most Americans knew very little about Japan and its history beyond caricatured and villainized depictions from World War II.[9] Owing to his studies at Harvard, Weidman felt that he had "a secret body of knowledge" that he could use to create an interesting and compelling theatrical work that would introduce New Yorkers to this exciting history and culture that he found so inspiring.[10] Weidman had met Harold Prince as a child when his father, the playwright Jerome Weidman, had worked with Prince on *Fiorello!* in 1959, but he had not spoken to Prince since. Knowing Prince's interest in experimental theater and desire to mentor and cultivate young artists, Weidman took a chance and sent Prince his working script. Prince clearly felt the script needed quite a bit of work, but he took Weidman under his wing, and they began working on the show as a straight play.[11]

The genesis of *Pacific Overtures* can be traced with particular clarity because Weidman and Prince began working on the book as a play two years before involving Sondheim. At least four full drafts of the script exist from various stages of development. The earliest extant draft of Weidman's straight play—available in the Boris Aronson archives at the Harry Ransom Center in Austin, Texas—is dated October 1973 and titled "Untitled Play About the Opening of Japan (Second Draft)."[12] (See the appendix for information about all drafts discussed.) By comparing this draft with the later drafts and the final production, we can trace Sondheim's influence on the show, as well as the way Prince helped Weidman develop his political and historical ideas into a compelling drama.

The October 1973 script reads like a morality play against the United States rather than a nuanced stage drama. Sondheim's biographer, Meryle Secrest, called it "a Brechtian polemic about what happens when capitalism and industrialism invade an ancient and poetic culture."[13] The play focused solely on Perry's interaction with the Japanese, lacking any critique of Japanese culture or positive proclamations of Western-influenced progress, which became more central in the final version. Unlike the complex ending of *Pacific Overtures*, the early draft casts Kayama as the clear hero of the story, which ends triumphantly when he keeps Perry from firing his cannons on Uraga by sitting in front of the guns and forcing Perry not to shoot.[14] *Pacific Overture*'s second act, which shows the results of American intervention after Perry has left, is completely absent from Weidman's untitled play.

Prince encouraged Weidman to use kabuki in the early draft to signal a shift from the U.S. point of view to the Japanese point of view. At first, the Americans speak alone and are represented in traditional Western sailor garb, but when they arrive in Japan and the audience is supposed to be viewing them from the Japanese perspective, the Americans are transformed with villainous kabuki costumes.[15] This change signals a new point of view, like a novelist changing narrators between chapters. Although this was jettisoned from the next draft owing to logistical difficulties, the technique would have afforded Weidman the ability to direct the audience's sympathies and move them in between worlds, declaring both points of view equally biased and unreliable.[16] More significant, this aspect of the early script shows that Prince and Weidman were already thinking about whose point of view to tell the story from and how to tell it. Eventually, the creators would attempt to make a musical *entirely* from a Japanese perspective, a reversal from previous East-meets-West theatrical productions.

This script also includes moments that reveal a critical understanding of the United States' imperialist expansion into the Pacific, inadvertently connecting the show with contemporary political discourse. First, the play connects this moment of American expansionism in Japan to later troubles, just as current activists connected colonialism, including Commodore Perry's expedition, with the war in Vietnam. The plan that the Japanese government adopts—both in real life and in the play—prefigures the cycle of violence that occurred when the country caught up technologically with the West. In Weidman's play, Hayashi, one of the governors, explains, "Now, when we are weak, we must give the westerners what they demand, but later on, when we are strong and have made the nation as united as one family, we will be able to give the westerners what they deserve."[17] This line strongly evokes Japanese imperialism throughout East Asia, as well as the bombing of Pearl Harbor and the Pacific theater during World War II, but places at least some of the blame on the United States for humiliating Japan.

Weidman makes space for the white ally, essentially writing himself (or the predominately white, liberal audience) into the play, a character type notably absent in the final script of *Pacific Overtures*. Colonel Williams, the interpreter for Commodore Perry, continually implores Perry to treat the Japanese with more respect. In the scene that introduces his character, Williams tells Perry, "It seems to me, sir, that we have a duty to these people to treat them as considerately as we can, and demand of them as little as possible. . . . I am convinced that the only thing we have seen today is an ill-considered and unprecedented violation of the sanctity of Japanese soil."[18] Unlike the other Americans, Williams shows empathy toward the Japanese people, and he sees the possible consequences of treating them poorly, though he is still somewhat paternalistic. One assumes this comes from Williams's experiences studying Japan and Japanese culture, as he is the only one who speaks Japanese on board the ship; therefore, Williams's voice could be interpreted as Weidman's. Williams does not serve completely as a white savior because it is Kayama who ultimately persuades Perry to back down with his act of selflessness, but Williams does assist Kayama and Manjiro. The removal of Williams from the musical further emphasizes the ways in which Prince, Weidman, and Sondheim wanted to make the show about Japan and the Japanese, attempting to completely decenter whiteness and Americanness and refocus on the Japanese point of view.

Although the original inclusion of Williams slightly shifts the good-bad dichotomy of the story, the ultimate conclusion of "The Untitled Play" is that the West's, and more specifically the United States', economic and political imperialism in East Asia caused and continues to cause unnecessary pain and suffering for people living in Asia and in the United States. Weidman also makes sure to point out that these aggressive actions do not go unanswered. In the final moments of the play, Perry makes an indirect reference to the creation of an American naval base in Hawaii, namely, Pearl Harbor:

> As you know, I have long advocated the expansion of American commercial and political interests in the Hawaiian Islands. If you are forced to lay over in Honolulu waiting for the mail steamer, I would very much appreciate your investigating the nature of the coastline in and around the city. I have been told that there is a natural harbor there which might make an ideal coaling station or naval base. Its name escapes me at the moment.[19]

This reminder of Japan's aggression in the 1930s and 1940s toward both its direct neighbors and the United States ensures that the audience would have connected what had just been seen on stage with more current events, perhaps even America's failed endeavor in Vietnam.

This notion continued into revisions and, ultimately, the final script of *Pacific Overtures*. In the penultimate scene the emperor declares, "We will organize an army and a navy, equipped with the most modern weapons . . . we will do for the rest of Asia what America has done for us!"[20] The implication that American imperialism provoked Japanese expansion, the bombing of Pearl Harbor, and the war in the Pacific theater during World War II paralleled other critiques made by the Asian American antiwar movement starting in the 1960s.

Most significant for the play's future trajectory as a musical, "The Untitled Play" overtly compares itself to Orientalist musicals by the inclusion of a bizarre minstrel show on Perry's ship. The white Americans sailing with Perry in 1854 actually did perform a minstrel show for the Japanese, and Weidman's show within a show made it into the first collaborative version of the musical with Sondheim. It was eventually cut only because they expanded the show to cover more of the after-effects of Perry's visit to Japan. The instructions for the minstrel show stated:

> It should be emphasized here that what takes place on stage during the succeeding minstrel show is a strange multi-leveled exercise in impersonation— orientals imitating whites imitating blacks. The performance should have none of the grace and charm of the "Uncle Tom's Cabin" sequence from "The King and I." On the contrary, it should be extremely awkward and slightly grotesque, reflecting some of the undertones of the imitation and exploitation of one racial group by another which runs through the play as a whole.[21]

The explicit mention of "The Small House of Uncle Thomas" from *The King and I* (1951) immediately gives a sense as to why Weidman wanted to include this moment and how he related it thematically to the rest of the show. While Jerome Robbins used this cross-cultural performance in the Rodgers and Hammerstein hit to dazzle audiences with Orientalist choreography and costumes (while also linking Tuptim's romantic desire to escape the king with that of enslaved African Americans seeking freedom), Weidman wanted something "extremely awkward and slightly grotesque," deromanticizing that iconic yet problematic scene from *The King and I*.

Weidman then goes further to explain that the play within a play represents the "imitation and exploitation of one racial group by another which runs through *the play as a whole*" [emphasis added]. Here, Weidman expands the play's larger critique to include all forms of racism, misrepresentation, and stereotyping common in American culture, from nineteenth-century minstrel shows to modern-day Broadway musicals. This imitation recalls the pervasive use of yellowface within *The King and I*, *South Pacific*, and other musicals, plays, and films during this period (and continuing today).

The play within a play also underscores the ways liberal white audiences were more accepting of racist and hurtful depictions of Asians than they were of blacks.[22] The minstrel show traffics in the worst stereotypes of blacks—unacceptable to most of the audience in the decade following the civil rights movement—including use of the n-word, as well as a thick dialect absent in the speech of the Japanese characters. This is the example of "American culture" presented to the Japanese in Weidman's play and therefore, simultaneously, to the audience: one based in exploitation and stereotypes. For those who enjoyed "The Little House of Uncle Thomas," this moment would have provided an opportunity for self-reflection. How was Robbins's creation any different from minstrelsy? Why does American culture continue to enjoy Orientalism in an unfettered way while at least giving lip service to challenging negative representations of blacks on stage? Weidman believed that at the time, most Americans had little to no experience with these differing cultures and that this ignorance is what allowed these negative representations to continue.[23]

One bit of this minstrel show does remain in the final production: Perry's "Lion Dance" at the end of Act I contains a cakewalk. The musical and dance genre, derived from practices of enslaved Africans and African Americans, became strongly associated with blackface minstrel shows, which often utilized the cakewalk in the finale.[24] When Perry performs it, the dance becomes an identifier of both Americanness and whiteness, while drawing on the historical ways in which imitating other races, such as in minstrel shows and yellowface, redrew and reestablished the boundaries of whiteness and white-as-Americanness.

Prince heavily influenced the later drafts of the play, bringing in the idea of using more of kabuki theater as inspiration and expanding the play's underlying political themes. Such themes included the benefits and drawbacks of progress, the consequences of the United States' expanding Manifest Destiny and the anti-Soviet campaign into a worldwide imperialist venture, and the continued racist representation of Asians in popular culture. These themes complemented Weidman's goal of introducing white New Yorkers to the history and people of Japan. Throughout the entire process, Prince helped Weidman considerably in crafting the book and included himself as co-author on at least two drafts (see the appendix). Weidman's original play ended when Perry and his crew left Japan, but Prince worked with him to expand the timeline, finally ending the show in 1976. Most significant, while working with scene designer Boris Aronson on the set, Prince decided that the show needed to be a musical and eventually convinced Sondheim to join the project, forcing the creative team to start the process over, even as casting for the straight play had already begun.[25]

As they worked on the script, Prince and Weidman began to conceive of the show as a mirror image of previous Orientalist works.[26] The story was to be told from the point of view of the Japanese, placing the Americans (and later, other Westerners) in the role of foreigners. The conceit was strengthened by Prince's decision to bring in Sondheim and make the show a musical, evoking *South Pacific* and *The King and I*. Initially, Sondheim was *not* interested in working on the show at all, but as Weidman joked, "Hal usually got what he wanted." Weidman guided Sondheim's research about Japan, eventually sparking Sondheim's interest in the minimalism of Japanese aesthetics. Sondheim's intense desire for character consistency and aesthetic cohesion inspired him to attempt to write a hybrid of Japanese and American music and lyrics that centered around what he could understand as the Japanese experience.[27]

## An Occidentalist Musical?

The setting of East Asia and the theme of Western influence in the area have a long history in Western theater. Yet even as these works provide a platform to challenge societal problems, they often simultaneously and unconsciously reinforce problematic depictions and narratives of those same marginalized communities. For example, *South Pacific* provided Hammerstein with a platform to critique racism within the United States by contrasting the racism of the white American characters with the racial tolerance of the Polynesian, Asian, and European ones, yet he also depicted the Tonkinese women in the show in an extremely stereotypical and problematic manner. Because these musicals have historically been created by white Westerners and aimed at their white audiences, this tension predominates.

Furthermore, Western stage works about Asia often performed political work for the benefit of U.S. foreign policy. Pearl S. Buck's novel *The Good Earth* (1931) turned into a play (1932), and a more successful film (1937) served to garner sympathy for Chinese allies during World War II and differentiate them in the mind of Americans from the Japanese and Japanese Americans, who were contrarily being turned into offensive cartoon enemies and forced into concentration camps. The Oriental musical, however, served to play an even more important role during the Cold War by offering an alternative, nonviolent mode of American expansion through cultural exportation, specifically in the stage musical and subsequent film *The King and I* (1951, 1956). As Christina Klein explains, "*The King and I* ... offers an exemplary instance of the culture of integration: it imagines that Others, rather than being exterminated, could be modernized through an intimate embrace."[28] Klein goes on to show how *The King and I* maps almost directly onto cold war policies and rhetoric with regard to using culture as a means to form connections and modernize countries in Southeast Asia. The underlying assumption is that these interventions would keep those countries from becoming communist by instilling the American values of individual rights and freedoms.

*Pacific Overtures* works in almost an entirely contrary way. Although both musicals are about a real historical event in which Westerners went to East Asia to "modernize" a culture, they frame the story in completely different ways. Anna is welcomed, even invited by the king, and though the king resists change, the eventual acceptance of Western values is celebrated. In *Pacific Overtures*, the Westerners force themselves on an unwilling population, and the result is at best ambivalent. *Pacific Overtures* offers little room for celebration of Western ideals or redemption for its white characters. The theater historian Joanne Gordon has argued, "Despite all the best intentions of its creators, the preponderant impact of the drama is undoubtedly anti-imperialist, and consequently anti-West."[29] Gordon correctly identifies the final product as anti-imperialist and anti-West, but it is not despite all the best intentions of its creators but *because* of their intentions—not, perhaps, to be anti-West, but to reverse historical precedent and create an Occidentalist (as opposed to Orientalist) musical.

By trying to create a show seen from the Japanese point of view, the team behind *Pacific Overtures* evoked contemporary debates about issues of minority representation and the consequences of American imperialism while never directly engaging with the contemporary world. Instead, *Pacific Overtures* used a historical event to comment on contemporary politics. This technique, derived from Brecht, among others, proved to be a favorite of Prince's. He envisioned *Cabaret* (1964) as a commentary on the civil rights movement and contemporary race relations in the United States, *Sweeney Todd* (1979) as a scathing critique of neoliberal policies, and *Evita* (1979) as condemning celebrity culture. Employed most recently and successfully in Lin-Manuel Miranda's *Hamilton* (2015), this approach allows audiences to choose to engage with the contemporary political undertones of the show while also foregrounding the possible future implications of current policies by comparing them to a past with known outcomes. It also allows for a show to potentially have a life after its contemporary moment, as most political issues and situations often resurface in different forms over time, whereas musicals too firmly rooted in the contemporary moment quickly lose their relevance and become difficult to revive.[30] *Pacific Overtures* contained a nuanced explanation and critique of American imperialist actions in East Asia in the distant and, by association, recent past.

The creators intended *Pacific Overtures* to be an inversion, a reversal of viewpoints, where the audience viewed Americans from a Japanese point of view rather than, for example, viewing Siam from Anna's point of view or the Pacific Islands from the view of American GIs.[31] Sondheim, Prince, and Weidman desired to create a more "authentic" Asian musical. In order to do this, they created a convoluted framing in which a hypothetical Japanese playwright creates a Japanese version of an American musical.[32] Although they desired to create a show that went beyond *The King and I* or *South Pacific* in its sympathetic and authentic portrayal of Southeast Asia and Asians, the creators never considered their whiteness as a fundamental impediment to achieving this goal.

## Sondheim's "Japanese" Experience

Sondheim's collaboration with and deference to the expertise of Weidman proved essential for a successful musical and lyrical contribution; as Weidman jokingly remarked, "A thing Steve doesn't do is research."[33] When discussing the show with Mark Eden Horowitz, Sondheim revealed the extent to which he had been influenced by negative representations of Asians in the media and the need for Weidman's assistance in correcting his assumptions. He explained the horrible racial stereotypes to which he was exposed: "I was brought up on movies, so I thought the Japanese were a lot of little people with buck teeth and glasses who tortured Americans. It was Weidman—being a sinophile, and having written this play—who introduced me, in that sense, to Japanese culture."[34] Before working on this project, Sondheim had little awareness of East Asian culture or interest in representations of Asians, as his misuse of the term "sinophile," which refers to one who is interested in Chinese culture, not Japanese culture, suggests. Weidman provided Sondheim with a few books, specifically Ernest W. Clement's *A Handbook of Modern Japan,* a turn-of-the-century book written from a Western point of view, and Japanese journalist Mock Joya's *Things Japanese* (1964), both easily digestible sources of information about the history and culture of Japan.[35]

In addition to Weidman's recommendations, Sondheim began his own studies in Japanese kabuki music. He relied primarily on a booklet from a three-LP set of Japanese music, the exact title of which is now lost.[36] Though he wanted to create an authentic Japanese score, Sondheim's notion of authenticity deviated from contemporary scholarly and cultural definitions. He notes,

> [The music of *Pacific Overtures*] *feels* like the music belongs in that show, that milieu, in that country. . . . That's my idea of authenticity. I think authenticity is useless otherwise . . . it doesn't matter whether it's true or not, it suggests something exotic—in the real sense of the word.[37]

Sondheim's statement indicates an attitude diagnosed by Edward Said as "Orientalism"—"suggests something exotic" implies an object for white audiences to consume rather than a culture to understand. This explanation for his less-than-authentic music demonstrates both the impossibility of Sondheim's being able to compose in a different musical language and that complete musical authenticity was never his desire or intent.[38] Sondheim became interested in creating a sonic atmosphere that would take the Broadway audience on a journey from a closed Japan to an open one. He explained, "As the score progresses, the language becomes more Western—as does the music—after the invasion."[39] Sondheim never claimed nor desired to be an expert on Japanese music, but rather, wanted to create a score that, he felt, fit the narrative of the drama appropriate for the Broadway stage.

Sondheim and Prince traveled to Japan, where they attended a variety of traditional Japanese theatrical productions. Ultimately, Prince decided to accomplish the goal of creating a Japanese-influenced American musical by synthesizing the two cultures, using the Broadway stage and Western conventions while simultaneously employing select characteristics of kabuki theater. Kabuki, along with the puppet theater *bunraku*, formed the basis of popular Japanese theater during the Edo period (1693–1868). Kabuki remains the most popular traditional theatrical form in Japan today. There are some obvious reasons why Prince might have wanted to draw on this style for *Pacific Overtures*. First, kabuki would have been the main type of theater in Japan during Commodore Perry's expedition, drawing a connection between the then of kabuki and the now of Broadway. Second, it developed almost exclusively during the period of Japan's isolation, making it a uniquely Japanese art form. Mixing it with Broadway would create a synthesis of one Japanese art form and one American art form. Third, music and dance are integral parts of kabuki. Japanese theater critic Masakatsu Gunji observed, "All in all, it can be said that the *Kabuki* resembles the musical of the West in certain ways. In that respect, therefore, the role of music in *Kabuki* is quite . . . important."[40] To combine kabuki with Broadway, then, would be more practical and intuitive than other types of Asian, and in particular, Japanese theater.[41]

The creators integrated kabuki elements, but they were adamant that *Pacific Overtures* was not a kabuki show nor a Broadway production, but a synthesis of the two.[42] Instead, they utilized some of the more recognizable parts of the tradition, including the use of a Reciter, who narrates the story; a *hanamichi*, or runway that goes through the audience, providing space for dramatic entrances and exits; kabuki-style costumes and makeup; and choreography inspired by the art form. This included a dance at the end of Act I choreographed and performed by Haruki Fujimoto, a Japanese-born American who was trained primarily in modern dance but who had some experience in kabuki.[43] It is striking that Weidman and Prince decided early on to follow the kabuki tradition of casting men, in particular Asian and Asian American men, to play all of the roles. They worked with Fujimoto, who is credited in Playbill as "*kabuki* consultant."[44] Sondheim concluded at the time of the show's opening, "The main thing about [*Pacific Overtures*] is that it is so *deeply* Japanese, as opposed to, say *The King and I* or *Madama Butterfly* which are merely Western treatments of Eastern subjects."[45] How "deeply Japanese" the final production was remains up for debate, but the creators' intentions were clear.

## Stereotyping Whites

In order to see things through the eyes of the other, the creators often simply took techniques found in popular Orientalist works and turned them around. Though their announced purpose was to make a musical from a hypothetical Japanese playwright's perspective, this move also highlighted white popular artists' conventional racist practices. For example, Weidman and Sondheim's reversal of the other ended up critiquing typical Asian stereotypes by reversing linguistic expectations within the musical. Unlike previous Orientalist musicals, in which the Asian characters spoke in broken, exaggerated, or quaintly wrong English, it was the foreigners, the Americans and other ambassadors, who were caricatured by speaking poor English in *Pacific Overtures*. The score states that the white Americans should speak in "Pidgin English." Historically, different Asian immigrant groups in America used pidgin English to communicate and organize together because they did not speak the same language.[46] The idea to reverse stereotypical language norms was Weidman's: "One of Weidman's most inventive ideas: the Japanese would speak elegant, formalized King's English, whereas all the foreigners would speak a pidgin form of their native language."[47] Sondheim followed suit in his lyrics, writing simple, incomplete sentences for the Americans, stereotyping the other Westerners, and giving the Japanese characters the most complex language and ideas.

In the opening of Act II, "Please Hello," Sondheim supports Weidman's linguistic frame while simultaneously demonstrating his lyrical and compositional skills. The number depicts foreign emissaries from the United States, Great Britain, the Netherlands, Russia, and France using gunboat diplomacy to force treaties with Lord Abe, the first councilor to the shogun. All of the ambassadors are presented as stereotypes, and Sondheim added greatly to Weidman's linguistic idea by caricaturing each of the ambassadors through music. Sondheim also aimed for historical accuracy by writing lyrics that followed the historical events as much as possible, including having the ambassadors enter in the proper order and having them ask for ports in specific cities. For Sondheim, however, this number was more of a creative puzzle than a political statement—he wanted to show off his talent as a composer and lyricist within very specific and difficult constraints. While he did contribute overall to Weidman's political goals, he also created a brilliant, clever, and historically (if narrowly) accurate comic number.

Sondheim had already proved himself an expert in parody in *Follies*, and he approached this song similarly. For example, the English ambassador sings a patter song reminiscent of a Gilbert and Sullivan operetta; Sondheim aimed to better W. S. Gilbert, whose lyrics Sondheim has continually found wanting.[48] The British number begins, "Hello, I come with letters from her Majesty Victoria / Who, learning how you're trading now, sang 'Hallelujah, Gloria!'" in a quick tempo. The American envoy is accompanied by a Sousa-like brass band march, and his lyrics include broken English such as "Last time we visit, too short. / This time we visit for slow. / Last time we come, come with warships, / Now with more ships—say hello!" Besides the poor grammar, the lyrics emphasize America's glorification of military violence. The Dutch admiral, who sings to a clog dance, brings stereotypical gifts of tulips, chocolate, windmills, and of course, wooden shoes. While providing a comic opening to an otherwise depressing act, this number also opens the door to commentary about contemporary practices of writing minority characters in popular culture—only here the groups being stereotyped are various powerful white nations.[49]

## Questioning Japanese Progress

The addition of Sondheim to the creative team coincided with a new second act that extended the show in time past Perry's initial expedition, focusing on the immediate and long-lasting effects of Western influence and so-called progress in

Japan. This theme necessarily complicated audiences' and critics' trying to place the show into any neat political box. The production that eventually ended up on stage at the Winter Garden was far more politically complex than Weidman's original concept. It still critiqued American foreign policy and domestic racism, but the second half's focus on the effects of Perry's invasion showed both the good and the bad of progress. Prince explained,

> What I want to say clearly is not that there was intended villainy on our part, not that the Japanese were party to their own corruption, but that we all had better pay attention because we are savaging the quality of life and the sensibilities of people in the name of technology and progress.[50]

Prince, then, placed equal blame—or perhaps no blame—on Japan and the United States by questioning the very fundamental ideal of progress that the West had supposedly brought to Japan and that the Japanese had so wholeheartedly embraced. This statement reflects Prince's continued questioning of a changing cultural norm that would eventually be recognized as neoliberalism, and he would continue to question the price of economic and technological progress in his next work with Sondheim, *Sweeney Todd* (1979).[51]

Yet as neoliberalism began to creep in and dominate political and economic culture, many Americans worried that the Japanese had adopted the values of technology and progress *too* well, particularly as globalization and the economic power of East Asia started to become central to foreign policy. Economic concerns were at the forefront of relations between Japan and the United States in the 1970s. At this point, just three decades after its defeat in World War II, Japan was the second largest economy in the world, and the United States had run up a huge trade deficit with the country.[52] Beginning with steel in the 1960s, then transistor radios, textiles, and color televisions, Japanese exports began to dominate trade throughout East Asia and within the United States.[53] By the mid-1970s the trade deficit with Japan was about $1.5 billion and would balloon to $18 billion by 1980.[54] The generally good relationship between Japan and the United States during the postwar era was severely affected by this trade deficit, and most Americans (wrongly) blamed Japanese political and economic policies. According to the economist Louis Mulkern, "[It was] comforting (and, therefore, popular) to believe that the chronic U.S. trade deficit with Japan [was] the product of unfair Japanese trade practices, such as dumping, and of artificial protectionist barriers in the Japanese marketplace."[55] As suggested in the musical's final scene, however, it was the Japanese work ethic, community-focused culture, and the ability to import, improve, and streamline technological development and production derived from the West that led to their economic dominance.[56] In the monologue leading into the final number of *Pacific Overtures*, the emperor proclaims, "Each of us will strive toward one great goal—the building of a modern Japan which will, in the community of nations, take a place second to none. . . . And we will do it—sooner than you think."[57] By 1976 Japan had reached this goal, leading technological advances with the international ascendance of companies such as Sony, Mitsubishi, Honda, and Toshiba.

Contrary to economists, with their worries in regard to Japanese economic dominance, the creators of *Pacific Overtures* questioned the positive narratives concerning the rise of Japan, specifically the way Western capitalism privileges labor and the attainment of wealth over the well-being of individual lives and communities. In his first draft, Weidman painted a picture of a pre-capitalist society interested in honor and family more than wealth, and then framed the Americans as greedy. This can be seen in one exchange between the Americans and the Japanese:

PERRY: I am sure your countrymen are eager to trade with us.
HAYASHI: Excuse me, but I do not think they are. . . . The day may come when we are forced into commerce with other nations, but that day is not here yet.[58]

Perry assumes that the Japanese would want to expand their wealth through trade, and he cannot understand why they would prefer isolation, highlighting the Americans' lack of understanding of the culture they were invading.

This critique continued into the final musical production. Act II, scene 5, consists of an American showing a Japanese merchant his invention, the rickshaw.[59] In this scene, the American is trying to secure investment in his invention, and as he shows the merchant his rickshaw, old men who are pulling it keep getting tired and collapsing, to be quickly replaced by other old men. The American explains, "The motor's self-contained, requires very little mainte-nance—and can be easily replaced."[60] By including this scene (which has been cut in subsequent productions), the show makes sure to highlight the negative aspects of American innovation being brought to Japan.

Yet, as Prince proclaimed, *Pacific Overtures* does not exonerate Japan. The show concludes with the most pointed questioning of the current situation in the final number, titled "Next," which demonstrates the way the Japanese govern-ment, after being forced to open and trade with others, chose to enthusiastically embrace Western capitalism. Weidman explained that this number highlighted and praised but also critiqued what had happened in Japan: "'Next' is the perfect word for a song which deals with the apocalyptic effect of Western cultures, es-pecially contemporary Western cultures blasting open a serene, self-contained society."[61] The number summarizes Japan's assimilation and domination of Western culture in economic, cultural, and military terms.[62] It does not only highlight how Japan became a capitalist power and how that had affected the nation both negatively and positively, but also includes Weidman's original claim that Japanese involvement in World War II was indirectly related to the humiliation the United States made them feel in 1853.

"Next" provides a frame for understanding the mixing of cultures that occurred during and after the Meiji period (1868–1912, when Japan opened to the West) by showing American imperialism not as ruining a culture but changing one—in contrast to Weidman's original play, which focused only on the negatives. Spoken examples illustrating the position of modern Japan, both the positive and the negative, are interjected throughout the number: "Fifty-seven percent of the Bicentennial souvenirs sold in Washington, D.C. in 1975 were made in Japan"; "1975 Weather Bureau statistics report 162 days on which the air quality in Tokyo is acceptable."[63] The first example shows Japan's economic dominance; the second, the cost. While proclaiming both the gains and losses made, the aggressive, driving song with the incessant repetition of "Next" satisfies the Western audience's need for progress and spectacle, something denied by the use of Prince's interpretations of kabuki throughout the production. The number has the entire cast embodying the changes to Japanese culture, with a wide variety of colorful contemporary Western costumes. This song fills the stage with movement and choreography. The sound also fulfilled Broadway's expectations, as women were used for this scene, creating an ensemble sound more in line with that of American musicals.

The show's opening number, "The Advantages of Floating," which introduces Japan as it was before Western intrusion, provides a foil to the finale. The two numbers form bookends that, when analyzed against one another, highlight the perceived changes in Japanese culture from the mid-nineteenth century to 1976. Weidman described "The Advantages of Floating" as depicting "an extraordinary culture that was overwhelming in purity . . . that no longer exists in that way." The use of parallel lyrics between the numbers allows for a direct comparison of where Japan was at the beginning of the show and where it is now. Sondheim uses similar imagery in both numbers to describe what is happening but does so in very different ways. For example, "The Advantages of Floating in the Middle of the Sea" uses water, in this case the ocean, as an image of stability and serenity. Floating implies not traveling forward or backward but a moment of stasis. "Next" opens with the lines "Streams are flowing / see what's coming / Next!" Here, water connotes movement, the stream constantly moving forward toward a specific goal. Another example is this line in the opener: "Kings are burning somewhere / not here!," implying the intentional isolation of Japan. In "Next," the line reappears as "Kings are burning, / sift the ashes / Next!" Rather than ignoring the outside world, the new Japan will take advantage of political violence for its own economic benefit. Sondheim deliberately reverses the imagery of the opening number to reveal the new Japanese culture.

Sondheim goes beyond lyrically juxtaposing these two numbers; they are strikingly similar and different in musical terms. Both are extremely quick (on the original cast recording, "The Advantages of Floating" runs between 130 and 140 beats per minute, and "Next" between 150 and 160 b.p.m.). However, "Next" feels much faster because each line of music and text is extremely short, between eight and twelve beats, before abruptly cutting off the phrase with silence. "The Advantages of Floating" uses much longer phrases, often between twenty and forty beats, before cadencing. Furthermore, the use of repetitive rhythmic figures and extremely slow harmonic movement makes "Floating" feel appreciably slower than "Next," as if the listener really is floating on top of the ostinato accompaniment. "Next" is frantic: short phrases ending with a rhythmically complicated accompaniment that includes different, almost independent instrumental lines creating cacophony, unlike the complex but carefully crafted counterpoint at the end of "The Advantages of Floating." Finally, each melodic line ascends to punctuate the shout of "Next!," as opposed to the typical descent toward a cadence in the opener. The extreme musical contrasts between the musical's opening and closing numbers emphasize on several levels the journey that the Japan of *Pacific Overtures* goes through over the course of the show. But the overwhelming, exhausting nature of "Next" could possibly leave one yearning simply to float.

Though artistically brilliant, these two numbers, "The Advantages of Floating" and "Next," exemplify an underlying limitation of *Pacific Overtures*. These white American creators can never fully leave their own subject positions as Westerners and, therefore, continue to bifurcate notions of East and West. They portray the East before the Meiji period as "serene" and "unchanging," when, as historians have demonstrated, societal changes were taking place during the Edo period, even as the country practiced severe isolationism.[64] Although the West is somewhat equally stereotyped in "Next," both the creators and the intended audience were Westerners, so the essentializing of Western culture held less power than did their portrayal of Japanese culture. They intended to reverse the problems of Orientalism, but the story being told was still one about the influence of Western culture *on* Japan, not about Japan itself.

## Asian American Reactions

Representations of Asians and Asian Americans in the media had become a central issue to the Asian American activist community by the 1970s.[65] In 1974, Asian Americans for a Fair Media published "Asian Images: A Message to the Media," a handbook "intended as a basic primer for all members of the media."[66] *Bridge: The Asian-American Magazine* published the handbook in its entirety

in its April 1974 issue. The handbook begins with a brief history of discrimination against Asians and Asian American in the United States starting in 1848 and
includes a timeline of major events. Beginning with children's books and songs,
the article details how the education system, advertising, and all media inun-
date Americans with negative stereotypes of Asians. The history of Asia and the
contributions of Asian Americans in the United States formed an entire section
of the handbook in order to educate white America about the history of Asia and
Asian America, an impulse that Weidman shared in writing *Pacific Overtures*.
Prince and Weidman were similarly responding to what they saw as problematic
depictions of Asians in the media.

One specific request in the handbook was for white writers to create Asian
characters who were more than stereotypes. Prince tried to take this a step further in *Pacific Overtures*. Desiring to do something new and more "authentic,"
Prince decided to center the Asian—specifically the Japanese—experience, and
by doing so, stereotyped the white characters instead. Perhaps more important,
his vision also included an all-Asian American cast, something that proved surprisingly difficult to achieve.[67]

Two years after *Pacific Overtures* received its premiere on Broadway,
Edward Said published his landmark study *Orientalism*, which discussed the
ways in which the "Orient" was primarily a product of the Western coloni-
alist imagination. His book questioned the ability of Westerners ever to create
representations of the other that had any sort of authentic validity outside
their own ethnocentric understandings. While Said never mentions musicals
explicitly, he pays considerable attention to the way cultural artefacts participate in the creation of the "Orient."[68] His ideas question the entire conceit of
*Pacific Overtures*, requiring a recentering of the discussion of the musical from
questions about Japanese culture to Weidman's, Prince's, and Sondheim's conception of the West.

To look through this window means to examine how and why Prince and
Weidman sought and understood the notion of authenticity. As W. Anthony
Sheppard poignantly inquired, "Were Sondheim and Prince attempting to express political solidarity with Asian and Asian American actors by avoiding
yellowface performance in this casting? Or were they motivated by a peculiar ideal of 'authenticity?'"[69] Clearly, their quest for authenticity inadvertently
resulted in their creating a work that happened to express solidarity with the
Asian American movement. Ultimately, their show spoke more to American
critiques of foreign intervention and to Asian American complaints concerning
representation than it did to kabuki or Japanese culture. While the abandonment
and critique of yellowface inherent in the show is commendable for its political
stance and the real, material opportunities it offered (and continues to offer)
Asian American actors, the show did little to alter the hegemony of white men in

the higher levels of the Broadway hierarchy, perpetuating the notion that Asian stories can be told by white men (if they do enough research).

One other unforeseen problem with Prince's vision was that it inadvertently reinforced problematic notions about Asians in the United States and erased the voices of Asian Americans from the stage. By writing a show about Japan seen through a "Japanese" lens, these white men were still marking the Asian body as foreign, even as most of the actors were Asian American. Their conceit ends up reflecting Asian American theater historian Karen Shimakawa's criticism of mainstream representations of Asianness: "To the degree Asian Americans are abjected in representation, they are frequently conflated with Asian foreigners. . . .as 'ordinary' Americans, Asian Americans are often simply incomprehensible or invisible."[70] The creators were attempting to write a show from an Asian point of view, but not from an Asian American point of view, even as they worked with American citizens and permanent residents of Asian descent throughout the project. Though Weidman and Prince tried to write a politically progressive show, they undermined their project by continuing to frame Asian American performers as other, as foreigners, and giving them little room to be considered part of the national psyche. *Pacific Overtures* remains a story of the other, despite the intentions of its creators, highlighting the need for space for Asian Americans to be able to tell their own stories.

That being said, both the Asian American community at large and the Japanese American community specifically responded positively to *Pacific Overtures* and found it to be an important breakthrough for Asian representation on the over-whelmingly white Broadway stage. On September 26, 1976, the Pacific/Asian-American Coalition of New York gave "The Producers and Cast of 'Pacific Overtures'" an award for "improving the image of Asian-American performing arts."[71] While the Asian American community focused primarily on the cast of the show, Prince also received some praise for his decision to mount a show with an all-Asian cast. In the review in the New York–based Asian American magazine *Bridge*, David Oyama wrote, "One must respect [Prince's] courage in putting this show together and breaking new ground." Oyama believed that *Pacific Overtures* provided an opportunity to demonstrate that Asian American actors "can carry a Broadway show alone—and in fine style."[72] Inclusion on the Broadway stage proved to be of primary importance for him.

Oyama did not praise Prince, Weidman, and Sondheim's endeavor unequiv-ocally. He continued, "Since I will have some uncomplimentary things to say about his production as well, one might as well give credit first where credit is due."[73] Oyama complained that although the show purports to be derived from kabuki and *noh*, it is still clearly a product of Broadway and the Western gaze. He wished that Sondheim and Prince "had only gone all the way and gotten more Asian or Asian American input into the writing and directing of the show as well as into the acting."[74] Oyama understood the necessity of having big names in the creative team for such a risky show, but he believed that rather than leaning on Weidman, a white "expert" on Japan, they should have gone one step further and collaborated with someone who was actually Japanese. They did consult, but consultation does not imply an equality of creative input that collaboration does. Perhaps if they had chosen a Japanese co-director, the show might have come closer to achieving their goal of authenticity through hybridity.

In the end, the interplay and support between *Pacific Overtures* and the Asian American theater community continues to have a lasting impact on Asian and Asian American representation in the theater. The review of the show in *Bridge* contains a post-script:

> Here in New York, one of the most considerable benefits of 'Pacific Overtures' [sic] run on Broadway has been the new interest and sense of possibility it has stirred among young Asian Americans headed for a career in the theater—whether in acting, writing, directing, or designing. Things seem to be happening. Mako [the actor who created the role of the Reciter] himself is conducting a workshop for beginning actors . . . at the Basement Workshop.[75]

Mako, with this workshop and with East West Players (which later produced a more critically successful run of *Pacific Overtures*), used the opportunity created by Weidman and Prince to break the cycle of underrepresentation of Asians in the media. He worked to train more Asian and Asian American artists, especially actors and to give them opportunities to learn the skills to step into the Broadway roles that Prince and Sondheim had provided.

*Pacific Overtures* is still one of the best opportunities for actors of Asian descent, as diversity continues to be a struggle in stories and casting on the Broadway and Off-Broadway stages. Forty years later, Jay Kuo's *Allegiance* (2015) became the first (and so far only) Broadway show with an all-Asian American creative team. George Takei, on whose childhood *Allegiance* was based, starred in the show, and he followed that role with the Classic Stage Company's Off-Broadway revival of *Pacific Overtures*, playing the Reciter. *Allegiance*'s second run was with the East West Players in the spring of 2018, also following the path of *Pacific Overtures*.

Even more in line with *Pacific Overtures* is David Henry Hwang and Jeanine Tesori's *Soft Power*, which opened in Los Angeles in 2018 and transferred to the Public in New York in September 2019. Like *Pacific Overtures*, Hwang viewed the show as a response to *The King and I*, specifically the 2015 revival at Lincoln Center.[76] As Arnab Banjeri noted in *Studies in Musical Theatre*, "[Hwang] puts a mirror in front of all Americans inviting them to evaluate themselves as imagined elsewhere," exactly what Weidman, Prince, and Sondheim were attempting to do in 1976.[77] Hwang's subject position, as a Chinese American, gives him an advantage over the white creators of *Pacific Overtures*, yet whether the production will be a financial success or have a broader impact has yet to be determined. Yet the work that *Pacific Overtures* did in the post-Vietnam period to make a space for Asian and Asian American stories and their actors in American musical theater eventually opened the door for Hwang's production, which will, ideally, spur better and more diverse stories about Asia and Asian America on the Broadway stage.

## Appendix: Archival Sources for the Original 1976 Production of *Pacific Overtures*

This appendix lists the surviving scripts for *Pacific Overtures* used in this chapter. The ones that I primarily consulted are listed first, with alternative copies in other archives listed second in parentheses.

**October 22, 1973 (Mislabeled February 1975):** "Untitled Play About the Opening of Japan (Second Draft)."

Harry Ransom Center at the University of Texas, Austin, Boris Aronson Papers, Box 4, Folder 2.

(New York Public Library for the Performing Arts, Billy Rose Theatre Collection, Script RM 2642.)

A straight play in three acts. This version does not contain lyrics for any musical numbers, though incidental music is sometimes indicated. The play concerns the story up to Perry's original exit from Japan (the end of Act I in the final production), and writes the story with Kayama as a hero, risking his life to keep Perry from shooting his cannons and scaring the Japanese.

The script contains two pages of typed notes from Prince to Weidman about how to improve the show. There is no mention of a musical.

**May 23, 1975:** *Pacific Overtures*, Music and Lyrics by Stephen Sondheim, book by John Weidman and Harold Prince.

Harry Ransom Center at the University of Texas, Austin, Boris Aronson Papers, Box 4, Folder 3.

(New York Public Library for the Performing Arts, Billy Rose Theatre Collection, Ruth Mitchell Papers, Box 17, Folder 3.)

This script documents the beginning of Sondheim's involvement with the show; the first two songs are present with lyrics, and a few other indicated numbers are scattered throughout the first act, but not the second act. The second act, however, more closely resembles the version in the final production, though it still contains a minstrel show. The show also continues to alternate between the American and Japanese points of view.

The first page of the script reads: "All the roles in <u>Pacific Overtures</u> will be played by Asians. The female roles, with the exception of Kayama's wife (the liberated woman), will be played by male members of the company."

The script has extensive edits in pen, probably by Prince, who is listed in this version as the book's co-author.

**August 7, 1975:** *Pacific Overtures*, Music and Lyrics by Stephen Sondheim, book by John Weidman and Harold Prince.

Harry Ransom Center at the University of Texas, Austin, Boris Aronson Papers, Box 4, Folder 4.

Act 1 of this script resembles the final version, but the second act still contains large deviances. The minstrel show has disappeared, and the Americans are no longer given private conversations, but the numbers "Pretty Lady," "Bowler Hat," and "Next" are still absent.

In the place of "Next" are two loose endings, one titled "Last Section (mélange)" that lists the scenes in a montage bringing the show up to the present, accompanied by "Civilization Song." The second section is a scripted realization of this list.

The script still opens with the note "All the roles in <u>Pacific Overtures</u> will be played by Asians. The female roles, with the exception of Kayama's wife (the liberated woman), will be played by male members of the company."

**September 29, 1975:** *Pacific Overtures*, Music and Lyrics by Stephen Sondheim, book by John Weidman.

Harry Ransom Center at the University of Texas, Austin, Boris Aronson Papers, Box 4, Folder 5.

(New York Public Library for the Performing Arts, Billy Rose Theatre Collection, Script RM 2603.)

This copy, though bound, still contains an incomplete Act II, with the appearance of a description of "Bowler Hat" but no "Pretty Lady." "Civilization Song" continues with the "mélange" in place of "Next." The copy is generally clean, with a handful of light pencil markings.

The first page is changed: "All the roles in <u>Pacific Overtures</u> will be played by Asians. The female roles will be played by male members of the company, until the 'mélange' sequence at the end when female roles will be assumed by actresses."

Harold Prince's name is removed as book co-author.

**January 11, 1976** (Opening night): "Final Playing Version"

New York Public Library for the Performing Arts, Billy Rose Theatre Collection, Script RM 2429.

(New York Public Library for the Performing Arts, Billy Rose Theatre Collection, Ruth Mitchell Papers, Box 17, Folder 4 [clean copy], Folder 5 [with stage manager cues].)

This script reflects the 1976 production, yet it contains handwritten stage directions from Prince and extensive edits in pencil, pen, and whiteout, with sections glued in. This was probably the version to be retyped for the final version; a clean, final version is available in the Ruth Mitchell Papers (see above).

# Notes

1. Special thanks go to the Music Department and American Culture Studies Program at Washington University in St. Louis, which provided the funds to do research in New York, and to Laurie B. Green at the University of Texas, Austin, in whose class I first began this project in 2012. Thank you to everyone at the Harry Ransom Center and New York Public Library for the Performing Arts. Large parts of this chapter are derived from my dissertation, a work indebted to Todd Decker. Thanks to Tony Sheppard for his expert input and keen eye. My understandings of Asian Americanness would not be where they are without the help of James McMaster and Donatella Galella. Finally, immense gratitude goes to John Weidman for taking the time to answer my pointed, obtrusive, and probably repetitive questions.

   Thomas P. Adler, "The Sung and the Said," in *Reading Stephen Sondheim: A Collection of Critical Essays*, ed. Sandor Goodhart (New York: Garland, 2000), 40.
2. I thank Elizabeth Wollman for bringing *The Lieutenant* to my attention and sharing it with me in her paper. Elizabeth Wollman, "Historiography and the Importance of Flops: The Case of *The Lieutenant*," at our panel at the Society for American Music conference in New Orleans, LA, March 2019.
3. John Weidman, interview by author, Zoom, May 10, 2020. News of the war was ubiquitous throughout the writing of *Pacific Overtures*. The fall of Saigon occurred on April 29, 1975, and *Pacific Overtures* opened on January 11, 1976.
4. Weidman interview. Meryle Secrest quotes Sondheim declaring that he "couldn't have been less interested in politics or in this kind of theatre [kabuki]." Meryle Secrest, *Stephen Sondheim: A Life* (New York: Knopf, distributed by Random House, 1998), 280.
5. Weidman interview.
6. Stephen Sondheim, "A Response from the Writer," *New York Times*, March 29, 2020.
7. *Company* is another show that began with Prince and the bookwriter, George Furth. Sondheim, however, was deeply involved in their initial work, as he was the one to send Furth's original manuscript to Prince. He was still interested in the material, even if it was not yet a musical. (On this topic, see Andrew Buchman's contribution in this volume.) This differs from *Pacific Overtures*; Sondheim did not know of the project's existence until approached by Prince far later in its development.
8. Weidman interview.
9. Ibid.
10. Ibid.
11. Ibid. The original play is available at Boris Aronson Scene Design Papers, Box 4, Folder 2, Harry Ransom Center, University of Texas, Austin (hereafter BASD).
12. Although the folder itself is labeled February 1975, the notes from Prince at the end of the script are labeled October 22, 1973. This earlier date makes more sense because this script is drastically different from the final project. The date on the folder most likely comes from the date when Aronson received the script.
13. Secrest, *Sondheim: A Life*, 279.
14. *Pacific Overtures*, Script by John Weidman, February 1975, BASD.
15. Ibid.

16. Notes on the draft from Harold Prince to John Weidman, in ibid.

17. Ibid., Act II, p. 47.

18. Ibid., Act II, p. 33.

19. Ibid., Act III, p. 36.

20. John Weidman and Stephen Sondheim, *Pacific Overtures* (New York: Dodd, Mead, 1977), 133.

21. *Pacific Overtures*, Script by John Weidman, February 1975, Act III, p. 16, BASD.

22. This is still often the case. See Donatella Galella, "Feeling Yellow: Responding to Contemporary Yellow Face in Musical Performance," *Journal of Dramatic Theory and Criticism* 32, no. 2 (Spring 2018): 66–77.

23. Weidman interview.

24. Claude Conyers, *Grove Music Online*, "Cakewalk," accessed February 27, 2019, http://www.oxfordmusiconline.com/grovemusic/view/10.1093/gmo/9781561592 630.001.0001/omo-9781561592630-e-1002092374.

25. Weidman interview.

26. *Pacific Overtures,* Script by John Weidman, May 1975, BASD.

27. The original Broadway production also included three Japanese musicians improvising on instruments such as the shamisen and nohkan. While there are a few cues in the introduction for the shamisen, this straightforward Japanese addition to the score was actually an innovation by Prince, not Sondheim, who hired the musicians. If one watches the original production, available on YouTube, these musicians are mostly used for underscoring during book scenes rather than integrated into the soundscape of the musical numbers.

28. Christina Klein, *Cold War Orientalism: Asia in the Middlebrow Imagination, 1945–1961* (Berkeley: University of California Press, 2017), 193–194.

29. Joanne Gordon, *Art Isn't Easy: The Achievement of Stephen Sondheim* (Carbondale: Southern Illinois University Press, 1990), 177.

30. Political shows that are contemporary often suffer from being too much "of their time" and feel obsolete after that specific political moment has passed, even if they are extremely popular during their initial runs. Examples include *Of Thee I Sing, Jelly's Last Jam*, and *Hair* (though significant revisions have allowed for that show to become about nostalgia rather than politics).

31. Secrest, *Sondheim: A Life*, 280.

32. J. Gordon, *Art Isn't Easy*, 174.

33. Weidman interview.

34. Mark Eden Horowitz, *Sondheim on Music: Minor Details and Major Decisions* (Lanham, MD: Scarecrow, 2003), 156.

35. Weidman, interview. I thank Weidman for providing me with photos of the exact copies used by Sondheim.

36. Horowitz, *Sondheim on Music*, 161–162.

37. Ibid.

38. W. Anthony Sheppard notes that this approach to Japanese authenticity had already been adopted by Hollywood in the 1950s and 1960s. W. Anthony Sheppard, *Extreme Exoticism: Japan in the American Musical Imagination* (New York: Oxford University Press, 2019), 246–257.

39. Craig Zadan, *Sondheim & Co.*, 2nd ed. (New York: Harper & Row, 1986), 212.

40. Masakatsu Gunji, *The Kabuki Guide*, trans. Christopher Holmes (Tokyo: Kodansha International, 1987), 57.

41. The show also includes a moment influenced by bunraku: a brief puppet show used to illustrate how the young emperor is a puppet of the Shogunate. At some point, they had planned to use a puppet show to depict the history of U.S.–Japan relations from the Meiji era to 1976.

42. J. Gordon, *Art Isn't Easy*, 176.

43. Sheppard, *Extreme Exoticism*, 373.

44. Playbill for the original production of *Pacific Overtures*, MWEZ + n.c. 27,575, Billy Rose Theatre Division, New York Public Library for the Performing Arts.

45. Zadan, *Sondheim & Co.*, 215.

46. Ronald Takaki, *Strangers from a Different Shore: A History of Asian Americans* (Boston: Little, Brown, 1998), 473.

47. Stephen Sondheim, *Finishing the Hat: Collected Lyrics (1954–1981) with Attendant Comments, Principles, Heresies, Grudges, Whines and Anecdotes* (New York: Knopf, 2010), 327.

48. Ibid., 324.

49. For more on this topic, see Todd Decker's contribution to this volume.

50. "A New Musical Brings Japan to Broadway," *Cue*, January 10, 1976.

51. For more, see Ashley M. Pribyl, "Sociocultural and Collaborative Antagonism in the Harold Prince–Stephen Sondheim Musicals (1970–1979)" (PhD diss., Washington University in St. Louis, 2019), 48–58.

52. Louis J. Mulkern, "U.S.–Japan Trade Relations: Economic and Strategic Implications," in *U.S.–Japan Economic Relations: A Symposium on Critical Issues*, ed. Thomas C. Smith (Berkeley: Institute of East Asian Studies, University of California Press, 1980), 23; Keiske Yawata, "Japanese Quality: How It Was Built and Maintained," in ibid., 35.

53. Mulkern, "U.S.–Japan Trade Relations," 28.

54. Federal Reserve Bank of San Francisco, "U.S.–Japan Trade," *FRB SF Weekly*, April 8, 1983, 2.

55. Mulkern, "U.S.–Japan Trade Relations," 24.

56. Ibid., 25.

57. *Pacific Overtures*, August 1975, Box 4, Folder BASD.

58. *Pacific Overtures*, Script by John Weidman, February 1975, Act III, p. 4, BASD.

59. *Pacific Overtures*, Script by John Weidman and Stephen Sondheim, May 1975, BASD.

60. Weidman and Sondheim, *Pacific Overtures*, 120.

61. Sondheim, *Finishing the Hat*, 329.

62. J. Gordon, *Art Isn't Easy*, 201.

63. Weidman and Sondheim, *Pacific Overtures*, 136–137. Also, these statements are usually updated with each revival.

64. This is not to say that "Floating" does not critique this way of being nor the problems of Edo Japan, including rampant inequality between genders and classes.

65. "Asian American" is a term generated by activists in the 1960s and 1970s as a way of bringing together multiple, disparate cultures for political influence. Most Asian

Americans still primarily identify with their ethnic, rather than racial, origin. Here, I discuss both this political and identity bloc and then, separately, Japanese Americans, who are included in the term but not synonymous with it. For more, see Daryl J. Maeda, *Chains of Babylon: The Rise of the Asian American Movement* (Minneapolis: University of Minnesota Press, 2009).

66. Asian Americans for a Fair Media, "Asian Images: A Message to the Media," *Bridge: The Asian-American Magazine* 3, no. 2 (April 1974): 25–30. I was unable to find the exact details of publication and dissemination of the original pamphlet that was republished in *Bridge*.

67. Ibid. In the end, Prince did use an entirely Asian but not necessarily Asian American cast, which caused a conflict between Equity and U.S. Immigration. For more, see Pribyl, "Sociocultural and Collaborative Antagonism," 78–79.

68. Edward Said, *Orientalism* (New York: Pantheon, 1978).

69. W. Anthony Sheppard, *Extreme Exoticism: Japan in the American Musical Imagination* (New York: Oxford University Press, 2019), 378.

70. Karen Shimakawa, *National Abjection: The Asian American Body on Stage* (Durham: Duke University Press, 2002), 17.

71. Plaque from the Pacific/Asian-American Coalition of New York, Harold Prince Papers, Box 164, Folder 10, Billy Rose Theatre Division, New York Public Library for the Performing Arts.

72. David Oyama, "Pacific Overtures," *Bridge: An Asian American Perspective* 4, no. 3 (July 1976): 46.

73. Ibid.

74. Ibid., 47.

75. Ibid., 47.

76. Arnab Banerji, "*Soft Power*: Hwang and Tesori's Reappropriation of *The King and I* in Representing Twenty-First-Century Diplomacy and the Dystopic Reality of Contemporary America," *Studies in Musical Theatre* 13, no. 3 (2019): 270.

77. Ibid., 275.

# 7

# Sexual Identity in *Company*, 1969–2019

*Andrew Buchman*

Have recent directors been right to follow Stephen Banfield's lead and "decline the scriptural authority of *Company's* original production"?[1] Will Robert's closeted sexual identity, so unsatisfying to many in our time, become a long-term liability?[2] In particular, is the finale too inconclusive for a less closeted era? Recall that Sondheim wrote four different musical endings for the show: "Marry Me a Little," "Multitudes of Amys," "Happily Ever After," and "Being Alive."[3]

This essay argues that the modernist ambiguities in the 1970 script were deliberate and might, over time, make the work more viable, not less, with the proviso that varying definitions of the protagonist's sexual identity have now become a firm part of the show's reception history.[4] Bobbie/Bobby's sexual identity could remain a mystery, like their occupation, in line with the ambiguous ending. Perhaps the work's twentieth-century modernisms will be more important to its survival onstage in the long run than its potential to be realigned with the history of the pursuit of gay rights among contemporary works, including the preceding Caffe Cino scene, *The Boys in the Band* (1967), and successors such as *The Faggot* (1973) and *Let My People Come* (1974).[5]

George Furth's unpublished notes on early story conferences reveal new angles on these issues without resolving them. It may be best to begin with the issue of the "concept," associated generally with the idea of abandoning a clear, coherent, conventional narrative arc. Banfield places *Company* along a line from *Tales of Hoffman* (1880) to *As Thousands Cheer* (1933), *Allegro* (1947), *Love Life* (1948), and other episodic narratives united by themes.[6] Some writers view director-producer Hal Prince as the innovative champion of the concept musical. Prince's *Fiddler on the Roof* (1964) focused on tradition, and *Company* focused on marriage. Certainly, Prince was the producer who paid the bills, with an auspicious record at the time of a string of commercial successes. These factors doubtless gave his opinions additional practical weight.

Furth's detailed notes and other contemporary documents strongly suggest that it was Sondheim who played a central part from the outset, in February 1969, in pushing the work toward becoming a nonlinear revue unified by common characters and thematic subject matter rather than a conventional narrative. The records discussed in this chapter establish that Sondheim contributed decisively

Andrew Buchman, *Sexual Identity in* Company, *1969–2019* In: *Sondheim in Our Time and His.*
Edited by: W. Anthony Sheppard, Oxford University Press. © Oxford University Press 2022.
DOI: 10.1093/oso/9780197603192.003.0008

to four crucial dramaturgical decisions in 1969 and 1970: the subject (or "concept") of the show, the avoidance of conventional narrative within the schematic plot, how the show began and ended, and Robert's ambiguous sexual identity.

The archives also detail Furth's contributions. He began his series of one-acts with the idea of building them into a sympathetic portrait of a single woman in middle age, to be played by Kim Stanley (1925–2001), who was forty-two at the time. He turned to an explicitly autobiographical rewrite of the scripts after connecting with Prince and Sondheim. Surprisingly, Furth also suggested that most of the cast should play musical instruments, although this suggestion was abandoned until John Doyle realized a new version of the idea for a 2006 revival (see figure 7.1). Although Sondheim, among others, has attributed the idea to Doyle, the May 1969 duplicated draft of the script included the prefatory note, "Wherever possible, every member of the company should play a musical instrument."[7] Thus, one of Doyle's independently devised directorial innovations was an echo of an early idea for *Company* vetted by Sondheim and Prince and executed by Furth, then withdrawn before rehearsals began.[8]

Documentary evidence in Furth's hand points to commitment, not marriage, as the theme of choice for both Furth and Sondheim. It was Prince who repeatedly invoked marriage, argued for its explicit inclusion in the plot, and even suggested that the topic begin and possibly end the show. Prince also appears to have problematized a gay subtext presented in one of Furth's early one-acts, persuading Furth and Sondheim that Bobby should not be "homosexual."[9] There is

**Figure 7.1.** Raúl Esparza (in background, atop a side table) as Bobby and Angel Desai (in foreground, holding a violin) as Marta in the 2007 Circle in the Square production of *Company* directed by John Doyle, performing "What Would We Do Without You?" Screenshot from *Company: A Musical Comedy* (Chatsworth, California: Image, 2007), DVD, at 1:21:00.

no record of the trio openly discussing the contemporary Stonewall riots of June 1969 or the popularity of *The Boys in the Band*, which was in the middle of a run of 1,001 performances Off-Broadway, although it is probable that the play did have a role in the genesis of *Company* as a model to avoid, as we will see.

The show is not plotless, as is sometimes claimed. "*Company* does have a story," wrote Sondheim, "the story of what happens inside Robert; it just doesn't have a chronological linear plot."[10] Evidence about Robert's character and state of mind accumulates as the evening progresses. Finally, circumstances, experiences, and his friends' urging bring him to the verge of a major decision: to set out on a conscious quest for a partner.

If director Harold Prince had had his choice, the show might, indeed, have ended with a wedding. In 1969 Sondheim resisted Prince's proposal that Robert pronounce his desire to marry in the opening scene, which would have given the show a far more accessible and conventional storyline from the get-go. Betwixt and between his two new partners, Furth drafted a version incorporating Prince's suggestion, but the idea was abandoned before the musical reached the stage. In contrast, after struggling to make a draft scene portraying Robert's bisexuality work, both Furth and Sondheim eventually consented to Prince's announced decision in February 1969 concerning Robert's sexual preference. Furth's version of either the trio's consensus or possibly Prince's words (the attribution is unclear) was to identify Robert as heterosexual.[11]

Evidently withdrawing his suggestion in late May 1969 that Robert announce his nuptial intentions in Act I, scene 1, Prince next proposed a more ambivalent Robert whose marital motives might be complicated. At several points, Sondheim suggested that the central subject of the show be not marriage but "the problem of commitment."[12] The distinction is significant because in 1969 legal marriage was an exclusively heterosexual institution.[13]

Nevertheless, Sondheim (according to Furth's notes) liked Prince's subsequent idea that Robert might marry someone in need of a partner as an act of mercy, rather than making his own choice—an idea that was incorporated into a scene with Amy. Prince also suggested that Robert might make an unsuitable choice from among his potential partners, leading to resistance from his circle of married friends.[14] This comment may have been the basis for Sondheim's ensemble in Act II for the wives, "Poor Baby," during which they find not one but all of Robert's lovers unsuitable as life partners.

## A Brief Reception History

Times have changed, and so has *Company*. After a hiatus of twenty-five years when *Company* was largely absent from commercial stages, Sondheim and

Furth, then Sondheim alone (after Furth's death in 2008) agreed to a series of interpretive revisions of *Company* encompassing words, music, lyrics, and casting. The protagonist of *Company*, variously named Robert, Bobby, or (since 2018) Bobbie, underwent both overt and tacit regenderings in major revivals in New York or London in 1995, 2006, 2011, 2013, and 2018. Explaining these surgeries adequately requires a trip back even further in time to Furth's original suite of one-acts, presented by Sondheim to Prince for his opinion in the winter of 1969. Furth rewrote his draft script extensively during 1969, replacing most of the original material in the process.

While Furth was alive, the duo continued to judiciously revise the book for *Company*. This may seem an unusual practice for an established, even canonical work, but it is the norm for Sondheim, who has participated in (sometimes extensive) revisions to several of his shows, including *Company*'s near contemporary *Follies* (1971) and *Merrily We Roll Along* (1981), his second show with a book by Furth. The cut finale "Marry Me a Little" was added to Act I for a New York revival in 1995 at director Scott Ellis's suggestion. Another significant dramaturgical change occurred later that year for a 1995 London revival at director Sam Mendes's suggestion: new lines revealing that Robert had slept with men as well as women. Despite its delayed public appearance, the genesis of this scene (presumably the impetus for Prince's emphatic rejection of a same-sex sexual identity for Robert in February 1969) dates back to the earliest drafts of the script by Furth, *before* he began collaborating with Sondheim and Prince. Director John Doyle's innovatively staged 2006 Broadway revival did not contain any script changes of comparable magnitude, but the issue of Bobby's sexual identity was raised indirectly by casting an actor as Robert who revealed his bisexuality to a *New York Times* interviewer during the run-up to opening night.[15]

After Furth's death Sondheim became editor as well as dramaturge, approving further revisions to the book and revising his own lyrics as well. For a concert performance in 2011 by the New York Philharmonic the action, score, and dialogue were condensed and Robert was played winningly by Neil Patrick Harris, who came out publicly as gay via an interview in *People* magazine in 2006.[16] When Peter spoke the first new line added in 1995 to Act II, scene 3, "Robert, did you ever have a homosexual experience?" the audience erupted in warm, knowing laughter and applause. After the concert in April the cast reassembled for a nationally broadcast performance at the 2011 Tony awards hosted by Harris, who opened the show with the hilarious original number "It's Not Just for Gays Anymore."[17] Thus, it seems fair to describe Robert in this production as tacitly gay, an identity made evident via casting rather than any further narrative revisions. In June, a film of the concert version opened at theaters; this production is currently probably the best-known video version of the show (see figure 7.2).[18]

**Figure 7.2.** The 2011 version of Act II, scene 3. *L–r:* Neil Patrick Harris, Anika Noni Rose, Jill Paice, and Craig Bierko in the 2011 concert performance of *Company* accompanied by the New York Philharmonic. Screenshot from *Stephen Sondheim's Company with the New York Philharmonic* (Chatsworth, California: Image Entertainment, 2011), DVD, at 1:52:35.

Sondheim approved a 2013 Off-Broadway workshop production directed by John Tiffany in which Robert was openly gay and the part of Joanne was played by Alan Cumming. A West End production with a straight female protagonist named Bobbie among other gender switches, directed by Marianne Elliott, premiered in London in 2018 (starring Rosalie Craig as Bobbie) and transferred to Broadway in 2020. This production was in previews and due to open on Sondheim's ninetieth birthday, March 22 (starring Katrina Lenk), but had to close prematurely due to the COVID-19 pandemic.

Three published versions of the book now exist along with the four musical finales and other cut materials, some of which are detailed in table 7.1.[19] Musicologists as well as directors have proposed further revisions; in 1993 Banfield suggested that "all four [final] songs ought to be in the score."[20] When a production is under way Sondheim always has made supportive statements, but how he really feels about updating *Company* is a mystery. Making the show topical may sell tickets, but it also may undercut the high modernist ambiguities that, along with the gorgeous modern set by Boris Aronson and a fine cast, helped make the original version of the show so distinctive. The documents

**Table 7.1.** Scene synopses for early scene drafts related to *Company*

---

Preserved in two full scripts titled *A Husband, a Wife, a Friend*, each divided into two acts, with four scenes each (in Furth 16.17 and 17.2 [i.e., Box 16, Folder 17, and Box 17, Folder 2], Furth Papers, NYPL), and one incomplete script prepared for producers Philip Van Zandt and Philip Mandelker, with one new scene and five retained scenes, retitled *Company* (Furth 18.1; one orphan scene is filed by itself in Furth 18.3).

Script #1: *A Husband, a Wife, a Friend* (Furth 16.7)

ACT I

I.1 *(1) SARAH AND HARRY [**karate scene**]—A couple bicker in front of a friend, and the wife demonstrates her martial arts skills on her husband.

I.2 (2) BERTHA AND ART—On the eve of Thanksgiving Day, a wife discovers that her husband and his partner spend their days on the vice squad entrapping gay men and sex workers, and throws him out of the house.

I.3 **(3) PETER AND GEORGIA [**"bi" scene**]—Peter lusts after a series of women named but not shown including Lila, Patty, and Elsie, and discusses his first wife, Marianne, and his current wife, Georgia. He's turned down by his next-door neighbor, Madeline. Next, Peter propositions the friend who is temporarily staying with him, named John. (With some rewriting, this is the scene that was removed before the show opened, but restored in 1996 and subsequent productions, in which Robert reveals that he has had sex with men.)

I.4 (4) MA AND PA—Just in time, an older woman is finally officially married to the father of her three grown children by a priest before dying onstage.

ACT II

II.1 (5) CYNTHIA AND WILLIAM—The morning after a wealthy couple liven up their sex lives with an overnight guest, the guest is put in his place.

II.2 (6) LARAINE AND ALLEN—During tryouts in New Haven, a star drinks and tries to talk her agent into firing her lover, the leading man.

II.3 *(7) JENNY AND DAVID [**pot scene**]—A couple and a guest experiment with pot.

II.4 (8) DOROTHY AND LOU—A couple mark their twenty-fifth wedding anniversary by fighting.

Script #2: *A Husband, a Wife, a Friend* [Furth 17.2]

The second script, also titled *A Husband, a Wife, a Friend* (Furth 17.2), has a one-page scenario for a ninth scene at the end of Act II:

II.5 (9) SALLY AND TIM AND AGNES AND GILL—An older couple, Agnes and Gill, watch a younger couple dance passionately and exit, locked in an embrace. Agnes says, "They were right to get divorced."

Script #3: *Company* [Furth 18.1], Van Zandt/Mandelker script

No songs, extensive penciled-in revisions, 6 unnumbered scenes, no acts indicated. Early producers Van Zandt and Mandelker are listed on the title page. No date. Scenes include SARAH AND HARRY (**karate scene**), JENNY AND DAVID (**pot scene**), CYNTHIA AND WILLIAM (as above in scripts for *A Husband, a Wife, a Friend*, Furth 16.7 and 17.2), LARAINE AND ALLEN (as above), DOROTHY AND LOU (as above), and a new tenth scene:

**Table 7.1.** *Continued*

---

(10) CLEOLA AND JOHN—A wealthy couple with a new servant with the same name as the husband try to make one another jealous.

*Script Fragment:* Orphan scene [filed within Furth 18.3 as a separate manuscript], an eleventh scene:

(11) DIANE AND BARRY—A former model on the day her first husband moves out and her new husband moves in.

---

* With revisions, included in the 1970 published libretto.

** With substantial revisions, included in the 1996 published, revised libretto.

discussed next suggest that, for Sondheim and Furth, the central theme of *Company* might also have remained intentionally generalized and blurred, the narrative fragmented and modernistic. Furth, however, began revising the series of one-acts that became *Company* with a very specific idea: modeling the central character on himself.

## Genesis of the Script

On March 3, 1969, Furth wrote a letter to Kim Stanley, a Broadway star in the 1950s with many film and television credits as well.[21] She was seriously considering starring in an upcoming Broadway production of a series of one-acts he had written with the working title *A Husband, a Wife, a Friend.*[22] In the letter he apologetically explained that the planned production had fallen apart due to "a polite disaster," irreconcilable differences between the director, George Morrison, and the producers Philip Van Zandt and Philip Mandelker.[23] Furth went on to describe a new direction for his script in which the central character would be a man, not a woman, and announced that Prince had optioned the play and proposed a musical version with songs by Sondheim. He explained that as a result "I put me into all the plays," regendering the protagonist as a single man in his mid-thirties, "someone pretending not to be alone." Furth described the "interplay and excitement" he felt with his new creative collaborators.[24]

The play remained a work of fiction. But by replacing his female central character with a fictionalized portrait of a talented man with close friends approaching forty in singleness with some trepidation, Furth was writing about a subject he knew well, a good strategy for any fledgling writer. Furth's protagonist, as noted, began as a role intended for a straight woman approaching middle age. But the new 1969 version of the yet-to-be-named Bobby was modeled upon a closeted single gay man with many friends, Furth himself.[25] Furth had found not only a promising new direction for a foundering project but two indispensable collaborators to help him reshape his one-acts into a single script. The first was Sondheim (like Furth, single at the time), a trusted friend with whom he had worked on *Hot Spot*, a 1963 Broadway musical. The other was Prince, a married producer-director who had compiled an impressive track record of critically esteemed commercial successes, including, in the 1960s alone, *A Funny Thing Happened on the Way to the Forum* (with Sondheim, 1962), *She Loves Me* (1963), *Fiddler on the Roof* (1964), *Cabaret* (1966), and *Zorbá* (1968).

Furth repeated the word *commitment* as his subject repeatedly. Although he presented "married friends" as subsidiary characters, he did not mention marriage at all, let alone as a central concept, theme, or subject. The show was a product of a time that was revolutionary in its acceptance of sex without marriage, a time "when sex mattered in a whole new way" according to American Studies scholar Jane Gerhard.[26] In the late 1960s, many young people viewed "sexual pleasure as empowering, as helping men become more human, and as a route out of patriarchal repression of the body."[27] Gerhard was referring to the era in general, not musicals in particular, but her point underlines how differently the depictions of sexuality in *Company* would have been received by most audience members in 1970. In her nuanced discussion of the issue of how audiences perceived Bobby's sexuality during the initial run Ashley Pribyl articulated the "unspeakableness of the topic [of gay identity]" in 1970, but also the insider knowledge various contemporary critics and audience members brought to bear to infer readings of Bobby as gay.[28] Pribyl describes such conflicts between authorial intentions and audience expectations as a sociocultural species of collaborative creation if, as in the case of Company, it led to successive revisions designed for later generations of theatergoers.[29]

Furth took careful handwritten notes at his meetings with Prince and Sondheim beginning in February 1969 and sometimes even went to the trouble of typing them up. He titled his typed-up notes of the first two meetings "Chapter One / (The New Era of my one-acts) / 20 Feb 1969." The notes display a useful habit: designating who said what at the meeting with initials at the beginning of a paragraph. But it is important to qualify Furth's attributions. His notes were almost certainly largely paraphrases of ideas, not verbatim quotations. What he recorded may not be what was said, in other words, but what he thought he heard.

Furth summarized the gist of this first story conference in his own words at the outset. The story was to center on a "young man" who was "uninvolved," until "conflicts and problems . . . FORCE HIM" to choose otherwise. He cited the 1963 surrealist feature film *8 1/2*, directed and co-written by Federico Fellini, as a comparable work. Furth then began paraphrasing his co-workers. According to Furth, Prince said that the central character's decision not to have sex with a male friend in a portion of the manuscript was "workable," but Prince also said (or, possibly, all three collaborators agreed): "Should the man be a homosexual? No, we say." This thought is set off as a separate paragraph (although still under the initials "HP"); thus, the "we" could mean either the royal we (i.e., Prince alone) or that all three collaborators agreed on this point.[30]

Sondheim made comments regarding the piece's overall form and content: *fluidity* in form and *commitment* (not marriage) as the nonlinear subject or theme (or concept, although that was not Sondheim's preferred term in his discussion of the show in his collected lyrics).[31] Recalling Furth's letter to Stanley, it is clear that Sondheim was supporting Furth's vision for the piece as well as his own by emphasizing commitment as the subject. Sondheim even predicted what would become the show's ending: a decision, rather than an action. In contrast, Prince's comments mostly concern actions and character traits. Prince defined the evening's subject in terms of marriage: "It's very hard to be married."[32] He picked out plot points that mattered to him: marriage and Robert's sexual preference. Furth emphasizes the importance of the opening scene, perhaps meeting Prince halfway by discussing specifics. But he also came up with a lovely aphoristic theme or metaphor for the show as a whole, emphasizing the importance of experience over received knowledge: "Unless you get your feet wet you aren't living."[33]

In retrospect, it is clear that at the start of their creative collaboration several issues that have dogged *Company* to this day had already surfaced: Robert's ambivalence about committed relationships, his ambiguous sexuality, and the lack of either a conventional or even a Fellini-esque climactic ending for the evening.[34] Even at this early stage Sondheim's dramaturgical comments could be pointed. He did not simply back up Furth at these meetings. For example, at the same February 20 meeting Sondheim suggested to Furth, "Never get specific regard[ing Robert's] occupation," again choosing ambiguity over narrative specificity.[35] Sondheim's invocation of what Furth said he called "a point of art, of theatre," points up his assumed role as dramaturge at this stage in the creative process. Sondheim got his wish and kept it in place for many years: In the most recent revised version of *Company* (2018), we have little idea what Bobbie does for a living, although she appears, like earlier Bobbies, to be in comfortable financial circumstances.[36]

## Shaping the Opening Scene: Birthday, No Wedding

An undated draft of a scene titled "YOU AND I AND GEORGE" may be the earliest extant version of the opening of *Company*.[37] Robert's friends throw a surprise birthday party for him as they do in the final 1970 version, but it is a gothic scene. Tapered candles held by each friend flicker in front of their faces, there is no cake, and Robert gives a maudlin, broken, somber speech about being single and feeling like "just an amusement . . . a filler-in" to his married friends.[38] In this version Robert is feeling his age and articulates unease at his single state. He says nothing about what he wishes for on his birthday. By late April Sondheim had begun work on the music for the opening and let Furth know in a letter that it would *not* come "specifically out of a dramatic situation," but presumably out of his avowed interest in a more experimental thematic approach rather than adherence to a conventional Broadway narrative.[39]

By May 1969, when Furth's first complete draft of the book (without lyrics) was duplicated and circulated among the creative team, birthday cake, candles, and wish are all present in Act I, scene 1. Robert turns his wish into a Manhattan real estate joke: He threatens to move in with one of the couples at the party. He says nothing about singleness or marriage. Three months after their first round of meetings, on May 26 Sondheim and Prince again sat down with Furth to discuss the current draft of the script. At that meeting Furth recorded that Prince suggested that Bobby (as the character was named by now) announce in the first scene of the show, "I'm getting married this year."[40]

If indeed Robert had said that line in the first birthday party scene, the audience would have known in the opening minutes of the show that the central character wanted to wed (or said he did) and would naturally be expecting that desire to be either fulfilled or frustrated by the end of the evening. This opening would have given the audience just what *Company* famously lacks: a linear narrative, establishing the central character's principal goal and priming the audience to expect complications, misunderstandings, but perhaps a happy wedding in the end.[41]

In any collaboration it is worth remembering who paid the bills. In this case that person was Prince, as producer, whose track record also spoke for itself. Thus, it comes as no surprise that at the end of the first scene in his personal copy of the May 1969 first draft of a full script, Furth, in pencil, put the following words into Robert's mouth: "Maybe I'm getting married."[42] In his handwritten revisions to the opening scene Furth executed a version of Prince's suggestion, but with a remaining degree of ambiguity ("*maybe* I'm getting married") that suggests that he and Sondheim had remained unconvinced by Prince's argument. Alternatively, Prince could have again been seeking to craft a compromise acceptable to both his collaborators. Regardless of these early disagreements, the collaborators were clearly all committed to the project. Some intriguing film footage of the creative trio discussing the genesis of the show in one of D.A. Pennebaker's remarkable documentaries suggests both their continuing strong rapport and their New York–style tendency to talk over one another (see figure 7.3). Sondheim recalls reacting to Prince's idea that Furth's one-acts might make a musical by saying that "it would be very peculiar," thereby obliquely suggesting

**Figure 7.3.** *L–r:* George Furth, Stephen Sondheim, and Hal Prince during a break in the all-night recording session for the original cast album of *Company,* on May 3, 1970. Screenshot from *Original Cast Album: Company,* directed by D. A. Pennebaker (New York: DocuRama, 2001), DVD, at 21:35.

that the novel thematic approach the trio had settled upon was also perhaps the best way to serve Furth's plays.

At the May 26 meeting Sondheim sought to change the direction of the discussion after Prince's suggestion that Robert announce his intention to marry, asking (in Furth's telegraphic version of Sondheim's words) "Let's not talk about [the] significance of [the] opening speech."[43] Instead, he urged the trio to step back and discuss "exactly what the play is about so, as Jim Goldman says, we can put it on our mirror."[44] At the time of these early planning sessions for *Company* Sondheim and Prince were concurrently working on another show (*The Girls Upstairs,* which became *Follies,* 1971) with a book by the established writer James Goldman.[45] Since Prince was *also* working with Goldman, this may explain why Sondheim as informal dramaturge invoked Goldman's name (note his use of the word *play* rather than *show* to describe the book at this point). Furth, in contrast to Goldman, an Oscar-winning screenwriter, was definitely the junior partner in this trio, just beginning his career as a playwright with the charm bracelet of one-acts that became, by many twists and turns, *Company.*

Sondheim may have been alone in differing with Prince at this juncture, but the evidence suggests that Furth and Sondheim preferred a more general and inclusive subject: commitment. In any case, these notes reveal that at this point, several months closer to casting and rehearsals, Prince was pushing for adding a narrative through-line to the relatively plotless evening, and Sondheim was pushing back, rather than vice versa, as is often assumed. Yet by now both Sondheim and Prince shared Jerome Robbins's often-expressed insistence that the success of a given show often depends on having the opening scene articulate not just plot, but theme: what "the show is about."[46]

The final version of the opening scene of *Company* in the running script (used by the stage manager to direct cues for the show), also a birthday party, ends with the main character, Robert, making a wish before he attempts to blow out the candles on his cake. But by opening night in 1970, Robert doesn't reveal his wish. One feature remains: He does not blow out all his candles, meaning that he will not get his wish anyway, as Jenny had warned earlier. Rather than describing his wish, Robert denies he even had one, saying, "Actually, I didn't wish for anything." Then the ensemble breaks into the title number.[47]

Sondheim, it appears, got his dramaturgical wish: The opening scene remains ambiguous, and Robert's wish becomes a piece of an ongoing puzzle: Who is Robert? Did he have a wish for himself, or not? What thoughts did he keep from his friends, and even, perhaps, from himself? The first musical number celebrates not Robert's determination to get married but his popularity, as he is serenaded by his lovers and his loving friends with a titular word more exhilarating but also more general than commitment: company.

## Developing the Subject and the Ending: Still No Wedding

At the same May 26, 1969, meeting, after Sondheim voiced his desire to talk through "exactly what the play is about" rather than what Robert wants in the opening scene, according to Furth's notes Prince came up with three more ways of thinking about the center of the story. Bobby could either (1) announce his intention to marry, (2) marry "a girl" to solve the problems they both experience regarding being single, or (3) marry a "nice, dumb girl" who is rejected by Bobby's friends as "unsuitable."[48] Once again Prince takes a somewhat reductive (and sexist, at least in Furth's paraphrase) approach to finding a central idea for the show, one predicated still on some decisive action taken by the character Robert that leads to conventional narrative conflict or resolution.

Prince did not suggest a clear theme, which is what Sondheim seemed to be asking for. "This is new!" Sondheim nonetheless replied, evidently in response to idea #2, marrying a girl who needs a willing partner, "that is a heroic act." Sondheim then made another attempt to get to the subject of the show as a whole (albeit centered on Robert) rather than Robert's desires and actions as envisioned by Prince, settling on the idea of an audition: "Is that what the evening is about [?]—he's examining or auditioning each of these ladies." Sondheim, Furth then wrote, suggested that the evening end with Bobby realizing that "he is a man who is unable to commit himself."[49]

Here we again see Sondheim the dramaturge being more conceptual than Prince, advancing a markedly different kind of Robert, ambivalent to the end. Perhaps as an offering to Prince, he did make ambivalence about the institution of marriage a specific component of Robert's personal struggles. At the show's end, Sondheim suggested, Robert might finally admit to himself that he is not only of two minds about the issue but is temperamentally unable to commit to a long-term relationship—the opposite of Prince's proposed three endings, all of them involving marriage.

After more conversation, Sondheim adds, "Opening number is Marriage is a Marvelous Thing—no, says Amy at the end—a <u>person</u> is a wonderful thing."[50] Once again Sondheim is seeing the idea of the show as a move away from marriage toward an ending in which Robert simply comes to understand himself more fully, via a more general definition of maturity: An adult is a self-aware person, and perhaps by implication also a person who is capable of caring for others. Further along in the notes Sondheim repeats a variation on this point: "The point is the <u>person</u>, not the <u>marriage</u>—he has committed himself to an idea."[51]

The debate about the show's ending did not stop, however, until Sondheim finally resorted to a more "'up'" ending after the Boston tryouts, replacing first "Marry Me a Little" and "Multitudes of Amys," then "Happily Ever After" with the anthem "Being Alive," a song which progresses "from complaint to prayer."[52] Once again Sondheim the dramaturge, it appears, got his wish for the most part: The ending scene remains ambiguous, and the last musical number, "Being Alive," celebrates not Robert's determination to get married but his newfound self-knowledge that he may at last be ready to give commitment a try, urged on via interjections from his lovers and his loving friends, drawn from drafts written by Furth.[53] In short, a decision rather than an action. Nevertheless, it is significant that Banfield, who had access to much of Sondheim's own records at the time, wrote that the show was "about marriage," not commitment.[54] Furth's notes may contradict this judgment only because his own views colored his interpretations of Sondheim's remarks at these meetings.

Furth's interjections bookend the comments by the couples added to the first scene, giving members of the ensemble a say at each end of the show. Among all fifteen of the various closing comments Furth drafted, not only those selected by Sondheim for inclusion in "Being Alive," there is no mention of marriage, family, or children. The theme of the show, by the book, as it were, remains something more general and less specific: commitment. Perhaps Furth helped Sondheim preserve his dramaturgical wish, even as the ending morphed into something more positive than they originally envisioned.

## Revisions for the 1995 London Revival: The "Bi" Scene

In order to understand Sondheim's role as co-dramaturge and editor with Furth in 1995 and as the sole surviving author in the years since Furth's death in 2008, it is now necessary to go back to the beginning, to Furth's collection of one-acts that became, over the course of a few furious months of collaborative revisions in 1969, the book for the musical *Company*.[55] While the revisions have been fewer since, the search for a commercially viable version of the show has led various directors to propose new directions, some drawn from these drafts. For a London revival in late 1995, in a bid to freshen up the show for changing times, the youthful director Sam Mendes approached Furth and Sondheim with a proposal to rewrite Act II, scene 3, set on an apartment terrace.[56] In the new version of the scene Peter (one of the five husbands) and Robert admit to one another that they both had had sex with men as well as women. Mendes edited Furth's original dialogue, in longhand, replacing the word *fag* with the word *gay.* Mendes also qualified Robert's final line to "*I guess, probably,* so have I" (that is, done it more than once with a man), adding the words in italics.[57]

In the libretto as published, Robert's last response becomes an even more guarded reply in the form of a question, "ROBERT: Is that a fact?"[58] It is certain that the idea for adding this "bi" dialogue to the scene occurred to neither Furth nor Sondheim, but to Mendes. He sent a twenty-page fax (a cover note, two pages of notes, and seventeen pages of script revisions) to Sondheim and Furth on October 20, 1995, suggesting six changes to the script, along with a declaration that he was an editor, not a writer, insisting that "It's all your work." He acknowledged that reincorporating the same-sex dialogue with Peter might be controversial, but added that he simply loved the scene due to its "unsettling nature" and "sheer <u>surprise</u> [underlined by Mendes]."[59]

The original one-act version of the "bi" scene, titled "PETER AND GEORGIA," predated the invention of Robert as a common character across a series of scenes (although it was revised in 1969, adding Robert by renaming the character originally named John). The scene was thus not reinstated into Act II, scene 3, as a reading of the two published librettos might imply. Rather, it was interpolated from a stand-alone one-act from a separate, earlier script, and it required major revisions in order to be repurposed to fit into Act II, scene 3. "PETER AND GEORGIA," Act I, scene 3, the earliest version of what I have labeled the "bi" scene, includes a similar discussion of same-sex love, much like the one reinserted into *Company* in the mid-1990s between Peter and a character named John.

In "PETER AND GEORGIA" both Peter and John say that they had sex with another man more than once, whereas in the 1996 published revised script, as noted earlier, only Peter, not Robert, admits to having sex with a man "more than once." Peter asks if the two men might also get together in this way, but John (as does Robert in later versions) turns him down. In both the 1970 and 1996 versions of the scene as staged in *Company*, Peter and his wife Susan are happily divorced and still cohabiting. In contrast, in the early drafts of Bobby's "bi" scene, Peter, who works in advertising, is in the throes of a difficult separation from his second wife Georgia and their three sons, who do not appear onstage.

Perhaps the longest version of the revised "bi" scene (fifteen pages) is preserved in a folder Furth topped with a note saying, "Original COMPANY stuff that was good and was cut." The character John is renamed Robert, indicating that Furth was trying to integrate the scene into the new version of the script with the male protagonist modeled on himself. It is part of a complete, bound duplicate of the revised script incorporating Robert as the main character in this folder.

The script, like others among Furth's papers, is described as a "FIRST DRAFT," dated May 1969, and hand-numbered #21 in what was presumably a small run of copies, containing no song lyrics—just suggestions for where songs might be inserted.[60] Incidentally, in another of Furth's multiple copies of the script, he marked in big cuts, including the visit to Robert's apartment by an African American female neighbor, Madeline, who says, suggestively, when Peter flirts with her, "I have a body like a boy. That's why I appeal to odd types." The existence of this altered version also suggests that Furth cut down this scene before it was cut out entirely after May 1969.[61]

There's no terrace in Furth's revised "bi" scene. We are indoors. Peter is staying with Robert, who enters the scene from the bathroom clad only in a towel. Bobby offers to feed Peter, but the latter exclaims, "Christ, I'm getting fat." Peter describes his lawyer as "homosexual," then adds, as proof, "I went to bed with him once." Bobby asks him if he wants a bath. Peter agrees, then, while Robert is offstage, arrays "dozens of candles and holders which he puts all over the room and lights." Peter strips to his shorts and "turns off the lights in the room." Peter hands Bobby a big drink, which he finishes, as requested, in three gulps. They both admit to having slept with men before. (As noted, this admission was narrowed down to Peter alone in the 1996 revised script as published.) Peter blows out the candles one by one and intimates that he and Bobby "might just go off and ball, and be better off for it." Bobby, turning him down, supplies Peter with bedclothes to make himself comfortable on the couch and wishes him a good night.[62]

There is no question that this scene appeals to contemporary sensibilities for its physicality—not to mention the panic attacks it might induce among stagehands just at the thought of having all those open flames onstage at once. But in 1969 it disappeared. Various scripts document earlier versions of the scene and numerous cuts and revisions along the way to the replacement text. These cuts mirror an extensive series of rewrites for the book as a whole. Only *two* scenes from Furth's first collection of eight full-length scene drafts were retained in the book for the musical (and they, too, were heavily revised). The eight original and three additional scenes, similar in format, are included among Furth's papers. They are listed in table 7.1. The two scenes retained from these eleven in the final script for the musical concern the sparring couple Sarah and Harry and the drug experimenters Jenny and David. Following Craig Zadan's example, I call these the karate scene and the pot scene.[63] The characters' names are retained in the final script along with much dialogue from the original drafts.

Furth's eleven one-acts are considerably more varied in content than the scenes in the final book for *Company*. They include working-class characters such as the vice squad cop whose wife is horrified when she realizes that he spends his day entrapping gay men in public bathrooms in "BERTHA AND ART" and poor, old, religious southerners in "MA AND PA." Dorothy and Lou are just getting by as they take care of a deaf brother-in-law, not a likely precursor for Bobby. Two scenes portray rich people involved in libertine sexual *ménages à trois*, "CYNTHIA AND WILLIAM" and "DIANE AND BARRY," although in the latter scene the threesome is implied but not depicted. *Company* ended up with a selection of vignettes all focused on apparently middle-class New Yorkers with the exception of one conspicuously wealthy couple, Joanne and Larry.

The new version of Act II, scene 3, derived from the old one-act at Mendes's suggestion in 1995, adds a potential piece to the puzzle of why Robert has not settled down with someone during an era when marriage and domestic partnerships of all kinds were narrowly defined (at least overtly) compared to our own era. It also offers something substantive to the many viewers and critics who since the show's debut in 1970 have divined a gay or bisexual subtext in Robert's character—an interpretation resoundingly dismissed by the show's creators but stoutly advocated and defended by some scholars and critics.[64] The question of Robert's sexual preference arose in the first place because few adults get through their twenties without coming to grips with their own sexual desires, whatever they may be. In 1970, this inference might be couched in harshly patriarchal language, as in the hostile review the show received in *Variety* during tryouts:

> Who cares what happens to Bobby—Bobby is only one of the problems affecting Harold Prince's unconventional musical. The songs are for the most part undistinguished. It is evident that the author George Furth hates femmes

and makes them all out to be conniving, cunning, cantankerous and cute. As it stands now it's for ladies' matinees, homos and misogynists.[65]

Forty-five years later attitudes expressed within the gay community were not yet becoming mainstream views but were nevertheless more likely to be expressed openly, as in this 2007 review in the *Advocate* (a magazine with a large LGBTQ readership) of the New York revival starring Raúl Esparza:

> This is a guy who isn't a kid anymore, who decorated his own apartment, who drinks heavily, who habitually deflects attention by asking questions, whose friends notice that he's always on the outside looking in, who beds women but never talks about commitment to anyone who isn't already married or otherwise clearly unavailable. . . . Hello?[66]

Many contemporary theatergoers would agree with the *Advocate*'s critic. And after all, as with "Being Alive," an ending that stops well short of being pat, adding these few lines into the script only broadens the canvas of Robert's sexuality, rather than limiting it to one pole of a binary or the other. This would seem to be consonant with Sondheim's original intent to make *Company* an "experiment in the commercial theater," akin in its "stylistic boldness" to Sondheim's first professional experience on Broadway as assistant to Oscar Hammerstein on *Allegro* (1947), a precursor to the concept musical that also was centered on a young man's coming of age.[67]

For Mendes, Furth approved changes to his script, but Sondheim also willingly revised lyrics and music in 1995 to suit the changing times (as previously mentioned) allowing director Scott Ellis to reinstate the cut song "Marry Me a Little" into the end of Act I for the New York production (the show's first revival on Broadway) a few months before Mendes's production opened in London.[68] With the addition of "Marry Me," Robert has an "I Want" number suggesting a linear narrative for Act II: Will he resolve his conflicted feelings, and maybe even find a partner?

Did Furth and Sondheim's approval of these successive changes fulfill their original artistic intentions, or were they simply allowing the book to be updated via timely additions? In 1995 Mendes was clearly after something more than timely updates—he wanted Bobby's bisexuality to be a moment of revelation for the audience. But by the twenty-first century the question became moot, at least for the reviewer in the *Advocate*, who asserted confidently that Bobby had always been not just bisexual, but predominantly gay.

The "bi" scene was certainly not the only "stuff that was good" that was cut.[69] Indeed, *most* of Furth's original script was discarded. Only two early scenes (those involving karate and pot) of eleven drafts were included in *Company* the musical; the ensemble "The Little Things You Do Together" and the husbands' "Sorry/Grateful" were incorporated into the karate scene, and the trio "You Could Drive a Person Crazy" adds a split-screen commentary by Robert's lovers to the pot scene.[70]

When Sondheim sent Furth's one-acts to Prince for review in 1969 the gay scene was included in the manuscript, indicating that Sondheim was open to Prince's considering it. Whether the decision to cut the scene was dictated by Prince or was a collective decision remains an open question. The sources I have found do not definitively explain why the "bi" scene was cut.[71] Although one reason for its replacement with a more ambiguous, shorter version in April 1970 might have been anxiety concerning portraying Bobby as bisexual to a mainstream Broadway audience, other motivations might have included the fact that it was fairly long, had no music or songs in it, involved subsidiary characters, and was unnecessary to the show as a whole.

Of course, *Company* famously successfully dispenses with most conventional plot devices. But the revised scene provides a comic reprise of an earlier scene, also set on Susan and Peter's apartment terrace, during which they reveal, to Robert's considerable surprise, their intention to divorce (but remain together afterward). Both Robert and the audience are invited to expand their definition of what a successful partnership can be to include divorced couples continuing to function amicably together as good parents (in Act I, scene 3), who may pursue sexual liaisons with other adults as Peter does when he propositions Robert (in the new version of Act II, scene 3).

Another possible reason springs to mind. The decision to cut the scene as originally written might also have been born of a desire to keep the new musical from seeming too openly derivative of a play that had opened off Broadway in 1968 and closed in September 1970: Mart Crowley's *The Boys in the Band*. A film version of the play was released on March 17 of that year, more than a month before *Company* opened. Both shows have plots centered on a birthday party for a thirty-something single man attended by lovers and friendly couples whose varied relationships are delineated with care. Both shows also contain scenes set on the terrace of a Manhattan apartment and feature thunderstorms and recreational cannabis use as plot points.[72] Perhaps the inclusion of this relatively intimate scene set in Robert's apartment might simply have brought *The Boys in the Band* too forcibly to mind, coming across not as revolutionary but unoriginal.

Furth was a prolific reviser, producing more than twenty possible one-acts, if one counts sketches and outlines, including the eleven distinct scene drafts described here. The Furth papers concerning *Company* are copious, duplicative, and sometimes inconclusive, leaving plenty of room for creative interpretations.[73] Elizabeth Wollman was probably the first scholar to consult manuscript sources for the "bi" scene from among Furth's papers, deposited at the New York

Public Library after his death. Wollman's forceful 2013 critique of outdated gender roles in *Company* pointed out some of the more dated aspects of the show's book, aspects that Marianne Elliott and Sondheim's radically regendered production addressed in 2018.[74]

## Retentions and Revisions for the 2011 New York, 2018 London, and 2020 New York Revivals

Fifty years on, the decision to keep Robert's wish in the opening scene an enigma—if he had one at all—may look like a wise choice. The spooky birthday party and consequent ensemble number "Company" are now one of the most celebrated openings of any Sondheim show. Likewise, the decision to keep the ending of *Company* ambiguous adds to the modernist allure of its reputation as a ground-breaking work that signaled a new turn in American musical theater toward greater abstraction in story-telling (and the common adoption of the term "concept musical" to describe such shows).

Both these elements were retained in the 2011 concert production, along with a striking subtraction (albeit one appropriate to a concert performance staged on the lip of an orchestral platform, without a fire curtain): a birthday cake in Scene 1 with only conceptual candles.[75] In this scene Bobby is presented with a sturdy cake-like prop with no candles; he mimes blowing out the nonexistent candles unsuccessfully. At show's end, *sans* cake, *sans* candles, Bobby simply sits down, alone, on his favorite easy chair, which has morphed over the course of the evening into a comfy, capacious couch big enough for two. He touches the empty seat tenderly, evidently thinking of past and future companions who did or might sit there, and smiles, a return to the final moment as portrayed in the original production and the published version of the 1970 book. In these early versions, it is the guests who prudently blow out the candles on the cake in the last scene before departing. Thus in 1970 and again in 2011, Robert begins and ends the show expressing ambivalence, although he is confronted repeatedly during the course of the show regarding not just Sondheim's preferred subject, commitment, but Prince's, marriage.

Prince (1928–2019) lived just long enough to see another director seek to restore a sense of urgency to Robert's search for a mate. This time Sondheim, acting as dramaturge and editor in Furth's absence, went along with a directorial choice that was similar in intention (if not in execution) to Prince's repeated suggestions around marriage back in 1969: desire not just for marriage but for children.[76] Making Bobby a female Bobbie whose biological clock is ticking is the central justification for Marianne Elliott's reimagined, regendered version of the show, which opened in London in 2018 and moved to Broadway in 2020.[77] As Elliott said in an interview two years prior to the London opening, "If it's a 35-year-old woman, and set now, then 35-year-old women are starting to think about settling down. They are thinking about the body clock and they think: Should they be with someone permanent? Suddenly, it became much more now."[78]

Note that Elliott was not saying that this must be the new focus of the musical; she was intending to add a dimension of backstory to the protagonist. Elliott related these thoughts to David Benedict, connecting her casting ideas to her own life experience. Benedict incorporated her thoughts into his introduction to the revised script published in 2019. For Elliott, marriage is the theme: "Marrying and having children create something of a crisis point for many, many women. . . . *Company* absolutely hits that nail on the head."[79] This "crisis point" is added on top of Bobbie's struggles with the idea of commitment to any long-term relationship (with or without children). Changing Bobby to Bobbie accomplishes this aim.

The show's lyricist, composer, and part-time dramaturge cautiously endorsed the idea of a female Bobby, saying, "What is there to lose? It can only make the play either interesting or, if you dislike it . . . dislikable."[80] Sondheim permitted the gender switch, but the implication that Bobbie will get hitched, and soon, was implied via casting, not by any direct changes to the book. As Ashley Pribyl has explained, the dance scene with music by David Shire, "Tick-Tock," was imaginatively reshaped into a dream ballet depicting Bobbie's possible futures of parenting with various mates, making Elliott's crisis point visible onstage.[81] But despite the existence of lines by Furth that could have altered the opening scene substantially (Bobbie could have announced her intention to marry, just as Prince wanted Bobby to originally and just as Furth had provisionally redrafted in manuscript), Sondheim authorized only minimal changes to the opening and concluding scenes.

Patti LuPone anchored the production in both London and New York, reprising her role as Joanne, a part she also played in John Doyle's 2006 New York production and in the New York 2011 concert production. Joanne's shocking proposition to Robert in Act II, scene 4, is altered in the 2019 published script. Instead of suggesting that she and Robert have sex, Joanne offers to help Bobbie set up a sexual tryst with Joanne's husband Larry. April's duet with Bobby, "Barcelona," is reassigned to a male character named Andy. Amy (who sings "Getting Married Today") becomes Jamie, who marries another man, named Paul, putting a new spin on the possibility that Jamie/Amy and Bobbie/Bobby are strongly attracted to one another, as were Amy and Bobby in 1970. The lines for two of the couples are swapped, making Susan the character playing the role of Peter, the male character who propositions Robert in the 1995 version of the book. In 2018 Susan makes no pass at Bobbie—the "bi" dialogue added in 1995 is deleted entirely. But Susan does reveal to Bobbie that she's divorced and pregnant at the end of Act II, scene 3, an analogous dramaturgical choice since it jolts Bobbie, just as Peter's revelation to Bobby that his committed relationship to Susan does not preclude the possibility of sexual liaisons (in the scene as revised in 1995) might force Robert to reassess his limited understanding of how family commitments can evolve and endure.

Sarah says "a woman's age" rather than "a person's age" in the last spoken line in the opening birthday party scene.[82] The stage directions for the ending of the musical are altered. A brief reprise of the "Bobbie" musical motif is sung by the cast at the opening of the final birthday party, after "Being Alive," as in the 1996 published libretto (this reprise is cut from the 2011 concert production). At the end of the show in 1970, Bobby's friends blow out the candles on his cake themselves before they hurriedly leave his apartment when he does not show up. In 1996, Bobby successfully blows out all the candles himself. In the 2019 version of the book new stage directions introducing comic uses of common kitchen appliances (a knife and a fire extinguisher) suggest that thirty-five is not so bad after all and that (since she does blow out the final candle successfully) Bobbie has finally gotten her wish.[83]

Perhaps Bobbie has triumphed over her feelings of loneliness, concluding that thirty-five is the new twenty-five and that "you're only as old as you feel," as the old cliché made doubly relevant by modern medical miracles goes.[84] As in all the previous versions with Robert, in 2018 and 2020 Bobbie is still alone at the end, with no marriage in the offing. Nevertheless, as with the addition of the "bi" scene and "Marry Me a Little" as a finale to Act I in 1995, the result is a decisively different version of *Company* offering something novel and saleable to a new generation of musicalgoers.

## Sondheim the Dramaturge

On April 24, 1969, Sondheim wrote to Furth to reassure him about his revisions to date, attributing the difficulties Furth was experiencing to "how good and tight the plays were in the first place," adding, "We'll clear up a lot in a couple of weeks."[85] Here we see not just Sondheim the dramaturge but Sondheim the mentor and warm, encouraging friend.[86]

In his chapter on *Company* in *Finishing the Hat* Sondheim dismisses the coinage of concept musical as "a meaningless umbrella term."[87] He then places *Company* in a much larger category, ironic plays, stretching back to Restoration comedies such as John Dryden's *Marriage à la Mode* (1672) through Bertolt Brecht's plays (some with music, such as *Threepenny Opera*, 1928, with a score by Kurt Weill) and Kander and Ebb's *Cabaret* (1966, directed by Prince): all authored by "purveyors of irony."[88] "*Cabaret* contained ironic moments," argued

Sondheim, "but *Company* was suffused with it."[89] Irony, then, was the style, non-linear was the form. In 2010 Sondheim also defined the subject: "All the songs would deal either with marriage in one sense or another, or with New York City."[90]

The central concept (or subject, to adopt the composer's preferred term) is generally interpreted as marriage, but we have seen that for Sondheim it was something else in 1969: "the problem of commitment."[91] But if marriage was not the concept Sondheim originally had in mind, it seems that by 2010 he was ready to embrace it as one of the two subjects at the heart of the show, while rejecting the "concept" label altogether. At the end of the chapter on *Company* Sondheim repeats an epigraph he quoted in *Sondheim & Co.* in 1974: "Chekhov wrote, 'If you're afraid of loneliness, don't marry.' Chekhov said in seven words what it took George and me two years and two and a half hours to say less profoundly."[92] In his typed-up notes from a story meeting on March 9, 1969, Furth had written at the end of a block of text attributed to "HP," all in caps, "IS IT WORTHWHILE TO BE MARRIED?"[93] The words may be less eloquent but the sentiment was similar; at these early story conferences both marriage and commitment were on the table as central subjects.

For his first professional musical, the unjustly neglected *Climb High* (1950–1953), Sondheim crafted not only his own lyrics and music but his own book, with a storyline and lyrics that anticipate those of *Merrily We Roll Along* (1981).[94] In his groundbreaking study of that first post-collegiate show Dominic McHugh quotes Stephen Banfield's question, "Might Broadway's recent history have been different had Sondheim chosen to persevere with a role for himself as overall *auteur* rather than go along with the collaborative model that he has helped to further?"[95]

Sondheim chose to collaborate instead of striking out on his own as an exceedingly rare triple threat (composer, lyricist, and author). His collaborations do not exclude further examinations of Sondheim's role as a dramaturge as well as a songwriter. Indeed, in the paper he presented at the March 2020 Williams College Sondheim symposium, John Weidman, the librettist for *Pacific Overtures*, *Assassins*, and *Road Show*, offered a detailed peek backstage at how putting two heads together on the book for *Assassins* meeting after meeting, month after month, delivered something more brilliant and effective than either might have delivered writing solo. Although McHugh finds a good deal of value in Sondheim's attempts at bookwriting for the early show *Climb High* and the sketches for a subsequent effort based on *Mary Poppins*, for Sondheim these efforts revealed "the real difficulties of playwriting, which is one of the reasons I'm not a playwright."[96]

"Good bookwriting is the most underdeveloped part of the musical theater," Sondheim has also said.[97] Through his collaborations with gifted writers

Sondheim has made a distinctive contribution to the state of the libretto art, comparable in some respects to Verdi's collaborations with Boito or Mozart's with da Ponte. He has helped give the comparatively obscure art of dramaturgy its due as an increasingly crucial part of the history and craft of the American musical. Sondheim was not only the composer and lyricist for *Company* but a sensitive, sensible dramaturge helping an inexperienced friend with a challenging project. He wanted Furth to succeed. He got his wish.

***

Perhaps the witty dialogue and lyrics, gorgeous score, and vivid characters of *Company* may matter more to audiences today than its thoroughly modern nonlinear narrative. Overdetermining Bobby (or Bobbie's) sexual preference may in the long run detract from the ambiguities that make *Company* an enduring work of art. In our own time, however, there's no question that deterministic gender play added via star power to the 2011 concert version and via casting in the 2018 London production helped make *Company* popular again nearly fifty years after it first opened on Broadway. What once was a social and professional necessity—the closet—is now perceived as sexual dishonesty. While the show *could* be about the problems of bisexuality (perhaps centered on the idea of no one thing or person ever making you complete), that would be a different story.

And yet, critics still consider the book weak, and the show in danger of losing its relevance.[98] One unaddressed problem in presenting *Company* in the present day is the predominant whiteness and wealth (or comfort, at least) of the cast (at least in major productions to date), all too familiar these days from syndicated reruns of television series featuring such characters, such as *Seinfeld* and *Friends.* In the London production directed by Mendes, Bobby was played by Adrian Lester, born in Birmingham of Jamaican descent (see figure 7.4). But Lester's racial identity is never explored as a possible dimension of Robert's identity, only his sexuality—a missed opportunity, perhaps, even if a tacit message was being delivered to the audience. One element in the score, Marta's bravura number "Another Hundred People," is certainly a potential anthem to migration and to cultural diversity. Marta was played with exuberance in Doyle's 2006-2007 production by Angel Desai, whose father is Indian and whose mother is Filipina (figure 7.1). In the 2011 concert production Marta was played by Anika Noni Rose, who won a Tony for creating the character Emmie Thibodeaux in *Caroline, or Change* (2004) and starred in the film version of *Dreamgirls* (2006). Susan's southern accent in Act II, scene 3 suddenly takes on a new edge as she and Peter recite with alacrity a whole series of Robert's previous partners in front of Marta, the only African American (and only person of color) in this cast (figure 7.2). Perhaps contemporary productions in Singapore (2012), Brazil (2001 and 2019),

**Figure 7.4.** The 1995 version of Act II, scene 3. *L-r*: Adrian Lester and Gareth Snook in the 1996 Donmar Warehouse production broadcast on BBC 2 on March 1, 1997. Screenshot from *Company Donmar Warehouse Stephen Sondheim 1996 (Entire show)* (YouTube posting of a videorecording of the BBC 2 broadcast, posted approximately 2015), at 1:51:10. Online at https://www.youtube.com/ watch?v=iamM_Qe7nbw.

and the Philippines (1997 and 2019) or elsewhere included more such moments of pointed performative relevance without changing a word or a note of the book, lyrics, or score.[99]

Whither *Company*? Over the next few years will Bobbie with an "ie" prove to be more believable, more contemporary, more moving than Bobby with a "y" could ever be? Or will this latest casting decision be viewed ultimately as a worthy (and publishable) reading suitable for today but not a definitive revision? Sondheim's decisions as dramaturge to approve casting changes and minor revisions to the book but no major revisions, suggest that this may be his view, along with a principled wish to defend Furth's work. When two *New York Times* critics denigrated Furth in an otherwise appreciative assessment of Sondheim's oeuvre, part of a bouquet of articles that appeared in the paper commemorating the composer's ninetieth birthday, Sondheim rose to "protest their dismissive underestimation" of his deceased partner in a letter to the editor, saying, "George was an actor, like many if not most of the best playwrights in history from Aeschylus to Shakespeare to O'Neill to Pinter."[100] Sondheim has been a faithful steward of Furth's legacy.

Furth and Sondheim's gracious accessions to requests from gifted directors for further revisions, far from compromising the work, have added to the story of a landmark in the history of American musical theater. The result is a show that, although it was devised during an era just beginning to discredit post-Victorian views of marriage as an "idealized vision of heterosexual stability, in which men and women took very clearly defined positions in the sexual order," has managed to change with the times.[101] Over the course of the past fifty years ingenious directors and varied casts have added new chapters to the saga of this historic show. The "story without a plot" that caused "both enthusiasm and dismay" in 1970 remains largely intact.[102] The ingenuity and topicality of the consequent series of careful, collaborative revisions discussed here suggest that *Company*, perhaps in yet more guises, may continue to play in commercial theaters as well as on nonprofit stages. As Banfield envisioned in 1993, *Company* may indeed "mature from a museum artifact (the original production) into a public domain text, complete with its variants and critical apparatus."[103]

# Notes

1. Stephen Banfield, *Sondheim's Broadway Musicals* (Ann Arbor: Michigan University Press, 1993), 164.
2. "To those of us who knew how hard it was to face the Great Unknown in 1970, *Company* was Truth." John Clum, *Something for the Boys: Musical Theater and Gay Culture* (New York: St. Martin's, 1999), 222.
3. See "The Four Last Songs," Banfield, *Sondheim's Broadway Musicals*, 166–173.
4. Profound thanks to two anonymous reviewers along with W. Anthony Sheppard, Dominic McHugh, and Geoffrey Block for their invaluable critiques and comments on drafts of this chapter. Thanks as well to Ashley Pribyl for our conversations at the Williams College conference from which this book emerged about Furth's story conference notes and other aspects of *Company*.
5. Astute scholars who have previously discussed the changes in sexual identity of characters in various versions of *Company* over the years include Elizabeth Wollman, *Hard Times: The Adult Musical in 1970s New York City* (New York: Oxford University Press, 2013), 40–61; Stacy Wolf, "Keeping Company with Sondheim's Women," in *The Oxford Handbook of Sondheim Studies*, ed. Robert Gordon (New York: Oxford University Press, 2014), 365–383; Ashley M. Pribyl, "Sociocultural and Collaborative Antagonism in the Harold Prince–Stephen Sondheim Musicals (1970–1979)" (PhD diss., Washington University in St. Louis, 2019), 180–240; and James Lovelock, "'A Peter sort of Susan': How Marianne Elliott's Adaptation of *Company* Queers and Straightens Gender and Sexuality" (unpublished conference paper, 2019), abstract online at https://songstageandscreen.com/past-conferences/song-stage-and-screen-xiv/programme/.
6. Banfield, *Sondheim's Broadway Musicals*, 147–148.

7. *Company*, duplicated script draft, Box 17, Folder 3, Furth Papers, Billy Rose Theatre Collection, New York Public Library (hereafter Furth Papers).

8. Doyle began equipping actors with instruments in 2004; he directed *Company* in his signature style at Sondheim's suggestion. See Stacy Wolf, "A Conversation with John Doyle About the Musicals of Stephen Sondheim," *Studies in Musical Theatre* 13, no. 2 (2019): 187–195. In 2010 Sondheim only drew attention to Esparza's "charismatic" performance and attributed this production's success primarily to "Doyle's theatrical metaphor" for Robert's emotional immaturity by making him the only cast member who doesn't play an instrument until the very end of the show, when he accompanies himself on piano as he sings "Being Alive." See Stephen Sondheim, *Finishing the Hat* (New York: Knopf, 2010), 166.

9. Photocopy of typed notes by Furth, dated February 20, 1969, Box 17, Folder 4, Furth Papers, c. 191–192. Whether this was the consensus view of all three collaborators or Prince employing the royal *we* is not clear.

10. Sondheim, *Finishing the Hat*, 166.

11. Furth notes, February 20, 1969, c. 191–192. Again, note that whether this was the consensus view of all three collaborators or the royal *we* is unclear.

12. Ibid.

13. See, for contemporary examples, Jane F. Gerhard, *Desiring Revolution: Second-Wave Feminism and the Rewriting of American Sexual Thought, 1920 to 1982* (New York: Columbia University Press, 2001), 81–117.

14. April, a flight attendant who sings a duet with Robert ("Barcelona") is a lover who might have been opposed as a fiancée for Robert by his cultured upper-class friends.

15. Raúl Esparza, the star of Doyle's 2006 revival (first produced in Cincinnati earlier that year), discussed his own bisexuality openly in a preview profile published on the front page of the *New York Times* Sunday Arts and Leisure section, thus providing readers with a potential identification of Robert as bisexual rather than predominantly heterosexual. This production was broadcast on PBS in 2007 and released on DVD in 2008. See Joyce Wadler, "Breaking Character for the First Time in His Life," *New York Times*, November 26, 2006, sec. 2, A1; and Don Shewey, "Is He or Isn't He?," *Advocate*, January 30, 2007, 58. A reference to Prozac was added to the book in 2006, and there may have been other changes. See Charles Isherwood, "Revisiting Sondheim's Odd Man Out," *New York Times*, March 21, 2006, E1.

16. People Staff, "Exclusive: Neil Patrick Harris Tells 'People' He Is Gay," November 3, 2006, accessed online on April 30, 2020 at https://people.com/celebrity/exclusive-neil-patrick-harris-tells-people-he-is-gay/. In addition to elisions, the cast ad libs many variations on the dialogue. Patti LuPone's up-tempo performance of "The Ladies Who Lunch" is remarkable not least for many rhythmic departures from Sondheim's score. But this essay focuses on intentional text and casting revisions rather than interpretive liberties.

17. Patrick Healy, "'Book of Mormon' and 'War Horse' Win Top Tonys," *New York Times*, June 13, 2011, C1. Composer Adam Schlesinger and lyricist David Javerbaum won an Emmy Award for Outstanding Music and Lyrics in 2012 for "It's Not Just for Gays

Anymore." See Eric Grode, "Did the Show Just Go There? Indeed," *New York Times*, June 5, 2020, C4–5.

18. The 2011 concert production was choreographed by Josh Rhodes and directed by Lonny Price with sets by James Noone. After debuting in movie theaters on June 15, 2011, the film of the performance was released on DVD in 2012.

19. See George Furth (book), Stephen Sondheim (music and lyrics), and Harold Prince (text copyright all three authors), *Company* (New York: Random House, 1970); George Furth (book), Stephen Sondheim (music and lyrics), and Harold Prince (text copyright all three authors), *Company*, in *Ten Great Musicals of the American Theatre*, ed. Stanley Richards, 643–719 (Radnor, PA: Chilton, 1973 [New York 1970 script]); George Furth (book), Stephen Sondheim (music and lyrics), and Harold Prince (text copyright all three authors), *Company* (New York: Theater Communications Group, 1996 [composite of the New York 1995 and London 1995 revised scripts]); and George Furth (book), Stephen Sondheim (music and lyrics), and Harold Prince (text copyright all three authors), *Company*, intro. by David Benedict (London: Nick Hern, 2019 [London 2018 revised script]).

20. Banfield, *Sondheim's Broadway Musicals*, 164.

21. Stanley appeared on Broadway in *Picnic* (1953) and *Bus Stop* (1955), received an Emmy Award for an appearance on the television series *Ben Casey* in 1963, and starred in the film *Séance on a Wet Afternoon* (1964).

22. This series is preserved in two full scripts titled *A Husband, A Wife, A Friend*, each divided into two acts with four scenes each (in Box 16, Folder 7 and Box 17, Folder 2, Furth Papers), and one incomplete script originally prepared for producers Philip Van Zandt and Philip Mandelker, with one new scene and five retained scenes, retitled *Company* (in Box 18, Folder 1, Furth Papers; one orphan scene is filed by itself in Box 18, Folder 3, Furth Papers).

23. George Furth, letter to Kim Stanley, Monday, March 3, 1969, Box 17, Folder 4, Furth Papers.

24. Ibid., emphasis in original.

25. Furth's letter to Stanley undercuts the assertion by Ethan Mordden that Anthony Perkins, the actor who the creative team hoped would create the role, was also the principal model for Robert; Perkins certainly could have inspired some later revisions. Ethan Mordden, *On Sondheim: An Opinionated Guide* (New York: Oxford University Press, 2016), 149. Perkins declared his willingness to continue in the show for at least a year. Sam Zolotow, "Perkins to Star in Stage Musical," *New York Times*, March 14, 1969, 48.

26. Gerhard, *Desiring Revolution*, 2.

27. Ibid.

28. Pribyl, "Sociocultural and Collaborative Antagonism," 187.

29. Ibid., 180.

30. Furth notes, February 20, 1969, c. 191–192.

31. Sondheim, *Finishing the Hat*, 166.

32. Furth notes, February 20, 1969, c. 191–192.

33. Ibid.

34. Toward the end of Fellini's *8 1/2* (1963) the protagonist, a film director, in a fantasy, imagines shooting himself in the head. He cancels the film he already has in production. We watch a crew dismantling an immense rocket-launching site set built for the film. Finally, in a daydream as his producer drones on monotonously beside him in a car, he experiences a change of heart something like Robert's in "Being Alive," directing, then joining a joyful final dance scene.

35. Furth notes, February 20, 1969.

36. The suggestions of class privilege in *Company* are considered briefly toward the conclusion of this chapter.

37. Furth notes, February 20, 1969. Odds are that Furth was referring to himself in the title of this draft, but on another occasion it would be interesting to explore the clear parallels between the protagonist's problems in *Company* and in *Sunday in the Park with George* (1984).

38. Carbon copy of typescript of Act I, scene 1 by Furth, n.d., four pages, Box 17, Folder 4, Furth Papers.

39. Letter from Sondheim to Furth, April 24, 1969, Box 17, Folder 4, Furth Papers, c. 61–63.

40. Handwritten notes by Furth on yellow lined paper, dated May 26, 1969, Box 17, Folder 4, Furth Papers.

41. The opening number, then, presumably would have had to support the dialogue and become a more conventional "I Want" song. "Marry Me a Little" (one of the first songs Sondheim composed) in the first act and "Being Alive" (the last major addition to the score) at the end of Act II could function as "I Want" songs, but to date are always placed later in the show.

42. "FIRST DRAFT—May 1969." Mimeographed typescript, Box 17, Folder 3, Furth Papers, 6.

43. Furth, notes, May 26, 1969.

44. Ibid.

45. James Goldman (1927–1998), not to be confused with William Goldman (1931–2018), his brother, also a screenwriter and novelist, won an Oscar for the script for *The Lion in Winter* (1966). James had previously written the book for the television musical *Evening Primrose* (1966) starring Anthony Perkins, with music and lyrics by Sondheim.

46. Sondheim and Prince had learned this lesson the hard way on their two most proximate collaborations, *A Funny Thing Happened on the Way to the Forum* (1962) and *Anyone Can Whistle* (1964). See Craig Zadan, *Sondheim & Co.*, 2nd. ed. (New York: Harper & Row, 1986), 71–72, 87. Sondheim's words "what the show is about" are quoted on page 87.

47. George Furth, "April 26, 1970, full script 'playing version,'" Box 18, Folder 5, Furth Papers.

48. Furth, notes, May 26, 1969.

49. Ibid.

50. Furth, notes, May 26, 1969.

51. Ibid.

52. "Up" [in mood] was Prince's term; "from complaint to prayer" is Sondheim's description of the song. Sondheim, *Finishing the Hat*, 196.

53. As previously mentioned, using the book as a source for lyrics has been a common practice for Sondheim and many other lyricists as well.

54. Banfield, *Sondheim's Broadway Musicals*, 147.

55. The materials in this section are adapted from my unpublished paper, "Early Scripts for *Company* (1970)," delivered at "Reading Musicals: Sources, Editions, Performance," a conference in honor of Geoffrey Block, organized by Dominic McHugh, hosted by the Great American Songbook Foundation, located in the Center for the Performing Arts, Carmel, Indiana, May 9–11, 2018. My thanks to all at that gathering for their questions, comments, and suggestions.

56. Although only thirty in 1995, Mendes had established his reputation with three West End stage credits, *Assassins* (1992), *Cabaret* (1993), and *Oliver!* (1994).

57. Copy of a twenty-page fax from Sam Mendes, October 20, 1995, in "Company—Notes, Clippings, 1969–1995," Box 17, Folder 1, Furth Papers.

58. Furth et al., *Company* (1996), 102.

59. Copy of Mendes fax, October 20, 1995.

60. George Furth, "*Company* script #21," Box 18, Folder 3, George Furth Papers, pp. 2-3-16 (Act I, scene 3, p. 16) to 2-3-30. In yet another copy of this script, the scene is twelve pages long and contains several interpolated pages suggesting that extensive additions may have been made *after* May 1969. See George Furth, "*Company* script #25," Box 18, Folder 2, Furth Papers, pp. 2-3-22 to 2-3-26 and 2-3-21, followed by pp. 2-3-28 to 2-3-33.

61. George Furth, "*Company* script #2, Box 17, Folder 3, Furth Papers, p. 2-3-25; and Furth et al., *Company* (1996), 100–104.

62. Furth, "*Company* script #21," pp. 2-3-16 to 2-3-30.

63. Zadan, *Sondheim & Co.*, 119.

64. Furth et al., *Company* (1996), 100–103. Before Act I, a note is inserted: "This script is an amalgamation of the Roundabout [New York, 1995] and Donmar Warehouse [London, 1995] productions of *Company*." The "bi" scene was reinserted only into the London production. See also Wollman, *Hard Times*, 47. Regarding denials and the reinserted scene, see Clum, *Something for the Boys*, 223–226, and Wollman, *Hard Times*, 44–51, especially 46 and 51. For examples of gay or bisexual readings, see John Rockwell, *All American Music* (New York: Knopf, 1983), 215, and Bruce Kirle, *Unfinished Show Business* (Carbondale: Southern Illinois University Press, 2005), 179–183.

65. Quoted in Stephen Citron, *Stephen Sondheim and Andrew Lloyd Webber: The New Musical* (Milwaukee: Applause Theatre and Cinema Books, 2014), 172.

66. Shewey, "Is He or Isn't He?," 58.

67. Sondheim, *Finishing the Hat*, 165.

68. The Off-Broadway revival of the show opened on October 5, 1995. The London production directed by Mendes opened on December 13, 1995. In *Finishing the Hat* Sondheim addresses his reasons for replacing the word "fag" with "gay," writing,

"By 1995 . . . it sounded not only offensive but old-fashioned." Sondheim, *Finishing the Hat*, 177.

69. George Furth, note in Furth's hand at head of folder reading "Original <u>COMPANY</u> stuff that was good and was cut" (Furth's underline), Box 18, Folder 3, Furth Papers.

70. Four other early scenes originally considered for *Company* were incorporated into Furth's play *Twigs*, which is centered on four female characters all played by one actor, in something close to his original conception for his one-acts: a female main character in each of the various stories to bind them together. *Twigs* opened on Broadway in 1971 and ran for 289 performances. The show was directed by Michael Bennett, with incidental music and one original song, "Hollywood and Vine," by Sondheim. George Furth, *Twigs: A Comedy* (New York: French, 1972).

71. Prince had recently faced this issue in working with Joe Masteroff, John Kander, and Fred Ebb regarding the sexual preferences of Clifford in *Cabaret*. See Carol Ilson, *Harold Prince: A Director's Journey* (New York: Limelight Editions, 2nd ed., 2000), 152.

72. Nor should we forget that Sondheim includes references to "a Pinter play" (perhaps *The Birthday Party*, written in 1958, remade as a film directed by William Friedkin released in 1968, also featuring a single man in uneasy negotiations with two kooky, indeed, scary couples), and to Gustav Mahler in "The Ladies Who Lunch." Friedkin also directed the film version of *The Boys in the Band* (1970).

73. Carol Ilson suggests (and the available documents support the idea) that much of the work was accomplished between May and July 1969, before Prince began work on a film in Europe; see Ilson, *Harold Prince*, 162. Sondheim visited Prince in Europe and played five songs for him in early September 1969: "The opening, a ballad for Robert, a song for Stritch in the first act, Amy's first act song—all marvelous. The fifth is a marvelous song, but not right for us. It's called 'Marry Me a Little.'" Letter from Prince to Furth, September 8, 1969, Folder 17, Box 4, c. 218, Furth Papers.

74. Wollman, *Hard Times*, 39–51. Wolf points out that it is the *men* in *Company* who are the most stereotypical. See Stacy Wolf, "Keeping Company with Sondheim's Women," in *The Oxford Handbook of Sondheim Studies*, ed. Robert Gordon (New York: Oxford University Press, 2014), 380, n.15.

75. Doyle also dispensed with the birthday cake in his 2005 Cincinnati and 2006 New York productions; see Wolf, "Conversation with John Doyle," 191.

76. Prince repeats a very similar suggestion on another page in Furth's notes, as follows: "Opening—he states (either in lines or in the number) Here's a toast to all the people here and the wonderful times we had—great times—*I want to get married*" (italics added). Furth, notes, n.d., Box 17, Folder 4, Furth Papers.

77. It is also worth recalling that a female central character was Furth's original choice when Kim Stanley was up for the role (although the substitute central character known as Robert had not yet been named or developed).

78. Baz Bamigboye, "Musical That Turns Rosalie into a Bobbie Dazzler: New Production and Company Will See the Show's Hero Become a Heroine," *Daily Mail*, November 24, 2016, accessed online on March 26, 2020, at https://www.dailymail.co.uk/

tvshowbiz/article-3969946/New-Company-production-Rosalie-Craig-play-s-hero-female-character.html

79. Quoted in David Benedict, introduction to Furth et al., *Company* (2019), 7–8.
80. Margaret Gray, "Sondheim on 'Sondheim on Sondheim's' New Orchestral Act at the Hollywood Bowl," *Los Angeles Times*, July 20, 2017. Accessed April 14, 2018. http://www.latimes.com/entertainment/arts/la-et-cm-sondheim-bowl-20170720-story.html
81. After 1970, "Tick-Tock" (music by David Shire) was removed from many subsequent productions, including both 1995 productions. Ashley M. Pribyl, "Performance Review: *Company* . . . London, UK, 9 October 2018," *Studies in Musical Theatre* 13, no. 2 (2019), 210. Pribyl's thoughtful review of this production also offers a discussion of how gender roles and plot points are revised scene by scene; see ibid., 209–211.
82. Not half, but all of Robert's candles stay lit after he attempts to blow them out in Act I, scene 1, but this minor change was already present in Furth et al., *Company* (1996).
83. Furth et al., *Company* (2019), 21, 111–112.
84. Paradoxically, perhaps most people do think of themselves as younger the older they actually are. See J. M. Montepare and M. E. Lachman, "'You're Only as Old as You Feel': Self-Perceptions of Age, Fears of Aging, and Life Satisfaction from Adolescence to Old Age," *Psychology and Aging* 4, no. 1 (1989): 73–78.
85. Letter from Sondheim to Furth, April 24, 1969, Box 17, Folder 4, Furth Papers, c. 61–63.
86. Years later Sondheim and Furth collaborated twice more, on *Merrily We Roll Along* (1981) and *Getting Away with Murder* (1997).
87. Sondheim, *Finishing the Hat*, 166.
88. Ibid.
89. Ibid., 166–167.
90. Ibid.,167.
91. Furth notes, February 20, 1969. Prince told Zadan that "for the last couple of years [1967–1969] we had been talking about doing a sort of autobiographical musical which was about marriage today . . . the plays [i.e., Furth's one-acts] weren't *all* about marriage, but some of them were." Zadan, *Sondheim & Co.*, 117. Perhaps the "we" here refers to Prince and his wife Judy Chaplin Prince.
92. Sondheim, *Finishing the Hat*, 196. See also Zadan, *Sondheim & Co.*, 117.
93. Photocopy of typed notes by Furth, dated March 9, 1969, Box 17, Folder 4, Furth Papers.
94. The Scottish toast sometimes attributed to Robert Burns, "Here's tae [to] us. Who's like us? Gey [Very] few," adapted by Sondheim into a refrain in *Merrily We Roll Along*, is discussed in McHugh, "*Climb High*," 113.
95. Ibid., 104; Banfield, *Sondheim's Broadway Musicals*, 25.
96. See McHugh's chapter on *Mary Poppins* in this volume; Zadan, *Sondheim & Co.*, 5.
97. Zadan, *Sondheim & Co.*, 61.
98. For critiques of the book as weak, see Hilton Als, "Brother Act: The Theatre," *New Yorker*, December 1, 2008, 85; John Lahr, "Sour Ball," *New Yorker*, December 11, 2006, 108–109; Margo Jefferson, "Sunday View: Listen to 'Company,' Tune out the

Book," *New York Times*, October 15, 1995, 2; and Walter Goodman, "Theater: A Revival of 'Company,'" *New York Times*, November 3, 1987, C15. For assessments of the book as dated, see Michael Schulman, "The Ascension," *New Yorker*, March 26, 2018, 22, and Patrick Healy, "Sondheim Working on Revised 'Company,'" *New York Times*, October 17, 2013, C3. Healy discusses the development of the 2013 workshop production in New York starring Daniel Evans as a Robert who is explicitly gay and Alan Cumming playing the character formerly known as Joanne mentioned at the outset of this chapter; Schulman states that it was Sondheim who refused to allow this production to go forward after the workshop performance in 2013.

99. "Company: International Productions" (Wikipedia), https://en.wikipedia.org/wiki/Company_(musical)#International_productions

100. Stephen Sondheim, "A Response from the Writer," *New York Times*, March 29, 2020, AR2. See also Stephen Sondheim, "Give the Book Writer Credit," *New York Times*, December 10, 2006, 4.

101. Gerhard, *Desiring Revolution*, 21.

102. Sondheim, *Finishing the Hat*, 166.

103. Banfield, *Sondheim's Broadway Musicals*, 164.

# 8

# Students Performing Gender with Sondheim's Musicals in the Age of #MeToo

*Stacy Wolf*

In 2018 Marianne Elliott's production of *Company* became the latest revisionist revival of a Sondheim musical. Recasting the beleaguered male bachelor Bobby as a female Bobbie not only gave the 1970 musical (sometimes labeled "dated") new life, it also renewed the show's relevance. Reviewers of the London production marveled over *Company*'s contemporary resonance, which emerged from Rosalie Craig's nuanced portrayal of the thirty-five-year-old heterosexual woman and from director Elliott's other choices. As *New York Times* critic Matt Wolf opened his review, "At last, *Company* has a human pulse and a proper dramatic core. And for that to happen, it took a woman."[1] Craig offered her own perspective: "I just love the fact that we have a female protagonist who is sexually active! That's quite a bold thing. . . . And somebody who is not shying away or trying to be sexy; it's warts and all up there. She's saying that she's not always nice, she doesn't treat people well all the time."[2]

Other dynamics shifted in this production, too. Joanne acted as a kind of mentor for Bobbie, as she expressed concern rather than attraction. And the wedding-anxious Amy became Jamie, a gay man whose breathless, lighting-speed, and hilarious rendition of "Getting Married Today" stole the show when I saw it in London. Elliott also interpolated a series of pantomimed "fantasy" vignettes of Bobbie's worst marriage nightmares into the number "Tick Tock." We first see Bobbie repeatedly lower the toilet seat lid, then teeter around with an alarmingly large pregnant belly, and finally soothe a fretful "baby" as her "husband" trots off to work. Set designer Bunny Christie created a series of small box-like rooms that conveyed Bobbie's entrapment; the production design was bright, intense, and exaggerated, including a huge mylar balloon shaped as the numerals 3 and 5, which served as a constant reminder of the threat of Bobbie's birthday. The production revealed how the text of this musical is more malleable than one might think. Writing of a 1995 revival, John Olson worried that the musical at that time was—twenty-five years out—hopelessly out of date and declared, "Its original 1970 setting is considered to be problematic and a barrier to successful revival."[3]

Stacy Wolf, *Students Performing Gender with Sondheim's Musicals in the Age of #MeToo* In: *Sondheim in Our Time and His*. Edited by: W. Anthony Sheppard, Oxford University Press. © Oxford University Press 2022. DOI: 10.1093/oso/9780197603192.003.0009

And yet, another twenty-five years later, changing Bobbie's gender reinvigorated this show.

The success of Elliott's production in London and its eagerly anticipated March 2020 opening on Broadway (which closed during previews owing to the COVID-19 pandemic) highlight the enduring interest in Sondheim's musicals in the United Kingdom, the United States, and around the world.[4] Sondheim and his collaborators wrote most of their shows in the 1970s and 1980s; the most recent was *Road Show* in 2008, which was first staged as a workshop and titled *Wise Guys* in 1999, then revised and renamed *Bounce*, which saw several productions from 2003 to 2006.[5] Still, theater artists return to Sondheim's musicals again and again. For example, John Doyle conceived of actor-musician productions of *Sweeney Todd* (2005), *Company* (2006), and others; the Fiasco Theatre Company reimagined *Into the Woods* (2015) and *Merrily We Roll Along* (2019); and Sarna Lapine reprised *Sunday in the Park with George*, starring Jake Gyllenhaal and Annaleigh Ashford, in 2017.

Sondheim praised most of these productions, welcoming restaging of his works. About Doyle's *Sweeney*, he said, "Of all the productions I've seen, this is the one that comes closest to Grand Guignol, closest to what I originally wanted to do." He praised Sarah Travis's new, minimalist, actor-musician–built orchestrations: "The variety of sounds she's gotten out of the instruments and also the practical way in which they allow John to work with the performers onstage is extraordinary." He noted how the orchestrations shaped "the play's atmosphere. These are wonderfully weird textures. The sound of an accordion playing with a violin—it's very creepy." Sondheim concluded, "What you gain is a swiftness and intensity that draws the audience into this macabre world, and that is created by a unified ensemble working in one tone. Here it's as if the audience is drawn into a tunnel."[6] He expressed similar appreciation of other revivals.

In addition to professional theaters, hundreds of high schools, community theaters, and colleges and universities produce Sondheim's musicals each season. Each of these productions is embedded in and received through its historical moment, filtered through both national politics and local issues. Even as Sondheim's musicals retain a high-art veneer, which presumes their timelessness and universality, each production reflects, converses with, and shapes its precise and specific historical context.

Similarly, all performance criticism and scholarship emerge from a specific historical moment and intellectual context. The late-twentieth and twenty-first-century articulation and development of, for example, feminist and queer theories, critical race studies and postcolonial critiques, disability studies, and Marxist analyses—to name a few—provide interpreters of musicals—both scholars and artists—with frameworks to analyze scripts and scores. In this way, all criticism is also "occasional," borne of a specific moment and shaped by local, national, and global politics. Both theatrical productions and critical writing, then, are time-based gestures, embedded in and responding to their place and time.[7]

This chapter is situated around the Trump presidency, the #MeToo movement, and what I will call "everyday feminism." It examines college students' perceptions of gender in Sondheim's musicals and performances of gender—especially of women and femininity—in several college productions of Sondheim's musicals from 2016 to 2020. By means of small group discussions and interviews, I learned how college-age theater makers navigate the complicated female characters in Sondheim's musicals. (As we will see, Sondheim's musicals appeal to college theater artists because many of the musicals in the traditional canon feel outdated and conservative, if not outright misogynist and racist.) Why do student directors want to work on Sondheim's shows? Why do women want to play these roles? How do they manage their complexity? And what do artistic approaches to these characters tell us about gender roles and gendered power dynamics on stage in our contemporary moment? The artistic choices and self-reflective comments of college theater directors (both faculty and students), musical directors, dramaturgs, designers, and actors reveal continued interest in Sondheim's musicals, ambivalence about his musicals' representations of gender and race, and eagerness to make these shows as relevant and resonant as Elliott's *Company*.[8]

## Occasion and Context

On January 21, 2017, more than three million people gathered in cities all over the world for the first Women's March.[9] The catalyst: Donald Trump's victory over Hillary Clinton for the office of President of the United States. This election, whose results surprised many, was a wake-up call for women and for minority groups who realized that their place in society was more precarious than they thought. During the campaign, more than twenty-five women accused Trump of sexual assault. When he spoke about women, he used sexist language, commenting on their looks. He suggested that journalist Megyn Kelly was harsh on him during a debate because she was menstruating. In terms of policy, President Trump blocked funding to Planned Parenthood, defunded a United Nations fund for family planning and reproductive services in 150 countries, and banned transgender individuals from serving in the U.S. military. Throughout his campaign, Trump frequently belittled ethnic minorities, immigrants, people with disabilities, and women, and yet almost 63 million Americans voted for him in 2016. Until his egregious mismanagement of the COVID-19 pandemic in the spring of 2020, Trump's approval ratings remained consistently above 40 percent.

Following the Women's March, there was at once a heightened awareness of misogyny across social institutions and a growing national divide between those who supported increased sensitivity to vulnerable communities and those who resented "political correctness." In 2017 the Merriam-Webster Dictionary declared *feminism* its "word-of-the-year," as feminist activism grew on a variety of fronts.[10] Some sought to correct the still-existent female pay gap and to equalize childcare, since working women continue to spend much more time on childcare than do men. Women, especially young women, got involved with politics, running for office with such role models as New York Representative Alexandria Ocasio-Cortez.

Gender-fluid or nonbinary people also gained more of a voice in society.[11] In the twenty-first century, gender nonconforming people (that is, those who do not identify as male or female) became more vocal about the need for a gender-neutral pronoun, and *they* became the default pronoun for nonbinary individuals, grammatically acceptable for referring to anyone. Just as *feminism* was the *Merriam-Webster Dictionary*'s word of the year in 2017, *they* earned the title in 2019; according to this dictionary, "It is increasingly common to see they and them as a person's pronouns in Twitter bios, email signatures, and conference nametags.[12] By 2019 it was customary for college students in classes or clubs to introduce themselves with their preferred gender pronouns and include them in their emails or nametags, and more colleges started indicating preferred pronouns on class rosters.[13]

The Me Too movement, founded in 2006 by Tarana Burke, exploded in 2017 into the #MeToo movement, which sought to "address both the dearth in resources for survivors of sexual violence and to build a community of advocates, driven by survivors, who will be at the forefront of creating solutions to interrupt sexual violence in their communities," according to its website.[14] Countless women across the world told their stories of sexual assault for the first time, and many prominent men were finally held accountable for their actions, such as the powerful movie producer Harvey Weinstein, who was convicted of rape and sent to prison for twenty-three years. His case inspired a reckoning in Hollywood.[15]

College campuses fueled the energy of #MeToo. The *Harvard Crimson* reported a 20 percent increase in sexual harassment reports in the few months following the complaints against Weinstein.[16] Across the country Title IX officers charged with ensuring that colleges comply with federal sexual harassment laws saw a rise in reports. A Title IX officer at Tulane University, for example, said, "For us [on college campuses], the #MeToo movement happened a few years ago, and it's like the country is catching up to us."[17] Students were on the front lines of activism, organizing campus groups to combat sexual assault with such tactics as boycotting fraternity parties, speaking with and making demands of university administrators, staging protests, and educating through social media.[18] At

Princeton in 2019, a weeks-long protest demanding clarity regarding Title IX policy was overseen by "open expression monitors," whom some saw as the opposite of their name, curtailing "free speech." A Princeton student who wrote "Title IX protects rapists" on the walkway in front of a campus gym was charged $2,700, which enraged many feminists on campus.[19]

In May 2020 Education Secretary Betsy DeVos announced plans to reform Title IX in favor of the accused. The new rules, which went into effect in August 2020, ensured that the accused party could cross-examine victims in live hearings and restricted the definition of *sexual harassment*. They also allowed universities to choose their standard of evidence—high or low. Critics said that the new regulations would discourage victims from coming forward, and by the summer of 2020, advocacy groups were working to change the course of Title IX. For example, the National Women's Law Center and the American Civil Liberties Union both filed lawsuits against the Department of Education in June.[20] The announcement of the rules came in the midst of the COVID-19 pandemic, limiting students' organizing power, but students responded. At Harvard, for example, a group advocating against sexual assault organized a "town hall" (that is, a community-wide discussion) to educate students, faculty, and staff about the guidelines, and a group member criticized the new policies as being "intended to silence survivors of sexual violence, and . . . intended to make filing a formal complaint that much harder."[21]

The arts world was also affected by and participated in everyday feminism's energy. In addition to dealing with the reality of sexual assault, the arts world grappled with the everyday inequalities that women face. On Broadway—the most visible and influential site of musical theatrical cultural production—only 13 percent of directors and 13 percent of writers were female in the 2018–2019 season, whereas the audience was 68 percent female.[22] At this moment, women do not control cultural production in any media, including theater.

The #MeToo movement led to broader conversations about representation and how it shapes social relations. More people asked why women are assumed to be sexually available to any man and acknowledged that this belief is due in part to how women are portrayed in movies, on television, and on stage. To counter such perceptions, a number of feminist television shows and movies including *RBG*, *The Handmaid's Tale*, and *Fleabag* were produced. Theatrical production (and change)—especially with regard to musicals—lags behind more popular media. This time lag is, in part, because of money: Producing a Broadway show is a multimillion-dollar prospect, and 80 percent of Broadway musicals fail financially, which means that it takes years of fund-raising and workshopping to open a show. In recent years, the streaming platforms HBO, Netflix, Hulu, Amazon, and many more have created feminist content quickly that speaks to the moment. In the midst of the #MeToo movement and a surge of interest in how gender and, more specifically, women are portrayed via representation, artists, including college theater makers, have been questioning how to handle revered older material that offends them.

Though musical theater is slowly becoming more diverse, most of the canon—"classic" musicals from the second half of the twentieth century—does not speak to the contemporary moment in terms of gender and race. All theater makers, from those on Broadway to community theaters to colleges to middle and high schools, must contend with a show's original script and score when they decide to perform it. For some, the challenge of making a show relevant and fresh in a new era of celebrating diversity is the exact reason why they choose a show. Director Ivo van Hove's 2020 Broadway revival of *West Side Story*, for example, deliberately cast a group of racially diverse actors, mixing up the brown-white dichotomy that we are used to seeing in the Sharks and the Jets.[23] And as noted earlier, Marianne Elliott's 2018/2020 *Company* with a gender-bent cast staged the extra pressures that women face today.

In other cases, the artistic team simply loves a show and must figure out how to make it work, as was the case with the Broadway revivals of *Carousel* (2017) and *Kiss Me Kate* (2019). Still, these productions (directed by men) did not escape scrutiny.[24] "It's frustrating that the material people seem to want to throw their energy into is old properties where women have no agency, and then there is the real scarcity of women on the creative teams," said composer Georgia Stitt in a 2018 interview. "And are these the shows I'm going to take my 12-year-old daughter to?"[25] Scott Rudin, the producer of the *Carousel* revival, told the *New York Times* that it is up to the audience to decide if they want to think about the abusive relationship in the show and #MeToo. "If people choose to look at it through that lens, that's great, and if they don't want to, that's their right," he said blithely.[26] As we will see, directors of college productions must deal with the offensive stereotypes in old shows as well, often with smaller (or nonexistent) budgets. And still, while young women at colleges are protesting in women's marches and advocating for reproductive rights, equal pay, and intersectional equality, some jump at the chance to perform in a show that portrays women as weak and dependent.

## Why Sondheim at College?

The theater departments and student-run theater organizations at colleges and universities choose to produce Sondheim's musicals for a variety of reasons, including the appeal of their challenging music, dense and specific lyrics, serious subject matter, unconventional narrative structures, and complex roles for actors. Sondheim himself wrote that "universities and schools are the most important bastion of keeping theatre alive today" and described the wonder of people sitting together in a room for a one-time-only experience.[27]

In order to gather information about productions and accounts of gendered experiences during this period, I met with a group of Princeton undergraduates across genders who participated in a showcase of scenes and songs from Sondheim's musicals as the culmination of a class on acting and directing in musical theater. I also interviewed colleagues who had recently directed undergraduates in a Sondheim show, in addition to student directors, musical directors, and actors, and saw several productions at colleges and universities from 2014 to early 2020. The accounts and observations were purposefully assembled for this occasion, for the writing of this essay at this time. My methods were neither scientific nor wide-ranging, but nonetheless, I think, the quotations offer a snapshot of student theater makers' attitudes toward gender in Sondheim's musicals during the Trump era.

In the fall of 2019 Musical Theatre International, which controls the rights to Sondheim's musicals, had licensed 685 upcoming full productions of Sondheim musicals in the United States. A number of junior shows (sixty-minute adaptations) and a few productions in the United Kingdom and Canada also were licensed. These amateur versions were planned at high schools, colleges, and community theaters. Music Theatre International issued 400 licenses for *Into the Woods*, by far the majority of productions planned. About 150 productions of *West Side Story* were planned, along with 50 *West Side Story JR.* productions. Other shows averaged about 25: *Company* had 26 productions planned, almost all in cities on the coasts, and, similarly, 25 productions of *A Funny Thing Happened on the Way to the Forum* were planned, all on the East Coast. *Sweeney Todd* was to see 24 productions in 2020 plus 12 "school editions" (full-length versions that edit out some sex and violence). Nineteen productions of *Assassins* were in the works, some of which would have been performed close to the November 2020 presidential election. Numbers dropped to fifteen for *Merrily We Roll Along*, most slated to be high school productions. Seven licenses were issued for *Sunday in the Park with George*, five for the revue *Side by Side by Sondheim*, four for *Follies*, two for *Passion*, and none for *Pacific Overtures*.[28]

Sondheim's musicals often top the list of desirable shows because they are considered serious fare and "high art." Participating in a Sondheim musical legitimates students' (and professors') passion for musical theater, which, at some colleges, is still suspect and considered to be frivolous and escapist. Sondheim ennobles musical theater for many college students. Because *Company, Assassins,* and the rest carry high cultural capital, the annual musical, which is sometimes met with disdain by one's colleagues, takes on a veneer of respectability.

This cultural capital is enhanced by the musicals' branding as "classic." That most of Sondheim's shows were written more than thirty years ago strengthens their value and, to some, excuses their conservative or retrograde representations of women. Yet many artists find the messages, characters, and music to be timeless; his work represents the expression of artistic genius, achieves ahistorical transcendence, and deserves universal acclaim. Like other artistic brands, Sondheim actively perpetuates his own value and singular genius (as much as he credits collaborators) in interviews and in his books of lyrics and commentary, *Finishing the Hat* and *Look, I Made a Hat*. These texts are useful analyses of the songs and shows, accounts of Sondheim's creative process and artistic self-fashioning. As Elizabeth L. Wollman explains, "He's a living legend, he actively bridges the gloried past to the present and (we hope) the future, and he has been actively shaping his own legacy and reputation for a long time, which only helps root him more strongly as a 'great' in a way that even . . . Rodgers and Hammerstein no longer can."[29]

Sondheim's musicals offer performance challenges that few musical theater composers can equal. The music is difficult to sing, and the acting requires psychological depth and emotional commitment. As Jeffrey Magee's essay in this volume demonstrates, Sondheim's visits to the Actors Studio in the 1950s exposed him to psychologically based Method acting techniques and compelled him to write characters' songs with subtext.

Themes are suited to adulthood in Sondheim's musicals; seriousness infuses the whole enterprise. Even *Into the Woods*, the lightest, most accessible and performable of them, deals with death, destruction, family loyalty, and marital infidelity. Many college students appreciate and are drawn to the sophistication of Sondheim's shows. His music, according to Todd Decker, "seldom requires a kind of razzle dazzle showmanship—and if he does it's usually meant as ironic. There's seldom a connection to pop culture or music."[30]

Since about 2010, Sondheim's musicals have experienced a resurgence in popularity. His well-known mentorship of Lin-Manuel Miranda links him to a younger generation. Revivals and revisals keep Sondheim's shows in the repertoire as living musicals, including, as noted, the 2020 Broadway revivals of *West Side Story* and *Company* and a new film version of *West Side Story* directed by Stephen Spielberg (2021). *Take Me to the World*, a celebrity-filled webcast tribute on the occasion of Sondheim's ninetieth birthday in April 2020, also contributed to Sondheim's popularity and fame, visibility and value.[31]

From a feminist perspective, Sondheim's musicals also hold appeal. First, women actors get excellent performance opportunities in most of them (see, for example, figure 8.1). Every student I interviewed talked about wanting to sing "On the Steps of the Palace," "Ladies Who Lunch," "A Little Priest," or other great songs in the repertoire. They are pleased and proud when they've mastered a Sondheim number—let alone an entire show—and can demonstrate their virtuosity as both singers and actors. Paige (white, she/her/hers), an actor, director,

**Figure 8.1.**  Sophie MacKay as the Witch in Muhlenberg College's 2019 production of Sondheim's *Into the Woods*. Photo: Ken Ek.

and dramaturg, said, "Sondheim's women get to have time on stage where they are dealing with issues and having opinions about the world and doing things, which seems very simple but that's not always the case. I think he writes about interesting people and interesting situations." Andrew (white, he/him/his), an actor, said, "I'm a man but I wish I could play a woman in Sondheim's musicals."

Student theater artists note the great divas who have played these roles and whose performances are preserved on video: Bernadette Peters as Dot in *Sunday in the Park with George* and as the Witch in *Into the Woods*; Angela Lansbury and later, Patti LuPone as Mrs. Lovett in *Sweeney Todd*; Donna Murphy (and Patti

LuPone in a concert version) as Fosca in *Passion*; Elaine Stritch, Barbara Walsh, and Patti LuPone (again) as Joanne in *Company*; and Meryl Streep as the Witch in the film of *Into the Woods*. Students want to emulate these actors' virtuosity and charisma.[32]

## Some Gender Trouble in Sondheim's Musicals

College students' attraction to Sondheim in the era of everyday feminism is tempered by anxiety and fretfulness, frustration and despair. For feminist theater makers, the high esteem with which many theater geeks hold Sondheim's musicals causes cognitive dissonance. As Gaea (white, she/her/hers), a student actor who participated in a group discussion of Sondheim's musicals and gender that took place in my office in January 2020, announced, "The problem is that we grew up with Sondheim as the god of musical theater. I think we should take him off that pedestal. The women are weak and that's all I have to say," and she walked out of the room. Gaea's anger echoes the sentiments of college theater makers of all genders in the age of #MeToo.

First, men are at the center of many of Sondheim's shows, and most shows are written from the male character's point of view. Paige said, "Mrs. Lovett is in relation to Sweeney. The role of Dot in *Sunday* is a great opportunity, but it's not her show." Even *Company*, which features a collection of memorable women, is built around Bobby. Violet (white, culturally Jewish, she/her/hers), a student actor, explained, "I'm attracted to Amy and Marta and April and especially Joanne. I can't even remember the names of the men! But the show is about Bobby." Sondheim and his collaborators have created a collection of strange, cruel, disappointed, vengeful, confused, unhappy men—negative representations, to be sure—but they nonetheless are at the center of most of the repertoire.

Second, a number of Sondheim's female characters focus their existence solely on a man, entirely motivated by their desire for him, such as Mrs. Lovett in *Sweeney*, Sally Durant in *Follies*, and Desiree in *A Little Night Music*. Some women do almost nothing in the musical other than pine for their man, including Dot in *Sunday*, Fosca in *Passion*, and the trio of girlfriends in *Company*. None of Sondheim's musicals—except, maybe, *Into the Woods*—pass the Bechdel test.[33] As Paige said during a discussion of *A Little Night Music*, which was about to open at Princeton in March 2020, "There's no woman who is not positioned in relation to a man in that show . . . the plot is constructed as a series of love triangles that then shimmy out and become pairs at the end like a Shakespearean comedy." Richard (Asian American, he/him/his), the production's director, said, "I think this show takes the perspective that this is 'Desiree's last chance' . . . the message is that a woman needs a man, a woman needs her husband." Allie (white, she/her/hers), the dramaturg for a production of *Into the Woods* at Muhlenberg College, wrote in a program note, "All the women in the show are given the right to pursue their own desires and learn about the world. However, in the process, they almost always end up adhering to a man."[34]

In addition to the female characters' limited dramatic purpose, many convey negative gender stereotypes, to which students are especially attentive. Squeaky Fromme in *Assassins*, according to a frustrated Kate (white, she/her/hers), who played her in a scene study, "was made to seem like a ditz." Allie wrote about *Into the Woods*, "The show does a good job at doing away with some of the old restrictions that constrained female characters in traditional narratives—but many fairytale archetypes and constructions still remain." Allie was especially critical of Cinderella's arc: "She has escaped cleaning for her wretched step-mother—only to end up cleaning for the Baker instead. . . . What does her un-dying role as care-giver suggest about female personalities?" Paige described the final couples in *A Little Night Music*: "Some of those pairings we're happy with, some of them we're concerned about, and some of them are actively bad. I mean, Charlotte and Carl Magnus are not a healthy relationship. And yet, we're meant to be happy that they get together, especially because they get together because he's jealous of her being with another man, and that's a good sign and that makes her happy. That's the most obviously toxic stuff that happens." Molly (white, she/her/hers), who played Petra, added, "Petra is this very, very, very sexualized character, which is a scary thing to approach." Emma (white, she/her/hers), who directed a scene from *Company*, said, "April's described as very stupid." To ex-plain why April changes her mind as she sings "Barcelona," Emma said, "It is kind of like he wears her down almost. If you think about it, it gets really like rape cul-ture-esque a little bit. . . . I think it plays into this trope that if a guy says enough of the right thing, that's what the girl wants to hear, so then she'll listen." All these examples reveal how rife Sondheim's musicals are with troubling gender stereo-types, how attuned students are to these representations, and how students assess characters in the context of their lives today.

## What's Appealing About Sondheim's Musicals

Even as the women in many Sondheim shows are weak, stupid, or obsessed with a man, they nonetheless appeal to student theater makers, in part because oppor-tunities for women performers are limited. In the 2018–2019 Broadway season, only 32 percent of leading roles were for women.[35] The scarcity of great female roles leads actors—even college-age ones—to settle for what they can get.

Moreover, other musicals' female characters are worse. Contemporary col-lege-age students are critical of the man-focused Nellies, Adelaides, and Elizas in "classic" Broadway musicals of the 1940s and 1950s (*South Pacific*, *Guys and Dolls*, and *My Fair Lady*, respectively), of the long-suffering "single girls" from the 1960s like Sally Bowles in *Cabaret* and Aldonza in *Man of La Mancha*, and of the pathetic women in 1980s and 1990s megamusicals such as Christine in *Phantom of the Opera*, Fantine, Eponine, and Cosette in *Les Misérables*, and Kim in *Miss Saigon*.[36] And as much as they love *Hamilton*, they are disappointed in the limited stereotypical roles of wife, muse, and whore that women play in that musical.[37] Compared to women in many other musicals, Sondheim's are more interesting, more complex, and less stereotypical.[38] Emma explained, "The way he writes the music really humanizes the characters in a way that I don't think a lot of the other musicals necessarily do for their female characters." Still, Kate said, "I feel very depressed by this conversation. We keep saying that at least his female characters are so much better than women in other musicals . . . why do we have to say 'at least'?"

Sondheim's women are undeniably compelling, and, as some students told me, the good outweighs the bad. Stacey (black, she/her/hers), referring to several female characters, said, "The character is weak and strong; she is dominant and submissive. She's both and that's what's interesting—the contradictions." Meghan (white, she/her/hers), a production dramaturg, noted that "the women of *Into the Woods* talk back." Beth (white, she/her/hers), the faculty director of Muhlenberg's production, wrote in her program note that the show "offers female-identified performers incredible leading roles, and it is vital to showcase a large number of challenging roles in which actresses can command a stage, tackle challenging physical demands, and carry the arc of an entire narrative forward." Paige summed up a feminist assessment of *A Little Night Music*: "There are a lot of women. They get a lot of stage time. They get a lot of songs. They seem to be driving the action most of the time. The men are kind of useless. They're all presented as dumb and more one-dimensional than the women . . . the women are trying to make things happen and are moving pieces."

Some students, compelled by a social realism argument, noted that the weak women in Sondheim's musicals illustrate society's strictures and pressures on women. When musicals show that a woman must be attached to a man and that women only find their identities through love and romance, theater can reveal the problems with the status of women in society. As Richard, the director of *A Little Night Music*, said, "We're showing how women suffer and are trapped." Paige echoed, "You see the limits on them because their power is almost entirely tied to their sexuality."

Comments by the famous actors who have played Sondheim's women stress the characters' layers. As Bernadette Peters said of playing Dot in *Sunday in the Park with George*, "Dot is trying so hard and trying so hard and trying so hard to get his attention. And it was heartbreaking, really. But, it's a love story."[39] Angela

Lansbury called Mrs. Lovett "a very resourceful woman, she didn't let anything go to waste, and I mean, after all, the meat pies were her idea . . . she was just being awfully clever and using available material." Playing her, Lansbury said, "was an opportunity . . . to do a character that I really would relish getting my teeth into."[40] On creating the Witch in the film version of *Into the Woods*, Meryl Streep said, "The issues that the Witch has, the idea that people do very bad things for sometimes very good reasons, felt very resonant. She loves, above everything, this little blossom of a girl that she never dreamed she would have. . . . She wants to protect her from all the bad things in the world, and that's something that every parent understands, to the extreme."[41] Musical theater icons who have performed in and who value Sondheim's musicals motivate college theater makers to do the same.

## Sondheim's Musicals in Production

Given these contradictions, what happens when young theater makers embark on a production and translate their ideas into artistic choices? They are not "cancelling" Sondheim's musicals, which they might do, but rather grappling with creating productions that align with their feminist values.[42] Three approaches to this problem follow, all from college or university theater programs. The first depends on acting and directing choices, the second relies on casting, and the third involves a production concept. But all of the productions mentioned—like any at a college—speak to and from the politics of gender of the #MeToo moment and everyday feminism.

## Female Characters with Agency

The solution to what students referred to as "the problematic women in Sondheim's musicals" that I heard most often was "to give agency." Directors and actors who worked on *Into the Woods*, *A Little Night Music*, *Assassins*, and *Company* aimed to interpret and to perform the characters to emphasize their strength, their conscious decision making and activity. Directors such as Richard scour the text for hints of a weak character's self-awareness. As he explained, "I think that if you look at this show [*A Little Night Music*] literally, it's easy to see a version or a world where the women have very little agency and very little self-awareness. And we are trying to steer clear of that as much as possible." As one example, he talked about Anne. "She's very bubbly. She speaks very fast. She has a lot going on," Richard said. "But . . . we've looked at her [as] a very self-conscious person. She does this kind of stuff because she knows what demeanor she's putting on." The director and actor make the character aware of her own performativity and hope the audience will notice Anne's choices, too.

Actors talked about developing psychological subtexts to bolster a character's strength. For example, for the "Barcelona" scene from *Company*, Lexie (white, she/her/hers), who played April, said, "I created an internal monologue in which the character was making self-reflexive choices with every lyric. It doesn't change what happens in the scene or Bobby's reaction to her decision to stay, but it gives her character agency and choice." For Lexie, whether the audience could perceive April's thoughtfulness mattered less than her integrity as an actor and her effort to infuse the character with agency. As Lexie and I continued the conversation, we agreed that April would probably lose her job by not showing up and that Bobby was not going to stay with her—a grim future for this character, even if she made a willing and conscious choice.

Directors and actors locate moments for women to connect or support each other. For example, the two women in *Assassins*, Squeaky Fromme and Sara Jane Moore, share one scene, which provides the show's comic relief. Moore is ridiculous and Fromme is a deluded child with a crush on cult leader and murderer Charles Manson. Neither garners the seriousness of (some of) the other assassins' political critiques. In a departmental production at Auburn University, Chase (white, he/him/his), a faculty director, tried to "ground" the women and to "avoid caricature." He worked with the actors to develop psychological subtext, motivation, and awareness and coached the two women to find moments of solidarity and agreement between them—to exchange looks, to empathize, to support each other—rather than allowing their scene to devolve into a silly catfight. Chase knew that he was directing "deconstructively" but hoped that the audience would perceive some strength in the female characters.

Musical directors coach actors to sing with strength, supported by character analysis and subtext. Maddie (Asian American, she/her/hers), music director for *A Little Night Music*, encouraged Billie Anna (white, she/her/hers), who played Desiree, to use different vocal qualities to amplify her "power" and, as Maddie described it, "the conviction that I feel like Desiree would have." Maddie explained, "Billie Anna is a wonderful actress, but has kind of a youthful voice, especially in her upper register. So I've been working with her to find that balance between the youthful side of Desiree, but also middle age, like she will stand up for herself." She went on, "For 'Send in the Clowns' we've been thinking about each lyric and the shifts between what she's grappling with: her love, but also the escape from her youthful side at that point." Billie Anna spoke some lines instead of singing them in order to give her more forcefulness. In Auburn's *Assassins*, the actor who played Moore possessed a strong voice, and she anchored the "Gun Song" quartet. Vocal quality, projection, and interpretation can convey a character's agency.

All actors (in any play or musical) aim to embody their character with physicalized commitment and to play each moment with high-stakes intensity. I observed such energy, which can communicate a character's determination and drive, in the cast of Muhlenberg's departmental production of *Into the Woods*. Beth (white, and the only female director I interviewed for this project; even in college settings, male directors dominate), wrote in her program note, "We're discovering ways to honor the original text's imagination while also embodying critically important new expressions for female-identified individuals." The production's costume design juxtaposed archetypal images with a flamboyant contemporary style, asking the audience to reflect on the connections between fairy tales and contemporary culture.

In all these examples, directors and actors explored ways to infuse characters' actions with consciousness and with self-determination. They relied on close analyses of music, lyrics, and script, attention to subtext, and classic feminist methods of "reading against the grain."

## Cross-Gender Casting

Another common solution is cross-gender casting, which is equally motivated by directors' desire to cast more women performers and by their intention to trouble gendered representations. Many women have played, for example, Jack or the Narrator in *Into the Woods*, Toby in *Sweeney Todd*, or the Proprietor in *Assassins*. Unlike Elliott's *Company*, though, these productions maintain the characters' masculine gender as written. They allow women and nonbinary actors to inhabit male roles but still normalize the representation of gender and gendered stereotypes in the show.

Still, cross-gender casting foregrounds gender as a performance. In her groundbreaking 1988 article "Brechtian Theory/Feminist Theory: Towards a Gestic Feminist Criticism," Elin Diamond argues that Brechtian theory's "alienation effect," which was created to denaturalize socioeconomic class relations, can also apply to gender. Diamond, Jill Dolan, and Sue-Ellen Case, among others, formulated what became classic tenets of feminist theater theory.[43] As Diamond writes, and as many theater makers have found, cross-gender casting can foster a productive Brechtian distancing. Diamond asserts that "when gender is 'alienated' or foregrounded, the spectator is enabled to see a sign system as a sign system—the appearance, words, gestures, ideas, attitudes, etc., that comprise the gender lexicon become so many illusionistic trappings to be put on or shed at will."[44]

The goal? To understand "gender as ideology—as a system of beliefs and behavior mapped across the bodies of females and males, which reinforces a social status quo."[45] The purpose? "To denaturalize and defamiliarize what ideology makes seem normal, acceptable, inescapable."[46] The role of the feminist theater scholar? To identify such theatrical choices and practice what Diamond calls "gestic criticism."[47]

For the production of *Assassins* at Auburn, for example, Chase cast a white woman as the Proprietor for political reasons.[48] He explained, "We produced it just before the 2016 presidential election, and it seemed all about toxic masculinity." Chase went on, "The Proprietor is sort of the overseer of everything. They set everything in motion. . . . [They're] the intermediary between the show and the audience. We were talking about the candidates during that time and having the proprietor be a female pointed out the ways in which toxic masculinity permeates the entire political system." In this production, the Proprietor "facilitates or creates" the situation and then "steps back and lets the action play out." Costumed in a pantsuit, which resonated with the "pantsuit nation" movement preceding the 2016 election,[49] high heels, and her own hair, the Proprietor "was decidedly modern. Of our time."

A 2018 departmental production at American University, for which faculty members Nathan (white, he/him/his) served as the musical director and Britta (white, she/her/hers) choreographed, women played Fromme, Moore, and the Housewife, and also Guiteau, Hinckley, Booth, and the Proprietor. With one-time-only permission from Sondheim and Weidman, they cast a trio of women as the Balladeer "like the trio of Sirens in *O Brother, Where Art Thou*" and strove to make each distinct vocally and choreographically (see figure 8.2). The Proprietor, Nathan explained, "was more like a Proprietress" and looked like "a coked-out beauty pageant contestant." Nathan felt that "Booth and Guiteau were electric. They were able to capture the flamboyance of each assassin compellingly, and our Booth was ready to turn on a dime to the ugliest parts of his beliefs." In this production, women playing men underlined how masculinity is a performance, thereby enhancing the story's effectiveness.

The argument for and strategy of cross-gender casting are not new, but in the seemingly intractable world of gendered musical theater casting (due in part to the constraints of vocal range), cross-gender performance can push against what Diamond, following Brecht, labels "iconicity." Though casting women in men's roles does not change the fundamental gender dynamics in the world of the play, characters seem different when embodied by differently gendered actors. Some college and university theater directors employ cross-gender casting, but this practice still has limits. We see women as Jack or the Narrator in *Into the Woods*, but not as the Baker; we see women as Toby or Pirelli in *Sweeney Todd* but not as Sweeney; we don't see a woman or nonbinary actor play George in *Sunday*. Vocal challenges notwithstanding, directors (who, as noted, are most often male-identified) cast men as leading men.

**Figure 8.2.** The cast of American University's 2018 production of *Assassins*.
Photo: Andrew L. Cohen.

## Directorial Concept

The third approach is a bold directorial concept, which, in the examples that
follow, either heightened gender or downplayed it. Like any canonical musical,
each original production (or significant revival) of a Sondheim musical is well-
known; many are widely available as recordings. These seminal productions,
directed by Harold Prince, James Lapine, and John Doyle, serve as referents for
all future productions, for theater makers and audiences alike. College theater
makers tend to be familiar with those productions, which "haunt" all future
versions.[50] A concept-driven production might not focus on gender specifically
but instead reframe the entire musical and compel new readings. Each of the
productions discussed here, knowingly or not, homed in on a specific theme of
the times: #MeToo, intersectionality, and gender queerness.

For *A Little Night Music* at Princeton (2020), for example, Richard, the director, created "a madcap comedy of romantic mismatches." Emphasizing the
musical's farcical qualities, Richard encouraged physical schtick among the actors. He "scored" the script to move between moments of realism and what he
called "spikes," or "exaggerated moments that are so far out of the baseline that
they are egregious to watch and don't fit into the show." The audience, temporarily startled, would question the characters' interactions and consider who had
power, who did not, who had agency, and who did not. Because heterosexual

desire structures the musical's triangulated romances, these "spikes" pointed to gender, to masculinity and femininity, and to the distances between this musical's nineteenth-century setting, its 1973 premiere, and its 2020 university performance context (see figure 8.3).

The designers enhanced these anachronisms. The costumes consisted of the muted colors and period-specific garb typical of many productions, but the set and lighting design eschewed the nostalgic tone that typically accompanies corsets and wide skirts for the women and close-fitting jackets for the men. Instead, the designers employed bright colors and sharp stylistic contrasts. Richard said, "Our lighting design also leans into this exaggerated idea and elevates us out of 'this is real.'" By building a production that stressed representation and unreality, Richard and the cast and design team were able to navigate the gender performances that they found "problematic."

An outdoor, immersive, site-specific Princeton production of *Sweeney Todd* in 2014 also used a strong directorial concept to offset the negative representation of women in the musical.[51] Eamon (white, he/him/his), the student director, set the production on a loading dock behind the gym, adjacent to the university's recycling center. Before the show, the audience members gathered in front of the gym and then were escorted in small groups along a path and down a hill around to the back of the building. A small wooden platform sat five feet off the ground, allowing spectators seated in the back (all fifty audience members sat on

**Figure 8.3.** Molly Bremer as Petra and Kateryn McReynolds as Anne in Princeton University's 2020 production of *A Little Night Music*. Photo: Bola Okoya.

folding chairs) to see. A higher platform upstage right held the small orchestra—keyboardist, percussionist, violinist—and a white sheet hung behind the stage, at first masking the concrete wall behind it and then serving as the surface on which blood appeared to splatter each time Sweeney cut someone's throat.

Some of the action took place on this main platform, but for many scenes, the actors moved around, over, and on all available surfaces, including a five-foot-high, 4' × 4' platform on wheels, a wide aisle between the two sections of audience seating, and the roof of the adjacent building. None of the scenes were "realistically" staged, and the actors were sometimes a considerable distance from one another, shouting to be heard. The effect was powerful, and it pulled in two directions: At once these characters seemed born of concrete, wood, and wire, all part of this industrial landscape, and, in addition, their human flesh, movement, and breath felt incongruous in this harsh setting, vulnerable and frail.

The lighting was do-it-yourself and hands-on, and like the set, seemed simple and spare but required intricate planning and set-up and precise execution. Several trees held lighting instruments that provided general illumination, and the actors constantly moved a number of spotlights on wheels to light specific areas of the space. Actors held industrial-sized flashlights to light their faces or others' faces and bodies. The shadowy lighting created a ghostly, haunted mood. The audience was constantly surprised by the next actor's appearance; we were on edge throughout the performance. The production emphasized the industrialization of society and the violence it compels. By requiring the audience to go to an industrial setting on the edge of campus on an early spring night, Eamon primed the audience to be attentive to the environment and to see the characters as buffeted about by the external forces that bore down on them.[52]

All of the characters in *Sweeney Todd* are broad and melodramatic, damaged or morally corrupt, but the three female characters are entirely defined in relation to men. Mrs. Lovett pines for Sweeney; Joanna suffers, entrapped by Judge Turpin until Anthony saves her; Lucy, once abused and now insane, begs (and dies) to be recognized by Sweeney. Mrs. Lovett comes up with the idea for the human meat pies and leads off "A Little Priest," the funniest, sharpest, word-full song in the musical (and maybe in any musical), but her super-objective in the musical is to get Sweeney to love her. Though the female characters' stereotypical roles are linked to genre (the scheming shrew, the helpless virgin, the witch wife), Eamon and his creative team refused to reproduce them without commentary.

Overall, Eamon's *Sweeney Todd* downplayed gender. At every turn, the larger themes of violence, exploitation, and cruelty rendered all of the characters victims of society.[53] The actor playing Joanna, for example, was often within a cage atop the rolling platform (see figure 8.4). This literalization of her entrapment made her seem less like the classic ingenue than an animal in a zoo, her dehumanization more extreme than gender's inequities. Mrs. Lovett was truly

**Figure 8.4.** Deirdre Ricaurte as Johanna in Grind Arts' 2014 immersive production of *Sweeney Todd* at Princeton University. Screenshot from production video, dir. Eamon Foley.

terrifying, as powerful as Sweeney, her comic blowsiness a mere shell over her ruthlessness. Her callousness and Sweeney's vengefulness were woven into the fabric of the society portrayed in this production. The characters were played with edgy desperation; all were in survival mode, their brutality and hard-heartedness inbred. This production reoriented my horizon of expectations to see all the characters trapped in their social context.

In the final example of a high-concept production that disrupted assumptions and troubled misogyny, student theater creator Andrew (black, TGNC [trans-gender and gender nonconforming]) directed a 2019 production of *Company* for the student-led AU Players at American University that emphasized gender as a theme. Though Andrew did not plan to direct what became, as Andrew said, "a very queer production" of the musical, a number of nonbinary actors auditioned, and Andrew decided to "cast everyone and see what happened." Through casting, acting, and costume design, Andrew and the team created a thoroughly gender-queer production, which Andrew described as a "liminal space."

Like the student-directed productions of *A Little Night Music* and *Sweeney Todd*, this production of *Company* grew from and conversed with 2010s culture. College students are on the leading edge of social, cultural, and political movements; the notion of gender as a social construction was well accepted by 2019, with increasing visibility of nonbinary gender identities. As noted earlier, introducing oneself with preferred gender pronouns was everyday practice on many college campuses.

All of the characters in *Company* maintained their assigned gender. The actors, though, were identified not as men or women or nonbinary but by descriptors of their embodiment. For example, Andrew said, "We cast someone with a quote unquote female body as Bobby" to allow the character to seem "less masculine and more feminine." Rather than describe this choice as "cross-gender casting," Andrew focused on gender's performative presence and acknowledged its corporeality and, as important, its corporeal fluidity. As Andrew said, "We decided to have the actors fluidly embody the genders of these characters so that the genders became more performances as opposed to something that has to be inherent to a male-female binary." In this way, the production expanded *Company*'s questioning of the institution of marriage to also query the social construction of gender itself.

Andrew and the creative team framed the production concept as an experiment, a series of questions about gender and relationships that each subsequent scene in the musical spun out. In the "Barcelona" scene, for example, the audience had to interpret the complex power dynamics they observed. Andrew said, "When Bobby got into bed and started listening to April talk, it entered into a different space as opposed to this guy listening to this woman ramble on. It became, well, what are these people talking about? Where are they trying to relate with one another? What kind of experience is this actually, and why is Bobby pursuing it in the way that Bobby does?"

Masculine bodies played both Joanne and her husband Larry, which raised more questions. Andrew said, "It became to the audience this experience of seeing homosexuality as a very typical thing. . . . And watching [Bobby's more] female body interact with these two masculine bodies in the final party scene set the ending in a place of genuine isolation." In this production, then, it was not a question of whether Bobby was straight or gay—which has been the subject of much critical and scholarly debate—but how the character operated within a larger sex-gender system.[54]

Costuming semiotically supported the production's interrogative stance regarding gender. Bobby's costume, for example, "was a blend of a traditionally masculine understanding of Bobby—a button-up shirt—but also a sort of softness. Bobby was wearing tight-fit leggings and in very delicate shoes," explained Andrew. Bobby's costume contrasted with other characters'; as Andrew said, "We had everyone else very clearly dressed in their gender almost to an absurd point. . . . Bobby's gender performance was so different from anyone in the show. And so this sort of dichotomy was very visually jarring." Every creative choice centered on gender, gender performance, and characterization by way of gender.

Among Sondheim's musicals, *Company* invites a gender-focused approach; one might argue that this musical is about gender. But Andrew's production understood the subject from a 2019 perspective in which gender binaries don't hold and gender itself can't be taken for granted. In most productions, Bobby coolly observes his friends' marriages and either avoids getting attached to or miscommunicates with his girlfriends. Bobby is at once the musical's protagonist and a cypher, as each marriage (or divorce or impending wedding) is revealed in turn. Andrew's production amplified Bobby's struggle beyond marriage per se to gender identity more broadly. Andrew said, "Our Bobby stayed on stage most of the time sort of swimming through the scenes, trying to learn what Bobby was doing wrong, why Bobby couldn't find that performance or presentation that gave Bobby closure." The production pointed out how the very notion of gender trapped Bobby. In the end, the creative team at American University created a queer, of-the-moment production that heightened and intensified what the musical is about: marriage, relationships, gender, and sexuality. These college theater makers are developing as artists in a culture where gender has expanded beyond binaries.

Though *Company* easily allows gender to be foregrounded aggressively, the time might be ripe for casting other Sondheim musicals across and through genders to bring new meanings to light. Sweeney Todd as a woman? All of the characters in *Into the Woods* as nonbinary? Or my favorite fantasy: *Road Show* with two sisters, which would not only offer two women fantastic parts but would feature sisters, a rarity in the Sondheim canon.[55]

## Sondheim and Gender at College: Now What?

My invitation to college theater directors, actors, designers, and dramaturgs to talk about the women in Sondheim did not surprise them. In fact, they were all already thinking about—or worrying about—gender in his musicals. At least in my limited case study, awareness of gender and of power in representation is part of twenty-first-century university culture. Further, making theater in a cloistered, noncommercial setting allows students to push on, critique, and deconstruct these texts.

What they do with that awareness varies. Grace (white, she/they), for example, told me:

> I mostly play men on this campus. When I auditioned for *Sweeney Todd*, I came in with the song "Johanna," and they asked, "Would you consider a woman's part?" and I said, "Not on this show." I'm pretty ferocious about it. Every show I auditioned for, I've looked at the characters and thought, "No, I can't. I can't feel right in my feminist mind playing this role."

Grace emphasized that she loves playing male roles and would like more opportunities to do so. Other female or nonbinary performers I spoke to also expressed the desire to play leading men, observing that actors have little choice in the supply-and-demand theater-making ecosystem; they can accept the role they are offered or elect not to perform at all. Even in the potentially experimental, free atmosphere of college theater, directors tend to cast conventionally.

Other students, like Paige, were similarly aggrieved by the limited supporting roles of women in Sondheim's musicals, but nonetheless grew as feminists from the experience. Paige told me, "I relate to Sondheim's women who often recognize that they are disempowered, that they are placing themselves in relation to a man, that they are loving a man who is abusive or unhealthy or just not good for them—there's something about that, for me, that feels very real to experiences of women I know and some of my own experiences." She mused, "Why do people stay with their abusers? Why do I find Sweeney sexy even if I can deconstruct all the messed-up power dynamics in the show? Why do I want George to be happy and fulfilled, and feel like if I were Dot I would want to make him happy, even when I can see how distant and emotionally abusive he is? I think by playing those roles and seeing those shows, I'm able to reflect on how I've been shaped by the world we live in."

Still other students describe a different experience; this is the kind of comment I heard repeatedly: "When I first read the script (or heard the song), I was upset. I didn't want to play a weak woman. But once I learned the song (or the role) and sang it, I loved it." Students describe how performance, especially singing, feels transformative and empowering. Might the pleasure of musical theater's over-the-top, direct-address, "sing out, Louise"-ness—its essence—temporarily override a feminist performer's discomfort with misogynist representations of women? Might Sondheim's songs—smart, sophisticated, complex—elicit even more of that delight? As Molly described it, "I feel like we might assume that a euphoric, powerful performance would reinforce underlying problematic politics, but in my experience, I haven't found that that is the case. Rather, I think that for this specific issue, the nature of musical theatre may even challenge the problematic aspects." She explained, "If the issue is a problematic/stereotypical female-presenting character and the song is an independent, powerful moment of taking the stage and captivating the audience, I usually find that the powerful performance moment and beautiful singing can overwhelm underlying messages." Moreover, she continued, "When I am on stage performing, I have to clear everything from my mind to be in the moment and deliver a present performance . . . so in that respect too, the analytical side of me takes a backseat to the creative in performance, and the result is usually a feeling of empowerment. Definitely an interesting clash of form and content that I think about a lot."[56]

Molly and the other students I spoke to readily admitted that "feeling empowered" while they perform does not alter gender relations or eliminate misogyny. One individual performance is not a strategy for social change. Still, they asserted, expressing the kinesthetic, embodied sense of strength in oneself is a feminist practice. Women taking up space on stage matters, whatever the gender of the character they are playing.

Where are we now? Should women and nonbinary artists make do with the canon of musical theater? The greatest composer and lyricist of our lifetime, Stephen Sondheim, leaves women both productively challenged and frustratingly compromised as actors, performers, musicians, and feminists. In the end, the problem of interpretation and embodiment in musical theater remains as pressing as it does for the canon of Western nonmusical drama. How do we take important dramatic literature and do something good for women and nonbinary people with it? How can we and our students take on the challenge? Looking at Sondheim's musicals through gender's lens not only opens up his shows to new and timely interpretations, and not only reminds us that these shows are and should be alive and well in the college theater repertoire, but also reveals the critical and creative interpretive practices of aspiring contemporary artists in an era of everyday feminism.

## Notes

1. I thank all of the students and colleagues who spoke to me and allowed me to quote their words. I have edited their comments for clarity (eliminated "like," "sort of," and unnecessary repetitions). Thanks to Tony Sheppard for inviting me to participate in the Sondheim@90@Williams symposium, which instigated this research and this chapter, and for the thoughtful and generous comments from that event's participants and audience. For reading drafts of the talk and this essay, my thanks to Paige Allen, Molly Bremer, Todd Decker, Jill Dolan, Deborah Paredez, the members of the Musical Theatre Forum (Doug Reside, Dominic Symonds, Elizabeth Wollman, Liza Gennaro, Jeff Magee, David Savran, Raymond Knapp, Tamsen Wolff, and Jessica Sternfeld), and the students in Jeff Magee's summer 2020 Sondheim course at the University of Illinois, Champaign-Urbana. Also, I thank Marissa Michaels for her excellent research assistance.

   Matt Wolf, "A Gender Swap Makes Sondheim's 'Company' Soar," *New York Times*, October 25, 2018, accessed July 9, 2020, https://www.nytimes.com/2018/10/25/theater/sondheim-company-london.html. Also see Matt Trueman, "West End Review: 'Company,'" *Variety*, October 17, 2018, accessed January 12, 2021, https://variety.com/2018/legit/reviews/company-review-gender-swap-marianne-elliott-1202981961/.
2. Rona Kelly, "BWW Interview: Rosalie Craig Talks *Company*," *Broadway World*, November 1, 2018, accessed July 27, 2021, https://www.broadwayworld.com/article/BWW-Interview-Rosalie-Craig-Talks-COMPANY-20181101.

3. John Olson, "*Company*—25 Years Later," in *Stephen Sondheim: A Casebook*, ed. Joanne Gordon (New York: Garland, 1999), 47.

4. *Follies*, for example, was performed in the former East Germany in January 2020; this was its first production in Germany since 1991. It moved to Dresden, then performances were halted, then plans were in place to resume in January 2021. See https://www.staatsoperette.de/spielplan/a-z/follies/. Accessed January 12, 2021. Scholar David Savran reviewed the production: David Savran, "'Follies' Set in Socialist East Germany: Sondheim at Staatsoperette Dresden," Operetta Research Center, January 8, 2020, accessed January 12, 2021, http://operetta-research-center. org/sondheims-follies-staatsoperette-dresden/.

5. Harry Haurn, "Exclusive! Sondheim Explains Evolution from *Bounce* to *Road Show*," *Playbill*, August 12, 2008, accessed July 9, 2020, https://www.playbill.com/article/ exclusive-sondheim-explains-evolution-from-bounce-to-road-show-com-152437.

6. Quoted in Charles Isherwood, "Cutting 'Sweeney' to the Bone," *New York Times*, October 30, 2005, accessed August 10, 2020, https://www.nytimes.com/2005/10/30/ theater/newsandfeatures/cutting-sweeney-todd-to-the-bone.html.

7. See, e.g., Nancy K. Miller, *Getting Personal: Feminist Occasions and Other Autobiographical Acts* (New York: Routledge, 1991).

8. The examples and interviewees for this chapter come from undergraduate, predominantly liberal arts theater programs, both student theater companies and departmental shows, but not from conservatory programs. It would be interesting to compare my interviewees' comments and theatrical solutions with those of students in conservatories who might anticipate navigating the conservative gender representations in professional musical theater.

9. Thanks to Marissa Michaels for researching and drafting this section. History.com Editors, "Women's March," January 21, 2017, accessed July 9, 2020, https://www.hist ory.com/this-day-in-history/womens-march.

10. "Word of the Year 2017: Feminism," Merriam-Webster, 2017, accessed May 14, 2020, https://www.merriam-webster.com/words-at-play/word-of-the-year-2017-feminism.

11. See, e.g., Dennis Baron (he/him/his), *What's Your Pronoun? Beyond He and She* (New York: Norton/Liveright, 2020).

12. "Word of the Year 2019," Merriam-Webster, 2019, accessed August 2, 2020, www. merriam-webster.com/words-at-play/word-of-the-year/they.

13. Jessica Yarmosky, "'I Can Exist Here': On Gender Identity, Some Colleges Are Opening Up," *NPR*, March 21, 2019, accessed August 2, 2020, www.npr.org/2019/03/ 21/693953037/i-can-exist-here-on-gender-identity-some-colleges-are-opening-up.

14. "About: Me Too Movement," accessed May 14, 2020, https://metoomvmt.org/about/ #history.

15. Eric Levinson, Lauren del Valle, and Sonia Moghe, "Harvey Weinstein Sentenced to 23 Years in Prison After Addressing His Accusers," March 11, 2020, accessed July 9, 2020 https://www.cnn.com/2020/03/11/us/harvey-weinstein-sentence/index.html.

16. Claire E. Parker, "Reports of Sexual Harassment at Harvard Increase amid National Movement," *Harvard Crimson*, July 21, 2020, accessed August 2, 2020, www.thecrimson. com/article/2017/12/13/title-ix-harvey-weinstein/#.WjFZ9Qe8ADw.twitter.

17. Lena Felton, "How Colleges Foretold the #MeToo Movement," *Atlantic*, January 17, 2018, accessed August 3, 2020, www.theatlantic.com/education/archive/2018/01/how-colleges-foretold-the-metoo-movement/550613/.

18. Anemona Hartocollis, "New Wave of Student Activism Presses Colleges on Sexual Assault," *New York Times*, June 8, 2019, accessed August 2, 2020, www.nytimes.com/2019/06/08/us/college-protests-dobetter.html.

19. Emily Spalding, "Students Protest Title IX Office at Firestone Plaza," *Daily Princetonian*, April 23, 2019, accessed September 5, 2020, https://www.dailyprincetonian.com/article/2019/04/students-protest-title-ix-office-at-firestone-plaza.

20. "NWLC Files Lawsuit Against Betsy DeVos, Trump Administration's Sexual Harassment Rules," NWLC, June 10, 2020, accessed August 2, 2020, nwlc.org/press-releases/nwlc-files-lawsuit-against-betsy-devos-trump-administrations-sexual-harassment-rules/.

21. Isabel L. Isselbacher, "Student Organizers Critique DeVos's New Title IX Regulations," *Harvard Crimson*, May 26, 2020, accessed August 2, 2020, www.thecrimson.com/article/2020/5/26/devos-guidelines-hgsu-our-harvard/.

22. Sean Patrick Henry, "Broadway by the Numbers," illustrated by I. Javier Ameijeras, produced by Alexander Libby, Bella Sotomayor, Florian Bouju, and Serene Lim (*Production Pro*, 2019), https://production.pro/broadway-by-the-numbers; Ryan McPhee, "New Broadway Demographics Research Shows Growth in Nonwhite and International Audiences," *Playbill*, January 13, 2020, accessed July 9, 2020, https://www.playbill.com/article/new-broadway-demographics-research-shows-growth-in-nonwhite-and-international-audiences.

23. Von Hove is a white man and also European. Some commentators observed that his not being American meant that he could not understand the racial dynamics of the musical. Similar questions arose about the Belgian choreographer Anne Teresa De Keersmaeker. See, e.g., Sasha Weiss, "How 'West Side Story' Was Reborn," *New York Times Magazine*, January 22, 2020, accessed August 22, 2020, https://www.nytimes.com/2020/01/22/magazine/west-side-story.html.

24. Michael Paulson, "The Problem with Broadway Revivals: They Revive Gender Stereotypes, Too," *New York Times*, February 22, 2018, accessed July 9, 2020, https://www.nytimes.com/2018/02/22/theater/gender-stereotypes-carousel-my-fair-lady-pretty-woman.html.

25. Ibid.

26. Ibid.

27. Stephen Sondheim, *Finishing the Hat: Collected Lyrics (1954–1981) with Attendant Comments, Principles, Heresies, Grudges, Whines and Anecdotes* (New York: Knopf, 2010), 287.

28. In 2011, MTI launched the MTI Musical Finder, a tool for finding shows playing near you. These statistics were found using the tool in the fall of 2019. Owing to its dynamic nature, however, these statistics kept changing. The Musical Finder became inactive in March 2020 because of live theater's pause during the coronavirus pandemic. Jason Cocovinis, "Introducing the Musical Finder—A Brand New Way to

Search for a Show Playing Near You!," April 3, 2011, accessed July 27, 2021, https://www.mtishows.com/news/introducing-the-mti-musical-finder-a-brand-new-way-to-search-for-a-show-playing-near-you.

29. Personal email, May 25, 2020.

30. Personal email, July 18, 2020.

31. See, e.g., Ben Brantley, "Review: For Sondheim's 90th Birthday, a Collage of Aching Voices," *New York Times*, April 27, 2020, accessed January 13, 2021, https://www.nytimes.com/2020/04/27/theater/take-me-to-the-world-sondheim-review.html.

32. See Marvin Carlson, *The Haunted Stage* (Ann Arbor: University of Michigan Press, 2001).

33. The Bechdel test was inspired by one of the comic strips in Alison Bechdel's "Dykes to Watch out For" series. In order to pass the Bechdel test, a movie (or television show, play, musical, or piece of fiction) must (1) feature at least two named female characters, who (2) speak to each other, (3) about something other than a man. See https://www.merriam-webster.com/dictionary/Bechdel%20Test, accessed July 14, 2020. To be sure, few if any musicals from creators of Sondheim's generation pass the Bechdel test, but Sondheim's perceived greatness leads students to expect that his musicals will align with their values.

34. Dramaturgs play an especially important role in college productions in support of research, interpretation, and the meaning of artistic choices.

35. Beth Schachter, program note, *Into the Woods*, Muhlenberg College, November 2019.

36. See Stacy Wolf, *Changed for Good: A Feminist History of the Broadway Musical* (New York: Oxford University Press, 2011).

37. See Stacy Wolf, "*Hamilton*'s Women," *Studies in Musical Theatre* 12, no. 2 (2018): 167–180.

38. See Laura Hanson, "Broadway Babies: Images of Women in the Musicals of Stephen Sondheim," in *Stephen Sondheim: A Casebook*, ed. Joanne Gordon, 13–34 (New York: Garland, 1997); Katherine Welsh, "An Interpretive Framework for Analyzing and Comparing the Women in Stephen Sondheim Musicals" (senior thesis, Princeton University, 2015); Laurie Winer, "Why Sondheim's Women Are Different," *New York Times*, November 26, 1989, 2: 1; Stacy Wolf, "Keeping Company with Sondheim's Women," in *The Oxford Handbook of Sondheim Studies*, ed. Robert Gordon (New York: Oxford University Press, 2014), 365–383.

39. Alexis Soloski, "Bernadette Peters: 'Every Role I've Played, I've Thought—That's Me!'," *Guardian*, May 30, 2019, accessed February 10, 2020, https://www.theguardian.com/stage/2019/may/30/bernadette-peters-broadway-sondheim. Peters said, "When I did 'Sunday in the Park,' I learned so much about life from that show. Especially when you get to that song 'Move On.'"

40. "Angela Lansbury Discusses 'Sweeney Todd'—TelevisionAcademy.com/Interviews," July 16, 2012, accessed July 27, 2021, https://www.youtube.com/watch?v=hW0g_HUlNik. Lansbury said, "For me, it was as if I had landed in the perfect spot for my talent. *Sweeney Todd* was an extraordinary opportunity to bring to the stage my London humor, which I was born to one day eventually show, and my ability to do a funny Cockney character."

41. Chris Hewett, "Meryl Streep on Why She's Finally Playing a Witch," *Next Avenue*, January 12, 2015, accessed July 27, 2021, https://www.nextavenue.org/8-meryl-str eep-quotes-why-shes-playing-witch-now/.

42. I put "cancel" in scare quotes because of its resonance at the time of this writing. See Aja Romano, "Why We Can't Stop Fighting About Cancel Culture," *Vox*, August 25, 2020, accessed June 22, 2020, https://www.vox.com/culture/2019/12/30/20879720/ what-is-cancel-culture-explained-history-debate.

43. Elin Diamond, "Brechtian Theory/Feminist Theory: Toward a Gestic Feminist Criticism," *Drama Review* 32, no. 1 (Spring 1988): 82–94. Also see Jill Dolan, *The Feminist Spectator as Critic* (Ann Arbor: University of Michigan Press, 1988); Sue-Ellen Case, *Feminism and Theatre* (New York: Methuen, 1988).

44. Diamond, "Brechtian Theory," 85.

45. Ibid.

46. Ibid.

47. Ibid., 83.

48. In the 2017 production of *Pacific Overtures* at the Classic Stage Company, director John Doyle eschewed the traditional kabuki all-male ensemble and featured women in the roles of the mother and the wife. Doyle's production made the critique of U.S. imperialism exceedingly clear.

49. Lexi Pandell, "How Clinton Supporters Made the Pantsuit a Serious Symbol of Power," *Wired*, November 8, 2016, accessed July 27, 202, https://www.wired.com/ 2016/11/clinton-pantsuits.

50. On the idea of original productions "haunting" future ones, see Carlson, *Haunted Stage*.

51. For a clip of this production, see https://www.youtube.com/watch?v=DZr9gQZTdXE.

52. These goals were similar to Prince's in the original production. See Ashley M. Pribyl, "Sociocultural and Collaborative Antagonism in the Harold Prince–Stephen Sondheim Musicals, 1970–1979" (PhD diss., Washington University in St Louis, 2019).

53. See Alosha Grinenko, "'Is That Just Disgusting?' Mapping the Social Geographies of Filth and Madness in *Sweeney Todd*," *Theatre Journal* 68, no. 2 (2016): 231–248.

54. On this subject, see Andrew Buchman's contribution to this volume.

55. Paige helpfully reminded me that while there are few women in *Road Show*, "the play is one of Sondheim's queerest shows, because it depicts gay men and centers on a somewhat 'queer' love between two brothers." My fantasy production would also cast Hollis as a woman, rendering the Addison-Hollis romance a lesbian one.

56. During this conversation, Molly also referred to my article about the women in *Company* and my book *Changed for Good*.

PART III

# VERSIONS, GENRES, AND COLLABORATIONS

# 9

# *Sweeney*'s Identity Crisis and the Dynamic Potential of Generic Hybridity

*Kim H. Kowalke*

After Hal Prince had left New York to direct *Evita* in London in 1978, Sondheim met with graphic artist Frank Verlizzo to fine-tune the artwork for *Sweeney Todd*. "It's pretty unusual to have the composer involved in poster art," the designer said, "but Steve's pretty much involved in everything that's going on, which is great. The advertising agency was concerned that there was too much blood and it would turn people off. But Steve felt pretty strongly that that was what the show was about and there was no reason to hide it. So we added blood to Mrs. Lovett's apron and blood on Sweeney's hands where originally it had just been on the razor."[1] The grotesquely exaggerated caricatures of Angela Lansbury wielding a rolling pin and Len Cariou his razor would perfectly convey the precarious balance between chills and laughs in a show not yet finished and still months away from the start of rehearsals (see figure 9.1). That was not Sondheim's only contribution to the poster. He also came up with the work's idiosyncratic generic subtitle, "A musical thriller," replacing the customary "a new musical" or "a new musical comedy" with which his and Prince's previous shows had been labeled.[2]

Thirty years later, in the first volume of his collected lyrics, Sondheim observed that "*Sweeney Todd* has been called by people who care about categories everything from an opera to a song cycle."[3] Indeed, during its long genesis the piece was announced as or described by at least one of its creators as melodrama, opera, chamber opera, musical comedy, comic musical, musical horror story, musical melodrama, epic theater, Jacobean tragedy, ballad opera, and Grand Guignol potboiler. No wonder Sondheim opted for the deceptive simplicity of "a musical thriller." Nevertheless, as he collected and annotated the lyrics of his life's work, he was still equivocating with two other oxymoronic labels for *Sweeney Todd*: "'Dark operetta' is the closest I can come, but that's as much a misnomer as any of the others. What *Sweeney* really is is a movie for the stage." But he acknowledges the issues that arise from such attempts to have your meat pie and eat it too: "Just as all baggage comes with labels, so do all labels come with baggage."[4]

Although many of Sondheim's other works are also generic hybrids, none carries nearly as much baggage as *Sweeney*.[5] Yet what might be called its generic instability

Kim H. Kowalke, Sweeney's *Identity Crisis and the Dynamic Potential of Generic Hybridity* In: *Sondheim in Our Time and His*. Edited by: W. Anthony Sheppard, Oxford University Press. © Oxford University Press 2022. DOI: 10.1093/oso/9780197603192.003.0010

**Figure 9.1.** Frank Verlizzo's window card for the original Broadway production of *Sweeney Todd* (1979) featuring caricatures of Lovett and Todd.

or promiscuity may actually have enabled it to be bent, adapted, or re-conceived again and again, sometimes radically, frequently with artistic and box-office success. This dynamic potential has prompted performances as provocatively divergent as the original "mega-Sweeney" at the Uris Theater in New York and the 2014 "tiny Todd" staged by the Tooting Arts Club in a London pie shop, with an "immersed" audience of thirty-five, a cast of eight, and a band of three.[6] Less than three years after the national tour of the Broadway production had closed in Los Angeles, the musical thriller started its ongoing global occupation of opera houses with productions directed by Prince in Houston and New York, with the State Opera of South Australia following in 1987, the 2,256-seat Royal Opera House in 2003, and Berlin's Komische Oper the following year. A parade of "Symphonic *Sweeneys*" commenced in 2000 with semi-staged concert performances by the New York Philharmonic and an all-star cast; PBS telecast the next year's edition by the San Francisco Symphony, which was then released as a DVD.

Meanwhile, in 1989 a fully staged "Teeny Todd" had debuted at Circle in the Square in New York, fifteen years before John Doyle downsized the piece even more by relocating the tale to an asylum inhabited by ten inmates who play, act, and sing a truncated score with "keyboard-and" instrumentation.[7] In contrast, Jonathan Tunick expanded his orchestration to seventy-eight players for Tim Burton's otherwise musically diminished 2007 film adaptation.[8] And, of course, in recent years there have been hundreds of performances of the School Edition, as well as Concert, College, and Community *Sweeneys*. What other Sondheim musical can claim to have won Tony and Drama Desk Awards for best musical, an Olivier Award for best musical plus two more for best revivals, an Emmy, a Golden Globe, and a Grammy in such diverse re-conceptualizations? Which other has taken up residence in such varied institutions and media with very different cast sizes and orchestral forces, types of performers, audience expectations, and its very content and length?

Sondheim now credits *Sweeney*'s surprising and continuing popularity to its telling of "a good story" that an audience will accept "no matter how bizarre and idiosyncratic it may be."[9] Numerous melodramatic and dramatic adaptations since the mid-nineteenth century certainly attest to the appeal of the urban tale about a murderous barber. But its being a good story cannot adequately account for the success of this musical thriller in its many guises, languages, and versions around the world. Might the show's ongoing popularity be attributable, at least in part, to the intersection and interaction of so many generic, idiomatic, and stylistic strands and layers inherent in the work? Examining *Sweeney*'s resultant (and ongoing) identity crisis may also raise some broader issues relating to sources, editions, and performances of core repertory of the American musical theater.

## Multitudes of *Sweeney*s

The oft-rehearsed genealogical account of Sondheim's six-year journey toward *Sweeney* begins in the spring of 1973, when he attended a production of *The Demon Barber of Fleet Street* at a small East End theater while in London for rehearsals of *Gypsy* starring Angela Lansbury. Though still billed a melodrama, what Sondheim saw and cheered was not George Dibdin Pitt's original 1847 melodrama but a 1968 adaptation by Christopher Bond: "It was something that just knocked me out. Bond's new version was a tiny play, still a melodrama, but also a legend, elegantly written, part in blank verse—which I didn't even recognize until I read the script."[10] In an attempt to rescue melodrama from the campy spectator sport it had become, Bond had taken elements from Dumas's *Count of Monte Christo*, several Jacobean tragedies (particularly *The Revenger's Tragedy*), and odds and ends from Shakespeare to transform the barber from a homicidal maniac, murdering only to rob his customers, into a quasi-sympathetic victim of cruel injustice gone mad with a lust for revenge.[11] Bond's tragic overlay further complicated *Sweeney Todd*'s generic identity by undermining some of the conventions of melodrama by making the young innocents Johanna and Anthony secondary to the two decidedly unheroic leading roles and by forgoing the customary victory of the virtuous poor or innocent over the villainy of the corrupt and cruel.

The day after seeing Bond's play, Sondheim had lunch with his friend, director John Dexter, and asked him "whether *Sweeney Todd* would be the basis of a good operatic piece. He had always been pushing me to write a through-composed piece. He said it would be perfect."[12] Because the play literally "sang" to him, Sondheim petitioned Bond and the two producers who had optioned it for a New York production to let him first attempt a musical version. They agreed, though the project would have to wait for the composer to finish *Pacific Overtures*, which did not open on Broadway until January 1976.[13] Seven months later the *New York Times* announced that Sondheim was writing music, lyrics, and book, not for an opera but for "a new comic musical" that would open in New York in the fall of 1977. The brief notice also contained a curious disclaimer: "It does not try to scare you."[14] Apparently Sondheim did not actually begin working on the piece in earnest until the summer of 1977: "I started trying to write everything myself because it was really all going to be sung . . . it was going to be virtually an opera."[15] Working directly from Bond's thirty-five page play, Sondheim retained its intricate plotting and all but one of its eleven characters, as well as Todd's reference to his razors as "his friends" and his exclamation "My right arm is complete again!" Two parallel passages shown in table 9.1 demonstrate how closely the final version of *Sweeney Todd* follows Bond's play in certain scenes.[16]

**Table 9.1.** Parallel passages from Bond's "melodrama" and Sondheim and Wheeler's "thriller"

*Sweeney Todd*

| Bond's play | Sondheim's lyrics (Wheeler) |
|---|---|
| | [No. 2, "No Place Like London"] |
| ANTHONY: I have sailed the world, beheld its fairest cities, Seen the pyramids, the wonders of the east. Yet it is true—there is no place like home. | ANTHONY (*sings*): I have sailed the world, beheld its wonders From the Dardanelles To the mountains of Peru, But there's no place like London! I feel home again. |
| TODD: None. | |
| ANTHONY: What's the matter? | I could hear the city bells |
| TODD: You are young. Life has been kind to you, And fortune smiles on your enterprises. | Ring whatever I would do. No, there's no pl— |
| May it always be so. My heart beats quicker, too, To find myself in London once again, But whether out of joy or fear I cannot say. | TODD (*sings grimly*): No, there's no place like London. ANTHONY (*speaks, surprised at the interruption*): Mr. Todd, sir? TODD (*sings*): You are young. Life has been kind to you. You will learn. |
| | [No. 3, "The Worst Pies in London"] |
| MRS. LOVETT: Are you a ghost? *Todd starts for the door, fearing he has been recognized* Hey, don't go running out the minute you get in. I only took you for a ghost 'cos you're the first customer I've seen for a fortnight. Sit you down. *Todd sits, warily* You'd think we had the plague, the way people avoid this shop. A pie, was it? | MRS. LOVETT (*singing*): Wait! What's yer rush? What's yer hurry? You gave me such a fright, I thought you was a ghost! Half-a-minute, can't-cher? Sit! Sit ye down! Sit! All I meant is that I haven't seen a customer for weeks. Did you come here for a pie, sir? (*flicks dust from a pie*) Do forgive me if my head's a little vague. Ugh! (*plucks something off a pie*) What is that? |
| TODD: A pie—yes. And some ale. | But you'd think we had the plague (*drops it on the floor, stomps on it*) from the way that people (*flicks at something on the counter*) keep avoiding (*spots it moving*) . . . No, you don't! |
| MRS. L (*getting the pie*): Mind you, you can't hardly blame them. There's no denying these are the most tasteless pies in London. I should know, I make 'em. (*She puts the pie on the table, then flicks a bit of dirt off the crust*) Ugh! What's that? But can you wonder, with meat the price it is? I mean, I never thought I'd see the day when grown men and good cooks, too, would dribble over a dead dog like it was a round of beef. (*She goes for some ale*) | (*smacks it with her hand*) Heaven knows I try, sir! (*looks at her hand*) Yich! But there's no-one comes in even to inhale. Tsk! (*blows dust off pie*) Right you are, sir, would you like a drop of ale? Mind you, I can hardly blame them. These are probably the worst pies in London. I know why nobody cares to take them. I should know, I make them, But good? No, The worst pies in London. Even that's polite. The worst pies in London. . . . And no wonder, with the price of meat what it is (*grunt*) when you get it. (*grunt*) Never (*grunt*) thought I'd live to see the day men'd think it was a Treat finding poor (*grunt*) animals (*grunt*) wot are dying in the street. |

Sondheim recalls that at first the piece was almost writing itself, but then he panicked about its probable length: "I did the first twenty minutes, the first seven songs, and I realized I was only on page five of Bond's script. . . . So at that rate, the show would possibly have been nine hours long. And I realized I didn't know how to cut it."[17] He also worried that what he had written was little more than a series of solo numbers: "I thought, Oh, God, you might as well have people come out in 'one' with a microphone and do a concert."[18] Indeed, the musical layout of the show's form in 1979 (see table 9.2) evinces that through number 11, Judge Turpin's "Johanna," the score is largely a succession of solo "I am" or "I want" numbers for the principals from Bond's play (with truncated, varied reprises of "The Ballad of Sweeney Todd" interpolated). At this point in its evolution, Sondheim's *Sweeney Todd* evidently did not diverge much from what Bond described as "really a quite small play, almost a domestic play."[19]

Sondheim decided to shift generic gears. He stopped calling it an opera: "I knew I wanted continuous music, but not necessarily continuously *sung* music."[20] His subsequent public statements routinely replaced "opera" or "chamber opera" with a new label. "What I wanted to write," he said, "was a horror movie. The whole point of the thing is that it's a background score for a horror film, which is what I intended to do and what it was."[21] Sondheim cited a specific model: "It's an open secret that the music for *Sweeney* is an homage to Bernard Herrmann's language. . . . I didn't consciously copy him, but it was *Hangover Square* that started that thought process in my head."[22] *Hangover Square* is that rare horror film with music as the focus of its plot rather than only its means of creating suspense. An unstable composer commits a series of murders while in the grip of amnesiac lapses, which are set off by discordant external sounds that trigger a sudden, high-pitched noise in his head and an urge to destroy anything that stands in his way. What popped into my head when I first heard Herrmann's unresolved dissonant chords at these moments in the film was the original ending of Sondheim's "Epiphany," after Sweeney has found his true calling: killing everyone. He sings ecstatically, "The work waits, I'm alive at last, And I'm full of joy!" with the orchestra then blasting a five-note *fortissimo* dissonant chord that dissolves eerily into a four-note *piano* crazed shadow chord (F♯–B–D–F), vividly signifying Todd's schizophrenic breakdown (see example 9.1).[23]

Although this is the ending that appeared in the first edition of the published piano-vocal score, it has seldom been heard in major productions or on recordings.[24] Sondheim explains that a similar result had occurred with Rose's "mad scene" in *Gypsy*:

I had persuaded Jule [Styne] to end the number on a high dissonant chord of eerie violin harmonics: a woman having a nervous breakdown would not end up on a triumphant tonic chord. . . . Oscar [Hammerstein] urged me to let the number come to a show-stopping climax to allow Ethel [Merman] to have her deserved thunderous ovation.[25]

**Table 9.2.** *Sweeney Todd*: musical layout

Italics indicate numbers cut from the original production but included in the published score and cast recording. Boldface is reserved for the eight occurrences of "The Ballad of Sweeney Todd." A line between numbers indicates intervening dialogue without underscoring.

ACT I

Prelude (Organ)

1   Prologue: **The Ballad of Sweeney Todd** [f♯ minor] (Todd, Company)

2   No Place Like London (Anthony, Todd, Beggar Woman)

2A   [m. 214ff] There Was a Barber and His Wife (Todd, Anthony)

2B   Transition Music

3   The Worst Pies in London (Mrs. Lovett)
—————

4   Poor Thing (Mrs. Lovett)
—————

5   My Friends (Todd, Mrs. Lovett)

5A   **Ballad of Sweeney Todd** (Lift Your Razor High) (Company)

6   Green Finch and Linnet Bird (Johanna)

7   Ah, Miss (Anthony, Johanna, Beggar Woman)

8A   Johanna, Part I (Anthony)

8B   Johanna, Part II (Anthony)

9   Pirelli's Miracle Elixir (Tobias, Crowd, Todd, Mrs. Lovett)

9A   Pirelli's Entrance (Pirelli)
—————

10   The Contest, Part I (Pirelli)
—————

10A   *The Contest, Part II* (Pirelli, Tobias)
—————

10B   **Ballad of Sweeney Todd** (Ensemble)

11   *Johanna* (Judge Turpin)

12   Wait (Mrs. Lovett, Beggar Woman, Todd)
—————

12A   Pirelli's Death (Pirelli)
—————

12B   Pirelli's Death Underscore

12C   **Ballad of Sweeney Todd** (3 Tenors)
—————

*(continued)*

**Table 9.2.** Continued

---

12D   Underscore

13   Kiss Me, Part I (Johanna, Anthony)

14   Ladies in Their Sensitivities (Beadle)

15   Kiss Me, Part II (Johanna, Anthony, Beadle, Judge)

15A   Underscore

16   Pretty Women, Part I (Judge, Todd)

16A   Pretty Women, Part II (Judge, Todd, Anthony)

17   Epiphany (Todd, Mrs. Lovett)

18   A Little Priest (Mrs. Lovett, Todd)

### ACT II

19   God, That's Good! (Tobias, Mrs. Lovett, Todd, Company)

20   Johanna ~ Act II Sequence (Anthony, Todd, Johanna, Beggar Woman)

20A   After Johanna Act II Sequence

21   By the Sea, Part I (Mrs. Lovett, Todd)

21A   By the Sea, Part II (Mrs. Lovett)

22   Wigmaker Sequence, Part I (Todd, Anthony)

**Ballad of Sweeney Todd** (Quintet)

Wigmaker Sequence, Part II (Anthony, Todd)

22A   The Letter (Quintet)

22B   After Letter Underscore

23   Not While I'm Around (Tobias, Mrs. Lovett)

23A   After Not While I'm Around

24   Parlor Songs, Part I (Beadle)

24A   Parlor Songs, Part II (Beadle, Mrs. Lovett, Tobias)

24B   Parlor Songs, Part III (Mrs. Lovett)

25   Fogg's Asylum (**Ballad of Sweeney Todd**) (Company)

25A   Fogg's Passacaglia

26   City on Fire! (Lunatics, Johanna)

27   Searching, Part I (Mrs. Lovett, Todd, Beggar Woman)

**Table 9.2.**  Continued

**Example 9.1.**  Original ending of No. 17, "Epiphany," mm. 78–83, *Sweeney Todd: The Demon Barber of Fleet Street* from Sondheim's published piano-vocal score (New York: Revelation Music and Rilting Music, 1981).

Sondheim recalls that twenty years later, "at the end of Todd's mad scene, Hal persuaded me that it was in the best interest of the actor. It was, but it allowed the audience a breather and dissipated the tension that I hoped would increase the humor of the next number, as tension always does."[26] In fact, the original ending of "Rose's Turn" portends Sweeney's: a five-note *fortissimo* explosive punch followed by a *pianissimo* four-note dissonant sonority (C–D♭–E♭–G), almost an inversion of Sweeney's.[27] Sondheim's attempt to avoid an applause-prompting finish for the actor playing Sweeney at *his* moment of epiphany, with the shadow chord "fading under dialogue," enables Mrs. Lovett to blithely break the tension with a deadpan delivery of "That's all very well." This invariably provokes a big laugh, followed by her urgent reminder, as she points to the chest containing Pirelli's corpse: "but all that matters now is him!" The cannibalistic idea that just pops into her head is *her* epiphany, which precipitates the stylistic and generic shift to musical comedy and "A Little Priest," the second half of the first-act double finale.

Apparently, Sondheim's attempt to write entirely on his own a horror movie for the stage hit a wall. In September 1977 the *New York Times* announced a change of plans: "Stephen Sondheim will not do the book for *Sweeney Todd*, but Hugh Wheeler will."[28] By then Sondheim also had finally convinced Harold Prince to stage the piece: "This show was the first time I sort of dragged Hal into sharing my vision. But Hal is not the fan of melodrama and farce that I am." Prince resisted: "I'm the wrong guy to direct it. Are we going to serve meat pies at intermission?"[29] But after reluctantly acquiescing, it was Prince who persuaded Sondheim to bring Wheeler on board as bookwriter. He, in turn, wanted to move *Sweeney Todd* even further away from the elements of "hiss-and-boo" melodrama: "We wanted to make it as nearly as we could into a sort of tragedy. I wrote it as a play, but I encouraged Steve to cannibalize it and make it nearly all music."[30]

Sondheim recalls the now collaborative process as largely "the three of us sitting in a room and pounding away at what it should and shouldn't be. . . . How in the hell do you tell that story and how large do you want it to be?" Prince had consented to direct the show only if he could expand it with the addition of an ensemble and an "epic" sociopolitical frame: "It could be about the class system, the industrial age, and the incursions of machinery on the spirit. . . . It was only when I realized the show was about revenge," Prince says, "that I knew how to do it." "For me," Sondheim countered, "what the show is really about is obsession. . . . Todd is the tragic hero in the classic sense that Oedipus is." "I suppose people who are collaborating should be after the same thing," Prince realized, "but Steve and I were obviously *not* with respect to *Sweeney*."[31] Sondheim reluctantly deferred to the director: "*Sweeney* was always conceived as a small piece, but Hal wanted to do it large and I wanted Hal to direct it. . . . Hal said you'll lose some of the scariness but I'll give it a large, epic feeling."[32] From the wings, Bond cautioned: "What's the matter with you people? Why don't you have a laugh? This is supposed to be funny."[33] And Sondheim had to agree with Bond: "There's an enormous advantage to comedy in melodrama; it's something Hitchcock made his reputation on. In every single one of his movies the laugh is immediately followed by the scream, or vice versa."[34] At first it seemed that Bond's play "would need little changing," Sondheim recalls, "but in fact as we got to work on it, much of the second half of the piece started to change in shape and in tone and in style."[35]

The absence of unanimity among the collaborators concerning the style, scale, and generic model for the piece did not augur favorably for a high-risk Broadway venture with a plot about mass murder and cannibalism. As writing progressed in 1978, three readings of what had been completed allowed the collaborators to assess their work in progress. At the first rehearsal of the Broadway cast of twenty-seven in January 1979 Prince articulated a mode of performance common to all the competing "larger-than-life" theatrical genres implicit in the work: "in the past the credo that governed the work Steve and I have done has been 'less is more.' This time I want more than anyone has ever seen before: if you don't chew up the scenery, we're going to be in trouble."[36] The show previewed at the cavernous 1,933-seat Uris Theatre in New York because designer Eugene Lee had dismantled an abandoned Rhode Island foundry and used it as the skeletal set, making out-of-town tryouts impossible. So much for Sondheim's "small piece."

Reviews of the March premiere were mixed, ranging from dismissive to "bloody good." Some critics concerned themselves with the question of whether the piece was actually a Broadway musical or an opera—an issue that is still being argued. Jack Kroll declared in *Newsweek*:

> *Sweeney Todd* is brilliant, even sensationally so, but its effect is very much a barrage of brilliancies, like flares fired aloft that dazzle and fade into something cold and dark. . . . Sondheim has been inching closer and closer to pure opera and *Sweeney Todd* is the closest he's come yet. . . . The problem is one of concept and unity: *Sweeney Todd* wants to make the same fusion of popular and high culture that Brecht and Weill made in *The Threepenny Opera*. But the fusion is never really made.[37]

Most of the major critics shared some of the reservations that Richard Eder expressed in the *New York Times*:

> The musical and dramatic achievements of Stephen Sondheim's black and bloody *Sweeney Todd* are so numerous and so clamorous that they trample and jam each other in that invisible but finite doorway that connects a stage and its audience, doing themselves some harm in the process. There is very little in "Sweeney Todd" that is not, in one way or another, a display of extraordinary

talent. . . . What keeps all its brilliance from coming together as a major work of art is a kind of confusion of purpose.[38]

A look at some key moments in the musical layout of *Sweeney Todd* will identify decisive instances of such collisions between competing generic conventions and stylistic idioms.

## Battling Ballads

*Sweeney Todd* begins with both a Prelude and a Prologue. "As the audience enters," the libretto reads, "an organist takes his place at a huge eccentric organ to the side of the stage and begins to play funeral music." Sondheim, however, now considers his Prelude "about as scary as an academic exercise" and recommends that it be omitted.[39] "The deafening shrill sound of a factory whistle blasts forth" to cue the initial blackout. "Lights come up to reveal the company, and a man steps forward" to open the Prologue by commanding the audience, "Attend the tale of Sweeney Todd."

In 2004, when *Sweeney Todd* debuted at the Komische Oper in Berlin in a production directed by Bond, some critics called "The Ballad of Sweeney Todd," a "Moritat." Like several of their New York colleagues twenty-five years earlier, they too described the moment as "Brechtian," an obvious descendant of the "Moritat vom Mackie Messer" ("Ballad of Mack the Knife"), which opens *Die Dreigroschenoper* (The Threepenny Opera). Bond concurred with that assessment:

> In my play there is no chorus. There is no, if you like, Brechtian commenting on the action; we're in the action and the story starts with the beginning and then goes to the end; it is not framed with comment by people. . . . There is no ballad of Sweeney Todd in the play. . . . The main addition [to the opera] is this "third eye chorus" which comments on the action.[40]

Sondheim's "Ballad of Sweeney Todd" indeed functions metadramatically rather than dramatically, in that it self-consciously addresses the audience, reminding them that what they are about to see is theater, a ritualistic reenactment of what Sondheim has called "an urban folktale." All but two of the actors in the show participate in the number, already in costume and makeup, but not in character. The last to appear is the actor playing Sweeney, who sings of the title character in third person: "Attend the tale of Sweeney Todd. He served a dark and a vengeful God. What happened then...well, that's the play, and he wouldn't want us to give it away."

Sondheim still bristles at the suggestion that his "Ballad" is in any way Brechtian: "*Sweeney* is entirely a plot piece which has a ballad running through as if there were a narrator. Brecht doesn't have a narrator. If anything, *Sweeney*'s closer to *Allegro*, which also had a chorus. . . . The show isn't Brechtian; it's a straightforward operetta with narration by the chorus."[41] Between its use as Prologue and Epilogue, abridged and varied versions of the Ballad intrude six times within the show (their placement is indicated in boldface in the musical layout presented in table 9.2); their function, however, is never "narrative" but rather, "descriptive" or "atmospheric."[42] These recurrences fill no gaps in the evening's storytelling, but instead function variously as a cinematic wipe or cross-fade for set changes, as markers articulating the show's substructure, or as transitions indicating passage of time or change of locale.[43] When the Ballad returns in full as the Epilogue, the actors, including recently deceased corpses, again address the audience directly. The framing numbers are identical in both music and lyrics up to m. 79, except that the Epilogue is in g minor, transposed up a semitone from the Prologue. After m. 79, new lyrics suggest that there are Sweeneys all around us, maybe even within us: "Perhaps today you gave a nod to Sweeney Todd" . . . "Isn't that Sweeney there beside you?" . . . "But everyone does it if seldom as well." The setting of the urban tale has abruptly shifted to the present, its putative function transformed from nineteenth-century potboiler into a cautionary sociological admonition to the audience, aspiring to an (unearned) Everyman significance.

I have long wondered whether "The Ballad of Sweeney Todd" was among the seven numbers Sondheim said that he had composed when he started writing his "chamber opera." He was working directly from Bond's play, where there is no hint of such a prologue, no chorus or ensemble, and no need for a "narrative" voice. And since such ballads belong to the generic conventions of neither melodrama nor horror movies, I thought it more plausible that the Ballad and its reprises might reify the impact on the score of Prince's later "epic" vision for the piece. So, when Mark Eden Horowitz asked if I had any burning questions for him to pose to Sondheim for inclusion in the "Encore" chapter appended to the second edition of *Sondheim on Music*, I submitted that puzzlement. Sondheim's answer appears on page 219 of the book. Horowitz states, "Regarding *Sweeney Todd*, one question came to me from a musicologist." Sondheim responds: "My stomach is tightening as you say that . . . but go on." Horowitz does so: "He is convinced that 'The Ballad of Sweeney Todd' was a late addition to the score, possibly suggested after Hugh Wheeler came on board with the show." Sondheim rebuts:

> No. It was the very first thing I wrote; absolutely. Once I decided that there was going to be some kind of storytelling thing, then I went right for it. And then the rest of the score was pretty well composed in sequence, starting with Anthony's entrance. But it started with "The Ballad of Sweeney Todd." Absolutely. The very first thing I wrote.[44]

Despite Sondheim's adamant denial, doubts about the chronology of composition persist. If he initially intended the piece to be small, a chamber opera for just ten characters, with a libretto closely tracking Bond's play, who was going to sing such a ballad? And at what point in the work's gestation was it decided that its recurrences would articulate the structure of the piece, with an ensemble singing these reprises and one of those calling for three solo tenors drawn from the ensemble? Might this be yet another instance of "how little there is to be sure of" about Sondheim's disclaimers, particularly when it comes to any influence of Weill or Brecht on his work?[45]

Whatever the evolution of the Prologue, there is actually another, but unlabeled, "ballad" in *Sweeney Todd*, which is indisputably narrative in function, as it initiates the telling of the tale to be attended. In a very long musical scene titled "No Place Like London" and identified in the piano-vocal score as "#2 & 2A," Todd responds to Anthony's curiosity about "what brought [him] to that sorry shipwreck" with "There was a barber and his wife" to begin an untitled ballad that will function much as Senta's does in *Die fliegende Holländer*.[46] When Mrs. Lovett starts the tale over again in number 4, she first replicates Todd's version of the backstory both musically and lyrically, except that the barber rather than his wife was "beautiful." But as Mrs. Lovett recounts what happened after Todd had been arrested and transported on trumped-up charges, she does so without empathy for Todd's wife Lucy or daughter Johanna. "Poor Thing" unfolds, paradoxically, first as a giddy beerhall waltz, then in a 6/8 quasi-tarantella, until Todd cuts her off with a screamed "No! Would no one have mercy on her?" The rest of the evening comprises a dramatization of the remainder of the second ballad, that of the barber and his wife. In the second-act finale, after Todd has waltzed Mrs. Lovett into her own oven, the music we hear as he cradles his dead wife in his arms is a reprise of "There was a barber and his wife." This is his Othello/Otello-like moment of recognition; his obsession with revenge has caused him to murder the very thing he loved most. If Todd is in any sense a tragic hero, this is his second epiphany: recognition of the cost of his first. Thus, the ballad of the barber and wife serves as the *dramatic* frame for the telling of the tale of Sweeney Todd, whereas "The Ballad of Sweeney Todd" and its reprise at the end of the show function as its *metadramatic* frame.

## Generic Juxtapositions

Sondheim bracketed Todd's broken-off ballad of the barber and his wife in number 2A with passages that he now labels "semi-recitative": "There's a hole in the world like a great black pit, / And the vermin of the world inhabit it, / And its morals aren't worth what a pig could spit."[47] (This is yet another "Brechtian" moment, one which several astute critics at its premiere recognized as derivative from lyrics in *The Threepenny Opera*.)[48] In example 9.2, compare m. 202, "There's a hole in the world," with m. 207, "I, too, have sailed." The entire intervening passage occurs over an F♯ pedal, and a cut from m. 201 to m. 207 can be made without any disruption to musical continuity or narrative flow. In example 9.3, the end of the scene, Sondheim reprises the first three lines of the semi-recitative, but here transposes it up a semitone, alternates 4/4 and 3/4 bars, and substitutes for the static pedal point an ostinato figure that he has called his "Stravinsky motif."[49] The lyric also intensifies: "There's a hole in the world like a great black pit / And it's filled with people who are filled with shit, / And the vermin of the world inhabit it." Note that the dynamics are still *sempre p* because Todd is only muttering to himself. This passage, too, is entirely expendable, if only in terms of musical syntax and continuity.

When the idea next occurs, in number 17, "Epiphany," which Sondheim called "Todd's breakdown" in his sketches, the ostinato, now marked *feroce* and *fortissimo*, reappears at the same pitch level as in example 9.3, but in doubled tempo and halved rhythmic values (see example 9.4). The pitches for "But not for long" are note-for-note the same as for "a foolish barber" at m. 218 in number 2A. This motivic connection cements the link between what had been a framing device for his ballad of a barber and his wife in the first scene to this penultimate number in Act I, when Todd decides "they all deserve to die," not merely Judge Turpin and the Beadle.[50] Might the first two occurrences of "There's a hole in the world" have been later insertions, back-patched into the show's first twenty minutes?

In number 2A this semi-recitative passage also serves another purpose. By appending the gesture to the end of Todd's telling of his tale to Anthony, Sondheim maximizes what Germans might call a *Stilbruch*, a disruptive stylistic break between that number and Mrs. Lovett's subsequent "Worst Pies in London," which signals an abrupt shift from one generic category of musical theater to a completely disparate one.[51] Paralleling the contrast in Bond's play between Todd's iambic blank verse and Mrs. Lovett's colloquialisms, "Worst Pies in London" emphasizes that she inhabits a musical world very different from Todd's semi-recitative. She sings "musical comedy numbers in a show that isn't a musical comedy."[52] After Mrs. Lovett's tour-de-force entrance number, the audience has been introduced to the two principal characters and been informed by their antithetical musical idioms that they are anything but "fated to be mated." Bond described this dichotomy to his cast at the Komische Oper Berlin: "This play is *Flying Dutchman* crossed with *Die Fledermaus*. Sweeney Todd is from *Flying Dutchman*, Mrs. Lovett is from *Fledermaus*. This is the tension of the story and the performance."[53]

**Example 9.2.** Number 2A, The ballad of the barber and his wife, mm. 201–208, Todd's "semi-recitative," *Sweeney Todd* (New York: Revelation Music and Rilting Music, 1981).

**Example 9.2.**  Continued

Nowhere are the vocal, linguistic, stylistic, and generic dichotomies between Sweeney's and Mrs. Lovett's manners more obvious and telling than in
the juxtaposition of Todd's alternations of keening and railing in the aria-like
"Epiphany" with the whimsical and wicked music-hall cleverness of "A Little
Priest." Prince describes the crucial function of the double finale: "The demonic
glee of 'A Little Priest,' coming right after the demonic hatred of 'Epiphany,'
provides a release for the audience. 'A Little Priest' is Mrs. Lovett's epiphany
in which she devises the money-making scheme of using Todd's victims as
the ingredients for her meat pies."[54] Had the audience been revolted by Mrs.
Lovett's recipes, many would not have returned after intermission. Therefore,
this list-song-on-steroids had to seduce the audience into subscribing on some
level to her scheme and somehow make cannibalism seem palatable. Sondheim
achieved this brilliantly by manipulating the audience into "getting her drift" a
full twenty-five measures before Sweeney does and thus into becoming de facto
accomplices to her plan. Once the distracted Sweeney does catch on, the ensuing
eight-minute "Little Priest" alternates between two dueling waltz idioms. Todd's
swirling aristocratic Viennese strains, which always begin with a reference to
the world at large, alternate with Mrs. Lovett's rag-tag clog waltz, which she always initiates in order to introduce the next flavor of the moment. Seven vamps,

**Example 9.3.** Todd's "semi-recitative," conclusion of no. 2A, The ballad of the barber and his wife, mm. 256–262, *Sweeney Todd* (New York: Revelation Music and Rilting Music, 1981).

six with spoken dialogue and one with merely convulsive laughter, articulate these binary alternations, which escalate lyrically, sexually, and dynamically to the final pose caricatured in the poster art (see figure 9.2). Alternating between B major and E♭ major, the pair finally meet in the middle, D♭ major, with mutual agreement to "take the customers that we can get," not discriminating great from small, serving anyone at all.

An audience inevitably finds itself cheering at the prospect—except in the film version, where Helena Bonham Carter's lackadaisical performance of this show-stopper manages to deprive the number of its vaudeville verve and slapstick humor. This curious internalized interpretation is exacerbated by director

**Example 9.4.** Todd's "semi-recitative," mm. 16–22 of no. 17, "Epiphany," *Sweeney Todd* (New York: Revelation Music and Rilting Music, 1981).

**Figure 9.2.** Photograph of the final pose of Act I, "A Little Priest," as it appeared on the back cover of the 2-LP RCA Red Seal original cast album of *Sweeney Todd*, as well as its reissue as a CD.

Burton's misguided mickey-mousing of each successive flavor of meat pie by having Lovett and Todd see them pass by on the street outside the pie shop's window, thereby robbing the number of both its improvisatory spontaneity and the humor dependent on the next offering on the bill of fare coming as a surprise. There could be no more vivid demonstration of Sondheim's assertion that stage and film musicals are entirely different genres or more persuasive counterargument to his hyperbolic claim that the film version of *Sweeney Todd* is the "first musical that has ever transferred successfully to the screen."[55]

These are but a few examples of generic and stylistic jostling and juxtaposition that energize the musical thriller. There are many more. The dazzling lyric and patter extravagance of Tobias's "Pirelli's Miracle Elixir" gives way to Pirelli's over-the-top parody of Italian comic opera barbers, which climaxes on a high

C, only for him to lose the shaving contest to the mute Todd. The retro oper-
etta-like vocalism of the naive innocents in "Green Finch and Linnet Bird" and
"Johanna" is dissected by the erratic gushing of "Ah, Miss" and then later all but
consummated in the breathless and brainless yet virtuosic "Kiss Me," whose bi-
partite structure in turn frames the Beadle's metrically unstable "Ladies in Their
Sensitivities."[56] Sondheim's abilities as collaborative dramatist manifest themselves even more virtuosically in the three disparate numbers sharing the title
"Johanna": Anthony's passionate profession of love at first sight, Judge Turpin's
twisted, self-flagellating lechery regarding his ward, and Todd's "paternal" lyrical counterpoint to Anthony's yearning reprise in number 20, as the now murdering barber sings "dreamily, benign and detached," while slashing the throats
of two customers and being denied a third because the customer brought along
his daughter. The juxtaposition in numbers 21–23 of the cozy metrical regularity of Mrs. Lovett's vision of domestic bliss, "By the Sea," with the maximal
surreal distortion of "The Letter" (sung by a quintet from the company and
addressed to Judge Turpin), is followed by the guileless diatonic simplicity of
Tobias's "Not While I'm Around." And most imposing of all, the final sequence
in Act II, numbers 26–29, where Sondheim generates maximal suspense and
tension by having virtually all of the principal musical ideas collide, coincides
with the serial murders of virtually all the remaining principal characters, with
the exception of Tobias, Anthony, and Johanna.[57] Sondheim remembers: "I had
a better time writing the last twenty minutes of *Sweeney Todd* than anything I've
done since the background music of *Stavisky*. It was just a matter of, 'Okay, let's
scare them.'"[58]

## Making Mincemeat of *Sweeney*

This sort of fertile hybridity seems to tempt, if not invite, directors to pick and
choose, privileging this or that generic or stylistic component over others. The
range of disparate productions mounted for more than four decades raises a fundamental question: Where does *Sweeney Todd* belong? Stylistically, generically,
institutionally, where is the tale attended most persuasively: in the opera house,
symphony hall, Broadway or West End theater, repertory companies, or even
real pie shops? That question is no more settled today than it was for the creative team in 1978–1979. In many of its incarnations, *Sweeney*'s identity has been
radically altered from its initial production, sometimes almost unrecognizably.
Substantial chunks of the score have been excised, particularly in productions
utilizing actor-musicians or lacking a choral ensemble. Performances by actor-
musicians have required reconsideration of what is diegetic and non-diegetic in
a mode of storytelling that is already extremely complex.[59] Orchestras have been

downsized to a trio (in the pie shop production) and expanded to as many as
sixty-five (in semi-staged symphonic versions). Smaller stagings have required
actors to play multiple roles, if not also instruments, sometimes as a corpse
resurrecting to impersonate another character without so much as a costume
change. Cross-gender doubling of Pirelli and the Beggar Woman has become almost commonplace, thereby adding a layer of gender identity and politics absent
from the original.

Although often marketed, and sometimes hailed, as bold reimaginings, most
of these *Sweeney*s have been motivated as much by financial as aesthetic considerations. And, remarkably, Sondheim has apparently tolerated, if not sanctioned,
virtually all of them. Implicit in that decision is an acceptance of the fluidity of
the "work," which continues to evolve as an open-ended series of provisional,
event-specific "scripts" without ever achieving an authoritative "text." Thus, if a
production opts to discard Jonathan Tunick's original orchestrations as if these
had been no less production-specific than sets, costumes, and lighting, they must
be, at least to Sondheim, inessential to *Sweeney*'s "work-identity." When asked,
for example, what he thought of Sarah Travis's Tony-winning orchestrations for
Doyle's Broadway production, Sondheim opined, "what she's done is absolutely
brilliant":

> Jonathan Tunick's original orchestrations may be the best ever heard on
> Broadway, but this is a whole other matter. The variety of sounds she's gotten
> out of the instruments and also the practical way in which they allow John
> [Doyle] to work with the performers onstage is extraordinary. But what got me
> most about the orchestrations is what they did for the play's atmosphere. These
> are wonderfully weird textures.... [But] there are certain things missing in this
> production—orchestral climaxes, choral climaxes—that are simply impossible
> because of the resources.[60]

I asked Tunick whether he had attended a performance. He said he hadn't and
made no attempt to conceal his disappointment with regard to the replacement
of his orchestrations with those played by the actor-musicians. He explained
that "Steve composes at the piano and hears his scores pianistically," an observation that Sondheim has confirmed.[61] That the published piano-vocal score
of *Sweeney Todd* was the first of Sondheim's stage works to be edited from his
piano draft rather than from a cued reduction of its orchestration is telling.[62]
As Stephen Banfield noted in 1993, "For Sondheim, the compositional process
ends with the complete pencil draft of a voice and piano copy in short score."[63]
It's hardly surprising, then, that certain passages seem to have been conceived
for performance by piano rather than orchestra, none more so than "Kiss Me,"
whose keyboard accompaniment rivals the technical demands of the "Toccata"

finale of *Le Tombeau de Couperin*, which, of course, Ravel omitted when he created the orchestral suite. The rapid repeated-note figurations, varied ostinato
patterns, cross-handed inner-voice melodic lines, and treacherous *perpetuum
mobile* of "Kiss Me" suggest that Ravel's "Toccata" may even have been a conscious model. Hearing Sondheim's piano accompaniment for the number played
(sans voices) at 132 quarter notes per minute that he specified for Part II of "Kiss
Me" demonstrates vividly why even Tunick couldn't preserve that sort of pianistic virtuosity, much less could it be retained in subsequent actor-musician
orchestrations.[64]

If Sondheim considers his own piano draft as the culminating urtext of his
score, any orchestration thereof remains provisional, adaptable if not dispos-
able, and production-specific, even when created with the composer's input and
right of approval. Though proudly self-identified as a collaborative *dramatist*,
Sondheim seems resistant to the possibility of being a collaborative *composer,*
although he relies on others to generate the score actually heard in productions.
The critic Terry Teachout has suggested that "Sondheim's inability to write directly for the orchestra is a major limitation of his work. Not only is much of
his 'orchestral' writing too obviously pianistic in origin, but the fact that he
allows the instrumental colors and textures of his music to be supplied by other
hands means that he cannot be given full credit for its creation."[65] For those of
us fortunate enough to have experienced the original Broadway productions of
Sondheim's and his collaborators' works, their sonic identities were indelibly established by their orchestrations and then widely disseminated on original cast
albums. Hasn't something intrinsic if not essential been abandoned when they
are replaced by the equivalent of a "continuo" of keyboard and bass, with additional obligato instruments joining only when released from cast-specific actors'
other obligations?

In 2005, shortly before Doyle's production opened in New York, Hal Leonard
published *The Complete "Follies" Collection: Author's Edition*, presenting the
"original Stephen Sondheim Piano/Vocal arrangements" of all thirty-three songs
from *Follies*. An "Author's Note" explains: "As these arrangements were made
from original manuscripts, there may be inconsistencies with the published
Vocal Score of *Follies* which is based on the orchestral arrangements, not the
original piano/vocal manuscripts. Additionally all tempos and dynamics are deliberate and are to be considered definitive as are all lyric emendations which
differ from any prior publications of the *Follies* score." Sondheim also contributed
a foreword in which he claims that "this compilation of music and lyrics is the
most complete publication to date of *Follies* either on record or in print."[66] Close
comparison of this collection with the piano-vocal reduction based on Tunick's
original orchestral arrangements demonstrates what is lost when his contribution has been discarded in favor of the piano-vocal urtext of a collaborative

dramatist-turned-auteur for the purposes of such a publication. Where would a similar approach leave us in an attempt at an authoritative scholarly edition of *Sweeney Todd*—or any of Sondheim's other musicals, for that matter? Is a "Sondheim Critical Edition" destined to be based on a piano-vocal draft, deprived of the dynamic collaborative experience and ongoing revision intrinsic to theatrical production?

Meanwhile, *Sweeney*'s identity continues to evolve, although its licensing agent, Music Theater International, has recently announced that henceforth licensees will be required to perform one of the authorized orchestrations or engage one of the approved orchestrators to make any alterations. It remains to be seen whether those horses can be successfully herded back into the corral. Perhaps to a greater extent than any work of the American musical theater, including *Show Boat* and *Porgy and Bess*, *Sweeney Todd* has managed not only to survive but to thrive without a unitary authorized *text* that fully conveys the *work*'s messy, dynamic, and endlessly fascinating generic and stylistic diversity. With so many *Sweeney*s all around us, will it ever be possible to ask a "real one" to reveal itself? The "Work" waits!

# Notes

1. Earlier versions of this chapter were presented at musicology symposia at Yale University and Cornell University in 2008–2009, and then a decade later as a keynote paper at the conference "Reading Musicals: Sources, Editions, Performance" at the Great American Songbook Foundation in Carmel, Indiana. I am grateful for responses and suggestions from colleagues at those events.

   Frank Verlizzo, who signed his work "Fraver," quoted in Craig Zadan, *Sondheim & Co.*, 2nd ed., updated (New York: Da Capo, 1994), 264.

2. "There were a number of reasons why I wanted to call the show a musical thriller and not a musical melodrama. . . . Thriller is one of those words that people take more seriously; it has all the implications of the colorful part of melodrama without any of the comic inferences that contemporary audiences would draw from the word." Stephen Sondheim, "Larger Than Life: Reflections on Melodrama and *Sweeney Todd*," in *Melodrama*, ed. Daniel Gerould (New York: New York Literary Forum, 1980), 7:7–8.

3. Stephen Sondheim, *Finishing the Hat: Collected Lyrics (1954–1981) with Attendant Comments, Principles, Heresies, Grudges, Whines and Anecdotes* (New York: Knopf, 2010), 332.

4. Ibid.

5. *West Side Story*, Sondheim's first Broadway show, may be a close second in terms of its generic hybridity. Most of the works emerging from the Prince-Sondheim collaboration challenged or collapsed generic boundaries and conventions: musical comedy and revue in *Company*, operetta and musical play in *A Little Night Music*, and a myriad

of Japanese, British, and American dramatic models in *Pacific Overtures*. Among Sondheim's subsequent works, *Assassins* may be the most wide-ranging amalgamation of generic prototypes.

6. The production transferred to the West End in 2015 and ran Off-Broadway at the 130-seat Barrow Street Theatre in 2017.

7. This highly influential production started life without authorization in the United Kingdom in 2004, but after Sondheim saw and approved the approach, it transferred to the West End and then to Broadway in November 2005 with Patti LuPone and Michael Cerveris for a 349-performance run, recouping after just nineteen weeks. Doyle's cost-saving practice of hiring a cast of actor-musicians was repeated the next season for his production of *Company*. It has subsequently become so ubiquitous that several colleges and conservatories, predominantly in the United Kingdom, offer actor-musicianship training programs. For a history of actor-musicians in the musical theater see Jeremy Harrison, *Actor-Musicianship* (London: Bloomsbury, 2016). For Sondheim's view of Doyle's production, see Charles Isherwood, "Cutting 'Sweeney Todd' to the Bone," interview with Sondheim, *New York Times*, October 30, 2005, https://www.nytimes.com/2005/10/30/theater/newsandfeatures/cutting-swee ney-todd-to-the-bone.html. Note that the original cast album contains significant cuts that were not made in the production itself, which did, however, omit all of nos. 10A and 24B, as well as substantial sections of nos. 9, 19, and 28.

8. While in London, a twenty-year-old animation major at CalArts named Timothy Burton spotted the poster for *Sweeney Todd*: "I didn't know anything about Stephen Sondheim," he said, "but the poster just looked kind of cool, kind of interesting. . . . I went to see it twice because I liked it so much." Terri Roberts, "The Work of a Fan: Screenwriter John Logan Talks About Adapting *Sweeney* for the Screen." *Sondheim Review* 14, no. 3 (Spring 2008): 14. See also Mark Salisbury, *Sweeney Todd: The Demon Barber of Fleet Street* [on the making of the film] (London: Titan, 2007), 13–14; and Sylviane Gold, "Demon Barber, Meat Pies and All, Sings on Screen," *New York Times*, November 4, 2007.

9. Sondheim, *Finishing the Hat*, 376.

10. Sondheim, quoted in Zadan, *Sondheim & Co.*, 243. See also Sondheim, "Larger Than Life," 3–14.

11. Interview with Christopher Bond, September 24, 2004, following the dress rehearsal of *Sweeney Todd*, which he was directing at the Komische Oper in Berlin. Published in English as an appendix in Marco Franke, *Stephen Sondheims "Sweeney Todd": Ein Werkporträt* (Hamburg: Diplomica, 2009): Anhang, 2–8. Bond recalled that Trevor Nunn's production of *The Revenger's Tragedy* (1606) for the Royal Shakespeare Company in 1966 had particularly influenced his adaptation of Pitt's melodrama, prompting him to treat the barber empathetically until halfway through the play.

12. Meryle Secrest, *Stephen Sondheim: A Life* (New York: Knopf, 1998), 290.

13. For a more detailed account of the interaction of Bond and Sondheim, see ibid., 289–291. Sondheim recalled in 1979 that when he saw Bond's play in London, his reaction was, "Oh, my goodness, an opera . . . as I realized it was composed of solos, duets, trios, etc. in terms of the structure of the piece." Harold Prince and Stephen

Sondheim, "On Collaboration Between Authors and Directors," moderated by Gretchen Cryer, in *Dramatists Guild Quarterly* 16, no. 3 (Summer 1979): 23.

14. *New York Times*, August 27, 1976, quoted in Zadan, *Sondheim & Co.*, 245.

15. Sondheim, quoted in ibid., 246.

16. For a comparison of several other parallel passages from Bond and from Wheeler and Sondheim, see Stephen Banfield's discussion of Sondheim's compositional process in *Sondheim's Broadway Musicals* (Ann Arbor: University of Michigan Press, 1993), 87–89, 283–285.

17. Sondheim, quoted in Zadan, *Sondheim & Co.*, 246.

18. Mark Eden Horowitz, *Sondheim on Music: Major Decisions and Minor Details*, 2nd ed. (Lanham, MD: Scarecrow, 2010), 138.

19. Bond, quoted in Franke, *Stephen Sondheims Sweeney Todd*, Anhang, 8.

20. Sondheim, quoted in June Wolfberg, "Attend the Tale: A Conversation with Stephen Sondheim," *Spotlight: The Magazine of the New York City Opera Guild* 16, no. 4 (Fall 1984): 13.

21. Sondheim, quoted in Zadan, *Sondheim & Co.*, 246.

22. Sondheim, quoted in Secrest, *Sondheim: A Life*, 295.

23. In *Sondheim on Music* he discusses what he had labeled in a sketch "Sweeney Chord" and its relation to the "Bernard Herrmann chord," which he spells D–E♭–F♭–B♭ and calls "one of the basic building blocks of the whole piece" (Horowitz, *Sondheim on Music*, 72, 127–128). The ear-shattering factory whistle that punctuated key moments of the original Broadway production may well have been inspired by one of the "triggers" in *Hangover Square*. See Craig M. McGill, "Sondheim's Use of the 'Herrmann Chord' in *Sweeney Todd*," *Studies in Musical Theatre* 6, no. 3 (2012): 291–312. On this moment in *Sweeney*, also see Jeffrey Magee's chapter in this volume.

24. The recording that best transmits Sondheim's original ending, though with a reduced orchestration, is the 2012 London Cast Album of the Olivier Award–winning production starring Michael Ball and Imelda Staunton, directed by Jonathan Kent and set in the 1930s.

25. Sondheim, *Finishing the Hat*, 77.

26. Ibid., 355.

27. See Jeffrey Magee, "Whose Turn Is It? Where *Gypsy*'s Finale Came from and Where It Went," *Studies in Musical Theatre* 13, no. 2 (2019): 117–132. Sondheim's sketch of this ending is included there on page 125.

28. *New York Times*, September 16, 1977, quoted in Zadan, *Sondheim & Co.*, 246. Sondheim recalls getting "panicky:" "I wish I'd stuck to my guns and just done it myself, but I couldn't. And Hugh had written murder mysteries under a pseudonym for a long time; and we'd worked together very happily; and he was British—he knew what Sweeney Todd was as a legend and all that. And I'm very glad, because he made some changes that are very important and very good for the show." Horowitz, *Sondheim on Music*, 149.

29. Zadan, *Sondheim & Co.*, 245.

30. Ibid., 246.

31. Prince and Sondheim, quoted in ibid., 245. See also Prince and Sondheim, "On Collaboration Between Authors and Directors," 14, 19.

32. David Savran, *In Their Own Words: Contemporary American Playwrights* (New York: Theatre Communications Group, 1988), 235.

33. Bond recalled that Prince had been "very keen to make this old story take place in a machine, saying that society was grinding people." See Franke, *Stephen Sondheims Sweeney Todd*, Anhang, 7.

34. Sondheim, quoted in Wolfberg, "Attend the Tale," 13.

35. Sondheim, in Prince and Sondheim, "On Collaboration Between Authors and Directors," 23.

36. Harold Prince, quoted in Foster Hirsch, *Harold Prince and the American Musical Theatre*, expanded ed. (New York: Applause Books, 2005), 124.

37. Jack Kroll, "The Blood Runs Cold," *Newsweek,* March 12, 1979), quoted in Zadan, *Sondheim & Co.*, 258. Many critics of the original production invoked "operatic" as a generic descriptive for the "musical thriller," and that controversial label became only more ubiquitous as *Sweeney* entered the repertory of American opera houses in the mid-1980s. New York City Opera confronted the question head-on in its advance publicity in 1984: "Is *Sweeney Todd* an opera?" Prince offered that "any piece that is 95% music must surely be an opera." Beverly Sills argued that it belonged in City Opera's repertory because she could cast it "without going outside this house." Sondheim famously sidestepped the generic issue by making it an institutional one, saying: "An opera is something performed in an opera house in front of an opera audience." Wolfberg, "Attend the Tale," 14. A review of the vast critical and scholarly literature on this topic, following on George Martin, "On the Verge of Opera: Stephen Sondheim," *Opera Quarterly* 6, no. 3 (Spring 1989): 76–85—as well as the changing "crossover" contexts for American musical theater and opera—would require massive research and a substantial publication of its own. Any conclusions concerning *Sweeney*'s operatic identity would, no doubt, depend as much on the institutions and performers presenting it and the audiences attending it as on any definitive evaluation of its attributes and demands. The debate may meanwhile have become moot. Michael John LaChiusa shrugged his shoulders to the question in *Opera News* almost twenty years ago: "Is it 'opera' or 'musical theater'? Who cares, as long as it's good?" ("Is It 'Opera' or 'Musical Theater'?" *Opera News*, August 2002, 12–15, 73). Nevertheless, the summer 2015 issue of the *Sondheim Review* is titled "Sondheim and Opera."

38. Richard Eder in the *New York Times*, March 2, 1979, quoted in Steven Suskin, *More Opening Nights on Broadway: A Critical Quotebook of the Musical Theatre, 1965–1981* (New York: Schirmer Books, 1997), 888–889.

39. Horowitz, *Sondheim on Music*, 127.

40. Bond, quoted in *Stephen Sondheims Sweeney Todd*, Anhang, 7–8.

41. Sondheim, quoted in Savran, *In Their Own Words*, 228–229.

42. This is a metadramatic device already used by Sondheim and Prince in *A Little Night Music* as the Liebeslieders sing and waltz in and out of scenes cinematically; they would attempt it again for transitions in *Merrily We Roll Along*.

43. Sondheim agreed to director Timothy Burton's proposal that "The Ballad of Sweeney Todd" be omitted from the film as essential to neither action nor characterization—in fact, in this context Sondheim recognized that "it interrupts the action." For his detailed explanation of the omission of all ensemble numbers in the film, see Horowitz, *Sondheim on Music*, 220.

44. Ibid., 219. Sondheim recalls that for backers' auditions for *Sweeney Todd*, he had "seven absolutely exemplary songs which covered all colors of the show, except that I didn't have a choral piece." Prince and Sondheim, "On Collaboration Between Authors and Directors," 24. Might this imply that "The Ballad of Sweeney Todd" had not yet been composed at that stage of the show's pre-production evolution? I do not recall suggesting to Horowitz that the Ballad may have postdated Wheeler's participation, but rather that it may have postdated Prince's.

45. Sondheim has repeatedly denied being influenced by Brecht or Weill, with the exception of the songs in *Company* being utilized in a Brechtian way as "comment and counterpoint." When asked point-blank by David Savran, "What about Kurt Weill and Bertolt Brecht?" Sondheim pulled no punches: "I'm not a Brecht-Weill fan. I'm one of those heretics who likes Weill's Broadway music better. . . . I do like the music in *Threepenny*. The rest of their work strikes me as repetition of the same stuff" (Savran, *In Their Own Words*, 228). Sondheim does not mention his collaboration in 1968 with Jerome Robbins, Leonard Bernstein, and John Guare on *A Pray by Blecht*, an adaptation of Brecht's *Lehrstück*, *The Exception and the Rule* (*Die Ausnahme und die Regel*, 1930).

46. The published piano-vocal score does not contain any indication of where #2A begins, nor does the conductor's score licensed by Music Theatre International. I have concluded that the most logical placement is the *meno mosso* at m. 214, labeled "intensely, molto rubato," preceding the lyric "There was a barber and his wife." Stephen Banfield also invokes "Senta's Ballad" but describes it as occupying a central structural position "converse" to the framing function of "The Ballad of Sweeney Todd." He does not make a connection between Wagner's and Todd's narrative ballads. See Banfield, *Sondheim's Broadway Musicals*, 304.

47. Horowitz, *Sondheim on Music*, 126.

48. See, e.g., Peachum's closing stanzas of the "First Threepenny Finale": "Of course that's all there is to it / The world is poor and man's a shit. We should aim high instead of low / But in our present state this can't be so. Which means He has us in a trap: The whole damn thing's a load of crap. The world is poor, and man's a shit / Of course that's all there is to it." *Bertolt Brecht: Collected Plays*, ed. Ralph Manheim and John Willett (New York: Vintage, 1977), 2:179. This new English translation had received its American premiere in a New York Shakespeare Festival production that ran for 307 performances at the Vivian Beaumont Theatre from May 1976 until January 1977 with Raul Julia as Macheath and C. K. Alexander as Peachum.

49. Horowitz, *Sondheim on Music*, 128.

50. Sondheim himself provides at his piano a detailed musical analysis of Todd's breakdown in an eighty-five-minute documentary about the London production titled "*Sweeney Todd*: Scenes from the Making of a Musical," which originally aired

on British television on July 26, 1980. It also includes commentary by Christopher Bond and Harold Prince. The complete film can be accessed in ten episodes at https://www.youtube.com/playlist?list=PLTvqeUCUx4UKsgTWyptg1kJHGs1lNhS_H.    In episode 2 Sondheim does the same with "The Ballad of Sweeney Todd," explaining the use of the "Dies irae" and the way his harmonies create the "creepy atmosphere" of the number. Ken Mandelbaum has provided a helpful inventory of the television film, which was never released commercially, in "Obscure Videos: *Sweeney* Special," *Sondheim Review* 12, no. 4 (Summer 2006): 44–45.

51. Sondheim exploits the generic and stylistic juxtaposition of Todd's and Lovett's music throughout the work, often to build and release suspense. For a brief and largely derivative summary of such procedures, see Millie Taylor, "*Sweeney Todd*: From Melodrama to Musical Tragedy," in *The Oxford Handbook of Sondheim Studies*, ed. Robert Gordon (New York: Oxford University Press, 2014), 335–349.

52. Choreographer Larry Fuller, quoted in Hirsch, *Harold Prince*, 125.

53. Bond, quoted in Franke, *Stephen Sondheims Sweeney Todd*, Anhang, 4.

54. Harold Prince, quoted in Hirsch, *Harold Prince*, 127.

55. Norman Lebrecht, quoting Sondheim's assertion at a London press conference, "When a Movie Outshines the Outstanding Original," *Scena*, February 12, 2008, http://www.scena.org/lsm.sm13-5/sm13_5_sweeneytodd_en.html. For a dissenting view of the "misguided" film, see David Thomson, "Attending the Tale of *Sweeney Todd*: The Stage Musical and Tim Burton's Film Version," in *The Oxford Handbook of Sondheim Studies*, ed. Robert Gordon (New York: Oxford University Press, 2014), 296–305. Thomson's comparison of the film with Hitchcock's *Psycho*, with music by Herrmann, is especially illuminating.

56. Sondheim and Wheeler thereby rendered Anthony and Johanna so inept and empty-headed that they in effect become a "secondary comic couple" in the dramatis personae of a musical comedy within the musical thriller—one of the most substantial departures from Bond's play.

57. See Banfield, *Sondheim's Broadway Musicals*, 288–289, for the diagram titled "Reprises of Musical Motifs and Numbers in *Sweeney Todd*."

58. Sondheim, quoted in Zadan, *Sondheim & Co.*, 251.

59. I recall asking Hal Prince what he thought of Doyle's production. With characteristic diplomacy, he responded that he was glad that he had directed the show himself before he saw the actor-musician version because he didn't think he would have been able to follow the plot if he didn't already know it.

60. Isherwood, "Cutting 'Sweeney Todd' to the Bone."

61. See Horowitz, *Sondheim on Music*, 129: "I think I hear pianistically."

62. The piano-vocal score published in 1981 by Rilting Music, edited by Frank Metis, contains the following prefatory note in bold type: "This score has been prepared from the composer's piano copy rather than the piano-conductor parts so that it can be more useful to the rehearsal pianist. As a result, when orchestral parts are utilized, some small musical discrepancies will be found." When I conducted a production of *Sweeney Todd* in 2003, however, I discovered this to be a rehearsal-busting understatement; the discrepancies between the rental piano-conductor score and

orchestral parts and the Rilting piano-vocal score were substantial enough to force rehearsal pianists to play from hastily assembled copies of the rental piano reduction of Tunick's orchestration and for me to reconcile instrumental parts with the Rilting score. All of the piano-vocal scores of Sondheim's shows thereafter follow this model, based on Sondheim's piano drafts and therefore uncued, with a similar prefatory disclaimer about "small musical discrepancies."

63. Banfield, *Sondheim's Broadway Musicals*, 76.

64. A "piano accompaniment/rehearsal track" of "Kiss Me (Part II) can be heard at https://www.youtube.com/watch?v=pVe_J9i7oFI.

65. Terry Teachout, "Sondheim's Operas," *Commentary*, May 2003, https://www.commentarymagazine.com/articles/terry-teachout/sondheims-operas/. Teachout suggests that a "compelling objection to *Sweeney Todd*'s acceptance as an opera is that it was orchestrated not by the composer but by Jonathan Tunick, who has scored most of Sondheim's Broadway shows." Of course, this sort of disparagement of Broadway composers' dependence on specialist orchestrators-for-hire was hardly original in critical discourse at the time.

66. Stephen Sondheim, *The Complete "Follies" Collection: Author's Edition* (Milwaukee: Hal Leonard, 2005), 1–2. Sondheim's claim about the completeness of this edition pertains only to the songs he wrote for *Follies*. It includes no other essential material such as the Prologue, Overture, dance expansions, and "routined" versions of vocal numbers (the "Loveland Sequence," for example, has been sliced up into its constituent songs and then presented alphabetically). The "complete collection" does include the four replacement numbers that Sondheim now regrets he wrote for the 1987 London production and nine numbers cut from the original production ("The Follies Notebook"). This publication essentially removes situation, plot, sequence, and character from *Follies* the stage work and instead presents a complete collection of only its songs.

# 10

# "A sad and listless affair"

## The Unsung Film Adaptation of Sondheim's
## *A Little Night Music*

*Geoffrey Block*

> The movie was a sad and listless affair, and a waste of everyone's time.
> Stephen Sondheim, *Finishing the Hat*

> I know people who openly loathe it, and I am at a loss to understand why. I find it [*A Little Night Music*] quite the most consistently stylish, intelligent and enchanting movie musical since *Gigi.*
> Rex Reed, *Daily News*

This essay explores the status, compositional history, content, flaws, and achievements of the little-known and more-often-than-not maligned film version of *A Little Night Music* (1978).[1] *Night Music* was by no means the only film musical adaptation subject to such criticism. In fact, with few exceptions film critics and scholars since the arrival of the sound film in the late 1920s have usually denigrated film adaptations in favor of original film musicals.[2] *Night Music*'s co-creator Stephen Sondheim shares this view. During the course of his 2007 interview with Jesse Green, in which he states that he found unsatisfactory the four film adaptations of his work prior to *Sweeney Todd* (*West Side Story*, *Gypsy*, *A Funny Thing Happened on the Way to the Forum*, and *Night Music*), Sondheim could think of only three film musicals of *any* type that he enjoyed. None were adaptations of stage musicals.[3]

The 1978 film version of *Night Music* was adapted from the musical of the same name, directed by Harold Prince (1928–2019), with a book by Hugh Wheeler (1916–1987) and lyrics and music by Sondheim (b. 1930), all of whom retained their assigned roles from the original successful version that opened on Broadway on February 25, 1973. After addressing the reasons why critics, scholars, and others were so disapproving of this particular film, this essay attempts to balance, in part, the negative critical barrage by exploring

Geoffrey Block, *"A sad and listless affair"* In: *Sondheim in Our Time and His.* Edited by: W. Anthony Sheppard, Oxford University Press. © Oxford University Press 2022. DOI: 10.1093/oso/9780197603192.003.0011

aspects of the film that some critics, including Prince (but not Sondheim), found worthy of merit or at least honorable mention. The chapter also focuses on how the film both follows and departs from the stage version, what Sondheim added to the film as lyricist and composer, how the finished film evolved from Wheeler's final screenplay draft, and the artistic consequences of these changes.

## Spoiler Alert

In his annotated lyrics, *Finishing the Hat* (2010), Sondheim credits Arthur Laurents with successfully conveying to him the importance of subtext.[4] Sondheim recalled his introduction to this important idea when he attended a session at the Actors Studio at Laurents's suggestion during the early stages of their collaboration on *West Side Story* (for which Laurents wrote the book and Sondheim the lyrics). Looking back on his development as a lyricist, Sondheim recalled in 2010 that "the idea of the actor as an instrument, and the uses of subtext—informed nearly everything I wrote after that session at the Studio."[5]

After writing about subtext in his 1974 essay "Theater Lyrics" Sondheim returned to this topic in "The World of Stephen Sondheim," one of several programs in the series *André Previn & the Pittsburgh Symphony Orchestra*, broadcast on PBS-TV on March 13, 1977.[6] About twenty-five minutes into his interview with Previn, Sondheim offered a clear and succinct definition of subtext to introduce a live performance of "Sorry-Grateful" from *Company*. After explaining to Previn that subtext is "saying one thing and having the music express something else," his host asked Sondheim to provide a more specific example. Sondheim quickly came up with the following: "When I'm talking to you right now, I'm thinking I'm going to kill you. That's subtext."

This chapter also has a subtext, in this case an underlying tension between what I think I *should* be saying about this film and what I'm really thinking. On one hand, it is tempting to join the bandwagon and bash the movie version of *A Little Night Music* as nearly everyone else has done, including its composer. My subtext, which I will now reveal (and will explain later in this essay) is that I enjoy much about this movie. Although I think the film could have been better had it retained some of the material cut during the latter stages in the filming and offered a more suitable leading lady, I maintain my position that this much-maligned and overlooked movie is one of the more successful Sondheim screen adaptations and a 1970s film musical worth getting to know. It offers an enjoyable mix of theatrical and cinematic elements, strong singing and acting from most of the leads (several retained from the stage version), the preservation of most of its glorious songs, a mostly new terrific song by Sondheim ("The Glamorous Life"), and the removal of another song ("The Miller's Son") that, I will argue, is better off unsung.

Perhaps more surprising than Sondheim's dissatisfaction with the film adaptation of *Night Music* is his unbridled enthusiasm for the film version of *Sweeney Todd*, especially given the absence of so much of its original music and the less-than-impressive singing voices of the fine leading actors, Johnny Depp as Sweeney and Helena Bonham Carter as Mrs. Lovett. Despite these drawbacks, not only did the film earn a profit of more than $100 million, it received Sondheim's public praise as the "most satisfying [film] version of a stage piece I've ever seen."[7] Sondheim did not say that the *Sweeney* adaptation from stage to film was also the *only* satisfying version of a stage piece that he has ever seen, but at a London press conference held shortly after the film was released he asserted precisely this when he praised director Tim Burton's *Sweeney Todd* as "the first musical that has ever transferred successfully to the screen."[8]

## Bergman Film to Stage Musical: The Backstory

In his valedictory memoir, *Sense of Occasion* (2017), Prince recalled an incident that had gone unmentioned in his remarks on the stage version of *A Little Night Music* published in his earlier memoir, *Contradictions* (1974).[9] In the later memoir Prince wrote that in response to a fine reading of Wheeler's libretto for *Night Music* Sondheim declared that "there was no need for it to be a musical," to which Prince's wife Judy "piped up, 'Of course it's a musical.'"[10] Forty-three years after *Contradictions* Prince confirmed that Judy "was right, of course."[11] The reason for Prince's earlier dismissive recollection of *A Little Night Music* seems to stem from the fact that he "suffered no sleepless nights" over it and "wasn't digging deep into [him]self."[12] Prince then cynically concluded his chapter on this show in *Contradictions* (but not in *Sense*) with the comment "mostly *Night Music* was about having a hit."[13] In *Finishing the Hat* Sondheim expressed his disagreement with Prince's earlier verdict (that *Night Music* was "all about having a hit") and offered a thoughtful explanation about where this was coming from: "First, the show wasn't daringly different enough, as *Company* and *Follies* had been, and second, *A Little Night Music* was a writer's piece rather than a director's—it lacked the chances for invention and spectacle called for by other musicals which he had directed."[14]

Also in *Finishing the Hat* Sondheim praises Prince for "bringing out the elegance and lightness of the show," an implicit retraction of his original assessment of the show as superfluous (a conclusion not unlike his original and often-repeated response to what he considered the superfluity of other musicals, including *My Fair Lady*).[15] Sondheim also offered high praise for Wheeler's contribution: "I underestimated Hugh's work shamefully when I first read it. After living with it through numerous productions for more than thirty-five years, I've come to the conclusion that it is one of the half dozen best books ever written for a musical."[16]

But at that early reading of Wheeler's book for *Night Music* Sondheim considered the idea of adapting for the stage *Smiles of a Summer Night* (1955) by the iconic Swedish director Ingmar Bergman much as he regarded the adaptation of George Bernard Shaw's *Pygmalion* into *My Fair Lady*. Although Sondheim regarded the Lerner and Loewe classic, which he enjoyed immensely, a "good show," his overall verdict was that it was essentially a "Why?" musical, that is, "a perfectly respectable show, based on a perfectly respectable source, that has no reason for being."[17] Similarly, he considered *A Little Night Music*, another "Why?" musical. In fact, *Smiles* was not the first choice of source material. Prince and Sondheim decided to adapt it only after failing for a second time to secure the rights to Jean Anouilh's play *Ring Round the Moon* (1948), first in 1959 and again in 1972.[18]

In the new millennium, nonmusical films have served as perhaps the most popular source material for stage musicals, but in the early 1970s the idea of adapting a film was still a relatively rare and novel phenomenon. A short list of notable stage musicals adapted from films prior to *Night Music* (and it is a short list) would include *Silk Stockings* (1955), *She Loves Me* (1963), *Sweet Charity* (1966), *Promises, Promises* (1968), and *Applause* (1970).[19] It was not until the 1980s and 1990s that stage adaptations of films began their exponential rise in popularity.

Before the video era, screenings of Bergman's films were typical repertory fare at such Manhattan "revival houses" as the Thalia, Waverley, and Theatre 80 St. Marks as well as the Museum of Modern Art, and the screenplay of *Smiles* had been translated into a Bergman collection in English and published in 1960.[20] Several years before Prince had secured the rights for *Night Music*, film critic Robin Wood wrote a major study of Bergman's work that demonstrates the musicality of *Smiles* and highlights numerous striking parallels between Bergman's film and Mozart's operas, in particular *The Marriage of Figaro* and *The Magic Flute*.[21] The year Prince and Sondheim started working on *Night Music* the film and theater critic John Simon published a penetrating analysis that explored the many theatrical qualities of *Smiles*.[22] Without articulating the reasons that prompted her to exclaim of *Smiles* that "of course, it's a musical," Judy Prince had quickly seen the potential to musicalize Bergman's film. Soon, Prince and Sondheim took advantage of its inherent musical and theatrical qualities as they adapted Bergman's musical film into a popular and critically acclaimed stage musical.[23]

## From Stage Musical to Film Musical

Shortly after the Broadway stage production closed on August 3, 1974, after 601 performances, Prince expressed his desire to direct a film version of this hit show.[24] In the spring of 1976 he was given the opportunity to fulfill this wish. It was only the second time Prince had directed a film. The first was the comedy *Something for Everyone* (1970), starring Angela Lansbury and Michael York with a screenplay by Wheeler. Despite this early success, many years later in *Sense of Occasion* Prince wrote that he was "ill suited" and lacked the patience to be a successful film director and that he "made a mess" of his second film after the "beginner's luck" he experienced with *Something for Everyone*.[25]

But in April 1977, when the film version of *Night Music* was recently completed and the producer was looking for a distributor, Prince stated in an interview that the adaptation offered an opportunity "to fix things that didn't work on stage" and, more surprisingly, that he liked the movie better than the stage version.[26] In the same interview he acknowledged having "a hard time working with Elizabeth Taylor" but didn't blame her for his own failure.[27] He even gave Taylor a compliment she seldom receives in connection with this film: "She knew how to act for the camera, and when she was good, she was very good."[28]

As stated earlier, Sondheim eventually came to appreciate what Wheeler and Prince accomplished in the stage version of *Night Music*. The film was another matter. For starters, as Prince reported in a letter to Wheeler dated March 9, 1976, regarding an early film draft, Sondheim was displeased by the decision to take advantage of a more favorable financial arrangement that would place the setting in Austria rather than Sweden.[29] Prince wrote: "In a surprising outburst he confided that he hates both Austrian and German culture, loathes German music, Viennese waltzes, schlag, oompah, etc., etc."[30] Considering that Sondheim had filled the music in the original Swedish stage setting with Viennese waltzes, his distaste for Teutonic culture might be mistaken as ironic. In the same letter, Prince also stated counterarguments to Sondheim's objection that their ideas for the film were insufficiently cinematic: "Another thing Steve assumes and I tend to disagree with as well is that the film script is so much like the stage script, it must still *be* a stage script."[31]

Again, in sharp contrast to his eventual appreciation of Wheeler's adaptation and Prince's staging of Bergman's source film, Sondheim's final thoughts on the film adaption of *Night Music*, expressed in *Finishing the Hat*, reinforce his original reservations, now at greater length. And as in his 2007 interview with Green, Sondheim considered only the film adaptation of *Sweeney Todd* (2007) a "satisfactory cinematic transposition."[32] The others, *West Side Story* (1961), *Gypsy* (1962), *A Funny Thing Happened on the Way to the Forum* (1966), and *A Little Night Music* (1978), all of which, while employing "cinematic techniques such as rapid cross-cutting," were, according to Sondheim, "essentially stage productions 'opened up' in terms of setting and spectacle."[33] In short, for Sondheim, the film version of *Night Music* more than fulfilled his prophecy in 1976 that the "film couldn't work without radical rethinking" and that the results justified his attempts to "persuade Hal and Hugh not to attempt it, but to no avail."[34] Sondheim's final word on the subject was that the 1978 film of *Night Music* was "the least successful" film adaptation of a Sondheim musical "in every way," a "sad and listless affair, and a waste of everyone's time."[35]

The film version of *Night Music* might be thought of as the cinematic equivalent of Sondheim's unpleasant stage collaboration as a lyricist for *Do I Hear a Waltz?* (1965) with a book by Laurents and a score by Richard Rodgers. For more than fifty years Sondheim has unwaveringly expressed in print and in interviews that the year he wasted on *Waltz* was his only creative regret and that, although it was a "respectable show," it was the one "real failure" of his professional life.[36] Whereas *Waltz* has had its share of public defenders, however, Sondheim enjoys considerable company in his assessment of the film adaptation of *Night Music*, which has enjoyed little critical support.[37]

## Critical Response to the Film Adaptation

Indeed, Craig Zadan in *Sondheim & Co.* describes the initial critical response to the film as "an avalanche of some of the worst reviews in motion-picture history."[38] Zadan goes on to quote from a range of negative reviews including those of Pauline Kael (*New Yorker*), Frank Rich (*Time*), and David Ansen (*Newsweek*), all of whom found little to praise. Vincent Canby of the *New York Times* summarized the most frequent complaints when he wrote that "Mr. Prince appears to have made every decision that could sabotage the music and the lyrics" and that Elizabeth Taylor "is an actress of more wit and character than *A Little Night Music* ever allows."[39]

Taylor, a major film star who happened to be Desiree's age (forty-four) at the time of filming, has perhaps received the brunt of the criticism, with Prince's directorial acumen a close second.[40] Whereas film critics and Sondheim specialists usually find Taylor dramatically unsuited for Desiree, especially in comparison with the original stage Desiree, Glynis Johns, most of the criticism centers on Taylor's appearance, captured in mercilessly unflattering camera close-ups. Even more than the close-ups, Taylor's weight, which seemed to fluctuate during the filming, came under particularly cruel scrutiny and condemnation. A few years earlier Lucille Ball was subjected to similar derision for the way the camera revealed her age (sixty-three), despite a translucent covering placed over the camera lens to disguise it, in the film adaptation of *Mame* (1974).[41]

To place some of these criticisms in more historical context, when the film musical *A Little Night Music* appeared, the genre in general had been in commercial decline since the mid-1960s following such blockbusters as *Gigi* (1958), *West Side Story* (1961), *Mary Poppins* (1964), *My Fair Lady* (1964), and *The Sound of Music* (1965). Looking back through the 1970s, it seems as though the decade could confidently boast but one major critical success, *Cabaret*, directed by Bob Fosse in 1972, and one financial bonanza, *Grease* ($396 million as of this writing), the latter released a couple of months after *Night Music*.[42] As for Taylor, in the 1960s she had regularly received positive reviews for her accomplished performances, especially in *Butterfield 8* (1960), *Who's Afraid of Virginia Woolf?* (1966), and *The Taming of the Shrew* (1967), the latter two among the eleven films she made with her on-and-off-again husband, Richard Burton. But in evaluations of her work in the 1970s, there is widespread critical consensus that Taylor's career had fallen into decline and that these later films, including *Night Music*, were not only undistinguished by comparison with her earlier successes but possibly more easily denigrated as an artifact of an outdated genre, namely the film musical (which would, fortunately, rise again several decades later).

Nevertheless, along with the disdain, some critics, including theater and film historian Foster Hirsch, have found qualities to admire in the film version of *Night Music*. That said, I must point out the harsh reality that aside from some IMDb user commentators who find "significant virtues" in this much-criticized film, which "may just steal your heart," I have so far uncovered only one *unequivocally* supportive review from a professional film critic. That critic is Rex Reed of the *New York Daily News*.[43]

In *Harold Prince and the American Musical* Foster Hirsch praises Prince's stage direction of *Night Music* for its "brisk pacing with its filmic transition."[44] In writing about the film, Hirsch lauds its opening "charming conceit" in the way it moves from stage to filmic space, Sondheim's (mostly) new version of "The Glamorous Life," and the filming of "A Weekend in the Country."[45] At the same time, Hirsch criticizes Prince's lack of consistency in his handling of cinematic techniques, including editing, and the film's unwelcome intrusion of realism:

> Opening the film with the actors performing on a stage and then shifting into real—filmic—space and time was a charming conceit, but realistic settings only made the songs seem disruptive. "The Glamorous Life" (for the film Sondheim wrote a new song with the same title) and "A Weekend in the Country," the shows' two elaborate ensemble numbers which had a film-like structure on stage, are in fact beautifully assembled, but for the most part the film's editing—the intercutting within scenes and the transitions between scenes—is stilted. . . . That the film is in no way a reflection of the pace and texture, the lush, confident theatricality, of Prince's original production only underscores his affinity for the stage.[46]

As for the cinematic treatment in the filming of "A Weekend in the Country," Prince himself found this to be "just as good as you can get."[47] Certainly, his filming of this number is especially well suited to the complexities of Sondheim's brilliantly conceived modern re-creation of an old-fashioned virtuosic operetta ensemble finale and arguably conveys these complexities more successfully than what Prince was able to manage on a stage, including the footage of automobiles traveling to Madame Armfeldt's estate and the rapid but unobtrusive cutting from the Egermans to the Mittelheims (see figure 10.1).[48]

There also seems to be universal critical agreement that the film treatment of Sondheim's new version of "The Glamorous Life," and the quality of the song itself, match if not surpass the stage version in effectiveness. The idea for the film conception most likely can be traced to Wheeler, who wrote in an undated letter (presumably March 1976) that "perhaps Steve could feel like writing a song for her [Fredericka][49] which reveals her ambiguous feelings for her mother, her present life, her perplexities about life etcetera."[50] The new version also continues with a variation of the pseudo-Clementi exercise in much of the accompaniment, including the prominent use of the piano exercises in the orchestration, a great touch.

The new melody for "The Glamorous Life" seems to subtly foreshadow the biological connection between Fredericka and her father Frederick. Since the pitches do not align, it may seem far-fetched to make such a claim, but the

**Figure 10.1.** Arriving at the Armfeldt estate for the weekend in the country, *A Little Night Music* (1977), screenshot.

*rhythm* of a key phrase in Fredericka's new song clearly anticipates the important musical phrase that Frederick sings to the words "which eliminates A" that is soon to follow in his opening internal dialogue "Now." It is first heard when Fredericka sings "see the children all year" and is repeated no fewer than four times in succession at the end of the song, culminating with "of the glamorous" (a rest followed by five quarter notes) and then a long-held note on "life." In short, when we hear Frederick sing "which eliminates A," attentive listeners might also be hearing Fredericka singing about her mother's glamorous life.

Concerning the casting, aside from their criticism of Taylor's performance, most commentators appreciated the fact that the film retained three of its original stage stars, Len Cariou as Fredrik (now Frederick) Egerman, Laurence Guittard as Count Carl-Magnus Mittelheim, and Hermione Gingold as Madame Armfeldt. Although some might rightly complain about the removal of Gingold's "Liaisons," which greatly diminishes her character, and the deletion of Guittard's "In Praise of Women," Carl-Magnus's only solo song, the opportunity to see and in most cases hear Cariou, Guittard, and Gingold in their original roles not long after their stage performances is most welcome.[51] Although several reviewers thought she looked too old at twenty-three to play the virginal eighteen-year-old Anne Egerman, Leslie-Ann Down, who had recently appeared regularly in the long-running British television series *Upstairs, Downstairs*, was widely regarded as a fine addition to the ensemble cast.

Commentators have also regularly and with justification singled out Diana Rigg for critical praise in the role of Charlotte, the wife of the boorish Count Carl-Magnus, implying and sometimes stating outright that she upstaged Taylor in her spirited, funny, but also poignant portrayal of a vibrant but unhappy woman dying a little death every day. Rigg was also the only female lead who did all of her own singing.[52] Steven Suskin suggests that her singing in the *Night Music* film led to her casting as Phyllis in the 1987 London revival of *Follies*.[53] The other females in the cast were either entirely (Fredericka, Anne, and Petra) or partly (Desiree) dubbed by Elaine Tomkinson.[54] In the case of Desiree, it seems likely that Taylor sang most of her notes, although perhaps not consecutively.[55]

## From Stage Script to Screenplay

Although in *Finishing the Hat* the show's lyricist and composer shared some of his indispensable later thoughts on the staged *Night Music* and its film version, the draft scripts of the screenplay from August and September 1976 add significantly to what Sondheim offered in this critical memoir regarding the latter text, including evidence of unused lyrical contributions that he does not mention.[56] More significant, the August 6 screenplay reveals that at the beginning of shooting Prince and Wheeler intended to retain nearly *all* of the songs from the stage version (with some to be reconceived). Contradicting this intention is a "Note" to Prince labeled "Timing of the Script" dated August 17. The "Note," written during the recording process but prior to the filming, indicates an approximate film time of 120 minutes, 52 seconds.[57] It must have soon become clear to Prince and his production staff that if they were to achieve this timing projection, several songs would need to be cut or greatly reduced.

After the recordings were completed, filming began at the end of August and concluded by early November, but as previously noted, the film's release was delayed until March 1978. As Ethan Mordden writes, "The completed movie had trouble finding a distributor and was released like a convict, in sullen spot appearances in a few cities."[58] A VHS followed in 1981, but the DVD did not become available until 2007.[59]

The stage version of *A Little Night Music* began with a group of five strolling singing players called Liebeslieders (a reference to the *Liebeslieder* Waltzes of Johannes Brahms) singing an overture that begins with vocalizations "*La la la*" before transitioning into "Remember," portions of "Soon" and "Now," and the "unpack the luggage" refrain of "The Glamorous Life." The choice of adding a five-member Greek chorus as a unifying dramatic device was perhaps the most theatrical new element in the transfer from Bergman's theatrical film to the musical stage. The idea of beginning a musical with a vocal overture is also a rare if not unprecedented "concept"-like feature of the stage version of the musical. After the sung components of the overture, the Liebeslieder Quintet dances a "Night Waltz." The dance gradually reveals the main characters as they waltz as couples, change partners, and recouple, all under the observant watch of Desiree's and (as we eventually learn) Fredrik's fourteen-year-old daughter, Fredrika. At various times throughout the stage musical the Liebeslieder Quintet will reappear to sing (1) a return of the "unpack the luggage" refrain in "The Glamorous Life," (2) a reprise of "Remember," which interrupts Desiree's theatrical performance in front of Fredrik and Anne, (3) the "Night Waltz" ("The Sun Won't Set") to open Act II, and (4) the swift and brief "Perpetual Anticipation" later in the second act.

The creative team agreed that, though *theatrically* effective, the Quintet was unsuitable for a *cinematic* adaptation. It was therefore removed from the screenplay, albeit with some of the musical material transferred to the central characters. Sondheim addressed this decision in *Finishing the Hat*, where he compared the problem of the Liebeslieders to the chorus in *Sweeney Todd*: "The chief problem in the score was to find an equivalent for the Quintet, who served both narrative and commentary functions in the show, but who would have been a clumsily abstract presence in the movie. (This was the reason that Tim Burton cut the choral commentary in the film of *Sweeney Todd*, a wise choice)."[60]

Aside from "Perpetual Anticipation," the Liebeslieders' "minute waltz" from Act II (the only song lyrics *not* present in the screenplay), Prince removed four songs that appear in the August 6 screenplay: the Liebeslieders' "Remember" (both in the opening of the show and during Desiree's theatrical performance), Madame Armfeldt's "Liaisons," Carl-Magnus's "In Praise of Women," and Petra's "The Miller's Son." This relatively small number of deletions stands in marked contrast to the musical butchering of the stage score for the filmed *Sweeney Todd* (2007) and the magical musical disappearances in the film version of *Into the Woods* (2014).[61]

In the most significant addition, a mostly new solo version of "The Glamorous Life," Fredrika (renamed Fredericka) alone sings the duet that Desiree and Madame Armfeldt, accompanied by the Quintet, had sung onstage. The updated "Glamorous Life" retains the opening mazurka-like melody but with new lyrics, after which Sondheim replaces the Quintet's "unpack the luggage" refrain with a brand-new song, a fast waltz. Interspersed within Fredericka's sung choruses are dramatic scenes that depict the faux glamorous life of Fredericka's mother in a film collage that is truly cinematic and imaginative. Its new placement before rather than after "Now/Later/Soon" (with Anne's "Soon" now appearing sooner than Erich's "Later") also makes for an effective departure from the stage narrative.[62]

Since at some point during the shooting the producers made the decision to stick to their announced two hours' traffic on the screen, something had to go. Aside from the music sung by the theatrical Quintet (and the Quintet itself), the relatively lengthy and potentially less cinematic monologues of Madame Armfeldt and Petra became central casualties, both to the score and to the characters. Carl-Magnus lost "In Praise of Women" but retained a slightly extended second-act duet with Frederick, "It Would Have Been Wonderful." Despite the loss of "Liaisons," Madame Armfeldt is given a fair share of dialogue, but Petra virtually disappears as a musical presence other than for a few lines in "A Weekend in the Country," an unsuccessful attempt to seduce Erich, and a consummated sexual union with Madame Armfeldt's servant Franz (Frid in the stage version).[63]

In *Finishing the Hat* Sondheim discusses and reprints several lyrical additions that made their way into the finished film, the most significant of which was the new version of "The Glamorous Life" now "told from Fredrika's point of view."[64] Another important new conception also occurred: "The opening number involved the same waltz that begins the show," he writes, "the principals dancing [and] exchanging partners with one another, presaging the romantic complications to follow, but in the film they sang as they danced."[65] What they sang was "Love Takes Time." Sondheim explains that the film's revised opening marked a return to the "first incarnation" of the show with its opening number called "Numbers," which, in the absence of the Quintet, introduced the main characters and their ages.[66] As in the introduction to the film, "Numbers" was to be "seen through Fredrika's eyes."[67] After a conversation about the three smiles of the summer night, the film, like the original stage production, would show Fredericka "practicing Clementi exercises on the spinet and singing to herself."[68]

Against his better judgment, at Prince's request Sondheim agreed to write an additional chorus of "Every Day a Little Death" for Charlotte to sing to herself in a carriage on the way to inform Anne about the sexual escapades of her husband Frederick and his former (and newfound) lover, Desiree.[69] He also deleted two choruses of "A Weekend in the Country" from the stage version and added two new ones. In *Finishing the Hat* he states that he made these changes at the request of the producer (Elliott Kastner) to shorten the length, but together they only managed a net savings of thirty-seven seconds in a substantial six-minute-long number.

Of special interest is that the added lyrics in "Weekend" include four new lines for Madame Armfeldt, who otherwise does not appear in the first-act finale, or virtually anywhere when singing, for that matter. This added portion gives something for Gingold (and more important, her character) to sing and partially assuages the loss of "Liaisons" and her disappearance in the new version of "The Glamorous Life." Still, Madame Armfeldt is deprived of her final conversation with Fredericka about the smiles of the summer night. The film doesn't even show her death immediately following the third smile. Curiously, neither at the time nor in 2010 did Sondheim complain publicly or in print about the loss of any of these songs, nor did he complain about the removal of songs in the future film adaptations of *Sweeney* and *Into the Woods* or the reduction of instruments in the stage pits of his shows. Despite his influence over final cutting decisions, he agreed to the Draconian cuts in both of these later projects. His acquiescence to the removal of "The Miller's Son" from the film is all the more surprising given his emphatic defense of its retention during the rehearsals of the stage version.[70]

## Shooting and Cutting the Film

Bergman's 1955 film and Prince's 1973 stage adaptation of it were set in Sweden, a location celebrated in the latter by the Liebeslieders, who remind audiences in the waltz at the beginning of Act II that the sun won't set. The change of locale from Sweden to Austria necessitated the removal of that lyric, but it took the heat off expenditures by providing a much-needed tax shelter and a $7.5 million budget not possible in its original location.

As filming costs took their toll, the production needed to cut financial corners. According to Peter E. Jones in his notes to the reissued CD soundtrack of the film, "financial and technical constraints would continue to plague the shoot, causing 'Remember' (also ambitiously rerouted by Sondheim for the film), 'In Praise of Women,' 'Liaisons' and 'The Miller's Son' to remain unfilmed."[71] Jones's assertion is only partly correct. In fact, the evidence offered in the daily production reports contained in the Hal Prince Collection necessitates further clarification and a partial rebuttal.

Although it does not address the question of whether the songs Jones mentions were *filmed*, the August 6, 1976, screenplay, New York Public Library (NYPL) no. 1738, clearly reveals the lyrics to all four of these songs.[72] This is the second screenplay dated August 6, 1976 (the first is NYPL no. 1740), ten days before the recordings of the songs had begun, that includes dated revisions from August 12 to September 28.[73] The lyrics to "Remember" appear in the screenplay no. 1738 between shooting scene no. 49 and no. 60, the lyrics to "Liaisons" on no. 149 and no. 149A, "In Praise of Women" on no. 196, no. 199, and no. 201, and "The Miller's Son" on no. 388, no. 389, and no. 389A. Based on the evidence offered in the daily production reports, the lyrics to the latter three songs" were all filmed.[74]

The one possible exception was the music set to "Remember." The word *possible* needs further clarification. Some of the numbered shots done during the scene that contains "Remember," which directly follows "The Glamorous Life," were indeed shot on September 25 (nos. 49–51 and no. 59). If the final shot had also been *recorded*, it would include one stanza of "Remember" sung by Desiree in voiceover. And if this stanza was shot and recorded, it would be the *only* portion of the lyrics to "Remember" to be listed as filmed in the production reports, an anomaly that seems unlikely but at least raises the question. Another possibility is that the song might have been abbreviated after the opening of the shot, which reveals a glimpse of the street by the theater where Desiree is playing. Since the "dailies" indicate that music of the song "Remember" was recorded on August 19, either scenario is possible.

Now that we know what was filmed, it is time to look at what remains in the released film from the remaining trio of cut songs: "In Praise of Women," "Liaisons," and "The Miller's Son." The short answer is, not much. The sole remnant of "In Praise of Women" in the finished film amounts to seven seconds of underscoring when Carl-Magnus arrives outside Desiree's "digs" (no. 174) and a few phrases of underscoring heard just before Frederick exits in Carl-Magnus's nightshirt when Desiree contradicts Carl-Magnus's claim that he is not hungry: "Of course you are. I'll be just a minute" (no. 194).[75] All that remained of "Liaisons" was a solitary phrase of orchestral underscoring. As for "The Miller's Son," not even a phrase of underscoring was used.

The decision to remove "The Miller's Son" apparently generated discussion for which there is some documentation beginning as early as July, one month before the songs were recorded and much of the filming began. In a letter to Wheeler dated July 12, Prince expresses some ambivalence about what to do about this song: "'The Miller's Son': I worry about the stretch of script without it. Would we miss the musical dynamics? I would not like to find out when I was cutting the picture that we were in trouble, so I intend to film the number and wait and see."[76]

The Prince papers contain an informative document titled "'A Little Night Music' Reel Breakdown," dated November 18, less than two weeks after the shooting was complete. The listing summarizes the main dramatic and musical contents of the rough cut of the film at this point, comprising eighteen reels of film (18 × 11 minutes = a whopping 3 hours and 18 minutes).[77] The file is extant in two copies, one completely clean and another containing brief annotations, including deletions. Two of the songs eventually discarded are noted, "Women" (i.e., "In Praise of Women") in reels 7 and 8 and "Miller's Son" in reel 15, but "Remember" is not. In the marked copy the words "Mme A. Liaisons" appears in cursive writing to the right of "Wife" in reel 6, and "Women" is placed in brackets in reel 6 (with the words "Mittleheim [sic] theme" in cursive writing to the right). Both "Women" and "Miller's Son" are crossed out, in reel 8 and reel 15 respectively.

The eventual deletion of the two last-named suggests that the decision was not made until after November 18, late in the creative process. Similarly, the *addition* of "Mme A. Liaisons" suggests that Prince was still contemplating keeping this song. Finally, in a handwritten set of notes dated December 6 (typed in an un-dated copy) Prince gave a final answer about what to do with "Liaisons" and "The Miller's Son" that supports his deletion and handwritten annotation in the "Reel Breakdown" of November 18.[78] The typed version of the breakdown is slightly clearer than the printed version with regard to "Liaisons": "Restore LIAISONS after 'What are good friends for.' Then after LIAISONS back to FREDERICK and DESIREE in bed." As for "The Miller's Son" the final verdict was simple and di-rect: "Take out MILLER'S SON."

Curiously, Sondheim did not mention the lyrical additions to "Remember" in *Finishing the Hat*. The typescript of the screenplay dated August 6, 1976, housed in the New York Public Library (no. 1738) nevertheless shows that Sondheim added new lyrics (what Jones referred to as "re-routing"). In the film that was released, viewers see Frederick Egerman, directly after "The Glamorous Life," noticing the theater poster announcing a performance that evening by "the one and only Desiree Armfeldt" in *Woman of the World* and purchasing two tickets (no. 49). The August 12 revisions to the screenplay (nos. 51–60) add an elab-orate duet between Frederick and Desiree to the music of "Remember" heard in voice-overs by each, while the film visually remembers by the use of cin-ematic flashbacks a scene between the lovers that took place fourteen years earlier. Following this montage the film moves to Egerman's house in a scene that culminates with the song trilogy "Now/Soon/Later." Later that evening, when Desiree recognizes Frederick in the audience from the stage and her face freezes (along with the play), the screenplay includes a short reprise of "Remember" sung by Desiree and "Audience." This corresponds to the brief interruption of Desiree's play by the Liebeslieders in the stage version of the show (no. 116) when Desiree notices Fredrik and "instantly 'all action' freezes."

In the scenes that follow the abandoned "Miller's Son" the film version departs considerably from the stage version. In the latter, Henrik's failed suicide, Anne's rescue, and their declaration of love (tellingly, without a love duet) *follow* "Send in the Clowns" and are in turn followed by "The Miller's Son," Petra's "11 o'clock number." In the film, Erich's suicide, rescue, and declaration of love (the latter underscored by snippets of "Later" and "Soon") now happen *before* they send in the "Clowns." Of the short scenes that follow "The Miller's Son" in the stage version, six are accompanied by brief song reprises. Most of these reprises are sung by one or more members of the Liebeslieders. The film as released retains all these scenes, but instead of the Liebeslieders singing a stanza for each of the vocal reprises, the music of these reprises is now heard *only* as snatches of orchestral underscoring until the reprise of "Send in the Clowns."[79] The August 6 screenplay (NYPL no. 1738) reveals that in some cases the original intention was to give the *stage* characters brief song reprises in voiceovers, but none of this material was used in the released film. Table 10.1 presents a brief comparative overview of the musical content of the stage and film versions during their respective final scenes.

**Table 10.1.** Comparative overview of the musical content of the final scenes of the stage and film versions

| Scene No. | Stage Version | Film Version |
| --- | --- | --- |
| 1 | Charlotte Malcolm explains to Fredrik that her attempted seduction was to make her husband Carl-Magnus jealous. Henrik and Anne "stealthily" depart with their suitcases toward the stables to elope, speak briefly, and kiss, but are deprived of a song. Instead, Mrs. Segstrom of the Quintet sings four lines of "Soon" (vocal score no. 26). | In the screenplay and in unreleased film shots Anne and Erich (Henrik) sneak off toward the stables to elope with the latter's suitcase and cello case, unseen by Charlotte and Frederick. After "Erich stops dead, throws his arms around her, kisses her" (no. 394), Anne sings a few lines of "Soon" as a voiceover (no. 394, filmed on September 11). In the released film (no. 396 to no. 398, also filmed on September 11), "Soon" is heard only as underscoring. |

*(continued)*

**Table 10.1.** Continued

| Scene No. | Stage Version | Film Version |
|-----------|---------------|--------------|
| 2 | Fredrik and Charlotte observe the elopement (vocal score no. 27, "You Must Meet My Wife," sung by Mr. Erlansen). | In the screenplay and unreleased film shots Frederick sings a few lines of "You Must Meet My Wife" as a voiceover (no. 401, filmed on August 31). In the released film the music of this song is heard only as underscoring. |
| 3 | Madame Armfeldt tells Fredrika about the man she discarded in her youth who might have been the love of her life (vocal score no. 28, "Liaisons," orchestral underscoring only). | As in the stage version, Madame Armfeldt reminisces about her first lover, a Croatian count who gave her a meaningful wooden ring that she regrettably failed to appreciate at the time. The dialogue is accompanied only by underscoring of "Liaisons" (no. 406, filmed on September 13). |
| 4 | Carl-Magnus challenges Fredrik to a game of Russian roulette (vocal score no. 29, "A Weekend in the Country," sung by the Liebeslieders). | In the screenplay and unreleased film shots the Company sings a few lines of "A Weekend in the Country" as a voiceover (no. 426, filmed on September 20). In the released film this portion of the screenplay was not shown, nor was the music of "Weekend" heard as underscoring. |
| 5 | Charlotte and Carl-Magnus kiss and make up after the latter's duel with Frederick (vocal score no. 30, "Every Day a Little Death" [B section], sung by Mrs. Anderssen and Mrs. Segstrom). | In the screenplay and unreleased film shots "Every Day a Little Death" is not reprised. Instead, when Charlotte remarks to Carl-Magnus in the released version that he "became a tiger for" her, the B section of this song is heard as underscoring (no. 429A, filmed on September 20). |
|  | Fredrik and Desiree sing a reprise of "Send in the Clowns" (vocal score, no. 31). | In the screenplay and released film Frederick and Desiree sing a reprise of "Send in the Clowns" (no. 430, filmed October 12). It is now about ninety-five minutes into the film, ten minutes after Desiree first sang the song. |

From the above comparisons between stage and screen versions we can observe that prior to filming, the screenplay closely resembled the finale of the stage version, in which snippets of songs, with the exception of "Liaisons," were mainly sung (by the main characters rather than the Liebeslieders). Somewhere between the screenplay and the film rolls, Prince and Co. replaced these sung passages with orchestral underscoring. As a consequence of this decision, text was replaced with subtext, in which the orchestra reveals thoughts and emotions that the characters no longer express in words and the Liebeslieders no longer express in song. In this way the theatricality of the stage *Night Music* gave way to a more cinematic approach.

## The *Night Music* Film Adaptation in Context

In order to understand the quandary that beset the creators of the film version of *A Little Night Music* concerning its length, some historical context may prove helpful. Between the 1930s and the early 1950s musical adaptations rarely ran longer than two hours and were almost invariably incomplete. In order to include more music from musicals in which the songs came to be regarded as integral to the works audiences now knew from cast albums, this practice began to change with the 1950s adaptations of Rodgers and Hammerstein shows, all of which ran at least a little longer: *Oklahoma!* (1955, 145 minutes); *Carousel* (1956, 128 minutes); *The King and I* (1956, 133 minutes); and *South Pacific* (1958, 171 minutes). On the other hand, the only major 1950s adaptation in this company that was not by Rodgers and Hammerstein is *Guys and Dolls* (1955), which, at 150 minutes, was surpassed in this decade only by *South Pacific*. By the early 1960s, however, adaptations began to approximate their original stage sources in fidelity, completeness, and therefore length, often in specially marketed road-show settings with intermissions to accommodate longer running times.[80] The following list of twelve major 1960s film adaptations (arranged in order of increasing length) range in running time between a little under two and a half hours to nearly three hours:[81]

> *Finian's Rainbow* (1968, 145 minutes)
> *Hello, Dolly!* (1969, 148 minutes)
> *Gypsy* (1962, 149 minutes)
> *The Music Man* (1962, 151 minutes)
> *West Side Story* (1961, 152 minutes)
> *Oliver!* (1968, 153 minutes)
> *Funny Girl* (1968, 154 minutes)
> *Sweet Charity* (1969, 157 minutes)
> *Paint Your Wagon* (1969, 166 minutes)
> *My Fair Lady* (1964, 170 minutes)
> *The Sound of Music* (1965, 174 minutes)
> *Camelot* (1967, 179 minutes)

After the lengthy adaptation of *Fiddler on the Roof* in 1971 (180 minutes), which slightly surpassed the longest of these 1960s films, followed one year later by the leisurely treatment of *1776* in 1972 (141 minutes), the approach to length changed dramatically and with some finality. Whether due to financial reasons or to better serve viewing audiences with reduced attention spans, for the rest of the 1970s and continuing until the present, it became rare for a film adaptation to run much longer than two hours. In fact, of the following 1970s musical films— *Cabaret, Man of La Mancha, Jesus Christ Superstar, Mame, A Little Night Music, Grease, The Wiz,* and *Hair*—only two, *Man of La Mancha* (132 minutes) and *The Wiz* (133 minutes), extend beyond 130 minutes.[82]

Exceptions to the newly self-imposed two-hour time-clock ruling among films that arrived after 1990 include *Evita* (1996, 134 minutes), *The Phantom of the Opera* (2004, 141 minutes), *Rent* (2005, 135 minutes), *The Producers* (2005, 135 minutes), *Dreamgirls* (2006, 130 minutes), and *Les Misérables* (2012, 158 minutes). But these remain exceptions. As far as Sondheim is concerned, the long-delayed film versions of *Sweeney Todd* (stage 1979, film 2007) and *Into the Woods* (stage 1987, film 2014) ran about the same length as the *Night Music* adaptation, 116 and 124 minutes respectively. Had the film version of *Night Music* included the deleted songs, its running time would have exceeded the magical two-hour length by at least another 15 minutes and perhaps by as much as 25 minutes.

Certainly, "Remember" and its reprise would add noticeable time, but "Perpetual Anticipation" breezes by in 58 seconds, leaving "Liaisons" (5:06), "In Praise of Women" (3:30), and "The Miller's Son" (4:28) as the major time savers. The loss of "Liaisons" is to be lamented, and we have noted that it was a decision Prince did not take lightly. Had the film combined a direct presentation with voiceovers and flashback reminiscences of Madame Armfeldt's youthful romantic adventures at the villa of Baron de Signac, the palace of the Duke of Ferrara, and the castle of the King of the Belgians, "Liaisons" might have been cinematically effective, but the screen directions focus exclusively and in detail on the "vast, sterile hoard of possessions" Madame Armfeldt has acquired over the years (nos. 147–151). The screenplay did not shed additional light on her relationships with her earlier lovers or how she felt about them in retrospect, including possible regrets, so perhaps its absence constitutes less of a loss than it might have. Without "In Praise of Women" the role of Carl-Magnus is dramatically as well as musically diminished and greatly missed. The verdict on "The Miller's Son" is more ambiguous and takes us back again to the debates about whether to keep the song in the stage version theater audiences apparently enjoyed, both the song and D. Jamin-Bartlett's bravura performance.

Sondheim may have considered "The Miller's Son" indispensable, but thoughtful writers such as David Craig and Kim Kowalke have seriously questioned why, by Sondheim's own well-known dramatic standards, he would have allowed a minor character (Petra, the sexually adventurous maid) to be showcased at length in the culminating 11 o'clock number near the end of the evening as she looks down on her new sleeping romantic partner, the servant Franz.[83] In his detailed and perceptive textual and musical analysis Kowalke asks whether Petra's song might be regarded as "a good but wrong song that impeded the flow of the story in its final minutes."[84] Arthur Laurents reinforces these doubts concerning the dramatic effectiveness of this song: "What that character is doing singing right before the [final] curtain I don't know. . . . But Steve told me that the song summed up the show."[85]

*West Side Story* contained an 11 o'clock number that offered comic relief toward the end of a tragic evening. The song was of course, "Gee, Officer Krupke," and it did (and still does) stop the show. At the time of its creation Sondheim argued that the song belonged in the first act and that "Cool" belonged in the second act. Twenty years ago I wrote that gradually "Sondheim came to accept [director-choreographer Jerome] Robbins's directorial decision and to acknowledge that 'Krupke' works wonderfully in Act II on the basis of its 'theatrical truth' rather than its 'literal truth.'"[86] In revisiting this decision in *Finishing the Hat* Sondheim explained that the reason his collaborators decided to place "Krupke" late in the show was based "on the traditional theatrical grounds that, as the drunken Porter in *Macbeth* exemplifies, comedy in the midst of melodrama makes the comedy more comic and the melodrama more melodramatic."[87]

Sondheim's acceptance of "Krupke's" placement was recorded much earlier, in a 1985 panel discussion that included Robbins, Laurents, Bernstein, and Sondheim.[88] In this session Laurents and Robbins both said that they applied "the old Shakespearean drunken-porter principle" to the placement of "Krupke." As Sondheim put it, "in the middle of a melodrama, you cut in with comedy." In his next utterance Sondheim added the distinction that "when Shakespeare does it, it's an irrelevant character." None of the creative principals mentioned that, in contrast to "Krupke," *Macbeth*'s drunken Porter interrupts the action relatively early (Act II, scene 3, lines 1–40) before vanishing from the rest of the play.

Further, unlike "Krupke" and most 11 o'clock numbers, Petra's song, performed by a minor character (albeit far less minor than Shakespeare's Porter), is fundamentally a serious song that does not offer the kind of comic relief found in "Krupke" or the Porter scene. Unfortunately, Sondheim did not explain in *Finishing the Hat* why he told Laurents that "The Miller's Son," which goes on far longer than the Porter's moment on the stage, "summed up the show" or why he not only allowed but *insisted* that a minor character intrude on an inevitable melodramatic resolution.[89] "The Miller's Son" also came at the expense of Anne and Henrik. Although the newly declared lovebirds are in a hurry to elope, the libretto regrettably does not give them even a brief chance to sing, only a few lines of dialogue and a kiss. Instead, the Liebeslieder Mrs. Segstrom sings a few lines of Anne's "Soon."

I confess to sharing my puzzlement as to why Sondheim was so insistent on keeping this song in the stage version, however brilliant on its own terms. Not only do I not miss it in the film version, I place its removal as one of the film's improvements over its stage source. Although we have witnessed the deliberations that occurred since July 1976 about whether "The Miller's Son" should remain in the film, we do not know what finally led Prince to delete it at the last moment in December. Perhaps in the end financial considerations outweighed artistic ones. In any event, the film was released at 124 minutes, a total that includes the removal of the potentially cinematic "Remember" and the noncinematic "Miller's Son."

## Reassessing Sondheim's Critical Contributions

In this chapter I have focused on the compositional process that led to the film version of *A Little Night Music* and how this version departs from its stage predecessor rather than arguing for or against its merits. Still, without overlooking its flaws, one might wonder, along with the IMDb user who speculated that "all the film critics secretly met and took a vote to hate it together," whether the critical response to the film version of *Night Music* stems in part from groupthink.[90] No doubt Prince is less comfortable outside of his theatrical milieu. Nevertheless, his first film musical frequently reveals a strong cinematic touch, especially in the new "Glamorous Life" and "A Weekend in the Country," the latter sequence prompting Prince to uncharacteristically boast that it "was just wonderful."[91]

One might also ask whether it is really such a misstep to allow the theatrical nature of the theatrical *Night Music* stage material to be retained in a film adaptation. As noted earlier in this essay, John Simon discusses numerous theatrical qualities in Bergman's film.[92] In contrast to Sondheim, Wheeler, in a March 1, 1976 letter to Prince, raised this critical choice when conveying his belief in the intrinsic merits of a film adaptation that is more rather than less faithful: "As you see, I am leaving great chunks of it exactly as it was in the theater because I see no reason to alter it—unless at some later point it is necessary to cut."[93] In a handwritten note at the top of the page Wheeler confirmed his position with regard to expanding the role of Desiree to accommodate Elizabeth Taylor's star status: "As was discussed I am making no plans to enlarge the Desiree part for Miss T. Sufficient unto the day!"[94]

The largely miscast Taylor is indeed overshadowed by the singing acumen of her fellow cast members, especially her two male lovers as performed by Cariou and Guittard, but perhaps even more by her female rival, played by

Rigg. Taylor also does not begin to do vocal justice to "Send in the Clowns." Nevertheless, I would contend that Taylor and Cariou create a believable chemistry when Desiree and Frederick ridicule the former's overly generous characterization of her "awful" dragoon as pea-brained and "laugh spontaneously, their old easy familiarity with each other returning."[95] (See figure 10.2.) This seems to be a good example of a time when Taylor, to use Prince's description, was indeed "very good."

Moving from subtext to text, I will reassert my original verdict that Sondheim's mostly unrecognized new work on the film is commendable: his lyrics to Charlotte's revealing new solo stanzas of "Every Day a Little Death" in the carriage, the way he brings Madame Armfeldt into "A Weekend in the Country," and the unused new voiceover lyrics and highly cinematic use of flashbacks of "Remember," preserved in the screenplay. Most welcome of all is Sondheim's newly-created version of "The Glamorous Life," filmed effectively and with cinematic imagination as it exposes the façade of Desiree's so-called glamorous life and in the process enriches the character of Fredericka and her relationship with her mother.[96]

Clearly, the film version of *Night Music* fell short of what critics and admirers of the stage version thought it could and should be. Unlike Sondheim, however, even those who find the film less cinematic or less convincing than their dream film version have found much to appreciate. Perhaps nothing I can say

**Figure 10.2.** "Isn't my dragoon awful?", Desiree Armfeldt (Elizabeth Taylor) and Frederick Egerman (Len Cariou), *A Little Night Music* (1977), screenshot.

will counteract what I perceive to be a genre bias that almost invariably starts and ends with the principle that a film adaptation of a stage show is inevitably destined to be less successful. According to this working principle, the film version of *Night Music* is presumed to be guilty without taking the trouble to explore its possible merits. Like most adaptations, it is imperfect, both on its own terms and as an adaptation. In any event, viewers are under no obligation to accept a predetermined verdict, handed down either by the film's creators or a consensus of its critics that inhibits us from seeing and deciding for ourselves. Personally, I'm glad Prince and Wheeler persuaded Sondheim to contribute to this little-loved and even lesser-known, but by no means unredeemable, movie. But don't take my word for it.

# Notes

1. Although the film was completed and copyrighted in 1977, it was not distributed until 1978. See Peter E. Jones, Notes to *A Little Night Music* Original Soundtrack Recording, Sony Music Entertainment, Masterworks 88883 72393 2 (2013); "The Stephen Sondheim Reference Guide, *A Little Night Music*," accessed July 23, 2021, http://www.sondheimguide.com/night.htm/html; and Craig Zadan, *Sondheim & Co.*, 2nd ed. (New York: Da Capo, 1986), 198. Zadan offers a date as well as month: "Finally, on March 8, 1978, Roger Corman, through his New World Pictures, released the Sascha-Wien Film very briefly to movie theaters" (ibid.). The movie soundtrack LP was released on April 14, 1978; a CD with three bonus tracks and notes by Jones was released in 2013.
2. Jeanine Basinger's magisterial history of the film musical from the early days of sound film to *La La Land* provides a recent demonstration of an author who manages to find much to admire in B musicals and the star vehicles of Bing Crosby, Elvis Presley, Shirley Temple, and Betty Grable but disparages film adaptations of stage musicals at every turn, primarily for their theatricality. Jeanine Basinger, *The Movie Musical* (New York: Knopf, 2019). In the course of six hundred pages Basinger finds only a few adaptations since the 1936 version of *Show Boat* (the one that features Paul Robeson) worthy of her praise and enthusiasm. What is somewhat troubling in Basinger's treatment of film adaptations in her otherwise measured and equanimous survey is not so much her pervasive criticism of film adaptations of stage musicals for not being sufficiently cinematic, but her resistance to acknowledging cinematic qualities when present and for exhibiting the appearance of a double critical standard by calling out an original film musical when it clearly demonstrates *theatrical* qualities. For more on this issue see Geoffrey Block, "The Movie Musical! Jeanine Basinger (2019)," *Studies in Musical Theatre* 14, no. 1 (2020): 230–233.
3. Jesse Green, "Sondheim Dismembers 'Sweeney' and 'Back Story,'" *New York Times*, December 16, 2007. The three musicals Sondheim singles out for praise appeared early in film history (between 1930 and 1932): *Under the Roofs of Paris* [Sous les Toits de

Paris] (1930), directed by René Clair; *The Smiling Lieutenant* (1931), directed by Ernst Lubitsch; and *Love Me Tonight* (1932), directed by Rouben Mamoulian. According to Green, all of these favorites, plus "a couple [unspecified] of the MGMs," were "those that were originally conceived for the screen."

4. Stephen Sondheim, *Finishing the Hat: Collected Lyrics (1954–1981) with Attendant Comments, Principles, Heresies, Grudges, Whines and Anecdotes* (New York: Knopf, 2010), 57. After *West Side Story* (music by Leonard Bernstein), Laurents (1917–2011) wrote the books to Sondheim's *Gypsy* (1959, music by Jule Styne), *Anyone Can Whistle* (1964, music by Sondheim), and *Do I Hear a Waltz?* (1965, music by Richard Rodgers).

5. Ibid. See the essay by Jeffrey Magee in this volume.

6. Available on YouTube as of this writing. In "Theater Lyrics" Sondheim relates how Laurents's "notion of sub-text" was "the major thing" he "got from Arthur." Stephen Sondheim, "Theater Lyrics," in *Playwrights, Lyricists, Composers Discuss Their Hits*, ed. Otis L. Guernsey (New York: Dodd, Mead, 1974), 70–72.

7. I am quoting Sondheim's words as he spoke them in a public conversation with former *New York Times* theater critic Frank Rich that took place in Portland, Oregon, on March 11, 2008. Several months later, the *Sondheim Review* offered the following summary of Sondheim's remarks: "Turning to the recent *Sweeney Todd* film, Sondheim reiterated that he didn't mind the loss of the play's musical numbers that 'didn't move the action forward.' Citing many differences between film and theatre, he added that a theatre audience is essentially a collaborator in the event, but a film audience is not. *Sweeney*, he believes, is the most satisfactory film made of any stage musical." Robert Sokol, Ken Kwartler, and Terri Roberts, "Side by Side: Rich and Sondheim," *Sondheim Review* 15, no. 1 (Fall 2008): 22–24.

8. David Thomson obtained this quote from Norman Lebrecht, "When a Movie Outshines the Outstanding Original," *Scena*, February 12, 2008, accessed February 11, 2021, http://www.scena.org/lsm/sm13-5/sm13_5_sweeneytodd_en.html. Thomson criticizes the film version of *Sweeney Todd* for drifting "towards being a horror film" and concludes that "the film is misguided, and often unpleasant in ways that might confirm the worst fears of Sondheim's critics." David Thomson, "Attending the Tale of *Sweeney Todd*: The Stage Musical and Tim Burton's Film Version," in *The Oxford Handbook to Sondheim Studies*, ed. Robert Gordon (New York: Oxford University Press, 2014), 302, 305.

9. Harold Prince, *Sense of Occasion* (New York: Applause Theatre and Cinema Books, 2017); Harold Prince, *Contradictions: Notes on Twenty-Six Years in the Theatre* (New York: Dodd, Mead, 1974).

10. Prince, *Sense of Occasion*, 179.

11. Ibid.

12. Prince, *Contradictions*, 183.

13. Ibid.

14. Sondheim, *Finishing the Hat*, 283.

15. Ibid.

16. Ibid., 253.

17. Ibid., 143.

18. Stephen Sondheim, "On Collaboration Between Authors and Directors," *Dramatists Guild Quarterly* 16, no. 2 (1979), 3.

19. *Silk Stockings* (lyrics and music by Cole Porter), based on Ernst Lubitsch's *Ninotchka* (1939); *She Loves Me* (lyrics by Sheldon Harnick, music by Jerry Bock), based mainly on Lubitsch's *The Shop Around the Corner* (1940), produced and directed by Prince; *Sweet Charity* (lyrics by Dorothy Fields, music by Cy Coleman), based on Federico Fellini's *Nights of Cabiria* (1957); *Promises, Promises* (lyrics by Hal David, music by Burt Bacharach), based on Billy Wilder's *The Apartment* (1960); and *Applause* (lyrics by Lee Adams, music by Charles Strouse), based on Joseph L. Mankiewicz's *All About Eve* (1950). Two decades after *Night Music* Sondheim adapted *Passion* (1994) with librettist-director James Lapine from the Italian director Ettore Scola's film *Passione d'Amore* (1981), which in turn was based on the novel *Fosca* (1869) by Iginio Ugo Tarchetti.

20. Ingmar Bergman, *Four Screenplays of Ingmar Bergman: "Smiles of a Summer Night," "The Seventh Seal," "Wild Strawberries," "The Magician"* (New York: Simon and Schuster, 1960). Regarding relevant revival houses see https://www.papermag.com/old-historic-nyc-movie-theaters-1958013380.html.

21. Robin Wood, "Ingmar Bergman: New Edition," in *Contemporary Approaches to Film and Media Studies*, ed. Barry Keith Grant (Detroit: Wayne State University Press, 2012), 78–85

22. John Simon, *Ingmar Bergman Directs* (New York: Harcourt Brace Jovanovich, 1972), 106–139, esp. 112–114.

23. On the adaptation from Bergman's *Smile of a Summer Night* to *A Little Night Music* see Geoffrey Block, "From Screen to Stage: *A Little Night Music* and *Passion*," in *The Oxford Handbook of Sondheim Studies*, ed. Robert Gordon, esp. 259–268, and Joseph Swain, "*A Little Night Music*: The Cynical Operetta," in ibid., 309–318. Swain argues persuasively that in contrast to the values espoused by the characters in Bergman's film, the characters in the stage adaptation lack the "essential presumption of the value of romantic fidelity" and "merely mock high society's behavior with respect to its professed proprieties about romantic and sexual norms" (310). According to Swain, "*A Little Night Music* is not merely farcical. It is cynical" (ibid.).

24. Meryle Secrest quotes Sondheim as saying that Prince and Wheeler were "desperate to make it." Meryle Secrest, *Stephen Sondheim: A Life* (New York: Knopf, 1998), 258; quoted in the Sondheim Guardian Lecture, *Biased* (Spring–Summer 1980), 48.

25. Prince, *Sense of Occasion*, 76.

26. Quoted in Zadan, *Sondheim & Co.*, 199.

27. Ibid. According to biographer Donald Spoto, Hermione Gingold recalled that Taylor "was divine to work with" and that the other cast members "found the star undemanding, untemperamental and entirely one of them." Donald Spoto, *A Passion for Life: The Biography of Elizabeth Taylor* (New York: HarperCollins, 1995), 269–270.

28. Prince, *Sense of Occasion*, 77. Prince leaves unstated the next phrase of Henry Wadsworth Longfellow's children's poem "There Was a Little Girl": "But when she was bad she was horrid."

29. Letter from Harold Prince to Hugh Wheeler, March 9, 1976, Hal Prince Collection, NYPL (hereafter HPC), *A Little Night Music,* Box 157, Folder 2, "Night Music Screenplay Correspondence."
30. Ibid.
31. Ibid.
32. Sondheim, *Finishing the Hat,* 280.
33. Ibid.
34. Ibid.
35. Ibid.
36. James Lapine, *Six by Sondheim* (New York: HBO Film, 2013). See Geoffrey Block, "The Last Word: Rewriting Musical Theatre History with Sondheim," *Studies in Musical Theatre* 13, no. 2 (2019): 140.
37. Peter Filichia, Ken Mandelbaum, Ethan Mordden, and Steven Suskin are among *Waltz's* most enthusiastic champions. See Peter Filichia, *Let's Put on a Musical!* (New York: Back Stage Books, 1993), 178; Peter Filichia, "Forgive Me, Stephen Sondheim," Masterworks Broadway, March 23, 2015, accessed March 27, 2017, https://www.masterworksbroadway.com/blog/forgive-me-stephen-sondheim/; Peter Filichia, "*Do I Hear a Waltz?* Encores, Encores!" Masterworks Broadway, May 10, 2016, accessed March 27, 2017, https://www.masterworksbroadway.com/blog/hear-waltz-encores-encores; Ken Mandelbaum, *"Not Since "Carrie": Forty Years of Broadway Musical Flops* (New York: St. Martin's, 1991), 255; Ethan Mordden, *Rodgers & Hammerstein* (New York: Abrams, 1992), 214; Ethan Mordden, *Open a New Window: The Broadway Musical in the 1960s* (New York: St. Martin's, 2001), 108; Steven Suskin, *Berlin, Kern, Rodgers, Hart, and Hammerstein: A Complete Song Catalogue* (Jefferson, NC: McFarland, 1990), 34. For more on these and other critical responses to *Waltz,* including Sondheim's longstanding antipathy to this show, see Geoffrey Block, *Richard Rodgers* (New Haven: Yale University Press, 2003), 213–225; Block, "Last Word," 133–150.
38. Zadan, *Sondheim & Co.,* 198.
39. Vincent Canby, "Film: *A Little Night Music*: Bergman-Inspired," *New York Times,* March 8, 1978, quoted in Zadan, *Sondheim & Co.,* 199.
40. By the time she made *Night Music* Taylor had been a film star renowned for her great beauty since her teen years in the 1940s.
41. The *Newsweek* review of *Mame* (March 29, 1974) is representative: "There she stands, her aging face practically a blur in the protective gauze of the softer than soft focus . . . looking alternately like any one of the seven deadly sins," quoted in Stephen Citron, *Jerry Herman: Poet of the Showtune* (New Haven: Yale University Press, 2004), 160. Canby is similarly cruel: "She [Ball] has been photographed in such soft focus that her face alternately looks beatific—all a religious glow—or like something sculptured from melting vanilla ice cream—a nylon tent" (Vincent Canby, "Mame Puts on New but Familiar Face—Lucille Ball," *New York Times,* March 8, 1974). Rex Reed, the only critic to bestow unequivocal praise on the film version of *Night Music,* quipped about *Mame* in the *Daily News* that someone must have spread chicken fat over the camera lens in an attempt to obscure Ball's age. "Mame (film)," accessed November 9, 2019,

https://en.wikipedia.org/wiki/Mame_(film). Body shaming did not end in the 1970s, but body shamers can no longer practice with impunity. As I write this chapter the nineteen-year old singer-songwriter Billie Eilish is making news for calling out the misogynistic body-shaming to which she has been subjected. Claire Shaffer, "Billie Eilish Addresses Body Shaming in Concert Interlude," *Rolling Stone*, March 10, 2020.

42. *Cabaret* was a notable financial success with a box office of $42.8 million on a budget of $4.6 million, but *Grease*'s total profit was truly staggering relative to its budget of $6 million.

43. Quoted in Zadan, *Sondheim & Co.*, 198. See note 41 for Reed's ridiculing of the film *Mame*.

44. Foster Hirsch, *Harold Prince and the American Musical Theatre* (New York: Applause Theatre & Cinema Books, rev. and expanded ed., 2005), 107.

45. Ibid., 108. In his introductory historical overview of film musicals Dominic McHugh concurs that the "'Glamorous Life' and 'Weekend in the Country' sequences [albeit only these sequences] truly do justice to the cinematic medium." Dominic McHugh, "'And I'll Sing Once More': A Historical Overview of the Broadway Musical on the Silver Screen," in *The Oxford Handbook of Musical Theatre Screen Adaptations*, ed. Dominic McHugh (New York: Oxford University Press, 2019), 20. This note offers a welcome opportunity to express my thanks to McHugh for his thoughtful and helpful reading of an earlier draft of this chapter.

46. Hirsch, *Harold Prince*, 108–109.

47. Quoted in Zadan, *Sondheim & Co.*, 199.

48. A note in the August 6, 1976, screenplay that appears during the "Weekend" number explains the process leading to the final cutting: "Each sequence will be shot in its entirety and the choice of which will be used will be decided during the editing. Although both the Egerman party and the Mittelheims will be singing at once, visually we will alternate between them, with the one not visible audible in Voice Over." Hugh Wheeler, *A Little Night Music: A Screenplay,* Music and Lyrics by Stephen Sondheim, HPC, no. 1738, August 6, 1976, no. 258. In Figure 10.1 the Egermans are in the car on the right, with the Count and Countess Mittelheim not far behind on the left.

49. The spelling of *Fredrika* in the published libretto of the stage version was changed in the film to *Fredericka* (although the screenplay spells her name *Frederika*). The *Fredericka* spelling matches Egerman's Frederick in the film, whereas in the stage version he's Fredrik. In *Finishing the Hat* Sondheim uses the spelling *Fredrika* for both the stage and the film character. The present essay will preserve the distinct stage and film spellings: Fredrik/Frederick and Fredrika/Fredericka.

50. HPC, *A Little Night Music,* Box 157, Folder 2, "*Night Music* Screenplay Correspondence."

51. Stage stars who have re-created their roles on film include the following: Ethel Merman, *Anything Goes* (1934; film 1936) and *Call Me Madam* (1950; film 1953); Ethel Waters, *Cabin in the Sky* (1940; film 1943); Vivian Blaine and Stubby Kaye, *Guys and Dolls* (1950; film 1955); Yul Brynner, *The King and I* (1951; film 1956); Gwen Verdon and Ray Walston, *Damn Yankees* (1955; film 1958); Judy Holliday, *Bells Are Ringing* (1956; film 1960); Robert Preston, *The Music Man* (1957; film 1962); Robert

Morse and Rudy Vallee, *How to Succeed in Business Without Really Trying* (1961; film 1967); Barbra Streisand, *Funny Girl* (1964; film 1968); Topol (London cast), *Fiddler on the Roof* (1964; film 1971); and nearly the entire original casts of *1776* (1969; film 1972) and *Rent* (1996; film 2005).

52. Gingold was deprived of her leading status when "Liaisons" was cut, but in her brief vocal moment in "A Weekend in the Country" she, too, did her own singing.

53. Steven Suskin, "On the Record: 'A Little Night Music' (Soundtrack) and the 1961 Revue *Seven Come Eleven*," September 15, 2013, accessed November 6, 2019, playbill. com/article/on-the-record-a-little-night-music-soundtrack-and-the-1961-revue-seven-come-eleven-com-209525.

54. Jones, Notes to the *A Little Night Music* Original Soundtrack Recording.

55. Len Cariou describes Taylor's recording session for "Send in the Clowns" in Zadan, *Sondheim & Co.*, 196.

56. Sondheim, *Finishing the Hat,* 250–83. Wheeler, *A Little Night Music*, HPC, no. 1738, "mimeographed copy with corrections and revised pages," August 6, 1976, 191 pages. Many thanks to the indispensable assistance of Andrew Buchman, who generously made this (and all) *Night Music* screenplays available to me, as well as the production materials and other papers housed in the Hal Prince Collection cited in this essay. The other NYPL film scripts are the following: no. 1744, March 4, 1976, "typescript with corrections, additions and notes from Mr. Wheeler" (no lyrics, but song positions indicated); no. 1745, June 3, 1976, "clean mimeographed copy"; no. 1740, August 6, 1976, "clean mimeographed copy").

57. HPC, Box 156, Folder 1, "*Night Music*—Film—Miscellaneous." The August 17 note indicates two timings, one for the dialogue and action (52 minutes, 52 seconds) and one for music and songs (68 minutes).

58. Ethan Mordden, *The Hollywood Musical* (New York: St. Martin's, 1981), 218.

59. *A Little Night Music,* Sascha-Wein Film, Hen's Tooth Video 4108 (June 2007), 124 minutes.

60. Sondheim, *Finishing the Hat*, 280.

61. Cuts in the film version of *Sweeney Todd* include all but the underscoring of "The Ballad of Sweeney Todd," all of "Ah, Miss," the Judge's version of "Johanna," the middle section of "Ladies in Their Sensitivities," nearly all of "God, That's Good," "The Letter," "Parlor Song," and the "City of Fire!" portion from the final sequence. Jesse Green reports that "in all fewer than 10 of the stage show's 25 major numbers survived substantially intact." Green, "Sondheim Dismembers 'Sweeney'" ("Slashing the Score"). Of the twenty songs in the stage version of *Into the Woods* six were cut in their entirety in the film version: "I Guess This Is Goodbye," "Maybe They're Magic," "First Midnight," "Ever After," "So Happy," and "No More." On those cuts see Mark Horowitz, "*Into the Woods* from Stage to Screen," in *The Oxford Handbook of Musical Theatre Screen Adaptations*, ed. Dominic McHugh, 107–24 (New York: Oxford University Press, 2019). In his interview for that essay Sondheim offered only the following: "I loved hearing the new rich orchestrations [by Jonathan Tunick]. It was the main pleasure of the film" (123). A few months prior to the film's release on Christmas 2014, however, Sondheim said a little more: "I can happily report that it is not only

a faithful adaptation of the show, it is a first-rate movie." Adam Hetrick, "Sondheim Issues Response Following Report of Disney *Into the Woods* Film Changes," *Playbill*, June 23, 2014.

62. Henrik's name was changed to Erich for the film. The reversal of "Later" and "Soon" in the film marks a *return* to the original order in the libretto drafts prior to the rehearsal draft of December 1972.

63. Although Petra was unsuccessful with Erich in the film, in their off-screen lives after the filming Lesley Dunlop and Christopher Guard married and produced two daughters, a great example, if one were needed, of life not imitating art.

64. Sondheim, *Finishing the Hat*, 281.

65. Ibid., 280.

66. Ibid., 254, 256.

67. Ibid., 254.

68. Ibid. As in the stage version, Mme. Armfeldt explains the three smiles in the following exchange:

MME ARMFELDT: "The first smile smiles for the young who know nothing. (*Looks down pointedly at Fredericka.*) The second for the fools who know too little like Desiree.

FREDERICKA (*suddenly defensive*): Mother isn't a fool.

MME ARMFELDT: Um hum [in the screenplay but not filmed]. And the third for the old who know too much like me." Wheeler, *A Little Night Music* HPC 1738, August 6, 1976, NYPL (no. 18).

69. The carriage portion of the song (*Finishing the Hat*, 267) was not released as part of the film soundtrack that appeared in 1978; it made its long-awaited debut as a bonus track on the release of the CD in 2013. At four minutes, the film version adds considerably to the initial release of the song, which lasted only 2 minutes, 28 seconds.

70. Kim H. Kowalke, "'Give Me Time': Sondheim, a Clever Maid and 'The Miller's Son,'" *Studies in Musical Theatre* 13, no. 2 (2019), 154.

71. Jones, Notes to the *A Little Night Music* Original Soundtrack Recording.

72. Wheeler, *A Little Night Music*, HPC, no. 1738, August 6, 1976.

73. Revisions were added on August 12–13, 16, 22, 24, and 28, and September 13–14, 21, and 28, 1976; in addition, several pages of revisions dated October 15 and 21 were placed at the beginning of the script.

74. The song "Liaisons" was filmed on September 28; "In Praise of Women" on October 19 (no. 196, no. 198, and no. 201), October 19 (no. 201), and October 25 (no. 199); and "The Miller's Son" on September 10 (no. 389) and September 13 (no. 388–389). HPC, Box 156, Folder 6, "*Night Music*—Production Reports."

75. The dialogue in the screenplay departs a little from the text, which reads, "Of course you are. After that long drive? It won't take a minute."

76. Letter from Harold Prince to Hugh Wheeler, July 12, 1976, HPC, Box 157, Folder 2, "*Night Music* Screenplay Correspondence" (this letter also appears in Box 154, Folder 7, "*Night Music* Movie Correspondence," with the Hal Prince letterhead cut off).

77. "'A Little Night Music' Reel Breakdown," November 10, 1976, HPC, Box 156, Folder 4 "Prince."

78. "Major Changes," Undated typescript (but dated December 6, 1976 in Prince's hand-written notes), HPC, Box 156, Folder 4, "Prince."

79. A full discussion of Tunick's underscoring is beyond the scope of this chapter, but it would be remiss to omit the importance that "Love Takes Time" plays in this important non-Sondheim musical component of the film. Not only does "Night Waltz" open and close the film, but it also is heard on five additional occasions. The fourth of these is particularly significant owing to its relative length. In the course of just under two minutes viewers observe a film montage that begins and ends with Desiree in her backstage dressing room on the closing night of *Woman of the World*, a scene in which Desiree plants the seeds of her invitation to Frederick and Anne for a weekend in her mother's country house. In between the dressing room bookends, the underscoring of the "Love Takes Time" Night Waltz supports the following scenes: (1) Frederick Egerman in his law office (no. 238b), (2) Carl-Magnus consorting with two whores (no. 238b), (3) Charlotte smashing her bedroom vanity mirror (no. 200), (4) Erich praying in church (no. 238d), and (5) Anne taking a doll from her childhood off a closet shelf (no. 238f). In an amusing touch of self-referentiality, Tunick was cast as the Conductor.

80. Roadshow movies were limited theatrical releases that opened in a select number of larger cities prior to their general release. During their heyday from the early 1950s to the early 1970s, roadshow movies tried to capture the trappings of a live stage show with reserved seats, elaborate souvenir programs, and fewer screenings each day. The film adaptation of *A Little Night Music* missed out on the roadshow era by just a few years. Matthew Kennedy, *Road-Show! The Fall of Film Musicals in the 1960s* (New York: Oxford University Press, 2014).

81. Films from the 1960s that ran closer to two hours include *Can-Can* (1960, 131 minutes); *Bells Are Ringing* (1960; 126 minutes); *Flower Drum Song* (1961; 133 minutes); *Jumbo* (1962; 125 minutes); *Bye Bye Birdie* (1963; 112 minutes); *The Unsinkable Molly Brown* (1964; 128 minutes); and *How to Succeed in Business without Really Trying* (1966; 121 minutes). Note that the latest film in this list appeared in 1966.

82. *Cabaret* (1972; 124 minutes); *Man of La Mancha* (1972; 132 minutes); *Jesus Christ Superstar* (1973; 106 minutes); *Mame* (1974, 132 minutes); *A Little Night Music* (1978; 124 minutes); *Grease* (1978; 110 minutes); *The Wiz* (1978; 133 minutes); and *Hair* (1979; 123 minutes).

83. David Craig, "On Performing Sondheim: *A Little Night Music* Revisited," in *Stephen Sondheim: A Casebook*, ed. Joanne Gordon (New York: Garland, 1993), 99; Kowalke, "Give Me Time," 151–168.

84. Kowalke, "Give Me Time," 153.

85. Quoted in Zadan, *Sondheim & Co.* (1974 ed. only, 237–238), quoted in Kowalke, "Give Me Time,"155.

86. Geoffrey Block, *Enchanted Evenings: The Broadway Musical from "Show Boat" to Sondheim and Lloyd Webber*, rev. and expanded 2nd ed. (New York: Oxford University Press, 2009), 289.

87. Sondheim, *Finishing the Hat*, 51.

88. *Broadway Song & Story: Playwrights/Lyricists/Composers Discuss Their Hits*, ed. Otis L. Guernsey Jr. (New York: Dodd, Mead, 1985), 50.

89. This paragraph is indebted to one of the helpful suggestions offered by W. Anthony Sheppard for improving an earlier draft of this essay. Sheppard expressed his view that "'The Miller's Son' feels somewhat Shakespearean, a final comic number infused with wisdom from the fool character, a number deliberately inserted before the final dramatic moments delaying the ending and thereby setting it up" (pers. comm., March 18, 2020). The suggestion caused me to recall Sondheim's reservations about the placement of "Gee, Officer Krupke," especially so near the conclusion of *West Side Story*. I still may not agree with Sondheim that "The Miller's Son" serves its intended purpose in the stage version, and I certainly do not think it serves its purposes as effectively as does "Gee, Officer Krupke," but I am grateful (rather than sorry) for the opportunity to consider possible parallels between "Krupke" and *Macbeth*'s drunken Porter scene.

90. bestactor, "Considering Everything It's Really Quite Good," IMDb User Comments for *A Little Night Music*, December 31, 2003, accessed July 24, 2021, http://www.imdb.com/review/rw0154097/?ref_=tt_urvt.

91. Zadan, *Sondheim & Co.*, 199.

92. Simon, *Ingmar Bergman Directs*, 112–114. Although the conventional wisdom among theater and film historians is that theatricality is invariably a negative attribute in a film adaptation of a stage musical, *New York Times* critic Jesse Green argues that "the best adaptations today relish the theatricality of their sources and try to enhance it." Jesse Green, "The Bumpy Road from Broadway to Hollywood," *New York Times*, December 20, 2020.

93. Letter from Hugh Wheeler to Harold Prince, March 1, 1976, HPC, Box 157, Folder 2, "*Night Music* Screenplay Correspondence."

94. Ibid. As a matter of possible interest, on the top left-hand margin Wheeler also inserted the suggestion, "How about Mia Farrow for Anne?"

95. Wheeler, *A Little Night Music: A Screenplay*, 140.

96. The 2008 London production directed by Trevor Nunn used the film version of "The Glamorous Life," which was also included as a bonus track in the CD 1998 reissue, Sony Classical/Columbia Legacy SK 65284. In his conversations with Mark Horowitz, Sondheim dismissed the use of this version on a regular basis, remarking that it should be reserved "for England" and "perfectly okay, but I prefer the original." Mark Eden Horowitz, *Sondheim on Music: Minor Details and Major Decisions* (Lanham, MD: Scarecrow, 2010), 123.

# PART IV
# RECONCEIVED STRUCTURES
# AND TECHNIQUES

# 11

# Time and Time Again

## Temporal Structures in Sondheim's Musicals

*Jim Lovensheimer*

In the second of the eight conversations with Stephen Sondheim that constitute most of Mark Eden Horowitz's book *Sondheim on Music: Minor Details and
Major Decisions*, Horowitz asked Sondheim if he thought it was important to
compose a score chronologically. Sondheim responded, "Absolutely. For me it is.
I almost always do it. . . . [It's] hard for me at the moment to think of a score since
*Forum* that I haven't composed from the beginning to the end." He went on to
recall a few exceptions—*Company*, for instance, and writing "It's Hot Up Here"
before anything else for *Sunday in the Park with George* ("because I thought it
was such a good idea, and I couldn't wait to write it"), noting that the rest of the
score was chronologically composed, as were the scores to *Sweeney Todd*, *Into
the Woods*, and *Assassins*. He started writing *Follies* chronologically, but the project developed in phases—it was put aside until *Company* was completed—the
result being that "the whole process was screwed up."[1] What is particularly interesting about this is that, from *Company* on, a number of the shows for which
Sondheim provided scores do not unfold in a linear, or chronological, progression. *Company* and *Assassins*, for instance, each take place in a kind of temporal
ambiguity. *Sunday in the Park with George* spends its first act following a fairly
straight line from beginning to intermission, but the second act begins in a kind
of temporal suspension in which the characters in Seurat's painting, caught there
for all time, sing the number mentioned above that Sondheim couldn't wait to
write. The script then jumps to the present, only to later introduce a character
from the first act—that is, the past—who helps the contemporary George find
his way back to his own art. (It makes far more sense in the show than it might
here.) *Merrily We Roll Along*, like the Kaufman and Hart play that inspired it,
has a linear plot; it simply moves backward through time. Or maybe not so
simply, depending on which audience member you talk to. Such structures make
Sondheim's preference for composing chronologically rather interesting.

Interesting though they may be, however, Sondheim's compositional practices
are not our primary concern. Rather, the temporal organizations of some of the
shows for which he wrote these scores are the main focus. Indeed, these treatments

Jim Lovensheimer, *Time and Time Again* In: *Sondheim in Our Time and His*. Edited by: W. Anthony Sheppard,
Oxford University Press. © Oxford University Press 2022. DOI: 10.1093/oso/9780197603192.003.0012

of time usually had more to do with the structures of the books than with any musical idea first thought of by Sondheim. I use the term *treatments of time* generally to describe what W. Anthony Sheppard has referred to as "different dramatic time zones" in the scores: a representation of the intersection of past and present in *Follies* and *Pacific Overtures*, the mosaic-like use of non-ordered time in *Company* and *Assassins*, or how what seems to be musical and emotional closure at the end of the first act of *Sunday* is delayed until late in the second act and, in terms of the plot, by over one hundred years.[2] Each of these musicals demonstrates a common characteristic that has been observed in many so-called concept musicals, and more particularly in those with scores by Sondheim, which present

> more freely conceived narrative modes, frequently described as "non-linear," which typically involve a predilection to superimpose or juxtapose different times or places. An important dramatic consequence of such a play is that it allows characters to interact onstage who could not actually do so within a realistic understanding of the story.[3]

*Treatments of time* also suggests the compositional techniques exploited by Sondheim to create these varied "time zones": motivic development, sometimes in reverse; pastiche to evoke the past within the present; minimally developing musical patterns that are repeated under sung passages of different songs; and so on. Given that the treatments of time are different in almost every one of these shows, Sondheim's responses to the challenges of each are impressive, especially when, as Sondheim noted, these scores tended to be written mostly in old-fashioned linear time. The result in each case, unsurprisingly, is unique from the rest while remaining unmistakably Sondheim. Each example also demonstrates the deep influence that a show's book has on the score that he creates for it. In terms of how these shows deal with and, in some cases, exploit humanly experienced time, the most complex of the lot is *Follies*, the book for which was written by the late James Goldman. In terms of music, *Sunday* demonstrates how the chronological composition of the score served to clarify and intensify the nonlinear aspects of its book. But before diving into those musicals, I shall start with two shows that are both situated in somewhat ambiguous temporal settings, the first of which also marked a keenly transitional moment in the development of the American musical.

## Temporal Twilight Zones

*Company*'s lack of a plot was one of the characteristics that set it off from shows that had preceded it. In his 1972 book *Words and Music*, the conductor and musical theater expert Lehmann Engel, not long after *Company*'s opening, noted the show's lack of linear structure with great interest. The penultimate chapter of Engel's book is titled "Non-Plot," and that is where he singled out the importance of *Company* in marking the move from the traditionally linear plot-driven musical theater to dramatic and structural trends already established in the nonmusical theater. He situated all this in an observation by George Pierce Baker in his 1919 book *Dramatic Technique*: "While action is popularly held to be central in drama, emotion is really the essential. . . . Accurately conveyed emotion is the fundamental in all good drama."[4] Accepting this idea, Engel used it to attack the "rock musicals" (*Hair*, *Salvation*, and *Promenade* in particular) that were short on plot and developed characters. Engel saw this as a fatal flaw: "The non-plot musicals have eschewed an important motivating theatrical element in being plotless and characterless because they have failed to furnish the audience with the sense of caring."[5] He then explored why many plotless works for the nonmusical stage are successful, crediting the "almost painful meticulous reliance on character development. This factor alone is enough to have created . . . interest, empathy, and deep concern."[6] Engel subsequently moved on to his discussion of *Company*, which he initially compared to *Applause*, another show running at the same time. He called *Applause* "a maze of plot" and *Company* "a succession of vignettes—storyless—pasted together by the presence of a single character and the employment of a single theme." *Applause*, he was careful to note, was the more commercially successful of the two shows, but *Company* was "by far the more important."[7] Noting that the show was important because it looked forward to the future of the genre, he specified that it demonstrated the difference between plot and situation, a differentiation that is also important to our discussion. Plot, Engel wrote, "occupies an over-all position in relation to . . . storytelling media," but situation, he explained, using a quotation from *Webster's Third New International Dictionary, Unabridged*, is "'a particular or striking complex of affairs at a stage in the action of a narrative of drama' . . . [that can] exist apart from plot in a number of contrasting or even related capsules." He concluded by stating that he had "come to believe that the future of musicals may lie in the situation-identity practice as opposed to the past-present method of plot and role."[8] And he felt that *Company* demonstrated how this could be done.

The often mordant Ethan Mordden summed it up nicely by noting that the show "is almost an imaginary piece, a sort of 'realism-but.' . . . Thus, the characters can irrupt into the action any time they want to: none of it is really happening."[9] This recalls Sondheim's comment in the book *Finishing the Hat* in which he affirmed that "the show takes place not over a period of time, but in an instant in Robert's mind, perhaps on a psychiatrist's couch, perhaps at the moment when he comes into his apartment on his thirty-fifth birthday. The framework is a surreal surprise birthday party for him. . . . The scenes which take place in between are all observations he makes about his married friends."[10] And about himself, I would add. This was later reinforced by what the actor Neil Patrick Harris recalled Sondheim telling him during the rehearsals for a 2011 Lincoln Center performance of the show: "The plot is all in [Bobby's] mind and you're sort of looking at all these photos on the wall. It totally is the existential musical."[11] And Stephen Banfield observed in 1993, before the show had been revived on Broadway or in the West End, that "the whole show can be seen as a fantasy taking place in an instant in his mind."[12] The most recent (2020) Broadway revival, a production directed by Marianne Elliott that opened in London in 2018 and closed in previews in March 2020 because of a pandemic-caused closing down of Broadway, kept to the idea that the entire musical was set inside Bobbie's head. (Robert became a woman called Bobbie in this production, which pulled off the various gender adjustments with complete plausibility.) This was aided by Bunny Christie and Chris Fisher's production design, which moved Bobbie through various *Alice-in-Wonderland*-like doorways that appeared before her on a set that was often in motion. Katrina Lenk's Bobbie seemed unsure of where she was headed at almost any given moment, and the effect worked beautifully.

No matter what the production concept, however, the "surreal" and "existential" elements of the show are what create its timelessness, which is expressed in part through Sondheim's score. The first music heard, for instance, is the "Bobby" theme sung by Robert's friends and soon expanded into a connective motive throughout the show. It also provides the motivic substance of the climactic song "Being Alive." This theme is the first thing we hear, and its initial incarnation is haunting. Indeed, the script calls it "ghostly."[13] (In the original production it was sung by unseen pit singers, which created a literal disembodiment of the theme.) It is also somewhat tonally ambiguous in this first presentation, and it grows increasingly dissonant as its implied tonality is further challenged. The lyrics consist solely of the name "Bobby" followed by the vocables "bah-bah bah bah bah bah bah bah." (Those syllables are replaced by nicknames for "Robert" as the theme is repeated.) The beginning of the scene that follows is equally ambiguous: the published script calls for Robert's friends, who are carrying wrapped birthday presents, to "look out front and speak tonelessly."[14] The scene slowly becomes more realistic and the actors "start becoming more human, looking and reacting to Robert and to each other."[15] It remains fairly realistic until Robert tries to blow out the candles on his birthday cake and they fail to go out. He tries again, and again they fail to go out. At this point, at least according to the published script, while the lines continue, the friends begin to exit until Robert is left alone. The music for the opening number begins, and the Bobby theme takes over. The lyrics alternate between the various nicknames for Robert and more personal comments to him—"We've been trying to reach you all day," "How about some Scrabble on Sunday," and so forth—but the friends do not sing any of this directly to him. Again, there is no specificity of time or place. Yet the number is so exuberant that the audience rarely realizes how disconnected everyone in it is, both from each other and from any point in time or space. The show continues to operate like this, its disconnected quality emphasized by numbers that do not grow organically out of a scene in any traditional way. Indeed, Sondheim has commented that the books for *Company* and *Follies* exist "in the twilight zone between a revue and a book."[16]

This last aspect was at first problematic for Sondheim. He has shared that, early on, he, George Furth (the author of the book whose one-act plays were the source for the show), and Harold Prince (the director), "realized . . . that the kind of song that would not work in the show was the Rodgers and Hammerstein kind of song in which the characters reach a certain point and then sing their emotions, because George writes the kind of people who do not sing."[17] Sondheim had learned from his mentor Oscar Hammerstein II how to write songs that were character- and plot-driven, but with this project that approach was not an option. Not only did Furth's characters not sing, but there was no plot. "All the songs had to be used," Sondheim realized, "in a Brechtian way as comment and counterpoint." This was despite his general distaste for Brecht's work. Nonetheless, he continued, "We had our songs interrupt the . . . [action] and be sung mostly by people outside the scene commenting on the action taking place."[18] This also facilitated songs that were not time-or space-specific. That it all worked and continues to work is demonstrated by *Company*'s stature in the repertory and its frequent revivals.

The quasi Brechtian approach is somewhat less surprising when we remember that, only four years earlier, Harold Prince had directed and helped develop the musical *Cabaret*, which exploited a similar use of musical numbers. Situated in what Prince called a spatial and temporal "limbo" outside the realistic settings of the plot, these numbers, performed by the Emcee of the cabaret, functioned "as ironic signposts, framing and pointedly disrupting book scenes. [The] limbo routines, like the songs in [Brecht's] *The Threepenny Opera*, use musical interludes in a self-conscious way to isolate and to enlarge the show's themes. As they fulfill the entertainment imperative of musical theatre the comment songs also create intellectual detachment."[19] This is how the musical numbers in *Company* functioned as well, minus the Emcee. In that the idea for *Company*'s structure, as well as *Cabaret*'s, was originally Prince's, this use of the musical numbers undoubtedly in part grew from that idea. Or, dare we say, "concept."

*Assassins*, which Sondheim, during its creation, referred to as a "surreal history,"[20] turned out to require a somewhat similar, though not exactly the same, approach to its musical numbers. Sondheim later recalled that "the structure of the show was to be a dreamlike vaudeville, skipping backward and forward in time (a hundred years' worth), and would incorporate a number of different theatrical models, from burlesque comedy to melodrama, with a few straight-forward stops in between."[21] It is a temporal and stylistic mosaic, in other words, not completely unlike *Company*, at least temporally and in the quality of being somewhat "dreamlike." *Assassins*, however, lacks a central character to corre-spond to *Company*'s Robert, which also suggests the need for a different musical approach. An argument might be made that the Balladeer, a contemporary folk-singer who introduces several numbers and is even acknowledged by Booth, fulfills that role, but, until he is forced off the stage by the assassins before the final chorus of "Another National Anthem," he serves principally in a narrative capacity and not as a character. Indeed, as Sondheim remarked to Mark Eden Horowitz, "*Assassins* is very much a collection of songs. . . . There is no attempt here to make a 'score' except insofar as relates to the characters. It's eclectic—different kinds of styles, reflecting the periods and reflecting the characters."[22] This structural approach necessitated numbers that do not so much comment on scenes as become scenes, which gives the show the added quality of a vaude-ville: The numbers are like individual acts held together by John Weidman's beautifully constructed book, which seamlessly flows through time and even brings together various characters from different time periods to encounter each other, at least one time to great comic effect. Sondheim later went a step further, noting that, unlike the "chronological revue" *Pacific Overtures* (an-other show with a book by Weidman), "*Assassins* was something more com-plicated and dangerous—a collage."[23] Late in the show, as Scott Miller has suggested, "when the assassins all materialize in the [Dallas] book depository scene to persuade [Lee Harvey] Oswald to join them [by shooting President Kennedy], the plastic nature of time throughout the show pays off . . . as past, present, and future collide in Oswald's brain. . . . This psychological and his-torical phenomenon is represented as an actual corporeal experience, making it so much clearer and more immediate to the audience."[24] A similar if less in-tense scene, minus Oswald, occurs early in the show and prepares us for this later simultaneous gathering of assassins: John Wilkes Booth, John Hinckley, Leon Czolgosz, Giuseppe Zangara, Samuel Byck, and an unidentified bartender are all assembled in a turn-of-the-century saloon that, the stage directions tell us, "could be on 14th Street in 1900, or on Columbus Avenue in 1991."[25] Sondheim also later noted that "the scenes which combined the characters from different time periods and played them off against one another tied the piece to-gether."[26] Perhaps this was in part because in these scenes, to paraphrase Ethan Mordden, Weidman and Sondheim's "surreal history" is motionless and, thus, ambiguous.[27]

## "Was It Ever Real?"

If *Company* and *Assassins* are "temporally ambiguous," as I have called them, *Follies* is far more explicit. Further, the show has an added layer of time and memory laid on it when, as in the superb 2017 revival at the National Theatre in London, it remains set in 1971, the time of the work's premiere. (Other revivals have suggested that the principal story line is contemporary with the production.) Whereas viewers of the original performance, like those at many subsequent productions, experienced at least one level of the work as a contemporaneous happening, viewers of the National Theatre production must begin their experience of the show by already looking backward to a specific time in the past, which is only the first step of the work's time-warped trajectory. What makes this phenomenon even more interesting and, in some ways, problematic, is that younger audiences, in addition to having no recollection of 1971, have drastically different constructs of memory than do older audience members. The period depicted is not only outside the boundaries of their memory, it is outside the way they experience memory. Their pasts are digitized and available for recall via the cloud, whereas the memories of those before them are "mostly trapped in analog formats . . . tangible and imperfect artifacts that degrade with age and can be lost irretrievably."[28] How might this younger digitized generation respond to a musical play that is based on characters' "imperfect" memories, on their lifelong lies about those memories, of the delusions that are only possible without any digitized record of them? This generational question in part informed my exploration of how memory and time are expressed in *Follies*, both in the dramatic text—that is, the work as written—and its performance text, specifically the aforementioned National Theatre revival as directed by Dominic Cooke. Both texts are uncomfortable and disturbing, perhaps even more so today than they were in 1971. But regardless of how each generation copes with the work's at times slippery slide through time and memory, those aspects of the show were present even in its gestation period. They also recall another literary work that might have influenced Prince's contributions, which will be discussed anon.

The initial concept for a show about a reunion of Ziegfeld Girls came to James Goldman in 1965. He and Sondheim tossed around ideas for it, and by the end of the year, Goldman had finished a first draft called *The Girls Upstairs*. After several more drafts and a rejection from producer David Merrick, the project was put on hold while Goldman and Sondheim wrote *Evening Primrose* for the television series *ABC Stage 67*, after which Sondheim became briefly involved with another project, which was ill-fated. He returned to *The Girls Upstairs*, which by now had attracted another producer. Meanwhile, Sondheim's friend George Furth showed Sondheim a series of one-act plays, which Sondheim in turn showed to Harold Prince, who thought they could be made into a musical. Furth and Sondheim then started work on the show that became *Company*, while *The Girls Upstairs* was still pending production with a second producer. But a little more than a month before rehearsals for *The Girls Upstairs* were to begin, the second producer also dropped the option. Sondheim showed *The Girls Upstairs* to Prince, who eventually agreed to produce it but only after *Company* opened. When Prince returned to the show, post-*Company*, he found things in it that he had not seen before, and, as Craig Zadan noted, he "went right to work . . . turning the naturalistic *Girls Upstairs* into the surrealistic, Fellini-esque *Follies*."[29]

The central story is about two very unhappily married couples—Ben and Phyllis, and Buddy and Sally (Sally and Phyllis were former Follies Girls)—whose relationships with each other in the past were also deeply problematic. Prince conceived of bringing their pasts into the plot to exist simultaneously with the present, and the result was stunning. As Foster Hirsch observed, Prince's

> suggestions of interweaving past events into the present action to make the characters confront their younger selves aimed at creating what Prince calls a "Proustian fracturing of time." A reunion of Follies girls provides an eerie symbolic frame against which the characters' follies—their self-delusions and misjudgments—are enacted.[30]

All the characters' "ghosts," as they are called, are seen from the very beginning of the show. Indeed, they are seen before their contemporary counterparts are and before we know specifically who they are. The direct intermingling of both sets of characters begins subtly: the host, Follies producer Dmitri Weismann, introduces a tenor who begins to sing "Beautiful Girls," the number that introduced the Follies Girls of old. He is accompanied by an onstage piano, but as the contemporary, and much older, Follies Girls make their entrances as in the past, now wearing banners announcing the years of their appearances in the Follies, the nondiegetic pit orchestra takes over. It is at this moment that, as Stephen Banfield observed, "the orchestra is already on a par with the ghosts."[31] And onstage, or more specifically upstage of the real-time action, the ghosts of the older chorus girls mirror their entrances in the costumes from the original Follies. They co-exist, although they do not as yet make any direct contact. But the individual identities of the ghosts start to emerge.

A closer proximity between past and present soon occurs in the musical number "Waiting for the Girls Upstairs," the third number in the show. The voices of Young Buddy and Young Ben, by now individually recognizable, start the introduction from offstage, but the older Ben and Buddy and, eventually, Phyllis and Sally sing the first section of the song. Following that, their younger selves appear and take over. It is important that there is no interaction yet between the sets of characters, although the stage directions suggest that when the young characters disappear "as suddenly as they appeared," the older couples "stand quite still for a moment, caught by the remembered joy of being young" before resuming and finishing the number.[32] It is in the following number, or, more precisely, suite of numbers, that the contact between the past and the present becomes corporeal. Emily and Theodore Whitman, an older dance team, begin performing "Rain on the Roof," one of their numbers from the past. They are immediately joined upstage by their younger selves, who mirror their number. At one point, at least in the Cooke production, the older Theodore is handed a prop umbrella by his ghost, which connects the past and the present in a quite literal way. Not long after that, the older Theodore returns the umbrella to his ghost as the number continues. It is an easy moment to miss, but a tremendously important one in that it creates a passage in time that continues to be physically crossed throughout the rest of the show, ultimately to terrifying results.

This connection between the present and the memory of the past recalls Prince's Proust reference. The Swiss-born British philosopher and writer Alain de Botton has noted that "one of the things that Proust brilliantly brings out is the way that suddenly a bit of our past, a bit of memory, can surge in front of us when we smell . . . or taste . . . [sensations] that we once had known. And these little stray moments can suddenly bring back to us a period of our lives that we thought was lost forever."[33] In *Follies*, it is not the sensation of a madeleine that unlocks memory and the past but the characters' presence in a place already full of memory—the theater that is about to be torn down—as well as the musical numbers that conjure up and re-enact the past, that draw the memories quite literally into the present. Or perhaps they sometimes draw the present back into the past. Before singing "Waiting for the Girls Upstairs," Buddy comments, "Just being together here, the four of us, I feel all the things I used to feel. Like it was yesterday." To which Phyllis responds, "Oh Buddy, that was 1941; that's thirty years ago." But Buddy continues, as a cue to beginning the song, "I see it all. It's like a movie in my head that plays and plays. It isn't just the bad things I remember. It's the whole show."[34] Two subsequent numbers—Ben's "The Road You Didn't Take" and Sally's "In Buddy's Eyes"—are each interrupted between verses by spoken scenes between Young Ben and Young Buddy in the first song and Young Ben and Young Sally in the second. But each set of characters remains unaware of the other with the exception, in Cooke's production, of Ben's seemingly bitter awareness of his younger self at the end of "The Road You Didn't Take," although it is fleeting. But the next number, "Who's That Woman," also often referred to as the "mirror number," brings together the ghosts of the showgirls and their older incarnations to dance together in what is perhaps the most memorable number of the show. This is especially effective because the older showgirls are actually performing the number in real time, seemingly on a dare from Weismann, and their ghosts appear first as mirrors of their dance and then, gradually, as actual participants in it, joining arms with the older women to form pinwheels and other choreographic executions. The number is basically a metaphor for the entire show—the ghosts' costumes literally have mirrors sewn into them—and its eerie comingling of past and present is unforgettable. Sondheim referred to the original staging as "one of the most brilliantly staged numbers in Broadway history."[35]

Two other moments in the show demonstrate the growing surreal presence of the past in the present. The song "Too Many Mornings," one of Sondheim's loveliest, is preceded by a scene that is initially between Ben and Sally but grows to include Young Ben and Young Sally. Then both Sallies begin speaking in unison and Ben responds with increasing directness to Young Sally, taking her in his arms as the older Sally is held by Young Ben. Ben sings the song to Young Sally and, as the script indicates, "both couples mirror each other's movements." At the end of the first chorus, "Young Ben and Young Sally leave their partners and slip back into each other's arms" as the older Sally and Ben finish the song. At the end of the song, "Sally falls into Ben's arms. The couples are in identical embraces."[36] The different planes of time have directly connected, just as the innocuous passing of the umbrella much earlier in the show suggested they could and would.

Once this direct connection between the present and the memory of the past has been firmly established, one last temporal confrontation remains, and it is staggering. The tension within each couple and between couples grows to a raging explosion. Present characters yell at their younger selves; the younger characters yell at each other, sometimes saying the same things at the same time that the older characters are saying. Eventually, according to the script, "all four speak simultaneously, each of them turning on their past self with mounting rage as if they mean to do physical violence to the memories. . . . It's now senseless, and frightening. . . . As the madness of the confrontation hits its peak, heavenly music is heard and we find ourselves transported to Loveland: a Ziegfeld extravaganza complete with costumed Chorus and a bevy of Showgirls."[37] This happens as both older couples stand in the middle of it, looking around in fear and wonder. They do not know what is happening (the audience isn't quite sure, either), and it is the one moment in the show when all four of them seem to sense that they might actually be completely mad. They then disappear, and the Follies, which consists of numbers representing each of their own personal follies, plays out. Eventually, Ben, whose Follies number is the last, breaks down before finishing the number and in desperation screams for Phyllis. The stage directions describe what happens next: "A flash of light and deafening sound as everything breaks apart and dissembles insanely. Bits and pieces of other songs shatter through. The Chorus line, although broken up, is still dancing, as if in a nightmare. The noise reaches a peak of madness before slowly starting to recede. Softer, softer . . .

leaving Ben kneeling on the stage as a solitary Showgirl drifts by."[38] Memory, the past, has receded along with the peak of madness. Or so it seems. But after all the guests have left, the Young Ben, Phyllis, Buddy, and Sally again appear and slowly sing the opening of "Waiting for the Girls Upstairs" as the stage goes black.

All of this again recalls Proust, whose last novel in the series of novels that constitute *À la recherche du temps perdu* climaxes with a party scene many years after most of the novel's action in which Marcel, the work's narrator, who is at the party, wonders where his friends are and who all the gray and faded guests might be. Of course, he eventually realizes that *they* are his friends and that they have simply grown old. Of this moment, Patrick Alexander has written that Marcel feels a "despair at the corroding effect of time, which makes all human feelings and experiences fade to nothing. [But Marcel eventually realizes] that past feelings and experiences, far from being lost, remain eternally present in the unconscious."[39] Marcel also realizes that their presence can be materialized in art, and he leaves the party to begin writing the book that the reader is just about to finish. The two couples in *Follies* leave the party not to create art but to reclaim their own lives in the present and the future, leaving their memories in the theater that is about to be torn down. *Follies*, as an early anonymous reader of this essay observed, is as much about the future as about the past. Still, as Alexander observed and as the last notes of Sondheim's score remind us, the past is still "eternally present."[40]

## "We Float"

*Pacific Overtures* began in 1973 as a nonmusical play by John Weidman, a third-year law student at Yale with an undergraduate degree in East Asian history from Harvard. Weidman's focus was the 1853–1854 expedition of Commodore Matthew Perry from the United States to Japan to open trade relations with Japan, which for approximately 250 years had been an isolated island country virtually uninfluenced by any outside culture. Perry, who arrived with four warships on what he claimed was a mission of peace, did not intend to take no for an answer, and the course of history, as well as Japan's insular culture, was forever altered. Weidman showed a draft of the play to Harold Prince, who was fascinated and asked the young playwright to write another draft. After several more drafts, Prince decided the play should be a musical, which did not much interest Weidman until Prince mentioned Sondheim as the composer-lyricist of the piece. But Sondheim was not initially enthusiastic, either: "At first I thought it could never work. I liked the play but I didn't see how the music would fit." Prince's idea was to create a "strange hybrid musical revue, with a story, but not particularly linear characters . . . a revue that told [a] nonlinear story."

The director played with this idea, wanting to incorporate various styles and influences, but he finally found the approach that guided the project: It would be an American kabuki.[41] And with that, they were on their way.

Prince's idea of a revue, which had been based on the use of consecutive scenes held together by a narrator, or Reciter, as he was called, continued to inform the concept for the show, but the scenes told a chronological story.[42] The somewhat traditional plot concerned the growth and ultimate destruction of a friendship between two men who initially came together in response to the presence of the Americans. Kayama is a minor samurai assigned to repel Perry—what Kayama sees as basically a suicide mission—and Manjiro is a commoner who has been to America and whose knowledge of Western ways Kayama finds useful. The story of the Americans' imposition of their trade and, eventually, their cultural values onto the Japanese covers a period of approximately fifteen years, during which the friendship of Kayama and Manjiro reflects two opposite Japanese responses: As Kayama begins a gradual but steady rejection of traditional Japanese culture in favor of an acculturation to Western ways, Manjiro becomes increasingly, and later violently, isolationist and conservative. Prince biographer Foster Hirsch provides a succinct summary of the show's concern with an idea as well as a story: "[In] *Pacific Overtures* history is the star; as the revue-like scenes advance a thesis of Japan's manifest destiny, the background moves to the foreground. . . . [Tradition] is both celebrated—it provides communal security—and criticized: it can be dangerously insular . . . and comes at a steep price in personal and cultural dislocation."[43] A number late in the second act titled "A Bowler Hat" follows the parallel developments of the two principal characters and demonstrates another way Sondheim, Weidman, and Prince manipulated time for dramatic purposes. It also demonstrates, as does the number "Someone in a Tree," the close relationship of Sondheim's work to that of his librettist.

"A Bowler Hat" is in part epistolary: The core of the number is a series of letters that Kayama writes to the Shogun over the course of fifteen years to apprise him (and the audience) of the effect of the Westerners—at this point not only Americans—on Japanese life. Sondheim, after discussing the scene with Weidman, asked the playwright to write the letters, which Sondheim would then turn into a song. But after reading what Weidman had written, Sondheim decided that "the crystalline formality of the prose"[44] would be undercut by his rhyming it, and he decided to retain the letters as spoken passages, read by the Reciter, between sung sections for Kayama. The sung sections, in turn, reveal Kayama's steady Westernization over the years. The song exploits what Raymond and Zelda Knapp have called "the manipulation of time and space through compression" by the use of letters.[45]

Kayama is first seen writing with a traditional brush, but, after the first section of the song, the brush is replaced with a pen. His increasing Westernization

is further demonstrated in the sung sections between segments of the read letters. His acquisition of the titular bowler hat is one of the earliest indications
of Kayama's cultural transformation. His final new possessions—a monocle and
a diplomat's cutaway coat—demonstrate Kayama's ultimate observation that,
"One must accommodate the times / As one lives them."[46]

On another part of the stage, however, during the reading of the letters and
Kayama's song, Manjiro performs the ritual tea ceremony and subsequently
dresses in samurai robes, ominously complete with sword.[47] Manjiro's graceful
and deliberate activities take place within a kind of temporal stillness that
contrasts with the compressed time span of Manjiro's Westernization. Frank
Rich wrote of this number, "In a few minutes, and with the use of only a few
details, Mr. Sondheim transforms a character's trivial autobiographical chron-
icle into a paradigm of an entire civilization's declining values."[48] Further, as
Sondheim even later wrote, the number "made for a memorable theatrical
moment, compressing fifteen extraordinary years into five extraordinary
minutes."[49] All this is accomplished while Manjiro demonstrates the timelessness of tradition.

The structure and setting of the show, along with the culture that inspired it,
also provided Sondheim, Weidman, and Prince with opportunities to exploit
other representations of time often outside traditional Western approaches. An
example of this comes near the end of the first act and, for the purposes of this
discussion, reflects an excellent observation of Paul Attinello's that although musical structure can often define or outline time through the creation of patterns
of repetitions, "it is also possible for music to refer to static views of time, apparently timeless states of being, and various constructions of eternity." Further,
Attinello insists that these timeless states "can also be embedded in, or at least
suggested by, music that uses relatively active rhythmic patterns."[50] "Someone
in a Tree" beautifully demonstrates this. The number is a recollection of the
first meeting between the Americans and the Japanese, which took place in an
isolated meeting house constructed solely for this purpose. It is sung by three
characters: an Old Man who corrects the Reciter's observation that there is no
account of the meeting ("Pardon me, I was there"); a Boy, who is a younger incarnation of the Old Man and reveals that, while he saw what happened from a
tree, he could not hear it; and a Warrior, who heard everything but saw nothing
because he was hidden beneath the floor to ensure that, if things went badly, he
could spring forth and protect the Japanese envoy. Sondheim has always spoken
fondly of the song. "[What] I love is its ambition, its attempt to collapse past,
present, and future into one packaged song form."[51] He also credits the idea for
this "ambitious invention" to John Weidman, who wrote a five-page scene that
Sondheim turned into the memorable number, demonstrating again his close
dependence on his collaborators.

Sondheim builds the song over a deceptively simple vamp based on a single chord. But he repeats it with very slight variations, so the audience does not necessarily notice that it is hearing the same chord for sixty measures. The "rhythm keeps changing," he explains, "and the texture keeps changing, and *where* the chord keeps being placed changes a little bit at a time. . . . Nothing's going on, but everything's going on. . . . It's an attempt musically to echo the visual—and the literal—of Japanese art."[52] Sondheim also acknowledges the similarities between this technique and that of composer Steve Reich. Of "Someone in a Tree," Sondheim notes "it's minimalist music. . . . It's phase music—in a very, very, very simplified form . . ."[53] The repeated vamp and its harmonic stasis are interrupted regularly by a repeated "chorus" of more melodic interest, the first of which begins, "It's the pebble, not the stream. / It's the ripple, not the sea." But it is the seemingly endless, yet never monotonous, vamp that suspends the number in what Attinello calls "split seconds of eternity" and "a nexus of transcendent perceptions."[54]

The lyrics reflect the past and present aspect of the narrative: After the Old Man begins a more historical description, the appearance of his younger self moves the descriptions into a kind of time-shifting reality. The Young Boy tells the Old Man, "Tell him [the Reciter] what I see," for instance, but the Old Man comments on the Young Boy (himself), "He was only ten," and the Boy says of the Old Man, "I was younger then." The Warrior introduces himself in the present tense—"Excuse me, I am here"—and the Reciter addresses him similarly—"Can you hear?" At one point the Old Man, the Boy, and the Reciter simultaneously command the Warrior, "Tell us what you see." Binding it all together is the idea, first sung by the Boy and then the Warrior, that each of them is "a fragment of the day." The Boy also sings, "It's the fragment not the day," which also begins the final chorus, sung by all four characters and which ends, "Only cups of tea / And history / And someone in a tree!" In this number, perhaps more than any other in the show, Sondheim succeeds in creating three simultaneous experiences of the past that co-exist in the present, which may be what prompted him to later say that "this song comes the closest to the heart of *Pacific Overtures*."[55]

## "How did you get to be here?"

The most notable fact about the temporal structure of *Merrily We Roll Along* is that the story, which has a traditional beginning, middle, and end, is told backward in time. This means that only the middle is where it might be expected. Each separate scene, however, moves forward in time, as we might expect. But another element of time is also at work in the show, or at least in Sondheim's creation of the score, and it has to do with our earlier discussion of *Follies* and

Proust. Concerning the conception of the show, Sondheim later wrote, "In truth, like the characters in the show, I was trying to roll myself back to my exuberant early days, to recapture the combination of sophistication and idealism that I'd shared with Hal Prince, Mary Rodgers, Jerry Bock and Sheldon Harnick, John Kander and Fred Ebb, and the rest of us show business supplicants, all stripped back to our innocence."[56] And in comments about the song "Opening Doors," which he admits to being one of the few songs in any of his work that is "drawn directly from life experience," he recalls, not without a trace of generally uncharacteristic sentiment, "although the details may vary, that song describes what the struggle was like for me and my generation of Broadway songwriters. I'm sure it must often have seemed frustrating at the time, but in retrospect it strikes me as the most exhilarating period of my professional life."[57] But in the musical, this exhilarating and youthful experience comes near the end of the show, long after we have met the bitter individuals that the three principal characters have turned into. It is no wonder, then, that this number is a part of what is probably Sondheim's most exuberant and, at the same time, most heartbreaking score.

Several compositional approaches were necessitated by the show's overall retrograde structure. Sondheim has spoken of how he wanted to use "conventional" song forms for the show since a lot of it takes place in the 1950s and 1960s, when the thirty-two-bar song form was standard. Perhaps because of the score's having been influenced by more conventional mid-century show tunes, its compositional complexity is sometimes easy to miss. For instance, Sondheim reminds us that in mid-century musicals, reprises of songs were expected and often had dramatic effect. But, he notes, "telling the story backwards suggested something unconventional: the possibility of reversing the usual presentation of [those reprises]. . . . The structure of *Merrily We Roll Along* suggested to me that the reprises could come first: the songs that had been important in the lives of the characters when they were younger would have different resonances as they aged." What is tricky here is that we experience those resonances before we know what is being resonated. Only after having experienced the entire score do we fully understand it and Sondheim's ingenuous development of themes and motives from beginning to end. Or would that be from end to beginning? For instance, the first time we hear the song "Not a Day Goes By," it is sung angrily by the principal character's betrayed wife. This is an example of a "reversed reprise," as Sondheim calls it. Sung in Act I, it is "a full chorus of a furious song that prefigures a rapturous version in Act II. In any other musical, the reprise [in Act II] would be the disillusionment; here it is the promise."[58] As we experience it, a promise is broken before it has been made.

Further, one motive, used at several key points of the score, provides a clear demonstration of how the reverse development of motives and themes is used throughout the score. (Although we should remember that, as Sondheim later pointed out, "if the score is listened to in reverse order—*although it wasn't written that way*—it develops traditionally.")[59] Originally, the show began with a contemporary graduation ceremony at Lake Forest High School, where Franklin Shepard and Charley Kringas, now a successful songwriting team and the show's two principal male characters, were students. The chorus is singing the end of the school anthem, "The Hills of Tomorrow," which Frank and Charley wrote at the infancy of their collaborative career. The original cast album features the entire song at this point, although Sondheim writes in *Finishing the Hat* that only the last part of the song was sung in the performance. However, having the entire song at the top of the show, at least on the recording, provides an important piece of musical information that is not immediately perceived as such: The opening phrase, sung to the words "Behold the hills of tomorrow," recurs throughout the show and is of great musical importance. Its presence in this early endeavor by the team shows it to be a very young kernel of what becomes the most important song of their career, one that also ultimately provides a sad coda to that career's demise.

The revised 1985 version of the show eliminated the opening commencement ceremony altogether. The song in which the motive in question finds its most successful incarnation, "Good Thing Going," is the last melody of the overture, which serves to plant it in the audience's ears. The next time it is heard is much later in Act I. Frank and Charley, along with Mary, a writer friend close to both, have just sung the number "Old Friends" and are about to go to a club to celebrate Frank's return from a long trip. But complications due to Frank's affair with a producer's wife necessitate his staying behind, much to Charley and Mary' disappointment. Left alone, he sits at a piano and starts playing some arpeggios, which become a chordal accompaniment to what we will later learn is "Good Thing Going." He whistles the melody and then sings a countermelody: "Thanks, old friends . . . / Keep reminding me . . . / Frank's old friends / Always seem to come through." The "Good Thing Going" melody is retained in the piano part, which Frank is playing.[60]

The next time we hear this motive is at the top of Act II. Gussie, the producer's wife with whom Frank later has an affair, sings it on opening night of Frank and Charley's first Broadway show, which her husband has produced. As the final section of a long musical sequence, Gussie sings part of "Good Thing Going," belting it in a bluesy style obviously intended to stop Frank and Charley's show. It has a completely different character than when we heard Frank playing it alone on the piano in Act I, but now we know what the melody was. A bit later in Act II, which is to say chronologically earlier, we see Frank and Charley somewhat uncomfortable at a party being hosted by Gussie, who is at this point already a star and promoting the team's work. She has them perform "Good Thing Going," which Frank plays and Charley sings. Here, it is a soft ballad, much more in character with Frank's reflective performance of it in Act I and completely un-like what it became when performed by Gussie. This is the central performance of the song and, given what we already know of the turbulent and ultimately sad end of Frank and Charley's friendship, its simplicity is deeply moving. Stephen Banfield sums it up nicely. He begins by noting how Sondheim "allows the song to be appreciated on many levels that shift back and forth between an intensely private role for the song and a markedly public one. . . . [On one level] a naïve but deserving hit, as a microcosm of their friendship and its fate . . . [and of] the unspoken or hidden thoughts . . . that can never be wholly satisfied except in the death wish of closure that the song's final words so poignantly act out."[61] Those final words are, "We had a good thing going, / Going, / Gone."[62]

Even later in the act, we hear the song in a chronologically earlier and comic setting. "Opening Doors" is the show's penultimate full number—there is a brief sung transition between this and "Our Time," the final number. "Opening Doors" is a masterful montage showing Frank, Charley, and Mary at the earliest stages of their careers in New York. It follows them through temp jobs, mutual support, mutual frustration, and auditions, and it winds up with them doing an original revue. The montage begins with Frank at a piano obsessively banging out the familiar motive that we by now know will eventually become his first hit. But here we see him trying, and failing, to turn the first phrase of a school anthem into something more useful. He extends it, he alters notes, he reharmonizes it, all while Charley is pounding his typewriter in rhythmic counterpoint and Mary is pecking at hers. Later in the sequence, Frank and Charley are auditioning mate-rial for producer Joe Josephson, who later will produce their first show (and lose his wife to Frank). The number we see them presenting is a jaunty and bouncing number that begins, "Who wants to live in New York," the opening melody for which is the very same motive that Frank was earlier obsessing over. Joe is some-what appreciative, but he is critical of this and the other songs he has heard: "There's not a tune you can hum." This is especially amusing in that we already know this particular tune will eventually be transformed into a hit.[63]

The original 1981 version of the show concluded with a return to the com-mencement and featured the full version of "The Hills of Tomorrow," which brought the well-used motive back to its origins. The reasons for cutting the framing commencement scenes in 1985 were undoubtedly defendable, but their excision deprived us of hearing a key musical element of the show make its way from beginning to end, or beginning to beginning, as the case might be. Even Sondheim acknowledges this is his notes on the original ending in *Finishing the Hat*: "The young Frank . . . turns and conducts the students in the Commencement song that he and Charley have written. We recognize the tune as the seed of 'Good Thing Going,' the song that launched their careers."[64] In other words, we hear how what "started out like a song" and ended regretfully had earlier extolled the promise of "the hills of tomorrow." Too bad we do not still have that moment of musical recognition.

## Moving On

In 1982 producer Lewis Allen encouraged Sondheim to meet with playwright-director James Lapine to discuss a potential collaboration, and in one of their early sessions Lapine asked Sondheim what kind of musical he would like to write. Sondheim mentioned theme and variation form and provided a visual example to Lapine by way of an issue of the French arts magazine *Bizarre*, which consisted solely of variations on the *Mona Lisa*. This led to a discussion that ended up with Lapine mentioning Georges Seurat's famous painting *Un dimanche après-midi à l'Île de la Grande Jatte* ("A Sunday Afternoon on the Island of the Grande Jatte"), which in turn led to the conception of *Sunday in the Park with George*. Despite Sondheim's initial thoughts of Lapine as one of the "off-Broadway playwrights of the sixties and their offspring . . . [who] lean toward lateral thinking, toward intuition rather than structural logic,"[65] Lapine's draft for the first act was a chronologically linear, and almost entirely fictitious, narrative based loosely on Seurat's life. More specifically, Lapine's focus was Seurat's obsession with his art and the difficulties this presented in his dealing with everyday life, especially his relationship with Dot, his model and lover whose love for him is frustrated by his lack of attention to her. George and Dot love each other deeply, but George cannot demonstrate his feelings enough to fulfill Dot's needs, and she ultimately leaves him (although she remains a key figure in the painting). The act ends with George finishing the painting, and its completion provides a sense of dramatic and, seemingly, musical closure.

Yet as Sondheim later noted, "the second act was entirely different" from the first.[66] After opening with a number vocalizing the uncomfortable stasis of the figures in the painting—"It's hot up here / Forever"[67]—the act jumps forward one hundred years and explores the artistic frustrations of another George, an American sculptor of "Chromolumes," or light machines, who is also the great-grandson of Seurat. Wearied by the grant writing and endless schmoozing necessary to get funding for new works, George is, as Craig Zadan commented, "unable to unlock his creative path."[68] Invited to the island of La Grande Jatte to display his latest Chromolume, George has time to contemplate the island that inspired his namesake as well as a recently acquired English primer that Dot had used a hundred years earlier. As he reads the primer and reflects on his dejected personal and artistic condition—"George looks within: / George is adrift. / George goes by guessing, / George looks behind: / He had a gift. / When did it fade?"[69]—he is visited by a specter of Dot, who addresses him as if he is his great-grandfather. This, as well as the quick change to a later time after the act's opening number, again demonstrates the sometimes abrupt juxtapositions of time and space that Sondheim and his collaborators have repeatedly been fond of. (The reappearance of Dot suggests the "ghosts" throughout *Follies*, and the abrupt time shift recalls *Assassins*, for instance.) Sondheim, because his previous musical had been *Merrily We Roll Along*, was also aware of the problems that shifts in time might present for an audience. He later told Mark Eden Horowitz, "I thought . . . these two acts are so different, and I know people are going to be discombobulated by the fact that the first act seems like the end of the play; and then we've got his whole other show to give them. And I thought one way to tie the two acts together would be to make . . . architectonic similarities . . . some kind of parallel structure."[70] Indeed, even more than the abrupt hundred-year leap after "It's Hot Up Here," Dot's reappearance is the principal temporal disruption in the show, the moment when the distinction between past and present is blurred in order to provide closure to the relationship between George and Dot and, as we soon hear, to the entire score.[71] This closure to the score is enabled by its having been composed from beginning to end, developing linearly within a book that does not always move in that direction.

Throughout the show, George and Dot sing what Craig Zadan calls "a continuous and continuing love song" that, when it reaches its fulfillment, becomes the emotional climax of the musical.[72] The climactic song that Dot and the contemporary George sing, "Move On," combines, extends, and develops material from earlier songs reaching back as far as "Sunday in the Park with George," the first song in the show. "All the musical themes of the love story," Sondheim explains, "culminate and intertwine in 'Move On,'" having been woven through one hundred years (and two acts). He is quick to add that this "long musical arc," as he calls it, is "something more apparent when . . . sung than on the printed page."[73] How Sondheim accomplishes this deft control of materials, and how their development is closely tied to his treatment of time in the score as well as his chronological composition of it, deserves investigation.[74]

Orchestrator Michael Starobin recalled that the only number in the show that gave him any trouble was the opening number. The problem was that it seemed "more musical theater than a lot of the rest of the show." But Starobin learned from Sondheim that this was exactly the intention: "It was supposed to be musical comedy to warm the audience up," Sondheim explained, "so they're not nervous, thinking they're in for a heavy artistic piece . . . that there was going to be humor in the show and there was going to be melody."[75] Perhaps "melodies" would be more appropriate, as the number contains two that reappear in the score. The first, a tongue-twisting patter section, is quoted almost exactly, while the second is developed and extended in its various reappearances. What's more, the latter plays an important part in the "long musical arc" of the ongoing love song.

The opening number is in three parts, the first and third of which reveal Dot's difficulty with concentrating and holding a pose. In the middle part, Dot imagines stepping out of her dress (which the actress playing Dot actually does) and moving freely about the stage, commenting on the frustrations of modeling as a profession and, increasingly, of her deep feelings for George. But the reality of being trapped in the dress overcomes her as the actress steps back into the costume and the third part of the song begins. The patter-like passage in question from the first and third sections of the song is not important to the developing love song, but it is used with comedic effect to express the frustration of immobility in two temporal settings, one at the beginning of each act. The passage for Dot begins, "Well, there are worse things than staring at the water on a Sunday" (mm. 5–6), and she repeats it in an extended version at the end of the third section (mm. 14–15).[76] At the end of "It's Hot Up Here," which opens the second act, Sondheim provides a clever musical correspondence by again using the same passage, even more intensified, for the characters in the painting (including Dot), all of whom complain of being stuck in their poses for perpetuity (mm. 143-145). It even begins with the same lyric as Dot's Act I version.

The use of material from the middle section of the opening number goes beyond being merely clever, however. It also demonstrates how Sondheim, at least in this one case, was able to draw from his chronological composition of the score to resolve the entire show. "When I got to 'Move on,'" Sondheim later recalled, "I thought: Okay, here's the culmination, what'll I do? I know, I'll take all the themes and put them together. And that's what I did." He had not started writing the score with this in mind, but by the time he reached the finish, he had the materials on hand to accomplish what he needed to do. "It's because for a year I'd been in this one country, and I'd spoken this one language. When it came to write 'Move On,' I used my entire vocabulary."[77] The lyrical middle section of "Sunday in the Park with George" provided the first utterances of that vocabulary.

Referring to George's painting, Dot begins the section in question with the lyric, "All it has to be is good. / And, George, you're good." She then uses images that refer to George both as artist and as lover—"George's stroke is tender. / George's touch is pure"—after which the thoughts are exclusively personal—"Your eyes, George, / I love your eyes, George." But she ends the section by returning to the art: "But most, George, of all / . . . I love your painting" (mm. 10–11). The music in this section, both in the vocal part and especially in the accompaniment, and to a lesser extent the lyrics, plant what Sondheim has called the "seeds" of the later numbers that in turn develop into the final ecstasy of "Move On."[78] As we shall see, the chordal accompaniment to the passage under the lyrics "Your eyes, George" (m. 10) will return several times in similar emotional settings, and the rolling pattern that begins under the lyrics "But most of all" (m. 11) becomes integral as the score unfolds.

Although the number "Color and Light" is the first subsequent vocal number to exploit material from the opening number, the scene change music before it quotes not only the rolling pattern in the accompaniment of the opening number but also the first two arpeggio figures that open the entire show (m. 1), both of which remain significant throughout the rest of the score. The orchestral introduction to "Color and Light," played under dialogue, introduces a rhythmic theme that is closely and repeatedly connected to George's painting technique and that alternates between the major and minor modes in quick succession, a compositional choice that Sondheim has pointed out as being "very important in the score." ("You hear that alternation . . . in the accompaniment [of 'Move On']; it's an echo of this.")[79] "Color and Light" is divided into numbered parts in the score, and Part II is where the first musical recollection occurs. Dot is making up at a dressing table while George is working, and when she starts to ponder her appearance—"If my legs were longer, / If my bust was smaller" m. (31)—the harmonies from the opening number (m. 10) recur. After this section, she launches into a brisk and comedic fantasy of being in the *Follies Bergère* that contains subtle orchestral quotes of the opening arpeggios. The chordal harmonies from the opening number then return as the tempo slows and Dot reconsiders being a "Follies girl." In Part III of the number, after George performs a bravura section of naming the colors that he is at the same time applying to his canvas, the same sustained harmonies again return to accompany Dot singing about George's eyes—"But it's warm inside his eyes" (m. 41)—which was the subject of her lyrics the first time the two chords appeared in the opening number. At this point, the melody is a simple e-minor arpeggio (E–G–B) followed by a sustained A that will be exactly repeated in "We Do Not Belong Together," the next song in the arc. Here it is repeated ten times with growing intensity, and the final vocal of the song line is an impassioned statement of this figure sung by Dot and George—"I could look at him/her forever" (m. 44). A forceful four-bar statement of the rolling accompaniment figure finishes the song.

"We Do Not Belong Together," George and Dot's final confrontation before she leaves for good, is rich in material from the characters' two earlier songs, which will also ultimately be exploited in "Move On." It begins with the familiar sustained two-chord figure, now played under dialogue (m. 105). But instead of underscoring Dot's gentle feelings for George, here they underscore a bitter argument. Anticipating the vocal entrance, the orchestra begins a pattern first heard in "Color and Light" under George's "It's getting hot . . . / It's getting orange" (m. 41), and repeated more extensively beginning just before when Dot sang "And you look inside the eyes" (m. 42). Dot's vocal line over the pattern in "We Do Not Belong Together" is the same as it was earlier—the minor triad followed by the fourth scale degree—although here the lyrics are more acrimonious ("What you care for is yourself"). The number swells, and a new melody that will later be recalled exactly in "Move On" is introduced starting with the lyric, "Tell me that you're hurt, Tell me you're relieved" (m. 107). Finally, the memorable phrase "We do not belong together" is introduced (m. 59) and repeated passionately, followed by the lyric "And we should have belonged together." But in the next repetition, Dot does not finish the phrase, singing only "And we'll never be-long—!" (m. 113). After noting that George has "a mission to see" and that she, too, has a mission, Dot again sings "And we should have belonged together." This is followed by the resigned statement of her "mission": "I have to move on" (m. 114), thus providing in its last two words the title and impetus for the climactic number in Act II. "We Do Not Belong Together" doesn't really end; it simply fades over the familiar two-chord figure (m. 115).

"Move On" follows "Lesson #8," a contemplative solo for George that grows from his reading Dot's English primer. As he finishes, Dot appears. Her entrance is underscored by a passage she sang in "We Do Not Belong Together": "Tell me that you're hurt, / Tell me you're relieved" (m. 107). The vamp before the vocal entrance repeats the principal vamp from "We Do Not Belong Together." In the earlier song, this accompaniment introduced George's lyric, "There's nothing to say," which is also, with one minor word change, the first lyric of "Move On": "I've nothing to say" (m. 219). Melodically, they are interchangeable. All this takes place on the first page of the song, which, with the second page, demonstrates Sondheim's manipulation of earlier material to recall an emotional exchange from the past between two characters in the present that do not—indeed, cannot—know each other.

Not until the third page does Sondheim introduce the phrase "Move on," the lyric for which recalls Dot's earlier conclusion ("I have to move on"). But even this new phrase floats over the same familiar vamp that started the song. At the end of the first chorus, the churning accompaniment vacillates between the major and minor modes before settling on a sustained chord, over which the vocal line returns to a passage from "We Do Not Belong Together" (m. 107), now with Dot instead singing, "Look at what you want, Not at where you are" (m. 223). Sondheim plays with this phrase, passing it back and forth between George and Dot, adding the melody from the first vocal entrance and building to a rhapsodic repeat of the "Move on" chorus. This subsides to the quiet repeat of the "Look at what you want" material (now on m. 228) that begins another build into what is one of Sondheim's most passionate musical utterances. George experiences a trans-formation brought about by Dot, which moves him from general observations of "Something in the light, / Something in the sky" (m. 228) to more specific things—"Flower on your hat / And your smile / and the color of your hair / And the way you catch the light, / And the care, / And the feeling, / And the life" (mm.

229–230). This entire passage exploits harmonies destabilized by their being built on inverted chords. Sondheim explained this to Mark Eden Horowitz as follows: "There's nothing on this page you haven't heard before. . . . This is a case where an inversion counts for a million bucks—at bar 119 the lyric 'and the care'—the fact that that's an inversion makes that whole chord work." He then explains how he continued this unstable harmony until the huge C-major climax on the word "life," where "it feels like you've entered a new kingdom—which you have."[80] The number continues from there and ends quietly with Dot singing to George, "Give us more to see," after which the orchestra softly recalls the fanfare that began the show. The musical ends with the characters from Seurat's painting appearing and bowing in acknowledgment of the young George, and reprising part of the first-act finale ("Sunday"), after which they disappear, followed by Dot. George is left alone in the present, facing a blank white canvas.

***

The foregoing discussions of some of the various temporal structures and the techniques through which they were developed are, if nothing else, indications of not only Stephen Sondheim's extraordinary craft and art but also of the deep connection in all his work between his scores and the books from which they grew. In one sense, the scores are solutions to temporal puzzles presented by the books: how to score a show that moves backward in time, for instance, or one that moves eerily between the present and pasts both real and imagined; how to create a perception of musical time for a book that takes place in the undefined instant of a character's mind or for one that works in three temporal settings before it is over (and into one of which a character from a hundred years before inexplicably appears). Inspired by the deep simplicities of Japanese art or the staggering detail of a late-nineteenth-century painting that contains no lines, Sondheim has always found the exact musical and lyric expression for the situation at hand. Although he probably never set out as a composer to deal with temporal perceptions that have given pause over the years to philosophers and physicists, among others, he has dealt with them with an almost unfailing artistry and a keen perception of the human condition. Time and time again.

# Notes

1. Mark Eden Horowitz, *Sondheim on Music: Minor Details and Major Decisions* (Lanham, MD: Scarecrow, 2003), 75–76.
2. I am grateful to W. Anthony Sheppard for suggesting this term and for other helpful comments toward the adaptation of this chapter from its origins as a conference paper to its present form.

3. Raymond Knapp and Zelda Knapp, "Going Postal: Collapsing Time and Space Through Sung Letters in Broadway Musicals," *Studies in Musical Theatre* 11, no. 3 (2017): 233.

4. In Lehman Engel, *Words and Music* (New York: Macmillan, 1972), 291.

5. Ibid., 292.

6. Ibid., 312.

7. Ibid., 313–314.

8. Ibid., 315, 316.

9. Ethan Mordden, *On Sondheim: An Opinionated Guide* (New York: Oxford University Press, 2016), 68.

10. Stephen Sondheim, *Finishing the Hat: Collected Lyrics (1954–1981) with Attendant Comments, Principles, Heresies, Grudges, Whines and Anecdotes* (New York: Knopf, 2010), 166.

11. Robert Sokol, "Neil Patrick Harris Describes Being Very Alive in *Company*," *Sondheim Review* 16, no. 1 (Fall 2011): 29–30.

12. Stephen Banfield, *Sondheim's Broadway Musicals* (Ann Arbor: University of Michigan Press, 1993), 164.

13. George Furth (book) and Stephen Sondheim (lyrics), *Company: A Musical Comedy* (New York: Theatre Communications Group, 1996), 4.

14. Ibid.

15. Ibid.

16. Foster Hirsch, *Harold Prince and the American Musical Theatre* (Cambridge: Cambridge University Press, 1989), 85.

17. Craig Zadan, *Sondheim & Co.*, 2nd ed. (New York: Da Capo, 1994), 117.

18. Ibid., 117.

19. Hirsch, *Harold Prince*, 61. Even earlier, Marc Blitzstein's *The Cradle Will Rock* (1937) consisted of a series of vignettes that were connected by their relations to a single event. They were in no particular chronological order and occurred at different points in time. In 1941 Moss Hart, Ira Gershwin, and Kurt Weill's *Lady in the Dark* exploited extended musical dream sequences to comment on psychological aspects of the central character. These long sequences occurred outside, but reflected on, the nonmusical dramatic structure of the play. And in 1948 Alan Jay Lerner and Kurt Weill's *Love Life* told the story of a married couple that spanned the years 1791 to 1947, during which the couple never aged. The plot was frequently interrupted by vaudeville-influenced numbers that commented on, while remaining outside, the plot.

20. Zadan, *Sondheim & Co.*, 382.

21. Stephen Sondheim, *Look, I Made a Hat: Collected Lyrics (1981–2011) with Attendant Comments, Amplifications, Dogmas, Harangues, Digressions, Anecdotes and Miscellany* (New York: Knopf, 2011), 113.

22. Horowitz, *Sondheim on Music*, 57.

23. Sondheim, *Look, I Made a Hat*, 113.

24. Scott Miller, "*Assassins* and the Concept Musical," in *Stephen Sondheim: A Casebook*, ed. Joanne Gordon (New York: Garland, 1997), 192.

25. John Weidman (book) and Stephen Sondheim (music and lyrics), *Assassins* (New York: Theatre Communications Group, 1991), 24.
26. Sondheim, *Look, I Made a Hat*, 113.
27. Mordden, *On Sondheim*, 129.
28. Edward Snowden, *Permanent Record* (New York: Holt, 2019), Kindle ed.
29. Zadan, *Sondheim & Co.*, 135.
30. Hirsch, *Harold Prince*, 93.
31. Banfield, *Sondheim's Broadway Musicals*, 188.
32. James Goldman (book) and Stephen Sondheim (music and lyrics), *Follies* (New York: Theatre Communications Group, 2001), 22.
33. Alain de Botton, "Time, Memory, and Marcel Proust," interview with Linda Wertheimer, NPR Weekend Edition, Saturday, December 31, 2005, accessed March 2, 2020, https://www.npr.org/templates/story/story.php?storyId=5077638.
34. Goldman and Sondheim, *Follies*, 15–16.
35. Sondheim, *Finishing the Hat*, 219. A video of the original staging can be found at https://www.youtube.com/watch?v=mgvoAr0_gt4&ab_channel=DavidFletcher.
36. Goldman and Sondheim, *Follies*, 43–44.
37. Ibid., 59–61.
38. Ibid., 85.
39. Patrick Alexander, *Marcel Proust's Search for Lost Time: A Reader's Guide to "The Remembrance of Things Past"* (New York: Vintage, 2009), 9.
40. *Merrily We Roll Along* later demonstrates this more personally.
41. Zadan, *Sondheim & Co.*, 210. For a detailed discussion of the development of this show, see Ashley M. Pribyl's chapter in this volume.
42. At the end of the show, however, Weidman and Sondheim unexpectedly leap into the present in the number "Next," which tells of Japan's rapid and massive industrialization from the late nineteenth century through 1976.
43. Hirsch, *Harold Prince*, 110.
44. Sondheim, *Finishing the Hat*, 328.
45. Knapp and Knapp, "Going Postal," 240. The Knapps were writing specifically about sung letters in musicals, but the idea of compression works for the use of a letter in this number as well.
46. Sondheim, *Finishing the Hat*, 328.
47. Ibid., 327–328.
48. In Zadan, *Sondheim & Co.*, 216.
49. Sondheim, *Finishing the Hat*, 329.
50. Paul Attinello, "The Universe Will Tell You What It Needs: Being, Time, Sondheim," in *Musicological Identities: Essays in Honor of Susan McClary*, ed. Steven Bauer, Raymond Knapp, and Jacqueline Warwick (Abingdon, UK: Routledge, 2008), 77.
51. Sondheim, *Look, I Made a Hat*, 323.
52. Horowitz, *Sondheim on Music*, 158.
53. Ibid.
54. Attinello, "The Universe Will Tell You," 82, 84.

55. Sondheim, *Finishing the Hat*, 323.

56. Ibid., 381.

57. Ibid., 408, 418.

58. Ibid., 397.

59. Zadan, *Sondheim & Co.*, 271. Emphasis added.

60. Stephen Sondheim, *Merrily We Roll Along*, piano/vocal score (New York: Rilting Music, 1991), 106–107.

61. Banfield, *Sondheim's Broadway Musicals*, 340.

62. Sondheim, *Merrily We Roll Along*, 202.

63. This comment of Joe's is also a little joke of Sondheim's in that his music was often accused of being cold and tuneless. Further, in trying to demonstrate "a tune you can hum," Joe misquotes the melody of "Some Enchanted Evening."

64. Sondheim, *Finishing the Hat*, 421.

65. Sondheim, *Look, I Made a Hat*, 4.

66. In Horowitz, *Sondheim on Music*, 100.

67. Sondheim, *Look, I Made a Hat*, 33.

68. Zadan, *Sondheim & Co.*, 297.

69. Sondheim, *Look, I Made a Hat*, 49.

70. In Horowitz, *Sondheim on Music*, 101.

71. James Lapine did not share Sondheim's concern about the second act. He later told Craig Zadan, "I love the second act and I think you wouldn't like the first act as much ultimately if you didn't see the second, because it puts it in an even stronger perspective." In Zadan, *Sondheim & Co.*, 307.

72. Ibid., 301.

73. Sondheim, *Look, I Made a Hat*, 52.

74. For more detailed and theoretical discussions of this, see especially Horowitz, *Sondheim on Music*, 93–103, and Banfield, *Sondheim's Broadway Musicals*, 375–379. And for an extended discussion of this musical's "architectonic" details, see Lara E. Housez's contribution in this volume.

75. Zadan, *Sondheim & Co.*, 310.

76. The measure numbers provided for each musical example are from the published piano-vocal score: Stephen Sondheim, *Sunday in the Park with George* (New York: Ritling Music, 2004).

77. Horowitz, *Sondheim on Music*, 94.

78. Sondheim, *Look, I Made a Hat*, 52.

79. Horowitz, *Sondheim on Music*, 93.

80. Although Sondheim calls this moment "a Rachmaninoff change" (Horowitz, *Sondheim on Music*, 97), this explosion of C major has also always reminded me of the shattering moment in Béla Bartók's opera *Bluebeard's Castle* when Judith opens the fifth door and the orchestra and Judith erupt from the previous dark harmonies into an overpowering C major.

# 12

# *Sunday in the Park* with Sondheim, Lapine, Seurat, and Babbitt

*Lara E. Housez*

"My God, this is all about music," Stephen Sondheim exclaimed, as he studied the paintings of nineteenth-century Neo-Impressionist artist Georges-Pierre Seurat (1859–1891). "He experimented with the color wheel the way one experiments with a scale."[1] Motivated by his study of scientific theories of color, vision, and perception, Seurat pioneered a technique that he referred to as "chromoluminarism" (known now as divisionism or pointillism): Rather than mix his paints on a palette, he meticulously juxtaposed thousands of tiny brushstrokes of color on a canvas, which the eye of the viewer combined optically. Seurat employed this laborious method to create the oil painting for which he is most famous, *Un dimanche après-midi à l'Île de la Grande Jatte* (A Sunday Afternoon on the Island of La Grande Jatte, figure 12.1). When seen from a distance, the pixel-like colors do indeed merge and impart to the painting and its subjects a shimmering luminosity. Sondheim studied a photograph of Seurat's canvas with playwright-director James Lapine (b. 1949). Seurat and his painting so captured their imaginations that he became the central figure in *Sunday in the Park with George* (hereafter *Sunday*), the first Sondheim-Lapine musical. Although few actual events from Seurat's biography ended up in the fictionalized plot, his chromoluminarism left significant marks on the conception of the show, its structure, characters, score, lyrics, and dialogue.

Sondheim recalls how, at first, he arranged the twelve notes of the chromatic scale in combinations of seconds, just as Seurat grouped his twelve colors into pairs: "I thought: Isn't this interesting that Seurat had, on his palette, eleven colors and white. And I thought, eleven and one make twelve. And how many notes are there in the scale? Twelve. And I thought, ooh, isn't that interesting. So I thought I would utilize that in some way, shape, or form."[2] Realizing that this approach would limit the score to successions or stacks of seconds, Sondheim looked for other ways—both musical and nonmusical—to emulate Seurat's technique.[3] The number twelve, for instance, appears in a variety of guises throughout the musical: Act I includes eleven different numbers plus the opening prelude, the narrative unfolds in a total of twelve settings, and the original orchestrations

Lara E. Housez, Sunday in the Park *with Sondheim, Lapine, Seurat, and Babbitt* In: *Sondheim in Our Time and His.*
Edited by: W. Anthony Sheppard, Oxford University Press. © Oxford University Press 2022.
DOI: 10.1093/oso/9780197603192.003.0013

**Figure 12.1.** Georges Seurat, *Un dimanche après-midi à l'Île de la Grande Jatte* (1884–1886), oil on canvas, 81 ¾ x 121 ¼ in. (207.5 x 308.1 cm), Helen Birch Bartlett Memorial Collection, 1926.224, The Art Institute of Chicago. Photography © The Art Institute of Chicago/Art Resource, NY.

consist of eleven instrumental "colors" plus the conductor.[4] Such instances of the number twelve are more than clever references to chromoluminarism; they represent a small sampling of the ways in which Sondheim and Lapine alluded to Seurat's technique and used those allusions to connect the two seemingly disparate acts of their musical. Some of the parallels that bridge the acts are well known, yet others are not, and none have been interpreted through the lens of chromoluminarism. In this essay I examine the origins of these large-scale similarities and unpack their significances as expressions and extensions of Seurat's painting and chromoluminarism.

Act I takes place on a series of Sundays from 1884 to 1886, with George (to avoid confusion, I will refer to the character in the musical as George and the actual painter as Seurat), a young man in his twenties, working on *Un dimanche après-midi à l'Île de la Grande Jatte*. George's tireless devotion to the pursuit of art pushes his pregnant mistress and model, aptly named Dot, into the arms of another man. Act II jumps ahead a century to 1984 and shifts across the Atlantic to urban America, where George's fictional great-grandson, also named George, struggles in the modern art establishment as a multimedia light sculptor. With the help of his ninety-eight-year-old grandmother Marie (Dot's daughter), George unveils his latest work, the seventh installment in a continuing series of

"Chromolumes," to an audience of curators, critics, patrons, fellow artists, and friends assembled in an art museum where Seurat's painting hangs. Despite his moderate success, George finds himself at creative crossroads and turns to his artistic roots for professional and personal renewal—to "connect," as the musical continually reiterates. *Sunday* closes as it begins with George reciting words that had become his great-grandfather's mantra: "Order. Design. Tension. Composition. Harmony . . . So many possibilities . . ." The words that frame the musical will provide this essay with its structural scaffolding. The first section, "Order," starts with Sondheim at Williams College, where he intended to study mathematics, more than three decades before *Sunday* would open on Broadway.

## Order

A freshman music course with professor Robert Barrow convinced Sondheim to veer from math to music. His decision paid off: At the end of his senior year at Williams College, Sondheim won the 1950 Hubbard Hutchinson Prize, a substantial cash award of $6,000, given to a member of the graduating class to support work in the creative and performing arts. In 1940, when Mrs. Eva W. Hutchinson established the prize in the memory of her son, the late Hubbard Hutchinson, she indicated how the money would be spent: "The student shall be given the income from the bequest for the two years succeeding his graduation, without any restrictions of any kind whatsoever."[5] Sondheim decided to return to New York and use the money for private composition lessons with Milton Babbitt. Babbitt may not seem like an obvious choice for Sondheim, but in addition to his profile as a skilled mathematician and total serialist, he was, as Sondheim described him, "a frustrated show composer."[6] Sondheim applied to his score for *Sunday* a concept that he had learned during these lessons. This concept, which Babbitt had called "architectonics," or large-scale structural parallels, helped Sondheim link Acts I and II in unusual and unexpected ways. He remembers:

> I thought, okay, these two acts are so different, and I know people are going to be discombobulated by the fact that the first act seems like the end of the play; and then we've got this whole other show to give them. And I thought one way to tie the two acts together would be to make—this is a word I learned from Milton Babbitt, and I loved it—architectonic similarities. . . . In *Sunday*, the second act is an entirely separate entity—it's another ship—so the way to link them together, it seemed to me, was to make some kind of parallel structure.[7]

That parallel structure connects the acts with an intricate web of character doublings, dramatic reflections, and musical and textual motives. The pairing of act openers, "Sunday in the Park with George" and "It's Hot Up Here," is an obvious example of architectonics. Although these musical numbers take place with various characters in different circumstances, they are both about posing uncomfortably for an artist. Sondheim's use of architectonics not only highlights similarities between Acts I and II but, from an abstract perspective, also reflects Seurat's chromoluminarism. The architectonics encourage audiences to *blend* the characters, musical numbers, dramatic events, and motives in order to connect the acts and see the elements of the musical as a larger whole, just as Seurat's viewer *blends* the small swirls of color on the canvas in order to perceive the figures and landscape in *La Grande Jatte*. In so doing, theatergoers may acquire a greater understanding and appreciation of the musical and see how the notoriously problematic second act, which so many of *Sunday*'s critics have dismissed as an unnecessary and disappointing postscript, fits within that larger framework.[8]

Perhaps another clear example of a large-scale relationship between the acts is character doublings.[9] Correspondences in the casting are both conceptual and practical. In the original 1984 Broadway production at the Booth Theatre, Mandy Patinkin, fresh from his Tony Award–winning portrayal of Che Guevara in *Evita*, played the older and younger Georges, and Bernadette Peters, whose most recent performance as Mabel in *Mack & Mabel* had earned her a Tony Award nomination, performed both Dot and her daughter Marie. Other couplings are similarly predictable: The actor playing George's mother in Act I returns in Act II as an opinionated art critic, and Jules, one of George's established but less-talented rivals, embodies the late-twentieth-century "art establishment" as museum director Bob Greenberg. Even so minor a character as the crass, culturally ignorant American tourist, referred to ambiguously as Mrs., has a logical counterpart; she becomes Harriet Pawling, a patron of the arts with dubious (or ap-*palling*) taste.[10] And baker Louis, Dot's sweet but insipid fiancé, returns as Harriet's clueless boyfriend Billy. In fact, all of the twelve singing characters in Act I have a recognizable double in Act II. Each pair represents a broad character type: artist, loved one, critic, competitor, prospective patron, or lackluster mate (see table 12.1).[11] *Sunday*'s character doublings do double duty: They put Babbitt's architectonics into practice by functioning as obvious connections between the acts, and, at the same time, analogize the twelve complementary colors on Seurat's palette. Whereas Seurat juxtaposed contrasting colors that the eye of the viewer, with the trick of perspective, recognizes as a single, uniform color, Sondheim and Lapine used a single actor to perform two corresponding characters, who, despite living on different continents more than a century apart, portray parallel identities and are thus made to seem far more similar than they first appear.

**Table 12.1.** Character doublings in Acts I and II of *Sunday in the Park with George* (as performed in 1984).

|  | Act I | Act II |
|---|---|---|
|  | George, an artist* ---------- | George, an artist* |
|  | Dot, his mistress* ---------- | Marie, his grandmother* |
|  | Old Lady, his mother* ---------- | Blair Daniels, an art critic* |
|  | Her Nurse* ---------- | Harriet Pawling, a patron of the arts* |
|  | Jules, another artist* ---------- | Bob Greenberg, a museum director* |
|  | Yvonne, his wife* ---------- | Naomi Eisen, a composer* |
|  | Louise, their daughter |  |
|  | A Boatman* ---------- | Charles Redmond, a visiting curator* |
|  | Franz, servant of Jules and Yvonne* ---------- | Dennis, a technician* |
|  | Frieda, his wife and cook of Jules and Yvonne* ---------- | Betty, an artist* |
|  | A Soldier* ---------- | Alex, an artist* |
| Mr. and Mrs., an American couple (Mrs. triples as Nurse) ---------- |  | Lee Randolph, the museum's publicist* (and Harriet) |
|  | Louis, a baker* ---------- | Billy Webster, Harriet's friend* |
|  | A Woman with baby carriage ---------- | A Photographer* |
|  | A Man with bicycle ---------- | A Museum Assistant* |
|  | A Little Girl |  |
|  | Celeste #1, a shop girl* ---------- | Elaine, George's ex-wife |
|  | Celeste #2, another shop girl* ---------- | A Waitress |
|  | A Boy bathing in the river |  |
|  | A Young Man sitting on the bank |  |
|  | A Man lying on the bank (played by Louis) |  |

* Singing characters

Within each act, many of the secondary characters appear in duos, some romantic, others platonic. Like the pairs of pigments on George's canvas that fuse to form a single color, these roles often represent two versions of the same archetype. Some of their names make the twosomes explicit (Celeste #1 and Celeste #2, Franz and Frieda, and Mr. and Mrs.) and others less so (the Soldier and his deaf-mute cutout companion, as well as the dog, Spot—whose name provides another nod to Seurat's technique—and the pug, Fifi). Sharing similar vocations and remarkably colorful names, museum director Bob Greenberg and the visiting curator Charles Redmond, also form a complementary pair. (In the initial workshop production at Playwrights Horizons, the two roles were designated somewhat differently as Robert Blackmun and Charles Green.)[12] The names of Louis and Louise, the daughter of Jules and Yvonne, seem to suggest a link between the two characters. Louis and Louise may be regarded as George's rivals, one romantic and the other professional. Louise, after all, claims that she too wants to be a painter when she grows up (II, 131).

Whereas *Sunday*'s character doublings across the acts may seem obvious, its twin plot developments require some explanation. In both acts, George loses a close friend who, in the end, returns in order to help him with one final creative endeavor. In Act I, Dot, despite her feelings for George, chooses to immigrate to America with their baby Marie and with Louis. But Dot comes back to take part in a beguiling moment of staging—an effect that looks back to Ben Ali Haggin's *tableaux vivants* in the *Ziegfeld Follies* of the late 1910s and 1920s—when Seurat's painting magically takes shape before the eyes of the audience. Dashing about the stage rearranging figures and trees, George transforms Dot and the other living characters promenading across the park into a frozen image that evokes *La Grande Jatte*. Perhaps from his devotion to Dot, George positions her downstage, or at the foreground of the painting. In Act II, Dennis, the technical mastermind behind the Chromolumes, tells George that he intends to leave the art world and resume his work at NASA. Dennis claims, "There is just too much pressure in this line of work" (II, 151).[13] Dennis, too, reappears in the story when George requires his expertise for a special performance of the Chromolume on the Parisian island that his great-grandfather had painted. What at first glance look like two unrelated incidents emerge as comparable turning points that help the two Georges attain a sense of resolution in their lives, despite their shared inability to connect with others. For George the painter, Dot's decision to leave pushes him further into his work and allows him to complete what would become his crowning achievement. For George the contemporary light sculptor, Dennis's compassion and his own desire to "move on" encourage George to forge a new path of his own.[14]

## Design

Musical, or aural, connections across the acts give cohesion and balance to the show. In addition to the obvious reprise of "Sunday" at the end of Act II, most of the music in the first act—from single numbers to sequences of numbers—finds a partner in the second. In fact, only two numbers in the score, one in each act, lack clear counterparts ("Opening Prelude" and "Lesson #8").[15] Table 12.2 lists the seven pairs that link the acts. The fourth pair, which groups five consecutive numbers in Act I, from "Gossip Sequence" through "Finishing the Hat," with the

**Table 12.2.** Seven pairs of musical numbers and sequences in *Sunday in the Park with George.*

|  | Act I | Act II |
|---|---|---|
| 1. | "Sunday in the Park with George" | "It's Hot Up Here" |
| 2. | "No Life" | "Eulogies" |
| 3. | "Color and Light" | "Chromolume #7" |
| 4. | "Gossip Sequence"<br>"The Day Off"<br>"Everybody Loves Louis"<br>"The One on the Left"<br>"Finishing the Hat" | "Putting It Together" |
| 5. | "We Do Not Belong Together" | "Move On"* |
| 6. | "Beautiful" | "Children and Art"* |
| 7. | "Sunday" | "Sunday" |

*In Act I, "We Do Not Belong Together" precedes "Beautiful," but their Act II complements, "Move On" and "Children and Art," unfold in reverse order, separated by "Lesson #8."

multisectional magnum opus "Putting It Together" in Act II, consists of a collection of short vignettes. The brief segments of music and dialogue unfolding in quick succession provide yet another analogy to chromoluminarism and its small, individual dabs of color on a canvas. (Present participles in two of the titles reinforce the connection between the two segments of the show.) In Act I, George sketches as he observes episodes that play out between various secondary characters; Act II mirrors these exchanges with a string of brief conversations between George and guests at a cocktail party in the museum where Seurat's painting hangs. Both fragmented structures fulfill a similar goal: They connect the Act I and II complements and invite spectators to recognize parallel and contradictory experiences between the two Georges, one who devotes himself entirely to the creation of his art at the expense of his personal life, and the other, who preoccupies himself with the business of art at the expense of his own art.

Sondheim has pointed out several of these reflections of Act I in Act II, including "Sunday in the Park with George"/"It's Hot Up Here" and "Color and Light"/"Chromolume #7." Some sets are more difficult to spot; as Sondheim has recounted, even Patinkin, singing the roles of both Georges, did not recognize that the notes setting the title phrase "Finishing the Hat" in Act I repeat an hour or so later in "Putting It Together" in Act II.[16] Sondheim, however, has been reluctant to explain *why* or *how* he coupled so many numbers.[17] Explaining *why* leads back to Babbitt: Parallels between musical numbers gave Sondheim yet another opportunity to highlight similarities between characters, contexts, and themes and thereby tie the two acts together with large-scale connections. Faced with the task of bridging distinct musical numbers that unfold more than an hour apart, Sondheim turned to the use of motives—the *how*—a technique that he had found increasingly useful for integrating his scores: "I'm very much a leit-motif man—I really like the notion that an audience will register certain tunes or rhythmic ideas, or even harmonies, with given characters. And you can build on that. It's very convenient. I don't know why more people don't do it."[18]

Motives, as Sondheim knows, give clues, depict surroundings, introduce characters, project correlations, convey subtext, and heighten the comprehensibility and expressivity of dramatic music even if the spectator fails to pick up on them on a cognitive level. "I believe in the subliminal power of music in theater," Sondheim asserts, "that you can play a theme that the audience associates with a character."[19] He saturated his *Sunday* score with so much repetition that the two acts sound far more similar than the plot synopsis, catalog of characters, or song list suggests. In *Sunday*, motives also provided Sondheim with another aural representation of Seurat's technique. Perhaps there is no better analogy to chromoluminarism than the palette of generative musical motives that help pair musical numbers and saturate virtually all of the musical material in the score (see example 12.1).

Example 12.1a–g. First statements of motives in *Sunday in the Park with George*.

Example 12.1a. "Creating" from "Opening Prelude," mm. 1–2.

Example 12.1b. "Dreaming" from "Sunday in the Park with George," mm. 77–78.

Example 12.1c. "Working" from "Color and Light," mm. 1–2.

**Example 12.1a–g.** Continued

**Example 12.1d.** "Gossiping" from "Gossip Sequence," m. 1.

**Example 12.1e.** "Relaxing" from "The Day Off" (I), mm. 49–50.

**Example 12.1f.** "Finishing" from "Finishing the Hat," mm. 27–28.

**Example 12.1g.** "Loving" from "We Do Not Belong Together," mm. 51–52.

Although he has referred to some of these motives in interviews, Sondheim has yet to identify or comment on their significance as a group. By the end of the tenth number, George and Dot's duet "We Do Not Belong Together," seven motives have been introduced, and four, including what I refer to as the "Creating," "Dreaming," "Working," and "Loving" motives, have appeared many times.[20] "Creating" and "Dreaming," in fact, permeate the musical texture of almost every number in the score (see table 12.3).

With seven pairs of numbers in the score (plus seven identified parts in "The Day Off" and the numerical reference in the song title "Chromolume #7"), one wonders whether Sondheim and Lapine had the number seven in mind as they wrote their musical. Sunday is, after all, one of the seven days of the week (indeed, the seventh by Christian reckoning: the Sabbath, or the day of rest). One of the earliest appearances of the number seven in Sondheim and Lapine's work on *Sunday* can be gleaned from an undated preliminary sketch of the scheme of the show, which survives among Sondheim's general notes for the project.[21] The outline lists seven sections, four in Act I (two promenades in the park

Table 12.3. Statements of motives in *Sunday in the Park with George*.

| Act I: A series of Sundays in 1884–1886 | | Act II: 1984 | |
| --- | --- | --- | --- |
| Musical Number | Motive(s) | Musical number | Motive(s) |
| "Opening Prelude" | Creating | "It's Hot Up Here" | Dreaming |
| "Sunday in the Park with George" | Creating, Dreaming | "Eulogies" | Dreaming |
| "No Life" | Dreaming | "Chromolume #7" | Working, Creating, Dreaming |
| "Color and Light" | Working, Dreaming | "Putting It Together" | Parts I, VII, IX, XIV: Cocktail music |
| "Gossip Sequence" "The Day Off" | Gossiping, Dreaming Part I: Working, Dreaming, Relaxing II: Creating, Relaxing III–V: Relaxing VI: Gossiping, Relaxing VII: Relaxing, Gossiping | | II–III: Gossiping IV: Relaxing, Gossiping V: Relaxing VI: Creating, Dreaming, Finishing, Working VIII: Creating, Finishing, Working X: Working, Finishing XI: Creating, Finishing, Working XII: Finishing XIII: Relaxing XV: Finishing XVI: Gossiping, Finishing XVII: Dreaming, Finishing, Gossiping, Relaxing |
| "Everybody Loves Louis" "The One on the Left" "Finishing the Hat" | Dreaming Working Relaxing, Dreaming, Working, Finishing | | |
| "We Do Not Belong Together" | Dreaming, Working, Creating, Loving | "Children and Art" "Lesson #8" | Dreaming, Working Dreaming |
| "Beautiful" | Working | "Move On" | Dreaming, Loving, Creating |
| "Sunday" | Creating, Working | "Sunday" | Creating, Working |

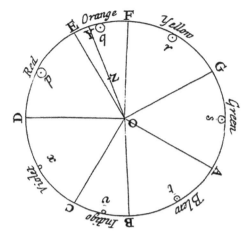

**Figure 12.2.**  Isaac Newton's color wheel, *Opticks*, 1704.

alternating with two interludes) and three in Act II (two promenades separated by one interlude).

The number seven offered Sondheim and Lapine a telling correlation between the visual arts and music: the seven colors of the spectrum and the seven notes of the diatonic scale. From his study of the color theories of Ogden N. Rood, Seurat was familiar with Isaac Newton's experiments, which showed that white light, when refracted through a prism, subdivided into seven discernible colors—in other words, that color was light. Newton organized the colors into a wheel and labeled each segment with the name of a color (Red, Orange, Yellow, and so on). At the points at which the pieces of the pie meet (that is, the spokes of the wheel), Newton added letter names of the seven "musical tones" of the scale (A, B, C, and so on).[22] (See figure 12.2.) When Newton undertook his "Opticks" experiments in the late seventeenth century, color wheels conventionally consisted of six colors, with three primary (red, blue, and yellow) and three secondary colors (green, orange, and violet), or twelve, with six tertiary colors. By including indigo, Newton brought the total number of colors to seven, perhaps in an attempt to have them correspond to such "givens" as the seven (at the time) known planets, the seven days of the week, and the seven notes of the diatonic scale or mode.[23]

## Tension

Sondheim seems to have extrapolated from his initial preoccupation with intervals of a second when he designed the underlying harmonic structure of

*Sunday.* Musical analysis unearths harmonic connections between several of the seven pairs of numbers, and this demonstrates further attempts to build tension and connect Acts I and II. "We Do Not Belong Together" and "Move On," for instance, unfold in keys separated by a minor second, C major and B major, respectively. "Beautiful" plays out in D major, whereas "Children and Art" starts in Db major and continues to descend chromatically with a final section in C major. The series of numbers in Act I, extending from "Gossip Sequence" through "Finishing the Hat," and its Act II counterpart, "Putting It Together," open in E major and Eb major, keys a minor second apart, and close in Gb major and Ab major, a major second apart.[24] Other numbers reveal interesting correlations: "Color and Light" and "Chromolume #7" both end in Eb major; "Sunday" and its reprise share the same tonic key so that both acts conclude in G major; and the acts and score as a whole begin and end in tonalities a third apart (Act I opens in Eb major, and Act II starts in Bb major). The four musical numbers that bookend the acts thus outline an Eb major triad. (See table 12.4 for the overall harmonic trajectory of the show.)

Chains of ascending and descending minor seconds play out at the beginning and end of the musical, reminding us again of Sondheim's fixation with close, tension-inducing intervals: from the initial Eb major sonority that launches the "Opening Prelude," the harmony rises by step to E major with the beginning of "Sunday in the Park with George" and, in the final pages of that number, shifts to F major, creating tension in harmonic motion with a series of rising minor seconds. In Act II, the tonal areas of "Children and Art" and "Lesson #8" descend by step from Db major to C major to B major. Although these harmonic relationships would be audible only to a highly trained musician, they form yet another bond between the acts—as if the characters living one hundred years apart inhabit the same aural landscape.

**Table 12.4.** Large-scale harmonic structure of *Sunday in the Park with George.*

| Act I | | Act II | |
|---|---|---|---|
| | | M3 | |
| Eb | G | Bb | G |
| M3 | | m3 | m3 |

## Composition

As he started to compose *Sunday*, Sondheim considered assigning a different pitch to each color in Seurat's painting as another way of analogizing the artist's technique; in other words, every time George sang the word "blue" he would sing the same note and the same would occur for red, yellow, green, and so on.[25] Sondheim, however, realized again that these mappings were too restrictive and, alternatively, tried to limit himself to short, monosyllabic words as a way of using lyrics to imitate chromoluminarism. "Color and Light" demonstrates best the effect of this constraint. Positioned on opposite sides of the studio, George and Dot immerse themselves in their private concerns. George, living in a world of specks, feverishly dabs paint on his canvas, while Dot, posed in a likeness of Seurat's painting *La Poudreuse*, prepares for an evening excursion. Sitting at a vanity and gazing at her reflection, she powders and plucks with the same rhythmic intensity with which George paints. Despite the physical distance and emotional disconnect separating the pair, they perform their duet with synchronous strokes. As he paints, George unleashes a passage of virtuoso patter:

Red red red red
Red red orange
Red red orange
Orange pick up blue
Pick up red
Pick up orange
From the blue-green blue-green
Blue-green circle
On the violet diagonal
Dia-ag-ag-ag-ag-ag-o-nal-nal
Yellow comma yellow comma
[ … ]
Blue blue blue blue
Blue still sitting
Red that perfume
Blue all night
Blue-green the window shut
Dut dut dut
Dot Dot sitting
Dot Dot waiting
Dot Dot getting fat fat fat

> More yellow
> Dot Dot waiting to go
> Out out out but
> No no no George
> Finish the hat finish the hat
> Have to finish the hat first
> Hat hat hat hat
> Hot hot hot it's hot in here . . .
> Sunday!
> Color and light! (I, 37–38)

In thirty lines George sings almost entirely monosyllabic words, with the exception of a few two- or three-syllable words (mostly present participles). The fragmented, repetitive lyrics and rhymes and, in the original cast recording, Patinkin's disjointed delivery mimic the application of tiny brushstrokes to a canvas.

Sondheim and Lapine saturated their Pulitzer prize–winning script with more overt allusions to pointillism as well. Characters speak of dabs, spots, specks, pigments, caring for a "dotty mother," connecting "the dots," and putting it together "bit by bit." And "point," the French translation of "dot," returns several times to create various ingenious puns: Jules tells George, "Let us get to the point" (I, 72), George fears he may be "straying from the point" (II, 130), George explains that Marie's mother had "pointed to this woman" (II, 138), Marie adds, "And she pointed to a couple in the back" (II, 138), and Alex and Betty sing, "There's not much point in arguing" (II, 157). Even the stage directions rely on the same word. In "The Day Off," the Boatman "points to his eyepatch," "points to George's eye," and "points to the other" (I, 57).

"Another aural equivalent of Seurat's color scheme," Sondheim has acknowledged, "was repeating certain key words and phrases."[26] He has referred to this textual way of analogizing Seurat's technique as "pointillist talk" and "pointillist phrases."[27] A close examination of the lyrics and book will demonstrate the accuracy of Sondheim's assertions and the extent to which he and Lapine relied on a relatively small palette of repeated words and textual phrases.[28] Several of George's lyrics in "Color and Light," for instance, recur elsewhere in *Sunday*. The words "color and light," which close the aforementioned excerpt, repeat 6 other times in Sondheim's lyrics and Lapine's book, and "color" and "light" appear independently 14 and 37 times, respectively. A conspicuously large number of instances of words relating to sight and the act of seeing figure in the text—unsurprising, perhaps, for a story about a visual artist: "look" (used as both a verb and noun) is uttered the most, with 69 references in the 123-page script, and "see" is heard 64 times. (For a list of word motives as well as a tally of the total

**Table 12.5.** Tallies of selected word motives
in *Sunday in the Park with George.*

| Word motive | Total |
| --- | --- |
| look | 69 |
| Sunday | 68 |
| see | 64 |
| paint | 60 |
| work | 58 |
| light | 37 |
| tree | 29 |
| hat | 28 |
| day | 27 |
| eye(s) | 26 |
| today | 22 |
| new | 18 |
| park | 15 |
| color | 14 |
| grass | 14 |
| Madame | 14 |
| week | 14 |
| art | 12 |
| water | 12 |
| connect | 10 |
| stare | 9 |
| point | 8 |
| vision | 8 |
| Monsieur | 7 |
| parasol | 7 |

number of times each one is delivered, see table 12.5.) Other words that apply to visual perception also pervade the text: "eye(s)," "stare," "vision," "watch," "notice," "view," "blind," "blink," "recognize," and "spy."

Textual motives permeate the lyrics and book of *Sunday* to such an extent that Sondheim and Lapine must have used them deliberately and intentionally.

Indeed, Sondheim admits, "I'd never used word and phrase motives so extensively [than in *Sunday*]."[29] For what purpose did the two collaborators return to the same group of textual motives? Perhaps for the same reasons Sondheim relied so much on musical motives: First, the collection of motives analogizes Seurat's technique, and second, they make the two acts sound connected even if the audience neglects to recognize the repetitions as such and absorbs them subliminally. The characters that populate *Sunday*'s two acts sing much of the same musical material and speak the same language—literally—despite their contrasting names, nationalities, and circumstances.

For their musical set in two different centuries, Sondheim and Lapine peppered the script with repeated references to the passage of and measures of time, one of the show's overarching themes.[30] "Sunday," in particular, recurs as a word motive and as a temporal setting. Much of *Sunday* takes place on Sundays: three of the scenes in Act I unfold on Sundays, and reference to a fourth Sunday arises in Act II, when Dennis informs George that he must wait until tomorrow for parts of the Chromolume to arrive ("They don't make deliveries on Sundays" [II, 164]). The word "Sunday," in addition, supplies the title for the only full reprise in the score as well as part of the title of the show, the title number, and George's light show, which he calls "Sunday: Island of Light" (II, 139). Other words that relate to aspects of time also abound: "day," "today," "week," and "yesterday."

George and the other characters utter the word "paint" and its variants ("painter," "painting," "painted," "repainted," and so on) a total of 60 times, almost as many as "Sunday." Specific objects in George's painting are also mentioned repeatedly; among the most prolific are "tree," "hat," "park," "grass," "water," and "flower." Other word motives include various French words, said and sung in scenes set on both sides of the Atlantic: "Madame," "Monsieur" (including Mr.'s bastardized version, "Excusez Masseur"), "parasol," "Mademoiselle," "La Grande Jatte," "rouge," "violet," "Bonjour" (literally "good day"), "nouveau," "Ansières," "cabaret," "gavotte," "La Coupole," "pardon," "passé," and "salon."

Some characters return to the same word motives; the Old Lady, for instance, circles around "tree" (10 examples plus 19 said by other characters), and George repeats the words "hat" and "connect" (6 examples plus 4 said by others), among others. Spot, the dog, reiterates his love of "grass" and when Jules, on three separate occasions, picks up the same word and expresses his longing for "tall grass," in particular, the shared vocabulary suggests a similarity between Jules and the Boatman's four-legged friend. Perhaps we are meant to think of Jules as a dog for philandering with his servant Frieda? Even she brings to mind Spot when she directs Jules to a secluded place for their next tryst: "I see a quiet spot over there" (I, 83).

The absence of certain word motives is just as significant as their prevalence. Nineteenth-century George evades completely the words "art" and "artist," whereas his great-grandson repeats the former 12 times and the latter 3 times. This modern George is preoccupied with arriving at something "new," a word mentioned only 3 times in Act I but 15 times in Act II (in addition to the 2 instances of the French equivalent, "nouveau"). The older George never utters the word "new" and prefers to focus on his "work," a term heard a total of 58 times, 28 in Act I and 30 in Act II.

Shared verbal motives and pointillist sentence fragments in the two musical numbers that open *Sunday*'s acts provide a clear link across the two halves. Dot's initial quips about the heat ("God, it's hot out here . . . God, I am so hot!" [I, 22, 25]) recur in "It's Hot Up Here."[31] Comparable declamatory formats also conjoin the numbers. In the former, Dot bursts forth with a long-winded, swift stream of thinly concealed indignation that recalls Amy's explosive rant in "Getting Married Today" from *Company*:

DOT:    Well, there are worse things
        Than staring at the water on a Sunday.
        There are worse things
        Than staring at the water
        As you're posing for a picture
        Being painted by your lover
        In the middle of the summer
        On an island in the river on a Sunday. (I, 25)

In "It's Hot Up Here," the disgruntled and hot-headed characters stuck in George's painting offer a slightly different version chronicling, instead, the trials and tribulations of being frozen in time as figures in an *objet d'art*:

ALL:        Well, there are worse things
            Than sweating by a river on a Sunday.
            There are worse things
            Than sweating by a river
BOATMAN:    When you're sweating in a picture
            That was painted by a genius
FRANZ:      And you know that you're immortal
FRIEDA:     And you'll always be remembered . . . (II, 128)

In addition to sharing similar subjects and structures with its predecessor, "It's Hot Up Here" adopts a fast-paced, three-note melodic turn accompanied by a dissonant staccato vamp first heard in "Sunday in the Park with George."

# Harmony

The two consecutive numbers, "Color and Light" and "Gossip Sequence," follow George as he works first on canvas in his studio and later with a sketchbook outside on the island. The pair thus focuses on the planning and working out of George's chromoluminarism. These two songs introduce to the score one new motive each played by the orchestra: the "Working" motive and "Gossiping" motive, which have several characteristics in common (example 12.1 notates these motives). Both consist of steady eighth-notes that continue without reprieve or rhythmic variety—as unrelenting as George engrossed in the repetitive physical act of applying precise strokes to his canvas and pad. Sondheim's detached articulation markings ("Working" is labeled *détaché* and notated with staccatos, and "Gossiping" is marked *secco*) and Michael Starobin's percussive orchestrations help project the cold, mechanical nature of George's work.

In the first 24 measures of "Color and Light," the "Working" motive repeats 6 times, and, in the first 18 measures of "Gossip Sequence," the "Gossiping" motive recurs 36 times. On the weak beats of each measure, slight changes to the shape of the "Working" motive gradually widen its narrow range upwards from a perfect fourth (B♭ to E♭) to a minor seventh (B♭ to A♭) and form new patterns and variations. But, just as the melodic line introduces new notes, it turns back to B♭, which keeps sounding four times per measure. At m. 50, when George calls for "color and light" for the first time, the "Working" motive adopts a somewhat new form that recurs, with slight variations, elsewhere in "Color and Light" (see example 12.2). With the same eighth-note rhythm, the texture increases to four parts that repeat a succession of alternating and slowly evolving chord clusters. This manifestation of the "Working" motive uses not only rhythm to imitate Seurat at his canvas but also clusters of notes to realize aurally his combinations of specks. The "Gossiping" motive, by contrast, undergoes fewer changes and repeats throughout virtually the entire length of the 82-bar score for "Gossip Sequence." The "Working" and "Gossiping" motives emerge as accompanimental patterns in several subsequent numbers (see tables 12.6a and 12.6b).

In each statement of the "Working" motive, George is visibly at work—painting, sketching, or observing—or he is referring to his work. At the outset of "We Do Not Belong Together," for instance, when Dot accuses him of caring only for things, not people, the orchestra starts playing a variation of the motive as he defends himself: "I cannot divide my feelings as neatly as you and, I am not hiding behind my canvas—I am living it" (I, 74). A similar situation takes place in "Putting It Together": On four separate occasions, remarks about George's work—which is now less about making art than about making money—trigger statements and variations of the "Working" motive as well as contrapuntal combinations with other motives.[32] When the orchestra plays the "Gossiping"

**Example 12.2.** "Color and Light," mm. 50–55, from *Sunday in the Park with George.* Words and music by Stephen Sondheim. © 1984 Rilting Music, Inc.

motive, George does not participate in the action; instead he adopts the role of observer and listens as others express their opinions.

The "Working" and "Gossiping" motives consist of a tetrachord rich in minor seconds. In terms of set theory, they constitute two pitch-class sets (pcsets): {321t} and {10e8}.[33] Comparing the normal forms of both pcsets—the most compact and compressed representations of the sets—makes it easy to see similarities between the two sonorities (see example 12.3).[34]

Both orderings contain the same interval succession 3-1-1. The "Working" and "Gossiping" motives thus are transpositionally equivalent pcsets, Set 2 = $T_{10}$ (Set 1), and have the same set class (sc), [0125].

A music sketch for *Sunday* evinces Sondheim's familiarity with twelve-tone music and its basic theoretical concepts (see example 12.4). Sondheim described this sketch as "some kind of attempt at a row. . . . I was experimenting with using tone rows to respond to the colors. These are early sketches where I'm feeling my way into the score."[35] And yet these two rows look similar to the one that emerges in "Eulogies," the axis point that marks the passage of time from 1891 (the year of Seurat's death) to 1984. This number follows the Act II opener, "It's Hot Up

**Table 12.6a.** "Working" motive in *Sunday in the Park with George*.

| Song | Incipit | Measures |
|---|---|---|
| "Color and Light" | (under action) "George stands on a scaffold, behind a large canvas" | Part I: 1–71 |
| | (under dialogue) Dot: "Nothing seems to fit me right" | Part II: 72–83 |
| | (under dialogue) George: "Are you proper today, Miss?" | Part II: 134–143 |
| | George: "Red red red red red red orange" | Part III: 151–191 |
| | (under dialogue) George: "The creamy skin" | Part III: 204ff. |
| | (under dialogue) George: "Damn" | Part IV: 222–251 |
| | (under scene change to park) | 11–23 |
| "The Day Off" | (under action) "George, who has been staring at his sketch of Spot, looks over and sees that Dot and Louis have left" | Part I: 1–5 |
| | George: "More like the parasol . . . Bum-bum bum" | Part I: 13–26 |
| "Finishing the Hat" | George: "As I always knew she would" | 16–22 |
| "We Do Not Belong Together" | (under dialogue) George: "I cannot divide my feelings as neatly as you" | 6a–15 |
| "Beautiful" | George: "Pretty isn't beautiful" | 43–54 |
| "Chromolume #7" | (under action) | Part II: 6 (II), 8 (Horn) |
| "Putting It Together" | George: "It's time to get to work" (then under dialogue) | Part VI: 13–18 |
| | George: "Start putting it together" (then under dialogue) | Part VIII: 10–17 |
| | George: "A vision's just a vision / If it's only in your head" (then under dialogue) | Part X: 11–17 |
| | George: "The art of making art" | Part XI: 45–48 |

**Table 12.6b.** "Gossiping" motive in *Sunday in the Park with George.*

| Song | Incipit | Measures |
|---|---|---|
| "Gossip Sequence" | (under dialogue) | 1–43 |
| | Old Lady: "Those girls are noisy" | 46–54 |
| | Boatman: "Over-privileged women" | 59–65 |
| "The Day Off" | Spot (George): "Piece of chicken" | Part I: 68–117 |
| | Chorus: "Taking the day on Sunday" | Part VII: 3–28 |
| "Bustle" (instruments only) | (under action) | 6–10 |
| "Chaos" (instruments only) | (under action) | 1–8 |
| "Chromolume #7" | (under action) | Part II: 8 |
| "Putting It Together" | Harriet: "I mean, I don't understand completely" | Part II: 1–10 |
| | Greenberg: "It's not enough" | Part III: 1–10 |

**Example 12.3.** The normal forms of the "Working" and "Gossiping" motives.

**Example 12.4.** Tone rows for *Sunday in the Park with George.* (These two rows come from the last two staves in example 4.14 of Horowitz, *Sondheim on Music*, 118.)

Here," and unfolds in a sort of limbo. Nineteenth-century George has died, and the figures in his painting take turns directly addressing to the audience their spoken reflections about the artist. Once they have completed their tributes, the characters exit, and pieces of scenery fly out until the stage is bare. The piano-vocal score for "Eulogies" includes the full spoken text of each remark above its thirteen unmetered measures. The synthesizer adds a new pitch as the characters begin to speak, and the pedal sustains each new note until the twelve-tone aggregate sounds simultaneously across more than four-and-one-half octaves.[36] With twelve pitches in the series and thirteen characters in the scene, the first pitch accompanies two characters, the Celestes. (The Boatman responds to Louise's and Frieda's remarks but he then waits for the penultimate pitch of the row before contributing the last miniature eulogy of George.) Table 12.7 compares the two aforementioned rows from Sondheim's sketches with the twelve-tone series in "Eulogies." The table also includes the order in which the characters speak as it suggests relationships and hierarchy. Reading the list of characters as two sets of six names reveals parallels: Franz and the Boatman, the two characters who question the value of George's work and exhibit a certain sense of integrity, occupy the fifth positions in each group of six, and Dot and George take up the sixth spots.

The twelfth note of the series in "Eulogies" ushers in a temporal shift to the auditorium of a modern museum and the entrance of contemporary George, who pushes his grandmother, Marie (played by the same actress who played Dot), in a wheelchair. The technician Dennis follows with a control console, and "an immense white machine" (II, 133)—George's Chromolume #7—takes center stage. With the row now complete and the aggregate still audible, the same series of notes repeats at an increasingly accelerated pace until George switches off his light machine (example 12.5).

**Table 12.7.** Series for *Sunday in the Park with George* with characters.

| | Celeste #1 and #2 | Soldier | Louise (and Boatman) | Frieda (and Boatman) | Franz | Dot | Old Lady | Nurse | Jules | Yvonne | Boatman | George (and Marie) | |
|---|---|---|---|---|---|---|---|---|---|---|---|---|---|
| Sketch 1 | A | G♯ | D♯ | A♯ | C♯ | B | E | A♮ | F♮ | C(♮) | F(♯) | B | G♮ |
| Sketch 2 | A | G♯ | D♯ | A♯ | C♯ | B | E | C♮ | G♮ | F♮ | D | F♮ | -- |
| "Eulogies" | A | G♯ | D♯ | A♯ | C♯ | B | E | C♮ | G | F | D | F♯ | -- |
| | | | | | | | | | | | | | -- |
| Characters | | | | | | | | | | | | | |

**Example 12.5.** "Eulogies," m. 13, from *Sunday in the Park with George.* Words and music by Stephen Sondheim. © 1984 Rilting Music, Inc.

**Table 12.8.** Tone row employed in "Eulogies" with hexachordal and tetrachordal relationships.

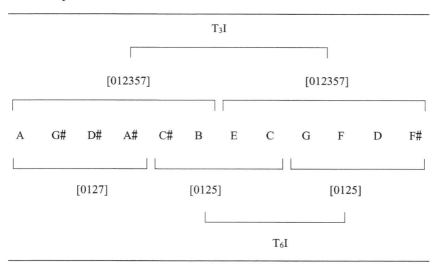

The "Eulogies" series subdivides into two self-complementary hexachords [012357] that relate by $T_3I$. One of the tetrachordal subsets of this hexachord and the last two tetrachords in the twelve-tone row share with the "Working" and "Gossiping" motives the same sc, [0125]. Table 12.8 organizes the "Eulogies" series into subsets and indicates its repetitive qualities and theoretical connections. Repetition of these set classes for the sake of establishing familiarity, even at a subconscious level, seems unlikely. Too much time and too many other musical numbers separate the earliest iterations of the tetrachord [0125], heard most prominently in "Color and Light" and "Gossip Sequence," from its statements in "Eulogies" to make the seemingly unrelated twelve-tone series sound remotely recognizable.

The ear is less likely to detect the use of set theory in "Color and Light" or "Gossip Sequence" than in "Eulogies." Although the title of the number suggests a connection to Seurat and the legacy of his work, contemporary George appears for the first time in the final measure, accompanied by straightforward repetitions of the twelve-tone series. Using set theory to mark his arrival indicates how the aesthetic has shifted for George. The real modernist George buried himself in his "work," whether in the creation of the hat or the parasol. Twentieth-century George concerns himself with only what is considered "new" and "art," not good or profound.

Sondheim envisioned the next number in the score, "Chromolume #7," as a piece of performance art, "Laurie Anderson's version of the Grande Jatte."[37] Yet instead of composing the piece himself, he passed the reins over to his orchestrator, Starobin. Sondheim had previously assigned the task of arranging dance music to an assortment of orchestrators and arrangers, including Betty Walberg (*Anyone Can Whistle*), David Shire (*Company*), John Berkman (*Follies*), and Daniel Troob (*Pacific Overtures*), but he had yet to leave such an authorial gap at such a structurally and dramatically significant point at the center of a score.

When Sondheim started writing *Sunday*, he was not looking for a new orchestrator. He had already worked with Jonathan Tunick on all six of the Harold Prince collaborations and *Into the Woods*. After *Sunday*, Tunick would orchestrate three more of Sondheim's scores and reorchestrate several others. Why didn't Sondheim hire Tunick to work on *Sunday*? What prompted him to pick Starobin, who had yet to contribute to a Broadway musical? *Sunday*'s genesis did not follow the "conventional" trajectory of a Broadway musical. It grew from a workshop production at Playwrights Horizons where Starobin worked as the house orchestrator and where he had met Lapine during *March of the Falsettos*. Lapine encouraged Sondheim to bring in Starobin for *Sunday*. With Tunick engaged with other projects, Sondheim agreed to give Starobin a chance. First, though, he would audition by orchestrating four of Sondheim's songs for *Sunday*.[38] When Sondheim heard the initial results, he was disappointed: "It was overorchestrated," he claimed. Then Sondheim asked Starobin for new orchestrations without extra contrapuntal lines or new harmonies. "And he slimmed down," Sondheim recalls, "and then he did this brilliant job."[39]

Starobin's audition pieces may have been brilliant, but "Chromolume #7" was not. When it came time to write the piece, Starobin faced a unique challenge. The presentation of the Chromolume needs to build excitement and reach a climax in order for theatergoers to sympathize with the modern George and invest interest in his journey as an artist; the audience must be able to take his work seriously.

And yet the machine has to be shown as an artistic failure big enough to trigger George's crisis. "Chromolume #7" is presented as diegetic music composed by George's friend and musical collaborator, Naomi Eisen, for the unveiling of the light machine. Starobin evoked the strength and soullessness of "Eisen," the surname of George's musical partner, which translates from German as "iron," by using synthesizers and sequencers that alter, repeat, and layer electronically fragments of motives, predominantly "Working," "Creating," and "Dreaming." The resulting piece of music, which spans only twenty-two seconds, tries so hard to project a modernist aesthetic that it becomes a parody of itself, and perhaps that is the point.[40] Even the most impressive pyrotechnical display usually fails to distract audiences from the inadequate musical accompaniment. "Chromolume #7" undermines the light sculpture and characterizes its creator as artistically inept and incapable of approaching the level of innovation that Seurat achieved or the degree of recognition that he earned posthumously. The perfunctory slide show, Marie's unscripted remarks, the electrical short, and Greenberg's bid for condo sales further undercut the Chromolume with scorn and ridicule.

For the Menier Chocolate Factory's 2005 production of *Sunday*, the 2006 London cast recording, and the subsequent 2008 Broadway revival, orchestrations by Jason Carr replaced Starobin's and earned Carr a Tony Award nomination for Best Orchestrations (and, presumably, an invitation to orchestrate the 2008 London revival of *A Little Night Music*, which transferred to Broadway the following year).[41] Sondheim again gave up the opportunity to compose his own "Chromolume #7." Why would he decline to write the definitive version of the number? Could he really find no solution to the problem of facing his own reflection? Although Carr's adaptation of Starobin's "Chromolume #7" stretches slightly longer with thirty-seven seconds of music, his is virtually subsumed by enthusiastic exclamations from the gallery of onlookers. For approximately two-thirds of the recording, the music is barely audible beneath the overpowering remarks from the people so eager to embrace George's latest piece. Their overt display of approval is unconditional, a reflective social gesture with no significance as a barometer for the artistically extraordinary. This alternative version thus mocks not only George and his artwork but also his audience, which extends metadramatically to include theatergoers and Sondheim and Lapine's own spectators. Perhaps the task of composing music for a predestined failure was an impossible one; Starobin and Carr succeeded well enough by creating mercifully brief versions.

At the dénouement, a more evocative repetition, rearrangement, and recombination of motives play out in "Move On." Disillusioned by the debut of his latest Chromolume and deeply affected by Marie's recent death, George makes a pilgrimage to his great-grandfather's world on the island of Grande Jatte, where he confronts his artistic limitations and personal failures in a surreal encounter with Dot, his deceased great-grandmother. In a nebulous space that blends the stories of the first and second acts, the living and dead, past and present, reality and imagination, Dot recognizes George as both the nineteenth-century painter and the modern light sculptor. George responds to her in the first person, as though inhabiting two personas simultaneously, one that expresses his present struggle in creating art and another that voices his great-grandfather's desires. In this strangely removed context, George can finally communicate his deep affection for Dot. She ultimately restores his creativity by reminding him of his part in the great family tradition of art making and encouraging him to keep looking for something new, to "Move On." The circumstances surrounding this otherwise quite wonderful song are contrived and improbable to such a degree that they challenge the suspension of disbelief with several questions: Was there no better way, no *logical* way, of resolving the plot's conflicts and finding an excuse to reunite the two leading actors for one final duet than relying on a deus ex machina? Is the problem of creating meaningful art in the late twentieth century so unsolvable and hopeless that George's artistic renewal must come from Dot, who—as a sort of wish-granting fairy—suddenly and unexpectedly resurrects herself so that *Sunday* may conclude conventionally with a happy, albeit artificially imposed, ending? Can the audience really believe that the same George who was responsible for the abominable Chromolume and who will continue working in the stifling conditions of the modern art world has the vision, talent, and wherewithal to create meaningful art? Does he even want to?

The bizarre conditions that bring together George and Dot have less to do with unimaginative storytelling than with one of Sondheim's peculiarities: that he only rarely has permitted himself to write heartfelt music and lyrics for characters to sing to one another directly, unambiguously; usually there has to be a gimmick. Sondheim relies on metaphor so his duets become more about ideas—in this case, the seemingly insurmountable challenges of making art—than characters. "Move On" exemplifies Sondheim's best attempt at composing a romantic duet, and yet the pair of characters singing could not possibly be mistaken as romantically involved. They make an unbelievable combination: a middle-aged great-grandson with his long-dead great-grandmother.

Despite the dramatic constraints that limit George and Dot's expression, "Move On" builds to a climax with the repetition of familiar motives. Sondheim remembers, "When I got to "Move On," I thought, 'Okay, here's the culmination, what'll I do? I know, I'll take all the themes and put them together.' And that's what I did."[42] Sondheim went a bit too far with this claim. While there is no doubt that "Move On" represents the pinnacle of *Sunday*, or, as Steve Swayne asserts, packs the most "emotional punch," it includes only a small number of motives, those associated with George and Dot: "Dreaming," "Creating," and "Loving."[43] (The same group also appears in George and Dot's earlier musical number, "We Do Not Belong Together"). In the last measures of the Act I duet, Dot foreshadows the title of "Move On" with the words, "I have to move on" (I, 76). A textual reprise in the closing section of the second duet, when Dot changes the familiar phrase "We do not belong together" to "We've *always* belonged together" (II, 171) makes the connection between the two songs obvious.

As George sings, "And the care, And the feeling, And the life" (II, 171), a powerful harmonic sequence, not heard elsewhere in the score, unfolds. A B♭ major first-inversion chord with a D in the bass functions as a "fake dominant," as Sondheim refers to it, and shifts to G, which tonicizes the Neapolitan chord on C in the tonic, B major.[44] The result is a straightforward progression of harmonies that outline the circle of fifths from D to G to C. When George utters the crucial words "Moving on!" and Dot overlaps with "We've always belonged together!" the harmony reaches a cadential $^6/_4$ and the resolution of a glorious cadence in B major (see example 12.6). At this point, George repeats the same words and, for the first time in the score, he and Dot sing in octave and rhythmic unison. Although the harmonic resolution and unison singing symbolize, in musical terms, reconciliation, without real characters or a believable situation the potential that the music and lyrics offer in heightening the emotions of and eliciting a poignant response from the audience is not fully realized. That George (or both Georges) and Dot unite at the level of artistic inspiration and creativity, not the "merely" personal level, undercuts the power of the music. For people who inhabit only the world of the arts, that aesthetic level is sometimes the only one, and that is perhaps what saves the number after all—and also gives the members of the audience a glimpse of a different kind of existence than their own.

According to Sondheim, the oscillation between major and minor that characterizes the motives in "Move On" makes an impact on the listener's ears. "When you're hearing ' . . . you have to move,' under the 'on,' after the cadence there, you hear the major and minor and they alternate. And what you get is a sense of *moire*. . . . I think it makes it satisfying."[45] Sondheim's terminology, borrowed from moiré patterns in physics, evokes a visual effect not unlike those prompted by Seurat's paintings that happens with an interference pattern in which, for instance, two grids (rather than colors) are superimposed and rotated at an angle. Sondheim explains why the "moire" elicits such a heightened emotional response:

> I really believe that in "Move On" when that alternation occurs—that little major/minor alternation—that the ear blends those two things and it comes out to be this unsettled, but very poignant chord. At least it does for me. I really hear it that way. . . . Ordinarily, that kind of uncertainty between major and minor would unsettle the audience. In "Move On," I think it feels like a cadence. And I think it's because it's been set up.[46]

**Example 12.6.** "Move On," mm. 118–132, from *Sunday in the Park with George.* Words and music by Stephen Sondheim. © 1984 Rilting Music, Inc.

The set-up to which Sondheim refers takes place most prominently in "We Do Not Belong Together," where, following Dot's final assertion, "I have to move on," the inner voice of the accompanying figure shifts between major and minor harmonies by articulating alternating E♮s and E♭s within the context of C major (example 12.7). (The pitch of E♭ and the pervasive use of thirds realize at the surface the score's underlying triadic harmonic progression.) After Dot sings "You have to move on" and "Just keep moving on," in "Move On," the same pattern emerges a minor second lower. For Dot, the thrill and strain of moving on translates musically into vacillating major and minor tonalities.

The crucial conflict between E♮ and E♭, the arpeggiated texture, and the technique of deconstructing and reassembling various repetitive patterns could have been lifted from Stravinsky's *Symphony of Psalms*, parts of which Sondheim, during his time at Williams College, sang informally with a small group of friends.[47] In 1980, when he appeared as a "castaway" on the BBC's "Desert Island Discs," Sondheim included *Symphony of Psalms* among his eight favorite pieces of music.[48] The same work would remain on his modified list of desert island discs when he returned to the program twenty years later.[49] Two similar passages for the piano, both from the first movement

Example 12.7. "We Do Not Belong Together," mm. 89–97, from *Sunday in the Park with George*. Words and music by Stephen Sondheim. © 1984 Rilting Music, Inc.

**Example 12.8a.**  Movement 1, mm. 12–21, from *Symphony of Psalms* by Igor Stravinsky. © Copyright 1948 by Hawkes & Son (London) Ltd.

**Example 12.8b.**  Movement 1, mm. 47–52, from *Symphony of Psalms* by Igor Stravinsky. © Copyright 1948 by Hawkes & Son (London) Ltd.

of *Symphony of Psalms*, bear a particularly striking resemblance to the bell-like sonorities and textures that pervade "Move On" (see examples 12.8a and 12.8b).

### "So many possibilities . . . "

Although the score for *Sunday* has been called "minimalist," the scope of Sondheim's interest in and knowledge of minimalism and its composers has yet to receive critical attention.[50] Sondheim owns multiple recordings of music by Philip Glass and Steve Reich, and he has stated that "Steve Reich is a personal hero to me."[51] Composer Ricky Ian Gordon claims to hear Reich's *Tehillim* in *Sunday*.[52] Sondheim himself has not been as candid. He has, however, pointed out, "When I met Steve Reich, he told me how much he loved *Pacific Overtures*. . . . It's similar to his own music, because so much of it is influenced by oriental music."[53] To which aspects, exactly, of "oriental music" is Sondheim referring? Do he and Reich share sources of influence, or have specific elements of Reich's compositions informed Sondheim's scores directly? Are there other minimalists who have left a mark on Sondheim's music? In short, just how much has minimalist music and its proponents shaped the development of Sondheim's voice?

The score for *Sunday* grew directly from the minimalist aesthetic that Sondheim had used for *Pacific Overtures* and his desire to translate into music the "less is more" aesthetic that provides the foundation of so much Japanese art. "Someone in a Tree," for instance, with its long sections of repetitive music articulating the same chord, rhythm, and accompanimental pattern (accentuated by Tunick's scoring for Asian instruments), seems to evoke some of the aesthetic qualities and additive techniques of music by Reich (*Four Organs*, 1970; *Music for 18 Musicians*, 1974–1976). Sondheim gives "Someone in a Tree" a sense of direction, momentum, and finally a point of arrival by making subtle changes over time to the rhythm, texture, and the placement of chords.

The size of *Sunday*'s orchestra seems to adhere to the same maxim that less is more: Starobin's orchestrations require only eleven musicians (2 reeds, 2 horns, percussion, piano/celeste, harp, synthesizer, 2 violins, 1 viola, and 1 cello)—roughly half as many players as required in Sondheim's eight previous Broadway musicals: *A Funny Thing Happened on the Way to the Forum* (26 musicians), *Anyone Can Whistle* (25), *Company* (26), *Follies* (28), *A Little Night Music* (25), *Pacific Overtures* (26), *Sweeney Todd* (26), and *Merrily We Roll Along* (20).[54] The unusually small number of *Sunday*'s accompanimental forces stems from its conception as a workshop production in a not-for-profit theater. The orchestrations started virtually as improvisations with a piano-vocal score distributed among players. When *Sunday* moved to Broadway, the number of musicians stayed small because the pit in the Booth Theatre holds only eleven players. For the 2005 production of *Sunday* at London's 169-seat Menier Chocolate Factory Theatre, Carr's new orchestrations reduced the orchestra to just five musicians (2 piano/synthesizers, 1 violin, 1 cello, and 1 flute/clarinet/bass clarinet/alto saxophone). Pianist Caroline Humphris doubled as musical director. With no trumpet or horn to play the "Sunday" melody, characterized by a rising minor sixth, Carr reassigned the memorable phrase to the alto saxophone, an especially misguided substitute for a part suggested by the bugler in Seurat's painting. When, in 2006, the production transferred to the West End, Carr's orchestrations—and lackluster saxophone—came with it.[55] That year, the London cast made an audio recording with the same five players plus three "additional musicians," which the liner notes list by name but not instruments. Although the synthesizer fills out the sound when the music calls for thicker textures, many numbers on the recording, particularly "Sunday," seem thin and lose some of their power. (The ensemble singing is weaker than on the Broadway album.)

The extent to which Sondheim employed pattern repetition in "Opening Prelude," "Color and Light," "Finishing the Hat," "We Do Not Belong Together,"

"Chromolume #7," "Putting It Together," "Move On," and selected music for scene changes reveals a conscious debt to minimalist music. "Putting It Together" exhibits best the application of minimalist techniques in generating large-scale structure. Its length alone—17 numbered sections, 47 pages in the 246-page vocal score (close to one-fifth of the entire score), and almost 7 minutes on the original cast recording—mimics, albeit on a smaller scale, the extended durations typical of many minimalist compositions. The perpetual motion of Sondheim's repetitive or slowly evolving eighth-note accompanimental figures articulating simple, alternating, and sometimes ambiguous harmonies evokes some of the music of John Adams. Compare, for instance, an excerpt of George's solo material from "Putting It Together" (XI) (example 12.9) with the opening of

**Example 12.9.** "Putting It Together" (XI), mm. 1–7 from *Sunday in the Park with George*. Words and music by Stephen Sondheim. © 1984 Rilting Music, Inc.

**Example 12.10.** *China Gates*, mm. 1–15, by John Adams. © Copyright 1977 by Associated Music Publishers Inc.

Adams's *China Gates* (1977) (example 12.10). "Putting It Together" (XI) unfolds in repetitive melodic patterns of four, six, and sixteen notes with an unremitting subtactile pulse (see table 12.9). Counting and grouping notes according to changes in melodic content or tonality reveals an intricate framework of alternating sections.

Pairing minimalism with chromoluminarism seems a compatible coupling. Minimalism depicts in music the repetitive nature of Seurat's (and nineteenth-century George's) approach to painting. As maximally repetitive music, minimalism also captures the spinning hamster wheel on which modern George runs, as he churns out Chromolume after Chromolume and performs the meaningless, creatively void, and yet all-consuming task that sustains his existence as an artist: Rigorously marketing himself within the climate of advanced capitalism in the hope of finding adequate financial

**Table 12.9.** Proportional design in "Putting It Together" (XI).

| Measures | Incipit | No. of eighth-note pulses | Groupings of eighth-note patterns | Tonalities | Form |
|---|---|---|---|---|---|
| 1–2 (safety) and 1a–6 | "Bit by bit" | 80 | ‖: 6, 6, 4:‖ 6, 6, 4, 4, 6, 6, 6, 6, 4 | G♭/A♭ | A |
| 7–16 | "Only way to make a work of art" | 80 | 6, 6, 4, 6, 6, 6, 6, 6, 6, 6, 6, 6, 6, 4 | G♭/C♭ | B |
| 17–28 | "Putting it together" | 96 | 6, 6, 6, 6, 6, 6, 6, 6, 6, 6, 4, 6, 6, 4, 6, 6, 4 | G♭/A♭ | A |
| 29–34 | "Adding up to make a work of art" | 48 | 6, 6, 4, 6, 6, 4, 6, 6, 4 | G♭/C♭ | B |
| 35–48 | "Take a little cocktail conversation" | 96 | 16, 16, 16, 16, 16, 16 | D♭/C♭ | C |
| 49–54 | "Is putting it together" | 48 | 6, 6, 4, 6, 6, 4, 6, 6, 4 | G♭/A♭ | A |

support for his artistic endeavors.[56] George tells the audience directly in "Putting It Together":

> Advancing art is easy . . .
> Financing it is not . . . (II, 146)

* * *

*Sunday* concludes as it began, with George standing in front of a white canvas (another interpretation of minimalist technique) and promising, "So many possibilities . . . " Sondheim has experienced this firsthand, of course, and his personal reflections echo George's cautious optimism: "Probably one of the most frightening things in the world is staring at a blank sheet of paper wondering how you're going to fill it. . . . But somehow you do."[57] By the end of *Sunday* George has learned that, in order to move on and create meaningful art, he needs to embrace his modernist roots; he cannot let the blank page scare him away from constantly pushing himself to try new things. With George as an Artist, a virtual stand-in for Sondheim and Lapine, his character invites such comparisons. Was Sondheim explicitly identifying with Seurat? Was he, like George, turning his back on commercialism and attempting to redefine himself as a modernist, searching for the new, moving on without regard to success or audience? Did Sondheim share George's mantra, and, ultimately, his optimism for future endeavors? Was *Sunday* Sondheim's *chef-d'oeuvre*, his *La Grande Jatte*? The show was, indeed, a turning point for Sondheim on several fronts as a collaborative musical dramatist. It marked a new first for him to work with Lapine instead of Harold Prince and introduced Sondheim to a different style of making theater. *Sunday* also gave Sondheim the chance to look back to what he had learned from Babbitt and use Babbitt's architectonics as an all-encompassing analogy to Seurat's chromoluminarism. Close to the canvas, Seurat's onlookers see distinct dabs of paint, like building blocks, and, from a distance, their eyes blend these individual elements into something new, "putting it together" to create larger images. Sondheim and Lapine encourage their audiences to adopt different perspectives, too, in order to grasp the large-scale connections that interweave throughout the show, whether putting together characters, circumstances, musical numbers, motives, tonal relationships, or collections of pitches. We, like Seurat's viewers, must work at putting it together in the hope that we, too, might follow George's instructions and "connect" to the musical and, ultimately, to ourselves.

# Notes

1. Portions of this chapter were presented as papers read at the annual meeting of the New York State–St. Lawrence Chapter of the American Musicological Society, London, Ontario, 2007; the Sagacious Sondheim Symposium, William Patterson University, Wayne, New Jersey, 2008; the annual meeting of the Society for American Music, San Antonio, Texas, 2008; and Music in Gotham/Song, Stage, and Screen III, New York, New York, 2008. I extend my gratitude to the following individuals: Katherine Axtell, Kim Kowalke, Ralph Locke, bruce mcclung, Steve Swayne, Graham Wood, and the anonymous readers for this book for their helpful suggestions.
   Craig Zadan, *Sondheim & Co.*, 2nd ed., updated (New York: Da Capo, 1994), 303.
2. Mark Eden Horowitz, *Sondheim on Music: Minor Details and Major Decisions*, 2nd ed. (Lanham, MD: Scarecrow, 2010), 91.
3. It is well known that Sondheim has a fondness for games and "loves the perennial puzzle." He is fascinated with words and numbers and has the ability to manipulate both. He has a large collection of antique puzzles and games, and has offered anecdotes about the games that he has designed over the years for his friends to play at parties. In 1968 Sondheim also contributed cryptic word games to *New York* magazine. Stephen Sondheim, *Finishing the Hat: Collected Lyrics (1954–1981) with Attendant Comments, Principles, Heresies, Grudges, Whines and Anecdotes* (New York: Knopf, 2010), 253; see also Stephen Sondheim, "How To Do a *Real* Crossword," *New York Magazine*, April 8, 1968, https://nymag.com/arts/all/features/46798/; Stephen Banfield, *Sondheim's Broadway Musicals* (Ann Arbor: University of Michigan Press, 1993), 43.

4. The original cast recording augmented the size of the orchestra from eleven to twenty-five. Stephen Sondheim and James Lapine, *Sunday in the Park with George*, Original Cast Recording, Paul Gemignani, music dir., RCA RCD1-5042, 1984. For a comparison of orchestrations in Sondheim's Broadway musicals, from *A Funny Thing Happened on the Way to the Forum* to *Into the Woods*, see Banfield, *Sondheim's Broadway Musicals*, 83.

5. "Hubbard Hutchison Prize Fund," Williams College, ca. 1940.

6. Milton Babbitt composed popular songs, film scores, and, in 1946, an unsuccessful musical, *Fabulous Voyage*. By the time Sondheim started studying composition with him in 1950, Babbitt had begun to work on a musical about Helen of Troy, which he hoped to develop into a star vehicle for Mary Martin. Banfield, *Sondheim's Broadway Musicals*, 20–22.

7. Horowitz, *Sondheim on Music*, 101.

8. For unfavorable reviews of *Sunday in the Park with George*, see, e.g., Clive Barnes, "Grass Could Be Greener in Sondheim's Sunday Park," *New York Post*, May 3, 1984, rpt. *New York Theatre Critics' Reviews* (45/7), 284–85; Howard Kissel, "Sunday in the Park with George," *Women's Wear Daily*, May 3, 1984, rpt. *New York Theatre Critics' Reviews* (45/7), 285; and John Simon, "What's the Point?," *New York*, May 14, 1984, 79.

9. Olaf Jubin has discussed character doublings in the casting of the Broadway production of *Sunday*, but his summary does not interpret them as embodiments of chromoluminarism, as I hope to do here. See Olaf Jubin, "'It Takes Two': The Doubling of Actors and Roles in *Sunday in the Park with George*," in *The Oxford Handbook of Sondheim Studies*, ed. Robert Gordon, 185–202 (New York: Oxford University Press, 2014).

10. The actress playing Mrs./Harriet triples as the Old Lady's Nurse.

11. If Louis, who sings negligibly in "It's Hot Up Here," is included, the tally reaches a baker's dozen.

12. These names, Bob Greenberg, Charles Redmond, Robert Blackmun, and Charles Green, are not only colorful but also similar to the names of art critic Clement Greenberg and painter Charles Blackman. Perhaps Lapine selected the names as allusions to these figures from the visual arts.

13. Quotations from the script will not have footnotes, but will be directly followed by a parenthetical note indicating the act and page number. Refer to Stephen Sondheim and James Lapine, *Sunday in the Park with George* (New York: Applause Theatre Book Publishers, 1991).

14. For a compelling reading of Dennis's role as not only George's employee but his lover, see Steve Swayne, *How Sondheim Found His Sound* (Ann Arbor: University of Michigan Press, 2005), 217–219.

15. "Opening Prelude" finds a partner of sorts at the end of *Sunday* when, in the last few measures of "Sunday" (reprise), a white canvas drops and George reiterates words from the beginning of the show (II, 174). "Lesson #8" also has a pair: the passage of dialogue that falls between "Gossip Sequence" and "The Day Off," in which Dot and George refer to the grammar book's "Lesson number eight" (I, 45–47).

16. Horowitz, *Sondheim on Music*, 99.

17. See ibid., 98–99; Zadan, *Sondheim & Co.*, 301–303.

18. Horowitz, *Sondheim on Music*, 73.

19. Steve Swayne, "Hearing Sondheim's Voices" (PhD diss., University of California, Berkeley, 1999), 334–335. Swayne and Stephen Banfield, perhaps taking cues from Sondheim, have discussed parallels between musical numbers in *Sunday*, and, in Swayne's case, he has traced selected motives through the score, but neither has read these motives as manifestations of Seurat's chromoluminarism. Swayne, *How Sondheim Found His Sound*, 197–256; Banfield, *Sondheim's Broadway Musicals*, 353–379.

20. What Swayne refers to as the "Reverie" motive, I have chosen to call "Dreaming." Swayne, *How Sondheim Found His Sound*, 236–238.

21. Banfield reproduced this draft layout for *Sunday* in his *Sondheim's Broadway Musicals*, 359.

22. Sir Isaac Newton, *Opticks: Or, a Treatise of the Reflections, Refractions, Inflections, and Colors of Light* (London: printed for Samuel Smith and Benjamin Walford, 1704), 154.

23. Hajo Düchting, *Georges Seurat, 1859–1891: The Master of Pointillism* (London: Taschen, 1999), 36–37. The number eight also figures prominently in *Sunday*. That it too appears in an Act II song title ("Lesson #8") and a total of four times in the script surely is not coincidental. Sondheim and Lapine's interest in the number may again derive from historical circumstances: in 1886, *Un dimanche après-midi à l'Île de la Grande Jatte* made its debut at the Eighth Impressionist Exhibition, a fact that Marie highlights in her presentation with George (II, 136). The number eight, as the new "first" in the cycle of seven musical notes and in the days of the week, also carries broader significance as the number of salvation, resurrection, and regeneration. Annemarie Schimmel, *The Mystery of Numbers* (New York: Oxford University Press, 1993), 156–163. As such, it symbolizes twentieth-century George's rebirth, literally, as the progeny of his great-grandfather's and Dot's, whose own act of creation has resulted in a child, Marie. (Dot is eight months pregnant when she visits George in the studio to ask him about a painting before she leaves for Charleston, North Carolina.) The number eight also signifies new endeavors in Dot's life; after leaving George, Dot learns how to read and write. In the park, he hears her reading aloud from a red grammar book, "Lesson number eight: Pro-nouns" (I, 45). When, in Act II, George reencounters Dot's grammar book, he adopts its simple, childlike language and third-person point of view to reflect on his professional and personal shortcomings ("Lesson #8"). From this objective perspective, George offers an introspective account of his situation. He decides to break from his seven-part cycle of Chromolumes and search for new creative undertakings—to find his new first.

24. Swayne has shown that a draft of the opening of "Putting It Together" (then titled "Party Sequence—Part I") shares with "Gossip Sequence" the key of E-flat major: "While this will be transposed to E major in the published score," Swayne asserts, "the manuscript's key makes the music's debt to Act I's 'Gossip Sequence' even clearer." Swayne, *How Sondheim Found His Sound*, 225.

25. For Sondheim's description of this abandoned idea, see Horowitz, *Sondheim on Music*, 117.

26. Zadan, *Sondheim & Co.*, 301.

27. Banfield, *Sondheim's Broadway Musicals*, 359.

28. For a compendium of examples, see Lara E. Housez, "Becoming Stephen Sondheim: *Anyone Can Whistle, A Pray by Blecht, Company,* and *Sunday in the Park with George*" (PhD diss., University of Rochester, 2013), 321–324, 327–328.

29. David Savran, *In Their Own Words: Contemporary American Playwrights* (New York: Theatre Communications Group, 1988), 231.

30. Sondheim and his collaborators have experimented with unconventional, nonlinear narratives and unusual combinations of a diegetic present and remembered past in several musicals. *Follies*, for instance, calls for multiple versions of the same character within the same scene, and *Merrily We Roll Along* unfolds in retrograde chronology. Sondheim would return to notions of time after *Sunday*, too, with *Assassins*, which brings together historical figures whose lifetimes never overlapped. For more on this subject, see Jim Lovensheimer's contribution in this volume.

31. "Sunday in the Park with George" and "It's Hot Up Here" join a group of Broadway act openers that use heat as a trope. In each one, characters comment on the climate: "Summertime" (*Porgy and Bess*), "Ain't It Awful the Heat" (*Street Scene*), "Too Darn Hot" (*Kiss Me, Kate*), and "Gonna Be Another Hot Day" (*110 in the Shade*).

32. For an analysis of the multiple motives at work in "Putting It Together," see Swayne, *How Sondheim Found His Sound*, 222–242.

33. For a discussion of pitch-class set terminology, see Allen Forte, *The Structure of Atonal Music*, 2d ed. (New Haven: Yale University Press, 1977).

34. Joseph N. Straus, *Introduction to Post-Tonal Theory*, 2d ed. (Upper Saddle River, NJ: Prentice Hall, 2000), 31.

35. Horowitz, *Sondheim on Music*, 118.

36. Banfield, *Sondheim's Broadway Musicals*, 356.

37. Ibid., 371.

38. Sean Patrick Flahaven, "Starobin Talks About *Sunday, Assassins,*" *Sondheim Review* 5, no. 2 (Fall 1998): 21–23.

39. Horowitz, *Sondheim on Music*, 229.

40. Sondheim and Lapine, *Sunday in the Park with George*, Original Cast Recording.

41. Stephen Sondheim and James Lapine, *Sunday in the Park with George*, London Cast Recording, Caroline Humphris, music dir., PS Classics PS-640, 2006.

42. Horowitz, *Sondheim on Music*, 94.

43. Swayne, *How Sondheim Found His Sound*, 201.

44. Horowitz, *Sondheim on Music*, 94.

45. Ibid., 93.

46. Ibid., 93–94.

47. Swayne has traced Sondheim's familiarity with *Symphony of Psalms* back to his college days, when Sondheim admits to having performed on street corners with like-minded friends the four-part chord progressions that set the four syllables of Psalm 150's "Al-le-lu-ia": "It's the only time I've ever indulged in such silliness," Sondheim claims. "But the whole piece is wonderful." Swayne, *How Sondheim Found His Sound*, 26. See also pp. 25 and 252.

48. Stephen Sondheim, "Desert Island Discs," BBC Radio 4, August 16, 1980. Sondheim also included on his list the following seven works: Ravel's *Valses nobles et sentimentales* and Piano Concerto in D Major for the Left Hand, Bartók's Concerto for Orchestra, Gershwin's *Porgy and Bess* (last-act trio), Brahms's Piano Concerto No. 2 in B♭ Major, and Sondheim's own "Poems" (*Pacific Overtures*) and "The Ballad of Sweeney Todd" (*Sweeney Todd*).

49. Stephen Sondheim, "Desert Island Discs," BBC Radio 4, December 31, 2000. This second compilation retained some of Sondheim's previous selections by Ravel (Piano Concerto in D Major for the Left Hand), Brahms (Piano Concerto No. 2 in B♭ Major), Stravinsky (*Symphony of Psalms*), and himself ("The Ballad of Sweeney Todd"). He changed his favorite number from *Porgy* to "Where Is Bess?" and added to the list Copland's Music for the Theatre and his own "The Advantages of Floating in the Middle of the Sea" (*Pacific Overtures*) and "Finishing the Hat" (*Sunday*).

50. Banfield, *Sondheim's Broadway Musicals*, 357–358, 366, and Martin Gottfried, *Sondheim*, enlarged and updated ed. (New York: Abrams, 2000), 156.

51. For an inventory of Sondheim's record collection, see Swayne, *How Sondheim Found His Sound*, 8–10. For Sondheim on Steve Reich, see Frank Rich, "Conversations with Sondheim," *New York Times Magazine*, March 12 2000, 40; Gottfried, *Sondheim*, 156; and "Reich and Sondheim: In Performance and Conversation," Lincoln Center's *American Songbook*, January 31, 2015, https://www.youtube.com/watch?v= 6Zbobkioa8E.

52. Ricky Ian Gordon, "If I Knew Then . . . ," *Sondheim Review* 19, no. 1 (Fall 2012): 21.

53. Horowitz, *Sondheim on Music*, 158.

54. Banfield, *Sondheim's Broadway Musicals*, 83.

55. Sondheim and Lapine, *Sunday in the Park with George*, London Cast Recording.

56. Minimal music as cultural practice in postwar America is the cornerstone of Robert Fink's fascinating monograph *Repeating Ourselves: American Minimal Music as Cultural Practice* (Berkeley: University of California Press, 2005), x.

57. Zadan, *Sondheim & Co.*, 394.

# 13

# Sondheim and the 11 O'clock Principle

*Elizabeth A. Wells*

Everyone knows when it is going to happen, but no one knows exactly what it is going to be—the 11 o'clock number in a musical. Designed to send the audience away with a toe-tapping extravaganza before the last train left, it sets up the ultimate ending of the show so that the *dénouement* seems not only inevitable but satisfying. The 11 o'clock number is a moment that Broadway producers, composers, and lyricists have relied on since the so-called Golden Age.[1] "Shall We Dance?" from *The King and I* serves as a perfect example, as does the show-stopping "Gee, Officer Krupke" from *West Side Story*. Like an "establishing song," a "production number," or an "I want" song, the 11 o'clock blowout was required fare for a great deal of Broadway's history, one of the song types identified and coded by everyone from author Richard Kislan to practitioner Bob Fosse.[2]

Most of the musical theater repertoire from the Golden Age and onward can be categorized based on the styles, types, and functions of songs in Broadway shows. Indeed, composers wrote to type, often using songs interchangeably between musicals, a kind of "borrowing" that was both common and encouraged. A song could be used in different shows because it served the same function, regardless of the specific characters involved. Certainly, of all the song types, the 11 o'clock number was key. As playwright John Weidman has said, "*Something* has to happen there."[3] No show should end anticlimactically; Broadway audiences looked forward to this penultimate moment in the show, their expectations high for creators and performers alike. Jack Viertel even refers to the 11 o'clock number as a collective "orgasm," so important was it to the climax of the show and the audience's enjoyment.[4]

The 11 o'clock number is undoubtedly iconic. But what purpose does it serve for an artist who defied conventional norms and rewrote the history and style of the Broadway musical? Composer and lyricist Stephen Sondheim, the ultimate theater man, was aware of the need for climax and closure at certain points in his shows. But how he handles and—ultimately—transforms this song type tells us a lot about his approaches to both art and innovation. From his unique approach in *Gypsy* to the finale of *Road Show*, looking at Sondheim's relationship to the 11 o'clock number reveals the interplay between form and genre in his work and demonstrates how his maturation as a creative artist affects his approach to some

Elizabeth A. Wells, *Sondheim and the 11 O'clock Principle* In: *Sondheim in Our Time and His*. Edited by: W. Anthony Sheppard, Oxford University Press. © Oxford University Press 2022. DOI: 10.1093/oso/9780197603192.003.0014

of Broadway's most deeply rooted traditions. It also gives us insight into how audience expectations of form affected the poor critical and popular reception of
his most underappreciated musicals.

## Sondheim's Precursors

The 11 o'clock number in a Broadway musical has a long and impressive history.
In Sondheim's own definition (from *Finishing the Hat*), he explains:

> In traditional musicals, there is a bookmark known as the eleven o'clock
> number. Dating back to the days when the curtain rose at eight thirty and
> musicals were essentially vehicles for star performers, the term meant a song
> performed by one or more of them just before the finale, calculated to bring
> down the house. It served as the climax of the show and was something the au-
> dience eagerly anticipated during the whole evening—and it usually involved a
> string of encores. ("Anything You Can Do" from *Annie Get Your Gun* is a classic
> example.)[5]

Some early examples in American musical theater come from musical revues
such as the Ziegfeld *Follies*, where comedy numbers, the occasional art song set,
and various musical acts culminated in an often patriotic blowout of massive
proportions. Later, the 11 o'clock number was specifically designed to showcase
the talents of the star of the show, a big-name performer such as Ethel Merman.
Indeed, as Sondheim suggests, the emphasis on the star was an important con-
tributor to this number's growing importance. At the end of her own long star
turn as Rose in the revival of *Gypsy*, Angela Lansbury remarked on the amount of
energy the show required from her: "I really do an 11 o'clock number at 7:45 and
another 11 o'clock number at the end of the show."[6]

As the genre developed and the musical matured, creators took different
approaches, from production numbers to songs such as "Oklahoma" in
*Oklahoma!* providing a recapitulation of the show's themes and featuring the
entire ensemble. However conceived, the number was an important part of the
warp and weft of any show, and producers and authors alike took it seriously as
an important climax. The 11 o'clock number is a showstopper when the show
does not need really to get going again. It differs from a finale in important ways,
although sometimes these two numbers get elided. Although musical theater
scholars and aficionados readily recognize this iconic song type, very little has
been written about it, suggesting that it has been more interesting to the creators
of Broadway musicals than it has to the people who study them. Indeed, few
scholars write about the formal aspects of the song types that we all take for

granted. The 11 o'clock number remains, even in the literature, a little-discussed phenomenon.[7]

As is well known, Sondheim was steeped in Broadway traditions and number types. He pushed the boundaries of the musical, but despite his many significant innovations, he still ran up against the traditional 11 o'clock moment. Here, he would need to provide the audience with a certain musical and dramatic climax, a sense of forward momentum that would lead to the end of the story. As we will see, he started to approach this juncture in the work as a place to stop the action—with few repercussions—in order to comment on the core themes of the musical. In his hands, these penultimate numbers became less a showcase for a particular star or character than a commentary on the show's larger themes.

Though the 11 o'clock number has received little critical attention, the few scholars involved in this discussion nonetheless still disagree about what numbers fill this slot in Sondheim's shows. At first glance, it is easy to argue that Sondheim abandons the song type early on and never looks back. In some shows the final blowout seems conspicuously absent. Other shows have numbers that fit the bill, if poorly: For instance, in *A Little Night Music*, Kim H. Kowalke and others have argued that "The Miller's Son" meets the need for an 11 o'clock number, and yet it does not act quite like one.[8] It does fill the penultimate position, yet in its placement and commentary on the plot, one could argue that it is simply a kind of "I am" number that occurs late in the game.[9] In addition, it is sung by a minor character, so it does not offer a stand-out moment to one of the stars. Alternatively, "Send in the Clowns" is often considered in this slot because of its placement, but it hardly stops the show. In *Gypsy*, "Rose's Turn" is generally considered the 11 o'clock number, yet it functions differently in its encapsulation of the show, especially when we consider the weight of the drama and music late in the second act.

In order to understand where Sondheim learned to write a true 11 o'clock number, we should look to his mentor and teacher, Oscar Hammerstein II, and how this kind of number worked in the Rodgers and Hammerstein shows. In these earlier musicals, the penultimate number is more presentational and lends itself to star turns and production numbers; it was also the place where "high art" (specifically ballet) also appeared. One could argue that the reprise of "If I Loved You" and "You'll Never Walk Alone" are 11 o'clock moments in *Carousel*, for instance, but the second act ballet acts as the musical's true climax. Yet *Carousel* is something of an outlier in the Rodgers and Hammerstein oeuvre because of its tragic plot, the fully composed overture, and the ballet sequence that had become popular in musicals such as *Pal Joey* and *On Your Toes* from the 1930s and 1940s. The song "Oklahoma!" is a more typical treatment of the 11 o'clock number. Here, the entire cast sings the show's title song while giving the raison d'être for their living so happily on the land. The darker aspects of the end of the

SONDHEIM AND THE 11 O'CLOCK PRINCIPLE 377

musical, such as Jud's death and the trial, are dealt with fairly quickly, so that the resonances of that penultimate musical number leave audiences happy as they file out of the theater. Similarly, in *The King and I*, "Shall We Dance" comes just before the final argument between the protagonists over the punishment of a slave. The audience's toes keep tapping—gently—as the musical winds to a more somber close with the death of the king. Putting something lighthearted, or at least exciting, in the penultimate position reminds critics and audiences of the show's entertainment value even while the creators explore such darkness.

Sondheim, as Oscar Hammerstein II's mentee, would have been very familiar with these works and would have understood both their formulae and content. Sondheim benefited from learning the rules before breaking them. His initial forays into writing demonstrate a more traditional approach to the penultimate number. One of his first collaborative 11 o'clock numbers is *West Side Story*'s appropriately orthodox "Gee, Officer Krupke," which occurs, as expected, in the penultimate position of its show. The song was moved out of this position in the film version, obscuring its role as a final showstopper for those who have never seen a live production of the musical. It was a welcome bit of comic relief in the midst of the tragedy; Arthur Laurents compared it to the comic scenes that pepper Shakespeare's tragedies. This is the 11 o'clock number at its best. It is fast and frenetic, it showcases the chorus (arguably the stars of this show), and it comes right before the swift *dénouement* of the show. In "Krupke," the Jets gang members discuss approaches to solving juvenile delinquency and how they are used by formal institutions. It is easy to see the song as a plea for more humane and effective ways of solving social problems; indeed, linking it to the general concerns of Jewish Broadway creators and audiences during this period is simple. That the authors approached such a difficult topic with humor, however, is not what we would expect in this very serious musical. Bernstein's attempt at a "great American opera"[10] hardly seems the place for comedic irreverence. Still, it is the vehicle itself, the way in which the song does its cultural work, that makes it particularly apt and, as I have argued elsewhere, particularly Jewish.[11]

"Krupke" is not only a funny song, it is a vaudeville song. This is one of the rare instances in this show in which the actors play more explicitly and self-consciously to the audience, not only to each other. And it worked, better than any other song in this show. "Krupke" was one of the most popular numbers in the musical, stopping the show every night with its comic genius, its energy, and its cathartic placement in the storyline. Its deliberately different musical "voice," a non-Latin, non-jazz, played-to-the-audience voice, is part of what makes it so successful as a penultimate climax. In the 11 o'clock repertoire, there seems to be a particular desire to make the music come out over the footlights–a signal to the audience that they are witnessing a highly performative moment blurring the diegetic and the non-diegetic. Robbins claims that he staged the number in record time, three hours on the clock. Although he claimed that he simply worked better under pressure, it seems likely that the attitude and the dramatic aesthetic of the song were so familiar to Robbins, a consummate theater professional, that he did not have to dig deep to figure out how it should be brought to life. As Sondheim's first big show, *West Side Story* must have impressed on the young composer in no uncertain terms that there was still something very important, and here very structurally satisfying, about an 11 o'clock number.

## *Gypsy* and the Development of an 11 O'clock Principle

Although *Gypsy*'s status as a Sondheim show is up for debate—must he have written the music for the show to qualify?—it provides an excellent starting place for a discussion of young Sondheim's unique experimentation with the 11 o'clock number. "Rose's Turn" is considered a canonical example of the Broadway climax. As Jeffrey Magee has argued, beyond his work as a lyricist, Sondheim had a big role in designing the form and content of the show under the more seasoned Jule Styne.[12] Sondheim even collaborated on "Rose's Turn" with Robbins in Styne's absence, which suggests his importance in shaping this moment of the show. As Jack Viertel describes it,

> Late in rehearsal, the director-choreographer Jerome Robbins, realized that the ballet he had planned, in which Rose would confront all the characters and crisis moments of her past, was wrong for the spot, so a new plan was concocted. Rose would sing about her gradual self-destruction, but defiantly, not reflectively. According to Stephen Sondheim, he and Robbins holed up one night in the long-abandoned rooftop theater that had once been home to Ziegfeld's Midnight Frolic shows. . . . Robbins played Rose, Sondheim played the piano and ad-libbed lyrics, which were refined over the next few days. Using snippets of music from the show by the composer Jule Styne (who was not present), they gradually stitched together what has become the signature 11 o'clock number of all time. Robbins moved around the stage, stalking Rose's past and present states of mind, while Sondheim plugged in jagged fragments of Styne's music, linking them with a few of his own inventions, until they had zeroed in on Rose's psychological profile—a woman abandoned by her mother, who had so tightly controlled her own children that they both have abandoned her, leaving her with nothing at all to cling to except scrapbooks and selective memory.[13]

Certainly, this and other documentary evidence suggests that Sondheim played an important role in the writing of this scene, and so we can allow that it is as much his creation as it was Jule Styne's.

Attention to *Gypsy* has focused not merely on the accomplishments of its male creators but on Ethel Merman's original performance as Rose, a complex character whom one New York critic called "the mastodon of all stage mothers."[14] Merman had made her name as a much younger woman in shows such as *Anything Goes*, *Annie Get Your Gun*, and *Something for the Boys*. *Gypsy* has become iconic in the literature because it seems to comment on the nature of performance, the nature of the diva and, ultimately, on Merman at a crucial point in her own career. It is a show about female characters, and it has a lot to say about the role of the feminine at this point in Broadway history. "Rose's Turn" is the final number. It is a mad scene for Rose and was also for Merman, a diva turn on a diva character. Feeling abandoned by her family, never having made it as a star herself, Rose sings what amounts to an aria in which textual and musical material from the whole of the show comes back in a nightmarish montage.[15] She sings alone to an imaginary audience of her pain, her shattered dreams, and the mother who abandoned her. Rose plays the role of the stripper, usurping in her mind the part her own daughter now plays. At the end she sings out manically, repeatedly, that this time is "for me, for me, for me." There is perhaps no bigger diva turn in the repertoire, and the applause that Rose imagines in her mind becomes the applause that the performer receives for this number. Rose's turn was Merman's turn. Reality and fantasy, diegetic and non-diegetic, come together.[16] It has many of the trappings of the 11 o'clock number: It is a star turn, it features the protagonist, it comes very near the end, and, crucially, it is played to the audience differently than any other number in this show. What is unique about this moment, though, is not that it is a diva turn but that the 11 o'clock number is manipulated to offset the balance of Act II. "Rose's Turn" throws the form out of its standard shape.

One could argue that *Gypsy* actually has *three* 11 o'clock numbers, presenting three different visions of the diva-as-stripper. The first is the show-stopping "Gotta Get a Gimmick," one of the funnier numbers in Sondheim's repertoire. In it, three aging (but still kicking) strippers show Rose's young daughter Louise how to put together a compelling strip act. For first-time audiences, this song seems to fit the bill for an 11 o'clock number. It has star power: three would-be divas gowned in over-the-top costumes and extreme gender performativity. It is extravagant: this number, if done right, should not simply be funny but should really stop the show. It comments on the themes of *Gypsy* in a highly performative manner that, although ostensibly sung to Louise, is really sung to the audience. For all intents and purposes, the 11 o'clock role has been well filled here. We could be forgiven for expecting to proceed to the finale.

Yet "Gotta Get a Gimmick" is swiftly topped by an unexpected *second* 11 o'clock number, Louise's rendition of "Let Me Entertain You," a grand stripper number that recasts one of the recurring signature tunes of the musical into its final form. Gypsy Rose Lee, the namesake of the show, contributes her star turn. This is the diva in full bloom, at the top of her game, showcased for the audience. This must be the last big number in the show; it is simply too grand *not* to be. And, if it did not stop the show, then one could argue that the creators have not done their job. This is an encore, after all, of the other iterations of this song. It features the title character, it is played more or less directly to the audience, and it has to be utterly convincing. We have to believe that Louise has completely transformed. The show should really stop here. Indeed, Robbins and his creative team argued over whether this was in itself the 11 o'clock number of the musical.[17]

But then comes "Rose's Turn." This is literally the *third* diva number of the show, the third 11 o'clock number, deconstructing and dismantling the diva and showing her as a fragmented, complex and ultimately sympathetic character. Suddenly the musical is over, ending very quietly as Louise and her mother leave the theater, Rose finally understanding that her turn has come and gone. The ending of this show in a backstage area forms a weird anticlimax: After such an explosion of emotion, there can be no more to say. It is as though the world of musical theater, and of the diva, comes to an end. So where does this leave us? The audience has just experienced three heavy climactic numbers, each one topping the last, and coming in fairly quick succession. What this suggests, then, is that there is not one 11 o'clock number, nor actually three, but an "11 o'clock complex," or more generally, "the 11 o'clock principle" in action. Each star turn outdoes the one that came before, which makes the final climax of this show in "Rose's Turn" even more shattering. The show is about divas, how they live, thrive, and survive. In these three takes on divadom (the new, the old, and the eternal) Sondheim and his collaborators explore the central themes of the show in tripartite form. "Rose's Turn" does not make sense without the two numbers that precede it. It grows with and into its characters.

## *Company* and *Follies*: The Principle Develops

Not every Sondheim show works as *Gypsy* does, but the 11 o'clock principle occurs in similar ways in Sondheim's other best-known and most-loved musicals. Instead of relying on one showstopper, Sondheim and his collaborators choose to extend and attenuate the moment of climax in a multipart form, building audience expectation and excitement while allowing different characters to express themselves about the meaning of the show as a whole. Although *Do I Hear a Waltz?*, *Anyone Can Whistle*, and *A Funny Thing Happened on the Way to the Forum* have a role to play in the story of the 11 o'clock number, they do not reveal the ways in which Sondheim has transformed this song type. For that, we must look to his first maturity in the early 1970s, with the iconic musicals *Company* and *Follies*. In them Sondheim actively dismantles the idea of musical theater in its traditional forms. This can be seen in both shows in his approach to narrative; it is also evident in the way the shows end.

In considering *Company*, a modular show with scenes that could play out in any order, we have to wonder where an 11 o'clock number would fit and whether it is necessary for the show's form and plot. If the scenes can take place in any order, or simultaneously in Bobby's mind, as many have suggested, why do we need a climax, and what would this climax achieve? As is common in Sondheim's works, *Company* uses musical genres and styles of the past mixed with liberal helpings of pastiche, allusion, and subtext. Sondheim, however, wraps up by bifurcating the ending of the show into an 11 o'clock complex. The song "What Would We Do Without You?" is one of Sondheim's longer production numbers, and its soft-shoe dance style and overall style suggest that it should come in an 11 o'clock position. The cast is on stage, they are all singing and dancing (at least a bit), and the focus remains on Robert, the star of the show. Yet the length and the over-the-topness of the number, along with its placement in the middle of the show after intermission, robs it of the right to work as a proper 11 o'clock number. It is almost as though Sondheim is saying, "I'm giving a bow to this tradition, but I'll do it *my* way." Instead, the traditional penultimate slot is filled by an 11 o'clock complex, providing perspectives from characters both male and female, married and single, novice and veteran, younger and older, in a show concerning itself entirely with these interpersonal issues.

Although "Being Alive" is often considered the 11 o'clock number of this musical, it cannot provide the audience with the expected climax on its own. Instead, the 11 o'clock principle is satisfied by the combination of "The Ladies Who Lunch" and "Being Alive."[18] These two related songs come one right after another; the book portion that separates the songs is barely two pages, which is in itself only a page or two from the end of the play. Joanne's solo is meant to be show-stopping, encapsulating the sardonic Sondheim worldview in a way that Bobby never could. By contrast, "Being Alive," despite its harmonic pump up in the middle of the song and its climactic conclusion, is far more a finale than a penultimate statement. Even then, "Being Alive" expresses too much emotional ambiguity to act as a convincing traditional finale, tying up the story in a tidy bow. As in *Gypsy*, the female perspective is given a kind of pride of place before turning to Bobby's male perspective. He ends the show with a semi-optimistic tone, but it is not really an 11 o'clock number on its own. Indeed, Sondheim describes "Ladies Who Lunch" in a way particularly suited to the 11 o'clock number. He writes in *Finishing the Hat*, "Privately, I had hoped that the number would be such a showstopper in Elaine's [Stritch] hands that the audience would actually get up on the 'Rise!' repetitions and give her a standing ovation. It was a showstopper all right, but not quite that big. My hope was probably a holdover from my Hollywood fantasies in which on opening nights black-tied men and bejeweled women stood up at anything."[19] It would not be too much to suggest that because the role was written for Elaine Stritch, "sewn on her," as people said about Merman's Rose, that it is a true 11 o'clock number. Joanne (especially in Stritch's hands) is, somewhat paradoxically, a star's role in an ensemble show. Yes, Bobby is the central character, but Joanne is the one on whom audiences often focus. The quality of a Joanne can make or break this show.

*Follies,* from the same era, takes the 11 o'clock complex even further. This show, more than any of Sondheim's other musicals, uses a mix of styles from musical theater and popular song history. Sondheim provides numbers for each of the major characters that express what they are taking away from their experience together. Most obviously 11 o'clock-ish in style, dance implications, and tempo are Buddy's number and Phyllis's number.

Mandy Patinkin's performance of "Buddy's Blues" in the live recorded version of *Follies* from the 1985 New York production is 11 o'clock from top to bottom.[20] The frenetic dancing, the pastiche of the song, and the show-stopping performance all point clearly to a penultimate number by a star. One cannot get bigger than this in a solo number without invoking the entire chorus-and-production treatment.

And yet all the principals are stars in this musical, and so each of them has an 11 o'clock number. Although one could argue that Sally's song falls far short of stopping the show, it provides a kind of slow movement to the structure of the 11 o'clock complex that highlights the dramatic aspects of the musical as its conclusion. Phyllis's "The Story of Lucy and Jessie" also rings in as a fast movement in the complex, is replete with pastiche of an earlier time period and musical style, and offers the show-stopping aspect of an 11 o'clock number. "Buddy's Blues," "Losing My Mind," "Lucy and Jessie," and "Live, Laugh, Love" form a four-movement complex in which the characters speak most clearly to the audience, as in many of Sondheim's other 11 o'clock numbers. Indeed, he seems to have considered these last four numbers a suite of sorts, since they all fall under the same number (19) in the score and flow one to the other.[21] "Buddy's Blues" starts in E♭ major and has a pump up throughout to end on F. "Losing My Mind," the slow movement, starts in A♭ major and moves up. The other movements are all on the flat side: C minor for "Lucy and Jessie," and a series of key areas for Ben. Each number is cued to begin on the applause from the previous song, suggesting that Sondheim also saw these as one large 11 o'clock complex. Each of the songs provides insight into the characters' emotional and psychological states after the events of the evening and provide a summation of the show's narrative so far.[22] The "Chaos" scene that ends this four-movement complex becomes the actual finale of the musical, and then the brief *dénouement* is what we expect from a dramatic work, whether by Sondheim or Shakespeare. What does it mean for the most important and authentic utterances of the musical to be delivered as pastiche? It seems to suggest that *Follies*, as many have claimed, is the post-musical musical, transmogrified into a site of emotional expression that transcends our understanding of musical theater form, style, and content. Sondheim has figured out how best to use this moment in the drama. The function of the penultimate number changes yet again, however, as we move farther through his oeuvre.

### *Sunday in the Park with George, Into the Woods,* and *Sweeney Todd*: More Explicit Thematic Connections

After *Company* and *Follies*, Sondheim moved away from the 11 o'clock principle a little more decisively, but he did create a few other 11 o'clock complexes. His new partnership with James Lapine (on parting ways with Harold Prince) suggests one possible reason for his new approach to form and genre. The change sparked new modes of production for Sondheim, who shifted from the typical Broadway show rehearsal period and opening to workshopping in off-Broadway milieus. This may be one reason why *Sunday in the Park with George* feels more experimental. Conceived almost as two distinct one-act plays, the musical ends with the modern George's realization that the legacy he leaves behind is his most important work. The resulting 11 o'clock complex contains two songs: "Children and Art" encapsulates the whole show, and "Move On" provides both male and female perspectives, both protagonist and secondary character, in the musical's final moments. It also supplies the quasi moral of the story while clarifying the characters' motivations. As *Company's* "The Ladies Who Lunch" distills an entire culture into a few verses without suggesting a course of action, and "Being Alive" serves to move the drama forward, so the pairing in *Sunday* does the same narrative work. Both "Being Alive" and "Move On," literally about moving on, are left open-ended, leaving audiences guessing what the character will do next but at least suggesting that some action will take place. "Being Alive" provides the main character of *Company* with some approaches to fixing what he has realized is his central problem. That he only imagines them in the second half of the song is typical of the ambivalence that Sondheim often includes in these emotional moments. In *Sunday*, "Children and Art" works in the same way; the song is reflective of the culture in which George finds himself. "Move On" then provides the action that the characters take and that brings the musical to an emotional and narrative conclusion. The fact that we do not know exactly how this will play out is part of what makes this sophisticated drama; we are left as an audience reflecting on the characters, their situations, and possible next steps.

*Into the Woods* has a similar complex, in which "No One Is Alone" provides the 11 o'clock function after the tour-de-force "No More." Here, the principle is used to encapsulate the entire meaning of the show, the "moral" after one character has stated that things cannot continue on as they have. Neither song has the qualities of a large production number or star turn, but the narrative of the show literally stops with the introduction of a stand-alone thematic number that sums up the musical and is performed specifically to the audience. The entirety of *Into the Woods* is a journey through the breakdown of moral and narrative tropes. Each character departs somehow from what is expected in the fairy tales that each originally inhabited. At the end of the show, both the audience and the characters need to bring events back into focus and control. "No More" thus serves to stop the action (as 11 o'clock complexes tend to do) and to signal that some higher meaning must come from the characters' tragedies. Just as "No More" asks a kind of question, "No One Is Alone" provides an answer, a reason for the characters and the audience to have hope. This becomes the new function of this number, or complex, in later Sondheim shows. "No One Is Alone" became a hit for a composer who does not specialize in hit songs, another clue that this moment in the musical is meant for alertness and attention on the part of the audience. It is not simply another number. It is *the* number to which the whole story has ultimately led.

*Sweeney Todd* departs perhaps most radically from some of our expectations of musicals in its time. Most of the show is sung operatically, if not in style, then certainly in scale. Because it is essentially a comic horror story with emotional overtones, the idea of a typical production number was not out of the question. Instead, Sondheim decided to almost completely musicalize the ending of the show, bringing back leitmotifs and other musical moments to provide the audience with clues as to how the story will end. Having the players move out of character to sing "The Ballad of Sweeney Todd" at the end is essentially the 11 o'clock principle at work. It is a reprise, it states very clearly the moral of the story, and it creates a sense of closure and climax after the particularly dramatic final moments of the plot. It is also sung blatantly to the audience. This direct breaking of the fourth wall is one thing that 11 o'clock principles in Sondheim shows seem to do repeatedly. To have ended (as the film version does) without the ballad would have left the audience with more questions than answers and a sense that the story was incomplete. The "Ballad" brings the story together and also serves as the finale of the musical, so that everything is wrapped up and everyone has been educated.

## Late Sondheim: The Demusicalization of the Climax

As Sondheim moved through his career, he continued to work with the 11 o'clock principle, and it is telling that he did so by gradually allowing the story itself, as developed by the bookwriter, to come across more directly. Two examples from later Sondheim demonstrate the ways in which the composer allowed the bookwriter to tell the tale without music, the most striking case being *Assassins*. In this show a series of vignettes featuring different assassins from America's history culminates in a scene in the Texas Book Depository where characters from the past appear anachronistically in order to convince Lee Harvey Oswald to shoot the president. After the fatal climax, the 11 o'clock complex becomes not a musicalized scene but a long spoken narrative without music. Although there is certainly a good balance of book time with music time in this show, it is astonishing that the soliloquy, "November 22, 1963," appears on the original cast recording as if it were a musical number, not an eleven-minute book scene. Here, the show stops to comment on the major themes of the musical in entirely nonmusical terms. Sondheim has, in effect, taken himself out of the equation in order to let the bookwriter (John Weidman) take the stage as the orchestrator of the drama. Yet questions remain as to whether this approach works and whether the collaborators were truly committed to this strategy. Weidman reports that "Steve wanted an 11 o'clock number" at the end, leading him to write a song that was later added for the 1992 London production ("Something Just Broke"). "Everybody's Got the Right," a reprise that comes from the beginning of the show, could be considered an 11 o'clock alternative.[23] Although this reprise does get played directly to the audience, and although it does deal directly with the themes of the show, it does not come across as strongly as "The Ballad of Sweeney Todd" and indeed, the style and structure of the show are very different from those of *Sweeney*. It is also a fairly short number and lacks the rousing effects of some of the other Sondheim songs used in this position. Therefore, the spoken soliloquy becomes the more-or-less-official 11 o'clock number, and audiences notice. We will soon discover the repercussions of this tension.

Sondheim continued to develop his daring sense of form and climax in this precise way in later musicals. *Passion* is a show that would not normally lend itself to a climactic production number or a broad solo turn. It is a serious and tragic love story, one that does not rely on production numbers or other traditional song types. Yet it still requires some form of climax and *dénouement*. The story revolves around the unrequited love of a plain, sickly woman (Fosca) for an attractive military man (Giorgio) who is having an affair with a married woman (Clara). At the end of the show, Giorgio and the Colonel take part in a duel over Fosca's honor. Although the duel is dramatic and takes place in an 11 o'clock position in the musical, the final letter-reading scene instead fulfills the 11 o'clock principle, again taking the composer out of the creative spotlight. The principal characters come to some kind of resolution in their relationships through letters to each other about love, either new (Fosca and Giorgio) or ending (Giorgio and Clara). Raymond Knapp and Zelda Knapp have written extensively about the "epistolary" musical that Sondheim and Lapine have created in this show.[24] The reading of the letters, whether musicalized or not, is the central conceit by which the story is told and the relationships are forged and expressed.[25] It therefore makes sense that the climax of the musical takes place in this way rather than in the singing of songs. The reading of letters from participants in the love triangle sums up the themes of the show, they seem more presentational to the audience, they are in a possible 11 o'clock position, and it is here that Sondheim allows his bookwriter (James Lapine) to take control of the scene. Although the end of the show is not left completely without music, the composer finally lets the drama itself assume center stage, taking up the space of what would traditionally be musicalized. By more or less discarding the 11 o'clock number and giving its power to the bookwriter, Sondheim demonstrates that the story itself is what needs to be told. He makes the drama a higher priority than keeping the audience entertained. The love scenes become the 11 o'clock complex and bring about the climax of a story that started in the bedroom. When we look at the span of Sondheim's output up to this point, it is interesting to note that his dramaturgy has developed from flashy showstoppers to musicalized psychological journeys to finally—in both *Assassins* and *Passion*—taking music out of these pivotal moments entirely.

## *Road Show* and the Hybrid Number

In his most recent musical, *Road Show*, Sondheim comes up with yet another approach to the musicalization and treatment of the 11 o'clock principle. After following the two entrepreneurial Mizner brothers through various adventures, the plot reaches its peak when they get caught up in a get-rich scheme of selling land to prospective investors in Boca Raton. A long musicalized radio commercial meant to entice investors to buy land in the idyllic Florida location slots itself neatly into the 11 o'clock position. We hear the commercial shilling the investment but eventually interrupted by Arthur Mizner's lover, who announces that the investment is a scam. It is a fairly complicated scene and a unique take on the 11 o'clock principle.

Just before the interruption, however, the ad features a musicalized portion full of patriotism and salesmanship, underscoring the announcer as he offers a great paean to American innovation, freedom, and frontiersmanship. Serving as a fascinating musical backdrop to this very over-the-top speech is music from

Sondheim's "The Flag Song," a number cut from *Assassins* but now known as a stand-alone Sondheim anthem. It is orthodox in its patriotism, and it eschews much of Sondheim's satiric and sardonic attitude. To find it here, almost hidden in the background of this very convincing but purple prose, shows Sondheim coming to terms with sentiment in a way that we rarely see in his work. The fact that the ad is a sham, and the audience knows it, does nothing to take away from the genuine sentiment we find in the announcer's text and the accompanying music; it is here that Sondheim finally plays all his emotional cards, albeit in his usual understated way. There is always a mask. The number also stops the show's singing and movement, focusing the audience on this moment in no uncertain dramatic terms. One might argue that the use of this music is sardonic, that since we as an audience know the ad is a sham, we cannot take it at face value. Yet I believe that this is how Sondheim tends to make some of his sincerest gestures: within a contested space.

What this does in an 11 o'clock position is provide musicalization that, though rousing, is divorced from lyrics and song-like characteristics. Instead, we are given a hybrid of what we found in *Assassins* or *Passion* and in Sondheim's earlier works. Sondheim and bookwriter Weidman share the spotlight, bringing the 11 o'clock principle into play with simultaneous spoken words and music and drawing the musical to a quick close as the Mizner brothers find themselves in the afterlife shortly thereafter. Indeed, the pioneering spirit featured in the ad becomes the final image of the show, as the brothers wonder what is down the road after death.

***

While the 11 o'clock principle gives important shape to musicals, it also plays a critical role in their commercial success. The failure to provide a strong 11 o'clock complex or principle has led to less successful popular and critical responses to Sondheim's musicals (see table 13.1). Although there are myriad reasons why shows succeed or fail, it is interesting to note that the numbers show a correlation between the presence of an 11 o'clock *something* and the number of performances each show has enjoyed in their original productions. Perhaps audiences and critics leave the theater reflecting on the last things they have seen and heard, coloring the way in which shows are assessed. Although there are many ways to define "success" in a musical theater work, scholars have traditionally used the number of performances not only to indicate a show's popular success but to identify the formation of a canon.[26] In this case, such successes as *Company* and *Follies*, for both audiences and critics, are easy to contrast with such obvious flops as *Do I Hear a Waltz?* and *Merrily We Roll Along*.

Although Sondheim has changed the character, structure, and form of the musical through his work, he has always done so in response to musicals of the

**Table 13.1.** Sondheim shows by number of performances

| | | |
|---|---|---|
| 1962 | *A Funny Thing Happened on the Way to the Forum* | 964 |
| 1987 | *Into the Woods* | 765+ |
| 1957 | *West Side Story* | 732+ |
| 1959 | *Gypsy* | 702+ |
| 1970 | *Company* | 690+ |
| 1973 | *A Little Night Music* | 601 |
| 1979 | *Sweeney Todd* | 558+ |
| 1984 | *Sunday in the Park with George* | 540+ |
| 1971 | *Follies* | 522+ |
| 1977 | *Side by Side by Sondheim* | 384 |
| 1994 | *Passion* | 280 |
| 1965 | *Do I Hear a Waltz?* | 220 |
| 1976 | *Pacific Overtures* | 193* |
| 1990 | *Assassins* | 73* |
| 1999 | *Road Show* | >40 |
| 1981 | *Merrily We Roll Along* | 16* |
| 1964 | *Anyone Can Whistle* | 9* |

+ strong 11 o'clock principle; * weak or no 11 o'clock principle.

past, to his training, and to the history of the genre. We can find evidence of this reactivity not only in the pastiche numbers that pepper such musicals as *Follies*, *Company*, and *Assassins* but also in the way he crafts the structures and endings of his works to support the drama. Although current musical theater composers have largely given up on some of the standard Broadway song genres, relying instead on more through-composed and sung-through works, 11 o'clock numbers continue to appear, as with "You Can't Stop the Beat" from *Hairspray* (2002), proving that climax and closure are still important parts of the audience experience. Although there is a large difference in structure and content between more mainstream musicals such as *Hairspray* and Sondheim's works, their related penultimate numbers point to the endurance of certain structural tropes. John Weidman's assertion that "*Something* has to happen there" relates not only to an iconoclast such as his collaborator Sondheim but to all dramatists who attempt to leave the audience with important thoughts, intense emotions, and narrative closure.

# Notes

1. The 11 o'clock number is not defined very well in the literature, except as an aside in many musical theater textbooks and as a passing mention in more general sources. Although the history of the 11 o'clock number and its significance in both literature and practice has yet to be written, this chapter will attempt to explore these numbers in the context of Stephen Sondheim's output, and, it is hoped, will lead to more scholarly attention for this important song type. I thank Lara Housez and Kaye Klapman for their comments on this chapter.

2. Richard Kislan, in his 1980 textbook, identifies a number of song types, including those used by choreographer and director Bob Fosse. Kislan, however, does not cite the source for these songs types, nor do they appear in any of Fosse's writings. They include the "I am" and the "I want" songs. See Richard Kislan, *The Musical: A Look at the American Musical Theater*, rev. ed. (New York: Applause Books, 1995), 228. A ProQuest Historical Newspapers search suggests that the first appearance of the term in the *New York Times* was not until 1977: "Fans Say 'Hello!' to Touring 'Dolly!'," *New York Times*, July 23, 1977, 10.

3. John Weidman, pers. comm. with the author, March 7, 2020.

4. Jack Viertel, *The Secret Life of the American Musical: How Broadway Shows Are Built* (New York: Sarah Crichton Books, 2016), 240.

5. Stephen Sondheim, *Finishing the Hat: Collected Lyrics (1954–1981) with Attendant Comments, Principles, Heresies, Grudges, Whines and Anecdotes* (New York: Knopf, 2011), 135.

6. Earl Wilson, "'Gypsy' Pays off Its Backers," *Hartford Courant*, January 2, 1975: 35. Surprisingly, the ProQuest Historical Newspapers database indicates that this was the first appearance of the term in a U.S. newspaper.

7. Lehman Engel calls it a "late lift." Lehman Engel, *The American Musical Theater*, rev. ed. (New York: MacMillan, 1975), 112–114.

8. Kim H. Kowale, "'Give Me Time: Sondheim, a Clever Maid and 'The Miller's Son,'" *Studies in Musical Theatre* 13, no. 2 (2019): 151–168. Others have designated "Send in the Clowns" as the 11 o'clock spot.

9. Engel, *American Musical Theater*, 114.

10. Bernstein wrote, "If I can write one real, moving American opera that any American can understand (and one that is, notwithstanding, a serious musical work), I shall be a happy man." Written in New York in 1948, quoted in Leonard Bernstein, *Findings* (New York: Knopf, 1982), 129.

11. "The Jewish West Side Story," manuscript in progress.

12. Jeffrey Magee, "Whose Turn Is It? Where *Gypsy's* Finale Came from, and Where It Went," *Studies in Musical Theatre* 13, no. 2 (2019): 117–132.

13. Viertel, *Secret Life*, 240.

14. Walter Kerr, quoted in Stacy Wolf, *A Problem Like Maria* (Ann Arbor: University of Michigan Press, 2002), 117.

15. I thank W. Anthony Sheppard for pointing out that this resembles in many ways Lucia's mad scene in Donizetti's opera *Lucia di Lammermoor*.

16. It was not until the 1970s that this moment was played in such a way that Rose imagines the applause is for her. My thanks to Lara Housez for pointing this out to me.

17. I am indebted to Ashley M. Pribyl, who notes that in the archival sources, the creators argued about whether this was the 11 o'clock number. Personal communication to the author, March 7, 2020.

18. Stephen Banfield notes that "Ladies Who Lunch" was originally positioned earlier in the musical, but was later moved. Stephen Banfield, *Sondheim's Broadway Musicals* (Ann Arbor: University of Michigan Press, 1993), 169.

19. Sondheim, *Finishing the Hat*, 193.

20. *Follies in Concert*, Avery Fisher Hall at Lincoln Center, 1985. Great Performances, Season 14, Episode 10. Aired 14 March, 1986.

21. Stephen Banfield also puts these numbers together in his chart of the follies that are explored in this part of the show. Banfield, *Sondheim's Broadway Musicals*, 191.

22. I thank Lara Housez for informing me that this harkens back to the Minstrel Show in Weill and Lerner's *Love Life*, which Sondheim saw as a young man.

23. Weidman discussed this topic in his paper on *Assassins* delivered at the March 2020 Williams College Sondheim symposium.

24. Raymond Knapp and Zelda Knapp, "Going Postal: Collapsing Time and Space Through Sung Letters in Broadway Musicals," *Studies in Musical Theatre* 11, no. 3 (2017): 233–246.

25. Raymond Knapp, *The American Musical and the Performance of Personal Identity* (Princeton: Princeton University Press, 2006), 303–308.

26. Geoffrey Block, "The Broadway Canon from *Show Boat* to *West Side Story* and the European Operatic Ideal," *Journal of Musicology* 11, no. 4 (Autumn 1993): 525–544.

# 14

# Finishing the Line

## Wit, Rhythm, and Rhyme in Sondheim

*W. Anthony Sheppard*

Over the decades, when Sondheim has spoken or written about his work he has repeatedly commented on one subject in particular: his use of rhyme. Looking back in 2010, he noted that "finding appropriate rhymes that haven't been used before is one of the few pleasures of lyric writing, an occupation consisting chiefly of tedious list-making and frustration."[1] He has both celebrated and been quite critical of his own rhyming and that of other lyricists.[2] I am interested in how poetic and musical rhythm and rhyme shape meaning in Sondheim's work, particularly in songs that feature surprising and witty line completion. As Stephen Banfield has noted:

> Even the conventional co-ordinates of rhymes and cadences, basic matter in song, are an undeveloped object of study. Do they accomplish the same and therefore redundant thing in their respective media? We hear a rhyme, on the one hand, as same sound/different sound; and on the other, as similar sound/ different sense. To a certain extent, these distinctions are simply reinforced when rhyme is accompanied by melodic cadence, as it is in basic lyrical genres like the nursery song (we actually call it "nursery rhyme").[3]

Though Sondheim's rhyming skills are consistently celebrated, the relation between his lyrical and musical rhyming remains worthy of study and proves to be not entirely straightforward.

In this chapter I first consider Sondheim's professed rules for rhyming and test the extent to which he has deviated from his own strictures. I then investigate sources of influence that shaped his use of rhyme and offer examples illustrating his range, exploring in detail how music may highlight rhyme, reinforce off-rhymes, and respond to contradictory lyrical meanings while maintaining coherence and flow. Pairs of words that Sondheim himself would not acknowledge as true rhymes are often made to rhyme through his musical setting—we experience such moments as analogous to rhyme, despite the rules. I find that our interpretation of witty rhythmic rhyming in terms of characterization depends

W. Anthony Sheppard, *Finishing the Line* In: *Sondheim in Our Time and His*. Edited by: W. Anthony Sheppard, Oxford University Press. © Oxford University Press 2022. DOI: 10.1093/oso/9780197603192.003.0015

predominately on the perceived diegetic status of that rhyming in our experience of a performance. These reflections lead to two culminating examples: a case of extreme musical/lyrical rhyming followed by an example of phantom rhyming, in which rhyme appears to have been deliberately avoided, thereby attracting our interpretive attention all the more. Finally, I touch briefly on the influence of Sondheim's rhyming on later songwriters in American musical theater.

## Sondheim's Rules for Rhymes, and Their Origins

In 1971 Sondheim delivered a lecture titled "Theater Lyrics" that was subsequently published and that, nearly four decades later, he drew on extensively for commentary in the two-volume publication of his collected lyrics.[4] Sondheim describes his song writing process as end-driven, placing emphasis on the final line in a song and claiming that he tends to "write backwards," nailing down the punch line first in the lyrics. As he put it: "Of course, I love twists, I love punchy last lines."[5] Sondheim has repeatedly offered a rather strict definition of true or perfect rhymes and has emphasized that perfect rhymes are essential for successful lyrics. He prefaced the first volume of his collection of lyrics with an introductory essay titled "Rhyme and Its Reasons" in which he once again laid out his dictums. For example, he stated:

> A perfect rhyme snaps the word, and with it the thought, vigorously into place, rendering it easily intelligible; a near rhyme blurs it. . . . An identity makes the word clear, but blunts the line's snap because the accented sound is not a fresh one. And both identities and false rhymes are death on wit. . . . Jokes work best with perfect rhymes.[6]

As Sondheim notes, to qualify as a perfect rhyme, the final accented syllables of multiple words must sound alike but must start with different accented consonant sounds. He does allow that identities, repeating the same word at the end of several lines, can effectively intensify feeling.[7] Likewise, though he tends to speak disparagingly of any reliance on assonance, consonance, and alliteration, he has employed all of these devices himself.[8] Note, for instance, the bumptious *b*s in the lines "You steal below, / And far behind / At the edge of day, / The bong of the bell of the buoy in the bay, / And the boat and the boy / And the bride are away!" from "Pretty Little Picture" in *A Funny Thing Happened on the Way to the Forum* (1962); or the sound of Cinderella stuck on *st* in "On the Steps of the Palace" (*Into the Woods*, 1987): "There's a lot that's at stake, / But you've stalled long enough, / 'Cause you're still standing stuck / In the stuff on the steps." Sondheim's study of the art of rhyming is frequently rather fine-grained. For example, he notes that rhymes with differently spelled endings are "more interesting than those which are spelled the same," and he repeatedly follows this guideline himself, as, for example, in the rhyming of "was"/"does"/"buzz" in "Children and Art" from *Sunday in the Park with George* (1984), "run"/"won"/"done" in the opening number of *Pacific Overtures* (1976), "dailies"/"ukuleles" in "I'm Still Here" (*Follies*, 1971), and "It's got flash! It's got flair! / It's got spectacle to spare! / People come from everywhere" in "Hades" (*The Frogs*, 1974).[9]

There has long been an evident tension in Sondheim's views concerning rhyme between a stated need to achieve intelligibility and avoid calling attention to the lyricist's craft versus an artistic desire to satisfy his love of puzzles and to express his wit through surprising word choice and clever rhymes.[10] There are numerous examples in his lyrics where reason takes a backseat to rhyme, where dramatic progress is put on hold, as though Sondheim the lyrical puzzler occasionally decides that "weighty affairs will just have to wait." Sondheim's reflections on rhyme are particularly instructive here:

> You try to make your rhyming seem fresh but inevitable . . . you try for surprise but not so wrenching that the listener loses the sense of the line. . . . The function of a rhyme is to point up the word that rhymes. . . . Also, rhyme helps shape the music, it helps the listener hear what the shape of the music is. Inner rhymes, which are fun to work out if you have a puzzle mind, have one essential function, which is to speed the line along.[11]

Here Sondheim points to the way rhyme influences our perception of the music, its melody and tempo, but I will also note examples in which the music shapes our experience of poetic rhymes.

Sondheim has consistently celebrated Clement Wood's 1936 rhyming dictionary as an essential tool for his art. Reading Wood's introduction reveals that this source directly shaped Sondheim's broader views of rhyming and its rules.[12] In fact, just as Sondheim found the strict, rule-based approach to music theory and composition of his Williams College professor Robert Barrow to be particularly congenial and influential, he was also enamored of Wood's narrow definitions for poetic rhyme. Indeed, some passages in Sondheim's several published statements about rhyme are clearly modeled on Wood, even in such details as noting that the word "month" has no real rhyme in English.[13]

We can go further in tracing the impact of Wood's dictionary on Sondheim's creative process, almost following his page turnings as he consulted this source.[14] For example, the song "Putting It Together" from *Sunday in the Park with George* displays an astonishing number of rhymes involving variations of the "SH'un" sound. Sondheim, noting a general overuse of this rhyme by lyricists, explains that the density of "SH'un" rhymes in these lyrics expresses George's increasing

394    W. ANTHONY SHEPPARD

tension and his attempt at an "intellectual rationale for his own glibness as an artist."[15] In this number, George, the contemporary artist, is attempting to keep his cool while recounting all of the cocktail party stratagems he is obligated to pursue in order to support his art. Considering just the words rhyming with "ĬSH'un" we find 162 options listed in Wood, all but three of which appear on page 424. Sondheim selected thirteen different words with this sound that he used a total of twenty-four times in the song, with the word "commission" appearing, not surprisingly, the most at five times. The word "suspicion" appears only once as the final word with this sound in the song. Most of the other 149 words in Wood clearly would not have worked for these lyrics or, in the case of such words as "recomposition" and "reposition," were perhaps too close to ones Sondheim did select. Yet there are at least nine words Sondheim passed over that, without much effort, I imagine might have led to other lines for George to sing such as:

> Always keep the focus on your mission!
> You must be the ultimate tactician,
> And be prepared for repetition,
> Letting them display their erudition.
> As you smile—indicating your submission,
> Avoiding any fatal omission—
> Remember, George, you must have funding for
> Electricians and need those acquisitions.
> Don't forget this is your big audition!

Though Sondheim consistently cites the dominant influence of his mentor Oscar Hammerstein II on his approach to creating musical theater, Hammerstein's views concerning rhyme were certainly not determinative for the younger lyricist. As Geoffrey Block has noted, in 1949 Hammerstein proclaimed a rather stringent approach to rhyme:

> There should not be too many rhymes. In fact, a rhyme should appear only where it is absolutely demanded to keep the pattern of the music. If a listener is made rhyme-conscious, his interest may be diverted from the story of the song.[16]

The phrase "keep the pattern of the music" might suggest a song writing process in which the music is composed first. In Sondheim's case, both in his collaborations with composers as a lyricist and as a solo songwriter, musical and lyrical patterning has emerged from a more coeval process.[17] Sondheim has frequently paraphrased Hammerstein's warnings regarding rhyme, but he almost entirely ignored this lesson even in his earliest works such as the 1954 *Saturday*

*Night,* a rhyme-infested musical that consistently employs clear rhyme patterns and a flexible approach to rhyming (as in "pure"/"sure"/"mature" in "Love's a Bond") and that demonstrates Sondheim's early interest in variant spellings in rhyming (as with "fox"/"stocks," "rye"/"cry"/"buy," and "heard"/"bird"/"preferred" from the same number). In the sophomoric song "Exhibit A" the rhyme is rather over-the-top and the double entendres could not be more blatant as a male character falsely claims to his buddies that he knows exactly how to trap and seduce (read: date rape) a girl with music and drink, getting her "supine" by employing the "fragrance of new pine" and coming out "on top" by putting "every prop in its proper place."

In 1949 Hammerstein had acknowledged that he employed a rhyming dictionary, but, unlike Sondheim, claimed he turned to it only rarely:

> A rhyming dictionary, however, should be used as a supplement to one's own ingenuity, and not a substitute for it. I do not open mine until I have exhausted my own memory and invention of rhymes for a word. Attractive combinations of words to make double and triple rhymes are not found in rhyming dictionaries, nor are modern words or colloquialisms which can be used with humorous effect in a song. A rhyming dictionary is of little use and may, in fact, be a handicap when one is writing a song which makes a feature of rhyming. If you would achieve the rhyming grace and facility of W. S. Gilbert or Lorenz Hart, my advice would be never to open a rhyming dictionary. Don't even own one.[18]

In reference to his more "primitive type of lyric," Hammerstein modestly pointed to his own "shortcomings as a wit and rhymester" and declared that a "rhyme should be unassertive, never standing out too noticeably."[19] In his approach to rhyme, as in other aspects of his work, Sondheim clearly swerved far away from the model of his surrogate father figure.

Considering his career as a whole, it appears that Sondheim most blatantly deviates from Hammerstein and breaks his own rules for rhyming in works involving pastiche of earlier song styles, as in *Assassins* (1990) in particular, where John Weidman's book prompted Sondheim to travel stylistically throughout American vernacular music history. Of course, Sondheim's wit and dexterity with trick rhymes is evident throughout his career, and it is tempting to revel in examples such as the extreme verbal efficiency of Jack's Mother's declaration "We've no time to sit and dither / while her withers wither with her" in reference to Jack's pathetic cow in *Into the Woods,* a line in which Sondheim milks three different meanings out of the same combination of letters (w-i-t-h-e-r), not to mention having the syllable "her" appear five times in a ten-syllable span. Or, as any opera buff will appreciate, the related quadruple syllabic echo in the line "Leontyne Price to sing her / *Meistersinger*" from "Bobby and Jackie and Jack" in *Merrily We Roll Along* (1981). Opening numbers tend to inspire Sondheim to pen witty rhymes, as in the "Beautiful Girls" lines "Faced with these Loreleis, / What man can moralize?" from *Follies*. Clever rhyming was even referenced directly in the original opening number for this show, "Bring on the Girls," which reflexively pointed to rhyming wit with the lines "Poets have tried, but try as they will, / They waste their time / Painting them in in- / Ternal rhyme," with "them in in-" rhymed with the word "feminine," appearing four lines earlier—the song does indeed feature some internal rhyming.[20]

The most compelling model for Sondheim's rhyming is found in the lyrics of Cole Porter, which, as Sondheim notes, exhibit an "ostentatious verbal dexterity."[21] As Steve Swayne has put it, Porter "is Sondheim's closest kindred spirit."[22] Specific song pairs support this claim. For example, the sardonic "Could I Leave You?" from *Follies*, an anti-love song ironically set as a waltz, appears to be wittily modeled on Porter's "Do I Love You?": Both songs have a question-and-answer setup in the lyrics, and both emphasize an F–G gesture in the melody with the G sustained in a short-long rhythm. As David Savran has noted, both songwriters revel in composing list songs in which rhyme makes us desire the next witty line ending again and again.[23] Sondheim has warned against the temptations of the list song form, disparaging some of his own but also admitting that he loves the game.[24] He has also acknowledged the influence of Porter on his work, indicating that his compositional process is similar to Porter's. Sondheim has cited Porter as saying that he "always wrote knowing exactly what the rhythmic structure of the melody was, even if he didn't know the notes," and Sondheim reports that this is how he proceeds as well: "I don't worry so much about the melodic line until I start to get the melodic rhythm of a lyric, so that the two will go together."[25] Furthermore, in an interview with Mark Eden Horowitz, Sondheim pointed to similarities between his songs and Porter's, noting that both have "little surprises scattered throughout" and that Porter's melodic line "keeps spinning it out in little tiny variations."[26] Despite his admiration for Porter, Sondheim has also expressed some ambivalence and has suggested that Porter's success relied less on his "facility with words" than on the fact that Porter "*believed* what he wrote," the one trait that Sondheim says Hammerstein exhibited as well.[27]

## Whose Mind? Rhyme and Diegesis

Sondheim's most interesting comments about rhyme tend to arise when he considers the impact of rhyming on the veracity of characterization and dramatic situation. For example, he has explained that he achieved a "conversational" and natural quality in the opening love scene of *Passion* (1994) by avoiding rhyme and regular rhythm in the lyrics, implying that rhyming would have pushed this scene toward the "bombast" of opera—but he observes that he "sprinkled the lyric with occasional rhymes" in order to avoid a recitative style that he finds anathema.[28] In contrast, he explains that Fosca's dictation to Giorgio of a letter addressed to herself in scene 7 called for "regular rhythms and neat rhymes," given that it was "calculated" and "crafty" on her part.[29] I note that the musical setting of these lyrics consistently calls our attention to the lyrical rhyming through musical repetition. Sondheim neglects to mention, however, that this scene appears to jumpstart rhyme for the rest of the show, including the dialogue for scene 8, in Clara's presumably heartfelt "Sunrise" letter to Giorgio in scene 10 (with "swear"/"stare"/"hair"/"unaware"/"bear" all set to the same pitch), and even in Giorgio's angry outburst at Fosca in scene 10, which we might reasonably assume would call for "natural," unrhymed and rhythmically irregular lyrics. Sondheim does reserve some of his most impressive rhyming for the vile, calculating seducer Ludovic, who delivers entwined rhyme chains, assonances, and alliteration, with expanding upward intervals setting up the sting of "rent," in the scene 9 flashback: "Well, let us part by mutual consent / And be content. / And so, good luck and goodbye, I must go. / Oh, and yes, we haven't paid the rent / Since July / Just so you know."

Sondheim stated in 1971 that "rhyme always implies education and mind working, and the more rhymes the sharper the mind."[30] To a certain extent, this proves true in his use of rhyme for characterization. For example, Fredrik, a lawyer, displays his brilliance in "Now" in *A Little Night Music* (1973) through tightly rhymed lines, though the tumbling eighth-note sequences in the relentless 6/8 meter indicate the frustrating and ridiculous situation he finds himself trapped in. The corollary of Sondheim's premise is that a lyricist should avoid extensive rhyming for characters of less brilliance. He explains that this holds true for Jack's song "I Guess This Is Goodbye" in *Into the Woods*, which he refers to as the only song he has written that entirely lacks rhyme: "It seemed fitting that innocent, empty-headed Jack be so dimwitted that he couldn't even rhyme. But it's not so easy to make nonrhymes work when the music rhymes—that is when the music has square and matching rhythms, as this ditty deliberately does."[31] Sondheim has repeatedly offered warnings about the use of rhyme in relation to characterization: "Unless a character is hyperarticulate for a reason (panic, defensiveness, exuberance, etc.), cleverly rhymed logorrheic patter draws attention to the lyricist, not the character."[32] Yet he has been a bit contradictory on this point, explaining, for example, that he avoided rhymes in "Getting Married Today" from *Company* in order to express Amy's hysteria but that the song switches to "rhyme with a vengeance" in order to avoid boredom and to represent another kind of dementia that she exhibits.[33] Sondheim has been more consistent in expressing his concern—one that echoes Hammerstein—that witty rhymes distract the audience from the drama and the characters and draw attention instead to the lyricist's sweat. Of course, this assumes a rather straightforward reception of lyrics by an audience.

In the course of performance, who does the audience deem responsible for rhyming? Or, better, where does an audience locate the source of lyrical wit? Does the audience assume that the character is aware of their rhyming or that the author is rhyming as a ventriloquist through the character and, thus, through the performer? I suggest that we perceive some rhyming as diegetic and other instances as nondiegetic. In some songs, particularly list songs, rhyme is framed diegetically; the characters know they are rhyming and, in such duets as Sweeney Todd's and Mrs. Lovett's "A Little Priest," are engaged in a conscious rhyming competition. This would also seem to describe how we experience a live performance of some of Porter's duet list songs such as "You're the Top" and "Friendship." In certain cases, characters even pause to consider what word to choose to end a line with or they seem knowingly to avoid a rhyme word that might land them in trouble. Sondheim's comments on Dot's rhymes in the title number "Sunday in the Park with George" suggest that this character has agency in her rhyming, that she is not only conscious of rhyming but of the register of her rhymes: "Dot, philosophizing, would not think in perfect rhymes but in imperfect ones if she were to try rhyming long words at all—which she would in her attempt to intellectualize the situation."[34] Similarly, Sondheim refers to the "calculated regularity of rhythm and rhyme" as revealing Mrs. Lovett's conniving in "Poor Thing" (*Sweeney Todd*, 1979), though we may well ask whether the audience credited Lovett, Angela Lansbury, or Sondheim with this cunning wit.[35]

I suspect that in many cases, audience members attribute the source of wit to the performers rather than to the author or character. The more virtuosic the rhyming, particularly in patter singing, the more likely our focus is directed to the seeming verbal wit of the performer. Some performers, of course, may deliberately adopt a bit of Brechtian alienation in their delivery in order to lay claim to the creative rhyming. I suspect that when Mandy Patinkin vocalized all of those "SH'un" rhymes in "Putting It Together" or when Bernadette Peters performed the "Greens" rap in *Into the Woods* the audience, consciously or not, felt that the performers were witty and verbally dexterous, rather than that "George" or "the Witch" or even Sondheim should be credited in those particular moments.

In light of his numerous published statements about his own rhyming, Sondheim appears both proud and embarrassed (one might say he is "regretful-happy") concerning his virtuosic rhyming. Of course, in the two-volume publication of his lyrics he is commenting as a lyricist and does not focus much on music's role in how rhymes are perceived, how his musical rhythms allow his rhyming to be appreciated. It is to the role of musical setting, particularly in terms of melodic shape and rhythm, in framing our experience of poetic rhyme that I now turn.

## The Roles of Musical Rhyming

First, what exactly is a musical rhyme? A strict definition might insist on two musical phrase endings that conclude with the same melodic gesture, with the exact same pitches and rhythmic values. Or, perhaps, that case would be equivalent to a verbal identity, and only a sequential repetition of a motive or phrase-ending gestures of similar rhythmic proportions and intervallic patterns would count. In discussing Sondheim's songs, I will refer to both exact and inexact repetition of musical gestures or motives as a form of rhyming, equivalent to poetic rhyme.

I have investigated the musical setting of lyrical rhymes throughout Sondheim's oeuvre in an attempt to arrive at some general observations. Sondheim typically reinforces lyrical rhymes with musical rhymes, repeating an exact musical gesture at pitch or slightly altering the gesture in the repetition to respond to or intensify lyrical meaning. In the simplest form, each rhyming word is set to the same pitch, as in "Bobby and Jackie and Jack" (*Merrily We Roll Along*) in which "the pill"/"Brazil"/"to fill" are each sung on an A♭–G, eighth–dotted quarter motive and "screaming"/"in"/"win" all land on C, or as in this show's title number, in which "it clear"/"of gear"/"from here" are all set with the same exact musical gesture. The musical pastiche of older styles encountered throughout *Follies* led Sondheim to emphasize rhyme, even including a good deal of triple rhymes as in "Don't Look at Me" where "the press"/"a mess"/"nevertheless" are all sung on D–F, and "eerie"/"party"/"dreary" are heard with an F♯–B motive, reinforcing these rhymes. In other cases, the rhymes are emphasized by the same melodic gestures, though at different pitches, as in "Beautiful Girls," "Ah! Paris!," "I'm Still Here," and "Broadway Baby." Repeating the same motive in a quadruple rhyme frequently intensifies meaning in Sondheim's songs, as in "Waiting for the Girls Upstairs" from *Follies*, in which "great"/"date"/"late"/"wait" each receive the same pitch and extended note value, making the listener wait for a melodic change. Direct musical and lyrical parallelism can also become monotonous for comic effect as, to take but one example, when in *The Frogs* Xanthias complains about traveling and sings a fifth leap from A to E each time to "the grippe"/"my hip"/"my lip"/"the pip," provoking Dionysus to declare: "You can stop rhyming right there." A similar case of diegetic rhyming supported musically is heard in "A Little Priest" when Mrs. Lovett attempts to suggest her diabolical plan to Sweeney as she sings "Think of it as thrift, / as a gift . . . / If you get my drift," repeating the pitch B with each rhyme as though to nudge the idea into his head, and again with the triple repetition of the word "it" on the pitch D, leading Todd finally to get it.[36] In the case of "Another 100 People" from *Company*, the lyrical emphasis on incessant linear growth is matched by a musical intensification as the rhyming words "vain"/"rain"/"explain" march up the scale (A♭–B♭–C) with increasing note durations. In other cases, rhythm highlights rhyming rather than pitch. This is true of the sixfold rhyme on the syllables "ies/ize" in "Maybe They're Magic" (*Into the Woods*) as the Baker's Wife sings the same three-note rhythm, and it is also frequently the case throughout *Assassins*.

Music repeatedly helps rhymes go down more easily in Sondheim, blending lyrical near rhymes, convincing the listener of the legitimacy of surprising line conclusions, and providing unification for rhymes with contradictory meanings. In fact, Sondheim's musical setting frequently allows words that sound only somewhat similar to function as rhymes in our experience of his songs in performance. Though Clement Wood clearly would not have approved, Sondheim rhymes "the news"/"to lose"/"abuse" in "Bring Me My Bride" from *Forum* and seems to acknowledge the imperfect rhyme by setting each word to different pitches but each with a short-long rhythm and punctuated by the same pitch in the accompaniment. Though in hearing a song we may briefly pause to ponder rhymes involving spelling variation, a rhymed musical setting of the words moves us forward to the next line, as in the exact repetition of the F–G gesture for "coming"/"drumming" and "armor"/"farmer" in the *Anyone Can Whistle* (1964) number "There Won't Be Trumpets." In "The Little Things You Do Together" from *Company*, the musical sequences lead the ear to accept the shocking third rhyme each time: "share together/swear together/wear together," "concerts you enjoy together/Neighbors you annoy together/Children you destroy together," sharing "winks"/"drinks"/"kinks" together; "shop together/Cigarettes you stop together/Clothing that you swap together," and "It's people that you hate together/Bait together/Date together." The fact that the musical sequences allow each third rhyming word of deviant or caustic surprise to slide right by, implying that all three rhyming words are equivalent, makes the song all the naughtier and, of course, all the funnier.[37] In "Sorry-Grateful," lyrical and musical rhymes poignantly hold together the contradictory descriptions of marriage, suggesting that rhyme reveals truth at the end of the line. In such cases, where lyrical rhyme yokes together contradictory terms, Sondheim often employs musical gestures that match in rhythm and intervallic pattern but that move in opposite melodic directions, as in "Comedy Tonight" (from *Forum*) and "A Weekend in the Country" (*A Little Night Music*).[38] In the case of "Comedy Tonight," "familiar"/ "peculiar" and "appealing"/"appalling" rhyme musically in opposite directions, starting and landing on the same pitches an octave apart and set with the same rhythms. This song eventually devolves into a list of rhymes, with rhyme taking over the music and lyrics entirely and the melody becoming increasingly stuck on the pitch D.

Actually, Sondheim's melodic style typically tends toward tight repetition, to the sound of being stuck. Swayne aptly refers to Sondheim's "remarkable degree of motivic compression" and notes that "the marvel of Sondheim's melodies is their close motivic unfolding rather than their expansive tunefulness."[39] Many of Sondheim's melodies rock between a couple of pitches or consist of repeated melodic fragments, slightly varied, that remain within a narrow range. Perhaps this melodic style leads to an even greater emphasis on rhyme, as rhyme is a tight repetition of sound and gesture. Furthermore, his motivic repetition and use of limited melodic material is intensely expressive for characters who feel alone and stuck without a clear sense of forward direction in life. This proves equally true for female characters ("Every Day a Little Death" and "Not a Day Goes By") and male characters ("Being Alive" and "Lesson #8").[40] I know of no better example of an intricate entangling of musical and poetic sound and sense than that encountered in "Getting Married Today," a song expressing a woman's hysterical reaction to being trapped in the social ritual of a church wedding.[41]

The lyrics of "Getting Married Today" are densely packed with poetic sound: end and internal rhyme, alliteration, assonance, consonance, repeated words, and so on. In table 14.1 I have attempted to use colors, font, and underlining to indicate the intricate connections of verbal sounds—pushing my analysis beyond rhyme, indicating every repetition of verbal sounds. In performance, this excerpt goes by in a mere twelve seconds. The excerpt consists of fifty syllables, forty-four words, and one surprising cultural allusion (to *Uncle Tom's Cabin*). We hear nine "I" sounds (only one of which is the word "I"). Some of the rhyming in this passage is exceedingly clever. Surely, Cole Porter would have gasped with delight on hearing the triple rhyme "perhaps"/"collapse"/"apse."

How does the musical setting respond to these poetic sounds? The added letters in table 14.1 refer to melodic pitches and I have used colors and capitalization to highlight corresponding points, spots where pitch and rhyme line up closely. The downbeats consistently emphasize the strong rhymes. "Shoes" is the only word falling on a downbeat without a rhyme, though perhaps it very distantly echoes "HU-man" which appeared at this spot in the first stanza of the song. I use the number 2 to indicate quarter notes, as all the other syllables are

Table 14.1. The density of poetic sound in "Getting Married Today"

heard with running eighth notes. Note how the long values, the quarter notes, fall on major rhymes. Almost all the rhymes and assonances in the first half of this stanza receive the pitch G and in the second half fall melodically on A. (In general, Amy's melody hammers out the rhymes in this song through pitch repetition.) Of course, Sondheim's tight motivic melodic style accounts in part for this synchronicity between rhyme and pitch. Finally, I should note that this particularly intricate musical/poetic sixteen-bar section is heard as part of a double song with Paul, her betrothed, who sings to a separate melody.[42] (See example 14.1.)

**Example 14.1.** Amy's and Paul's double song in "Getting Married Today,"
Stephen Sondheim, *The Complete "Company" Collection* (Milwaukee: Hal Leonard,
2009), 48–50.

## Hearing Phantom Rhymes

What happens when an expected rhyme fails to arrive at the end of the line? Sondheim has referred to the value of sometimes not rhyming "even when the music calls for it."[43] He has explained that by avoiding a conclusive rhyme he is able to "intensify the emotion at the end of a song" and thereby make it "seem as if the character's feelings are getting out of hand, since rhymes, being verbally self-conscious, imply control."[44] The implication in such statements is that Sondheim occasionally deliberately decides to avoid a poetic rhyme despite having composed a musical one. These surprising moments in his songs often prove poignant or otherwise significant. I will introduce two such moments that are perhaps more subtle than other potential examples but that are no less meaningful in their implications.

One of the most common rhymes in musical theater lyrics, including in Sondheim's works, is "life" with "wife."[45] Sondheim has declared that "two of the hardest words in the language to rhyme are life and love."[46] Indeed, Clement Wood lists only twelve words for the "ĪF" sound, and he even cheats a bit since, in addition to "life" and "wife," three of the words he lists end with the syllable "wife" and two end with "life," so legitimately Wood only lists "bowie-knife," "fife," "knife," "rife," and "strife" as other potential rhymes for this sound.[47] Though I will forgo tracing all of the "wife"/"life" rhymes and their musical settings in Sondheim's works here, I can report that Sondheim uses this particular rhyme a great many times (very often with a negative twist), and he almost always supports it with a musical rhyme.[48]

In the number "No Life" from *Sunday in the Park with George,* however, the rhyme seems conspicuously avoided as Jules and his *wife* Yvonne criticize George's painting and seem to compete with each other in finishing their lines with biting rhymes. They are playing the poet and they know it, creating rhymes rather mechanically. On one hand, Sondheim supports their rhyming with melodic rhymes. For example, for the critical barb "Just density / Without intensity" the rhyme is highlighted by repeating the same three pitches. On the other, Sondheim seems to undercut or mock his own characters here by consistently juxtaposing their chromatic melodic lines dissonantly with the accompanying harmony. In fact, I suspect Sondheim modeled this number on another satirical scene involving the critical appraisal of objects for potential purchase: the auction scene in Stravinsky's *The Rake's Progress,* an opera that Sondheim has commented on several times in print.[49] Both numbers are in 3/4, feature dissonance (more so in Sondheim), have a low C as the first pitch in the accompaniment (C and B sounding simultaneously in Sondheim, successively in Stravinsky) and a G–A clash on the downbeat of bar two, and have an embedded B–A–G descending melodic structure; moreover, the words "go high" are set with a G–G octave upward leap in *The Rake,* and "no life" is set with a G–G octave

**Example 14.2.** The auction scene, reh. 62–65, Igor Stravinsky, *The Rake's Progress* (London: Boosey & Hawkes, 1951), 184.

fall in *Sunday*. (Compare examples 14.2 and 14.3.) Perhaps the most audible similarities are the vocal interjections such as "mmm" and "Ahh" in *Sunday* and "hmm!" and "poof!" in *The Rake*. I should note that the last item auctioned off in the Stravinsky scene is Baba the Turk, the rake's *wife*, and that both Stravinsky's

**Example 14.3.** "No Life," mm. 1–12, Stephen Sondheim, *Sunday in the Park with George* (New York: Rilting Music, Inc., 1987), 18–19.

opera and Sondheim's musical were inspired by works of art that each composer encountered at the Art Institute of Chicago.

Jules and Yvonne conclude their critique of George and his art with the lines "All mind, no heart. / No life in his art. / No life in his life! / No—Life." Before that final word "life" they "giggle and chortle." Surely, it is rather lame of them to repeat the word "life" four times here and to follow their pregnant pause with the seventh utterance of this word in this short song rather than with the obvious expected concluding rhyming word, "wife." We hear this phantom word in our heads or, at least, Jules and Yvonne appear to. Indeed, in their giggles I assume they are thinking about George's most obvious personal flaw: his inability to sustain a relationship, sacrificing his life for his art and losing Dot in the first act. This failure to secure a wife is framed as a genetic flaw, for in the second act, his great-grandson, also an artist named George, is divorced and laments his lack of a family. This phantom rhyme is, to my mind, hugely significant, drawing pointed attention to the bourgeois proposition that "life" equals "wife" by avoiding this conventional rhyme at the very end of the song.

**Example 14.4.**  "Poor Baby," mm. 5–10, Stephen Sondheim, *The Complete "Company" Collection* (Milwaukee: Hal Leonard, 2009), 76.

I cannot resist briefly raising a directly related second instance of a resonant phantom rhyme in *Company*, another musical focused on a lone male character lacking a significant other in his life and with rather clear autobiographical implications. In "Poor Baby," the several wife characters lament to their husbands about Bobby's loner status: "There's no one . . . In his life . . . Robert ought to have a woman." Here we even get the "w" sound but Sondheim avoids the "wife" rhyme; indeed, rhyming does not begin in this song until after "woman" is sung. The one-syllable word "wife" set to the pitch A♭ would have sounded like a natural climax to this melodic line. Instead, we get the rather moody setting of "wo-man" with its descending minor third interval (see example 14.4).

## Further Down the Line: Sondheim's Influence

I began this chapter by considering the possible influences that shaped Sondheim's approach to lyrical and musical rhyming. I now conclude by very briefly pointing further down the line to suggest just how influential Sondheim has been. Numerous lyricists and composers active in Broadway over the course of the past fifty years have cited him as a major influence. For example, William Finn has repeatedly mentioned the impact of Sondheim on his own work, and Stephen Schwartz has testified that Sondheim's early musicals were a major early influence on him and that he has found "the precision and deft wordplay of [Sondheim's] lyrics" particularly inspiring throughout his own career.[50] I will briefly note two works that reveal the influence of Sondheim's lyrical and musical rhyming and for which Sondheim served as a direct mentor.

Exhibit A: It is well known that Sondheim mentored Jonathan Larson, as is clear in several numbers in the 1996 musical *Rent*. Even the opening voice machine messages in *Rent* seem an allusion to the opening of Sondheim's *Company*. The opening numbers, "Tune Up" and "Rent," also resemble several complex multipart Sondheim numbers that efficiently cover much ground in terms of character and plot introduction (*Into the Woods* offers one example). Some of Larson's lyrics strike me as Sondheim-like in terms of their wit and repetition of verbal sound. Consider all the "īne" sounds (which all land on the pitch G) and the "-ead" rhymes throughout the second lyric in the title number ("Headlines, bread lines blow my mind and now this dead line; eviction or pay"), not to mention the "fiction"/"eviction" and "day"/"pay" rhymes that tie the opening lines neatly together. This intricate rhyme design is maintained in verses 2 and 4. Larson's "You light up a mean blaze / with posters and screen plays" in verse 3 reminds me of Sondheim's love for multiple rhymes with different spellings. And then, in the show-stopping list number "La vie boheme," we get seven "SH'un" sounds in the following feisty passage that might remind us of George's frustration in "Putting it Together":

> To loving tension, no pension
> To more than one dimension
> To starving for attention
> Hating convention
> Hating pretension
> Not to mention, of course
> Hating dear old Mom and Dad

And Larson clearly drew on the wit and attitude of both Sondheim and Porter in the lines

> To hand-crafted beers made in local breweries
> To yoga, to yogurt, to rice and beans and cheese
> To leather, to dildos, to curry vindaloo
> To huevos rancheros and Maya Angelou

And then comes the shout-out:

> Compassion, to fashion, to passion
> When it's new
> To Sontag
> To Sondheim
> To anything taboo

Larson had already paid homage to Sondheim in *Tick, Tick . . . Boom!* (1990/2001). This autobiographical musical, originally performed solo by Larson himself, explores the anxiety of an aspiring Broadway composer as he faces his thirtieth birthday, a parallel with Robert's situation in *Company* as he faces the prospect of a surprise party in celebration of his thirty-fifth. Larson's references to Sondheim in this show are also more explicit, both in the number "Sunday"—which offers a reworking of the title number in *Sunday in the Park with George*, now from the perspective of a waiter working in a diner, rather than of a painter painting in a park—and in the use of Sondheim's pre-recorded voice in an encouraging phone call that the protagonist receives late in the show.

Exhibit B: Lin-Manuel Miranda has repeatedly acknowledged the mentoring he received when writing *Hamilton* (2015) from both Sondheim and John Weidman. The prologue to *Hamilton* is modeled on the opening of *Sweeney*

*Todd*, with each character singing about the title character before the title character speaks. As with Larson's opening number in *Rent*, the opening number in *Hamilton* also recalls the efficiency of *Company* and *Into the Woods* in setting up the relationships between the characters. Miranda's number "The Room Where It Happens," which he refers to as a *Rashomon* sequence, is similar in subject to the powerful Sondheim-Weidman number "Someone in a Tree" from *Pacific Overtures*.[51] Like Sondheim, Miranda creates extended numbers that efficiently introduce a lot of plot information and characters. Also like Sondheim, and in response to the older lyricist-composer's direct encouragement, Miranda includes, in addition to hip-hop, a variety of musical styles and even pastiche of older forms of American music in this period piece. Miranda tips his hat to Sondheim's own mentor, Oscar Hammerstein II, in "My Shot" with the line "You've got to be carefully taught" and makes his own tour of "SH'un" sounds: "conventional," "revolutionary," "manumission," "abolitionists," "position," "ammunition is." Finally, in certain lines Miranda is clearly competing directly with his mentor. When Hamilton meets Burr we hear an ouroboros string of rhymes in their exchange. (I have added italics and underling to indicate the dense sound repetition in these lyrics.)

H:   Pardon me, are you Aaron *Burr, sir*?
B:   That depends, who's asking?
H:   Oh, *sure, sir*
     I'm Alexan*der* Hamilton, I'm at *your* <u>ser</u>v<u>ice</u>, *sir*
     I have been looking for you
B:   I'm getting *<u>nervous</u>*
H:   *Sir*, I heard your name at Princeton
     I was seeking an accelerated course of <u>study</u>
     When I got sort of out of sorts with a <u>buddy</u> of yours
     I may have punched him it's a *blur, sir*
     He handles the financials?
B:   You punched the *bursar*?

Miranda reported that when Sondheim heard these lines he laughed and Miranda tweeted that he wished he could bottle that laugh forever, recapitulating Sondheim's own feelings when Cole Porter famously gasped after hearing one of his quadruple rhymes in *Gypsy* (in "Together Wherever We Go").[52] Sondheim would also likely recognize a kindred spirit in Miranda's punning in "Schuyler Sisters": Angelica: "Burr, you disgust me"; Burr: "Ah, so you've discussed me, I'm a trust fund, baby, you can trust me!" And, finally, in "You'll Be Back" King George delivers shocking rhymes, to a deliberately peppy tune, that seem quite in line with Sondheim's dark comedic personality: "Cuz when push comes to shove / I will kill your friends and family to remind you of my love."

\*\*\*

Throughout his career Sondheim has rhymed so extensively and with such variety in both lyrical and musical terms that almost any generalization I could offer on this topic would be at least partly true. He has created numerous unique and surprising rhymes resembling those of Cole Porter. He also frequently employs tried and true conventional rhymes and identities, as did Oscar Hammerstein. He uses both simple and complex rhyming patterns. He prefers perfect end rhymes but has also written intricate lyrics infested with internal rhymes, near rhymes, and alliteration. Rhyme is intended in his musicals to indicate the brilliance and control of certain characters and, in other cases, excessive rhyme indicates that a character is desperate or has lost their mind. His musical settings most often rhyme right along with lyrics unless they move in an opposite direction to suggest other meanings. Frequently, Sondheim composes melodies that compel us to hear more lyrical rhyming than is actually present on the page. Despite Sondheim's stated rather rigid rules for rhyme that he inherited from Wood and Hammerstein, he has explored all forms of rhyme, and his work reveals the great many ways in which musical setting and lyrical rhyme may intersect. As he once put it in the cut number "Invocation," originally from *Forum*, Sondheim's songs repeatedly invite us to "frown on reason, smile on rhyme."

## Notes

1. Stephen Sondheim, *Finishing the Hat: Collected Lyrics (1954–1981) with Attendant Comments, Principles, Heresies, Grudges, Whines and Anecdotes* (New York: Knopf, 2010), 5.
2. For instance, see the potshots he aimed at his own use of rhyme in *Saturday Night* (1954) and his oft-repeated disparagement of his rhyming for Maria's "I Feel Pretty" in *West Side Story* (1957), as they appear in ibid., 7 and 13; 48. Along these lines, he criticizes "The Little Things You Do Together" from *Company* (1970) for his "use of multiple rhymes to conceal poverty of thought—rhyming poison. Tight rhyme schemes may make for surface brilliance, but they can be as tiresome as they are elaborate," and he deplores "crowded and incessant rhyming" in general, noting that this is something he is "not always able to avoid" himself (175). All quotations of Sondheim's lyrics in this chapter will be from this publication or from his second volume of lyrics: Stephen Sondheim, *Look, I Made a Hat: Collected Lyrics (1981—2011) with Attendant Comments, Amplifications, Dogmas, Harangues, Digressions, Anecdotes and Miscellany* (New York: Knopf, 2011).

3. Stephen Banfield, "Sondheim and the Art that Has No Name," in *Approaches to the American Musical*, ed. Robert Lawson-Peebles (Exeter: University of Exeter Press, 1996), 143.

4. Stephen Sondheim, "Theater Lyrics," in *Playwrights, Lyricists, Composers on Theater*, ed. Otis L. Guernsey Jr. (New York: Dodd, Mead, 1974), 61–97. The section focused on rhyme appears on pp. 83–86. Also see his "Rhyme and Its Reasons" in Sondheim, *Finishing the Hat*, xxv–xxvii.

5. Sondheim, "Theater Lyrics," 81.

6. Sondheim, *Finishing the Hat*, xxvii.

7. Sondheim, however, frequently includes an internal rhyme when the final word or words in different lines are identities, as in "Agony" in *Into the Woods* (1987): "Why does she run from me?" and "The heart she has won from me?" In addition, when Sondheim repeats a word exactly he tends, unlike Oscar Hammerstein II, to twist the word's meaning, to set up puns, and to aim for irony, rather than simply tugging the listener forward by the hand toward an emotional response or for ease of comprehension.

8. For a catalog of Sondheim's use of such techniques, see Sheila Davis, "No Rhyme Before Its Time: Sondheim's Lyrics Are Repetitive Devices," *Sondheim Review* 13, no. 1 (2006): 29–31.

9. Sondheim, *Finishing the Hat*, xxvii. Though Sondheim suggests that this creates interest, one might counter that these moments of rhyming surprise might well distract the listener, presenting the mind with something to ponder and appreciate that has more to do with the lyricist's witty word choice than with the character and narrative. This is something that Sondheim has otherwise warned against.

10. Sondheim explained that "lyric writing is an elegant form of puzzle, and I am a great puzzle fan." Sondheim, "Theater Lyrics," 66. On Sondheim's skillful rhyming, also see Thomas P. Adler, "The Sung and the Said: Literary Value in the Musical Dramas of Stephen Sondheim," in *Reading Stephen Sondheim: A Collection of Critical Essays*, ed. Sandor Goodhart (New York: Garland, 2000), 44–45. As Adler notes, though Sondheim's rhyming is profuse in numerous numbers, ultimately the "quality of rhyme takes precedence over mere quantity" (45).

11. Sondheim, "Theater Lyrics," 83–84. In considering our experience of song in live performance, he refers to music as "a relentless engine [that] keeps the lyrics going" (64) and notes that the lyrics "also help shape the music, just as the music shapes them" (66).

12. Clement Wood, ed., *The Complete Rhyming Dictionary and Poet's Craft Book* (New York: Halcyon House, 1936).

13. See ibid., 25, 29. For an example of Sondheim's mention of the difficulties of rhyming the word "month," see Sondheim, *Finishing the Hat*, 5.

14. For a detailed manuscript-based study of Sondheim's process in the creation of rhymes for one song, see Mark Eden Horowitz, "Biography of a Song: 'Please Hello,'" *Sondheim Review* 14, no. 3 (Spring 2008): 25–33.

15. See Sondheim, *Look, I Made a Hat*, 43. Sondheim included a facsimile page from his drafts for this song that reveals his listing in the margins potential "ĀSH'un" rhymes

(38). For his use of SH'un rhymes in several other versions of this number, see 46–48. Dot also employs several words with this sound in the show's opening number: "attention"/"connection"/"profession"/"expression"/"affection." In addition, Sondheim frequently employs long strings of rhymed words for characterization, as in *The Frogs* as Dionysus introduces Shaw: "generosity"/"virtuosity"/"animosity"/"velocity"/ "pomposity"/"verbosity."

16. Quoted in Geoffrey Block, *Enchanted Evenings: The Broadway Musical from "Show Boat" to Sondheim and Lloyd Webber* (New York: Oxford University Press, 2014), 339. On Hammerstein's and Sondheim's approaches to rhyme, also see Andrew Milner, "'Let the Pupil Show the Master': Stephen Sondheim and Oscar Hammerstein II," in *Stephen Sondheim: A Casebook*, ed. Joanne Gordon (New York: Garland, 1997), 156–157.

17. *Gypsy* (1959), with music by Jule Styne, and *West Side Story* (1957), with music by Leonard Bernstein, do not actually offer test cases for determining how Sondheim's own musical setting of his lyrics might differ from that of other composers, given that he so closely collaborated with both Styne and Bernstein. It is therefore not surprising that the relationship between rhyme and musical setting in these works resembles that found in musicals for which he served as both composer and lyricist. Sondheim has explained that for both *Gypsy* and *West Side Story* he frequently created lyrics to fit preexistent music and that for *Gypsy* he even suggested melodic and rhythmic material to Styne for specific songs. See Sondheim, *Finishing the Hat*, 142.

18. Oscar Hammerstein II, *Lyrics* (New York: Simon and Schuster, 1949), 19–20. It is noteworthy that Hammerstein cites the work of two lyricists whom Sondheim has disparaged.

19. Ibid., 20–21.

20. Sondheim discusses rhyme in the two versions of this number in *Finishing the Hat*, 203.

21. Ibid., 212. On the ways in which Porter's rhythm and rhyme work wittily together see Rob Kapilow, "Which Comes First, the Music or the Lyrics? 'You're the Top,'" in *A Cole Porter Companion*, ed. Don M. Randel, Matthew Shaftel, and Susan Forscher Weiss (Urbana: University of Illinois Press, 2016), 86–97.

22. Steve Swayne, *How Sondheim Found His Sound* (Ann Arbor: University of Michigan Press, 2005), 58. Swayne discusses Porter's influence on Sondheim on 58–60.

23. David Savran, "'You've Got That Thing': Cole Porter, Stephen Sondheim, and the Erotics of the List Song," *Theatre Journal*, 64, no. 4 (December 2012), 533–548. As Savran explains: "Because the list song is a desiring machine, it produces desires that oscillate between revealed and concealed, carnivalesque and closet" (534). He also points out that in Sondheim's *Company* "every song (save one, 'Barcelona') happens to be a list song. . . . But unlike Porter's list songs, Sondheim's are exercises in futility, frustration, and anger, more likely to evoke anxiety than joy. *Company*'s list songs may be desiring-machines, but they produce something very different from the swarming abundance of Porter's" (541).

24. See, e.g., Sondheim, *Finishing the Hat*, 63. Here Sondheim disparages his lyrics for the song "Have an Egg Roll, Mr. Goldstone" (*Gypsy*), referring to it as a list song at its

"most egregious" and one that "sweats with effort." His verdict on this song form is blunt: "At their best, list songs are endlessly inventive, at their worst merely endless." One could argue that this list song perfectly expresses Rose's uncontrolled excitement at this moment as she stumbles over her words, making a hash of word order and verging on a patter song format. Rose sounds rather like a Dr. Seuss character here.

25. See Sondheim's remarks as quoted in Craig Zadan, *Sondheim & Co.*, 2nd ed., updated (New York: Da Capo, 1994), 234. Sondheim makes similar remarks about the primacy of establishing the rhythm inspired by the character in his songwriting in Mark Eden Horowitz, *Sondheim on Music: Minor Details and Major Decisions*, 2nd ed. (Lanham, MD: Scarecrow, 2010), 204, 211.

26. Horowitz, *Sondheim on Music*, 8–9.

27. Sondheim, "Theater Lyrics," 79.

28. Sondheim, *Look, I Made a Hat*, 149–150.

29. Ibid., 162.

30. Sondheim, "Theater Lyrics," 85. As Joanne Gordon notes: "Sondheim emphasizes his conviction that rhyme suggests education. The quality of language must match the character." Joanne Gordon, *Art Isn't Easy: The Achievement of Stephen Sondheim* (Carbondale: Southern Illinois University Press, 1990), 15.

31. Sondheim, *Look, I Made a Hat*, 66. I should note, however, that Jack's alliterations substitute somewhat for the lack of clear rhyming. In addition, given that the music rhymes exactly for the lines "been a perfect friend" and "day I'll buy you back," we are surprised by the missing rhyme and therefore are eager to accept the delayed "I'll see you soon again" as a slight lyrical rhyme ("friend"/"again"), as though Jack has sensed his mistake and then sings this off-rhymed phrase to the same musical gesture transposed higher, thus offering an approximate musical rhyme as well.

32. Sondheim, *Finishing the Hat*, 6. He also states that the use of trick rhymes can undermine realistic depiction of a character (158) but that "trick rhymes invest the character who sings them with a certain amount of wit" (177).

33. Ibid., 184–185. Sondheim's remarks on rhyming and characterization have led some of his commentators to offer similar contradictory explanations. See, e.g., Max Adams, "Pointing Sense," *Sondheim Review* 21, no. 3 (Summer 2015): 30–32.

34. Sondheim, *Look, I Made a Hat*, 11.

35. Sondheim, *Finishing the Hat*, 340.

36. A more elaborate example of melodic and rhyming insistence is encountered in "Chrysanthemum Tea" (*Pacific Overtures*) as the Shogun's Mother employs intense motivic repetition allied with rhyme to prod the Shogun to action. The same melodic gesture and rhyme appear seven times in the first verse and ten times in her second verse.

37. As Joanne Gordon puts it, in "Little Things" the "tone becomes progressively more ironic" as we move through the song. Gordon, *Art Isn't Easy*, 51.

38. Desiree's increasingly impatient and sardonic rhyming responses to Fredrik in "You Must Meet My Wife" (*Night Music*), one of Sondheim's several ironic waltzes, emphasize stinging tritone sonorities between successive rhyming words: "How nice"/ "whatever the price," "my word"/"a bird," and "unversed"/"her first." Sondheim had

employed rhyme to similar effect, yoking together sharply contradictory viewpoints, in the verbal battle between Rosalia and Anita in "America" (*West Side Story*).

39. Swayne, *How Sondheim Found His Sound*, 103, 108. Swayne also discusses Sondheim's use of vamps as accompaniments (115–117). Sondheim has noted that in composing a song, the accompaniment's vamp often comes first for him. Sondheim, "Theater Lyrics," 72.

40. When Beth sings "Not a Day Goes By" near the end of Act I of *Merrily We Roll Along*, her frustration and yearning are poignantly clear as she becomes stuck on a triplet figure and a list of "-ing" rhyming words. (This reminds me somewhat of the "yearning"/"burning" expressed by the protagonist in Porter's "Night and Day").

41. "Ladies Who Lunch" is another example from *Company* of Sondheim's use of alliteration and intricate inner and end rhymes that, for the most part, receive musical support. On his use of hidden inner rhymes in this song, see Sondheim, "Theater Lyrics," 84. For a related analytical approach to the one that I will offer here, detailing a songwriter's coordination of lyrical and musical sounds, see Don M. Randel, "About Cole Porter's Songs," in *A Cole Porter Companion*, ed. Don M. Randel, Matthew Shaftel, and Susan Forscher Weiss (Urbana: University of Illinois Press, 2016), 225–226.

42. The musical rhyming that parallels the Church Lady's inner and end rhymes in her inserted hymn-like statements in this number highlights the humor of her subsequent shocking turn to negative lyrics ("tragedy of life"/"yoked to wife" and "feels dead"/"This dreadful day"), resulting in a bit of Brechtian alienation between the words and their musical setting.

43. Sondheim, *Look, I Made a Hat*, 55. Sondheim also discusses the potential power of avoiding an expected rhyme in Horowitz, *Sondheim on Music*, 236–237.

44. Sondheim, *Finishing the Hat*, 144.

45. On the wife/life rhyme in musicals, including those by Sondheim, see Peter Filichia, "The Most Used Musical Theater Lyric," *Playbill*, May 12, 1999, https://www.playbill.com/article/stagestruck-by-peter-filichia-the-most-used-musical-theater-lyric-com-81857. On the musical emphasis placed on the wife/life rhyme in "Getting Married Today," see Adams, "Pointing Sense," 30.

46. James Lipton, "Stephen Sondheim: The Art of the Musical," *Paris Review* 39, no. 142 (Spring 1997): 265.

47. Wood, *Complete Rhyming Dictionary*, 186–187.

48. Examples of Sondheim's use of this rhyme appear in "Miracle Song" (*Anyone Can Whistle*), "Getting Married Today" and "Ladies Who Lunch" (*Company*), "You Must Meet My Wife" (*A Little Night Music*), "A Bowler Hat" (*Pacific Overtures*), "The Barber and His Wife" and "Poor Thing" (*Sweeney Todd*), "Rich and Happy" (*Merrily We Roll Along*), "Prologue" (*Into the Woods*), "Unworthy of Your Love" (*Assassins*), and the Mistress and Colonel numbers in scene 9 of *Passion*. I note that Sondheim also uses the knife/life and knife/wife rhymes in several numbers, including in "You Must Meet My Wife" (*A Little Night Music*), "Poor Thing" (*Sweeney Todd*), "Agony" (*Into the Woods*), and in Fosca's dictated letter in scene 7 in *Passion*. In addition, he rhymes "lives" with "wives" in "The Glamorous Life" (*A Little Night Music*).

49. Sondheim has stated that the Auden/Kallman lyrics for *The Rake's Progress* "read gracefully and sing unintelligibly, not only because Stravinsky distorts them but because they're too packed for the listener to comprehend in the time allotted for hearing them." Sondheim, *Finishing the Hat*, xix. An earlier critical statement about the opera appeared in Sondheim, "Theater Lyrics," 65.

50. Stephen Schwartz, "Learning from Sondheim," *Sondheim Review* 17, no. 1 (2010): 33–34.

51. Lin-Manuel Miranda and Jeremy McCarter, *Hamilton: The Revolution* (New York: Grand Central Publishing, 2016), 187. Miranda cites the influence of Weidman as well (173). In addition, the paired numbers "Helpless" and "Satisfied" present multiple perspectives on the same event and suggest a form of time travel through song in much the same way as we encounter in Sondheim's and Weidman's "Someone in a Tree" (*Pacific Overtures*).

52. Lin-Manuel Miranda, Twitter, February 5, 2015, https://twitter.com/lin_manuel/status/563206245751193602?lang=en

# Afterword

## Moving on with Sondheim

*Kristen Anderson-Lopez*

It is impossible to identify the moment Sondheim's work started shaping who I was and who I would become. Before I could tie my own shoes, I had absorbed through osmosis (or the television?) multiple lyrics from *West Side Story* and *Gypsy*. I would sing a bastardized version of "Comedy Tonight" while swinging on our backyard swing set. Judy Collins sang "Send in the Clowns" on *The Muppet Show*. My wonderful elementary music teachers had us sing various pieces in Sondheim's songbook, reading the handwritten lyrics projected on the wall from a transparency sheet on the overhead projector. My high school boyfriend scored major points when he and his family flew us up from North Carolina to New York to see *Into the Woods* on Broadway for my sixteenth birthday. By the time I was in college making the annual back-to-school commute from Charlotte to Williamstown, Massachusetts, my reverence for Sondheim had crystalized into a personal tradition. It's worth noting that during those years I had no idea I would later channel this love of the art form and become a songwriter myself. At the time, all I knew was that Sondheim was the measure of intellectual artistic excellence. And every September I would pack up my Dodge Caravan (with classy wood siding) and next to me, in the plastic CD holder on the passenger seat, was every Sondheim original cast album as well as my all-time favorite compilation, *Live Celebration of Sondheim at Carnegie Hall*. I would drive up I-95 to my academic year at Williams, propelled North by Sondheim's sophisticated body of work.

To say I have put Sondheim on a pedestal would be an understatement. He is the genius of all geniuses. The Father, Son, and Holy Ghost of my chosen religion: musical theater. As has been explored in multiple chapters in this book, Sondheim's monolithic greatness—to my mind and in the Broadway community at large—is connected to his ability to capture the nuanced paradoxes of the human heart and mind. Whereas musical theater was once the land of Meredith Willson's "Till There Was You," Sondheim moved the needle to "Marry Me a Little." Bawdy charm songs such as *Oliver*'s "Oom-pah-pah" were obliviated by the ghoulish, punning genius of Sweeney and Mrs. Lovett's "A Little Priest." In

Kristen Anderson-Lopez, *Afterword* In: *Sondheim in Our Time and His*. Edited by: W. Anthony Sheppard, Oxford University Press. © Oxford University Press 2022. DOI: 10.1093/oso/9780197603192.003.0016

Sondheim's musical world, expressions of love always have a nuanced dark side. Expressions of pure evil are all laced with a vein of joy. Who can forget this anthem to the ambivalence of love?

> You're sorry-grateful,
> Regretful-happy,
> Why look for answers where none occur?
> You'll always be what you always were,
> Which has nothing to do with,
> All to do with her.

He wrote love songs to murder weapons and can-cans for colonialism. Sondheim's unflinching, penetrating pen had transformed the sentimental Broadway musical into a sophisticated, cerebral exploration of human foible and contradiction. And this was the picture, in my mind, of Sondheim for quite some time. Until one day, beneath the ever-contradictory Janus face, I saw something new.

Again, I can't point to when it happened. Maybe it was the day I read the first bad review of my own work in the *New York Times*. Or maybe it was that first good review. Maybe it happened during one of the long, torturous nights spent rewriting an opening number that *please oh please* had to work before previews were over. Maybe the shift came the first time I spoke to a room full of young people and realized I had a responsibility not only to my own work but to whatever future work they would create. Whenever it happened, it was like looking at one of those Magic Eye pictures they used to sell at the mall. Once my eyes focused and I saw the picture hidden inside the picture, I couldn't *unsee* it.

Sondheim, this master of our craft, this god of our industry, this creator of intricate, sophisticated lyrics sung by complicated paradoxical characters is also (*gasp!*) a vulnerable artist.

Whether it's a Victorian actress, a vaudevillian mother, a trio of mid-century creative dreamers, a famous French impressionist, a bloodthirsty British barber, a Civil War–era actor, or a group of aging show girls, Sondheim's stories are full of artists trying to make sense of the idealists they were when they began and the wounds they've sustained along the way. As noted in this book's introduction, these characters are often multifaceted, looking at the beginning through the end or the end through the beginning. But through the lens of someone working and struggling every day as an artist myself, I suddenly saw a consistent face—one that whispered truths about many of my own fears and challenges as a writer.

Now, it is very important that I clarify something. It would be unfair to Sondheim, and patently untrue for me, to claim I know what he felt or experienced at any given moment in his life. I do not possess secret journals, transcripts of therapy sessions, or cosmic mind-reading techniques that could give me access to anyone else's innermost thoughts or feelings. I cannot claim to have traveled the same exact path—nobody could! Rather, I am sharing my *own* experiences and highlighting moments or aspects of his work that resonate differently for me now that I've been a working musical theater songwriter for twenty years.

Let's look at Bobby from *Company*. There are many angles from which to view Bobby's outsider role in this show. But I'd like to shed some light on a dynamic very few people know about that exists within the "company" of a new musical. When you become the composer of a show, nobody tells you that it comes with a price. As a child you are drawn to theater because you love dancing and singing. You are pulled into the world because you find a community of like-minded theater kids who are all similarly sensitive, hyper, and drama-seeking. You learn you can channel these feelings into writing songs and one day, if you are very lucky, your dream comes true when someone takes a chance and you are professionally produced. And it's then that you realize there's a catch. The cast, choreographer, and director get to romp and explore the playground you built as you watch from a cold metal folding chair on the side. You observe, decide what must change, and write those changes at night. Alone. You hand those changes to the stage manager and go back to your metal folding chair on the side again. Sure, you can banter pleasantly with the cast when they are on their ten-minute break, but you can never be one of them. Your job is to watch and learn and use your critical thinking. If it will improve the show, you may have to cut your favorite actor's song or recast your beloved actress-friend's role. The closer you get to opening night, the further away the cast and crew are. They settle into their backstage home and you sit with your laptop out in the empty rows of velvet seats trying to build the strongest, sturdiest, prettiest house—a house in which you will never truly live. So I can't help but be curious about whether Sondheim was channeling this unique writers' experience when he wrote Joanne's penultimate verse:

And here's to the girls who just watch—
Aren't they the best?
When they get depressed, it's a bottle of Scotch,
Plus a little jest.

Another chance to disapprove,
Another brilliant zinger,
Another reason not to move,
Another vodka stinger —

Anyone who has sat in the back row with a yellow pad and a long night ahead can drink to that.

As writers, we get used to sitting on the side, watching, judging, coming up with the right line. But there's always a part of us in awe of the actors up there under the lights dancing, singing, making mistakes, but up there all together "crowded with love." On some level, I wonder if "Being Alive" is informed by Sondheim's admiration and, perhaps, possible longing to be one of the company members living so boldly and collaboratively on the other side of the footlights.

Speaking of footlights, let's turn to Desiree Armfeldt of *A Little Night Music*, a prominent actress whom we meet through an "I am" song titled "The Glamorous Life" as she tours from small town to small town.

> Mother's surviving, la la la!
> Leading the glamorous life!
> Cracks in the plaster, la la la!
> Youngish admirers, la la la!
> Which one was that one? la la la!
> Hi-ho, the glamorous life!
>
> Bring up the curtain, la la la!
> Bring down the curtain, la la la!
> Bring up the curtain, la la la!
> Hi-ho, the glamorous life.

By the time *A Little Night Music* opened on February 25, 1973, Sondheim had been through the grueling process of developing and opening *eight* Broadway musicals, two major films, and an original musical for television in eighteen years. Now, it is one thing for us to look at a timeline and think to ourselves "This is what a prolific writer does." It is another to imagine the logistics and personal sacrifices involved in packing up for an out-of-town tryout every twelve to twenty-four months. Not wanting to be mired in fact finding, I crowd-sourced my wide network of Sondheim-expert friends to get an idea of just how many such tryouts Sondheim would have experienced prior to opening *A Little Night Music*. Table A.1 presents the picture I was able to piece together.

The industry has changed a great deal since the 1960s and 1970s. Most shows today are developed mainly in New York City via multiple workshops in partnership with a producer or non-profit theater or both. I have had to survive just two out-of-town tryouts myself. In both cases, it felt like being shot into space for ten to twelve weeks only to return to life in New York dazed, drained, and in dire need of rebuilding my neglected friendships. It is a brutal process that demands putting the rest of your life into a state of suspended animation. You move to a new city, live in a hotel or short-term rental, and spend every waking moment in the theater rehearsing. When not in rehearsal, you're in a room by yourself or

**Table A.1.** Sondheim and the "Glamorous Life," 1957–1973

| Show | Out-of-town tryout(s) |
| --- | --- |
| *West Side Story*<br>Opened September 1957 | Washington, Philadelphia |
| *Gypsy*<br>Opened May 1959 | Philadelphia |
| *West Side Story* (movie)<br>Opened October 1961 | |
| *A Funny Thing Happened on the Way to the Forum*<br>Opened May 1962 | New Haven, Washington |
| *Anyone Can Whistle*<br>Opened April 1964 | Philadelphia |
| *Do I Hear A Waltz?*<br>Opened March 1965 | Boston, New Haven |
| *A Funny Thing Happened on the Way to the Forum* (movie)<br>1966 | |
| *Evening Primrose* (television)<br>November 1966 | |
| *Company*<br>Opened April 1970 | Boston |
| *Follies*<br>Opened April 1971 | Boston |
| *A Little Night Music*<br>Opened February 1973 | Boston |

with the creative team tinkering, rewriting—all with a giant clock ticking. It is indeed, as Desiree sings, a state of "surviving." It is no life.

Over the course of *Night Music*, Desiree realizes something has to change. As she assesses the damage the demands of her artistic life has done to her personal life, she corrects course and with courage and humility reunites her family. Happy ending. Curtain.

Alternatively, in *Gypsy*, Rose loses Herbie when she chooses the constant road and quest for Stardom over giving up and settling down. Mental breakdown, tragic ending. Curtain.

As I write this paragraph, I am realizing the role that these cautionary tales must have played in the very conscious choice my husband and I made early in our careers to collaborate and navigate this career together as a family. For both of the out-of-town tryouts we've survived, we were there as a couple—with our children—all on the same adventure. So, while our normal domestic lives were temporarily suspended, our most important connections continued (a little more stressed out than usual, but present and intact.) I'm now curious how many mistakes and hard decisions we were able to avoid because we had so fully learned from Rose and Herbie's heartbreak or from Desiree and Fredrik's "farce." And through this work, or perhaps through the simple fact that he was drawn to tell stories about artists on the road, was Sondheim sharing hard-won wisdom? Did he have a need to share stories about the toll that so much time on the road would take on personal connections? And if so, how many other artists like us have benefited from this wisdom?

Let's turn to Mary, Charley, and Frank of *Merrily We Roll Along*. I was one of the lucky ones able to experience the stunning revival in New York City Center's 2012 Encores! season (starring a pre-Hamilton Lin-Manuel Miranda). I was not very familiar with this particular show. But as I watched from the steep City Center balcony, I had a creeping visceral response. As the story unfolded and I got to know the three main characters, I recognized problems I was facing and trying to balance every day in my own life. There was the "Frank" side of me, working for a large Hollywood studio, who needed to meet deadlines, be professional, and show up like someone deserving of a seat at the table within a corporate structure. There was the "Charley" part of me, longing to add something completely honest, fresh, and artistically meaningful to the musical theater art form. And there was the "Mary" part of me—the mollusk—developing a tough outer shell to protect the most fragile, precious part of any creative: the part that feels things. I now call these parts of myself "The Executive," "The Artist," and "The Human." All three of these selves are important to keep in balance in any creative career. What good is a great idea if it doesn't resonate emotionally and illuminate something about the human experience? What good is a groundbreaking song if you don't meet the deadline or have the relationships to get it out in the world? As artists, we need to keep all three parts in a balance resembling a Calder mobile. When I look through this lens, I see *Merrily* as Sondheim's exploration of how easily this fragile harmony can be upended.

And then, two years later in *Sunday in the Park with George* he showed us how to find and protect that harmony.

But before we go there, let's talk about reviews. Specifically, let's talk about all the myriad ways in which reviews can wound. First, there's the fun of not getting mentioned at all. I went back and read Brooks Atkinson's original review of *West Side Story*'s 1957 Broadway premiere (*New York Times*, September 27, 1957). It's positive! Arthur Laurents, Leonard Bernstein, and Jerome Robbins are all cited multiple times. And Sondheim's name does not appear once. The second form of cruelty is the casual dismissal, or damning with faint praise. In his *New York Times* review of *Anyone Can Whistle*, Howard Taubman snipes, "Sondheim has written some pleasing songs but not enough of them to give the musical wing" (*New York Times*, April 6, 1964). As for negative reviews, there is a spectrum of cruelty that can run from bad to scathing to personal. And then there is the kind of review that can close a show after sixteen performances. Frank Rich, the "Butcher of Broadway," penned a notorious pan of *Merrily* in the *New York Times* in 1981 that not only closed the show but was a very personal reprimand aimed directly at Sondheim: "But what's really being wasted here is Mr. Sondheim's talent. And that's why we watch 'Merrily We Roll Along' with an ever-mounting—and finally upsetting—sense of regret" (*New York Times*, November 17, 1981).

For me, when a show closes, there is tremendous grief from losing something ephemeral that was years in the making and can never be built again. There is also a heavy feeling that I have let down the cast, the crew, the producers. There is deep shame and there are perseverating questions. What should I have done differently? What didn't I see? Should I have spoken up louder that time? Should I have kept my mouth shut and listened that other time? And there is an urgency to make it all stop. If an artist lives in the shame headspace for too long, it can lead to paralysis, bitterness, even rage.

It could perhaps lead to a deeper understanding of someone like John Wilkes Booth and to new insights regarding Lincoln's assassin.

> Some say it was your voice had gone,
> Some say it was booze.
> They say you killed a country, John,
> Because of bad reviews.

A public failure like a musical flop or a scathing review, especially in our insular industry, can often lead to a hard journey finding your way back to facing "a blank page or canvas." In her 2015 bestseller *Rising Strong: The Reckoning, the Rumble, the Revolution*, Brené Brown writes about how when we find ourselves "face-down in the arena" the way forward is to own, learn, and find our way to frame our disappointments or failures. She writes, "Our job is not to deny the story, but to defy the ending—to rise strong, recognize our story, and rumble with the truth until we get to a place where we think, Yes. This is what happened. This is my truth. And I will choose how this story ends."[1]

Unfortunately, in 1981 Sondheim did not have the benefit of knowing Brown's *Rising Strong* wisdom. He did not have the benefit of knowing this work would eventually become a beloved cult favorite. After the seeming failure of *Merrily* and implosion of his collaboration with Hal Prince, Sondheim was ready to quit the business. As he has said of this time, "I want to find something to satisfy myself that does not involve Broadway and dealing with all those people who hate me and hate Hal."[2] And yet it is in this state that, somehow, over the course of the next two years he birthed perhaps the most powerful, emotionally rich hit of his career. *Sunday in the Park with George* tells the story of an artist reckoning and rumbling with his detractors, disappointments, and doubts. And it is in this show that Sondheim "rises strong" with the revolution that is "Move On."

> Stop worrying where you're going—
> Move on.
> If you can know where you're going,
> You've gone.
> Just keep moving on.
>
> I chose, and my world was shaken—
> So what?
> The choice may have been mistaken,
> The choosing was not.
> You have to move on.
> . . .
> Stop worrying if your vision
> Is new.
> Let others make that decision—
> They usually do,
> You keep moving on.
> . . .
> Anything you do,
> Let it come from you.
> Then it will be new.
>
> Give us more to see

Without a doubt, every musical theater songwriter I know has a deep personal connection to this lyric. I have turned to it as a balm time and time again—after a tough workshop, after a big success, after reading a snarky post about my work on social media. It is a carefully drawn map for an artist to find their way back to their true North. It's the lyric that I was most excited to celebrate in this afterword. Though I am unable to quote the entire lyric here, the power of this song is the struggle and the eventual breakthrough to "something new" that George discovers *because* of the struggle.

From a musicological perspective, Sondheim's musical and lyrical form supports storytelling function. The prosody—the rhythm and pattern of the lyric—acts like a small toy boat struggling to make its way smoothly down the twisting stream of the accompaniment. On the longer phrases that touch on the ways fear or worry can stop the creative flow, it's as if our lyrical toy boat gets tangled and caught in a pile of sticks. But then it always finds its way back to a smooth flow with the two-syllable lines "Move on." Later in the song, when George and Dot's voices join together, the stop-and-start quality of the lyric gives over to a new fluid expansiveness. We literally hear our main character find his flow as he melds with the inspiration he finds in giving over to his love for "the light" and "the feeling and the life!" The boat, untangled from reviews, opinions, and petty concerns, is now sailing smoothly down the river.

As for lyrical content, there are many valuable pieces of advice in this number that we all should tattoo on the back of our hands. Whenever I find myself struggling with a creative problem—a line I can't quite land, a character decision I can't quite capture—it's usually because I'm approaching it with someone else's eyes. Perhaps I'm stymied by something someone told me to do in a notes session. Or I'm imagining what some critic might write about me at some future date. That's when I pull out the magical four lines at the end of this song. "Anything you do, / Let it come from you. / Then it will be new. / Give us more to see." With these four lines, Sondheim frees us from worrying about comparison or the critical voices in our head. He gives us a simple way to navigate out of the weeds and move forward in the present moment. Go inside. See what's there. Be honest. Share it. That's all we have to do, and it will be new.

Perhaps through writing "Move On" for George and Dot, Sondheim was able to move forward himself. *Sunday* was the beginning of a fertile new chapter with bookwriter-director James Lapine. But the gift of *Sunday* for all of us is that Sondheim used his craft to share his breakthrough. It's Sondheim the mentor, the teacher, generously showing us by example how we write ourselves out of our own way.

Stop worrying if your vision
Is new.
Let others make that decision—
They usually do,
You keep moving on.

It is a fair assumption that Sondheim may never read this book. He's on his own journey to understand what it all means. But this book is not *for* him. It's for all of us who have been forever changed by his genius, for when we get to experience his words and music looking through a new lens, we get the gift of experiencing it and growing from it in new ways. And we realize it's not Dot's voice but our own as we turn to this volume of new insights about Sondheim's rich, multifaceted, layered body of work and, on bended knee, implore, "Give us more to see."

# Notes

1. Brené Brown, *Rising Strong: The Reckoning, the Rumble, the Revolution* (New York: Random House, 2015), 50.
2. Martin Gottfried, *Sondheim* (New York: Abrams, 1993), 153.

# Works Cited

Adams, Max. "Pointing Sense." *Sondheim Review* 21, no. 3 (Summer 2015): 30–32.

Adler, Thomas P. "The Musical Dramas of Stephen Sondheim: Some Critical Approaches." *Journal of Popular Culture* 12, no. 3 (Winter 1978): 513–525.

Adler, Thomas P. "The Sung and the Said: Literary Value in the Musical Dramas of Stephen Sondheim." In *Reading Stephen Sondheim: A Collection of Critical Essays*, edited by Sandor Goodhart, 37–60. New York: Garland, 2000.

Alexander, Patrick. *Marcel Proust's Search for Lost Time: A Reader's Guide to "The Remembrance of Things Past"*. New York: Vintage, 2009.

Als, Hilton. "Brother Act: The Theatre." *New Yorker*, December 1, 2008.

Attinello, Paul. "The Universe Will Tell You What It Needs: Being, Time, Sondheim." In *Musicological Identities: Essays in Honor of Susan McClary*, edited by Steven Bauer, Raymond Knapp, and Jacqueline Warwick, 77–92. Abingdon, UK: Routledge, 2008.

Banerji, Arnab. "*Soft Power*: Hwang and Tesori's Reappropriation of *The King and I* in Representing Twenty-First-Century Diplomacy and the Dystopic Reality of Contemporary America." *Studies in Musical Theatre* 13, no. 3 (2019): 269–282.

Banfield, Stephen. "Sondheim and the Art That Has No Name." In *Approaches to the American Musical*, edited by Robert Lawson-Peebles, 137–160. Exeter: University of Exeter Press, 1996.

Banfield, Stephen. *Sondheim's Broadway Musicals*. Ann Arbor: University of Michigan Press, 1993.

Banfield, Stephen. "Sondheim's Genius." In *The Oxford Handbook of Sondheim Studies*, edited by Robert Gordon, 11–25. New York: Oxford University Press, 2014.

Baron, Dennis. *What's Your Pronoun? Beyond He and She*. New York: Norton/Liveright, 2020.

Basinger, Jeanine. *The Movie Musical*. New York: Knopf, 2019.

Bergman, Ingmar. *Four Screenplays of Ingmar Bergman: "Smiles of a Summer Night," "The Seventh Seal," "Wild Strawberries," "The Magician."* New York: Simon and Schuster, 1960.

Bernstein, Leonard. *Findings*. New York: Knopf, 1982.

Bial, Henry. *Acting Jewish: Negotiating Ethnicity on the American Stage and Screen*. Ann Arbor: University of Michigan Press, 2005.

Block, Geoffrey. "The Broadway Canon from *Show Boat* to *West Side Story* and the European Operatic Ideal." *Journal of Musicology* 11, no. 4 (Autumn 1993): 525–544.

Block, Geoffrey. *Enchanted Evenings: The Broadway Musical from "Show Boat" to Sondheim and Lloyd Webber*. New York: Oxford University Press, 2009.

Block, Geoffrey. "From Screen to Stage: *A Little Night Music* and *Passion*." In *The Oxford Handbook of Sondheim Studies*, edited by Robert Gordon, 258–277. New York: Oxford University Press, 2014.

Block, Geoffrey. "Integration." In *The Oxford Handbook of the American Musical*, edited by Raymond Knapp, Mitchell Morris, and Stacy Wolf, 97–110. New York: Oxford University Press, 2011.

Block, Geoffrey. "The Last Word: Rewriting Musical Theatre History with Sondheim." *Studies in Musical Theatre* 13, no. 2 (2019): 133–150.

Block, Geoffrey. Review of *On Sondheim: An Opinionated Guide*, Ethan Mordden. *Studies in Musical Theatre* 10, no. 1 (2016): 143–145.

Block, Geoffrey. Review of *The Movie Musical!*, Jeanine Basinger (2019). *Studies in Musical Theatre* 14, no. 1 (2020): 230–233.

Block, Geoffrey. *Richard Rodgers*. New Haven: Yale University Press, 2003.

Bradley, Ian. *You've Got to Have a Dream: The Message of the Musical*. Louisville: Westminster John Knox Press, 2004.

Bristow, Eugene K., and J. Kevin Butler. "*Company*, About Face! The Show That Revolutionized the American Musical." *American Music* 5, no. 3 (Autumn 1987): 241–254.

Brodkin, Karen. *How Jews Became White Folks and What That Says About Race in America*. New Brunswick, NJ: Rutgers University Press, 1998.

Brown, John Russell. *Shakespeare's Plays in Performance*. New York: St. Martin's, 1967.

Burton, Humphrey. *Leonard Bernstein*. New York: Doubleday, 1994.

Caplin, William E. *Classical Form: A Theory of Formal Functions for the Instrumental Music of Haydn, Mozart, and Beethoven*. Oxford: Oxford University Press, 1998.

Carlson, Marvin. *The Haunted Stage*. Ann Arbor: University of Michigan Press, 2001.

Carnelia, Craig. "In Conversation with Stephen Sondheim." *Sondheim Review* 15, no. 1 (Fall 2008): 15–20.

Case, Sue-Ellen. *Feminism and Theatre*. New York: Methuen, 1988.

Chandler, John W. *The Rise and Fall of Fraternities at Williams College: Clashing Cultures and the Transformation of a Liberal Arts College*. Williamstown, MA: Williams College Press, 2014.

Chapin, Theodore. *Everything Was Possible: The Birth of the Musical "Follies"*. New York: Applause Books, 2003.

Citron, Stephen. *Jerry Herman: Poet of the Showtune*. New Haven: Yale University Press, 2004.

Citron, Stephen. *Sondheim and Lloyd Webber: The New Musical*. New York: Oxford University Press, 2001; repr., Milwaukee: Applause Theatre & Cinema Books, 2014.

Clum, John. *Something for the Boys: Musical Theater and Gay Culture*. New York: St. Martin's, 1999.

Clum, John. *The Works of Arthur Laurents: Politics, Love, and Betrayal*. Amherst, NY: Cambria, 2014.

Clurman, Harold. *The Fervent Years: The Group Theatre and the '30s*. New York: Da Capo, 1983.

Comden, Betty, Adolph Green, and Jule Styne. *Bells Are Ringing*. New York: Random House, 1957.

Cone, Edward T. *The Composer's Voice*. Berkeley: University of California Press, 1974.

Conyers, Claude. "Cakewalk." In *Grove Music Online*. Accessed February 27, 2019. http://www.oxfordmusiconline.com/grovemusic/view/10.1093/gmo/9781561592 630.001.0001/omo-9781561592630-e-1002092374.

Cox, Karen. *Dreaming of Dixie: How the South Was Created in American Popular Culture*. Chapel Hill: University of North Carolina Press, 2013.

Craig, David. "On Performing Sondheim: *A Little Night Music* Revisited." In *Stephen Sondheim: A Casebook*, edited by Joanne Gordon, 93–106. New York: Garland, 1993.

Davis, Sheila. "No Rhyme Before Its Time: Sondheim's Lyrics Are Repetitive Devices." *Sondheim Review* 13, no. 1 (2006): 29–31.

Decker, Todd. "'Big, as in Large, as in Huge': *Dreamgirls* and Difference in the Performance of Gender, Blackness, and Popular Music History." In *Twenty-First Century Musicals from Stage to Screen*, edited by George Rodosthenous, 94–109. New York: Routledge, 2018.

Decker, Todd. "Broadway in Blue: Gershwin's Musical Theater Scores and Songs." In *The Cambridge Companion to George Gershwin*, edited by Anna Harwell Celenza, 80–101. New York: Cambridge University Press, 2019.

Decker, Todd. "'Do You Want to Hear a Mammy Song?': A Historiography of *Show Boat*." *Contemporary Theater Review* 19, no. 1 (2009): 8–21.

Decker, Todd. "Race, Ethnicity, Performance." In *The Oxford Handbook of the American Musical*, edited by Raymond Knapp, Mitchell Morris, and Stacy Wolf, 197–210. New York: Oxford University Press, 2011.

Decker, Todd. "Remembering the American Tribal Love-Rock Musical Before It Got Old: Broadway's 'Hair' in Its Times Square Time." March 2, 2021. https://commonreader.wustl.edu/c/remembering-the-american-tribal-love-rock-musical-before-it-got-old/.

Decker, Todd. *"Show Boat": Performing Race in an American Musical*. New York: Oxford University Press, 2013.

Diamond, Elin. "Brechtian Theory/Feminist Theory: Toward a Gestic Feminist Criticism." *Drama Review* 32, no. 1 (Spring 1988): 82–94.

Dinero, Dan. "A Big Black Lady Stops the Show: Black Women, Performances of Excess and the Power of Saying No." *Studies in Musical Theater* 6, no. 1 (March 2012): 29–41.

DiPiero, Thomas. *White Men Aren't*. Durham: Duke University Press, 2002.

Dolan, Jill. *The Feminist Spectator as Critic*. Ann Arbor: University of Michigan Press, 1988.

Draper, Ellen Dooling, and Jenny Koralek, eds. *A Lively Oracle: A Centennial Celebration of P. L. Travers*. New York: Larson, 1999.

Düchting, Hajo. *Georges Seurat, 1859–1891: The Master of Pointillism*. London: Taschen, 1999.

Dyer, Richard. *White*. London: Routledge, 1997.

Elem. "Strawhat Reviews: *The Life of the Party*." *Variety*, July 19, 1950.

Engel, Lehman. *The American Musical Theater*. Rev. ed. New York: Macmillan, 1975.

Engel, Lehman. *Words and Music*. New York: Macmillan, 1972.

Felton, Lena. "How Colleges Foretold the #MeToo Movement." *Atlantic*, January 17, 2018. www.theatlantic.com/education/archive/2018/01/how-colleges-foretold-the-metoo-movement/550613/.

Filichia, Peter. *Let's Put on a Musical!* New York: Back Stage Books, 1993.

Filichia, Peter. "The Most Used Musical Theater Lyric." *Playbill*, May 12, 1999. https://www.playbill.com/article/stagestruck-by-peter-filichia-the-most-used-musical-theater-lyric-com-81857.

Fink, Robert. *Repeating Ourselves: American Minimal Music as Cultural Practice*. Berkeley: University of California Press, 2005.

Flahaven, Sean Patrick. "Starobin Talks About *Sunday, Assassins*." *Sondheim Review* 5, no. 2 (Fall 1998): 21–23.

Flatley, Guy. "When Stephen Sondheim Writes Words and Music, Some Critics Don't Leave the Theater Humming." *People*, April 5, 1976.

Forte, Allen. "Milton Babbitt's *Three Theatrical Songs* in Perspective." *Perspectives of New Music* 35, no. 2 (1997): 65–84.

Forte, Allen. *The Structure of Atonal Music*. 2nd ed. New Haven: Yale University Press, 1977.

Franke, Marco. *Stephen Sondheims "Sweeney Todd": Ein Werkporträt*. Hamburg: Diplomica, 2009.

Freedman, Gerald. "My Life in Art: A 21st Century Riff on Stanislavsky." Address presented at the John F. Kennedy Center for the Performing Arts, April 20, 2008.

Fromm, Erich. *Escape from Freedom*. New York: Avon, 1941.

Furth, George. *Twigs: A Comedy*. New York: French, 1972.

Galella, Donatella. *America in the Round: Capital, Race and Nation at Washington, DC's Arena Stage*. Iowa City: University of Iowa Press, 2019.

Galella, Donatella. "Feeling Yellow: Responding to Contemporary Yellow Face in Musical Performance." *Journal of Dramatic Theory and Criticism* 32, no. 2 (Spring 2018): 66–77.

Galella, Donatella. "Playing in the Dark: Musicalizing *A Raisin in the Sun*." *Continuum* 1, no. 2 (January 2015). https://continuumjournal.org/index.php/33-volumes/issues/vol-1-no-2-content/ysc-1-2/95-playing-in-the-dark-musicalizing-a-raisin-in-the-sun.

Garfield, David. *A Player's Place: The Story of the Actors Studio*. New York: Macmillan, 1980.

Gerhard, Jane F. *Desiring Revolution: Second-Wave Feminism and the Rewriting of American Sexual Thought, 1920 to 1982*. New York: Columbia University Press, 2001.

Goldman, James, and Stephen Sondheim. *Follies*. New York: Theatre Communications Group, 2001. First published 1971.

Goldschmitt, K. E. *Bossa Mundo: Brazilian Music in Transnational Media Industries*. New York: Oxford University Press, 2020.

Gordon, Joanne. *Art Isn't Easy: The Achievement of Stephen Sondheim*. Carbondale: Southern Illinois University Press, 1990.

Gordon, Joanne. *Art Isn't Easy: The Theater of Stephen Sondheim*. New York: Da Capo, 1992.

Gordon, Mel. *Stanislavsky in America: An Actor's Workbook*. New York: Routledge, 2010.

Gordon, Ricky Ian. "If I Knew Then . . . " *Sondheim Review* 19, no. 1 (Fall 2012): 19–22.

Gordon, Robert. "Old Situations, New Complications." In *The Oxford Handbook of Sondheim Studies*, edited by Robert Gordon, 63–80. New York: Oxford University Press, 2014.

Gordon, Robert. "Sondheim Scholarship: An Overview." *Studies in Musical Theatre* 13, no. 2 (2019): 187–204.

Gottfried, Martin. *Sondheim*. Enlarged and updated ed. New York: Abrams, 2000. First published 1993.

Granade, Andrew. "Decoding Harry Partch's Aesthetic: Satire, Duality, and *Water! Water!*" *American Music* 35, no. 2 (Summer 2017): 172–196.

Grinenko, Aleksei. "'Is That Just Disgusting?' Mapping the Social Geographies of Filth and Madness in *Sweeney Todd*." *Theatre Journal* 68, no. 2 (2016): 231–248.

Grinenko, Aleksei. "Madness and the Broadway Musical, 1940s–2000s." PhD diss., City University of New York, 2019.

Guernsey Jr., Otis L., ed. *Broadway Song and Story: Playwrights, Lyricists, Composers Discuss Their Hits*. New York: Dodd, Mead, 1985.

Gunji, Masakatsu. *The Kabuki Guide*. Translated by Christopher Holmes. Tokyo: Kodansha International, 1987.

Hanson, Laura. "Broadway Babies: Images of Women in the Musicals of Stephen Sondheim." In *Stephen Sondheim: A Casebook*, edited by Joanne Gordon, 13–33. New York: Garland, 1997.

Harrison, Jeremy. *Actor-Musicianship*. London: Bloomsbury, 2016.

Hathaway, Brad. "Church Had a Real Good Time in *Gypsy*." *Everything Sondheim*, October 10, 2017. https://www.everythingsondheim.org/church-real-good-time-gypsy/.

Haurn, Harry. "Exclusive! Sondheim Explains Evolution from *Bounce* to *Road Show*." *Playbill*, August 12, 2008, https://www.playbill.com/article/exclusive-sondheim-explains-evolution-from-bounce-to-road-show-com-152437.

Henry, Sean Patrick. "Broadway by the Numbers." Illustrated by I. Javier Ameijeras, produced by Alexander Libby, Bella Sotomayor, Florian Bouju, and Serene Lim. *Production Pro*, 2019. https://production.pro/broadway-by-the-numbers.

Hethmon, Robert H., ed. *Strasberg at the Actors Studio*. New York: Viking, 1965.

Hetrick, Adam. "Sondheim Issues Response Following Report of Disney *Into the Woods* Film Changes." *Playbill*, June 23, 2014.

Hirsch, Foster. *Harold Prince and the American Musical Theatre*. Expanded ed. New York: Applause Books, 2005.

Hoffman, Warren. *The Great White Way: Race and the Broadway Musical*. New Brunswick, NJ: Rutgers University Press, 2014.

Homes, A. M. "On the Road: Rich Evenings with Sondheim." *Vanity Fair*, February 22, 2008, https://www.vanityfair.com/news/2008/03/ontheroad200803.

Horowitz, Mark Eden. "Biography of a Song: 'Please Hello.'" *Sondheim Review* 14, no. 3 (Spring 2008): 25–33.

Horowitz, Mark Eden. "Biography of a Song: 'Send in the Clowns.'" *Sondheim Review* 11, no. 3 (Spring 2005): 15–20.

Horowitz, Mark Eden. "*Into the Woods* from Stage to Screen." In *The Oxford Handbook of Musical Theatre Screen Adaptations*, edited by Dominic McHugh, 107–124. New York: Oxford University Press, 2019.

Horowitz, Mark Eden. "'Really Weird': The Story of *Anyone Can Whistle* with Lots of Details." *Sondheim Review* 17, no. 2 (Winter 2010): 7–11.

Horowitz, Mark Eden. *Sondheim on Music: Major Decisions and Minor Details*. 2nd ed. Lanham, MD: Scarecrow, 2010. First published 2003.

Housez, Lara. "Becoming Stephen Sondheim: *Anyone Can Whistle, A Pray by Blecht, Company,* and *Sunday in the Park with George*." PhD diss., Eastman School of Music, University of Rochester, 2013.

Howe, Irving. "This Age of Conformity: Notes on an Endless Theme, or, a Catalogue of Complaints." *Partisan Review* 21, no. 1 (January–February 1954): 7–33.

Hunt, Robert, ed. *Gulielmensian*. North Adams, MA: Miller, Lamb, and Hunter, 1950.

Ilson, Carol. *Harold Prince: A Director's Journey*. 2nd ed. New York: Limelight Editions 2000.

Jones, John Bush. *Our Musicals, Ourselves: A Social History of the American Musical Theatre*. Hanover, NH: Brandeis University Press, 2003.

Jubin, Olaf. "'It Takes Two': The Doubling of Actors and Roles in *Sunday in the Park with George*." In *The Oxford Handbook of Sondheim Studies*, edited by Robert Gordon, 185–202. New York: Oxford University Press, 2014.

Kajikawa, Loren. "The Possessive Investment in Classical Music: Confronting Legacies of White Supremacy in U.S. Schools and Departments of Music." In *Seeing Race*

*Again: Countering Colorblindness Across the Disciplines*, edited by Kimberlé Williams Crenshaw, Luke Charles Harris, Daniel Martinez HoSang, and George Lipsitz, 155–174. Berkeley: University of California Press, 2019.

Kapilow, Rob. "Which Comes First, the Music or the Lyrics? 'You're the Top.'" In *A Cole Porter Companion*, edited by Don M. Randel, Matthew Shaftel, and Susan Forscher Weiss, 86–97. Urbana: University of Illinois Press, 2016.

Kellner, Douglas. "Introduction to the Second Edition." In *One-Dimensional Man: Studies in the Ideology of Advanced Industrial Society* by Herbert Marcuse, xi–xxxviii. London: Routledge Classics, 2002.

Kennedy, Matthew. *Road-Show! The Fall of Film Musicals in the 1960s*. New York: Oxford University Press, 2014.

Kirle, Bruce. *Unfinished Show Business: Broadway Musicals as Works-in-Process*. Carbondale: Southern Illinois University Press, 2005.

Kislan, Richard. *The Musical: A Look at the American Musical Theater*. Rev. ed. New York: Applause Books, 1995.

Klein, Christina. *Cold War Orientalism: Asia in the Middlebrow Imagination, 1945–1961*. Berkeley: University of California Press, 2017.

Knapp, Raymond. *The American Musical and the Formation of National Identity*. Princeton: Princeton University Press, 2005.

Knapp, Raymond. "History, *The Sound of Music*, and Us." *American Music* 22, no. 1 (Spring 2004): 133–144.

Knapp, Raymond. "Sondheim's America; America's Sondheim." In *The Oxford Handbook of Sondheim Studies*, edited by Robert Gordon, 432–450. New York: Oxford University Press, 2014.

Knapp, Raymond, and Zelda Knapp. "Going Postal: Collapsing Time and Space Through Sung Letters in Broadway Musicals." *Studies in Musical Theatre* 11, no. 3 (2017): 233–246.

Kowalke, Kim H. "'Give Me Time': Sondheim, a Clever Maid and 'The Miller's Son.'" *Studies in Musical Theatre* 13, no. 2 (2019): 151–168.

Krampner, Jon. *Female Brando: The Legend of Kim Stanley*. New York: Back Stage Books, 2006.

Krasner, David. "Stanislavsky's System, Sense-Emotion Memory, and Physical Action/Active Analysis: American Interpretations of the System's Legacy." In *The Routledge Companion to Stanislavsky*, edited by Andrew R. White, 195–212. New York: Routledge, 2014.

Kroll, Jack. "The Blood Runs Cold." *Newsweek*, March 12, 1979.

LaChiusa, Michael John. "Is It 'Opera' or 'Musical Theater'?" *Opera News*, August 2002.

LaFontaine, David. "Merrily He Strolled Along." *Gay & Lesbian Review* 26, no. 2 (March–April 2019): 19–22.

Lahr, John. "Sour Ball." *New Yorker*, December 11, 2006.

Laurents, Arthur. *Mainly on Directing: "Gypsy," "West Side Story" and Other Musicals*. New York: Knopf, 2009.

Laurents, Arthur. *Original Story By: A Memoir of Broadway and Hollywood*. New York: Knopf, 2000.

Laurents, Arthur. *The Rest of the Story: A Life Completed*. Milwaukee: Applause Theatre and Cinema Books, 2011.

Laurents, Arthur, and Stephen Sondheim. *Anyone Can Whistle: A Musical Fable*. New York: Random House, 1965.

Lebrecht, Norman. "When a Movie Outshines the Outstanding Original." *Scena*, February 12, 2008, http://www.scena. org/lsm/sm13-5/sm13_5_sweeneytodd_en.html.

Lewis, Hannah. "*Love Me Tonight* (1932) and the Development of the Integrated Film Musical." *Musical Quarterly* 100, no. 1 (2017): 3–32.

Lewis, R. Cragin, ed. *Williams 1793–1993: A Pictorial History*. Williamstown, MA: Williams College Bicentennial Commission, 1993.

Lipton, James. "Stephen Sondheim: The Art of the Musical." *Paris Review* 39, no. 142 (Spring 1997): 258–278.

Mackintosh, Cameron. "Why You'll Love this Book." Introduction to *Mary Poppins: The Complete Collection* by P. L. Travers. London: HarperCollins, 2008.

Maeda, Daryl J. *Chains of Babylon: The Rise of the Asian American Movement*. Minneapolis: University of Minnesota Press, 2009.

Magee, Jeffrey. *Irving Berlin's American Musical Theater*. New York: Oxford University Press, 2012.

Magee, Jeffrey. "Rodgers and Hammerstein's Musical Metatheatre, or: Why Billy Bigelow Had to Die." *Studies in Musical Theatre* 8, no. 3 (2014): 215–223.

Magee, Jeffrey. "Whose Turn Is It? Where *Gypsy*'s Finale Came from, and Where It Went." *Studies in Musical Theatre* 13, no. 2 (2019): 117–132.

Mandelbaum, Ken. *Not Since "Carrie": Forty Years of Broadway Musical Flops*. New York: St. Martin's, 1991.

Mandelbaum, Ken. "Obscure Videos: *Sweeney* Special." *Sondheim Review* 12, no. 4 (Summer 2006): 44–45.

Manheim, Ralph, and John Willett, eds. *Bertolt Brecht: Collected Plays*. Vol. 2. New York: Vintage Books, 1977.

Marcuse, Herbert. *One-Dimensional Man: Studies in the Ideology of Advanced Industrial Society*. London: Routledge Classics, 2002.

Martin, George. "On the Verge of Opera: Stephen Sondheim." *Opera Quarterly* 6, no. 3 (Spring 1989): 76–85.

McConachie, Bruce. *American Theater in the Culture of the Cold War*. Iowa City: University of Iowa Press, 2003.

McGill, Craig M. "Sondheim's Use of the 'Herrmann Chord' in *Sweeney Todd*." *Studies in Musical Theatre* 6, no. 3 (2012): 291–312.

McHugh, Dominic. "'And I'll Sing Once More': A Historical Overview of the Broadway Musical on the Silver Screen." In *The Oxford Handbook of Musical Theatre Screen Adaptations*, edited by Dominic McHugh, 13–27. New York: Oxford University Press, 2019.

McHugh, Dominic. "*Climb High*: Sondheim at the Gateway to His Career." *Studies in Musical Theatre* 13, no. 2 (June 2019): 103–115.

McLaughlin, Robert L. "Sondheim and Postmodernism." In *The Oxford Handbook of Sondheim Studies*, edited by Robert Gordon, 25–39. New York: Oxford University Press, 2014.

McLaughlin, Robert L. *Stephen Sondheim and the Reinvention of the American Musical*. Jackson: University Press of Mississippi, 2016.

McMillin, Scott. *The Musical as Drama: A Study of the Principles and Conventions Behind Musical Shows from Kern to Sondheim*. Princeton: Princeton University Press, 2006.

McPhee, Ryan. "New Broadway Demographics Research Shows Growth in Nonwhite and International Audiences." *Playbill*, 2020, https://www.playbill.com/article/new-broadway-demographics-research-shows-growth-in-nonwhite-and-international-audiences.

Miller, Nancy K. *Getting Personal: Feminist Occasions and Other Autobiographical Acts.* New York: Routledge, 1991.

Miller, Scott. "*Assassins* and the Concept Musical." In *Stephen Sondheim: A Casebook*, edited by Joanne Gordon, 187–205. New York: Garland, 1997.

Milner, Andrew. "'Let the Pupil Show the Master': Stephen Sondheim and Oscar Hammerstein II." In *Stephen Sondheim: A Casebook*, edited by Joanne Gordon, 153–171. New York: Garland, 1997.

Miranda, Lin-Manuel, and Jeremy McCarter. *Hamilton: The Revolution.* New York: Grand Central Publishing, 2016.

Mitgang, Herbert. "Actors' Studio: Classroom for Our Stars." *Town & Country*, May 1953.

Montepare, J. M., and M. E. Lachman. "'You're Only as Old as You Feel': Self-Perceptions of Age, Fears of Aging, and Life Satisfaction from Adolescence to Old Age." *Psychology and Aging* 4, no. 1 (1989): 73–78.

Mordden, Ethan. *The Hollywood Musical.* New York: St. Martin's, 1981.

Mordden, Ethan. *On Sondheim: An Opinionated Guide.* New York: Oxford University Press, 2016.

Mordden, Ethan. *Open a New Window: The Broadway Musical in the 1960s.* New York: St. Martin's, 2001.

Mordden, Ethan. *Rodgers and Hammerstein.* New York: Abrams, 1992.

Most, Andrea. *Making Americans: Jews and the Broadway Musical.* Cambridge, MA: Harvard University Press, 2004.

Mulkern, Louis J. "U.S.–Japan Trade Relations: Economic and Strategic Implications." In *U.S.–Japan Economic Relations: A Symposium on Critical Issues*, ed. Thomas C. Smith, 26–27. Berkeley: Institute of East Asian Studies, University of California Press, 1980.

Newman, Harry. "The Theater's Resistance to Non-Traditional Casting." *Drama Review* 33, no. 3 (Autumn 1989): 22–36.

Newton, Isaac. *Opticks: Or, a Treatise of the Reflections, Refractions, Inflections, and Colors of Light.* London: Printed for Samuel Smith and Benjamin Walford, 1704.

Oja, Carol J. *Bernstein Meets Broadway: Collaborative Art in a Time of War.* New York: Oxford University Press, 2016.

Oja, Carol J. "*West Side Story* and *The Music Man*: Whiteness, Immigration, and Race in the US During the Late 1950s." *Studies in Musical Theater* 3, no. 1 (2009): 13–30.

Olson, John. "*Company*—25 Years Later." In *Stephen Sondheim: A Casebook*, edited by Joanne Gordon, 47–67. New York: Garland, 1999.

Pao, Angela C. *No Safe Spaces: Re-Casting Race, Ethnicity, and Nationality in American Theater.* Ann Arbor: University of Michigan Press, 2010.

Peyankov, Yasen. "In Search of Truth: Stanislavsky and Strasberg." In *The Routledge Companion to Stanislavsky*, edited by Andrew R. White, 506–514. New York: Routledge, 2014.

Pribyl, Ashley M. "Performance Review: *Company* . . . London, UK, 9 October 2018." *Studies in Musical Theatre* 13, no. 2 (2019): 209–211.

Pribyl, Ashley M. "Sociocultural and Collaborative Antagonism in the Harold Prince–Stephen Sondheim Musicals, 1970–1979." PhD diss., Washington University in St. Louis, 2019.

Prince, Harold. *Contradictions: Notes on Twenty-Six Years in the Theatre.* New York: Dodd, Mead, 1974.

Prince, Harold. *Sense of Occasion.* New York: Applause Theatre and Cinema Books, 2017.

Randel, Don M. "About Cole Porter's Songs." In *A Cole Porter Companion*, edited by Don M. Randel, Matthew Shaftel, and Susan Forscher Weiss, 222–242. Urbana: University of Illinois Press, 2016.

Reisman, David, with Nathan Glazer and Reuel Denny. *The Lonely Crowd: A Study of the Changing American Character*. New Haven: Yale Nota Bene, 2001.

Rich, Frank. *Hot Seat: Theater Criticism for the* New York Times, *1980–1993*. New York: Random House, 1998.

Riley, James Whitcomb. *James Whitcomb Riley's Complete Works*. Vol. 1. Indianapolis: Bobbs-Merrill, 1916.

Rockwell, John. *All American Music*. New York: Knopf, 1983.

Romano, Aja. "Why We Can't Stop Fighting About Cancel Culture." *Vox*, August 25, 2020, https://www.vox.com/culture/2019/12/30/20879720/what-is-cancel-culture-explai ned-history-debate.

Row, Jess. *White Flights: Race, Fiction, and the American Imagination*. Minneapolis: Gray Wolf, 2019.

Russ. "College Show: *All That Glitters*." *Variety*, March 23, 1949.

Said, Edward. *Orientalism*. New York: Pantheon, 1978.

Savran, David. "'Follies' Set in Socialist East Germany: Sondheim at Staatsoperette Dresden." *Operetta Research Center*, January 8, 2020. http://operetta-research-center. org/sondheims-folliesstaatsoperette-dresden/.

Savran, David. *In Their Own Words: Contemporary American Playwrights*. New York: Theatre Communications Group, 1988.

Savran, David. "'You've Got That Thing': Cole Porter, Stephen Sondheim, and the Erotics of the List Song." *Theatre Journal* 64, no. 4 (2012): 533–548.

Savran, David, and Daniel Gundlachtt. "*Anyone Can Whistle* as Experimental Theater." In *The Oxford Handbook of Sondheim Studies*, ed. Robert Gordon, 81–94. Oxford: Oxford University Press, 2014.

Schimmel, Annemarie. *The Mystery of Numbers*. New York: Oxford University Press, 1993.

Schmalfeldt, Janet. "Cadential Processes: The Evaded Cadence and the 'One More Time' Technique." *Journal of Musicological Research* 12, nos. 1–2 (1992): 1–52.

Schulman, Michael. "The Ascension." *New Yorker*, March 26, 2018.

Schwartz, Stephen. "Learning from Sondheim." *Sondheim Review* 17, no. 1 (2010): 33–54.

Secrest, Meryle. *Stephen Sondheim: A Life*. New York: Knopf; London: Bloomsbury, 1998.

Shephardson, Francis W. *The Beta Book: The Story and Manual of Beta Theta Pi*. Menasha, WI: George Banta, 1927.

Sheppard, W. Anthony. *Extreme Exoticism: Japan in the American Musical Imagination*. New York: Oxford University Press, 2019.

Shimakawa, Karen. *National Abjection: The Asian American Body on Stage*. Durham: Duke University Press, 2002.

Simon, John. *Ingmar Bergman Directs*. New York: Harcourt Brace Jovanovich, 1972.

Smith, Thomas C., ed. *U.S.–Japan Economic Relations: A Symposium on Critical Issues*. Berkley: Institute of East Asian Studies, University of California, 1980.

Smith, Wendy. "Good Thing Going: Stephen Sondheim Only Looks Better with Time." *American Scholar* 76, no. 4 (Autumn 2007): 109–116.

Snowden, Edward. *Permanent Record*. New York: Holt, 2019.

Sokol, Robert. "Neil Patrick Harris Describes Being Very Alive in *Company*." *Sondheim Review* 16, no. 1 (Fall 2011): 29–30.

Sokol, Robert, Ken Kwartler, and Terri Roberts. "Side by Side: Rich and Sondheim." *Sondheim Review* 15, no. 1 (Fall 2008): 22–24.

Sondheim, Stephen. *The Almost Unknown Stephen Sondheim: 39 Previously Unpublished Songs from 17 Shows and Films*. New York: Rilting Music, 2016.

Sondheim, Stephen. *The Complete "Follies" Collection: Author's Edition*. Milwaukee: Hal Leonard, 2005.

Sondheim, Stephen. *Finishing the Hat: Collected Lyrics (1954–1981) with Attendant Comments, Principles, Heresies, Grudges, Whines and Anecdotes*. New York: Knopf, 2010.

Sondheim, Stephen. "How to Do a Real Crossword." *New York*, April 8, 1968. http://nymag.com/arts/all/features/46798.

Sondheim, Stephen. "Larger Than Life: Reflections on Melodrama and *Sweeney Todd*." In *Melodrama*. Vol. 7, edited by Daniel Gerould, 3–14. New York: New York Literary Forum, 1980.

Sondheim, Stephen. *Look, I Made a Hat: Collected Lyrics (1981–2011) with Attendant Comments, Amplifications, Harangues, Digressions, Anecdotes and Miscellany*. New York: Knopf, 2011.

Sondheim, Stephen. "The Musical Theater." In *Broadway Song and Story: Broadway Playwrights, Lyricists, Composers Discuss Their Hits*, edited by Otis L. Guernsey Jr., 228–250. New York: Dodd, Mead, 1985.

Sondheim, Stephen. "The Musical Theater: A Talk by Stephen Sondheim." *Dramatists Guild Quarterly* 15, no. 3 (Autumn 1978): 6–29.

Sondheim, Stephen. "On Collaboration Between Authors and Directors." *Dramatists Guild Quarterly* 16, no. 2 (1979): 14–34.

Sondheim, Stephen. "Theater Lyrics." In *Playwrights, Lyricists, Composers on Theater*, edited by Otis L. Guernsey Jr., 61–97. New York: Dodd, Mead, 1974.

Spoto, Donald. *A Passion for Life: The Biography of Elizabeth Taylor*. New York: HarperCollins, 1995.

Stanislavsky, Konstantin. *Building a Character*. Translated by Elizabeth Reynolds Hapgood. London: Methuen, 2001. First published 1949.

Stempel, Larry. *Showtime: A History of the Broadway Musical Theater*. New York: Norton, 2010.

Stewart Jr., Sidney A., ed. *Gulielmensian*. North Adams, MA: Miller, Lamb, and Hunter, 1949.

Stoddart, Scott Frederick. "Visions and Re-Visions: The Postmodern Challenge of *Merrily We Roll Along*." In *Reading Stephen Sondheim: A Collection of Critical Essays*, edited by Sandor Goodhart, 187–198. New York: Garland, 2000.

Strasberg, Lee. *A Dream of Passion: The Development of the Method*. Edited by Evangeline Morphos. Boston: Little, Brown, 1987.

Straus, Joseph N. *Introduction to Post-Tonal Theory*. 2nd ed. Upper Saddle River, NJ: Prentice Hall, 2000.

Sullivan, Shannon. *Revealing Whiteness: The Unconscious Habits of Racial Privilege*. Bloomington: Indiana University Press, 2006.

Suskin, Steven. *Berlin, Kern, Rodgers, Hart, and Hammerstein: A Complete Song Catalogue*. Jefferson, NC: McFarland, 1990.

Suskin, Steven. *More Opening Nights on Broadway: A Critical Quotebook of the Musical Theatre, 1965–1981*. New York: Schirmer Books, 1997.

Swain, Joseph. "*A Little Night Music*: The Cynical Operetta." In *The Oxford Handbook of Sondheim Studies*, edited by Robert Gordon, 309–318. New York: Oxford University Press, 2014.

Swayne, Steve. "Hearing Sondheim's Voices." PhD diss., University of California, Berkeley, 1999.

Swayne, Steve. *How Sondheim Found His Sound*. Ann Arbor: University of Michigan Press, 2005.

Swayne, Steve. "*Music for the Theatre*, the Young Copland, and the Younger Sondheim." *American Music* 20, no. 1 (Spring 2002): 80–101.

Swayne, Steve. "Sondheim's Piano Sonata." *Journal of the Royal Musical Association* 127, no. 2 (2002): 258–304.

Symonds, Dominic. "'You've Got to Be Carefully Taught': Oscar Hammerstein's Influence on Sondheim." In *The Oxford Handbook of Sondheim Studies*, edited by Robert Gordon, 39–63. New York: Oxford University Press, 2014.

Takaki, Ronald. *Strangers from a Different Shore: A History of Asian Americans*. Boston: Little, Brown, 1998.

Taylor, Millie. "*Sweeney Todd*: From Melodrama to Musical Tragedy." In *The Oxford Handbook of Sondheim Studies*, edited by Robert Gordon, 335–349. New York: Oxford University Press, 2014.

Teachout, Terry. "Sondheim's Operas." *Commentary*, May 2003. https://www.commentarymagazine.com/articles/terry-teachout/sondheims-operas/.

Thomson, David. "Attending the Tale of *Sweeney Todd*: The Stage Musical and Tim Burton's Film Version." In *The Oxford Handbook to Sondheim Studies*, edited by Robert Gordon, 296–305. New York: Oxford University Press, 2014.

Tomo. "The Mad Show." *Variety,* January 19, 1966.

Travers, P. L. *Mary Poppins: The Complete Collection*. London: HarperCollins, 2008.

Trueman, Matt. "West End Review: 'Company.'" *Variety*, October 17, 2018. https://variety.com/2018/legit/reviews/company-review-gender-swap-marianne-elliott-1202981961/.

Viertel, Jack. *The Secret Life of the American Musical: How Broadway Shows are Built*. New York: Sarah Crichton Books, 2016.

Weidman, John, and Stephen Sondheim. *Pacific Overtures*. New York: Dodd, Mead, 1977.

Wells, Elizabeth A. "*West Side Story*": *Cultural Perspectives on an American Musical*. Lanham, MD: Scarecrow, 2011.

Welsh, Katherine. "An Interpretive Framework for Analyzing and Comparing the Women in Stephen Sondheim Musicals." Senior thesis, Princeton University, 2015.

Wheeler, Hugh, and Stephen Sondheim. *Sweeney Todd: The Demon Barber of Fleet Street; A Musical Thriller*. New York: Dodd, Mead, 1979.

White, Andrew R., ed. *The Routledge Companion to Stanislavsky*. New York: Routledge, 2014.

Whitfield, Stephen J. *In Search of American Jewish Culture*. Hanover, NH: Brandeis University Press, 1999.

Whyte, William H. *The Organization Man*. Philadelphia: University of Pennsylvania Press, 2002.

Wolf, Stacy. *Changed for Good: A Feminist History of the Broadway Musical*. New York: Oxford University Press, 2011.

Wolf, Stacy. "A Conversation with John Doyle About the Musicals of Stephen Sondheim." *Studies in Musical Theatre* 13, no. 2 (2019): 187–195.

Wolf, Stacy. "*Hamilton*'s Women." *Studies in Musical Theatre* 12, no. 2 (2018): 167–180.

Wolf, Stacy. "Keeping Company with Sondheim's Women." In *The Oxford Handbook of Sondheim Studies*, edited by Robert Gordon, 365–383. New York: Oxford University Press, 2014.

Wolf, Stacy. *A Problem Like Maria*. Ann Arbor: University of Michigan Press, 2002.

Wolfberg, June. "Attend the Tale: A Conversation with Stephen Sondheim." *Spotlight: The Magazine of the New York City Opera Guild* 16, no. 4 (Fall 1984): 11–14.

Wollman, Elizabeth. *Hard Times: The Adult Musical in 1970s New York City*. New York: Oxford University Press, 2013.

Wood, Clement, ed. *The Complete Rhyming Dictionary and Poet's Craft Book*. New York: Halcyon House, 1936.

Wood, Graham. "The Development of Song Forms in the Broadway and Hollywood Musicals of Richard Rodgers, 1919–1943." PhD diss., University of Minnesota, 2000.

Wood, Robin. "Ingmar Bergman: New Edition." In *Contemporary Approaches to Film and Media Studies*, edited by Barry Keith Grant, 78–85. Detroit: Wayne State University Press, 2012. First published 1969.

Wurgaft, Benjamin Aldes. *Jews at Williams: Inclusion, Exclusion, and Class at a New England Liberal Arts College*. Williamstown, MA: Williams College Press, 2013.

Yarmosky, Jessica. "'I Can Exist Here': On Gender Identity, Some Colleges Are Opening Up." *NPR*, March 21, 2019. www.npr.org/2019/03/21/693953037/i-can-exist-here-on-gender-identity-some-colleges-are-opening-up.

Yawata, Keiske. "Japanese Quality: How It Was Built and Maintained." In *U.S.–Japan Economic Relations: A Symposium on Critical Issues*. Edited by Thomas C. Smith, 31–38. Berkeley: Institute of East Asian Studies, University of California Press, 1980.

Zadan, Craig. *Sondheim & Co.* 2nd ed., updated. New York: Da Capo, 1994. A second edition was also published by Harper and Row, 1986, and by Da Capo, 1986. First published 1974.

# Index